THE WORLD OF SUGAR

D1615786

THE WORLD OF
Sugar

How the Sweet Stuff Transformed
Our Politics, Health, and
Environment over 2,000 Years

ULBE BOSMA

THE BELKNAP PRESS OF
HARVARD UNIVERSITY PRESS

Cambridge, Massachusetts
London, England
2023

First printing

Library of Congress Cataloging-in-Publication Data

Names: Bosma, Ulbe, 1962– author.
Title: The world of sugar : how the sweet stuff transformed our politics,
health, and environment over 2,000 years / Ulbe Bosma.
Description: Cambridge, Massachusetts : The Belknap Press
of Harvard University Press, 2023. | Includes index.
Identifiers: LCCN 2022036216 | ISBN 9780674279391 (cloth)
Subjects: LCSH: Sugar—History. | Sugar trade—History.
Classification: LCC TX560.S9 B67 2023 | DDC 641.3/36—dc23/eng/20221007
LC record available at https://lccn.loc.gov/2022036216

Contents

Timeline

Dramatis Personae

Karl Franz Achard (1753–1821): German inventor who devised a process for efficiently extracting sugar from beet root.

Francisco Arango y Parreño (1765–1837): Architect of Cuba's ascendency as the world's largest exporter of cane sugar.

Edwin F. Atkins (1850–1926): Boston trader who became one of Cuba's largest sugar producers and an influential US government lobbyist.

William Banting (1796–1878): British undertaker who developed the low-carbohydrate Banting Diet.

Ghanshyam Das Birla (1894–1983): Founder of India's Birla Industrial Group and of the Birla Sugar Company.

Jean-François Cail (1804–1871): French manufacturer of steam-driven machines, including Derosne & Cail vacuum pans.

John Middleton (Jock) Campbell (1912–1994): British Labour politician and chairman of UK food wholesaler Booker McConnell, who negotiated the Commonwealth Sugar Agreement.

Thomas Lincoln Chadbourne (1871–1938): Wall Street lawyer and architect of the 1931 Chadbourne Agreement regulating the global sugar market.

Charles Derosne (1780–1846): French chemist, pioneer in beet sugar manufacturing, and, together with Jean-François Cail, inventor of the Derosne & Cail vacuum pan.

John Gladstone (1764–1851): Liverpudlian merchant and Demerara plantation-owner who initiated Indian indentured migration to the West Indies.

Henry O. Havemeyer (1847–1907): Leader of the third generation of US sugar refiners and president of American Sugar Refining Company, known as the Sugar Trust.

Elizabeth (Coltman) Heyrick (1769–1831): British anti-slavery activist and author of the influential 1824 pamphlet "Immediate not Gradual Abolition."

Père Jean-Baptiste Labat (1663–1738): Dominican priest, botanist, and West Indies plantation-owner whose six-volume Caribbean travelogue chronicled the region's sugar industry.

Edwin Lascelles, 1st Baron Harewood (1713–1795): Member of the Lascelles sugar dynasty of Barbados, powerful financier of sugar commerce, and one of the largest sugar plantation owners in the West Indies.

W. Arthur Lewis (1915–1991): Saint Lucia–born economist who won the Nobel Prize for pioneering work on economic development and poverty in plantation societies.

Julio Lobo y Olavarria (1898–1983): Cuban trader who became the world's most powerful sugar broker before his exile in 1960.

Zachary Macaulay (1768–1838): Governor of Sierra Leone, cofounder of the Anti-Slavery Society, and editor of *Anti-Slavery Reporter.*

James Mylne (1815–1899): Scottish railway engineer and landlord in India, coinventor of the portable Beheea mill together with his partner Walter Thomson.

Herbert Myrick (1860–1927): Populist advocate of the US beet sugar industry and publisher of agricultural journals.

Henry T. Oxnard (1860–1922): French-born American beet sugar producer and president of American Beet Sugar Company.

Pierre Poivre (1719–1786): Botanist and founder of Pamplemousses Botanical Garden on Isle de France (Mauritius).

Hendrik Coenraad Prinsen Geerligs (1864–1953): Dutch chemist and renowned sugar expert.

Norbert Rillieux (1806–1894): Louisiana-born chemical engineer and inventor of the multiple-effect vacuum pan.

Manuel Rionda (1854–1943): Spanish-born sugar baron in Cuba, cofounder of the Czarnikow-Rionda Company.

Adolph Claus J. Spreckels (1828–1908): German sugar refiner in San Francisco and owner of extensive sugar plantations in Hawaii.

Henri Tate (1819–1899): Founder of the Tate & Lyle sugar empire—introducer of sugar cubes—and of what is now the Tate Britain art museum.

François-Dominique Toussaint L'Ouverture (1743–1803): Leader of the successful Haitian slave rebellion and war of independence.

Rafael Trujillo (1891–1961): Brutal dictator of the Dominican Republic from 1930 until his assassination, who appropriated most of the country's sugar industry.

Johannes van den Bosch (1780–1844): Dutch governor-general of Java, who introduced the forced cultivation system that turned the island into the world's second largest cane sugar exporter.

Joseph Martial Wetzell (1793–1857): Chemical engineer and inventor of the Wetzell boiling pan, a low-cost, high-efficiency sugar-refining system.

William Wilberforce (1759–1833): Leading British abolitionist and parliamentarian who spearheaded the legislative campaign to ban the slave trade.

Harvey Washington Wiley (1844–1930): American chemist, sugar expert, father of the Pure Food and Drug Act (1906), and key contributor to *Good Housekeeping* magazine.

John Yudkin (1910–1995): Controversial British nutritionist who warned against the dangers of sugar consumption in works such as *Pure, White and Deadly* (1972).

THE WORLD OF SUGAR

Introduction

To SEE HOW IMPORTANT SUGAR has become in our lives, we need only take some packaged food from our kitchen shelves and read the ingredient labels. Sugar is listed on almost every one. Sugar has fundamentally changed how we feed ourselves, has deeply affected human relations through its close relationship with slavery, and has caused extensive environmental degradation. These are stunning facts given that sugar was unknown for most of human history.

It took time for our simple white sugar to be become quotidian because it is difficult to make. Much more difficult than salt, for instance. It requires ingenuity and patience to extract from plant material the complex sucrose molecule $C_{12}H_{22}O_{11}$, a disaccharide or compound sugar that couples sweeter fructose and less sweet glucose molecules. The resulting white table sugar was a luxury 200 years ago and could only be produced in small quantities, through costly and time-consuming artisanal manufacturing. Today, huge factories with gigantic crushers, boilers, and centrifuges turn massive volumes of sugar beet or cane into crystalline sugar within a matter of hours.

Granulated sugar is no more than 2,500 years old, and white crystalline sugar started its career even more recently, about 1,500 years ago, in Asia as a pure luxury, a sign of power and wealth. Sugar initially had no purpose beyond royal banquets and ceremonies or in tiny medicinal doses. Royal sugar consumption percolated over time into the elites in the growing cities of China and India, as well as much of Central Asia and North Africa, before reaching Europe. By the thirteenth century, sugar-making skills had developed sufficiently for sugar to take off as a major commercial item throughout Eurasia. The history of sugar capitalism began in Asia, where most of the world's sugar was produced until the 1870s.

Sugar's widespread commercial success fostered a chain of small innovations in cane crushing and juice boiling, which further lowered the price. Over the past seven hundred years sugar has showed up in a rapidly growing number of recipes across the world and increasingly became part of daily diets. It was Europeans who turned sugar into a globally cultivated commodity, precisely because they were incapable of growing much of it on their own continent, at least not prior to the introduction of the sugar beet. When Europe learned to love sugar, its demand had to be met from overseas and from the Americas in particular. What followed was a story of deeply shocking cruelty at a scale beyond imagination. Between half and two-thirds of the 12.5 million Africans shipped across the Atlantic Ocean in the course of the slave trade were destined for sugar plantations. The labor regimes on sugar plantations were exhaustive and lethal, far more than those of tobacco and coffee production, for instance. By the late 1860s, when Karl Marx was writing his monumental *Capital,* half of the sugar consumed by the industrial proletariat in Europe and North America was produced by enslaved people.[1]

In the mid-nineteenth century, sugar was what oil would become in the twentieth: the Global South's most valuable export commodity.[2] The crucial difference from oil, however, is that almost every country has been able to produce sugar. Since Europe was cut off from Caribbean sugar under Napoleon Bonaparte's rule, beet sugar became a viable alternative. From these roots the same white crystals could be extracted, but never as cheaply as from cane. Powerful beet sugar cartels in wealthy countries convinced their governments to establish protectionist policies, not only shielding them from competition from poorer cane sugar–producing countries but also enabling them to dump their excess production abroad. The marriage between expansive global capitalism and increasingly powerful nation-states artificially cheapened sugar. This in turn facilitated sugar's introduction, in massive quantities, into industrially produced food and beverages. Today, the scale and economic clout of the sugar industry makes it incredibly difficult to address market inefficiencies, overproduction, and overconsumption.

In his classic work *Sweetness and Power* (1985), the anthropologist Sidney Mintz argued that the history of sugar shows how modern consumption, global inequalities, and the emergence of modern capitalism are all part of the same massive transformation of our world.[3] The history of capitalism is indeed Janus-faced, as it involved immense material progress but also caused social misery, unhealthy consumption patterns, and environmental destruction.[4] The environmental consequences alone should make us rethink sugar production. Currently, the average annual sugar and sweetener consumption of a person living in Western Europe is 40 kilograms; in North America, that number is almost 60 kilograms. Now imagine if the entire world were to consume the same amount of sugar as the Europeans. Global production would have to increase from the present 180 million tons to 308 million tons. This would cause an almost-proportionate gobbling up of land, since increasing productivity per acre is rarely possible these days. And keep in mind that ever more land is already being used for cane cultivation, to produce ethanol as a so-called biofuel.

The industry that disgorges sugar in immense volumes has emerged as a formidable adversary to the medical profession, which spent the past century warning against excessive sugar consumption.[5] Human metabolism evolved in light of food scarcity, not calorie abundance, and today we suffer the consequences. Sugar has already ruined the health of many, and matters are poised to grow worse. Incidence of type 2 diabetes—associated with obesity, a condition to which excessive sugar consumption contributes heavily— is expected to rise at an alarming rate over the next decades.[6] The World Health Organization had every reason to declare obesity a pandemic in 1999, but the announcement went largely unnoticed. Sugar is not a virus, after all, and was allowed to quietly continue wreaking havoc.

This book is not only about sugar but also its history, which is made by people. It is the story of millions of workers doing exhausting labor, from field to factory, to produce sugar. It is a history of resistance by the enslaved and by contemporary cane and beet sugar workers, and by millions of farmers who persisted in making their own raw sugar rather than bringing their cane to the big industrialists. These industrialists, who typically operated in tight family networks, are also crucial actors. Big producers came from diverse national and ethnic backgrounds, but, if they were cane sugar producers, they were often born and raised in the tropics. They were among the first in the world to apply steam power and revolutionary insights from physics and chemistry to the manufacture refined sugar. They were truly a *colonial sugar bourgeoisie* spreading industrial modernity, although their progressiveness was confined to their narrow class interests. They created huge cartels and ruthlessly exploited labor and nature.[7] We will meet the members of the world's most important sugar dynasties: the

Karimis of Egypt, the Venetian Corner family in Cyprus, the Lascelles of Barbados, the Havemeyers and Fanjuls in the United States, and the Birla family in India. In the front of this book, the reader can find a list of the dramatis personae in the world of sugar.

Sugar's ascendency is a remarkable and globe-spanning story that covers more than two thousand years, the most important moments of which are indicated on a timeline included in the opening of this book. Over the centuries, humans have perfected the art of making sugar and unraveled the miracles of chemistry in service of the loftiest industrial and commercial goals. Sugar, once a soluble white gold, is omnipresent in every conceivable edible item today. This reality contains within it a history of human ingenuity—the transformation of something sweeter than nature into a bulk commodity. The ubiquity of sugar tells us about progress but also reveals a darker story of human exploitation, racism, obesity, and environmental destruction. Since sugar is a relatively recent phenomenon, we have not yet learned how to control it and bring it back to what it once was: a sweet luxury.

1

Asia's World of Sugar

ON A HOT SEPTEMBER DAY in 1826, Robert Mignan, a young British Army officer, stood at the banks of the Karoon River in the Persian province of Khuzestan. He had just left an unappealing small town built with stones cobbled together from the immense ruins stretching miles along the river. In old (probably Persian) documents he had read that the ruins related to a city pillaged during the Mongol invasion in the early thirteenth century. The army officer saw ruins of aqueducts, bridges, temples, and palaces but also objects that he found hard to identify: "In every direction I found vast heaps of circular flat stones, perforated in the centre, apparently used for the purpose of grinding grain; though rather *colossal,* indeed, for such a purpose, as they generally measured four, five, and six feet in diameter; and some exhibited characters upon them."[1] These stones, Mignan conjectured, could not have been for grain but must have belonged to "sugar manufactories." They came from a large number of mills that had ground the cane grown in fields along the river, which had been returned to forest long ago. Indeed, Mignan had stumbled on the ruins of an immensely important but forgotten sugar industry.[2]

Early nineteenth-century European explorers, linguists, historians, and geographers uncovered the depth and reach of the sugar economy of Asia. They already knew that Indian and Chinese manufacturers made sugar of equal or even superior quality to the sugar from the Atlantic realm, and that it was traded throughout Asia and even to Europe and North America. Chinese sugar, for example, reached almost every corner of Asia without a single European trader involved. One of these itineraries is described by an astonished Alexander Burnes, the diplomat, explorer, and contemporary of Mignan, in his bestselling travelogue on Central Asia: "The sugar had been first brought from China to Bombay, shipped from thence to Bushire, and then sent inland to Tehran and the banks of the Caspian, where it was a third time embarked, and transported across a desert to Khiva. It would there meet the sugar of our West India possessions, which is exported by the Russians, which would place the products of America and China in competition with each other in the centre of Asia."[3] Burnes, Mignan, and other scouts of the British Empire encountered a world of sugar that was older and much larger than the Atlantic sugar economy they knew.

The ruins visited by Mignan belonged to an industry producing crystal-line sugar, which had existed since the fifth century A.D. Not far from Abwaz, at the hospital of Gundisabur, sugar makers may have found out how to crystallize the boiling cane juice by elevating its pH level through adding lime or another alkaloid (this prevented the inversion of sucrose into glu-cose and fructose). The cooling and solidifying mass was subsequently shov-eled into pots, which might have had small holes in the bottom. The holes allowed the molasses—consisting of nonsucrose particles and noncrystal-lizable sucrose—to drip out while the white sugar crystals stayed behind.[4] From Abwaz and Gundisabur, the knowledge of how to cultivate cane and extract sugar from it traveled toward the Tigris-Euphrates Delta and fur-ther to Syria. As a result, the east coast of the Mediterranean Sea became the center of sugar cultivation by the ninth century.[5] Branching southward, sugar making reached the Nile Delta, which soon became the hub of sugar production for much of the Arab world as well as medieval Europe. Arabs and Berbers disseminated it throughout their Mediterranean territories and along the coast of East Africa, as far down as Zanzibar and Madagascar. Barbosa, the sixteenth-century Portuguese globetrotter, saw the cane abun-dantly growing on the latter island, although the knowledge of how to make sugar from it seemed to have been lost.[6] Cane was even cultivated in the Lake Regions of Central Africa and at the foot of the Kilimanjaro in East Africa, as the great Victorian explorers Livingstone, Burton, and Thornton documented.

India, Where It All Began . . .

White crystalline sugar was once a precious delicacy. For most of its exis-tence, it has been a luxury only affordable by the wealthiest on earth. Cane, by contrast, grew ubiquitously in many parts of Asia. From there it was introduced to North Africa, Southern Europe, and the New World. One only needs a big sharp knife to obtain a cane stalk for chewing. People in the countryside picked the stalks from the field, whereas in the cities they could buy them from street vendors. As the geographer Carl Ritter noted, children all over the tropical world, from Manila to the Sandwich Islands to Rio de Janeiro, had a sugar cane in their hands to chew on as a candy.[7]

The first step in processing cane was to press a juice from it, a delight which is still sold by vendors in South Asia today. This delicious raw juice has to be drunk within a day because cane starts fermenting immediately after harvesting. By boiling the juice into a solid mass, however, it could be stored for a few months. Somewhere in northern India, peasants must have begun to do this thousands of years ago. They kept the juice over a fire long enough for it to solidify into crude brown sugar, known as gur, and ate a chunk of it each winter morning before putting the plough to their fields. In addition to being a peasant's breakfast in the winter, chunks of gur were highly valued as energy bars. Exhausted pilgrims counted on hospitable villagers for some gur to recuperate; travelers passing the icy heights of the Hindu Kush toward Central Asia ate gur to ease their breathing; and

Street vendors selling sugar cane in Java, circa 1915. Cane stalks remain popular today, sold across the globe as a sweet delight to chew on.

soldiers were given it in their rations. Even animals shared in this consumption. Horses or oxen pulling carts over long distances were fed with gur, and elephants in palace stables chewed hay mixed with it.[8]

In northern India, the harvesting of cane and the boiling of its juice into a crude mass was solidly embedded in the agricultural cycle. Milling started in November, right after the harvest of paddy or other crops. Five to ten families, usually the richer villagers because cane was a luxury crop, combined their cattle and labor. The mill to grind the cane was often in common ownership within a village since few cultivators had enough land to make such a possession worthwhile. Workers without a plot of cane land were generally paid in kind with gur. In fact, gur was the currency for all kinds of village services, including the barber, the priest, the bard, the carpenter, and the blacksmith. Gur smoothened the village economy. And as long as gur was not sold outside the village, usually no money was involved.[9]

India's rural sugar was a sticky brown mass and utterly different from the white crystalline sugar we know today. But as we have seen, the art of making such granulated sugar was known already in Persia in the fifth century. And there is evidence of its manufacture in northern India three hundred years before that. The development of granular sugar is again a few hundred years older, since the Sanskrit word *sakkara,* which means gritty particles, came into use somewhere between 500 B.C. and 300 B.C.[10] Through extensive contacts between India and the Sassanid Empire, the knowledge of how to make granular sugar arrived in Gundisabur in Persia, from where it further spread to the west.[11] In the eastern direction, Indian sugar may have arrived in China as early as 200 B.C. Eight hundred years later, Buddhist monks from India made the long journey to teach the art of sugar making to the emperor's court, after which it percolated into urban environments.[12]

While white sugar had become known throughout Asia by the end of the first millennium A.D., it took another couple of centuries before it evolved into a commercial item as part of nascent capitalist economies in Eurasia. White sugar had to be paid for in gold as long as its manufacturing required so much effort. Most people at the time had no idea what sugar was, neither did they need it as they had access to a host of nonsucrose or largely nonsucrose sweeteners such as honey, glutinous rice, or barley. White sugar for centuries continued to be a luxury item and a sign of royal wealth and power among Chinese emperors, Indian rajas, Egyptian caliphs, the Persian courts and, later on, European monarchs and princes.

Today, cane or beet can be turned into white crystalline sugar within a matter of hours, but until the mid-nineteenth century the process took weeks, and it was an art not understood by many. In some Indian principalities, the manufacturing of white sugar was still a royal privilege at the time of Francis (Hamilton) Buchanan (1762–1829), the Scottish traveler, physician, and botanist. He informs us about local rulers who had their own sugar manufacturers working with secret recipes handed down from father to son for many generations.[13] Nonetheless, Buchanan was able to describe a variety of methods throughout India. These ranged from pressing the molasses out of a sack of raw sugar to putting the sugar mass in earthen pots with holes in the bottom. To remove the remaining molasses, sugar refiners in India placed waterweed on top of the sugar mass. From here water trickled down, rinsing out the molasses, which is more soluble than the crystals.[14] About a third remained as white sugar; the rest was molasses, still fit for human consumption, for cattle fodder, or for distilling spirits.

The refineries obtained their sugar through their agents who went to the countryside and made advance payments after an inspection of the cane standing in the field. Although the manufacturer charged 17–20 percent interest for a half-year advance, for the peasant families it was still a welcome additional income. It came at little economic cost, moreover, since they produced their gur in their slack season after other crops had been harvested.[15] While this raw sugar was still full of plant fibers and hence prone to rotting, the urban refineries removed most of these perishable particles. Fine *khandsari* (sugar manufactured using the waterweed refining method), or *quand* as it was alternatively called, could be stored for years if pure enough. Thus sugar became part of India's market economy.

Marco Polo found commercial sugar production thriving in Bengal, where cane was raised in abundance. At the time of his visit in the late thirteenth century, cane cultivation had already spread throughout northern India, and Delhi had a large sugar market. Firoz Shah Tugluq, the sultan of Bengal, would push sugar cultivation further through his canal construction projects in the Indus and Ganges plains in the second half of the fourteenth century.[16] The processing of cane developed in response to soaring demand; in Bengal the old laborious method of pressing cane by hand gave way to the pestle and mortar mill turned by cattle. Some of the oldest mills still survive today, sometimes with beautiful carvings in the stone mortars. Sugar making became an art organized through its own caste of sugar boilers.[17] Refining had become a professional occupation, and sugar commerce thrived—sugar capitalism had firmly taken root in urban India. From the refineries, sugar capitalism stretched out into the countryside via the purchasing of peasant sugar. It brought money into the village economy, and by the time of Marco Polo's visit wage labor and monetization had certainly taken hold.[18] If we define capitalism as a continuously advancing commodification of labor and nature for profit by private entrepreneurs, then India's sugar sector clearly exhibited a capitalist dynamic.

Initially, India's sugar trade was mainly overland. Caravans departed from India for Central Asia and traveled through Afghanistan to Herat, Kandahar, or Kabul, the hub of Indian-Central Asian trade. From here the caravans moved further into contemporary Uzbekistan: to Bukhara and Samarkand. Extensive caravans brought among their many products highly refined candy sugars deep into Central Asia and as far as in contemporary Turkmenistan.[19] When cane cultivation expanded, cheaper maritime transport began to overshadow India's overland trade. Barbosa noticed in the sixteenth century that white sugar was no longer an exquisite item but had emerged as a principal item of trade for Bengal. Along the Ganges, 500 kilometers into the interior cane grew everywhere, as François Bernier, physician at the court of India's Mughal emperor, noted in the seventeenth century. The Bengal River system carried many boats with different grades of sugar as well as molasses and alcoholic beverages. Reloaded on seaworthy ships, sugar reached Ceylon in the south and on to the west coast of India, which maintained a substantial sugar trade with the Persian Gulf and the Gulf of Aden.[20]

Bengal was not the only region in India where cane cultivation had expanded since the days of Marco Polo. The Dutch topographer Johannes de Laet, another seventeenth-century traveler of South Asia, observed that an extensive irrigation system served many of the thousands of square miles of farm land between Agra and Lahore, which allowed for the cultivation of a host of crops, and sugar in particular.[21] Cane was also to be found in India's Vijayanagara or Karnataka Empire, that stretched from the east to the west coast of the southern subcontinent and where ancient inscriptions attest to irrigated sugar cultivation.[22] As in Bengal, new crushing technology developed from an expanding demand for sugar in southern India. Here, a mill with two horizontal rollers dominated, and it produced a much cleaner juice that was less fibrous than the pestle and mortar, which continued to be used in northern India. Later on, via the Portuguese enclave of Goa, came another innovation: a three-roller vertical mill originating from the Iberian colonies in the Americas, which pushed the sugar sector in some parts of the south further ahead of northern India.[23]

The best sugar of India, according to Abbé Barthélemy Carré, an emissary and spy for the French king Louis XIV, was sold in the Portuguese city of Bassein, near today's Mumbai. It was exported at great profit to Persia and Arabia. Nodal points in this maritime sugar commerce were Baticala, Surat, and Cambay, famous port cities along the northwestern coast of India. Surat's hinterland, Gujarat, produced large quantities of sugar, as John Fryer, a surgeon employed by the East India Company, reported in the 1670s. In the Gujarati town of Ahmadabad, sugar refiners made sugar-loaves of powdered white sugar that were shipped west as far as to the Hadramaut coast, where caravans carried it into the interior of the Arabian Peninsula. In the east, sugar went to Malacca to be further distributed by its considerable Gujarati merchant community.[24] Indian khandsari sugar would serve European markets into the nineteenth century. Widely advocated by the British abolitionist movement, a trickle of India's immense sugar production reached England as an alternative to the increasingly controversial sugar produced by enslaved workers in the West Indies.

Chinese Sugar and Its Commerce

When the Berber Maghrebi scholar and explorer Ibn Battuta arrived in China, probably in 1346, he noticed that "there is abundant sugar-cane, equal, nay superior, in quality to that of Egypt."[25] Ibn Battuta was qualified to judge because he had visited both countries. China's Fujian province, Marco Polo had claimed, was the largest cane-growing area in the world, with the expansion of commercial sugar production crowding out rice cultivation.[26] Under the Sung Dynasty (960–1279), sugar consumption had spread from the court to populace and was used in medicines, pastries, conserves, and beverages. In Marco Polo's day, sugar featured in many pages of Chinese cookery books and appeared in the form of confectionery and edible sculptures. Sweetmeat sellers became a common sight in city life. Sugar consumption spread even to the countryside, albeit as a luxury for festive occasions. More than a century before Marco Polo came to China, candy sugar was already being shipped from Fujian—especially the city of Fuzhou—to Cambodia, Thailand, Srivijaya (Sumatra), the northern cities of the Malay Peninsula, and possibly even Japan.[27]

As had been the case in India, expanding sugar commerce resulted in less labor-intensive production methods. In the fourteenth century these replaced the exquisite craftsmanship that had developed under the Sung Dynasty, when Chinese sugar boilers had learned to manufacture crystalline sugar directly from syrup. They had chopped, peeled, squashed, and then boiled the cane before its juice was pressed out of it. Boiling of the squashed cane allowed sucrose to leave via the cell walls. As a final step, the juice was sieved through a piece of cloth. An exceptionally clean sugar mass was the result and when put aside for a couple of weeks, large, transparent, and almost white sugar crystals grew in it. These large crystals were highly sought after by the Sung court.[28] This labor-intensive production was already failing to keep up with the growing consumer market at the time Marco Polo visited China. He described how urban manufacturers refined the rough brown peasant sugar with charcoal, a process to which they had been introduced by foreigners. These foreigners, it has been suggested by scholars, were Egyptians.[29] Indeed, technology from the Arabian world had been smoothly transferred to China thanks to extensive contacts between the Chinese and Arabian empires since the seventh century. Chinese ships sailed as far as the Persian Gulf, and Iranian and Arabian merchants, some of whom traded in sugar, had premises in Canton.[30]

Under the Ming Dynasty (1368–1644), sugar production in Fujian rapidly expanded, catering to a growing number of cities with a hundred thousand inhabitants or more in the vast region south of the Yangzi River. Merchants went into the countryside and handed out advances to peasants to grow cane. Meanwhile, markets in Southeast Asia were also growing, and the Portuguese began to trade sugar with Japan. Later on, the Dutch engaged in this commerce as well. The growth of the sugar commerce encouraged further innovations to speed up the separation of the molasses from crystals. In a variation of the Indian method of putting waterweed on top of the sugar mass placed in cones, the Chinese used clay, which also released water slowly along the sugar crystals, separating them from the molasses. This procedure spread widely not only in China but also in the Mediterranean and Atlantic regions. In principle, a white refined sugar was the result, but there was some risk of the clay flavor persisting, and hence in Europe this product may have been used predominantly for preserving fruits.[31]

In southeast China, where sugar cultivation buoyed during the late Ming period (the early seventeenth century), the wooden-roller mill replaced the edge-runner mill with two mill stones. Similar to debates about the provenance of the printing press, the jury is still out on whether this particular Chinese mill was adopted by Europeans for their plantations in the New World or it was introduced in China as a European innovation by Jesuit priests. It is not unlikely either that the Chinese and Europeans developed their mills independently from each other.[32] At any rate, in China the cheap mills, which were easily transportable by cart or boat, stood the test of time remarkably well, and Chinese migrants disseminated them all over Southeast Asia.

The boiling process underwent radical innovations as well because the increase in sugar manufacturing quickly turned fuel wood into a scarce resource. Searching for ways to save energy, Chinese sugar makers developed a battery of cauldrons on top of a flue that ran from a single fire to a chimney. Sucheta Mazumdar suggests that this device, or at least the prototype of a "multi aperture stove," was soon copied by the Dutch, who might have seen it in operation in Java. They introduced it at their plantations in Brazil, whence it spread throughout the Caribbean region.[33] Sugar technology traveled remarkably fast in the seventeenth century across every thinkable cultural boundary, and if new mills or any other equipment were not adopted, it was usually for perfectly sound economic reasons.

The expanding acreage under cane as well as improved milling and boiling techniques turned Fujian into a major sugar exporter to Southeast Asia.[34] Japan was another destination for Fujian sugar, the Japanese having become acquainted with sugar in the seventh or eighth century when ambassadors of the Chinese Tang emperors and Buddhist priests brought it with them, probably for medicinal purposes. Consumption really expanded when the Portuguese introduced candies, caramels, and cookies to Japan in the sixteenth century, and when sugar entered the traditional rice cakes and dumplings.[35] In the early seventeenth century, in order to capitalize on the growing demand for sugar in Japan, a fleet of about one hundred Chinese vessels defied the Ming ban on sugar trading and unloaded up to three thousand tons annually at the port of Nagasaki, the only Japanese port they were allowed to call.[36]

Without doubt, the sugar production of southeast China and India's Gangetic plains widely surpassed that of the Atlantic colonies in the seventeenth century. None of these sites were colonial export enclaves like in the Atlantic realm, however—with one notable exception. The world's largest sugar-exporting colony in the early eighteenth century was not located in the Atlantic world, as one might expect, but near China on the island of Taiwan. This new sugar frontier emerged in response to the strains that commercial production of sugar and other crops had put on the population of southeast China. As the most densely populated region of the world at that time, it entered a phase of precarity. Tenants' debts accumulated and peasants rose up in droves against their exploitative landlords in the 1620s and 1630s, plunging the region in chaos, pulling the rug from under the Ming Dynasty, and opening the door to their Xing successors.[37]

For the Dutch East India Company (Dutch: Vereenigde Oostindische Compagnie [VOC]), this turmoil came as a serious setback, because it had planned to buy sugar from southeast China to sell in Japan. In 1609, it had become the only European company to secure the permission of the Tokugawa shogunate, Japan's military rulers, to call at the port of Nagasaki. Now, it reverted to an alternative scheme that turned Taiwan into one of the world's most important preindustrial sugar frontiers. After the VOC had gained a foothold on this thinly populated and fertile island, its governor introduced sugar cane and attracted Chinese workers skilled in cane cultivation. The Dutch were expelled in 1662, but their pioneering presence ultimately led to the emergence of Taiwan as the world's largest sugar exporter. In the early eighteenth century, more than a thousand mills produced an estimated sixty thousand tons of sugar in Taiwan, widely exceeding the output of Brazil, which was by far the largest Atlantic producer at that time. The workforce consisted overwhelmingly of male migrant labor from mainland China organized into *kongsis* or companies—the general model for Chinese migrant workers on plantations and in mines throughout Southeast Asia.[38] To mill the cane, farmers formed cooperatives, combining their oxen to turn the mills. Alternatively, private entrepreneurs engaged in sugar manufacturing by contracting with fifty to a hundred peasants to supply their mills with cane. In both models, wholesale dealers who oversaw the export of sugar and rice to mainland China stood at the top of chain.[39]

Sugar mill from Liu-shi-qi's *Illustrations of Taiwan Savage Villages* (1744–1747). In the early eighteenth century, Taiwan was the world's largest sugar exporter.

Taiwan's sugar exports stagnated by the mid-eighteenth century, by which time sugar production in Guangdong had recovered and sugar had emerged as one of the most important commodities—if not the most important—in China's coastal commerce, where it became interwoven with the cotton trade. Smaller quantities were traded throughout the Indian Ocean, and some of it even reached Europe. Well into the nineteenth century, sugar in Guangdong and Fujian remained a crop more popular and more commercially rewarding than rice. In some Guangdong counties at least one in every two households grew cane.[40] Yet despite this intense commercialization, sugar cane continued to be a peasant crop just like in India and, in contrast to the Atlantic world, cultivation and milling were not combined on a single estate. Since the root cause of the widespread rebellions against the Ming rulers had been the enserfing of the smallholders, the Xing emperors were keen to prevent the emergence of large sugar estates and protected the small peasantry, but obviously without stopping the commercialization of production in the countryside and the exploitation of its population.

Urban capitalists exploited the peasantry via high-interest advances, low prices for cane, and stiff charges for milling and boiling. These merchants sent their agents to provide advances on the basis of the cane standing in fields and often organized milling and boiling teams. The cane was brought from the field to the riverside, where the sugar makers, according to the eighteenth-century traveler Charles Gustavus Eckeberg, built "a hut of bamboo and mats, at one end of which they make a furnace with two great iron boilers; and at the other an even floor of considerable size laid with planks, over which two oxen draw an angulated roller of hard wood."[41] Here, the simple and easily transportable two-roller mills proved their value, because merchants could send them with the boilers to the fields, often using local waterways. While the refineries of northern Europe burned ever more wood, peat, and even coal to reboil the sugar and skim off more non-sucrose particles, Chinese refiners, who were short of fuel wood, dried and bleached their sugar in the sun. Thanks to the skill and resourcefulness of its craftsmen, Chinese sugar continued to be appreciated across the globe well into the nineteenth century.

Meanwhile, Japan brought its sugar sector in line with its autarkic trajectory. Worried about the nation's growing sugar consumption, its rulers encouraged domestic production and put a ceiling on sugar imports. In the early eighteenth century, the shogun of Japan gained control over the Ryukyu Islands—the string of islands between Taiwan and Japan, where the Chinese had introduced sugar cultivation—and encouraged the islanders to provide sugar for the Japanese market. The shogun also ordered the import of cane seedlings from these islands and had them distributed in Japan's warmer southern islands.[42] Shikoku Island, located in the southern region of Japan, became renowned for its *wasanbon,* a fine-grained sugar used for sweets. This sugar was procured by putting raw sugar in cloth and kneading it with water to remove the molasses. After repeating this process three times, it was dried for a week. Mixed with rice flours and shaped in molds, it was served as a delicacy. During tea ceremonies the participants put these sweets *(wagashi)* in their mouth before sipping their bitter tea. Since sugar was not used in dishes, consumption stayed at less than two hundred grams per capita, per year. Thus, Japan was able to dispense with sugar imports for most of the nineteenth century.[43]

Chinese Sugar in Southeast Asia

Chinese sugar cultivators not only crossed the sea lane to Taiwan; over time they could be found all over Southeast Asia. Facilitated by Chinese merchant networks, farmers from the overcrowded counties of southeast China spread the art of sugar making over land and sea.[44] In much of Southeast Asia there was some trade in sugar, but it was probably not locally produced before Chinese immigrants introduced their milling and refining technology.[45] As noted above, in mainland China, sugar was a peasant crop integrated in the rice cycle and linked to urban refiners, but this was not the case in Taiwan or in Southeast Asia, at least not initially. Overseas, sugar estates emerged that integrated field and mill. The Chinese millers around Batavia, for instance, hired workers via Javanese headmen or recruited enslaved people in addition to Chinese migrants, who predominantly had supervising roles and operated the crushing and boiling equipment.[46]

This overseas expansion continued into the nineteenth century and traveled as far as Hawaii. Shortly after Captain Cook had visited those islands as the first European in 1778, they became a destination for Chinese traders in sandalwood. One ship involved in this commerce carried a mill and boilers to Hawaii in 1802, and more would follow, all owned and operated by Chinese who had acquired plots of land via their Hawaiian wives. This was, however, just the final chapter in a long story of widely spreading Chinese sugar production that had begun well before the first European vessels reached East and Southeast Asia. The migration of Chinese cane cultivators and sugar manufacturers may have already been underway at the time Ibn Battuta visited Fujian and noted its growing sugar exports.

The bustling fourteenth-century hub of Chinese traders on the Ryukyu Islands was probably the first overseas Chinese sugar frontier, followed by mainland Southeast Asia and the western tip of Java. Chinese migrants settling in the Philippines brought sugar to the large island of Luzon in the north, but this probably did not happen before the Spanish came in the early sixteenth century.[47] Under Spanish rule, Chinese settlers confined themselves to refining and repacking sugar from one of the thousands of small mills that crushed sugar with stone rollers that were mostly turned by cattle.[48] In *farderias* (places for the drying and packing of sugar), Chinese sugar merchants in Manila prepared this sugar for export. Thanks also to British and American merchants, export volumes quadrupled between 1789 and 1831 to over thirteen thousand tons, an output comparable to that of a middling Caribbean producer such as Barbados.[49]

Chinese entrepreneurs established their sugar estates throughout Southeast Asia, and most of their output catered to the international sugar trade. Chinese immigrant sugar makers turned Siam into a supplier of sugar to the VOC, for instance.[50] Pierre Poivre, the famous French botanist who visited Cochin-China—the southern part of present-day Vietnam— reported a flourishing Chinese sugar industry in 1749–1750, which in his estimation produced forty-six thousand tons of sugar annually. Although this was probably an exaggeration, he indubitably witnessed a thriving sector that served an expanding Chinese market.[51] A few decades after Poivre's visit, political turmoil and military conflicts caused a severe decline of production in Siam and Cochin-China, which produced not more than a few thousand tons of a brown, unrefined quality by the early nineteenth century.[52]

However, since famine and violence held southeast China in their grip during these years, thousands of peasants traveled to Siam to regenerate its sugar sector.[53] Bishop Jean-Baptiste Pallegoix, vicar apostolic in Siam, noted dozens of sugar plantations that were owned by Chinese. He describes one of these Chinese estates as being equipped with two-cylinder crushers of ironwood and two huge sheds, in which a remarkably white sugar was manufactured by about two hundred workers.[54] By the late 1850s, sugar had become Siam's leading export, with about twelve thousand tons reaching markets from North America to Germany annually. This was all achieved with traditional mills as the first two steam-driven sugar crushers only arrived in Siam in the 1860s. It is telling that the global competitiveness of Chinese sugar making persisted at a time when the Industrial Revolution had already significantly reshaped global sugar production.[55]

European observers held Chinese sugar makers in high esteem. Pierre Poivre was deeply impressed by the Chinese sugar millers he saw in Cochin-

China and by the abundance and quality of sugar they produced at a much better price than the Caribbean region. Poivre concluded that each free worker could produce twice as much sugar as an enslaved one in the New World, and after his trip to Cochin-China in 1749 he therefore advocated importing Chinese workers and artisans to Mauritius.[56] Actually, in western Sumatra such an estate with Chinese labor was established in 1777 by Henry Botham, a planter who had first tried to make a career in the West Indies but had become deeply disturbed by how the enslaved workers were abused. His experiment in Sumatra drew a lot of attention, including from the British Parliament's committee debating the abolition of slavery. Called to testify, Botham praised his Chinese labor gangs for working diligently without supervision, very different from his experience in the West Indies.[57]

Not long after Botham had established a plantation in Sumatra, the British East India Company invited Chinese sugar makers to Penang, their newly acquired island just off the coast of the Malaccan Peninsula. Soon, a Chinese labor force of around two thousand immigrants, probably from Guangdong, worked in the fields and processed cane in well-constructed stone sheds. After each milling season, workers returned home from this prosperous venture with their pockets filled.[58] The expanding number of immigrants enabled Chinese pioneers to cross the sea lane between Penang into the Malaccan Peninsula, drain the swamps of the province of Wellesley, and start sugar cultivation there as well.

The Dutch had already set the example, of course. They had seen the great potential of Chinese sugar making for their fledgling trading empire from the very moment they set foot on Javanese soil in 1596. In the marketplace of Banten, at the most western tip of the island, they found sugar, and at the city of Jacatra they encountered Chinese mills producing arrack (a rum-like drink made from fermented cane).[59] The VOC wasted no time inserting itself into the local sugar trade. It had barely erased the city of Jacatra and replaced it with its own Asian capital, Batavia, when the first fifty tons of sugar left for Amsterdam. This sugar came from the land south of Batavia, which VOC officials had appropriated and rented out to Chinese millers. By the early eighteenth century, sugar production for the VOC spread further along Java's north coast and emerged together with coffee as one of the company's new core commodities after profits from of its spice trade shrank.

The aforementioned Taiwan sugar frontier was more or less an offshoot of the Sino-Dutch collaboration in Java. After the VOC's governor of Taiwan had pushed the frontier into the interior at the expense of the aborigines in 1636, he issued a call for immigrants from China's mainland, promising them a four-year tax exemption and land ownership. A key role in bringing this message across had been assigned to Su Minggang, the leader of the Chinese community in the VOC capital, Batavia. He originated from Fujian and was a close friend of Governor-General Jan Pieterszoon Coen, Batavia's founder. Su Minggang sold his beautiful Batavia mansion in 1636 to start sugar plantations in Taiwan and act as the VOC agent in Fujian, in which he seems not to have been very successful. Nonetheless, a steady stream of migrants, mills, and planks for sugar boxes must have entered the island in the 1640s.[60] A bigger problem was that the immigrant sugar workers were being exploited by the Chinese merchants who organized the sugar production in Taiwan and who charged excessive interest rates for their advances. A severe drought in 1652 was the last straw, and they rose up in a revolt that was suppressed by the Dutch, who butchered between 2,500 and 4,000 poorly armed rebels. The Chinese workers rose up again when Zheng Chenggong (known as Koxinga by Europeans) invaded Taiwan in 1661. This was for them an opportunity to rid themselves from their Dutch oppressors.[61]

This would not be the last time the Dutch found out that relying on Chinese entrepreneurship and immigrant communities was like trying to ride a tiger. Whereas in Taiwan they had struggled to recruit Chinese immigrants, sugar production south of Batavia by far exceeded VOC demand, which had reserved for itself the sole right of purchase. Overproduction prompted the VOC to set a draconian ceiling on its purchases, resulting in a sharp decline in the number of mills. Batavia nonetheless still attracted so many Chinese immigrants that the Dutch residents of the city became increasingly worried. Rumors about a conspiracy brewing among the Chinese population were enough to bring the Dutch to a state of murderous frenzy, and the infamous Chinese massacre of 1740 was the result. Terrible as this act was, it did not destroy Chinese sugar production in Java. Thirty years later, output had not only recovered but reached a record level of four to five thousand tons, and would even have expanded further if it had not come up against the ecological limits of soil exhaustion and fuel wood shortages.[62]

Asian Sugar Crossing the Oceans

The European trading companies played a junior role in Asia's world of sugar, but it was still a lucrative one precisely because sugar was so widely traded and consumed in this part of the world. The VOC was particularly active in this commerce since it had developed into a trading multinational for whom European markets became of diminishing importance. Some Asian sugar reached Europe, but most of the sugar the VOC vessels took on board was sold for other items that found willing markets in Europe: initially spices and later on tea and bone china. The VOC bought sugar of a variety of qualities to serve different markets. It could sell, for example, its poor-quality Bengal sugar to Japan, while calling at the port of Surat with higher-quality sugar from the Chinese millers around Batavia.[63]

Persia was a major market for both the VOC and the British West India Company, which together brought in hundreds of tons of khandsari from Bengal and later on sugar from Batavia. But their involvement proved temporary, and in the course of the eighteenth century VOC sugar sales at Red Sea and Persian Gulf ports declined, allowing the Gujarati merchants in West India to take over this trade. They transported not only increasing volumes of sugar from their own hinterland and Bengal but also sugar that originated from Java and even from the Philippines. Ships under a variety of flags unloaded their sugar in Bandar Abbas, located at the entrance of the Persian Gulf and, subsequently, further into the Gulf at the port of Basra.[64]

These growing volumes easily found their way to the many sherbet (lemonade) houses that existed in all major cities of the Ottoman Empire. Some of these such as Baghdad, were true metropoles with over half a million inhabitants.[65] Meanwhile, French trading houses, particularly those located in Marseille, brought Caribbean sugar to Smyrna, Izmir, Istanbul, and Aleppo, as well as to Persia by the end of the eighteenth century, where it arrived alongside sugar from India and Egypt. Most of the Caribbean sugar was probably *muscovado* and much cheaper than more refined sugars from Egypt. Price mattered since sugar became ever more popular with the growing consumption of coffee.[66] At the same time, Russian refineries were exporting their processed Caribbean sugar deep into Central Asia. Highly valued by wealthier consumers, it competed with sugar arriving with the caravans from India.[67]

Asian sugar trade appears as less prominent in the historical record than the associated Atlantic commerce by around 1800, but that is not a true reflection of the surviving evidence. From India, for instance, exports to the United States, Britain, Persia, and Arabia amounted to about twenty thousand tons by 1805. Fifteen years later, from the port of Calcutta alone, about 12,800 tons left for ports as far away as Cape Town and Australia, and over seven thousand tons for Britain.[68] Apart from Jamaica and Cuba, none of the Caribbean islands exported more than ten to fifteen thousand tons at that time. In addition to increasing volumes destined for Europe and the United States, considerable quantities of sugar left from Bombay for various ports along the Western Indian Ocean coast and further to the Red Sea, from where Persian merchants took them as far as Turkmenistan in the north and Arab traders to Mozambique in the south.[69]

In the bustling port of Bombay, sugar was the single largest item of trade in terms of value in the early nineteenth century, as it was in Cambay—located in present-day Gujarat—where annual imports of different grades of sugar may have amounted to twelve thousand tons.[70] Sugar arriving in the port of Bombay not only came from Bengal but also from China—about 6,600 tons in 1805—and was sold along the Malabar Coast. Madras and Calcutta exported a substantial volume of sugar in various qualities themselves, while importing high-quality candy sugar from China and some sugar from Batavia.[71] However odd this crisscrossing trading pattern may seem, it perfectly suited the taste of consumers for different grades and grains of either Chinese or Indian sugars.

The sugar belts of Southeast China easily sustained substantial maritime and overland trade. British and American ships purchased annually several tons of sugar in Canton in the early nineteenth century, and the British acquired as much as 7,500 tons in 1831.[72] Chinese traders catered to markets located as far west as in Yarkand, which bordered on the Himalayas. Penang, Batavia, and Cochin-China all exported sugar manufactured by Chinese millers to India, including to the harbor of Calcutta. The new port of Singapore received Chinese sugar from Siam, Cochin-China, and possibly Batavia. From this port traders carried sugar along the east coast of the Malaccan Peninsula toward the Sulu archipelago north of Borneo. Finally, via Bombay, Chinese sugar reached the most remote destinations in Central Asia.[73]

Until the final decades of the nineteenth century, sugar exports from southeast China, Taiwan, Siam, and India thrived. Taiwan's sugar exports boomed thanks to growing demand from Japan, Australia, the Hong Kong refineries, and even from California.[74] In 1856, the American firm Robinet & Co. was the first Western firm since the VOC had been expelled from Taiwan to do business on the island. It exported sugar to California until Claus Spreckels, the leading San Francisco refiner, built his own plantation empire in Hawaii in the 1870s. In some districts of Guangdong in southeast China, 90 percent of exports was accounted for by sugar, thanks also to modern sugar refineries that emerged in some of the coastal cities. The prominent Hong Kong trading firm Jardine Matheson, with its offices in various Chinese cities and Japan, opened a refinery in Huangpu in 1869 and another a few years later in Shantou (Swatow). It built a third one in Hong Kong, where the powerful Butterfield & Swire Taikoo firm had already established a gigantic refinery. Chinese sugar, produced by peasants but increasingly industrially refined, continued to be competitive on the world market until the very end of the nineteenth century.[75]

2

Sugar Going West

WHEN THE ART OF SUGAR MAKING traveled from India eastward to China 1,500 years ago, it moved west from Persia to Mesopotamia and onward to the eastern shores of the Mediterranean Sea and Egypt. After being introduced in the Nile Delta in the eighth century, cultivation gradually moved up along the river to upper Egypt. Two hundred years later, Egypt was the main supplier for both the Muslim and Christian worlds. Thousands of smallholders grew cane, usually combining it with other crops. They tended thousands of hectares under cane, each of which might have produced about one to two tons of raw sugar annually. They drew their water from the Nile, and when the river was low their oxen turned the water wheels to feed the irrigation channels. Overarching mud dams around the cane fields served to keep mice out.[1]

The Egyptian peasants delivered their cane to a caliph's or, later on, sultan's official or directly to the government-licensed holder of the press.[2] These Egyptian sugar mills are among the oldest that have been described in detail. They were actually identical to the olive oil mills in use since antiquity and equipped with a horizontally positioned under-stone on which a vertically placed upper-stone was turned via a horizontal beam using animal power. Since these implements could not crush entire stalks the cane first had to be cleaned and cut into small pieces. The mash was shoveled into baskets and put under a stone roller to squeeze out the remaining juice, which was then sieved through a piece of cloth before boiling. The resulting sugar mass was subsequently put in cones with small holes on top and placed upside down to allow molasses to drip out, a procedure that may have originated from Persia but was further developed in Egypt. The upside-down cones were also covered with mud, which had the same effect as clay or waterweed. In urban refineries, this still raw sugar was dissolved in water and milk—containing the necessary egg white—was added to purify the sugar.[3]

Egypt's major cities hosted dozens of sugar refineries that made a highly and widely appreciated white sugar. Caravans of hundreds of camels, carrying as much as 150 tons of sugar, left Egypt for other parts of the Arabian world.[4] This commerce relied on skilled sugar masters and particularly on the Karimi, a powerful merchant network that was predominantly but not exclusively Muslim as it counted some Jewish members. Often of humble descent, these famously wealthy Karimi—portrayed as true bourgeois by the historian Eliyahu Ashtor—controlled the spice and slave trades. They now engaged in the sugar trade and even bought or established sugar factories.[5] Their network expanded with Egypt's sugar production and followed the territorial conquests of the Mamluk sultans, who ruled the country after the thirteenth century. These sultans added the high-quality sugar production along the east coast of the Mediterranean Sea and in the Jordan Valley to their already considerable production in the Nile Valley and Delta.

With the advent of the Crusades in the Levant—the eastern shoreline of the Mediterranean Sea—a period of nearly two hundred years began that would play a crucial role in familiarizing Europe with sugar, which was scarcely known in the Christian world at that time. The knights of the Teutonic Order, the Templars, and the Hospitallers appropriated sugarcane fields on the domains of Muslim landlords near Tripoli (in today's Israel) and Tiberias (in today's Lebanon). They expeditiously turned sugar into a major source of income to underwrite their orders, which had been established by the pope to facilitate the pilgrimage to Jerusalem. In addition, the Hospitallers used sugar abundantly to treat their patients.[6]

The Hospitallers and Templars expanded sugar production in the Levant and the Jordan Valley, put their Muslim prisoners of war to the fields and advanced sugar production technologically. Canals guided water to waterwheels with sufficient velocity and volume to turn the heavy milling stones around. The squeezed cane went to a room where a press extracted more juice, instead of putting the mangled stalks in a sack and putting them under a roller again as was the practice in Egypt. In large copper cauldrons, the syrup was boiled until the point of crystallization and then put in the well-known conical pots. These have been excavated in large numbers by archaeologists, who determined that large sugar refineries were in operation at the outskirts of Acre or Akko, the capital of the Second Latin Kingdom, which was established by the Crusaders in 1192.[7]

The Crusaders' sugar production in the Levant ended when they were driven from the last vestiges of their conquests in 1291, but it did not stop the flow of sugar to Europe. Under Mamluk rule, exports from Egypt and its dependencies reached new heights despite a papal ban on trading with Muslim nations. Venice and Genoa simply dodged the ban or paid the Vatican a dispensation for their transgressions.[8] The Mamluk government and powerful Egyptian families further developed the sugar belt in the Jordan Valley.[9] Alexandria affirmed its position as the central hub connecting the spice trade from the Indian Ocean, Egypt's sugar trade, and commodities exported from Europe. The "Frankish" (Italian, French, and Catalan) merchants in Alexandria operated under protection of the sultan. In 1327, he did not hesitate to send an army to the city to ruthlessly suppress mob violence against the European traders, which was probably incited by the Karimi in response to foreign competition.[10]

Meanwhile, Venice and Genoa had developed other sources than Egypt, drawing growing amounts of sugar from Cyprus where Crusaders had started cane cultivation in the wake of the island's conquest by Richard Lionheart. After the expulsion of the Crusaders from the Levant in 1291, the island became a major provider of sugar for the European market. Many traders from various Italian cities based their operations in the Cypriot port of Famagusta. The Lusignan kings of Cyprus derived a substantial income from sugar exports, although over time they had to concede to the Genoese and Venetians much of their economic power.[11]

One branch of the famously wealthy and powerful Venetian Corner family obtained a large domain in return for their loans to the House of Lusignan, which had incurred large debts fighting off the Mamluk Empire. On this domain, which was near the village of Piskopi, they established a huge plantation in 1361.[12] Three to four hundred workers tended and harvested the cane, making it one of Europe's largest agro-industrial enterprises at the time. Archaeologists have reconstructed the sophisticated water-powered mills in Cyprus. At the heart of such a complex stood a central mill that drew its water from an aqueduct that ended in a pressure channel to propel the waterwheel. After having gone through the classical runner-stone mill, the mashed cane was squeezed again by water power, which turned two smaller stones with a horizontal runner-stone. Like the

Excavation of the cane sugar refinery at Kouklia-Stavros, Cyprus. In the late thirteenth and fourteenth centuries, the Mediterranean island was a major producer of cane sugar, which reached Europe via Italian traders.

Crusaders in Akko, the Corners refined their sugar on the spot, for which purpose they had imported copper boilers from Venice.[13] A Venetian pilgrim visiting this estate on his way to Jerusalem marveled at the impressive volumes of sugar leaving the mill, which he thought would be enough for the entire world.[14]

The Venetian traveler obviously exaggerated; the flourishing of the Cypriot plantations did not eliminate the sugar trade between the Mamluk territories and European merchants. It certainly received a heavy blow when the Black Death reached Egypt in 1348 and killed between a third and half of its population. Many cane fields were deserted and intricate irrigation systems became dilapidated.[15] On top of this, raiding desert tribes upset the agricultural rhythm, while droughts brought waterwheels to a halt. Of the sixty-six sugar mills that were in operation in Egypt's sugar center, Fusṭāṭ, only nineteen still produced sugar after the first wave of the Plague. Elsewhere in Egypt's sugar producing regions the situation was not less dramatic.[16]

Egypt's sugar production did recover, however, and its exports to Europe flourished again after a Genoese-Venetian delegation obtained a peace treaty with the sultan in Cairo in 1370. The Vatican granted dispensations to a host of European merchants for trade with Cairo and Syria, which turned out to be attractive sources of income for the church. The Mamluk rulers continued to be favorably disposed to European traders, some of whom had acquired fluency in Arabic. Cog ships, which could traverse longer distances and had larger holds than galleys, gave this commerce additional momentum. The Genoese cog trade with Alexandria overshadowed those of all other European nations and was also directly connected with England and Flanders, whence was brought linen for the Levant. In these years also, the Genoese merchants created the basis for their expansion into the Atlantic realm.[17]

This expansion into the Atlantic Ocean followed a movement of production toward the western Mediterranean in the wake of a severe decline of the vitally important Mamluk sugar economy in the early fifteenth century. The Turco-Mongol troops of Tamerlane overran the Jordan Valley and went on to destroy the great city of Damascus in 1401. Meanwhile, changes in the climate had led to more droughts, and the recurring Plague severely diminished agricultural output. While the Mamluk sultans desperately tried to shore up their shattered revenues by creating monopolies, including of sugar, they eliminated the independent sugar traders and producers, and thus a vibrant sugar bourgeoisie.[18] The once thriving sugar economy of the Middle East crumbled, and, although Egypt's sugar industry again recovered in the sixteenth century, its trade with the Christian world had ended.[19]

The destruction caused by the Black Death and Tamerlane's invasion was of crucial geopolitical significance as it ushered in the detachment of Europe from the Asian sugar economy.[20] European merchant houses expanded existing sites of sugar production or sought new ones. The Venetians, for instance, attempted to cultivate cane in its Chania kingdom on Crete, which was famous for its exports of grain and wine, but sugar never became a successful crop there. Old sites of sugar production that were established centuries before by Muslim rulers were revived with greater success. In the wake of the Arab conquests in the western Mediterranean region in the seventh century, sugar production had spread through the western Maghreb and crossed into Spain and Sicily. Via this route, the technology that had been developed in Persia and Egypt arrived on the Iberian Peninsula.[21] Cane was grown in small quantities in the Andalusian Muslim kingdom of Granada, for instance, where it served as a source of income for its rulers, the builders of the magnificent Alhambra. Genoese traders disseminated the exports from Granada's port cities to the still small but rapidly growing European market.[22] On the east coast of Spain, the Kingdom of Valencia established a thriving sugar belt serving markets in southern France and even southern Germany.

Sicily also became a sugar producer of some consequence at this time. In the thirteenth century Frederick Barbarossa, the famous German emperor and crusader who held court in Sicily, revived the island's languishing cultivation that had been introduced by the Arabs three centuries before. He hired Syrian sugar makers because as a crusader he had seen with his own eyes the sophisticated level of sugar manufacturing in the Levant.[23] The modest sugar production of Sicily was reinvigorated when the decline of Egyptian sugar production encouraged rich Sicilians to make major investments in their estates. Aqueducts arose to transfer water over considerable distances to irrigate the fields and provide water power for milling.[24] The mills employed used the same stones that had pressed oil from olives since the days of the Roman Empire. Known as the *siculi trapetum,* it was in use throughout the Mediterranean region. Since Sicily did not have enough workers to tend and mill the cane, landlords brought workers from as far away as present-day Albania.[25]

While the quality of sugar in Egypt, the Levant, and Cyprus might have matched the best Chinese and Indian product, the sugar from the western Mediterranean region, while being much cheaper, was also much inferior.[26] For the galley trade, this was a serious problem because in a raw condition sugar needed about twice as much space than when refined, making its long-distance transport prohibitively expensive. The cog ships, however, made it profitable to bring relatively raw sugar to the refineries in northern Italy, northern Europe, and Antwerp in particular. By the mid-fifteenth century, just a few decades after the demise of the Egyptian sugar belt, these ships started to bring sugar from Madeira to Europe. The Atlantic age had begun.

Mediterranean Afterglow

Europe's rise to become the center of global capitalism began in the Mediterranean Basin, and sugar played a key role in this. The history of sugar also demonstrates, however, that this capitalism began as part of a much larger Eurasian system. From Shantou to Surat and from Cairo to Antwerp, merchants loaded their ships or caravans with ever-growing volumes of sugar. The international sugar trade involved merchant classes from China, India, Egypt, and the Spanish province of Málaga. It crossed religious divides and even filled the Vatican's coffers via dispensations and absolutions. Sugar became a crucial source of revenue for rulers. Trade between Persia, Egypt, and the Levant and the Venetians, Genoese, and other European trading communities flourished until the early fifteenth century. The establishment of sugar-making expertise in the Iberian Peninsula, Portuguese explorations in the Atlantic, and the long-distance trade of the Genoese played a crucial role in bringing sugar into the Atlantic realm.

The fourteenth century had seen powerful merchant networks such as the aforementioned Karimi dominating the long-distance routes of the sugar trade. To control trade routes, eliminate competition, and increase profits, the local urban bourgeoisie forged regional networks, a phenomenon that reappears time and again in the history of sugar. Members of influential families were sent to overseas ports to control the sugar trade. The Humpis family, which dominated the sugar trade of Valencia, had Ravensburg as its economic and political base but was also present in the great city of Avignon, which was for a while the papal seat. This family played a leading role in the Great Ravensburg Trading Company, a merger of several family networks spread across southern Germany.[27] Like other less renowned trading networks, the Humpis family and their partners secured their monopolies through kinship bonds, which were extended and underwritten by marriages.

Nonetheless, the assembled economic power of these family networks did not make them less dependent on the policies and whims of powerful rulers. The Karimi network had experienced this to its detriment when the Mamluk rulers tightened economic control under pressure of climate change, the Plague, and the incursion of Tamerlane. The Great Ravensburg Trading Company, which commercially linked southern Germany with the Mediterranean region, saw its fortunes dwindle in the late fifteenth century, when Europe's economic center of gravity rapidly shifted from the Mediterranean Sea to the north and increasing volumes of sugar traveled directly from Madeira to Bruges and Antwerp.[28] The Portuguese and Spanish courts emerged as the key actors in a new era of capitalism moving into and across the Atlantic Ocean. At that time the Great Ravensburg Trading Company was dissolved and the Humpis family retreated to the countryside as landed aristocrats.

That the courts of Lisbon and Madrid involved themselves directly in the international sugar production and trade was a sign of the times. Because of its high commercial value, sugar was a commodity of geopolitical importance. In contrast to grain, olive oil, and wine, the refining and trading of sugar was tightly controlled by the ruling elites who nevertheless depended on merchant communities to provide capital and reach distant markets.[29] The Mamluk sultans of Egypt cooperated with the Karimi and Frankish merchants, the Crusader States with the Venetians and Genoese, the Muslim Granada kingdom with the Genoese, and the Kingdom of Valencia with the Great Ravensburg Trading Company. Genoese merchants helped to save the Nasrid princes, and the Venetian Corner family even obtained the royal crown of Cyprus as a result of their financial ties with the island's rulers, the House of Lusignan. Likewise, the Iberian Christian kings knew that only by harnessing Florentine and Genoese capital would they be able to develop sugar production in Madeira and the Canary Islands and have the sugar shipped off to the ports of Flanders.[30] On the Canary Islands, the Portuguese and Genoese, seconded by Catalans and Florentines with the Welsers and Fuggers—the powerful Augsburg bankers—in the background, set the tone as owners of sugar estates. Although Flemish merchants did not own estates, their ships did call on these islands to load sugar.[31]

In contrast to India, China, and Egypt, sugar production in the Christian principalities involved not individual peasants but large estates. It was driven by a close collaboration between merchants and princes, and it pushed aside food crops and viticulture in its relentless quest for fertile land and water. The most powerful actors of medieval Christendom clashed in their competition for precious natural resources, often requiring the intervention of royals and even the pope. The pontiff himself had to settle a conflict between the Templars and Hospitallers who operated estates near Acre and who vied for water to power their mills and grow their cane.[32] In Cyprus, the Corner family's estate near Piskopi and the neighboring plantation of the Hospitallers fiercely competed for water from the same river. Royal officials eventually had to intervene and diverted the water toward the Hospitallers' estate. Since the diversion destroyed part of the Venetian estate's cane, it must have created a crisis between the Lusignan king and his Venetian financiers.[33]

On the Christian Mediterranean sugar estates, the mills were built on-site and production relied on imported workers—this again in complete contrast to mainland China and India where the mills were brought to the fields. Madeira had seen small landowners growing cane for capitalist mill owners, but over time they were pushed aside by the mill owners in the struggle for shrinking natural resources.[34] On the Canary Islands, water was scarce, and the Spanish government, keen to turn their colonial conquest into a sugar frontier, restricted the land that had access to water to capitalists with the means to build a mill. Large land grants were made to ensure owners would have jurisdiction over a river from its fountainhead to the sea.[35] Sugar capitalism entailed a relentless struggle for resources that usually ended in the subjugation or expulsion of small landowners and the integration of field and mill. It started in the Mediterranean Basin, continued in the eastern Atlantic islands, and adopted its most radical shape in the small Caribbean islands. Although the integration of field and mill was not unique and was to be found in overseas Chinese sugar plantations, the driving force in the Mediterranean regions and eastern Atlantic islands was competition for scarce natural resources, and water in particular.

The Caribbean sugar plantation complex, so often cited as a revolutionary chapter in European capitalism, was deeply rooted in this older Mediterranean capitalist mode of sugar production, in which the estate's mill was the central unit that monopolized natural resources and recruited its own labor force. The Caribbean plantation was the result of centuries of knowledge transfer. Sugar makers traveled from Egypt and Syria to Cyprus and Sicily, from where their knowledge and skills crossed into Valencia and reached Madeira. Portuguese sugar masters learned their art from the Muslims in Andalusia and brought it to Madeira and also the Canary Islands. Terminology traveled with the technology: the Sicilian word *trapetto* (olive mill) became the Valencian word *trapig* and later on *trapiche* in the Iberian Atlantic world.[36]

Indeed, technologically speaking, the basic features of the Atlantic sugar industry were already developed on the Mediterranean islands. Archaeologists have been able to reconstruct the workings of the sugar factories in Cyprus via an eighteenth-century description of Caribbean estates.[37] Aqueducts and canalizations enhanced the pressing power of the watermills, and fertilizer was applied to cane fields throughout the Mediterranean Basin from Egypt to Sicily to Andalusia and the Canary Islands.[38] In Egypt, where deforestation was complete by 1300, palm leaves, bagasse (dried pressed sugar cane) and especially straw served as fuel to spare the forests, which the Mamluk rulers were keen to preserve.[39]

The continuities between the Mediterranean and Atlantic sugar production are many and their histories overlap because until the late eighteenth century productivity growth in the sugar sector was a matter of slow incremental change. Transport was expensive, and hence ecologically and climatically disadvantaged regions with strong traditions of sugar production continued to cultivate cane longer than one might expect. Despite severe ecological limitations and the rapid emergence of sugar production in Brazil, the Canary Islands and Madeira produced sugar throughout the sixteenth century.[40] Egypt's sugar production rebounded again and was still qualitatively competitive with Caribbean sugar in the eighteenth century. Along the southern coast of Spain and in Cyprus sugar production continued as well, although it was of marginal significance compared to Egypt's.[41]

The real rupture between the Mediterranean to Atlantic systems of sugar production came with African slavery. Slavery remained the exception rather than the rule at Mediterranean estates, even after waves of the Plague that caused severe labor shortages. After the devastating ninth-century rebellion by thousands of enslaved East Africans who toiled the cane fields and maintained the irrigation works of the Euphrates Delta, the risks of putting large groups of enslaved people in the cane fields had become all too obvious. The Egyptian cane fields or mills wisely did not use enslaved people and in fact had no need for them.[42]

The crusaders put prisoners of war on their cane fields but presumably just as an additional workforce. In Cyprus, the labor force consisted mainly of free and servile workers, although later on the Plague must have forced the estates to resort to enslaved labor on a more structural basis.[43] In Morocco, peasants were forced to grow cane and work in the mills, but enslaved workers do not appear to have been involved. In Valencia they could be found in the fields, but they were never the dominant workforce.[44] Neither was slavery introduced on a structural basis at sugar estates in the eastern Atlantic islands. In Madeira and the Canary Islands, cane was still grown by smallholders and sharecroppers, with some African slave labor employed in the mills. Only in São Tomé, the uninhabited island off the coast of West Africa, was African slave labor used in its sixteenth-century sugar plantations in a way comparable to the Americas.[45]

From Medicine to Delicacy

White crystalline sugar began its history in princely courts. When it eventually did reach the masses, it was usually as a medicinal ingredient at first.[46]
This is how it happened in India, Persia, China, and Egypt, and subsequently in Europe. Medieval pharmacopoeias and inventories of apothecaries throughout the Persian, Christian, and Muslim worlds all praised
sugar highly. The trust in the medical power of sugar was embedded in the
teachings of the Greek Claudius Galenus (Galen) who lived in the second
century A.D. and considered sugar as one of the means to restore imbal-
ances in the bodily tempers. His medical philosophy traveled westward
through the cultivation of sugar, and eastward to China through Sino-
Arabic contacts.[47] Europe became acquainted with it through the highly
influential medical compendium of the seventh-century Greek physician
Paulus Aegineta and via the Arab world through Avicenna and Constan-
tinus Africanus.[48]

    In Europe honey was already known to be effective with bad coughs, but
sugar was sweeter and was therefore attributed a superior potency. Moreover, since sugar can be easily absorbed by the human body, sugar water
helped keep patients suffering from chronic diarrhea alive. Joining the sugar
waters, syrups as well as comfitures became widely used medicines for
stomach pains and respiratory diseases.[49] Sugar was extensively used in hospitals in the Arabic world from Cairo to the Iberian Peninsula, and of
course by the Hospitallers in Jerusalem. Crusader chronicler William of
Tyre described sugar in the late twelfth century as "so much needed for
people's health."[50] No doubt, he was alluding to sugar's potential to keep
people with serious intestinal problems alive. Travelers always encounter
new bacteria and viruses to which they are particularly susceptible. While
traveling in Mesopotamia in the seventeenth-century, the Frenchman Abbé
Carré, a trained physician, concluded that sherbets—lemonades of rose
water, limes, and pomegranates—was the best medicine against intestinal
infections caused by polluted water.[51]

    In India, Central Asia, and the Arab world, sugar water or rose water
gradually developed into the forerunners of lemonade. Initially only appreciated as delights among the wealthiest and most powerful, the consumption of sugar waters reached the masses over time. Mixed with ice, sherbets
became sorbets, developed in Italy as early as the seventeenth century.[52]

Pierre Paul Sevin's *Banquet Table with Trionfi, Arranged for Cardinal Leopold de Medici* (1667) depicts sugar sculptures adorning a nobleman's table. Decorating with cast sugar was for centuries a fashionable practice among European, Mediterranean, and Chinese dignitaries.

Serving sweet delicacies acted as a status symbol and became a fixture of royal audiences and diplomacy. No ceremonial entrance or departure of a grand magistrate in Persia could not involve sweets, for instance.[53]

The most fanciful application of sugar, however, was sculpture, for which the material lends itself excellently. European travelers who visited China in the sixteenth century reported that high dignitaries displayed sugar sculptures at their banquets.[54] In Egypt, the caliphs and their successors, the Mamluk sultans, had sugar sculptures adorning their banquets during Islamic festive days. A Fatimid caliph, for example, organized a procession with a diorama of 152 cast sugar figures and seven castles through the streets of Cairo at the end of Ramadan. Mamluk rulers on many occasions displayed their sugar wealth, sometimes so ostentatiously—as at the wedding of the sultan's son in 1332—that it met with condemnation from a prominent member of Cairo's ulama. The Ottoman rulers in Istanbul displayed hundreds of cast sugar figures at their court, a practice they in all likelihood had inherited from their Byzantine predecessors.[55]

European princes followed this tradition. The ruler of Perugia had his wedding banquet adorned with a splendid array of sugar-crafted animals. Even more enthralling might have been the sculptures at the farewell banquet for Catherine de Medici before her marriage to Henry II of France. When their son, King Henry III of France, visited Venice in 1574, he was received with equal splendor and sugar ornaments designed by an apothecary and an architect. By that time, Atlantic sugar production had begun and the art of making sugar sculptures spread to the north as well as to the west of Europe. The court of Brussels witnessed a magnificent display of this craft at the occasion of the marriage of Alexander Farnese to Princess Maria of Portugal in 1565.[56]

Sugar consumption spread beyond the aristocracy first in China, India, and then Egypt, where cane cultivation thrived as early as the thirteenth century. When Ibn Battuta, the Berber Maghrebi scholar and explorer we met in Chapter 1, visited China and Egypt in the fourteenth century, he found sugar already in the urban markets. He might even have seen shopkeepers in Cairo hanging sugar candies cast in all kinds of shapes in front of their stores in the two months before Ramadan up until its celebratory end, the Eid al-Fitr.[57]

At that time, sugar was still practically absent from northern Europe. In 1226, the English king Henry III asked the mayor of Winchester to obtain for him three pounds of sugar from Alexandria "if so much could be got." Fifty years later, imports from Egypt, the Levant, and Cyprus had grown substantially, and sugar entered the wealthiest English households by the kilogram.[58] Over time, increasing volumes reached northern Europe via Venetian, Genoese, Florentine, and Ravensburger merchants.[59] Sugar became avidly consumed by European aristocrats, and various Habsburg rulers suffered from painful tooth decay as a consequence.[60] Queen Elizabeth I of England had black teeth by the end of her life, which, according to a German visitor to her court, was a direct consequence of her sugar consumption. Indeed, at that time what sugar did to one's teeth was already known, and for French apothecary Theophilus de Garancières, who practiced most of his life in England, sugar was a curse and better sent back to India.[61]

Caries must have begun to affect non-royal Europeans too in the course of the sixteenth century. At the time of Columbus's voyages across the Atlantic, a mere five thousand tons of sugar reached the various markets in Europe annually, but that volume tripled in the century that followed. By

1700, Europe was importing about sixty thousand tons of sugar.[62] Insignificant as this amount may seem in comparison to the production of the Chinese mainland, Bengal, and Punjab, it was still of some consequence considering that the total population of western Europe was much smaller than that of China and India. Yet even in the eighteenth century, for most of Europe sugar was still far from quotidian. Honey was a common sweetener in coffee and tea, for instance, as long as it remained cheaper than imported cane sugar.

Most Europeans did not see much pure sugar; they were more likely to encounter it in the form of comfitures or confectioneries. Both these words are derived from the French *confiserie* (literally, "putting together"), which in turn comes from the Italian *colleazione,* meaning a lavish and expensive assemblage of sweetmeats.[63] In Europe as well as in many other parts of the world, bakers discovered that sugar was easier to work with than honey for confectioneries and pastries.[64] But still, the only place in Europe that enjoyed sugar in abundance was the wealthy Dutch Republic, where in the early seventeenth century half of Europe's sugar was refined. Here, sugar sculptures, that once only adorned aristocratic tables, now became popular items at the festivities of wealthy commoners. A prohibition by the municipality of Amsterdam in 1655 on such conspicuous consumption was simply ignored, despite the heavy fine of hundred guilders, which was half a workman's yearly wage. For Dutch citizens, Saint Nicholas feasts, Epiphany, courting, weddings, and baptisms became unthinkable without serious amounts of sugar. This consumption was not confined to the urbanites; wealthy farmers invited their neighbors to celebrate the baptism of a child with generous amounts of sugar.[65]

Recipes that applied sugar in pastries and other dishes traveled widely across Eurasia and the Americas, often in the slipstream of military conquests. The rather poor Arab cuisine was upgraded when the Abbasid rulers came to power in 750 and located their caliphate in Baghdad, until then part of the culinarily sophisticated and sugar-loving Persian Empire. Ottoman cuisine developed into a melting pot of sweet traditions of the Persian and Arabic worlds, and here Eid al-Fitr became the "sugar feast."[66] Meanwhile, the enriched Arab cuisine revolutionized kitchens with many sweet delicacies from Baghdad and the Iberian Peninsula. The art of making small sweets and pastries that had matured within the Arabic-Andalusian tradition was exported by the Spanish and Portuguese to their colonies. The

Iberian convents with their predilection for sweets spread the art of making
them throughout Latin America, the Philippines, and their colonial settlements of South Asia. In Spanish American cities sweets and cakes were sold
by street vendors from the seventeenth century and sugar soon became a
common item in grocery shops.[67]

In the eastern direction, the Portuguese brought the skills of confectionery making all the way to Japan. So-called southern barbarian sweets—
"barbarian" referred to their European provenance—found willing consumers, particularly as an accompaniment to the tea ceremony. From
Japan, confectionery making arrived in Siam. Marie Guyemar de Pinha
(1664–1728), or Marie Guimard, as she is known in French, introduced sugar
into Siamese cuisine. She was the wife of Constantin Phaulkon, the Siamese
king's prime minister, who was executed together with his monarch during a
palace coup in 1688. Marie had learned to cook Japanese-Portuguese dishes
from her mother, a Catholic Japanese who had fled her country during the
persecutions of Christians. In Siam as well, the consumption of sweets
trickled down from the royal court to the streets of Bangkok in the course
of the eighteenth century.[68]

In spite of its global spread, in most of the world cane sugar was just
one of the available sweeteners. In India sugars from fruits and flowers
existed alongside palm and cane sugar, although sugar from flowers especially must have been a delicacy rather than an ordinary consumption
item.[69] Actually, throughout the Malay world palm sugar continued to be
the dominant sugar even after Chinese immigrants had introduced sugar
manufacturing. Whereas in Persia the court and well-to-do urban homes
were avid consumers of sugar, local sweeteners as honey, dates, grapes, and
manna dominated in ordinary Persian households.[70] In Bukhara (in contemporary Uzbekistan) as well as elsewhere in the Central Asia and the
Arab world, the juice of grapes, melons and other fruits, as well as juice from
the *turunjbeen* (or *taranjabin*)—that is, honeydew left by leafhoppers—was
consumed rather than cane sugar.[71] In the Mamluk territories, carob beans,
widely cultivated around Nablus, were highly appreciated as a sweetener
and exported to Cairo and Damascus, according to Ibn Battuta.[72] Even in
the Ottoman Empire, where sugar was well known and confectioneries
and candies widely popular, sugar did not become a common item. Grape
syrup was abundantly available and even cheaper than honey, which in turn
was half as expensive as sugar. This only changed after the arrival of the

Caribbean sugar in this part of the world at the end of the eighteenth century.[73]

The populations of pre-Columbian America too were familiar with many sweets made from a variety of fruits. The Aztecs, moreover, made a syrup extracted from maize, which Cortés, writing to Charles V, said was as sweet as cane sugar, although this seems unlikely; it must have contained glucose, which is less sweet than the sucrose obtained from sugar cane.[74] In temperate zones, what came closest to pure sucrose was maple sugar. Since time immemorial, Algonquin-speaking Native Americans near the Hudson Bay had extracted maple sugar by boring into the maple tree during springtime when the fluids move up into the bark of the tree.[75] However, in temperate climates honey as well as glucose syrups from barley or sorghum were the most common peasant sweeteners. In northern China they must have been consumed for thousands of years and are still used today. Rice-growing societies, finally, often made their sweets from glutinous rice, which later on would be mixed with sugar.[76] All these different sweeteners had their own taste that enriched local dishes, and they continue to exist even after white crystalline sugar conquered most the world in the twentieth century.

Sugar in Urban and Industrial Europe

By the mid-eighteenth century, sugar had become part of urban consumption culture almost everywhere in the world. Thanks to the abundance of sugar from Taiwan and the recovery of sugar production in southeast China, for instance, sugar consumption and the making of confectioneries had moved up along the Chinese coast to Shanghai and the neighboring city of Suzhou by the mid-eighteenth century.[77] Sugar also came within reach of the European urban middle classes as annual production in the Americas exceeded the 150,000-ton mark by 1750 and grew another 60 percent by 1790. Annual per capita sugar consumption in Western Europe rose from a tiny 87 grams in 1600 to 614 grams in 1700 to 2 kilograms on the eve of the French Revolution.[78] By 1800 sugar consumption in this part of the world approximated that of China, where it ranged from 1.5 to 2.5 kilograms per capita. This was still far behind India, however, where people on average consumed 4 kilograms of raw sugar every year.[79]

By the eighteenth century, sugar consumption had spread from Europe's bourgeois urban quarters to the more plebeian neighborhoods, and in

Britain and the Dutch Republic even to the countryside. The lower classes for whom crystalline sugar was still out of their budget resorted to treacle (i.e., molasses).[80] Many hogsheads of it arrived not only in Britain but also in the thirteen British colonies of North America, where it was consumed with little restraint.[81] In western Europe and North America sugar appeared as a common ingredient in cookbooks, while manuals on the preparation of sweets, ice cream, marmalade, and deserts proliferated. Sugar was applied in increasing volumes to confectioneries and candies, fudge, and marzipan, which consists of sugar and ground almonds. In North America, Philadelphia emerged as a center of sweet making, thanks to the skills of its Dutch and German immigrants. Quaker women proved themselves particularly proficient in pastry baking; they crafted confectioneries and their creations adorned the dinner tables of the city's high society. Newspaper advertisements played their part in making Philadelphia the "capital of sweets."[82]

As sugar spread, warnings by doctors against its consumption became more frequent too. They wrote about the dangers to human metabolism and pointed to the risk of caries, scurvy, and even lung diseases.[83] Prominent among the critics was the seventeenth-century Dutch medical doctor Steven Blankaart, who fulminated against brown sugar and the syrups (probably treacle) consumed by common people. He claimed that the best doctors in the Dutch Republic no longer prescribed sugar and syrups and urged their removal from apothecaries' shelves. He also strongly advised moderation with regard to sweets made from sugar such as macarons, marzipan, "banquet letters,"[84] and sugared almonds—all beloved items in the Dutch Republic. Last but not least, he warned that excessive sugar consumption might cause fat bellies and scurvy among children.[85]

Sugar also elicited some scrutiny for being a stimulant, but it escaped religious condemnation, let alone an outright ban like alcohol in Islam. For the Catholic clergy, indulgence in sweets did count as intemperance and therefore was a sin of minor consequence; most people could only afford sugar in tiny quantities anyway.[86] The temperance proclaimed by early (Protestant) Enlightenment bourgeois culture might have been stricter, but, in this milieu, sugar was considered far less of a problem than excessive drinking. Moreover, whatever the clerics might have said, the flow of delicate pastries, cakes, and confectioneries had become unstoppable. The art of casting sugar had spread from the royal courts to sugar bakers, and its secrets were available on booksellers' shelves.

In France, Antonin Carême, who cooked for the French top diplomat Charles-Maurice de Talleyrand and Czar Alexander I, lifted baking to a new level. His book *Le pâtissier pitoresque* (The Picturesque Pastry Chef) (1815) was one of a long list of pastry cookbooks that started with *Le Cannameliste français* (The French Confectioner), published by Joseph Gilliers in 1768. By that time, the consumption of tobacco, coffee, and tea had spread throughout western Europe and appealed to both genders. These tropical stimulants shaped new standards of consumption and new trading patterns, creating a more globalized economy and cosmopolitan culinary practices. Sugar accompanied tea in England and tea ceremonies in Kyoto and Edo, where the confectioneries made from the fine *wasanbon* sugar went well with the bitter tea.[87]

Meanwhile, sugar consumption per capita varied widely in Eurasia, with India ranking highest, followed by China, Persia, and the Ottoman Empire, with Europe far behind.[88] Within Europe, many people would never see sugar, while for others it had become quotidian. Whereas in Austria sugar consumption was still restricted to Vienna's urbanites, in the Dutch Republic a spoonful of sugar in a cup of coffee had become common even in the countryside. In Britain sugar became particularly popular with per capita consumption rising from about five pounds in 1700 to over sixteen pounds in 1775, a quantity seen nowhere else in Europe and elsewhere in the world matched only by India.[89] Beyond the wealthier classes, consumers could be found in the emerging industrial centers of Britain, where wages rose significantly, but also in the countryside, where grocery shops had considerable quantities of sugar in their stores from the early eighteenth century. There were tens of thousands or perhaps even more than a hundred thousand such shops in Britain at that time.[90]

By contrast, in France sugar consumption remained predominantly an urban habit, partly because its rural population was much poorer than Britain's and because its warmer climate facilitated ample alternative sweeteners. Parisians had definitely become accustomed to sugar and their consumption per head may have been around twenty-three kilograms annually on the eve of the French Revolution.[91] In one of six hundred-odd cafés or at home, Parisians of all walks of life took their café au lait with some sugar in the morning.[92] When the people rioted in Paris in 1792, it is well known that they were protesting against the doubling of the sugar prices, which heavily affected their daily lives.[93] While it has been argued that Parisian workers disliked sugar until the late nineteenth century, finding it effeminate and weakening, this may have been restricted to newcomers from the countryside. The urbanites clearly thought otherwise.[94]

What drove sugar consumption in Europe's cities too was the gradual replacement of beer and wine for daily consumption. For centuries these alcoholic beverages were widely consumed because they were rightfully considered to be safer than water, which tend to be heavily polluted, particularly in urban centers. Coffee and tea made with boiled water proved to be a perfect alternative. Meanwhile, in the United States piety and the preaching of sobriety by dissenters such as the Quakers saw sweetened drinks and sweeteners move into the countryside. This spread toward rural areas probably happened in some German principalities too. Although these did not receive the large colonial supplies of sugar that came to the British and French ports, their per capita consumption came on par with that of France in the course of the eighteenth century. Thriving manufacturing sectors, such as weaving, raised the incomes of large segments of the German population.[95]

Sugar bakeries could be found all over Germany after recipes for flans with marmalade or rice porridge entered the country via Flanders and the southern provinces of the Dutch Republic. Soon the Germans too had developed the habit of drinking sugared coffee. In cities such as Hamburg, Leipzig, and Cologne, sugar may have entered the daily diet. Domestic servants returning from their positions in the cities to marry in the countryside may have got used to a spoonful of sugar in coffee or tea and introduced this habit in village households.[96] This was all made possible by twelve thousand tons of sugar coming from Holland via the Rhine and another thirty thousand tons being unloaded in Hamburg, most of it originating from the French Antilles. Although German refiners and traders shipped their sugar as far as Russia, thirty to forty thousand tons may have supplied the domestic a market of about twenty million consumers. This amounts to between 1.5 and 2 kilograms per capita annually, which was indeed comparable to average French consumption at that time.[97]

In the late eighteenth century, the use of sugar for sweets, cakes, and as a condiment for coffee and tea spread among the urban bourgeoisie throughout western Europe and North America, and from there to wealthier rural households. In England, even servants consumed it.[98] Again, in terms of per capita sugar consumption, these parts of the world now matched China. Europe and North America only equaled India for consumption in the course of the nineteenth century, however, when their rapidly urbanizing and industrializing societies generated an almost insatiable demand for sugar. Tragically, this soaring demand would lead to the mass enslavement of Africans.

3

War and Slavery

EUROPE HAD JUST LEARNED to love sugar in the early fifteenth century when its production in Egypt collapsed. It was a crucial moment that would link sugar and Europe's Atlantic history for centuries to come. Initially, old sites of production in the western Mediterranean were revived and new ones opened up. This expansion rapidly met its limits, however, because Europe's climate confined sugar cultivation to its southernmost islands and shores of the Mediterranean Sea. Soon, Madeira emerged as the largest sugar provider for the European market. This is typical for capitalist commodity production: it overcomes local ecological constraints by relocating, a phenomenon for which the geographer David Harvey coined the expression "spatial fix."[1] Maybe the most momentous spatial fix in the history of the sugar industry happened when supplies from Madeira declined. New sugar frontiers made headway in a world only recently known to Europeans. Just before 1500, on his second voyage, Columbus had planted some cane on Hispaniola and enthusiastically reported back that on this island it grew sweeter and thicker than in Sicily or Andalusia.[2] Twenty years later, the first sugar from Hispaniola came to Spain, just in time to reach King Ferdinand on his deathbed.

Sugar connected the various nodal points in the immense empire of Ferdinand's grandson, Charles V. When the nineteen-year-old monarch was crowned emperor of the German Holy Roman Empire in 1519, he became indebted to the Welser and Fugger families, banking dynasties who had generously financed his campaign for this crown. The Welsers also sponsored Charles V's expansion in the Americas, for which they obtained important commercial privileges in return, namely a virtual monopoly on the slave trade for Spanish America. In addition, they maintained a trading establishment in Hispaniola's capital Santo Domingo, from where they shipped sugar and brought thousands of enslaved to the sugar mills of the island.[3]

The plantations on Hispaniola were the largest of their time and employed a new type of mill with a crushing capacity twice that of the *trapetto,* the ancient edge-runner mill. It was a two-roller horizontal mill, a model which had emerged in west India in the thirteenth or fourteenth century. It has been suggested that it may have come to Hispaniola via the Portuguese, who had a settlement in Goa. It is, however, more likely that the two-roller horizontal mill originated in Madeira and was brought via the Canary Islands to Hispaniola. The horizontal rollers with protruding iron bars to enhance crushing power were excellently suited for water power, and the Hispaniola mills were preferably located along rivers, which also served transport purposes.[4]

Mills proliferated in New Spain—contemporary Mexico, Columbia, and Peru—as well as in Puerto Rico. After their ruthless advance, the conquistadores ordered sugar stalks to be planted on their newly founded estates.[5] By the mid-sixteenth century, the Spanish possessions in the Americas together may have yielded 2,000–2,500 tons of sugar, which still did not exceed the output of the Canary Islands or the Portuguese sugar island of São Tomé, in the Gulf of Guinee.[6] Production in Hispaniola was intensely resisted by enslaved and those who had escaped slavery (known as maroons), who set mills on fire and captured cattle. French and British corsairs regularly preyed upon the island and destroyed sugar estates. Meanwhile, planters circumvented the Seville monopoly of Spanish sugar purchases by selling to British smugglers who brought sugar to London. Together these factors explain why after the mid-sixteenth century, Spain's sugar imports from the Americas stagnated.[7]

The Portuguese, not the far more powerful Spanish, emerged as the dominant sugar producers in the Atlantic. Early on in the sixteenth century, the Portuguese royals and their courtiers had attracted German and Antwerp merchant capital to develop São Tomé and turn it into a major slave-based sugar producer, much like Hispaniola.[8] One might wonder why sugar production did not move from São Tomé to West Africa instead of crossing the Atlantic, particularly because plantation agriculture did exist in West Africa. However, most of the region proved to be ecologically unfit for sugar, as precipitation throughout the year soaked the soil and turned it acidic. Such soil was fine for palms but ruined sugar cane, which grows best in a

monsoon climate with a dry season. And on top of this, horses that turned
the mills perished in equatorial Africa, infected by the tsetse fly.[9] It seems
ecology pushed sugar production across the Atlantic, and, as we all know,
millions of Africans followed in captivity.

The long coastline of Brazil emerged as the dominant sugar cane belt of
the Atlantic world. The extensive area of coastal Brazil offered opportunities for many, and within a century after the first Portuguese had set foot
on its soil, Brazil was producing about 7,500 tons of sugar annually, which
was about 1.5 times of what Sicily, the Iberian Peninsula, and the Spanish
and Portuguese colonies produced combined. Hundreds of ships carried
sugar from Brazil to Portugal and from there to other European ports,
Antwerp in particular. In fact, the Brazilian sugar frontier owed much of
its momentum to the merchants of this city, who had obtained the sugar
monopoly for the Low Countries from the Portuguese Crown and had
made their city the center of sugar refining in northern Europe. These merchants provided much of the capital for the plantations in Brazil and

Brazilian sugar mill, circa 1816. The three vertically positioned rollers are characteristic
of a design that contributed to Brazil's emergence as a dominant sugar-producing colony
in the sixteenth and seventeenth centuries.

shipped half of the sugar produced there to Europe. Quite a few plantations, particularly those in Pernambuco and Bahia—the main sites of sugar production—had owners from the Low Countries as well. Their ranks were strengthened by Jewish merchants who had escaped persecution on the Iberian Peninsula and built a new life in Brazil.[10]

The opening up of the Brazilian sugar frontier, with its abundance of fertile land and tropical conditions, led to investors building huge mills that had a crushing capacity far beyond what the world had seen up until that point. These mills consisted of three *vertically* positioned rollers, a system that probably originated in Spanish America. This design processed cane faster and more thoroughly and thus produced more juice.[11] Most planters could not afford such a high-powered mill, but fertile land was plentiful, and thus Brazil replicated the initial situation in Madeira, with large milling operations surrounded by smallholders. By the mid-seventeenth century, about 87 percent of the cane milled in Pernambuco was grown by Portuguese *lavradores* (workers), who owned some land, enslaved, and cattle and delivered their cane to the nearest *engenho* (mill).[12] The abundance of natural resources allowed for a less advanced form of capitalism than at the Canary Islands, Hispaniola, and São Tomé, where land with water was predominantly granted to merchants who could finance a mill, not leaving any room for European smallholders.

Brazil's demand for enslaved labor was relentless. By the mid-seventeenth century, production had soared to thirty thousand tons annually, and each ton of sugar required the labor of two or three slaves to produce. Only a minority of them were Amerindians, and over the entire century a million Africans were kidnapped and transported to the Brazilian sugar frontier.[13]

The Dutch Pursue a European Sugar Monopoly

As French and British corsairs preyed upon Spanish possessions in the Caribbean in their war against the dominance of the Habsburg rulers over Europe, sugar emerged as a critical commodity. The conflict would reconfigure the Atlantic world into an arena attracting merchants from all over Europe. The combatants engaged in violent struggles driven by the belief that destroying the colonies of their adversaries was at least as important as developing their own. The grand prize was the sugar monopoly, which was practically unattainable—although the Dutch Republic came close.

Antwerp, the largest city of the Low Countries, had been the center of European sugar commerce for most of the sixteenth century, but it was also the heroic leader of the Protestant revolt against King Philip II of Spain, which began in 1568. Antwerp's role as the capital of the rebellion severely undermined its position in the European sugar market, particularly after it was taken by the Spanish Army in 1585. Sugar merchants and refiners moved to other, less turbulent places such as Cologne and Hamburg. Antwerp also began to feel the heat from Amsterdam, which was already the staple market of the European grain trade and possessed a technologically superior fleet. Even during the most ferocious years of the Dutch Eighty Years' War (1568–1648) against their Spanish overlords, trade with the Iberian Peninsula continued. Dutch ships delivered grain to Lisbon and returned with salt and sugar on board. The Portuguese capital had a population of 165,000 in the 1620s, who could by no means be fed by its hinterland. Merchant networks that had settled in multiple locations in Europe such as Lisbon, Antwerp, Amsterdam, Cologne, and Hamburg circumvented embargos and the maritime sugar trade flourished in spite of mercenaries pillaging the European countryside in the wars against the House of Habsburg.

When the war between the Dutch Republic and Spain reached a stalemate at the turn of the seventeenth century, Antwerp was left under Spanish rule. Its access to the sea was blocked by the Dutch Republic's ships, meaning it could no longer be Europe's center of the sugar trade. When the Dutch signed a truce with Spain in 1609, Amsterdam already processed half of Brazil's sugar exports.[14] But the Dutch wanted more, and when in 1621 their Twelve Years' Truce with Spain ended, they established the Dutch West India Company (Geoctrooieerde West-Indische Compagnie [WIC]), which considered the rich sugar lands of Brazil as an obvious target in addition to the Spanish fleets that carried the silver from Potosí. After a short occupation of Bahia in 1624–1625, the WIC secured the more permanent conquest of Recife in 1630, and sugar supplies seemed to be guaranteed when in 1637 the WIC captured Recife's hinterland, Pernambuco. It also took El Mina, the central Portuguese entrepôt in West Africa, ensuring a constant flow of African slaves. Simultaneously, the Dutch East India Company (Vereenigde Oostindische Compagnie [VOC]) opened up its sugar frontier in Taiwan, and its directors, known as the Gentlemen XVII, informed Batavia that they would take any amount of their sugar for export to the Netherlands.[15]

In the seventeenth and eighteenth centuries, Amsterdam was Europe's hub of sugar refining. The interior of de Granaatappel, the refinery in this 1812 depiction, was typical of the city's hundred or so such facilities, many of which were located along canals.

These conquests added to Amsterdam's success in European sugar commerce, but a crucial role was played by its Sephardic Jewish community, which stood in close contact with the Crypto-Jewish communities in Bahia and Antwerp. Perhaps not coincidentally, two years after the WIC conquest of Recife, Jews became eligible for Amsterdam citizenship, another encouragement for them to engage in the sugar trade and invest in refineries in particular. By the mid-seventeenth century, the Dutch refineries, three-quarters of them located in Amsterdam, supplied half of the sugar to European consumers.[16] Six- or seven-story factories with tall chimneys appeared along Amsterdam's canals, despite the great risk of fire due to the huge amounts of fuel being burned. Quite a few went up in fires that destroyed an expensive building and even more valuable sugar stock.[17]

When the WIC conquered parts of Portuguese Brazil, it might not have realized that it was on its way to becoming a slaveholder: the notion of slavery was in fact alien to the Dutch at the time. While enslavement practices lingered on in the Mediterranean Basin and slavery still existed as an

institution in Spain and Portugal, it had disappeared in Europe's north-
western nations in the course of the Middle Ages. At the time that the
Dutch Republic began building its immense maritime empire, slavery was
moreover a notion antithetical to the freedom for which the Dutch fought
so hard. William of Orange, the father of the Dutch nation, motivated the
secession of the Netherlands among other things by accusing the Spanish
overlords of being enslavers and having killed twenty million Amerindians.
This explains why in its early years the WIC was not yet the notorious
enslaver it would later become and still held that selling slaves was not
permitted to Christians.[18]

However, without enslaved workers the sugar mills of Brazil would stop
running. The WIC set aside its moral scruples against slave holding and
even became a major slave trader itself.[19] The Dutch soon turned out to be
ruthless slaveholders unhindered by any laws protecting the enslaved. In
contrast to Spaniards and Portuguese, they were not bound to medieval
Iberian legal regulations regarding the treatment of enslaved, nor Catholic
laws prescribing baptism. While Spanish and Portuguese plantations often
ignored medieval and Catholic regulations, for the Dutch, and the British
for that matter, these simply did not exist; they knew no boundaries,
treating enslaved people as commodities and denying them personhood
and possession of human souls.

The Dutch substantially extended sugar production—reaching a peak of
6,600 tons annually—in Pernambuco under the rule of Johan Maurits, the
governor of Dutch Brazil from 1637 to 1644.[20] Their hard-won central
position in the global sugar trade would not last long, however. A large
uprising of severely indebted Portuguese planters in Dutch-occupied Brazil
in 1645 squeezed sugar supplies to Amsterdam to a mere thousand tons.[21]
Meanwhile, Taiwan's sugar frontier became a disappointment. The VOC
never obtained more than 2,100 tons of sugar per annum from this island,
far less than what Brazil could deliver by the mid-seventeenth century.[22]
The VOC now set its sights on increasing sugar production in Java and
Mauritius. The latter effort failed, however, and by no means could Java
compensate the loss of Dutch sugar production in Brazil.

The Dutch Republic's chances of monopolizing Europe's sugar commerce
had dwindled by the mid-seventeenth century—it had by now fallen from
its zenith as a global economic and maritime power. In the Atlantic realm
it faced mounting competition from the French and British. In 1626, French

corsairs took the Caribbean island of Saint Christophe from Spain with the blessing of Cardinal Richelieu, Louis XIII's chief minister. Nine years later, Martinique and some smaller islands followed. In the year between the Dutch conquest of Bahia and the French capture of Saint Christophe, Henry Powell set foot on the still densely forested island of Barbados, carrying a range of crops with him including tobacco, indigo, and sugar cane.[23]

Initially, the Dutch and British collaborated in the Caribbean region, which resulted in the astonishingly rapid emergence of Barbados as a sugar island. For the Dutch, Barbados offered new opportunities after extensive rebellions in the 1640s had made their position in Brazil increasingly precarious. They had been forced to find new suppliers for their Amsterdam refineries as well as new buyers for the captives from Africa. After all, at that time the WIC had captured 20 percent of the Atlantic slave trade.[24] Declining exports from Brazil encouraged planters in Barbados to abandon indigo and tobacco for sugar. And thus James Drax and some of his fellow Barbadian planters turned to Pernambuco to obtain some cane and advice from the Dutch on how to build a small sugar mill.[25] Within a few years Barbados became a true sugar island, employing improved mills with iron protruded or iron plated rollers, boiling houses with batteries of cauldrons, and racks carrying sugar cones releasing their molasses.[26]

The Anglo-Dutch partnership fell apart, however, once Oliver Cromwell was fully in charge of the Commonwealth of England. He saw his country and the Dutch Republic as Protestant brother nations united in a common cause against Catholicism. In this struggle he envisaged a division of the world in which the British would conquer the West from the Spanish and the Dutch the Iberian possessions in Asia and Africa. However, the Dutch learned to their surprise and annoyance that their English brethren had assigned them a junior role in this grand scheme. Rebuffed by the Dutch, England issued the Navigation Act in 1651 aimed at banning the highly competitive Dutch ships from its harbors and those of its colonies, which in turn ushered in the First Anglo-Dutch War of 1652–1654. This war not only exhausted the resources of both the British and the Dutch, but also created the perfect opportunity for the Portuguese to recapture Dutch-occupied Brazil. After desperate pleas by a delegation from Recife, the capital of Dutch Brazil, the Dutch Estates General had sent a hastily convened fleet to Pernambuco, but it came too late and could do no more than evacuate the Dutch residents on overcrowded ships.

Yet neither the loss of Brazil nor the English Navigation Act seriously diminished Amsterdam's role in Europe's sugar commerce. In fact, all these wars to monopolize sugar production and markets disrupted rather than fundamentally changed commodity chains that continued to run across borders. Amsterdam's sugar commerce relied not on maritime conquest but on its strong Sephardic trading network that had spread throughout the Caribbean to the Azores and London.[27] Moreover, since London had only a few refineries at that time, Amsterdam absorbed substantial volumes of West Indian sugar, either via London traders or via Caribbean smuggling routes dodging the Navigation Act. The deputy governor of Barbados, Christopher Codrington, himself was a major participant in this illicit trade. He not only used his own five ships but also the navy ships under his command to trade with Curaçao and the other Dutch colony, Saint Eustatius, a nodal point in the sugar commerce of the region.[28]

By about 1660, a fleet of one hundred ships was carrying sugar to Amsterdam, and the sugar industry was still the largest sector of its economy.[29] Almost ten thousand tons of sugar came from London and a further 3,500 tons from Brazil and the French and British Caribbean islands via various routes; varying quantities also arrived from Asia aboard VOC ships. Although Amsterdam would lose its role as a refiner of West Indian sugar by 1713, this would eventually be compensated by a massive flow of raw sugar from the French Antilles, and Saint Domingue in particular. These cargos were either legally purchased in France or illicitly obtained in the Caribbean region.[30] The extensive smuggling and trading diasporas of the bourgeoisie did much to undo mercantilist policies.

The British and French Sugar Revolutions

The war waged against the Habsburgs by the French, British, and Dutch, and the presence and expulsion of the latter from Brazil, opened a new chapter of sugar production by enslaved Africans in the Caribbean islands. Barbados rapidly changed from an island with a variety of crops grown by British settlers and convict labors into a sugar island relying on enslaved Africans. In the 1660s it had become the second largest Atlantic sugar exporter after Brazil, but it had also reached its limit, being too small to accommodate the rapidly expanding British plantocracy, who therefore began settling other Caribbean islands.

That Barbados was not simply ecologically exhausted and abandoned within a couple of decades was only because planters managed to overcome its natural limitations, thereby turning it into a model for the entire Caribbean region.[31] Timber shortages on this rapidly deforested island were partly solved by importing lumber from New England for construction purposes and coal from England for heating. Using sun-dried bagasse as fuel was another fix enabled by the relatively dry climate of Barbados. Equally important was the introduction of powerful windmills. About four hundred pairs of wings turned the crushing rollers of Barbados by 1670, allowing to largely dispense with the extensive rearing of cattle, for which the island had little space.[32] The windmills would survive the Industrial Revolution, which saw steam-driven cane crushers spread across the globe. As late as the eve of World War I, 219 sugar estates in Barbados were still operated with wind power.[33]

In addition to solving their energy problem by using windmills, burning bagasse, and importing lumber and even coal, the Barbadian planters also surmounted formidable ecological obstacles. To stem the dwindling yields caused by rapid soil degradation and erosion, they introduced "cane holing," which involved the digging of two-directional ridges. This meant manure could be better used as well. Holing as a technique spread throughout the West Indies and with it came the division of enslaved workers in labor gangs moving over the field in a particular rhythm, which rapidly evolved into a standard practice in Caribbean sugar plantations.[34] Rotation with food crops (such as yams) allowed the land to recover from the exhaustive cane cultivation, although it was not enough to stem soil exhaustion. Barbadian planters went to desperate lengths to maintain production; they even resorted to the importation of compost from Suriname, which for a short while was in British hands.[35]

In Barbados, the skills and experience of five centuries of sugar production converged. The three-roller mills came from Portuguese Brazil, and the use of multiple cauldrons to save fuel was probably developed by the Dutch, who were alarmed by rapid deforestation in Pernambuco and who in turn may have learned about this technique from Chinese sugar boilers in their Asian possessions.[36] In the field, practices such as crop rotation and manuring were already widely used in medieval Egypt and China. Bagasse burning was not in use in Brazil where forests were still abundant, but it had probably been practiced many centuries before in Egypt.[37]

The Barbadian planters added their own innovations to squeeze the maximum out of this tiny island and their enslaved workers. Their total integration of mill and field and the rigid division and timing of labor marked an important turning point. It was also completely different from the way in which Henry Drax and other planters had organized tobacco production. Tobacco cultivation tended to involve small parcels of land farmed by indentured white workers, who were to be had at half the price of enslaved Africans. However, a rebellion by disgruntled indentured workers for whom there was no longer space to become farmers themselves had made this source of labor less attractive. The abundant supplies of enslaved Africans soon tilted the balance toward excluding white workers from the plantations.[38] In contrast to Brazil, white cane farmers did not become part of the Barbadian sugar economy.

Barbados returned to the old Mediterranean model, in which ecological limitations had already enforced a subjugation of labor by capital. But now it happened with complete commodification and thus depersonalization of the workers. This was, according to B. W. Higman, a "sugar revolution" and above all a revolution in racial relations.[39] While slave imports more than doubled in the 1660s, a substantial part of the white settler population who could no longer find employment in Barbados moved to other Caribbean islands and North America. A solid racial line emerged between plantation owners and their white supervisors on the one hand and their workers on the other: capital was white and labor black. Dutch supplies of enslaved Africans, British planters leaving Barbados, and Sephardic Jews expelled from Brazil extended the Barbados sugar revolution further into the Caribbean region. First it spread to Dutch Suriname, which was in British hands between 1652 and 1667, and then to Jamaica, which had been captured from the Spaniards in 1655 and which would become Britain's most important plantation island.[40] Other prominent Barbadian planters, including the aforementioned Christopher Codrington, moved to Antigua.

Meanwhile, Jewish and Dutch refugees from Brazil established new colonies along the Guiana coast, a process that had already started when hundreds of Sephardic Jews who had reconverted to their original religion— being allowed to do so in Dutch Pernambuco—left Brazil fearing for their future when the governor Johan Maurits was called back in 1644. A second group of Sephardic Jews departed ten years later when the WIC vacated Brazil and left either for the Dutch Republic, the Dutch colonies at the

Guiana coast, or the Caribbean islands—most notably Barbados and the French Antilles. In this diaspora they were joined by Jewish emigrants who came from the Iberian Peninsula fleeing a new wave of persecutions, and by Jews from Hamburg and Leghorn.[41]

In the end, Dutch Brazil and the diaspora that followed upon its fall set in motion a sugar revolution in the French Antilles, which initially produced tobacco, cacao, and indigo like Barbados. A French sugar maker residing in Pernambuco was engaged by the governor of the French Antilles to build a sugar plantation on the island of Saint Christophe. In 1646, the plantation was up and running with about one hundred enslaved and two hundred artisans, indentured laborers, and other workers.[42] Eight years later, Dutch ships crammed with evacuees from Pernambuco arrived at Martinique, where an intervention by the Jesuits on the island pushed these skilled sugar producers further into the French Antilles. Not happy with the presence of these prominent Protestant Dutch and Sephardic Jewish sugar producers, they forced the governor to expel them to a more welcoming Guadeloupe.[43]

Much like Barbados, the French Antilles were initially populated with European coerced laborers—called *engagés*—who had to work for a number of years for a tobacco or indigo planter before being entitled to their own plot. This was part of the French policy to consolidate these vulnerable colonies with settlers. With the conversion to sugar and the influx of enslaved Africans provided by the Dutch, these *engagés* were pushed out of the production system and lost their access to land in the French Antilles. Soon Guadeloupe's sugar production became so abundant that Jean François Colbert, Louis XIV's finance minister and father of French mercantilism, was briefed about a pending shortage of vessels to transport the sugar to France. Smugglers may have helped solve this problem; what really put a brake on the soaring sugar output of the French Antilles was that there were not enough slave ships to meet the planters' growing demand for enslaved workers.[44]

As sugar production in the Caribbean region took off, Brazil's sugar industry was entering what turned out to be a century of stagnation. Thus far in the history of sugar either ecological limits, climate changes, or military invasions had halted or even destroyed sugar frontiers, but none of this applied to Brazil. Its planters simply failed to take further advantage of fertile land, abundant water power, and numerous draught animals, as well as the million enslaved Africans who were shipped to Brazil between 1700 and 1760—almost as many as to the French Antilles and British West Indies together.[45] Most of these enslaved in fact went to gold and diamond mines. Nor were the Brazilian planters able to profit from rising sugar prices or from their neutrality in the frequent wars in which the British, French, and Spanish were embroiled. The Brazilian sugar estates had lost much of their markets in France, Britain, and the Netherlands. These countries, and Britain in particular, were interested in gold and diamonds but not in sugar, for which they had their own Caribbean colonies.[46]

When demand for Brazilian sugar finally recovered by the end of the eighteenth century, only 5 percent of the mills of Pernambuco were water-driven and few rollers were iron clad; processing capacity and crushing power were thus compromised.[47] Instead of resorting to bagasse burning, the Brazilian planters responded to depleted forests by moving further into the interior, destroying even more trees regardless of the quality of their wood. The practice of burning a forest just before planting saved manuring but forced planters to use even more land, with large areas being left fallow for years in order to recover. This not only caused widespread deforestation, it was also highly uneconomical. The enslaved workers had to walk longer distances to the cane fields at a time when sugar estates had to compete with the gold and diamond mines for labor, and for scarce fuel wood with the leather tanning industry. Profitability declined, and many mills were forced to close down in the 1780s.[48] By that time Brazil as a sugar exporter was surpassed by Saint Domingue and Jamaica.

The Enslaved

As a consequence of the wars against the Habsburg hegemony, slavery, which was introduced by the Iberians in the Americas, had spread to the colonies of the Dutch, British, and French nations. For the Iberians, slavery was an old institution, in which the Church had somewhat mitigated the harshest depersonalizing effects of people turned into property. In the Americas, the Catholic Church continued to reverse the depersonalization of the enslaved under the regime of plantation capitalism by demanding from its Catholic kings to facilitate the baptism of its enslaved subjects. Protestant slaveholders were under no obligation, however, to care for the souls of their enslaved people which, against the backdrop of a deeply religious Europe at that time, gives us a shocking insight in the thoroughly dehumanizing character of this new capitalist system of slavery.

The main destination for enslaved Africans was the sugar plantations, where at least half and perhaps two-thirds of the approximately 12.5 million people who were kidnapped in Africa and survived their transport across the Atlantic ended up.[49] Due to the rapidly growing demand for sugar in Europe, slave ships could not keep up with the demand for enslaved people and this was particularly true during the heyday of Saint Domingue production in the late eighteenth century, when French slavers sailed all the way to the east coast of Africa to purchase captives.[50]

In an average year in the second half of the eighteenth century, well over six hundred thousand enslaved people worked on the Caribbean and Brazilian sugar plantations or performed auxiliary tasks, such as grazing the cattle that turned the mills or transporting sugar to the port and tending provision fields. Only 30–40 percent of the land of an average West Indian sugar estate might have been under cane; the rest was given over to provisions and cattle.[51] The enslaved workers also had to construct and maintain infrastructure, including irrigation or drainage works. If possible, this was done outside the peak time of the harvest, which was the bottleneck in the plantation calendar when labor-intensive manual cane cutting, haulage, crushing of the cane, and boiling of the juice all had to be handled simultaneously. In preindustrial plantations, little could be done to reduce the need for labor during the milling season.

Brutally severed from their families, from their communities, and from their land, the enslaved lived a "modern life," as C. L. R. James, the famous Trinidadian historian, has pointed out. He meant modern in the sense that their kinship relations were destroyed, that much of their food and clothes were imported, and that the minute division of labor and time management bound them even closer together than proletarians in Europe at that time.[52] The kidnapped Africans must have considered their condition as the grim result of a lost war or the consequence of a raid on their village or city back home. The enslaved women were worse off than the men. Contrary to what the modern reader might expect, the arduous field work employed a majority of women. Coopers, masons, and carpenters as well as sugar boilers were usually men, however. The work was exhausting, the days in the fields backbreaking, and the heat in the boiling houses unbearable. Women who had given birth were back in the field after four-teen days, often carrying their child on their back.[53]

Sugar planters in the Atlantic world not only squeezed the maximum of labor from their enslaved workers but also preferred them to grow their own food. This had to be done in the evenings or on Sundays, although beyond the milling season it might have included Saturday afternoons as well. Co-lonial authorities acknowledged that this was by no means sufficient for a proper feeding. When Johan Maurits saw how the sugar monoculture in Pernambuco engendered malnutrition and even starvation, he ordered sugar lords to plant two hundred cassava shrubs per enslaved, which however had little effect.[54] In the French Antilles, Colbert tried to improve the nutri-tional conditions of the enslaved by including in his Code Noir of 1685 an article making masters fully responsible for the maintenance of their enslaved. But this again had little positive impact. According to the Dominican Père Jean-Baptiste Labat, enslaved workers had barely time to eat let alone plant during the milling season.[55] He knew because besides being a priest he was a sugar planter, engineer, and expert on Caribbean affairs in the late seven-teenth century. The appalling conditions in the Caribbean sugar islands were no secret in Europe and were even a cause of some concern. An inves-tigative report sent to British Parliament in 1737 concluded that the feeding of the enslaved left much to be desired and was a cause of the diminishing profitability in the sugar colonies.[56]

Poor nutritional standards, if not outright malnourishment, increased the enslaved's susceptibility to a range of diseases, including beriberi, to which female enslaved in particular were exposed during childrearing. Mortality spiked each year in August, which was known as the hunger month because at that time of the year the yields of the provision grounds were utterly inadequate. The teeth of exhumed skeletons attest to these periods of hunger and to starvation caused by diets of corn and molasses, with very little meat provided.[57] The enslaved would consume rats, lizards, or snakes, which they had to exterminate for the planters, if they had the chance to do so. Père Labat, who abhorred the eating of such animals, recounts how he set rat traps in the cane fields to diminish the threat of this ubiquitous vermin that reproduced itself at an alarming rate and attacked the cane cutters. To discourage the enslaved from making a business out of selling the captured animals, he gave financial compensation for each rat the assigned enslaved workers found in the traps.

Incidentally, Labat's story is one out of the many revealing that a monetary economy existed among the enslaved.[58]

Enslaved workers often succeeded in creating a food economy to counteract the regime of malnutrition imposed by the planters. Manioc and plantains (cooking bananas) might be the only foods that enslaved were given by the planters, the Scottish-Dutch military officer John Gabriel Stedman noted in Suriname in the 1770s.[59] However, enslaved Africans managed to introduce the cultivation of yams, sorghum, millet, rice, and peanuts. They turned the small yards around their huts into vegetable gardens, kept poultry, and sometimes even goats and hogs. If they were lucky, as was the case for those on estates near the coast in Barbados, they might catch some crabs or fish.[60] How enslaved Africans brought seeds and crops to the Americas is a mystery; they might have smuggled seeds, including rice, on board in their hair or perhaps collected plant material disposed of by slave ships sailing from the Caribbean ports.[61] At any rate, thanks to their knowledge of vegetables and fruits, enslaved at least got some vitamins, a necessity the planters often did not even care about for themselves.[62] Gradually, a creole cuisine emerged with cooking oil and vegetables that also entered the planters' households; indeed, without the expertise of their enslaved servants, Europeans arguably would not have survived in their sugar colonies.

Although the time allowed to take care of their own subsistence was wholly insufficient, enslaved people managed to successfully grow and even sell food. In the course of the eighteenth century, America's plantation owners often recognized the possession rights of the yards that had been cultivated by enslaved and which could even be bequeathed to friends or relatives. In whatever time the enslaved had left when they were not working or tending their own yards, they might do extra work for the plantations, such as collecting firewood or rope making. In addition, they could earn some cash by plaiting baskets or crafting pottery.[63] This gave rise to urban market economies on the Caribbean plantation islands, which also offered a space for women who had deserted their plantations to make a living and stay out of the hands of their masters.[64]

While it was already hard for the plantation workers born in the West Indies to survive, mortality among the newly arrived Africans was truly devastating. According to Reverend Robert Robertson, who was based at the island of Nevis in the early eighteenth century, about two-fifths of the enslaved Africans died within the first year. Many arrived in terrible conditions. Stedman, for instance, saw with his own eyes that the enslaved disembarking in Suriname were skin and bone.[65] Already traumatized upon arrival, conditions at the plantations made many enslaved suicidal. The Englishman and exiled royalist Richard Ligon, who lived in Barbados in the mid-seventeenth century, appeared to be puzzled that the enslaved did not seem to care for their lives at all. Quite a few committed suicide to deliver themselves from their terrible fate, he reported, to return their souls to their land of ancestry.[66] As William Beckford, a planter in late eighteenth-century Jamaica, wrote, "Some indeed will dare the terrors of the boiling cauldron, some attach themselves to the trees and doors, some plunge into the rapid torrent, and some will end their desperate existence with a knife."[67] Stedman, Beckford's contemporary, reports the same horrific events in Suriname, where enslaved jumped into the boiling sugar pans to free themselves from cruel masters, which gave them at least the grim satisfaction that it would cause financial loss to these torturers.[68]

The pervasive misery, the sadism of the overseers, chronic hunger, and excessively long working days did not go unresisted, however. The enslaved circumvented the planters' practice of giving them plantation names by keeping their African names for their own use. They also maintained and preserved their funeral rites, their singing, dancing, medicine, food preparation, weaning patterns, and religious systems. Inter-African syncretism emerged amidst the joint experience of rupture from Africa, racist oppression, and capitalist exploitation.[69] Women preserved their autonomy over their bodies by resorting to abortifacients to avoid giving birth to unfree children or after having been raped by an overseer.[70]

Resistance was not confined to the mental and cultural domains, and the enslaved's own bodies, but also frequently included setting fire to dry cane. Although the burned cane could still be milled, this had to be done without delay, which could not always be organized. Such incinerations made the lives of the cane cutters a bit easier, however, as it destroyed or at least expelled the rats.[71] If they saw an opportunity, the enslaved workers might also sabotage the mill, if only to have a moment of rest during the grueling eighteen-hour-plus days they had to work during harvest. If they had a place in the household, they might avenge their mistreatment by poisoning their masters' family members.[72] But above all they rebelled and deserted, as enslaved workers had already done in the early sixteenth-century plantations of

São Tomé and Hispaniola.[73] Resistance was always there and would culminate in the massive slave revolts of Saint Domingue in 1791 and of Jamaica in 1832, both of which played such a crucial role in the abolition of slavery.

The level of organized resistance varied according to the extent to which enslaved people were able to communicate with each other. The diverse ethnic and linguistic origins of the newly arrived enslaved mitigated the risk of rebellion, but it never took long before organized resistance emerged. In Barbados, a widespread plot was uncovered as early as 1675. It had been in the planning stages for three years, and the planters only learned about it after the betrayal of one enslaved woman.[74] From then on, slave owners in Barbados were permanently on the lookout for insurrections. They turned their houses into fortresses, formed a militia, and introduced written passes that their enslaved always had to carry when away from their plantation. In practice it was impossible to uphold such a rule and passes were often counterfeited by enslaved who tried to escape to Barbados's capital, Bridgetown.[75] In the French colonies, the article in the Code Noir of 1685 that forbade any contact between enslaved people from different masters to prevent or at least impede rebellious conspiracies was equally ineffective. Living under the constant fear of insurrection meant that even the beating of drums of the enslaved frightened the planters, who suspected hidden signals in the rhythms and often forbade these instruments as a result.[76]

In Brazil, the Guianas, or Jamaica, where desertion was easier than on the small and intensely cultivated island of Barbados, maroons soon numbered in the thousands. In Jamaica, military expeditions to subjugate them ended disastrously for the British. Not only was the landscape largely inaccessible, but the maroons also proved themselves to be capable military tacticians; many had been sold as slaves after being taken prisoners of war in their homelands. The British had no other option than to recognize the independence of some of the most powerful maroon communities, who in return assisted in upholding the plantation system by capturing and returning deserters. In the 1760, Tacky, a Fante prince from what is today Ghana, and Apongo, a headman from Dahomay, managed to organize an island-wide rebellion, which could have brought the end of British rule over Jamaica if maroon communities had not come to the aid of the British Army.[77]

Resistance in the Dutch Guianas was no less vehement and challenging to colonial rule. John Gabriel Stedman's account of his regiment's expeditions in Suriname against maroons gives us an impression of the sophistication and resilience of their communities, which colonial troops could not destroy and only drive deeper into the forests. In 1760, the Dutch government had no option but acknowledge the independence of these maroon communities. Meanwhile, deserting enslaved could expect the most gruesome punishments, such as the severing of a leg, which many did not survive.[78] In Saint Domingue, thousands of maroons lived in the mountains, posing a real threat to the planters, particularly since the chances of enslaved and free populations making common cause increased. The latter became more and more disgruntled, when in 1763 the *sang mêlés,* the descendants of enslaved Africans and their masters, some of whom had become successful indigo planters, were debarred not only from public service but also from learned professions, a restriction that was extended to include education in France.[79]

Cruel punishment was omnipresent and continued until the very end of plantation slavery. To ensure compliance, freshly arrived plantation over-seers were forced to participate in torturing enslaved workers for the mi-nutest transgressions. Newcomers from Europe would soon abandon their sense of humanity and become immersed in the gruesome realities of the plantation.[80] This happened to the Scotsman Zachary Macaulay, who was sent off to a Jamaica plantation in 1784 as a sixteen-year-old. According to a biographer, he went through the usual trajectory from shock and regret about the fate of the enslaved to being "callous and indifferent, and could allude to them with a levity which sufficiently marked my depravity."[81] Back in England, his brother-in-law Thomas Babington Macaulay managed to bring him over to the right side of history via the anti-slavery movement. Zachary served this cause with distinction: first as governor of Sierra Leone in the 1790s and subsequently as a leading abolitionist in England and founding editor of the *Anti-Slavery Monthly Reporter.*

Increasingly significant slave resistance and the emerging abolitionist movement in Britain made slaveholders aware that the slave trade posed a political problem for them. Meanwhile, their profits were shrinking because of rising prices on the slave markets spurred by growing demand for sugar and the high mortality rates on the plantations. The planters realized fur-ther that in the British colonies in North America the slave population was increasing without new shipments of captives from Africa. This gave abo-litionists the argument that banning the slave trade would force slave holders to treat their enslaved more humanely in order to stay competitive in the longer run. The planters felt the change in the wind, and were left with no option but to bring the death rates down and birth rates up. In Barbados, planters authored a manifesto in 1786 outlining measures to improve the lot of the enslaved and encourage enslaved women to have more children.[82] In the final quarter of the eighteenth century, Barbados was actually the only Caribbean island where the enslaved population almost stabilized without external supplies.

It is important to note that sugar plantations were far more deadly than tobacco and cotton estates, experiencing an annual mortality ranging from 4 to 6 percent by the end of the eighteenth century.[83] Malnutrition combined with an exhaustive labor regime resulted in an infant mortality that was extreme even for an era used to most children not reaching the age of five. Many newborns died from tetany due to a lack of calcium and magnesium, which led to a spasm of the jaw, which in turn meant the baby was unable to take the breast.[84] Tetanus, meanwhile, killed scores because of the high use of manure in the fields and because of slaves' proximity to cattle pens. Workers also had to carry manure in large baskets on their heads into the fields.[85] In addition, rats and snakes attacked the cane cutters. Mortality was also excessive because of improper clothing, inadequate housing, absence of shoes, severe burns, and accidents with the cane crushers. During the harvest, exhausted enslaved workers fell asleep while feeding the mill with cane, leading to horrific injuries when the rollers caught their hands or sleeves. Usually, an overseer was nearby with an axe to chop off the arm to prevent the enslaved from being completely pulled between the rollers.

Enslaved people were also in permanent danger because of the extreme violence that affected the whole Caribbean region. Almost every European war spilled over to this part of the world, where the smaller islands were an easy prey and the larger ones impossible to protect against raids. The French invasion of Jamaica in 1694, for example, destroyed more than fifty sugar mills and captured two thousand enslaved. The War of Succession (1701–1714) was a time of extreme anxiety for the planters and had horrific consequences for their enslaved who were put in harm's way during British bombardments of Guadeloupe, a French landing in Jamaica, French depredations of St. Kitts, and the ransacking of Nevis and Montserrat. During each war, buccaneers who operated with permission of their sovereigns took many ships. For instance, in a single month of 1704, of the 108 ships departing from Barbados and the Leeward Islands, forty-three were taken by the French.[86]

The Seven Years' War (1756–1763) and the French-British War (1778–1783) again disrupted maritime connections. When ships were lost, sugar rotted on the waterfront and food did not come in. In the 1780s, devastating hurricanes took an immense toll on the region's populations, and tens of thousands of enslaved died.[87] These decades marked the peak of casualties during the long period between 1688 and 1813 of almost permanent war. The Caribbean region was the frontier of colonial capitalism—an inferno of bullets, whips, hunger, and disease, in which most involuntary participants suffered and perished, and only a lucky few became fabulously wealthy.

Planters

The few planters who both survived and made a fortune unsurprisingly preferred to enjoy their wealth in a healthier environment. Prominent planters from Barbados, for instance, took their families and capital to New England, and to South Carolina in particular, where half of the white settlers originated in the West Indies.[88] They made slavery common in their new home and many led the pleasant life of a nobleman. While the North American colonies offered the space for overseas British societies to develop, the West Indies remained culturally and economically dependent upon Britain. None of the Dutch, French, or British Caribbean communities were large enough to sustain a center of higher learning. As early as the seventeenth century, successful planters' families sent their sons to Cambridge or Oxford University in England or to Harvard College in Massachusetts, which had opened its doors in 1636. These university-educated planters climbed to the highest administrative ranks.

Christopher Codrington, who was introduced above, was one of them. His grandfather, born into a family of English magnates, had become a successful Barbadian planter. His father was commander in chief of the Leeward Islands, and Christopher followed in his footsteps as governor of the same. Born in 1668 in Barbados, he studied at Oxford University and was fluent in French. He fought on the side of the Dutch stadholder and English King William III in Flanders against the army of the French "Sun King" Louis XIV before grudgingly returning to the West Indies to take up the post assigned to him. He had hoped to return to England at the earliest opportunity with fame and even more wealth than he had already inherited, but it was not to be, and he died in Barbados in 1710 at the age of forty-one. His body was interred in All Souls Chapel of Oxford University, the university to which he bequeathed a magnificent library.[89]

Even though Codrington deplored his tour of duty in the West Indies, he lived there like a prince. The Dominican planter Père Labat describes how Codrington moved around with a retinue of eight servants, trumpeters, and enslaved men who were positioned in front of the trumpeters and had to keep pace with the horses.[90] This seems to have been standard practice for how rich planters shuttled to their social events, a baffled Daniel Defoe reported.[91] The wealth of the white populations of the West Indies exceeded by far that of the North American colonists and made the West Indies economically far more important than Chesapeake for the United Kingdom. Even after the bank crisis of 1772, the War of Independence of the United States, and disasters such as the hurricanes of the 1780s, the white residents of the West Indies remained by far the richest of any British settlement in the Americas.[92]

Bridgetown, the second largest city in the English-speaking Americas, remained the center from where planters embarked on risky ventures to start new sugar plantations in the Caribbean region. Prominent among them was Gedney Clarke Sr., who came from Salem in Massachusetts and established himself in Bridgetown in the early 1730s. In 1742 he visited London, where he entered into a business partnership with Henry Lascelles, the prominent financier of the sugar business with roots and possessions in Barbados. In 1762, Gedney Clarke Jr. married into the Lascelles family and later succeeded his father as an associate in Henry Lascelles's firm.[93] Ties with New England were maintained. In 1751 Gedney Clarke Sr. received George Washington and his brother at his house in Barbados, who belonged to a prosperous Virginia slaveholding family themselves.[94]

Gedney Clarke Sr. heavily invested in Berbice and Demerara, the Dutch colonies on the Guiana coast, a new and violent frontier where over 450 plantations arose in the eighteenth century. He and his son were among the most prominent British and American investors, having sunk between £80,000 and £100,000 into eleven plantations. For centuries, merchants and entrepreneurs had crossed national boundaries in search of new investment opportunities and the production of sugar, but from the mid-seventeenth century they increasingly had to adapt or work around mercantilist economic policies. Gedney Clarke Sr. thought he had solved this problem by sending his son to Amsterdam in 1755 to learn Dutch and acquire Dutch citizenship. Gedney Clarke Jr. eventually settled in Middelburg, and thus he and his father handsomely profited from their binational base, which allowed them to supply enslaved Africans to Dutch Guiana and gave them access to low-interest Dutch loans. However, the disadvantage here was that, in return, sugar financed with Dutch money had to be consigned to the mortgage holder in the Dutch Republic against a fixed price. Another problem was that British customs considered Demerara sugar as foreign and thus subject to higher duties. Hence, planters such as the Clarkes sold some Demerara sugar as Barbadian to circumvent British duties on foreign sugar and also smuggled some of their sugar financed with Dutch money to Barbados at the expense of their Dutch consignees.[95] They had more problems with the devastating slave rebellions in 1763 and in 1765 that raged through Berbice. The inability of the Dutch to contain them compelled the Clarkes to send in troops at their own expense. Clearly disappointed by the Dutch attitude, they started to invest in Tobago, another frontier, in 1765. Four years later, after the death of his father, Gedney Clarke Jr. sold most of his eleven plantations in the two Dutch colonies.[96]

While the Clarkes invested in the frontiers, took the risks, and incurred losses, their Lascelles relatives reaped the profits, as merchants and refiners based in England earned the most from the sugar commodity chain.[97] The Lascelles were a singularly successful dynasty among Barbadian planters. The first member of the family arrived in Barbados in 1648 and the last two family plantations in Barbados were not sold until 1975. Henry Lascelles (1690–1753), who lived part of his life in Barbados, was an astute businessman widely engaged in supplying loans and mortgages to West Indian planters and slave traders. He was also one of the twenty-four directors of the British East India Company (EIC).[98] His son, the Cambridge-educated Edwin Lascelles (1713–1795), became the first Baron Harewood and built the magnificent Harewood House in West Yorkshire. Edwin and his brothers abandoned the family's resistance to investing directly plantation ownership when plantations came on the market at a bargain in the wake of the London and Amsterdam bank crisis of 1772–1773. They rapidly acquired estates from defaulting debtors, including plantations of Gedney Clarke Jr., who had to beg his Lascelles relatives for support to ensure his family's survival.[99]

Another outstanding member of this generation of Jamaica planters was William Beckford, who rose to one of Britain's most powerful positions. As a young man, William studied medicine in Leiden and Paris, and went to Jamaica at the age of twenty-seven to supervise the family property, soon enlarging it by taking over the plantations of his defaulting debtors. He ended his illustrious career as mayor of London and befriended Prime Minister William Pitt Sr. Two of Beckford's siblings married into the aristocracy, as would his son and only heir, William.[100] Less visible, but still pervasive, was the power of the roughly seventy members of Parliament who either owned plantations, had substantial investments in slave-based commerce, or issued loans in the West Indies. The largest proportion of their interests were related to Jamaica, followed by Barbados, St. Christopher, and Antigua. Although a small minority in Parliament, they exerted an outsized influence thanks to their remarkably professional lobby machine.[101]

Jane Austen's *Mansfield Park* (1814) and Charlotte Brontë's *Jane Eyre* (1847) offer us literary glimpses into how deeply the British ruling class had become involved in the West Indian economy, and how West Indian planters had become part of the British ruling classes, right up to the Royal family. Henry Lascelles, the sixth Earl of Harewood, married Princess Mary, daughter of King George V. The 2019 film that tied into the popular BBC series *Downtown Abbey* (2010–2015) was partly set at Harewood Castle, but the viewer is kept entirely unaware that each and every stone of it was paid for by slave labor.[102]

Since the thirteenth century, almost five hundred years of sugar capitalism had been driven by a combination of the immense profitability of the sugar commerce, the presence of skilled sugar masters, the necessary capital to build mills, ruthless exploitation of labor, and governments keen to further the industry to enlarge their revenue basis. Capital and expertise had traveled in East, Southeast, and South Asia, extensively in the Mediterranean, across the Atlantic, and from Brazil to the West Indies, as well as the French Antilles. But while the French and British governments reconfigured sugar as national projects and legislated tariffs, they did not involve themselves in its production and marketing, in contrast to the Crusaders, the Mamluks, and the Iberian courts, as we have seen in earlier chapters.

The Atlantic economy thrived on the circulation of people, goods, finance, and knowledge, transgressing international trading bans of the most powerful European states. The widespread smuggling undertaken was often a matter of survival to obtain food and other necessary goods.[103] Families such as the Clarkes were involved in the Carolina slave trade as well as in businesses in Salem, Middelburg, and London. With the drums of war sounding, Christopher Codrington and Père Labat convivially enjoyed their dinner conversing in French. Planters were drawn into national interests, but the grandees among them saw politics as having to serve their profitable way of life and not the other way around.

Europe's Profits from Sugar

Major European port cities thrived thanks to their Atlantic connections. England's second city, Bristol, for instance, obtained 40 percent of its wealth from slave-based activities by 1790, most of which pertained to sugar.[104] Bristol's Queens Square, like the impressive eighteenth-century buildings in Bordeaux and Nantes, or Rodney Street in Liverpool, is still there to provide evidence of the wealth accrued from this commerce. Dozens of houses along the gorgeous Amsterdam canals were built with money earned from enslaved plantation labor or from the processing of sugar, coffee, or tobacco. London, Glasgow, and Middelburg in the Netherlands need to be added to this list, but also cities that are not immediately associated with slave-based wealth such as Hamburg or Belgium's Ostend, where merchants displayed through splendid mansions their affluence accumulated from Atlantic slave-based commerce. And of course, merchants and plantation owners not only had lavish houses in the cities but also ostentatious manors in the countryside.[105]

The economic importance of the Atlantic slave-based commerce went far beyond the mercantile elites of the port cities. By about 1800, the West Indian sugar economy, for instance, exploited over three hundred thousand enslaved and employed tens of thousands in British refineries, shipping, and brokerage. In terms of employment within the British realm, only the wool sector surpassed this number.[106] The refiners in particular took a big share of the added value, benefiting from their position as the gatekeepers for the British market that was practically closed to sugar imports from other European countries.[107] The father of classical economics, Adam Smith, believed that this gigantic sector was only profitable thanks to its monopoly and hence at the expense of the consumer, an argument reiterated by some historians two centuries later. The burst of the colonial speculation bubble of 1773, the high level of protectionism for West Indian sugar, and the formidable military expenditures maintaining Britain's position in the Americas appeared to underwrite the argument that the colonies had thrown a millstone around Britain's neck.[108]

In reality, the rapidly growing and overwhelmingly slave-based Atlantic commerce contributed tremendously to Britain's economic stamina. It helped to finance the country's soaring government debt caused by its global conquests, in which foreign holdings, mainly by Dutch financiers, amounted to less than 10 percent in the 1780s.[109] For its exports, Britain's Atlantic orientation was vital after its access to the European market was closed off by France, a country three times as populous and militarily far more powerful. While Britain's largest sector, the wool industry, lost its customers on the other side of the Channel, it found new ones in the West Indies and among Britain's rapidly growing North American populations. Exports to Africa and the Americas accounted for more than a third of Britain's exports and more than half of its imports by 1776, when the United States declared their independence. Meanwhile, Britain's dependency on the slave-based Atlantic imports not only pertained to tobacco, sugar, cotton, and indigo from its own colonies but also included extensive gold imports from Brazil.[110]

Moreover, the Atlantic slave-based commerce offered high returns on investment. Barbara Solow concluded that these were four to seven times higher in the West Indies than at home in Britain.[111] In the capital-abundant Dutch Republic, the Atlantic commerce likewise promised much higher rewards than the domestic interest rates of around 2.5 percent. For France as well, long-distance trade appears to have offered higher returns on investment than domestic activities.[112] In these countries, more than in Portugal and Spain, the Atlantic economy was closely connected to the most dynamic parts of the metropolitan economy, such as shipbuilding, the processing of tropical products, and the banking and insurance sectors.[113]

Britain, North America, and the West Indies uniquely constituted a triangular economy, in which Britain produced industrial goods and services, North America provided timber, food, and other basic commodities for the West Indies, and the West Indies cultivated the tropical commodities.[114] In absolute figures, the international commerce of France widely overshadowed that of Britain, and exports from the French Antilles were over 2.5 times those of the West Indies on the eve of the French Revolution. In fact, the Antillean commerce's share of the French gross domestic product (GDP) in the 1780s may have amounted to an impressive 9 percent.[115] Still, the synergetic effects of the Atlantic economy were less for France than for England.

Sugar was the most important of the tropical commodities reaching Europe, and here we see how the Atlantic synergies worked. The British sugar sector probably accounted for over 3 percent of the nation's GDP in 1794–1795 and a comparable 3.5 percent for France on the eve of the French Revolution.[116] However, in France the sugar sector had not been developed to its full potential. To their own detriment, French cities competed with each other for tax privileges from the French government. The haphazard and localized fiscal policies of Ancien Régime France resulted in a decline of the once prominent sugar industry of Nantes. French refining capacity was at best stagnating when Saint Domingue became the largest sugar exporter in the world.[117]

A considerable share of the sugar from Saint Domingue went to refineries in Amsterdam. The Dutch Republic had the distinct advantage of their superior ships and abundance of low-interest capital.[118] Moreover, the Dutch Estates General had seen an opportunity in the floundering French refinery sector to restore the Republic's prominence in Europe's sugar trade and slashed the import duties on foreign sugar by 80 percent in 1771. This move was somewhat at the expense of its own planters in Suriname and the Dutch Guianas. However, in spite of the fortune the Dutch had invested in their sugar and coffee plantations in Suriname and adjacent Berbice, Essequibo, and Demerara, supplies had stagnated, whereas Saint Domingue managed to produce sugar—as well as coffee—in enormous quantities and at a lower price. Amsterdam's sugar imports from Suriname and Dutch Guiana amounted to about ten thousand tons in the 1770s, whereas from France imports peaked at about thirty-six thousand tons in that decade.[119]

The Dutch Republic had therefore made a wise decision to sharply reduce the import tariffs on foreign sugar and continue its policy of duty-free exports of sugar refined within its borders. During the 1770s, Amsterdam refineries employed four thousand workers and processed fifty thousand tons of sugar.[120] Dordrecht, a Dutch city with a direct river connection with Germany, must have employed hundreds of workers in its seventeen sugar refineries. Most of these were established by German Lutherans in the first half of the eighteenth century.[121] In total, the Dutch Republic's exports of Atlantic slave-produced sugar amounted to ten million guilders per year, rapidly growing volumes of sugar reached consumers deep down into Germany, particularly via the Rhine. When Adam Smith wrote in his *Wealth of Nations* that the Dutch Republic was the wealthiest nation in the world, the Atlantic slave-based commerce accounted for over 5 percent of its GDP.[122]

Indeed, while Britain enjoyed the full synergy of its Atlantic sugar commerce, on the Continent it was divided between more countries than just France and the Dutch Republic. After the 1770s the sugar imports of the Dutch Republic would actually stagnate, whereas those of Hamburg rapidly increased.[123] Since France and Hamburg concluded their trade agreement in 1769, the latter had become the gateway for French sugar exports destined for Central Europe and Russia. After the Dutch Republic was occupied by the French in 1795, Hamburg took over almost the entire Dutch sugar industry, and its imports reached almost fifty thousand tons annually by 1800.[124]

Saint Domingue, British India, and the Ban on the Slave Trade

Sugar production in the late eighteenth-century Atlantic realm was propelled by popular consumption of coffee, tea, lemonades, candies, and pastries spreading like an inkblot over northwestern Europe as well as New England and the cities of the Ottoman Empire.[125] Through the relentless abduction of Africans and the relocation of plantations to new fertile land, the output in the Caribbean region kept pace with this growth. The expansion of production in Saint Domingue and Jamaica more than compensated the stagnating production in Brazil and the smaller Caribbean islands. The marvelously fertile island of Saint Domingue alone produced almost eighty thousand tons of sugar per year, nearly a third of what Europe consumed at the time.[126]

But the massive importation of enslaved Africans also fueled resistance on the plantations, which earned increasing moral support from colonial free burghers (free people of color, some of them formerly enslaved), who learned from newspapers and other sources about growing criticism back in England as well as in North America about the institution of slavery.

One of the earliest, or perhaps the earliest, petitions requesting abolition that we know of circulated in the Quaker colony of Pennsylvania in 1688. The Quakers' engagement with abolition ironically had its roots in Barbados. Here, the most prominent early abolitionist and Quaker Benjamin Lay had run his shop that catered to enslaved as well. He saw how severely malnourished and mistreated they were and became an early and ardent advocate of abolition, waging a one-man crusade after he settled in Pennsylvania in 1731. After the death of his wife, he lived as a vegetarian hermit in a converted cave and tended a vegetable garden.[127]

The idea of boycotting slave-made products and rejecting them as sinful luxuries continuously resonated among Quakers. John Woolman wrote in his *Plea for the Poor* in 1764—not published until 1793—about the relationship between slavery and consumption society: plain and coarse cloths made people free and wearing such attire in itself was already a sign of protest against slavery.[128] Although most fellow Quakers did not yet share Lay and Woolman's comprehensive rejection of slave-based products, they did consider alternatives, and some even started to buy land for maple syrup production. As one of them pointed out in a newspaper article, the country could make its own maple sugar and save a lot of money.[129] Benjamin Rush, father of American psychiatry and one of the fifty-six signatories of the Declaration of Independence, claimed that millions of acres could be planted with maple trees and be tapped by small farmers. He wrote about it in an open letter addressed in 1793 to Secretary of State Thomas Jefferson. Rush had carefully chosen his addressee, because among the Founding Fathers it was Jefferson who propagated a decentralized state with small farmers as its backbone.[130]

Rush's letter to Jefferson was accompanied by a postscript that included the report by Henry Botham, the planter in Sumatra whom we met in Chapter 1, on Chinese sugar manufacturing near Java's capital, Batavia. Rush advanced this as another argument to abandon West Indian sugar.[131] Twenty years earlier, in 1773, Rush had quoted from the travelogue by the famous French botanist Pierre Poivre also mentioned in Chapter 1—of which almost immediately an English translation circulated—in which he stated that Chinese workers "would have produced double the quantity that is now procured from the labor of the unfortunate Negroes."[132] In the same pamphlet, Rush had condemned slavery, which involved "every violation of the Law and the Gospel," although at that time he still held a enslaved servant himself and was of the peculiar opinion that having a black skin was the result of a disease.[133]

Pamphlets such as Rush's traveled swiftly across the Atlantic via the commercial links between Quakers in Philadelphia and London, helping to turn abolitionism into the most prominent popular movement in Britain in the 1780s. Quakers started petitioning Parliament in 1783 and widened it to an ecumenical movement grounded in fact-finding and Smithian economics. Adam Smith, after all, had already disavowed agricultural servitude as backward and had included, although not persuasively, black slavery in this point of view.[134] The protests against the consumption of slave sugar became a genuine popular movement. William Fox's pamphlet of 1791 condemning the consumption of sugar "stained with spots of human blood" was printed in twenty-five editions totaling fifty thousand copies—and it has been assumed that, including bootlegged versions, that number rose to almost 250,000. Its message was clear and simple: "If we purchase the commodity, we participate in the crime."[135]

The phrase "stained with spots of human blood" entailed an awkward visualization with an almost cannibalistic connotation and was particularly powerful in the case of sugar.[136] As the Cuban Fernando Ortiz wrote in his famous book on tobacco and sugar as each other's counterpoints, "Sugar comes into this world without a last name."[137] Indeed, sugar never had the positive attributes associated with the provenance of tobacco, like a specific flavor that can be uniquely related to where it was produced. As a rule, preindustrial sugars were ranked according to their level of refinement and grain. While groceries in Europe at the time of abolition advertised their items through their provenance, such as Dijon mustard, Castile soap, or Jamaica rum, they merely wrapped their sugars in different colored papers to denote their respective grades of refinement.[138]

Fox's urgent request to consumers also contained a direct and resonating appeal to women. As William Wilberforce, the most prominent British abolitionist, prophesied in the 1790s, women's role in the abolition movement would eventually further their own emancipation.[139] Abstinence reverberated nationally and apparently right up to the royal house, if we can believe a cartoon showing the English king, queen, and their daughters around the table bravely sipping their bitter sugar-free tea. However, alternatives were available. Like Rush had done before, Fox alluded in the American version of his famous pamphlet to Botham's observations, who in the meantime had testified in the British Parliament that sugar grown by Chinese millers in Java could be obtained more cheaply than sugar from the West Indies.[140]

At this juncture, a realistic—and formidable—alternative to slave sugar emerged. Since 1772 the British had ruled over Bengal, where they found a once thriving sugar economy that had been shattered by war and famine. The EIC (East India Company) quickly lowered taxes on sugar and sent its functionaries around to provide advance payments to local merchants. These in turn had their agents in the countryside to buy the cane standing in the field shortly before the harvest.[141] Within a few years' time, Bengal would be shipping about ten thousand tons of sugar to England. Although still of minor importance in comparison to the 157,000 tons coming from the West Indies by 1800, it was a start at least, and more would come since it was just a fraction of the estimated five hundred thousand tons of raw sugar milled annually in India at the time.[142]

Moreover, India's potential was outrageously underutilized, according to enthusiastic entrepreneurs. Among these was John Prinsep, a man of rather humble origins who had made his incredible fortune in India, engaging in copper mining and coinage, indigo and chintz production, and shipping. He took up the pen to advocate the opening up of trade with India and emphasized the vast potential of Bengal's sugar production.[143] Others saw opportunities to produce sugar with the latest equipment and methods from the West in this immense, populous and largely fertile subcontinent. William Fitzmaurice, for instance, introduced himself in a memorandum to the Court of Directors of the EIC as having been a manager of sugar estates in Jamaica. To him, it was clear why Bengal performed poorly as a sugar exporter. To begin with, the pestle and mortar mills used were obsolete pieces of equipment producing a juice so dirty that it was already in a "forward state of fermentation before the process of boiling is commenced."[144] Importing the sugar manufacturing practices of the West Indies could immensely enhance India's sugar production, Fitzmaurice concluded.

The EIC began to facilitate experiments with West Indian equipment and assigned the eminent botanist William Roxburgh to the botanical garden in Calcutta to test foreign, mainly Chinese, cane varieties. Yet despite India's excellent climate and soil conditions, experiments to start a West Indian type of sugar manufacturing came to nothing. Until the 1820s, European sugar technology had not yet sufficiently progressed to outdo traditional Indian sugar making. British planters did not have estates and enslaved workers at their disposal as they had in the West Indies and had to buy cane from farmers. They found it hard to compete with the urban refineries, the khandsari workshops, which had their dense networks of agents stretching out into the countryside to buy the cane standing in the fields. The EIC administration in Calcutta did consider sending its own moneylenders to the cane fields in order to obtain cane for British sugar mills, but Governor-General Charles Cornwallis, who was in office from 1786 to 1794, decided against it. He could not easily perceive sugar in India as of strategic British interest, in contrast to opium, which was exported to China to pay for the tea for British households.[145]

While in Britain and Pennsylvania people engaged in lively discussions about ways to replace slave sugar, in France, slavery was only questioned by a small and dedicated group of French writers who prided themselves on being at the vanguard of the Enlightenment. The most notable example of the literature they produced is *L'Histoire philosophique et politique des établissements et du commerce des Européens dans les deux Indes* (A Philosophical and Political History of the Settlements and Trade of the Europeans in the East and West Indies) (1777), which was edited by Guillaume-Thomas Raynal and included a blistering critique on slavery by the radical and leading Enlightenment philosopher Denis Diderot. This work was widely disseminated, reprinted dozens of times, and translated into English and Dutch, but it did not inspire a broad abolitionist movement in France; in the Dutch Republic it did not resonate at all. Nonetheless, the very fact that the abolitionist movement in France never gained the same popular traction as in England might explain how it became more radical than its counterpart, demanding the immediate abolition of slavery. Its chance came with the French Revolution. The French abolitionists petitioned in 1791 to the revolutionary National Assembly for immediate abolition, a cause the Republic would embrace by banning slavery throughout the French domain in 1793.

Meanwhile, the British Parliament moved toward the far less radical measure of the abolition of the slave trade. By about 1790, even business interests affiliated with West Indian planters admitted that the ongoing human trafficking was not sustainable and that amelioration of enslaved's living conditions was an urgent matter. In 1792, the House of Commons voted for the abolition of the British slave trade within four years—which in fact would still allow for a final massive capturing of Africans to increase the enslaved population in the West Indies. Yet Thomas Babington wrote to

his brother-in-law Zachary Macaulay, acting governor of Sierra Leone, ju-
bilantly: "Gisborne and I sat till six this morning in the gallery of the House.
Gradual Abolition is resolved on by a majority of 238 to 85. The number of
petitions which come up every day must make an impression on the minds
of the members."[146]

While the Act was being debated in Parliament, a full-scale rebellion
among the largest slave population of the Caribbean was underway. The
enslaved and free black populations of Saint Domingue rose up, sending a
shockwave through the West Indian planters. Fleeing French residents
brought the terrifying news that their proud capital Port au Prince, with
its beautiful houses, a theatre, and many other hallmarks of European civilization, had gone up in flames.[147] They were warmly received by the British
residents of the West Indies out of solidarity, at least until in 1793 when
British and French declared war on each other. The Act to ban the slave
trade, despite gaining a large majority in the House of Commons and being
the subject of a glowing speech by Prime Minister William Pitt Jr., became
stranded in the House of Lords, which first postponed the bill and then in
1793 defeated it. By that time the revolution in Saint Domingue seemed
inextinguishable, and the British West Indies were the main beneficiaries
of the ruin of their most powerful competitor. Jamaica rapidly increased its
slave imports.[148]

Pitt Jr. now did his utmost to crush the French Revolution in the Caribbean, determined as he was to use Britain's naval superiority to turn the
region into an auxiliary front against revolutionary France. His government
dispatched a huge military force to Saint Domingue, but Toussaint L'Ouverture managed to hold his own with the moral backing of the revolutionary
French National Convention in Paris. Between 1793 and 1796 Pitt's government sent a total of sixty thousand soldiers to the Caribbean islands, of
whom a third went to Saint Domingue. Almost two-thirds of this army
died, mostly from yellow fever.[149]

While thousands of British soldiers died and the British government
wasted about £20 million on its Caribbean military campaign, West Indian planters—many of whom stayed safely in their British mansions—did
very well. This did not make them popular in the eyes of the British public.[150]
In 1794, one could read in English newspapers alarming messages such as
that "unless a speedy reinforcement arrives from England, it is much to be
apprehended that the British will be obliged to evacuate all the newly-taken

possessions in Domingo; as so great has been the mortality in Jamaica, occasioned by the yellow fever among the soldiers and sailors, that there are not left sufficient to do the duty of the latter island."[151]

While Britain's soldiers succumbed in huge numbers on the other side of the Atlantic Ocean and the sugar business prospered, the abolition of the slave trade disappeared from the political agenda. For most of the years between 1793 and 1806, Britain was able to add the sugar from Martinique and Guadeloupe as well as the sharply diminished production of Saint Domingue to its imperial output. In addition, the British captured the Dutch Guianas, Trinidad, and Tobago. As a result, sugar imports into Britain reached their highest peak of two hundred thousand tons on the eve of the Peace of Amiens in 1802. The British had practically achieved a sugar monopoly for the European market. Even after some French sugar islands were returned as part of this peace treaty, Britain controlled most of the Caribbean sugar commerce, and British planters and merchants were confident that they could easily sell the vast volumes at home and in continental Europe. But for this they needed fresh supplies of enslaved Africans, and were therefore not at all interested in a ban on the slave trade.[152]

But then, in 1806, Napoleon's imposition of the Continental System blockaded, among other British goods, its sugar imports to the entire European continent. Moreover, Cuba and Puerto Rico emerged as serious sugar producers, and the state of Louisiana had begun to produce sugar as well. Not prone to be captured by France and its allies, neutral American shipping proved to be cheaper than its British equivalent during these years of Napoleonic Wars. This also loosened Britain's hold on the global European sugar market. In addition to dwindling sugar prices and lack of access to European markets, there was yet another incentive for British planters to no longer oppose abolishing the slave trade. They now reckoned that a general ban on the Atlantic slave trade would hurt the new and fledgling plantations of Cuba far more than the British possessions. The British planters may well have felt that they had sufficient enslaved workers now to dispense with the slave trade.[153]

For East Indian sugar, meanwhile, oversupply from the Caribbean region on the British market spelled bad news just at the moment that its shipments had risen from a negligible few hundred tons to about ten thousand. These imports collapsed and would only fully recover after the abolition of slavery in the British Empire in 1834.[154] The West Indies were still by far Britain's most important and profitable overseas possession, and its planters were still firmly entrenched in Parliament and able to uphold discriminatory import duties against East Indian sugar. They received support from Britain's refiners who were equally interested in punishing duties for the traditional East Indian sugars, the khandsaris, that could be directly retailed without further refining. Meanwhile, in 1813 an additional 25 percent duty was imposed on all sugar imports from outside the West Indies to protect the slaveholders who were having to accommodate the end of the slave trade. Obviously, this was aimed against the cheaper sugar from India. Tariffs were a mighty weapon in the hands of the defenders of West Indian sugar in Parliament.[155]

But it was not all bad news for Indian sugar exports, as these still found growing export markets, including continental Europe. Since Indian sugar hardly passed through British customs in the first two decades after 1813, British merchants shipped it to Hamburg and replaced France as the main supplier to Germany. In these years, 70 percent of the sugar unloaded in this German sugar hub came from Britain, and half of this volume was from India, alongside increasing quantities from Cuba and Brazil. Hamburg maintained its position as one the largest centers of sugar refining in the world and through the sugar trade its patrician families, such as the Schröders, would lay the foundations for their world-spanning banking network. They established themselves in half a dozen European cities, and their firms extended into the Americas as well Batavia and Singapore. The London branch of this family firm assumed a major role in the Cuban sugar trade and the island's railway construction. In the first half of the nineteenth century, a growing share of the sugar arriving in Hamburg came from Cuba, first via the United States and then, from the 1820s onward, directly. In addition, Hamburg received increasing quantities from Brazil.[156]

Thus an entirely new trade configuration came into existence, in which the French Antilles and the British West Indies rapidly lost their position as leading sugar suppliers for the European market. New sugar belts that would cater to the North Atlantic market emerged in the Spanish Caribbean islands, India, and Louisiana. Last, but not least, a serious competitor for cane sugar made its appearance: beet sugar. The world of sugar was about to enter an entirely new era of industrialization, driven by a new spirit: that of the industrial and colonial sugar bourgeoisie.

4

Science and Steam

BY THE END OF THE EIGHTEENTH CENTURY, sugar from the Americas had reached the urban lower classes in Europe. It was traded deep into Russia and Central Asia, where it competed with imports from China and India. Opportunities to sell sugar abounded as markets around the globe buoyed and catered to the growing demand, from pastry bakers in Philadelphia and sherbet houses in Baghdad to coffeehouses in Vienna. This rapidly growing consumption had stopped the decline of Brazilian sugar production and pushed its frontier far into the interior toward the border with contemporary Bolivia, defying staggering transportation costs.[1]

Thus far, expansion had been the only viable response to declining yields and soil exhaustion in particular, and the frontiers of the Guianas, Jamaica, and Saint Domingue had emerged as a result. However, at the end of the eighteenth century higher-yielding canes were introduced followed by the advent of steam power, which reversed the trend of declining yields per worker. An impressive 40 percent increase in the amount of sugar produced per worker between 1770 and 1840 matched the productivity growth of Great Britain as a whole, at that time economically the most advanced nation in the world.[2]

In the course of the eighteenth century, experiments in chemistry, physics, and botany initiated a transformation of tropical commercial agriculture and changed the world of sugar beyond recognition. The first botanical garden in the tropics was laid out in Batavia (Java) in 1757, which was soon followed by half a dozen more sprinkled around the equator, setting in motion multiple crop transfers across the globe. The first steam technology to mill cane was tested in Jamaica in 1767—an inauspicious and isolated event at the time, but, together with dozens of other patents, it would pave the way for a complete industrialization of cane milling. While cotton weaving was famously crucial for the breakthrough of the Industrial Revolution, the sugar crushers were among the first machines driven by steam power in the tropics.[3] Early on in the nineteenth century, hundreds of these machines entered sugar estates across the globe.

Meanwhile, with its many wars and revolutions the Napoleonic era proved to be a phase of creative destruction, generating multiple diasporas of planters that crossed the rapidly shifting imperial boundaries between the British, French, Spanish, Dutch, and American domains. Planters transferred their skills to Java, Sumatra, Penang, India, or the Philippines. A planter from Saint Domingue, for example, traveled all the way to Batavia in 1804 to offer his services to revive waning sugar estates near the city, while others traveled from the West Indies to British India. Such journeys accelerated the circulation of knowledge and forged a global community of sugar experts.

Crucially, around the turn of the nineteenth century, in the midst of the Napoleonic Wars, pharmacists and chemists developed a viable production process for extracting sugar from beet by boiling it under vacuum, which would also revolutionize the cane sugar sector. Industrialists in France and Britain together with the colonial bourgeoisie would metamorphosize Ancien Régime plantation enclaves into agro-industries dominating large frontiers equipped with railroads and massive steam-driven factories. The colonial bourgeoisie dominated this transition period from water- or cattle-powered mills to factories with steel skeletons, corrugated roofs, and machines fully driven by steam. These developments would comprehensively change the nature of sugar from an agricultural and artisanal item into an agro-industrial bulk commodity made from two different and competing crops.

This industrialization was embedded in a broader societal transformation, in which discussions about human rights and human progress came to the fore. Freedom became a central notion of these debates, both among the people who rebelled against their enslavement and among consumers who refused to be complicit in slavery and its atrocities. Concepts of progress and freedom shaped new bourgeois values that foregrounded industrial development as the means of liberating humanity from arduous manual work and ultimately from slavery itself.[4] The most progressive and educated members of the colonial sugar bourgeoisie were definitely aware of the glaring contradiction between modernity and slavery and prepared themselves for a gradual phasing out of slavery. They began investing in mechanization, considered alternative sources of labor, and focused their sights on sugar production in Asia. However, the majority of the planters likely fortified themselves in a racism that denied progress to most of mankind. Tragically, slavery and labor coercion would not disappear under the regime of industrial capitalism and the global spread of industrial sugar production—it would actually expand.

Science and Tropical Agriculture

The Seven Years' War (1756–1763) was the first conflict that involved four continents and marked the beginning of a period in which Britain established itself as the world's hegemonic power. It turned India, the world's largest sugar producer, into the most important British colonial possession. For France and Spain, this global war ended in a humiliating defeat at the hands of Britain. France, the most populous country of Europe, and Spain, which still had its immense empire in the Americas, realized that unless they generated more revenue from their colonies, Britain's maritime superiority would soon relegate them to second-rank colonizers. The war forced them to rethink the economies of their diminished empires. Tropical agriculture would play a key role in their pursuits, which were informed by physiocratic notions. The physiocrats were originally a group of French economists who insisted that agriculture was the source of all wealth and argued that agricultural products should be highly priced. They condemned costly colonial wars, which in their view stemmed from the misguided protectionism and the mercantilist doctrine that one nation's economic loss was another's gain. Among the physiocrats were influential colonial administrators such as Martinique's intendant Pierre-Paul Le Mercier de la Rivière, who lifted the mercantilist trade bans with New England far more comprehensively than Paris had allowed him to do.[5]

The Spanish Crown likewise dismantled the bans on foreign commercial relations it had imposed upon its imperial possessions and their residents. It now acknowledged that local initiatives deserved its full support. Moreover, the English had unintentionally done the Spanish a big favor by conquering Havana in 1762, because it opened Cuba up for English and Chesapeake commerce. Eleven months of British occupation made the island's Spanish creole population realize that being under the Spanish Empire had nullified their advantageous proximity to the settlers' colonies of North America. When Havana's port received the blessing of the Spanish Crown in 1776 to welcome ships under foreign flags, it turned out to be excellent timing. In that very year, the thirteen American colonies declared their independence from Britain. The United States of America became the most important trading partner of Havana. Spain's joining of France and the American rebels in their war against Britain definitely advanced commercial contacts between Cuba and the United States. The wealth accumulated in this commerce flowed into Cuba's now buoyant plantation agriculture.[6]

Concomitant to weakening imperial mercantilist reflexes, which allowed for intensifying international trade and contacts, sugar production saw more innovations in the latter part of the eighteenth century than in the two preceding centuries combined. Not that progress had been entirely absent—the many measures taken to put Barbadian sugar production on an ecologically sustainable basis proved otherwise.[7] New was the notion, however, that knowledge was something not exclusively obtainable through experience on the spot. Publications on best practices and even on the application of scientific insights therefore found a keen readership. William Belgrove's *Treatise on Husbandry and Planting* (1755), for instance, enjoyed seven reprints.[8] Professionalism increased, also because quite a few of the wealthiest sugar planters of the West Indies and the French Antilles had studied at European or American universities, and some of them were advanced amateur scientists.[9]

Innovation was also driven by the rising prices planters had to pay for enslaved Africans, declining margins of profits, growing demand in Europe, and the pending abolition of the slave trade. These combining factors changed the calculus for planters, who began to show some concern about their slaves' health.[10] Sure, many of the medical explorations by plantation doctors were tainted by white prejudice, for instance blaming enslaved mothers for the high infant mortality rate. Still, the masters learned to appreciate the sophisticated knowledge of herbal medicine, including the application of quinine, among their enslaved.[11] Particularly influential became James Grainger's *Essay on the West Indian Diseases* published in the wake of the Seven Years' War. It urged planters to organize weekly inspections of fingers and toes and to be constantly on the lookout for parasites.

Grainger explored cures for the many different worms in circulation and deplored the fact that enslaved had to walk barefooted, particularly if they had ulcers on their feet and ankles.[12] In terms of prevention, crucial progress was made with the introduction of variolation to combat smallpox in the West Indies in the 1760s. Around 1800, Jennerian vaccination against this disease may have started in Cuba as part of the global tour of the vaccine mission sent out by the Spanish king, which also made mainland Latin America and the Philippines early adopters. This must have resulted in a substantial reduction of mortality; during previous epidemics about 10–20 percent of newly arrived West African enslaved had died from smallpox.[13]

A range of infrastructural and managerial innovations, as well as large investment, also boosted productivity. Planters in St. Domingue undertook irrigation works, and the Dutch built dikes and drainage systems in Dutch Guiana and Suriname, allowing them to exploit the fertile swamps, use water mills, and transport sugar over water. To save labor, planters throughout the Caribbean region sought to streamline the logistics of their estates; they improved and relocated mills, dug canals, or constructed rudimentary tramways to facilitate transport. They established new estates close to the sea to expeditiously ship their sugar and thus save precious labor and draught animals. Planters converted from cattle to water mills, and, in Suriname, this happened almost entirely thanks to money flowing from the Dutch Republic. Some planters in the Caribbean region built aqueducts to generate water power. Antigua and Guadeloupe extensively converted to windmills, which had a higher capacity per hour than water or cattle mills and thus allowed planters to dispense with night shifts, which had beneficial effects of the enslaved's health.[14]

Nonetheless, life for the enslaved continued to be hard, particularly because mechanization in the field stalled. Cane harvesting was grueling labor, and the plough rarely entered the cane fields of slave plantations. Planters were, moreover, usually not interested in saving labor beyond the harvesting season. On some islands, hills were so steep that ploughing caused erosion. In Trinidad the soil was too wet, whereas in Guiana the drainage system of the polder prohibited ploughing.[15] Innovations and improvements did little to diminish severe exploitation. As a consequence, birth rates stayed low, and while in most of the West Indies mortality rates declined from 6 percent in the eighteenth century to 3 percent between 1800

An 1823 depiction of enslaved workers in Antigua planting cane stalks in a prepared field. The fortress in the background underlines the violent character of the Caribbean sugar economy.

and 1830. This was insufficient for enslaved populations to grow. Food imports may have mitigated the effects of the hunger month of August, when the provision grounds did not yield sufficient food. Planters allowing their enslaved more time to tend these provision grounds may have raised nutritional conditions too. Nonetheless, malnutrition persisted as a serious problem in the Caribbean plantations and increased enslaved's vulnerability to diseases. An influenza epidemic in the early nineteenth century and whooping cough carried away many, and dysentery was still a tremendous killer.[16]

Botany

Attendant upon the rise of the colonial bourgeoisie and spread of physiocratic notions, a lively transfer of knowledge and expertise occurred across imperial boundaries, marking a significant rupture with the era of mercantilism. Charles-Theodore Mozard, a book printer in Saint Domingue's capital Port au Prince, member of learned societies, and amateur meteorologist, noted in 1788 upon the return of a French ship from Jamaica with plant species: ". . . the time has passed where nations try to monopolize certain of nature's riches."[17] Botany was indeed one of the rays of Enlightenment that pierced through the darkness of endless European wars. The oldest botanical garden on the Caribbean island of St. Vincent, established shortly after the Seven Years' War by the island's garrison surgeon George Young, was maintained without any support from London and relied solely on contacts crossing imperial boundaries. Plants received from Guadeloupe and South and Southeast Asia contributed to a botanic treasury that boasted thirty different commercial crops by 1773.[18] Two years later, a similar garden was created on Jamaica, from where a variety of new crops spread over the island, ranging from mango to cinnamon.[19] Some of these species also arrived in Saint Domingue, as Mozard witnessed.

A pivotal figure cementing connections between a string of botanical gardens in British colonies was Joseph Banks, a high-ranking Londoner but also a man with bourgeois credentials; he only became a baronet later in life. He obtained the peerage through the merit of his academic career, which he had started by serving as the botanist on Captain James Cook's first voyage to the Pacific (1768–1771).[20] Banks, a landowner who had embraced physiocratic notions, reached the most prestigious positions of Privy Council to the King and President of the Royal Society of London for the Improvement of Natural Knowledge. Through his personal interventions he smoothed the transfer of plant material and under his long leadership Kew Gardens would emerge as the center of global botany.

Smooth migration of plant specimens also enabled the rapid spread of a new type of cane throughout the Americas. In the wake of the Seven Years' War, botanists set their eyes on the Pacific islands and the Indonesian archipelago for wild "noble" (meaning thick and high-yielding) canes. Louis-Antoine Comte de Bougainville's voyage around the world in 1766–1769 was an astounding success in terms of the botanical knowledge gathered. Moreover, it resulted in the discovery of a new sugar cane variety, the Otaheite or Bourbon cane. De Bougainville discovered it on the Island of Tahiti and handed it over to Pierre Poivre—we met him as advocate of Chinese sugar in Chapter 1—the intendant of the botanical gardens of Île de France and Bourbon, and a key figure in the spread of tropical crops throughout the French colonies.

Poivre took care of further disseminating the Otaheite—the fact that he was based in Bourbon (later Réunion) gave the cane its other name: Bourbon. In the early 1780s, it arrived in the French Antilles, and then in Suriname in 1789 and St. Vincent and Cuba in 1793.[21] Meanwhile, Captain William Bligh brought Otaheite cane from the Pacific to the British West Indies, from where it spread across the Latin American mainland in the nineteenth century.[22] It owed its rapid dissemination to its 15–20 percent higher yields than the Creole variant that had been brought from the Canary Islands centuries before by Columbus on his second voyage. As an additional advantage, Otaheite left a bagasse after milling that burnt much better in the mill's furnaces than that of the Creole cane. This was a particularly important quality on Caribbean islands, where sugar plantations had caused widespread deforestation.[23]

Higher-yielding canes became of strategic importance, and it was clearly perceived as such also by the EIC in India. Banks was involved in finding the appropriate cane for India, not due to any abolitionist inclinations but because he had designated India as the ideal supplier of raw material to Britain on economic and agronomic grounds.[24] William Roxburgh, the Scottish surgeon, botanist, and specialist on Indian sugar cane cultivation, tested different types of cane for Indian conditions at the Calcutta botanical garden, and he stayed in close contact with Banks.[25] His appointment came in 1793, not coincidentally two years after the revolution in Saint Domingue and one year after the British Parliament had adopted the Act to abolish the slave trade, which was ultimately defeated in the House of Lords (see Chapter 3).

Learned and Economic Societies

In late eighteenth-century European colonial settlements, scientific explorations were followed as keenly as today's latest technological developments. Learned societies mushroomed in the French, British, Spanish, and Dutch colonies. In 1784, a group of nine surgeons, physicians, and merchants based in Saint Domingue established the Cercle des Philadelphes (Circle of Philadelphians). The name was an homage to Benjamin Franklin, whose book on electricity was well known among Caribbean planters.[26] Franklin was still not an obvious choice, however, as he had manumitted his enslaved in 1781 and condemned the misery and death caused by slavery, as well as the degeneration inherent to slave-holding societies.[27] He nonetheless accepted honorary membership in the Circle of Philadelphians. Together with the rapid spread of Freemasonry, the burgeoning interest in science reflected an emancipated bourgeoisie that asserted themselves as leaders of social progress, despite having no qualms about branding their names on the skin of their enslaved.[28]

The Circle of Philadelphians had much in common with the oldest learned society in the tropics, the Batavia Society of Arts and Sciences, which was established in 1778. The Batavia Society soon counted about two hundred members and enlisted among its foreign-corresponding members the aforementioned Joseph Banks as well as the French Enlightenment icon Marquis de Condorcet.[29] This learned society was clearly imbued by the spirit of Enlightenment, as was its initiator Jacobus Radermacher, a high-ranking VOC official who was also founder of one of the first masonic lodges in Asia. The ambitions of the Batavia Society were eminently practical, however. Java had a small but incredibly wealthy colonial bourgeoisie and considerable sums of their illicitly obtained riches were sunk into agricultural pursuits. One of the Batavia Society's most active members was Johannes Hooyman, who was a Lutheran pastor but above all a landlord—he seemed more interested in developing commercial agriculture than in matters of the soul. His most important treatise was probably not on the Holy Scriptures but on the sugar mills in the lands surrounding Batavia. In this respect, Hooyman was representative of the Batavia Society, which despite carrying the illustrious words "arts and sciences" in its name, devoted itself to the mundane ambitions of furthering agriculture and industry. In fact, the members of the Circle of Philadelphians had set the same practical priorities for their own planters' society.[30]

Sugar was a prominent topic for debate in Batavia, a matter of urgency even, because the local industry was floundering due to soil exhaustion and a shortage of firewood.[31] These concerns about sugar resulted in active interventions by European landlords and the VOC, who were no longer willing to rely exclusively on the expertise of their Chinese millers. They introduced, for instance, the fuel-saving Jamaica Train process, which was probably brought over from Mauritius. Gaudin Dutail, a former planter in Saint Domingue, came to Batavia in 1804 to demonstrate a boiling device he had constructed, claiming that it could run solely on bagasse, which, if true, would solve a nagging problem.[32] Although a failure, it was still a significant step in the transformation of Java's sugar production away from Chinese to European knowledge.

The Society for the Encouragement of Arts, Manufacturers and Commerce established in Barbados in 1781 was probably the first planters' association to advance the quality of the cultivation and processing methods and to issue guidelines on how to improve the living conditions of the enslaved. That said, it may have been preceded by planters in Jamaica who had convened in 1767 to launch a patriotic society to improve their island's cultivation and commerce, driven by envy of the rapid progress of the neighboring French islands. Jamaican plantation managers obtained one patent after another concerning improved grinding and boiling. This included the design that prefigured the nineteenth-century steam-driven cane mill with three horizontally placed crushers. This machine was crafted by John Smeaton in 1754 and served as the basis for John Stewart's project of a steam-driven mill, for which he obtained a patent thirteen years later. Both men lived in Jamaica.[33]

In Havana, the merchant and land-owning classes who saw their wealth rapidly growing thanks to the expanding trade with the newly independent United States were now ready for more than cattle raising and tobacco growing and began reshaping the island's backward sugar sector. The driving force behind this transition was the intellectual Francisco Arango y Parreño, born in 1765 in Havana into a creole bourgeois family. As one of Cuba's most respected sons, he received many honorable and prestigious assignments, but as a true bourgeois he refused a noble title.[34] As a student, Arango y Parreño read and must have appreciated *Les deux Indes* (The Two Indies), indeed a famous book in his day, whose editor Guillaume Thomas Raynal had recommended that the Spanish king develop Cuba as a sugar plantation island, arguing that the white crystals could replace gold and silver as the empire's primary source of wealth.[35] Returning home in 1788, Arango y Parreño made a stopover in Britain to inform himself about the organization of the slave trade. Back in Cuba, he developed together with fellow members of the Cuban elite a methodical approach to develop the interior of Cuba: from scientifically informed colonization schemes for inhabitants of overcrowded Havana to a megalomaniacal plan to dig a canal from Havana across the island all the way down to the southern harbor city of Batabanó. He also convinced the Spanish court to allow Cuba's residents to import slaves on their own account, releasing the slave trade from the monopoly of the Spanish Crown, or in his own words from "mercantilist restrictions."[36]

When, two years later, the revolution in the neighboring colony of Saint Domingue broke out, Arango y Parreño, who was in Madrid at the time, hastened to write a memorandum to the Spanish Council of State as he feared that Spain would get cold feet about the liberalization of Cuba's slave trade. He pointed out that the risk of the revolution jumping to Cuba was negligible, claiming that on his island treatment of the enslaved workers was much better than in Saint Domingue, which also had to cope with a disgruntled and politically vocal free colored population. He urged the Spanish government not to miss the opportunity for Cuba offered by the collapse of the world's largest sugar exporter. It could be just temporary, after all.[37]

The next year, in 1792, Arango y Parreño wrote a famous essay on how Cuba, at that time still almost entirely covered by forests, could develop its agricultural potential. It led to the establishment in Havana of the Consulado de Agricultura y Comercio (Consulate of Agriculture and Commerce), which would play a key role in Cuba's ascendancy as a sugar exporter.[38] Besides Arango y Parreño's enormous ambition, sugar production in Cuba benefited greatly from the influx of French planters—together with their employees and eighteen thousand enslaved people—who escaped from the revolution in Saint Domingue.[39] The French refugees taught the Cuban planters to build state-of-the-art sugar mills. In the decade after the revolution in Haiti, Cuba's sugar exports jumped from almost nothing to more than thirty thousand tons and subsequently doubled in the first quarter of the nineteenth century.[40]

To enable this expansion, the Consulate of Agriculture and Commerce wrestled part of the jurisdiction over Cuba's forests from the navy wharfs, which had used the forest to build some of Spain's best warships. While the navy respected the forests as a renewable resource, the sugar barons in their predatory frenzy only saw inexhaustible raw material for the wear and tear of their factories as well as for fuel, carelessly felling tall cedars eminently suitable for shipbuilding. When private landowners obtained the right to indiscriminately fell trees on their property in 1815, it unleashed an unhinged spatial expansion of Cuba's sugar frontier that greedily devoured the island's forests.

A few years after winning the battle for land, Arango y Parreño and his fellow planters won the fight to keep slavery firmly in place. From 1810 to 1814, as a last bulwark against Napoleon's occupation of most of Spain, representatives from the entire Spanish Empire convened the Spanish Cortes (parliament) in Cádiz. Dominated by liberals, it discussed the issue of slavery, a debate dreaded by the Cuban planters who saw it as the opening of a Pandora's box. Arango y Parreño warned that the "barbarian king of Haiti" was lying in wait to bring all the Africans in the Caribbean region under his flag. Arango y Parreño considered himself no less a liberal and progressive than the members of the Cortes of Cádiz, but for him in liberal societies property ought to be sacrosanct, and enslaved were property after all.[41]

Arango y Parreño's allegation about the intention of Haiti's rulers to liberate the entire Caribbean enslaved population was definitely not exaggerated. Only one year after his stern warning a conspiracy was uncovered, led by the free carpenter and black militia corporal José-Antonio Aponte, who was joined by Cubans of African descent, black militia men, and enslaved Cubans, and assisted by a high-ranking Haitian military officer. The Aponte conspiracy was encouraged by the rumor that the Cortes of Cádiz was in favor of slave emancipation but that the Cuban whites had not obeyed its order. Anyway, Aponte's rebellion failed, slavery was preserved, and slave trafficking to Cuba would continue for another half century.[42]

Considering Arango y Parreño's disrespect for both nature and human rights, it is remarkable that he became such good friends with Alexander von Humboldt, the father of modern ecology, who visited Cuba from December 1800 to March 1801 and again for a short stint in 1804. Together they traveled to various parts of the island and von Humboldt studied the emerging sugar industry as well as the institution of slavery, which he condemned as the greatest of all evils that had ever been inflicted upon mankind, and which he hoped would gradually disappear.[43] Von Humboldt argued that Spanish law offered some hope in this regard, since it gave the enslaved the rights to marry, to seek better masters in case of cruel treatment (*pedir papeles*), to own some property and to buy themselves free (*coartación*). Moreover, rules existed about proper clothing and food. Yet he knew very well that in the context of ruthless exploitation, most of these legal obligations, some dating from thirteenth-century Castile others introduced in Cuba by the Spanish king in 1789, were being flouted.[44]

Apparently, von Humboldt took a gradualist approach to abolition, counting on the progress of civilization and industrialization to phase out slavery.

The Arrival of Steam Engines

In 1794, on his way back home from Spain, Arango y Parreño visited Augustín de Betancourt, the director of Spain's Royal Cabinet of Machines who resided in England at that time. De Betancourt, one of the most gifted engineers of his day, had just designed a steam-driven cane crusher. Arango y Parreño gave the Reynolds firm the order to build this machine after Boulton & Watt refused, accusing Betancourt of having plagiarized the design from them after visiting their atelier. The machine arrived in Cuba in 1797 to become the first steam-driven crusher installed in the Americas, albeit one that did not yet perform satisfactorily.[45]

Cane crushers stood in the vanguard of the Industrial Revolution and would gradually improve in terms of strength and pressing efficiency until they obtained their final shape in 1871.[46] In the early nineteenth century these still experimental machines consumed a growing share of Britain's soaring coal output, of which more than 15 percent was exported to the West Indies.[47] By 1820, at least two hundred steam-driven cane crushers had been shipped across the Atlantic Ocean, half of which were installed in the three former Dutch but now British colonies: Berbice, Essequibo, and Demerara (which were later merged into British Guiana) and another third in Jamaica.[48] Cuba, from where von Humboldt received report of twenty-five steam-powered crushers as early as 1817, was among the early adopters too. Thirty years later, over a third of Cuba's sugar mills employed them, and by 1860 the proportion had risen to 70 percent.[49]

Steam-powered crushers also made rapid headway in Louisiana. The first granulated sugar was made by Etienne de Boré, born in Illinois but educated in France, where he had worn the uniform of a captain in the French king's palace guard. Louisiana was still a French colony at this time, and Boré had started to grow cane there in desperation after pests had ruined his indigo plantation. He bought a sugar mill in 1793, planted cane, and hired specialists who had just arrived with the planters' diaspora from Saint Domingue. Boré's first sugar-making experiment attracted a crowd of the colony's notables, impatiently waiting to see the boiling sugar mass granulating. True to his former profession, Boré organized his plantation as if it were a military base. Fellow Louisiana planters followed the martial design of his estate when they shifted from indigo to sugar.[50]

After the first Louisiana cane crusher was installed in 1822 by Edmund J. Forstall, the prominent industrialist and politician in New Orleans, an impressive eighty-one would follow within the next six years. By the early 1840s, over four hundred of the almost seven hundred Louisiana sugar estates operated steam-driven crushers, many of which had come from Forstall's forge. He managed to produce these machines for $6,000—still a lot of money but half the price of some machines on the market. Duties imposed on Cuban sugar in 1832 turned investments in Louisiana sugar highly profitable and spurred the dissemination of Forstall's cane crushers.[51] Indispensable too was Louisiana's banking system, ranking third in the United States after New York and Massachusetts. The banker Thomas Baring, a friend of Forstall, participated behind the scenes as co-financer of the Consolidated Association of the Planters of Louisiana, the land bank of the sugar planters, which opened its doors in 1827.[52]

By the 1840s, steam mills had proliferated in Cuba, Louisiana, Trinidad, and British Guiana. They rapidly spread in St. Kits, and in Tobago and Jamaica about a third of the mills were steam-powered. At that time also, seventy-eight steam-driven cane crushers were in operation in India.[53] While the noisy machines could be heard in hundreds of places around the world in the 1830s, they were practically absent in Barbados, Antigua and Guadeloupe because those islands' strong winds kept the windmills in operation.[54] Java, standing in the vanguard of global sugar production in the nineteenth century, welcomed its first cane crusher in 1820, but it remained an isolated experiment as sugar mills continued to use water power well into the 1870s.[55] Where wind and water power were abundant, little incentive existed to buy an expensive steam-driven crusher, which voraciously consumed coal and needed the close attention of skilled technicians as well repair shops stocked with spare parts.

Beet Sugar

When in the late 1820s a Cuban delegation toured the West Indies to gather information about best practices for sugar production, one plantation in Demerara attracted their interest in particular. Here, a revolutionary machine was in operation, a vacuum pan that reduced the boiling temperature of the cane juice to just below 100 degrees Celsius, which substantially diminished the risk of scourging and produced a higher-quality sugar. This was the first major change in the boiling process since the introduction of batteries of cauldrons at the turn of the seventeenth century. Designed originally for refining purposes, this vacuum pan was built by Edward Charles Howard, credited as the first British chemical engineer. The owner of Demerara's vacuum pan, John Gladstone—father of the famous Victorian prime minister—was a wealthy Liverpudlian merchant who not only extensively traded with India but also owned several plantations in the West Indies. Thanks to his expensive new device he could send a more refined sugar to Europe that not only fetched a better price but also survived ocean transport in better shape as it contained less plant fibers and hence was less prone to rotting.[56]

The vacuum pan had not started its career in the tropics, however. In its early stages of development it was intimately connected to sugar refining and the emergence of the beet sugar industry. In Europe, apothecaries, who for a long time had dominated sugar retail, would apply their knowledge of chemistry to extracting sucrose from alternative materials. Cane is just one of the many sources from which sweeteners can be manufactured, after all; maple trees and dates had long been the most notable alternatives but were of limited importance on the global scale. In 1747, the apothecary Andreas Sigismund Marggraf discovered how to extract sugar from beet roots. His pupil and successor Franz Karl Achard further developed Marggraf's work into an operational process. Achard had already acquired some fame as an inventor for launching a weather balloon from Berlin Zoo, and, like his contemporary Benjamin Franklin, he was determined to understand the phenomena of lightning and electricity.

The Prussian government, which struggled to develop its own refining industry in competition with Hamburg, recognized the economic value of Achard's beet sugar experiments and sponsored his small factory and its few hectares planted with beet roots. In 1799, Achard reported the successful production of beet sugar, the news of which spread quickly to Vienna, London, Paris, and St. Petersburg. West Indian sugar planters were so alarmed that they reportedly tried to bribe Achard into abandoning his venture, fearing a devastating blow to their business, as the French duly acknowledged. In 1801, the Prussian king enabled Achard to build an experimental sugar factory in Silesia, which was joined by another, gigantic, factory, built by Achard's friend Moritz Freiherr von Koppy, four years later.[57]

The momentum behind beet sugar was such that the burning down of Achard's and von Koppy's factories by Napoleon's troops in 1806 was only a brief setback. In the same year that his army raged through Prussia, the emperor introduced the Continental System, which banned British products from mainland Europe, including West Indian sugar, thereby creating a unique opportunity for beet sugar to break through. Achard received help to rebuild his destroyed factory from the Prussian government. In the years that followed, his star rapidly rose thanks to his widely read book on deriving sugar from beet roots. Skyrocketing sugar prices—caused by the Continental System—spurred the building of beet sugar factories throughout Europe. Achard's own rebuilt experimental factory opened its doors in 1811, and students from all over Europe attended his classes.[58] Information about potentially revolutionary innovations traveled faster than even Napoleon's armies in these years. Beet sugar was revolutionary, Achard underlined in his monumental book on the subject, as it had the long-term political benefit of making Prussia independent from British supplies, which was crucially important since England, as master of the Caribbean, could set the sugar price. Above all, he also pointed out, it was an excellent way to destroy the slave trade.[59]

For Napoleon, beet sugar became an urgent matter after his expedition to Saint Domingue to restore it as a slave-based plantation island failed miserably, and after he lost Martinique and Guadeloupe to the British in 1810. French chemists at that time tried to extract liquid sugar from apples and pears, as they were not immediately converted to the beet root. Moreover, Napoleon had already promised wealth and fame for anyone who could lift experiments with grape sugar to the scale of national production.[60] In an official report—published in the semigovernmental *Le Moniteur* of June 22, 1810—the chemist Antoine Augustin Parmentier, famous for having convinced his countrymen that the potato was edible, advised against beet roots for sugar making and instead recommended using grapes, which were already cultivated in abundance.[61] Meanwhile, throughout Europe there were frantic attempts to produce sugar from potatoes and even mushrooms. Germans were more realistic in their attempt to extract sugar from ahorn (maple) trees, although disappointment soon set in because the German species did not produce a palatable syrup. This spelled the end of the experiment, as importing seeds of the right species would have taken decades to result in mature trees.[62]

Meanwhile in France, a feverish search for the best production methods for beet sugar started, closely watched by the emperor. The story goes that as soon as Napoleon heard about a successful experiment by Benjamin Delessert in Passy, near Paris, he shouted, "Let us go!" and rushed to the workshop. Seeing the sugar crystals, he tore the *croix de honeur* from his own uniform and pinned it on the coat of the inventor. While who was the first in France to procure sugar from beet is still undecided, there is no doubt that all successful experiments in this direction captured the emperor's immediate and full attention.[63] *Le Moniteur* wrote about the production of France's first refined beet sugar thus: "France will collect it on her own soil, and our refineries will no longer depend on the greed of our enemies."[64]

Napoleon ordered further experiments in 1811 and gave instructions to have a hundred thousand acres planted with sugar beets. He sent specialists to the factories of Achard and von Koppy and further decreed the recruitment of a hundred students from schools of medicine, pharmacy, and chemistry for his beet sugar schools. Although Napoleon's first beet harvest yielded only a pitiful 1,500 tons, this was more than compensated for by the fact that Achard had brought his work to the attention of all the prefects in the territories under Napoleon's rule. Beet sugar factories were up and running all over Europe by 1812.[65]

However, the bright future for European beet sugar became frozen in the Russian winter, along with Napoleon's Grande Armée. Indeed, after the emperor's downfall in 1814, its production was no longer profitable, and manufacturers were not yet influential enough to convince their governments to establish protectionist tariff walls around their infant industry. The recovery of maritime connections, the return of Martinique and Guadeloupe to France, and the emergence of Cuba, Louisiana, and India as major sugar exporters all but destroyed the beet sugar industry in France and Germany.

Some beet sugar producers survived against all odds, however, and among them was Louis François Xavier Joseph Crespel, who in 1810 had established what was probably France's first beet sugar factory. Ten years later, he introduced steam power at every stage of the process with equipment from Britain, which in all likelihood included the Howard vacuum boiling pan.

Thanks largely to Crespel's incredible perseverance, France emerged as a major beet sugar producer, and he himself became a rich man, at one point owning eight beet sugar factories before losing three million francs due to a failed beet sugar harvest in 1862–1863. Actually, Crespel's friends prodded the French emperor Napoleon III into showing his gratitude, and he awarded Crespel a state pension.[66] Two years after his death, in 1867, a monument was erected in Arras to honor this pioneer of the French beet sugar industry. Crespel had not just served the French sugar industry but also Germany's, and even the cane sugar industry of Java, as we will see.

The French beet sugar industry also owed its survival to the stagnant cane sugar production in the French sugar colonies, which had a hard time finding sufficient workers after the British ban on the slave trade. To help the French sugar colonies, the French king had introduced stiff duties in 1822, which however not only protected cane but also the country's domestic beet sugar from Cuban and Brazilian competition, as Prince Louis-Napoleon, who would later be emperor, noted in 1842. He used his time in prison for his failed coup d'état to write a treatise on the sugar question. Inspired by the technocratic ideology of Claude Henri Comte de Saint-Simon, who foresaw a future in which the productive classes such as industrialists and bankers would be society's leaders, Louis-Napoleon in his later capacity of dictator and emperor ardently supported the industrialization of both French beet and cane sugar production.[67]

A few years before Louis-Napoleon wrote his treatise, the beet sugar industry had received a major blow when the Antillean planters convinced the government to impose a tax on French beet sugar. This bankrupted many factories and wiped out most beet sugar regions, except for northwestern France.[68] Had not railway construction forged ahead in France, the beet sugar industry would have perished. Now, bulk transport over larger distances facilitated the concentration of production in a declining number of factories located in northwestern France. The output of raw beet sugar grew so rapidly that by the 1850s it already accounted for half of the sugar consumed in France.[69]

Meanwhile, Germany emerged as the main competitor of the French beet sugar industry, driven by brilliant technical pioneers such as Ernst Ludwig Schubarth and Justus von Liebig. Their work greatly benefited, however, from the French pioneers, who had generously shared their knowledge with them. Schubarth was trained as a chemist in France on a stipend granted by the Grand Duke of Hessen, which enabled him to publish his book on the beet sugar industry in France in 1837. Von Liebig visited the factory of Crespel in Arras in 1828 and later some of his German colleagues visited this plant in preparation for the building of their factory, as did the owners of the factory in Quedlinburg. This ancient city in the Harz belonged to Saxony, which had already proven its particular suitability for sugar cultivation during the interlude of Napoleon's Continental System. In the 1830s, Saxony already counted thirty-one beet sugar factories.[70]

German scientists' innovations and Prussia's creation of the German Customs Union, which imposed stiff import duties on cane sugar imports, decisively contributed to the emergence of a thriving beet sugar industry and dealt a severe blow to Hamburg as the hub of cane sugar imports. With colonial cane sugar being restricted, Germany's beet sugar production advanced even faster than in France. German industrialists unstintingly raised the efficiency of their production processes. In the 1840s, for instance, one factory owner started experiments with diffusion technology by slicing beets and throwing them in hot water, a technology that Ernst Ludwig Schubarth must have observed at the factory of Mathieu de Dombasle in France. After many years of experimenting, the first successful production round took place in 1865. Fifteen years later, all German factories employed this diffusion technology, which substantially enhanced the extraction of sucrose from the beets. Cane sugar producers watched in envy and tried to emulate the process but did not succeed, as we will see in Chapter 7. The beet sugar industry, meanwhile, would become a pioneering force in botany and chemistry. The laboratory in Berlin that was built by the Beet Sugar Industry Association and opened its doors in 1867, for instance, played a foundational role in German chemistry. One of its scholars, ironically, was Constantin Fahlberg, the discoverer of the artificial sweetener saccharin, a serious competitor of sugar.[71]

The production of beet sugar was also subject of keen interest to the other major powers of continental Europe, especially Russia. Czar Alexander I steadfastly encouraged a beet sugar industry after its first successful experiments on Russian soil in 1800. In contrast to almost everywhere else, this industry survived after 1814. Protection and cheap enserfed labor, as well as low wheat prices, made up for a lack of technological sophistication. However, the end of serfdom in 1861 destroyed probably half of the four hundred or so Russian sugar factories. From then on, the aristocracy, mainly in the Ukraine, started to invest in more advanced equipment, which enabled the industry not only to serve the markets of the Russian Empire but also export to Central Asia.[72]

In the United States, the Quakers in Philadelphia, not surprisingly, were keen to procure beet sugar to replace slave sugar, but lack of knowledge about cultivation and extraction doomed their venture.[73] More promising was the initiative by Maximin Isnard, the former superintendent of Napoleon's sugar school in Strasbourg, which was destroyed by allied forces while defeating Napoleon on his own soil. He built a new life in the United States and became an advocate for a beet sugar industry in the state of Massachusetts. This resonated with Edward Church, a former consul in France, who raised funding to send Isnard to his mother country to obtain seedlings.[74] Church's *Notices on Beet Sugar* was published in 1836, and was bold enough to state "that the introduction of the beet culture and its manufacture into sugar is destined to create a memorable epoch in the prosperity of our Republic, not inferior probably, to the cotton culture."[75] Church and Isnard's Northampton Sugar Company was generously stocked with capital, much of which probably came from American abolitionists, but it was not sufficient to make it a viable enterprise.[76]

The Mormon followers of the Church of Jesus Christ and Latter-day Saints were next to try. Encouraged by the progress of the French beet sugar industry, they sent a mission to France to bring the technology to Salt Lake Valley. In the 1840s, however, this was tantamount to a logistical nightmare. Shipping the machinery across the Atlantic was by far the easiest part; it then had to be transported up the Mississippi and subsequently carried overland to Utah, a trip of just sixty-four kilometers that nevertheless took eight weeks. With the Mormons lacking any experience in handling a vacuum boiling pan, the whole venture was doomed to fail.[77] This marked the end of beet sugar production in the United States for the next thirty years, basically because its cultivation and harvesting was too labor-intensive in this still thinly populated land.[78]

Sugar production was by now well on its way to becoming an industrial process carried out by huge and expensive machines—but it still required a massive input of agricultural labor. In contrast to cotton, the key commodity in the Industrial Revolution, sugar cane could not be grown in one part of the world and processed in another. Hence, whereas cotton revolutionized industry in Britain, steam and steel came to the sugar mills and revolutionized tropical agriculture. While the most famous intellectuals of the day, from Benjamin Franklin to Alexander von Humboldt, were in touch with the centers of cane sugar production, Napoleon and the Prussian king personally encouraged beet sugar experiments. Defying the permanent threat of pillaging armies during the Napoleonic Wars, beet sugar factories thrived. After the departure of Napoleon to Saint Helena, these factories could only survive through protectionism, because tropical sugar cultivation rapidly moved from the old capitalism of monopolies into a new era of shared knowledge, steam power, and transporting plant specimens. After hundreds of cane crushers had been shipped to cane fields, the pharmacists and engineers who had devoted their attention to beets would sell their machines to tropical sugar colonies as well, as we will see in the next chapter. Beet sugar producers in France and Prussia could only look on in envy.

5

State and Industry

WHEN IN 1848 THE SPIRIT of revolution spread throughout Europe, new ideas and new technologies had begun to change every aspect of life in many parts of the world. This new world was however still heavily inscribed by the past. In the middle of the nineteenth century, more than half of the sugar shipped to Europe and North America was still slave-produced, and Chinese and Indian peasants produced more sugar than the rest of the world together. Although completely steam-driven sugar factories had spread widely, most of the sugar in the world was still made with simple implements; animal power would turn mills for another forty years. Not confined to China and India, traditional production methods were also to be widely seen in the Caribbean region, despite the precocious adoption of new technologies there. In 1850, the more than sixty preindustrial estates on the island of Tobago were producing less than the four state-of-the-art factories in nearby Guadeloupe. Thus, two highly different but at the same time overlapping epochs of industrial and preindustrial production coexisted.

The European methods of sugar production escaped their confinement to the Caribbean area and spread in India, Indonesia, and the Philippines. Entrepreneurs such as Francisco de Arango y Parreño and John Gladstone represented a new era that defined sugar making as an industrial process. Whereas most of the plantation capital was accrued in enslaved until the early nineteenth century, from then on impressive sums were also invested in steam-driven machinery. Crucial in this phase was the role of the state, which hitherto had either been absent or destructively present, and had often been circumvented by planters. The collaboration of industrialists and crowned heads to transform the sugar mill into the sugar factory as an integrated unit of steam and steel proved revolutionary. Governments facilitated the construction of railroads and harbors, regulated financial operations, designed labor contracts, and legislated the appropriation of land by sugar estates.

In the meantime, the bourgeois sugar industrialists were well aware of the fact that the Enlightenment had produced new humanitarian ideals that were incompatible with slavery. They nonetheless hoped to reconcile morality and profitability in the long run and bet on the power of industrialization to reduce the labor intensity of sugar manufacturing, thereby diminishing their reliance on slave labor. Some utopians, such as the German agronomist and abolitionist Conrad Friedrich Stollmeyer, who lived in Trinidad in 1844, spoke about the massive employment of the "iron slaves"—a metaphor for steam power—and that God had given sun and water energy as well as sweet maize for a brighter future without hard manual labor. Maize sugar, or high-fructose corn syrup, would indeed massively change the global market for sweeteners, but only in the 1980s. In Stollmeyer's days, people at the helm of British colonial policies found him a peculiar person and not entirely coherent.[1] He was indeed an eccentric thinker steeped in the utopian thinking of Charles Fourier and Henri de Saint-Simon, but he was not completely out of sync with the mood of his day. In fact, the Saint-Simonian spirit captured the new sugar frontiers of Cuba and Java. From the end of the nineteenth century to the late 1920s, these two islands accounted for half of the world's cane sugar exports, a dominance that was only interrupted by Cuba's devastating War of Independence (1895–1898) against Spain.[2]

The Vacuum Pan

By 1840, Europe's beet sugar industry had technologically advanced far beyond that of the cane sugar producers. The planters' pride, a lack of investment capital, and labor shortages after the abolition of the slave trade and then slavery itself delayed innovations on plantations that were once the most precocious vehicles of capitalism. Indeed, with about two hundred enslaved on three hundred to five hundred acres of land, a regimented division of labor, and highly integrated stages of production, the Caribbean sugar estates had belonged to the largest and most tightly organized units of Europe's preindustrial manufacturing. But in the early nineteenth century, these estates proved to be too small to employ expensive steam-driven equipment on a profitable basis.

Besides the intimidating price tags of the newfangled machines, investment in the latest steam-driven technology entailed enormous risks for Caribbean planters. The quality of iron was often not up to the immense strain of cane crushing around the clock for several consecutive months. Crushers breaking down during the sugar campaign drove planters to despair, as the forges needed to repair the machinery were seldom nearby. Cane would be left rotting at the mill compound, and delays could be devastating: in Louisiana, a single overnight frost was enough to ruin the cane in the field.[3] Operating in tropical environments often close to the seashore, the machines would suffer corrosion in the humid, salty air. Under these circumstances, even the slow-turning cattle mills with their low juice extraction were preferable to steam-driven ones. Considering all this, the presence of hundreds of steam engines in the tropics was a miracle.

Nonetheless, until the 1840s most planters still trudged on with their pre-industrial mills, even if they had the opportunity to sell their cane to their wealthier, better-equipped colleagues. In societies with sharp racial and class divisions, giving up a mill was tantamount to a demotion from aristocracy to peasantry. Tellingly, Sidney Mintz attributed the downfall of Puerto Rico as the second largest sugar producer of the Caribbean region to this conservatism.[4] The old guard's resistance could be vehement, and Auguste Vincent, the owner of St. Marie plantation in Réunion, would pay the ultimate price for underestimating it. Being the first French cane sugar planter with a vacuum pan, he felt so encouraged by its performance that he planned to build a series of *usines centrales,* or sugar centrals (large sugar factories that process sugar from many farms) capable of processing most of his island's cane. His scheme would demote his fellow planters to cane farmers. Before he could execute his scheme, however, Vincent disappeared from the scene without a trace. Rumor pointed to his jealous colleagues as complicit in his vanishing.[5]

Whereas in the late eighteenth century many innovations still originated in the sugar colonies, now the main incentives for industrialization came from equipment manufacturers and innovators in the beet sugar industry. French and Belgian farmers happily grew beets for sugar factories because they were more profitable than wheat, and Central and Eastern European landlords either built their own factories or joined forces with neighbors.

The most influential pioneer in beet sugar technology was the chemist and industrialist Louis Charles Derosne (1780–1846), born in Paris into a family of pharmacists. His career bridged the time that the apothecaries still had an important role in sugar retailing and the industrial age of steam and steel. In the winter of 1809–1810, Derosne produced his first few kilograms of brown sugar from beets. One year later, he learned about Achard's methods (see Chapter 4), which he felt deserved to be brought to the attention of a wider audience.[6] He wrote the preface to the French translation of the latter's book on beet sugar, which appeared in 1812. Derosne also gained some of his expertise at Crespel's pioneering factory, where he stayed during the beet campaign of late 1812.[7]

Derosne would become an industrial celebrity, a status he would share with a twenty-year-old boiler maker from humble rural origin who came to his Paris workshop in 1824. Jean-François Cail (1804–1871) arrived at the perfect time, as Derosne was on the brink of inventing new sugar boiling technology based on the distilling of grapes, potatoes, and beets.[8] Partly by stealing an invention from his engineer colleagues, Derosne succeeded in substantially improving the design of the pioneering British Howard vacuum pan in the early 1830s. Cail, the young man from the countryside, became a full partner of Derosne, and the two industrialists extended their operations over the French border to Brussels, where they established a plant in 1838. A few years later, Derosne & Cail employed 2,500 workers of different nationalities—an impressively sized industrial establishment for the time.[9]

An indefatigable self-promoter, Derosne turned his factory into the market leader for vacuum pans.[10] Initially, he only sold equipment to the struggling beet sugar industry before the unfortunate Auguste Vincent of Réunion became the first to install his equipment in the tropics. From then on, business expanded rapidly. By 1844, the Derosne & Cail pan was in operation in eight factories in Cuba, seven in Java, five in Guadeloupe, four in Bourbon, one in Suriname, and one in Mexico. This involved incredible sums of money for the time. A complete set of equipment cost about £10,000, equivalent to $50,000, and a factory required twice this investment. Since credit to buy their machines was hard to come by, Derosne & Cail arranged for payment to be spread over four years and was also prepared to receive payment in sugar.[11] Across the globe, this French firm overcame the massive obstacles of planters' capital shortage and their unfamiliarity with the technological intricacies of its boiling technology by co-financing installations and by sending its own engineers over to its customers. Cail even bought an estate himself and started a sugar factory to set an example. In 1857, he bought an estate in Trostianetz, in the Ukraine, where he built his own beet sugar factory.[12]

For his first vacuum pan sold in Cuba, Derosne himself traveled to the estate of the plantation magnate Don Wenceslao de Villa-Urrutia in 1841. He oversaw the adaptation of his equipment, which was originally designed for the European beet sugar factories, to the specific conditions of Cuba. Once the equipment performed properly, he wrote a brochure that was translated into Spanish by José Luis Casaseca, the head of the Chemistry Department of the University of Havana, and a protégé of Arango y Parreño. Casaseca wrote a preface under the title "Cuba's Industrial Revolution." A thousand copies were printed and within three years another seven Derosne & Cail vacuum pans had arrived in Cuba.[13]

In Java, the conversion to vacuum pans was a project of the colonial government, which had introduced the forced cultivation system in 1830, forcing 60 percent of Javanese rural households to relinquish part of their land and time to grow crops, including cane, for a meager wage.[14] While this was a government monopoly, the government itself did not build mills for cane processing but offered contracts to private persons to do the milling, contracts that made the use of a vacuum pan mandatory but which also included a subsidy. Crucial to the rapid spread of this arrangement were two brothers-in-law, one a high-ranking officer in the military and the other a prominent colonial civil servant, who convinced the Ministry for the Colonies to introduce the Derosne & Cail vacuum pan in Java. In the early 1840s, they toured Belgium and France accompanied by the Dutch engineer Hubertus Hoevenaer, who not coincidentally had worked at the Crespel factory in Arras. The factory of this eminent French beet sugar pioneer received visits from many Europeans, including scientists from Germany, and even the king of France, but these were usually short. The Dutch visitors, however, stayed for some time. They were allowed to test the processes and received a lot of advice.[15]

The visit of the Dutch delegation to France and Belgium must have been of tremendous importance to Derosne & Cail, because in Java British merchant houses were well represented and offered an excellent avenue for the importation of the British Howard vacuum pan. The first was installed as early as in 1835 at the estate of the Englishman Charles Etty in East Java. If only to reduce the influence of the British in Java, the Dutch were more than willing to team up with Derosne & Cail. Probably to improve access to this crucial Java market, Derosne & Cail partnered with Paul van Vlissingen to establish a factory in Amsterdam in 1847. He was a prominent Amsterdam industrialist who after a stint in Java had started a dock in Amsterdam to repair steamships. Thanks to this collaboration and active Dutch government support, fifteen Derosne & Cail vacuum pans were in operation in Java by 1852 in addition to nine Howard pans. Five years later, two-thirds of Java's sugar exports were produced with vacuum pan technology, leaving the world's other sugar producers far behind in this respect.[16]

While British merchants were far from side-lined in the development of Java's sugar industry, the Indo-Chinese, who had dominated the local industry for two hundred years, gradually became a minority among the sugar industrialists. The colonial government recruited a sugar bourgeoisie from a party of former government officials, retired army officers. And a few rich Indo-Chinese merchants. A new class of entrepreneurs emerged, who in the words of Roger Knight were "singularly fortunate," as they did not have to buy slaves and received government advances for their operations. The only obligation imposed on these manufacturers was to invest in state-of-the-art equipment, including vacuum pans.[17] Not all sugar manufacturers were part of this coterie of contractors. In the 1870s, 25 percent of Java's sugar came from the Principalities, a semiautonomous area in Central Java, where the forced cultivation system was not implemented. Here, export agriculture was developed by European sons or grandsons of European sergeants and officers and Javanese mothers or grandmothers. These entrepreneurs had close ties to the local Javanese courts, from whom they rented land and servile labor.[18]

Like Cuba, Mauritius, British Guiana, and India, Java was a new frontier for European sugar entrepreneurs, who were most receptive to the new industrial spirit. They were the first to convert to the expensive vacuum pans, which saw their operations advance well beyond those of the older planters. In India, British merchant capital had found a new outlet, and by 1847 a third of India's sugar exports to Great Britain came from vacuum pans, a share comparable to that of Java and larger than the advanced sugar producers Cuba and Mauritius.[19] One would therefore have expected the vacuum pan to advance in Louisiana at least as rapidly as in Java, because this was a new frontier as well and all the necessary conditions appeared to be in place. The steam-driven cane crushers indeed had been expeditiously introduced, and the first vacuum pan was installed quite early, in 1832—a Howard presumably—in the same year that the introduction of US tariffs on Cuban sugar encouraged investments in Louisiana's sugar industry.[20] Louisiana's planters were not discouraged through stiff US tariffs on higher-grade sugars as were those in Cuba and the West Indies. Louisiana's capital New Orleans, the third largest city of the United States in the 1840s, was a hub of industry and commerce.[21] The most prominent among the planters were well-educated capitalists and highly responsive to innovation. They founded the Agriculturalists' and Mechanics' Association of Louisiana in 1842, a name that left nothing to the imagination about their industrial ambitions. In the same year, the first Derosne & Cail vacuum pan arrived at Louisiana's Bayou Laforche estate, followed by two others in 1845 and 1846. Through the extensive contacts of planters with France and French-educated scientists, all the existing knowledge about sugar boiling was available in Louisiana. As a further sign of an advancing innovative spirit, the publisher and statistician J. D. B. DeBow launched *DeBow's Review* to disseminate scientific and technological information among planters.[22]

There was no lack of entrepreneurial energy and scientific enthusiasm, and yet by 1860 only 11 percent of Louisiana's sugar was produced by vacuum pans.[23] Nor can capital shortage explain the limping introduction of the vacuum pan. Sure, a severe financial crisis hit the United States in the late 1830s and caused an almost complete credit crunch. The famous industrialist Edmund Forstall, who happened to be the acting governor of Louisiana at that time, was forced to reduce the sugar estates' options to secure mortgages from banks. Nonetheless, well-run plantations encountered no difficulty in obtaining loans and planters even succeeded in obtaining mortgages on their enslaved, who in the case of larger plantations represented formidable capital. Moreover, many Louisiana mills invested in bagasse-burning technology, which also required substantial investments.[24]

What makes the sluggish introduction of the vacuum pan even more puzzling is that perhaps the most brilliant sugar engineer of the nineteenth century, Norbert Rillieux, was born and lived in Louisiana. After his training in Paris, where he also lectured on steam technology, he returned home to develop a vacuum pan superior to Derosne & Cail's. It was more energy-efficient as it reused steam twice, for which it called "a multiple-effect" or "triple-effect" pan. Yet in Louisiana only eighteen estates had installed his device by the eve of the Civil War. Significantly, Forstall, was doing good business with his own cane crusher and was not a fan of the vacuum pan. He deemed the device too complicated to be operated by African enslaved.[25] An additional explanation is that Rillieux's mother was a "woman of color"; he must have suffered from racial prejudice himself and this may have prevented Louisiana playing a leading role in vacuum pan technology. Meanwhile, Rillieux's vacuum pan was introduced in Cuba and even in Europe. This happened after he had advised, apparently for free, an engineer of Germany's Magdeburg Steamship Company to adapt his system for the beet sugar industry. The engineer sold the design without scruple to his employer, which in turn sold it to the company Cail & Cie. This company integrated Rillieux's design into its own apparatus under the name "triple-effect."[26] It became the standard in the most advanced sugar factories, while Louisiana was still boiling most of its sugar in open pans.

Saint-Simonism and Abolitionism

In the early nineteenth century, the industrial spirit of the age was expressed most radically and eloquently by Henri de Saint-Simon, who claimed that engineers ought to be leading the nation politically and that the state had a prominent role to play in industrialization. In the Netherlands Indies, the semigovernmental Netherlands Trading Society, the largest financial facilitator of colonial agriculture, played the role of vanguard industrializer, with Saint-Simonians in leading positions.[27] This massive colonial enterprise was established in 1824 under the auspices of the Dutch king, and was chartered with a monopoly on the transport and auctioning of the tropical products in the Netherlands, including sugar. It was a state intervention that aimed to enhance the profitability of the Dutch colonial possessions and simultaneously counter the influence of British commercial interests in the Netherlands Indies.

In Cuba, India, and Java, metropolitan industrialists, wealthy and influential colonial bourgeois, and imperial governments joined forces to bring an industrial revolution to the cane sugar colonies. In France high-ranking government officials and industrialists tried to overcome the conservatism of the French sugar planters, who strongly rejected the introduction of the vacuum pan and procrastinated even with respect to steam-driven crushers.[28] In metropolitan France, the slaveholders' mentality was held responsible for the lack of economic progress in its overseas territories and abolition and industrial progress became inexorably linked.[29]

The connection between abolition and industrialization was particularly emphasized by Victor Schoelcher, the most prominent French abolitionist, and, in 1848, the spokesperson for abolition within the provisional revolutionary government. A comprehensive modernization of tropical sugar production was in order, Schoelcher insisted, and he approvingly cited P. Daubrée's *Questions Coloniales sous le rapport industriel* (The Colonial Question from the Industrial Point of View) (1841).[30] Daubrée, an engineer in a sugar factory in Guadeloupe, reckoned that steam-driven crushers with their high extraction rate could easily double the sugar output of the French Antilles. But most plantations were simply too small for an investment in steam power and, according to Daubrée, they urgently needed sugar centrals that could handle greater volume. Daubrée praised "King Guillaume" of the Netherlands, who oversaw the introduction of the vacuum pan in Java, and Auguste Vincent, the vanished planter from Réunion, for understanding the economies of scale and the need for investment banking.[31]

Charles Alphonse, Comte de Chazelles, the first planter in Guadeloupe who installed Derosne & Cail's equipment, approached the colonial sugar question from a slightly different angle but came to the same conclusion. He showed himself acutely aware of the shrinking supply of enslaved Africans and their pending emancipation. His message was clear: do not repeat the costly mistake made by the British, otherwise so innovative and intelligent, who had abolished slavery without being able to fully replace manual labor by machines.[32] De Chazelles did not want to wait; he started building a class of small farmers consisting of enslaved people to be gradually emancipated and given a piece of land in property, while simultaneously importing European colonists.[33] He was on the same page as the French abolitionists, and reckoned that industrialization would lure white skilled staff, a bourgeoisie of white workers so glaringly absent from planter society. De Chazelles was also a planter, however, and did not put all his money on white immigration; he also advocated measures to ensure that the emancipated slaves continued to work on the plantations, insisting that "repressive regulations on vagrancy are urgently needed."[34]

De Chazelles was actively involved in an ambitious project to modernize Guadeloupe's sugar industry. A severe earthquake that struck the island in 1843 provided an ideal opportunity. In response to a request by the Ministry for the Colonies, Derosne & Cail submitted a plan to industrialize the island's cane processing, and, thanks to the intervention of Derosne's son-in-law, a banker, this eventually resulted in the formation of the Compagnie des Antilles (Antilles Company), stocked with private and banking capital. On the day of abolition in all French colonies, April 27, 1848, Guadeloupe counted twelve centrals, two of which were owned by Daubrée and four by the Antilles Company, of which de Chazelles was a director.[35] The French had avoided the mistake the British had made in Jamaica, but still could not prevent a disaster. The Revolution of 1848 ruined the main financiers of the company. Adding to this misfortune, the millions of francs to compensate the planters for the abolition did not go to the heavily indebted estates but ended up in the hands of their creditors. Daubrée and most of his colleagues were ruined.[36]

Nonetheless, without an earthquake and the intervention by the metropolitan government, industry and banking, Guadeloupe's sugar industry would have remained overwhelmingly in a preindustrial state. It would have languished the same way Tobago's sugar sector did when it was struck by a fierce hurricane in 1847 that destroyed almost half of its sugar mills and damaged the rest. Britain's transfer of a £20,000 loan to this shattered island was hopelessly inadequate, compared to the capital of six million francs—equivalent to £240,000—assembled by the Antilles Company. As a result, about sixty estates in Tobago produced less than the four of the company's in Guadeloupe.[37] If this company had fared better, all French sugar colonies might have rapidly moved in the same direction as Cuba and Java. Instead, planters' conservatism coupled with a lack of capital would make them seek out intermediate technologies.

Intermediate Technologies

Although many planters dreaded social change and disliked putting themselves at the mercy of metropolitan industrialists and banks, they were also desperate to keep their estates competitive. By the mid-1840s, Louisiana had its *DeBow's Review* and the planters in British Guiana, Jamaica, and Barbados had all established agricultural societies to improve the technological and botanical levels of their estates. Interest among planters and their staff in agricultural innovations was impressive. In 1846, for instance, five thousand people visited an agricultural show in the parish of Cornwall, Jamaica.[38]

An innovative spirit also imbued the planters of Réunion, where an intermediate boiling technology was developed that would spread to other sugar colonies as well. Here, a former associate of Derosne, Joseph Martial Wetzell would go on to design and give his name to a boiling apparatus much simpler and cheaper than the vacuum pan. In the year of the Battle of Waterloo, 1815, he decided to give up his studies at the École Polytechnique and traveled to Réunion to teach hydrography to planters' sons for a couple of years. Back in France, he took sugar courses and worked with Derosne. In 1828, Wetzell declined a highly attractive offer to become director of a beet sugar factory in northern France because his loyalty lay with his planter friends in Réunion.[39] They were keen to upgrade industry but not through building sugar centrals, and they definitely did not want to accept metropolitan capital and the concomitant oversight and closer scrutiny of their business practices. These included, after all, illicit imports of enslaved from Africa's east coast and Madagascar, a sizable trafficking operation that involved a total of 45,000 victims between 1817 and 1835.[40]

Wetzell developed his low-temperature boiling system that yielded 25–33 percent more sugar than the Jamaica Train, which had dominated since the eighteenth century, and he was able to supply his equipment at only a quarter of the cost of Derosne & Cail's vacuum pans. Wetzell himself emphasized that thanks to his technology plantations with less financial muscle and no nearby maintenance facilities could prosper too. The Wetzell pans spread to Mauritius, Natal, Madagascar, Penang, Antilles, Brazil, and Puerto Rico as a piece of intermediate technology favored by the colonial sugar bourgeoisie.[41]

This was not at all to the liking of Cail, whose partner Derosne had died in 1845. Cail convinced Napoleon III in 1860 to establish a bank, a successor of the failed Antilles Company, to finance the dissemination of his vacuum pans. As a Saint-Simonian, the emperor always lent his ear to what the country's prominent industrialists had to say. Urged on by Cail, he encouraged the wealthy financiers of Paris to establish the Colonial Credit Society (renamed as the Crédit Foncier Colonial or Colonial Credit Bank in 1863) to provide planters with long-term loans using their plantations as collateral.[42] In the 1860s, this bank invested over thirty-seven million francs in the industrialization of sugar production in Guadeloupe, Martinique, and Réunion.[43] Still, the result must have disappointed Cail, because of the fifteen new factories in Guadeloupe sponsored by this bank, eleven still used Wetzell pans.[44]

The French Empire exhibited most sharply the division between the Saint-Simonian industrialization ideology and the plantocracies who distrusted new technology as a threat to their autonomy and the existing social order. Moreover, planters were accustomed to making cost-benefit calculations, in which status preservation but also tariff systems played an important role. West Indian producers continued working with open pans since the British refiners managed to keep the higher-grade sugars under a higher tariff regime. Some planters in Barbados worked with pans invented by the London refiner August Gadesden, which like the Wetzell pan functioned under normal atmospheric conditions.[45] This in contrast to the wealthy British merchants who installed vacuum pans in the factories of British Guiana at the same time they were being installed in Java and Cuba. The Barbadian planters were still comfortable producing a crude brown sugar.[46] When the British postal officer and novelist Anthony Trollope, who toured the West Indies in 1858, asked them about their primitive methods he was told that given the existing British duty system that punished refined sugar, this was the most profitable operation for them.[47] With outdated technology, a few Gadesden pans, and four vacuum pans, they had managed to increase their sugar exports by more than 60 percent in the twenty years after emancipation.[48] The resistance against the vacuum pan made sense in the West Indies far more than it did in Louisiana.

While planters selectively applied new technologies, one innovation achieved a startling and universal ascendancy and even reached the peasant cane fields in India by the turn of the twentieth century. At a Paris exhibition in 1839, a new machine was demonstrated for drying textile goods that would ignite a revolution in sugar manufacturing. Until the 1830s, draining was the only way to rid sugar crystals from molasses. Waterweed and clay were the first widespread means to draw the molasses from the sugar mass, but this took weeks (see Chapter 1). Used globally for about thirteen hundred years, these techniques became obsolete overnight thanks to the centrifuge, which separated molasses from crystals in no time. The Cossipore factory near Calcutta was the first sugar factory to adopt it. From there it spread to Magdeburg in 1844, Cuba and Belgium in 1850, Mauritius in 1851, and Java in 1853.[49] The advantages of the centrifuge even managed to mollify the die-hard technological conservatism of the Barbadian planters.

Mills, Technicians, and Capitalists

While the planters of old sugar colonies reluctantly entered the era of industrialization, in Cuba and Java giant sugar complexes emerged that would dominate the world of cane sugar until the Great Depression of the 1930s. In Cuba it was a powerful bourgeoisie and in Java colonial administrators who led the industrialization process, which mirrored the diametrically different character of the two colonies. In 1817, 45 percent of Cuba's population of 572,363 was classified as white, a percentage comparable to that of Louisiana. In Java, however, about fifteen thousand Europeans constituted a tiny presence among an overwhelmingly Indonesian population of 7.5 million.[50] While the Dutch Ministry for the Colonies and the Dutch king set themselves the task of creating a colonial bourgeoisie—by among other things subsidizing the introduction of the vacuum pan—Cuba already had a self-conscious economic elite.[51] This class only gained in strength through an influx of merchants, engineers, and planters from North America, from other Caribbean islands, from Latin America's mainland, and of course from Europe.[52]

Cuba's position at the vanguard of tropical agriculture was also the fruit of a close collaboration between the Cuban bourgeoisie, the Spanish court, and international banks. With a loan guaranteed by the Spanish queen, for instance, the first railway opened on November 19, 1837, and reduced transportation costs tenfold. It was constructed by an American engineer and financed by the English Robertson bank. From the 1850s onward, the Schroder house, with its provenance in the eighteenth-century Hamburg sugar trade, dominated railway expansion, building a 1,262-kilometer network that enabled plantations to move deep into the island. The introduction of narrow-gauge tracks within the estates enabled factories to draw their cane from much larger areas. Steamships transported the sugar to foreign destinations, and telegraph cables provided instant business news as early as in 1844. The discovery near Havana of coal layers, which greatly facilitated the expansion of the Cuban railroad network, further boosted the good fortunes of the planters.[53] Sugar production became a story of steam and steel in all aspects. Nonetheless, the tariffs imposed by Britain and the United States discouraged the production of higher grades sugar. This slowed the introduction of the vacuum pan; by 1863, only 20 percent of Cuba's sugar was produced using such equipment, much less than in Java, although that percentage would increase in the decades to follow. The technological prowess of the elite of the Cuban planters was showcased in Justo Germán Cantero's beautifully illustrated *Los Ingenios* (The Sugar Mills).[54]

Cuba's machines needed technicians to maintain them, and many travelled to the island from Britain, the center of the Industrial Revolution. Cuba employed more than six hundred mostly British engineers by the early 1850s, and in excess of eight hundred in the 1860s. This small army played a strategic role not only in the Cuban economy, but also in the global development of tropical agriculture in general because they enabled Cuba to outcompete most other sugar exporters. Java likewise saw a steadily rising influx of technically trained personnel from abroad.[55] These mechanics were ranked as engineers and paid accordingly. In Java their wages were comparable to that of a senior colonial civil servant. In antebellum Louisiana, engineers could earn $150 or even more per month, and quite a few came from the Upper Mississippi Valley, Indiana, Ohio, or Illinois just for the milling season.[56]

In addition to the importation of engineers, local repair workshops appeared. At the instigation of the Amsterdam industrialist Paul van Vlissingen—who would later become a partner in Derosne & Cail—the Dutch government had sent Jacob Baijer to Java together with two other experts on cast iron in 1835. In addition to Baijer's workshop in Surabaya, which employed 750 people by 1860, quite a few factories had their own forges, which often served their neighbors as well. Most factories now employed steam engines for at least part of their processes. By 1870, all of them were equipped with vacuum pans. Java's sugar factory owners now began to consider themselves as industrialists, and accordingly established the Netherlands-Indies Industrial Society. At that time, the French Antilles could only have their broken machines fixed if the engineers on ships in port were available.[57]

Meanwhile, in the French sugar colonies a new generation of better-educated sugar producers assisted by a squad of metropolitan engineers quickly advanced the technological level of their factories. These technicians called the shots and were mostly affiliated with Cail & Cie, which often co-financed the placement of its machines in the upgraded factories of the creole families in the French Antilles. The Wetzell pans were disposed of and sugar centrals arose with vacuum pans, each drawing their cane from the nearby estates. French observers reported that these centrals democratized agricultural relations as they serviced both the small and large cane farmers with state-of-the-art industrial technology.[58] Indeed, technological progress and social change were inextricably linked.

Financing Plantations

As a rule, plantation commerce financed its expansion from its own profits. Securing fresh bank capital was hindered by imperial legislation that usually limited the liability of estates to creditors, a legal practice that went back to the time the first mills appeared in the Americas.[59] The legislation existed both to encourage pioneers to build mills and to prevent creditors destroying defaulting estates by splitting up and selling slave populations.[60] The British gave less protection to mills than the French, Portuguese, and Spanish, but as the pioneering historian on eighteenth-century West Indian commerce Richard Pares concluded, "Nothing could altogether counteract the tendency of the colonial communities to favor the interests of the resident debtor against those of the creditor in Europe."[61] Therefore, only highly powerful planters-cum-merchants such as the Lascelles, the Beckfords, and the Pinneys had enough leverage to expropriate debtors, and hence could afford to act as bankers circulating capital among plantation owners.[62]

Plantation mortgages based on the value of the estate were an exception until the mid-nineteenth century. The Dutch had introduced their revolutionary financial instrument of negotiation loans for Suriname and Dutch Guiana in the eighteenth century, but this scheme practically collapsed because of overrated appraisals of the value of the collateral during a boom. Planters soon proved to be incapable of paying the interest when conditions worsened.[63] In the early nineteenth century, Louisiana banks extended plantation mortgages for up to 50 percent of the value of the property at interest rates of 6–8 percent, but Louisiana was an exceptional case, and the financial crisis of 1837 put an end to these arrangements.[64]

By the mid-nineteenth century, practically all governments prohibited banks from extended mortgages with plantation property as surety because of wanting legal protection from creditors.[65] Merchant houses stepped in to provide advances on harvests, issue mortgages on slave ships, or, in the case of Louisiana, accept enslaved as collateral. Firms in Europe providing advances compelled their debtors to consign their harvest to them. However, consistently declining sugar prices severely diminished the profitability of the sugar estates, and to hedge against the increased risks merchant houses pushed up the interest rates, which further indebted planters and thus further enhanced their risk of defaulting.[66] The obvious answer to this vicious circle was to strengthen the creditor's position through facilitating moneylending based upon the plantation equipment, which became increasingly valuable. Spain, Brazil, Britain, and France had done so by the mid-nineteenth century, but this was not enough to produce new capital flows to the sugar colonies.[67]

Most Cuban planters, for instance, continued to be deeply mortgaged to US, English, Spanish, and Latin-American merchants, and slave traders who charged interest rates of up to 20 percent, still with the crop as collateral. Only in 1880 did a new law allow mortgages on land.[68] Cuba's new bankruptcy legislation did not have the desired effect of increasing the capital flowing to the sugar estates. Instead, it accelerated the transfer of estates into the hands of a class of wealthy planters, who were often also merchants. Tomás Terry Adan was one such a Cuban sugar magnate, who had arrived penniless from Caracas (Venezuela) to become probably the island's richest man and one of the richest persons in the world. He had made his first fortune in the slave trade, and in particular through a convalescence facility for enslaved who arrived ill and malnourished in Cuba.[69] He became a Cuban Croesus—a magnified example of a broader trend of the island's sugar industry: large plantations emerged with more than five hundred enslaved and more than a thousand hectares of land, which led to the rapid introduction of vacuum pans.

Whereas in Cuba and the West Indies the state and metropolitan banks largely refrained from financing the colonial sugar factories, in the Dutch and French realms they played a leading role. As we have seen, the Netherlands Trading Society—a bundling of merchant capital under the king's auspices designed to revive the country's colonial empire—directly

Interior of a Réunion sugar factory, 1911. The Crédit Foncier (Colonial Credit Bank), established in 1863 to modernize sugar production in the French colonies, owned many factories, including this one.

promoted the industrialization of Java's sugar production. In the French colonies, new capital had been infused in the sugar colonies through the establishment of the Colonial Credit Bank (Crédit Foncier Colonial) at the urging the industrialist Cail, which led to a restructuring of the sector. In Réunion, for instance, this bank rapidly took over the plantations of defaulting debtors until it had expropriated twelve estates, with a total acreage of 5,761 hectares, by 1873. It hired the engineers of Cail & Cie to replace Wetzell's equipment, which they condemned as hopelessly out-dated. Réunion's sugar sector was then almost entirely in the hands of two actors. Alongside the Colonial Credit Bank, there was the almost equally extensive property empire of the sugar magnate Kervéguen, who even in-troduced his own currency, the "kervéguen," which was in fact a supply of obsolete silver coins bought from Austria-Hungary.[70]

Meanwhile, the British government was conspicuously absent in the in-dustrialization of its sugar colonies. Under pressure of the refiners, it even hindered industrialization by imposing tariff policies that put additional duties on higher-grade sugar. Plantation property rapidly changed hands, increasing concentration of ownership but again without bringing new investments. In Jamaica, sugar production was actually abandoned: creditors in England were not inclined to invest new capital in what they considered to be a declining industry.[71] Likewise, much of the compensation money that slaveholders had received was not reinvested in sugar estates. This included key beneficiaries such as John and Francis Baring and John Gladstone, who were generously compensated but invested these considerable sums elsewhere.[72] Gladstone would start sugar production in India, whereas the Baring brothers participated in Louisiana banking and Cuban railway construction, thereby contributing to the prolongation of slave-produced sugar.

Only the wealthy Glasgow merchant Colin Campbell continued his extensive estates in British Guiana. In the twentieth century, his descendants would merge their estates with Booker McConnell as the dominant sugar business up until the early years of Guyana's independence in the 1970s.[73] The Bookers, Liverpudlians like the Gladstones, started with a shipping line between Liverpool and Georgetown, the capital of British Guiana. Like other metropolitan firms such as Cavan Bross and the Colonial Company, they managed considerable plantations in British Guiana and Trinidad, where they rapidly introduced vacuum pans. These firms were also capable of obtaining the finances for a railroad for British Guiana, which ran along the seashore and served the dual purpose of a dike and a means of transport.[74]

Barbadian planters, however, saw their railway project fail because both the compensation money and plantation profits mostly ended up in the pockets of the absentee owners in Britain. This had not happened in Mauritius, originally a British colony but now dominated by French planters' families (the island had been in French hands in the eighteenth century). The island's settler plantocracy kept investing their capital in their sugar estates instead of remitting it to France. Moreover, the compensation money was not doled out but put in a government's reserve fund, of which £200,000 was channeled toward a railway connection between the port town St. Louis and the hinterland. The government of Mauritius obtained an additional £800,000 through bonds issued on the London capital market.[75] In the early 1860s Mauritius' planters had their railway and also produced a third of their sugar by vacuum pans, while most of the remaining production was done with the Wetzell technology imported from Réunion.[76]

The British Empire's tendency to leave sugar planters to their own devices would also be experienced by the ambitious governor of St. Lucia, George William Des Vœux, when he launched a project to build a sugar central on his island to crush the cane from various estates. Des Vœux noticed that in Martinique such a factory allowed the smaller planters to continue while not having to incur massive expenditures on machines. He toured Martinique—separated by just thirty miles of water from his own St. Lucia—and admired its well-developed sugar industry and well-maintained roads, which strengthened his resolve to establish a sugar central himself. He sailed to France, where he was warmly welcomed to the Cail factory in Paris. Impressed by this huge workplace, he was convinced that this company should build the factory envisaged. It would be convenient for the planters on St. Lucia who spoke French and, very importantly, in case of repairs Cail's engineers were only thirty miles away in Martinique. But then came disappointment: during his extensive fundraising tour in England, Des Vœux discovered that wealthy investors had little appetite to invest in the West Indies. Eventually, a British construction enterprise was prepared to build a factory on credit, filling the gap in Des Vœux's budget, who consequently had to abandon his plan to engage Cail & Cie. Des Vœux gave St. Lucia its first sugar central at great personal expense, but he had the satisfaction of seeing his factory soon joined by two others.[77] Des Vœux was exceptional among the civil servants of the British Empire, where in contrast to France, the Netherlands, and Cuba, the Saint-Simonian notion of industrial policies had not taken root.

New Sugar Capitalism and an Old Monarchy

Princes were always prominent in the world of sugar. Because of sugar's high value, the most eminent medieval worldly and religious authorities had intervened to regulate access to precious and fragile natural resources. Later on, sugar colonies had been the most prized objects of the perennial wars between the major European powers. By the mid-nineteenth century, a new relationship emerged between the modern, increasingly powerful state bureaucracies and industrial sugar capitalism in which the state even began to arrange the financing of the industrialization. This was a necessary intervention at a time of declining profit margins. As we have seen, planters in the British colonies in particular, but also in Réunion and the French Antilles, tried to maintain profits by limiting their investments and thus debt. But this proved to be the wrong strategy as imperial governments and colonial administrations advanced industrialization, further reducing sugar prices and rendering intermediate technologies uncompetitive.

From the mid-nineteenth century, crowned heads, powerful industrialists, wealthy merchants, and planter magnates pushed sugar production into a new phase by building sugar centrals to process cane from multiple estates. This also happened in Brazil and Egypt. The Brazilian government tried to modernize the chronically undercapitalized Brazilian sugar industry by attracting British, French, and Dutch investors to build sugar centrals by guaranteeing them a fixed return on their capital—without much success.[78] In Egypt, by contrast, the world's largest project of state-led sugar industrialization took place. Industrial ambitions guided the rulers of Egypt to resurrect their once so prominent sugar manufacturing.

In 1818, Khedive Muhammad Ali ordered the building of a factory based on Jamaican technology. This was part of his Saint-Simonian ambition, strengthened by the presence of French doctors and engineers in his country, to have Egypt join the ranks of industrializing nations. His son and successor Ibrahim arranged for the construction of four sugar factories between 1840 and 1845, which was carried out by the same French engineer who had installed sugar factories in Guadeloupe in the service of Derosne & Cail.[79] When the resuscitation of the cotton production after Civil War in the United States put an end to the cotton boom in Egypt, Ibrahim's son Isma'il decided on a huge expansion of Egypt's industrial sugar production using the 132,556 hectares he had either seized from villagers or converted from waste land, and on which he could direct the *fellahs* (peasants) to grow the crops he desired.[80] For the building of his giant sugar complex, he commissioned Cail & Cie in partnership with the locomotives and railroad builder Fives-Lille.

This transaction was facilitated by a state banquet during the Paris World's Fair of 1867, where Napoleon III strategically had put Khedive Isma'il and Jean-François Cail at the same table. The khedive closely watched over his massive Egyptian sugar project, arranged for the importation of cane varieties, invited the world's leading sugar engineers, and even gave directions for the design of the crusher rollers. Cail & Cie and Fives-Lille built sixteen factories and constructed 522 kilometers of narrow-gauge railway for cane haulage as part of the Egyptian project. The result was a hundred-mile-long sugar belt along the Nile.[81]

The building of the Egyptian sugar factories was not only part of the largest industrial project of the time; it was also the largest single project ever conducted by Cail & Cie, according to their brochure distributed in 1878. It proudly proclaimed its responsibility for fifty factories in Cuba with a joint capacity of seventy thousand tons of sugar; twenty-five factories in the French colonies disgorging sixty thousand tons; and sixteen factories in Egypt with a joint capacity of a hundred thousand tons. These Egyptian factories became the model for the universal design of sugar factories, as they were the first with an iron skeleton and a corrugated iron roof. Incidentally, the same iron skeleton building appeared in Cail's contribution to the 1867 World's Fair.[82] The humble country boy Cail had become an industrial legend in France. He would survive his partner Derosne by twenty-five years and leave twenty-eight million francs at his death. Fortunately for him, he did not live long enough to see some of his real estate in downtown Paris demolished during the revolution of 1871 that followed the France's defeat to Prussia. It was a symbolic reversal of his success, which had been so closely tied to the industrial ambitions of Napoleon III, the imperial Saint-Simonian, who at that time was already in exile.[83]

Khedive Isma'il's great dream of stripping Egypt away from the Ottoman Empire and turning it into a European nation, for which he earned the epithet "The Magnificent," ended six years after the spectacular opening of the Suez Canal in a nightmare of towering debts, bankruptcy, and total economic dependence on Britain. As a consequence, not only Egypt's Suez shares but the entire sugar complex would be sold off as well, in this case to a French and Levantine group of investors. And it would stay in foreign hands.[84]

Nonetheless, the interventions of crowned heads signaled that the age of laisser-faire was over in the world of sugar. Industrial sugar capitalism moved ahead thanks to direct involvement of the state. The exceptions to the rule were the British colonies, where such initiatives were confined to a handful of strong metropolitan companies and a single local administrator.

Overall, sugar production had gone through a crucial period of transition that had begun with French physiocrats in the wake of the Seven Years' War and ended with the Saint-Simonian industrial and state-led projects of the 1840s. The state, as we will see in Chapter 6, would also play an indispensable role in guaranteeing supply of workers, who almost invariably labored under coerced conditions.

6

Slavery Stays

FIFTY YEARS AFTER THE REVOLUTION led by Toussaint L'Ouverture in Saint Domingue (now known as Haiti), the map of global sugar exports had changed beyond recognition. Cuba now dominated with an output almost equal to what was exported from the entire set of French and British Caribbean islands. The exports of Brazil, India, Java, Louisiana, Mauritius, Puerto Rico, and British Guiana followed Cuba's output in descending order and at some distance.[1] Unchanged, however, was the dominant role of slavery in the cane fields. This persistence had immense consequences for the societies involved and exacerbated the legacies and traumas of slavery that continue until this very day.

Slavery persisted particularly because in the cane fields, as well as the cotton fields for that matter, mechanization did not at all replace grueling manual harvesting and thus failed to turn labor into less of a determinant of the cost price. This was also to the advantage of Asia, where, as the prominent abolitionist Zachary Macaulay had already noticed in 1823, living expenditures and the cost of necessary materials to cultivate and process cane were so much lower than in the Americas.[2] Asia's peasant sugar was moreover often produced in the slack months after other crops had been harvested. Meanwhile, producers in the Americas had to cope with relatively unaccomplished but intimidatingly expensive technology, perennial labor shortages, and the still primitive state of agronomics, particularly with respect to plant physiology. India's sugar production might have stagnated in the first half of the nineteenth century, but it continued to be the largest in the world, followed by China. In addition, India had a thriving palm sugar sector, producing an annual eighty thousand tons of gur in Bengal alone in the 1870s.[3] At that time China and India together still accounted for half of the world's sugar production, predominantly for their own markets, but substantial volumes were nonetheless still shipped across the globe.[4]

When Britain outlawed the slave trade for its colonial possessions in 1807, it marked the beginning of a long strong struggle against international human trafficking rather than the beginning of the end of slavery. Despite the fact that Britain succeeded in having most other European colonial powers follow its ban by 1820, it struggled to contain the Atlantic slave trade in Cuba and Brazil. Cuba emerged as the world's largest sugar exporter through massive importation of enslaved Africans. In spite of heroic slave resistance and unstinting efforts by abolitionists, slavery continued to dominate in the cane fields of the Americas.

Other labor systems that gradually replaced or emerged alongside enslaved labor usually involved coercion too. This was definitely true for Java, where the colonial government summoned 60 percent of the island's peasant households to grow cane, indigo, or coffee for a minimal remuneration. Cuba and Java emerged as giant cane sugar exporters, accounting for almost half of the world's cane sugar exports between the 1860s and 1920s.[5] Both pulled off a tropical industrial revolution that would have been impossible without slavery or forced labor.

Amelioration and Resistance

After the ban on the slave trade by the United Kingdom, the authorities of the British and Dutch West Indies as well as the French Antilles had implemented regulations to improve the conditions of enslaved, policies that received the name "amelioration" and softened the harshest depersonalizing aspects of capitalist slavery. The recognition of the enslaved as persons was a key element, which entailed a ban on the splitting up of families with prepubescent children. Amelioration also recognized enslaved persons as witnesses in court and allowed them to own property. Another crucial change was the admittance of religious services to the plantations, since most Dutch and British plantations had barred the clergy until the late eighteenth century.

Free black communities, house slaves, and the church in particular influenced the culture of plantation slaves toward adopting European music, European clothes, and Christian names.[6] The vocal harmonies of African creole music deeply impressed visitors from Europe attending church services in the West Indies. Plantations began to integrate festive moments in their harvesting cycle. In the West Indies, the Harvest Home—the end of the milling season—was introduced probably in 1819 as a day off with a good meal.[7] In Louisiana, planters allowed their enslaved to celebrate the end of the harvest and the Fourth of July with quadrilles and square dances. It was a reworking of French and European entertainment—not the latest fashions, of course—and helped to tear down the boundaries of white exclusiveness.[8] In Suriname, three or four times per year enslaved workers could hold feasts wearing their best clothes instead of their plantation rags.[9] In the French Antilles, enslaved could wear for their finest clothes on Sundays, as Victor Schoelcher noted: "We see them on Sundays in frock coats or in very well-made clothes, with satin waistcoat, frilled shirt, boots, and the indispensable umbrella; they completely adopt our costume, and once dressed, become almost unrecognizable."[10]

Wearing these clothes was an escape from the daily reality of wearing rags. On the sugar plantations in Louisiana, for instance, enslaved were clad in coarse jute. Children wore just a jute bag with holes for their neck and arms, and the adults walked on unbearably hard shoes.[11] Enslaved's Sunday clothes and their quotidian rags were the perfect metaphor for the growing rift between aspirations and reality. The gradual appropriation of the European paraphernalia, the incorporation in the Christian religion in colonies where previously clergymen were not welcome, and feeble recognitions of personhood by colonial authorities and planters did not chime with the pressure to produce more sugar—pressure that was exerted on a shrinking enslaved population and therefore exacerbated plantation suffering. Meanwhile, growing literacy among free black populations and the percolation of news about the advance of the abolitionist movement into plantations created an atmosphere of expectation.

News of the uprising in Saint Domingue in 1791 spread immediately across the Caribbean islands as well as Suriname, as did the abolition of slavery in the French colonies two years later.[12] A rebellion in Barbados in 1816, which ended in hundreds of enslaved losing their lives, was triggered by news about the Imperial Registry of Slaves Bill, introduced into Parliament by the leading abolitionist William Wilberforce the year before to block the persistent illicit slave trade.[13] The bill did not pass, but the anger of the planters was splashed over the pages of the Barbadian newspapers.

The news unavoidably reached the island's enslaved population and mixed with swirling rumors that soldiers from Haiti stood ready to help them with any insurrection.[14]

In Demerara, the news of resistance by planters' circles against a London amelioration circular issued in 1823 sparked a massive revolt, which involved dozens of plantations.[15] It would radicalize the British abolitionist movement. Apart from the sheer size of the revolt, the fact that it had started on an estate owned by John Gladstone, the high-profile Liverpudlian merchant, incited a new round of public debate.[16] He and his sons had obtained six estates in Demerara—as well as five in Jamaica, for that matter—from defaulting debtors and had left the management to attorneys who ruthlessly exploited the enslaved under extremely primitive and unhealthy conditions, causing massive outbreaks of dysentery. In general, conditions at sugar estates in Demerara, a rough sugar frontier, were appalling, with mortality rates two to three times higher than those on most other West Indian plantations. There was clearly no consideration for the health of the enslaved workers—only for increased production from a shrinking enslaved population.[17]

From Amelioration to Abolition

The revolt in Demerara reverberated in Britain and gave new momentum to the abolitionist movement thanks largely to James Cropper, a Quaker merchant from Liverpool. His coming into the limelight came with a tinge of drama because Cropper happened to be a friend of Gladstone when he gave the clarion call with his newspaper article on the "Impolicy of Slavery" in the fall of 1823. Although not attacking Gladstone directly, Cropper alluded so obviously to the cruelty and violence of slavery and the pernicious role of absentee planters that readers could hardly not connect the dots.

The ensuing polemical contest between Gladstone and Cropper gave a new, more radical twist to the abolitionist movement, making the abolition of slavery itself the objective. It diverged from Wilberforce's gradualism, which counted on the support of the planters in the British Parliament to push the government to clamp down on the illicit slave trade by other European nations, such as by their main competitor Spain in Cuba, and to ameliorate the conditions of the enslaved in the West Indies. Cropper's line became dominant, however, initially thanks to his friend Zachary Macaulay, the former governor of Sierra Leone and a leading abolitionist. Together with Wilberforce, Macaulay had founded the Society for the Mitigation and Gradual Abolition of Slavery (later the Anti-Slavery Society), but now he sided with Cropper. In late 1822, he had already pointed out that the protection of West Indian sugar only served to keep East Indian sugar out of the country, because, as everyone could see, Indians produced sugar at lower cost.[18] Macaulay was right. In the port of Calcutta the cheapest sugar on earth was for sale, but the British government erased this advantage by adding a stiff additional duty at British ports.[19] Meanwhile, prices on the London market rose because of stagnating imports from the West Indies, the proponents of East India sugar pointed out.[20] According to Cropper, "the great bulk of the poor do obtain [sugar] in but very limited quantity." Indians could produce both sugar and cloth for Britain more cheaply. Britain stood to gain as it could sell its cloth in new markets, and Asian farmers would benefit as well.[21]

Cropper's naming and shaming of plantation owners coupled with advocating East Indian sugar was turned into a sustained effort by Macaulay who started the *Anti-Slavery Monthly Reporter* in 1825. This journal documented atrocities against enslaved across the British Empire, at sugar plantations from Berbice to Mauritius, and destroyed the myth that civil servants and planters cared for enslaved workers. It described, for example, in detail how enslaved workers were tortured at sugar plantations in Mauritius, and how the increase of the enslaved population on this island could not have been the result of natural growth; it was the dire consequence of illicit slave imports from Madagascar and the east coast of Africa.[22]

In the turn away from Wilberforce's moderation, women now played a key role. They propagated and practiced abstinence from West Indian sugar and advertised East Indian sugar whenever they could. Many households put sugar bowls on the table with a label saying "East India Sugar not made by slaves."[23] In a famous pamphlet, Elizabeth Heyrick—a painter, schoolteacher, converted Quaker, and one of the early members of the Anti-Slavery Society—decried the trepidation of Wilberforce and his associates as well as their consideration for the arrogant West Indies planters. No one could be unclear about the objective of her pamphlet, published in 1824, "Immediate not Gradual Abolition," nor about what had to be done: "Abstinence from *one single article* of luxury would annihilate the West Indian slavery!!"

But *abstinence* it cannot be called;—we only need substitute *East* India for *West* India sugar,—and the British atmosphere would be purified at once, from the poisonous infection of slavery."[24]

The call for substitution now replaced the call for abstinence, which had originally been championed by the Quakers in the late eighteenth century. In 1791, the radical pamphleteer William Fox had published *An Address to the People of Great Britain, on the Propriety of Refraining from the Use of West India Sugar and Rum,* which had urged a boycott of slave sugar and reached a circulation of fifty thousand copies within a few months, garnering Fox an estimated three hundred thousand followers. Abstinence at that time was about the sacrifice of drinking bitter tea for a just cause. The slogan of the 1820s was substitution and was far more comfortable to practice and thus more feasible. Heyrick's pamphlet not only widely resonated in Britain but also found its way to Pennsylvania, where its message of substitution inspired the local Free Produce movement to establish its own shops. These looked for alternative suppliers of sugar produced with free labor in Haiti, the Philippines, and closer to home in Florida; they even sought sugar made from other crops than cane.[25] On both sides of the Atlantic, people discovered their power as consumers too.

Cropper, Macaulay, and Heyrick shifted the battle from the purely moral to the economic and factual. The words "mitigation and gradual" disappeared from the texts of the Anti-Slavery Society. In the early 1830s, about five thousand petitions flooded Parliament signed by a total of four hundred thousand women and nine hundred thousand men. This movement was sustained by Britain's rapid urbanization and the ever-growing circulation of newspapers. Quaker entrepreneurs such as Josiah Wedgewood were ardent abolitionists and from his and other factories sugar bowls imprinted with "East India Sugar Not Made by Slaves" entered British households.[26]

Developments in Britain did encourage enslaved to liberate themselves. News about inconclusive emancipation debates in the British Parliament probably spread via free black residents to the plantation quarters. The bomb burst on Christmas Day 1831 in the form of a widespread revolt in Jamaica that lasted for eleven days; about thirty thousand enslaved people were involved and many plantations and planters' mansions were torched. It entered the history books as the Baptist War, or Christmas Rebellion, and was only suppressed after two hundred casualties and the mass execution of five

During the massive abolitionist campaign of the 1820s, many Brits
served sugar in bowls bearing a message designed to reassure guests
that their contents were not produced by enslaved workers.

hundred enslaved. The sheer numbers involved in this resurrection and the
massacre that followed were the writing—in blood—on the wall.

This tragedy convinced London that emancipation could be delayed no
longer, and in 1834 slavery was abolished throughout the British Empire.
This had potentially immense consequences for sugar production as the majority of the 667,925 enslaved in the British West Indies worked on sugar

On Christmas Day, 1831, enslaved Jamaicans began torching plantations and planters' mansions. The revolt, which involved 30,000 laborers, was bloodily suppressed but nonetheless proved a turning point in the campaign to abolish slavery within the British Empire.

plantations, predominantly in Jamaica and Barbados, and to a lesser extent in British Guiana.[27] However, abolition did not grant enslaved workers immediate freedom. They first had to undergo a period of apprenticeship lasting until 1838, in which they still had to work on the estates of their former masters. After this apprenticeship, most workers only wanted to flee. Almost everywhere in the West Indies labor became in short supply, with the notable exception of Barbados where nearly all arable land was in the hands of the planters. Wages on this island were lower than almost anywhere else in the West Indies and amounted to only a third of those of British Guiana, for instance. Rampant poverty struck the eyes of any visitor walking through the dilapidated streets of Bridgetown. Emigration and seeking employment, such as on the construction of the Panama Railway, seemed to be the only way out of such misery.[28]

In Jamaica, the largest West Indian island, there was far more space to establish free villages and homesteads than in Barbados. At the end of the 1840s, already two-thirds of former slaves had removed themselves from the estates.[29] The wealthiest estate owners tried to overcome labor shortages by mechanization and ordered light rail and expensive equipment to be sent over from England, even though the reliability of the machines left much to be desired. The planters were still confident about their future, trusting that they were protected from competition by foreign sugar on the British market. They therefore felt seriously betrayed when the British government lifted this protection in 1846, pushing global sugar prices toward a collapse. Additional calamities came in the shape of devastating drought, followed by cholera as well as smallpox, which carried away 10 percent of Jamaica's population.[30]

Jamaica's sugar production, which was still almost ninety thousand tons in the 1820s, had fallen to just a quarter of that amount thirty years later.[31] Plantations were abandoned or split up in parcels and sold to Jamaicans who bought them from savings made from their work on the Panama Railroad. By 1860, Jamaica counted fifty thousand smallholdings and their numbers continued to grow in the following decades. Still, many Jamaican families were not able to survive as farmers, and the demise of the sugar sector caused widespread destitution.[32] The misery was exacerbated by the island's planters and authorities who refused to modernize the plantation system and, in contrast to French abolitionists, could not see how smallholder cane growing and modern factories could work together. In 1865, impoverished and desperate Jamaicans rose up in the Morant Bay Rebellion, which was brutally suppressed, resulting in hundreds of casualties.

Peasant production eventually made Jamaica's rural economy less vulnerable and steered it away from the monocrop economy that continued to dominate in other West Indian islands. Many descendants of the former slaves began growing fruits for the US market, which made them much better off than workers on sugar estates, as the British Royal Commission concluded during its investigation of the appalling conditions in the West Indies in 1897.[33] The demise of Jamaica's sugar sector happened because planters had mistakenly believed that they could control labor and continue to be protected by British tariffs, as they had been for the past two centuries. However, Britain had changed into an industrial society with a basic interest in cheap sugar, as Cropper had emphasized. In 1846, it opened its markets to new producers, including those that held slaves in Cuba, to replace Jamaica, once the most important British sugar island. It also would destroy the investments the British had made in India introducing industrial sugar production with steam crushers and vacuum pans.

Boom and Bust of India's Industrial Sugar Manufacturing

In the 1790s, British traders began to export the first meaningful volumes of sugar from India. Most of this had not arrived at British customs but been diverted to markets in Europe, Hamburg in particular. The abolition of slavery within the British Empire completely changed things. In 1834, Liverpudlian merchants with ties to the British cotton industry stepped in as investors in India, which they were eyeing as an important market for their cheap industrially manufactured cloth. John Gladstone stood out among them, although his reorientation toward India may seem surprising after having been the first to introduce the vacuum pan in his Demerara factories and among the first to bring indentured labor from India to the Caribbean. However, Gladstone may have considered that, rather than bringing Indians to his factories, it was safer and probably more profitable to bring his factories to India. In 1840, therefore, he sold most of his Demerara and Jamaica estates and brought many of his West Indian staff to India for his new state-of-the-art palm sugar factory in Chowgutcha. It was the largest sugar factory in the world at the time with an annual production capacity of seven thousand tons. This was tantamount to a third of the entire production of Barbados in these years.[34]

British sugar industrialists in India experienced a golden decade from the mid-1830s. Like their counterparts in Barbados and Jamaica, they trusted that Prime Minister Robert Peel would unwaveringly stand for colonial interests and maintain the ban on Cuban and Brazilian slave-produced sugar from the British market. Provided with abundant capital from the merchant houses of Liverpool and Calcutta, dozens of factories emerged in India, all with state-of-the-art equipment. A contributor to the *Friend of India* newspaper claimed not without justification that the West Indies plantations, which owed their survival to the "preposterous" system of importing labor from India, would soon belong to the past.[35]

However, money and machines were not enough to alter the fact that sugar in India had always been produced by peasants who milled their own cane. Even a powerful local landowner such as Dwarkanath Tagore, grandfather of the Nobel Prize–winning poet, was unable to force them to grow cane and bring it to his factory. All the money Tagore invested in the 1840s, his hiring of the best British technicians with West Indies' experience, and the ships he sent to bring cane from Mauritius were to no avail. Indian peasants had to pay rent to their landlords but were under no obligation to grow particular crops for them. They continued to produce their own raw sugar, their gur, and resolutely preserved their independence, snubbing the factories when they offered a price for cane almost equal to what they could obtain for their cane or palm gur. Capitalism was rebuffed here, and industrialists could only survive by converting from cane milling to processing peasant sugar.

There was, however, one exception. In Tirhut, a district bordering Nepal, planters obtained servile labor as part of their land lease contracts with the local maharajas. Soon, nineteen factories emerged, their tall chimneys peeking over the horizon. But Tirhut was not yet connected to Calcutta by rail and its sugar could only leave India via the River Ganges, "suffering heavily from wastage by theft and leakage in ill-found boats, while there was no infrequent loss of boat and cargo," as one contemporary observed.[36]

In their quest for alternative locations to produce sugar, British investors had few other options in Asia beyond India. Mauritius exhibited suitable conditions but was in the hands of a Franco-Mauritian plantocracy. Ceylon proved to be unsuitable for sugar production, and the Malaccan Peninsula was a promising but still undeveloped territory. Leonard Wray, the indefatigable advocate for transferring the Caribbean plantation model to Asia, did try his luck in the Malay Province of Wellesley, but he was met with a hazardous coast full of swamps and pirates. Until the end of the nineteenth century, most of the sugar in the Malay Peninsula and Penang came from Chinese millers, and Europeans played merely a marginal role. Wray himself left for South Africa and would eventually turn up in the United States.[37]

While a substantial relocation of sugar production from the Atlantic region to Asia did happen, it was not as fast as the British abolitionists had expected. This became a problem because the British market was closed to slave sugar after the Slavery Abolition Act of 1834. Sugar therefore continued to be an expensive item for ordinary people at a time when famine and high food prices already generated unrest among the rapidly growing urban proletariat.[38] Industrial interests and food riots coalesced into a movement for free trade, and particularly for lowering duties on food imports, a movement known as Cobdenism, after the industrialist and statesman Richard Cobden. Sensitive to his country's needs, Tory prime minister Robert Peel trashed his reputation as a strong defender of West Indian interests and pushed a reduction of the duties on non-slave-produced sugar from outside the British Colonies through Parliament in 1844. Two years later, the Whig prime minister John Russell crossed a red line, unthinkable ten years before, by including in this reduction slave-produced sugar. This step was motivated by the necessity to keep the British manufacturing competitive with Germany's rising industrial economy. But the consequence was that by 1856 enslaved workers were producing 40 percent of the sugar consumed in Britain.[39]

The equalization of the duties in 1846 rapidly pushed sugar prices down on the London market and threw the already struggling Jamaica sugar industry into a tailspin. In India, factories were in no position to bring down their cost price as they had to compete for cane with representatives of the khandsari workshops, who had their middlemen in every village to buy the cane in the field. As a result, the great expectations that India's industrial sugar would replace slave sugar were dashed. The signing away of the British sugar factories in both India and Jamaica, the largest West Indian sugar colony, in favor of the opening up of the British market for slave sugar is an almost forgotten chapter in history. The planters in Jamaica never forgot and felt utterly betrayed. To them, Robert Peel was nothing but a traitor.[40]

Some factories in India survived the slump of the sugar prices of the mid-nineteenth century. In South Bengal, resilient entrepreneurs processed gur from palm sugar, which came from trees along roads and bordering fields that were not liable to the high land rent.[41] A few others pulled through thanks to excellent contacts with the most important landlords around their factories. Among them was Frederick Minchin, an Irishman married to an Indian woman and owner of the Aska sugar factory in Orissa. Unlike the traditionally refined cane or palm sugars from India, Minchin's sugar did not reach England. Again, these so-called khandsaris were not counted as refined sugar and therefore—like the rather raw Barbados sugar—were subject to lower duties. They were readily imported in Britain until they were pushed out of this market by the dumping of German beet sugar in the 1880s.

Britain's Global Search for Sugar

That Britain allowed slave-produced sugar from Brazil and Cuba on its market seemed to be justifiable as a tactical move to obtain additional leverage to stop the ongoing Atlantic slave trade. After all, in 1845 Britain had signed a new bilateral treaty with Spain to ban the slave trade, renewing the mostly ignored first treaty of 1817 and the second of 1835, which was also heavily dodged. The new Anglo-Spanish treaty contained an important concession made by the Spanish government allowing the British Navy to intercept and punish slave ships heading for Cuba, but it was still far from effective. While Britain sent its navy ships to raid Brazil's territorial waters and forced the country to stop its slave trade with a second treaty against the slave trade in 1851, it took a softer stance on Cuba. Britain did not want to drive the Cuban elite into the arms of the United States, where prominent politicians had already expressed their desire to buy the island from Spain. Britain had little leverage apart from Spain needing its support to stave off the threat of the United States annexing Cuba.[42]

Although the British government had made serious efforts to renew bans on the Atlantic slave trade while opening its markets to slave-based sugar, those efforts nonetheless represented a capitulation. In hindsight, the abolitionist political agenda that combined free trade, industrialization, and emancipation personified by Cobden—himself a liberal abolitionist—had rested on a fragile basis. It had to be upheld with prohibitive duties, which drove up sugar prices in Britain. These duties were moreover not consistently applied—they were never extended to coffee or cotton, for example. Some abolitionists gave up resisting the removal of additional duties on slave-produced sugar, believing, or hoping, that coerced labor was unable to survive the rigors of the free market because of its inherent inefficiency. They speculated that increasing commerce between Britain and Brazil, under the condition of sharpened observance of the ban on the slave trade, would rationalize and industrialize Brazilian production and ultimately phase out slavery. However, no consensus existed on that account and, in contrast to the days of Adam Smith, few abolitionists still dared to say that free labor was cheaper than slave labor.[43]

Meanwhile, the quest for cheap cereals and sugar, as well as markets for its industrial commodities, directed Britain's imperial policies. It used its maritime supremacy and rapidly maturing financial sector to open up new markets for its industrial goods and tie new suppliers of commodities to its commercial empire. Britain's dispatch of vessels to Brazil, its military subjugation of Burma, the treaty it enforced upon Siam to produce rice for Britain, and the opening up of the Philippine island of Negros to produce sugar for the British market all happened in the 1850s. These actions all emanated from the same grand design to have the periphery in Latin America and Southeast Asia produce food for the British consumers while also serving as markets for Britain's manufactures. The Cobdenist policies of low import tariffs on agricultural commodities clearly met its objectives with respect to sugar. Coupled with rising wages, it resulted in a rapid growth of sugar consumption after decades of stagnation.[44]

The emergence of the Negros sugar plantation belt in the Philippines was the direct result of these British policies. It began in 1855 with the opening up of the port city of Iloilo on the adjacent island of Panay to foreign commerce. The British established a vice-consulate in this city and the first to be entrusted with this office was Nicholas Loney, an agent for several Manchester textile firms. He found a partner in the Liverpudlian John Higgin, who happened to be a nephew of Richard Cobden himself. While politically and personally connected to Cobden, economically Loney was supported by Russell and Sturgis, the biggest trading house of the Philippines, which in turn was backed by the prominent London house of Baring.[45]

Loney aggressively encouraged sugar production in Negros and the retailing of cotton on his and other islands of the Philippine Visayas. He supplied both crop loans at a decent interest rate and sold equipment such as steam-driven cane crushers that could be paid for in instalments. The monastic order of the Recollects played a key role in mediating between Loney and the planters, and even acted as guarantors for repayment of loans. In addition, textile producers from Iloilo, mostly ethnic Chinese, invested profits made in their workshops in the sugar frontier of Negros just twenty miles across the sea. Much of the land was cleared by immigrants from Iloilo, but they were dispossessed by the capitalist investors who turned themselves into landlords, or *hacenderos,* ruling over tenants who did the cultivation. For harvesting and haulage, these landlords began to rely on seasonal laborers, who came in gangs of twenty or so from increasing distances, led by their own foremen. By 1886, Negros had become a sugar island with two hundred steam-driven and five hundred animal-driven iron crushers, as well as thirty water-powered mills.[46]

Brazil, once the world's largest sugar exporter, benefited remarkably little from its access to the British market. Lack of capital, fuel depletion, and soil exhaustion were partly to blame, but the most important factor was the emerging coffee frontier in southeast Brazil competing vigorously for the shrinking enslaved labor force in the final decades before abolition in 1888.[47] Although Pernambuco managed to double its output in these years, growth could have been much more impressive. Cane fields were still dominated by the seventeenth-century mill, the *engenho,* as the attempts by the Brazilian government to introduce sugar centrals had failed. The Pernambuco planters had gobbled up vast tracts of land, which allowed them to plant on virgin soil and ratoon (i.e., allow the cane to grow up again from the same stubbles instead of planting new stalks) for up to six years. After that time the soil would be exhausted, and they would relocate their cane fields together with the cattle mills. This delayed the introduction of steam and steel and kept Brazil's sugar output per ton of cane far below Java's or Cuba's.[48]

Slavery Stays: Cuba, Brazil, and Louisiana

Geopolitics played a crucial part in Cuba's successful dodging of the British ban on slavery and thus its ascendency as the world's largest sugar exporter. That slavery still existed in the United States and that its presidents regularly expressed their interest in the annexation of this island gave the Cuban plantocracy a powerful weapon against any abolitionist intentions of Spain. In defiance of the Anglo-Spanish treaty of 1845 that renewed and improved the earlier bans on the slave trade to Spanish colonies, the annual number of trafficking of enslaved Africans to Cuba would reach a peak of 25,000 in 1859. Existing estimates suggest that at least 323,800 enslaved arrived between 1835 and 1864.[49]

But even this massive illicit slave trade did not stop the decline in Cuba's enslaved population from 436,500 in 1841 to 363,288 in 1868.[50] The fact that the enslaved, who came directly from Africa and were susceptible to the deadly diseases of the Americas, definitely played a role, but extreme exploitation did its devastating work too. Cuban enslaved worked at least twelve hours most days; their workday could increase to eighteen hours during the harvest. Annual mortality among the enslaved population in Cuba amounted to 6.3 percent in the years 1835–1841, which was higher than in most of the West Indies on the eve of abolition. While excruciatingly long workdays must have reduced life expectancy, the gender imbalance (men outnumbered women 2:1) reduced birth rates.[51]

The exhausting enslaved work was performed under very harsh supervision in Cuba, which represented a complete reversal of the amelioration policies of the early nineteenth century. While in most Caribbean colonies, slaves had their own plots of land to grow vegetables, which they brought to the market, in Cuba—as well as Puerto Rico—the enslaved lost their subsistence plots, and opportunities to buy their freedom were reduced. They were fed by their masters and confined to their estates. This was both to avoid comingling of enslaved people from different plantations at food markets and to prevent them from developing an independent food economy that would help them to buy themselves free.[52] The entire slavery regime was one of institutionalized cruelty, as appears from a description by the abolitionist British consul in Cuba David Turnbull. He wrote about the horrendous use of whipping posts: "Although by means of the parapets, the authorities have succeeded in shutting out the inquisitive glances of the passers by, excluding from public view the streaming blood and lacerated flesh of the sufferers, they have totally failed in shutting in their piercing screams and piteous shrieks for mercy."[53] This factory of punishment and torture stood at the apex of a system designed for maximum control, which came close to imprisonment as many enslaved were shut up in barracks in the evening.[54]

Most enslaved people in Brazil lived in less prison-like conditions, but the country was still the largest slave importer in the nineteenth century, involving the trafficking of almost two million Africans, many of whom were destined for sugar estates, and the physical and psychological abuse of enslaved did not abate. The English-American Thomas Ewbank, who traveled Brazil in the 1850s, described the torture of enslaved in graphic detail, with drawings of torture instruments accompanying his text. The spirit of resistance was nonetheless inextinguishable, leading to frequent killings of masters, arson and sabotage of mills, suicides, and of course periodic rebellions. Resistance was vehement in Cuba as well, fueled by news about abolition in other Caribbean colonies that was spread by the free black population and peddlers.[55]

Confronted with a declining and rebellious enslaved population, Cuban planters desperately tried to source labor beyond Africa, which they treated almost as harshly as their enslaved workers, regardless of their provenance. Chinese contract workers and many laborers from Ireland, Mexico's Yucatan, the Canary Islands, and Spanish Galicia were more or less treated as merchandise. Quite a few Galicians were kidnapped in the 1840s and sold at less than half of the price of enslaved Africans.[56]

The oppressive work regime on Louisiana's sugar plantations also killed enslaved in large numbers in the nineteenth century. Whatever measures Louisiana's planters might have taken to increase birth rates, these were undone by the short-term consideration of obtaining as much labor as they could from their enslaved. In contrast to Cuba, however, the growing sugar economy of Louisiana did not have to resort to labor imports from Africa, China, Mexico, and Europe. Between 1820 and 1860, approximately 875,000 enslaved were transferred from the northern states to the lower south of Louisiana for the cultivation of sugar and cotton. They came from Virginia, for instance, where soil exhaustion had brought about the conversion from tobacco to cereals, which needed far less labor. It was not until in the 1850s that the need for slave imports in Louisiana diminished due to the combination of mechanization and slightly improved living conditions.[57]

Improvements in enslaved's conditions in Louisiana meant they were allowed to wear shoes; in some cases they were even prescribed.[58] A month's convalescence for women after giving birth was another minor amelioration, because giving birth to a new generation of enslaved was considered to be of the utmost importance. Louisiana's planters introduced crisp money (money tokens), which enslaved workers could earn from extra work such as collecting wood at night, selling poultry or vegetables from their yards, or selling pumpkins, potatoes, and hay from their plots of land outside the plantation to their estate's management. Crisp money was only valid in the plantation shops so as to block commercial dealings between slaves and peddlers, who allegedly encouraged enslaved to pilfer (e.g., machinery parts), which would be an effective means of sabotage.[59]

Defenders of slavery seized upon these limited improvements to compare the living conditions of the enslaved in the southern states of the United States favorably with those of industrial workers. Obviously, the material conditions of workers in northern cities of the country could be bad, but they were by no means comparable to the abuse inflicted on enslaved. The eyewitness accounts of torture, maiming, and blood hounds being set on enslaved are numerous. Whipping facilities like that described by Turn-

bull in Cuba also existed in Louisiana.[60] Any romanticizing of the conditions at plantations, such as in nostalgic stories of antebellum Louisiana,
obscures the words of Herbert Aptheker, one of the pioneers of slavery
studies in the United States: "Slavery was a chronic state of warfare, and all
men who were not Negroes were, *by law,* part of the standing army of
oppressors."[61]

Indentured Labor on the Sugar Estates

The abolition of slavery in the British and French colonial empires happened in the name of freedom, but the freedom of plantation workers would
turn out to be heavily circumscribed. First, planters, who dominated local
assemblies in the colonies, convinced their governments to enact legislation that would force emancipated populations back on the plantations, as
Charles Alphonse, Comte de Chazelles, had suggested for the French Antilles (see Chapter 5). Just a few years after emancipation in the French
Empire, Martinique and Guadeloupe adopted regulations that included an
onerous taxation on smallholdings and stiff regulations against vagabondism
to coerce the emancipated to return to the plantations. Similar legislation
was implemented in Mauritius, where a Francophone sugar plantocracy
dominated the island's assembly. Victor Schoelcher, the great French abolitionist, fulminated against these regulations as purposeful measures to
make the labor of the emancipated former enslaved population cheaply
available to planters.[62]

In addition, an old coercive labor system dating from the time of the
severe labor shortages in the aftermath of the medieval Black Death was
dusted off. The indenture system involved a document that gave the master
legal authority over the life of the servant for the duration of the contract.
This quickly became the basis for labor contracts used in colonial plantations and mines. The contracts invariably made it a criminal act for workers
to abandon their work before they had served their contractual term. As
has been noted in Chapter 3, indentureship had preceded slavery in the
West Indies and the French Antilles. Almost immediately after emancipation, indentured workers reappeared in the West Indies and Mauritius, and
engagés resurfaced in the French colonies. The hundreds of thousands of
Asian workers who came to work at sugar plantations came almost invariably under such indentured contracts. In fact, these contracts were a

universal phenomenon in the world's cane fields, including those of Hawaii and the Spanish colonies, and did not exempt Europeans.[63]

Chinese workers had been identified as an ideal labor force to replace enslaved well before the abolition of the slave trade. Pierre Poivre, Benjamin Rush, Henry Botham, and others had written in glowing terms about their performance. Joseph Foster Barham II, the owner of the Mesopotamia plantation in Jamaica, had heard about the hardworking and frugal character of the Chinese and planned to establish a company to hire them in fourteen-year indentures, a contract that came very close to slavery. But it would be Robert Farquhar who went down in history as the architect of the Asian-Caribbean indentured labor system. During his term as lieutenant-governor of Penang (1804 to 1805), he had seen the accomplished Chinese sugar producers running plantations and organized the first voyage of 192 Chinese migrant laborers from Macao to Trinidad. It was not a success; but when the end of the apprenticeship period neared the plantation owners of British Guiana, led by John Gladstone, tried again and organized the first shipment of 396 Indian contract laborers.[64] Apparently, Gladstone had not much confidence in this solution; he sold his factories in Demerara and started again in India in 1840. That proved to be a wise decision because one year later John Russell, the secretary for the colonies, famously denounced this "coolie trade" as "a new system of slavery" and stopped it.[65]

Yet Gladstone might have been too hasty because the recruitment ban was lifted in 1844. In Mauritius, the planter-dominated legislative council levied taxes on wine and liquor to pay for the immigration, on which it spent £423,579 between 1844 and 1848 alone.[66] In Trinidad, planters plundered the exchequer of the colony to finance the recruitment of indentured laborers, which did not go unresisted, however. Colored Trinidadians petitioned against this importation, denouncing the way in which £250,000 were cobbled together by raising taxes and cutting wages at plantations. They were outraged that Trinidad's desperately needed public funds for infrastructure and services were being diverted to serve the plantocracy. Colored members of the Jamaican legislature and Baptist missionaries sought to stop planters using Jamaica's government funding to subsidize the importation of Indian contract workers.[67] They were fueled by anger about former enslaved having to pay for the recruitment of contract workers, as this would intentionally depress their wages.

Planters frantically undertook the recruitment of indentured laborers, which soon became big business. First, recruiters from British Guiana and Trinidad paid on a bounty basis went to smaller West Indian islands and hired 18,000 laborers.[68] They also imported labor from Sierra Leone and St. Helena, as well as black and white workers from the Portuguese Atlantic islands. A lesser known fact is that almost forty thousand Africans liberated from slave ships were landed in British Guiana, Trinidad, and Jamaica to be put to work as indentured laborers, mostly on sugar plantations.[69] Powerful British businessmen engaged in the transport of Indian contract laborers, to British Guiana in particular. Since they had made major investments in British Guiana and Trinidad, 85 percent of the Indian indentured laborers for the West Indies ended up at these two destinations, whereas only 10 percent disembarked in the much larger sugar colony of Jamaica.[70]

Meanwhile, in Asia overpopulation and conflict offered growing opportunities for labor recruiters. The desperate situation in southeast China during the years of the Taiping Rebellion (1850–1864) fed migration to the cane fields of Cuba and Peru as well as Hawaii. It also explains the buoyant immigrant Chinese sugar cultivation in Thailand and in the Malaccan Peninsula. Most of the three hundred thousand Chinese contract laborers for sugar plantations came to Cuba, Peru, or Hawaii. If they were not simply kidnapped, they were often clueless about where they were heading. Quite a few thought, according to one witness, that the golden mountains—the gold mining—of California were waiting for them. Conditions on board were almost as crammed as on slave ships, and 25 percent of the passengers did not survive the journey.[71] Those who did arrive in Cuba were treated as chattel slaves and brought to auctions, where planters could buy them for less than enslaved Africans. Planters spoke about "buying coolies," humiliated them by cutting off their queues and, as an act of depersonalization, gave them Spanish names. There are many tragic stories of Chinese committing suicide by jumping in a cauldron of boiling sugar juice. Mistreated, tortured, and sometimes maimed, about half of the Chinese coolies died before their eight-year contract expired.[72] Not much better was the fate of the ninety thousand Chinese coolies, also taken via Macao, to replace slave labor on Peru's sugar estates after emancipation in 1854. Although the British stopped the supply of Chinese workers from Macao in 1874, their soaring sales of opium to Peru helped to keep the resident Chinese workers in peonage, a condition almost equivalent to slavery.[73]

Java's Forced Cultivation System (1830–1870)

Coercion continued to dominate the world's cane fields for most of the nineteenth century. While the Americas experienced a "Second Slavery" and an influx of indentured laborers, in Java 60 percent of the rural population had to relinquish part of their land and time to grow sugar, alongside coffee, indigo, and other crops for the colonial government. The man who designed and implemented this forced cultivation system was general Johannes van den Bosch, an army engineer. Born into a bourgeois milieu, the charismatic and impatient Van den Bosch had demonstrated his impressive organizational capabilities when he stirred up a nation-wide movement for pauper colonies in the present-day Netherlands and Belgium in the late 1810s. Five of these colonies, intended to relieve poverty, were awarded UNESCO World Heritage status in 2021. A few years later, Van den Bosch departed as commissioner-general for the Dutch West Indies, which included Suriname, which was still a sugar producer of some consequence. He reorganized the administration of these colonies and—similar to the amelioration policies of the British—ensured that enslaved people were granted personhood. Although opposed to slavery himself, this was the best he could achieve given the almost complete absence of an abolitionist movement in the Dutch Kingdom.

Appointed as governor-general of the Netherlands Indies in 1829, Van den Bosch's assignment was to restore the profitability of the severely loss-making Dutch colonial empire in Asia. When he arrived in Java, sugar production was still mainly left to the Chinese millers. In the early years after Britain's abolition of the slave trade, Van den Bosch believed that Java's sugar mills would now be able to serve European markets. He reckoned that the end of the slave trade would force plantation owners in the Americas to improve labor conditions and that the ensuing higher operational costs would eventually bring about the end of slavery. But when he sailed to Asia in 1830, he realized that the ban on the slave trade was far from effective, and that slavery would continue to exist for the foreseeable future. In that case, Java sugar stood no chance on the European market, particularly because it had to make the long journey around the Cape of Good Hope, which more than doubled its price.[74]

As we have repeatedly seen, sugar producers could only survive if they were able to keep labor costs to the bare minimum, just enough to keep their workers alive. Even in Java, with its low living standards, people willing to work under these conditions were hard to find, because, Van den Bosch argued, the Javanese had no incentive to work harder than they already did to subsist on their own small plots of land. Although a considerable proportion of Javanese peasants did not own their land, or possessed only a tiny plot, they usually made their living as dependents working on the fields of wealthier farmers and receiving part of the harvest. Also preventing a large proletariat from emerging was a government ban on land purchases by Europeans, Chinese, and their descendants. This was issued in 1823 to prevent Javanese peasants being driven from their land, which could be a cause for unrest and threaten colonial rule. In the absence of a rural proletariat, sugar estates with wage workers that were started by British merchant houses in the early nineteenth century collapsed because of labor shortages.[75]

To solve this deadlock, at least from a colonial perspective, Van den Bosch proposed to kindle a capitalist economy by forcing Javanese peasants to grow crops for financial remuneration from which they had to pay their taxation on their land, thus turning them into taxpayers and consumers dependent on monetary income. Although this was against the colonial government's stated objective, it already had made a major exception for the forced cultivation to coffee, its most important export crop. Moreover, Van den Bosch had no philosophical objections against forced labor. To King William I of the Netherlands, who held the sole authority over the Dutch colonies, he wrote that the concept of free labor did not mean anything for most of mankind, for whom idleness meant starvation. Since people *had* to work, labor was forced by definition.[76] Sailing to take up his position in the Dutch East Indies in 1830, Van den Bosch held his king's approval to implement his forced cultivation system, which would solve the problem of labor shortages that had ruined the earlier plantation experiments by British merchant houses in Java. Supervised by European and Javanese officials, the coerced labor of 125,000 Javanese secured a steady flow of cane to private factories. Their labor, Van den Bosch proudly claimed, was four times cheaper than of the enslaved in the Caribbean region.[77]

Van den Bosch envisaged his forced cultivation system as a temporary set of measures to be phased out once Java's rural economy was sufficiently monetized and enough Javanese had to work for wages. To accelerate this process, the colonial government engineered an enormous influx of small copper coins into Java in the early 1830s. A crucial task was assigned to the semigovernmental Netherlands Trading Society, which, as we have seen in Chapter 5, played a key role in the industrialization of Java's sugar sector. It also provided the liquidity to pay the peasantry and took care of the shipment and auctioning in the Netherlands of the colonial products.[78] In all this, Van den Bosch had the full support of his King William I, referred to in Dutch history books as the king-merchant. Again, like the three successive khedives of Egypt and Napoleon III, this Dutch king explicitly furthered tropical agro-industrial capitalism as a national project under his own direct responsibility.

While Dutch colonial civil servants supervised and enforced the cultivation of cash crops for the European markets, its implementation was put in the hands of the traditional Javanese rulers and village heads who became gradually integrated into the colonial bureaucracy. As a reward, they received a share in the profits, giving them a stake in maximizing the production of cash crops. Landowning farmers were conscripted to make their labor and land available for a low plant wage, with which they were supposed to pay their land rent. In theory, the system was meant to be fair and tolerable. In practice, the burdens of the forced cultivation system were spread unevenly over the different parts of rural Java, and within each village wealthier farmers shifted the work to the many small and landless peasants who depended upon them for their livelihood.

Many marginalized peasants tried to escape from the burdens imposed upon them and start new homesteads in less densely populated parts of Java. Extensive migrations are recorded from the regions where conscription fell particularly heavily on the peasantry.[79] These often must have been secretive as Javanese were not allowed to travel beyond their own district without permission from the village head and colonial officials. Travel permits would continue to exist until the end of the cultivation system, and for anyone caught without a pass a beating with the rattan or imprisonment would be waiting. Indeed, the measures that were in place to enforce conscription stemmed from the same ideology and the same cynical practicality of the ruthless postslavery anti-vagrancy laws of the Caribbean islands and Mauritius intended to drive people to the plantations.[80]

Java's forced cultivation of cane led to widespread desertion and was actively resisted. In some instances overburdened and disgruntled peasants marched en masse to the mansion of the Resident (the provincial administrative head), something utterly unthinkable in Cuba. Many cane fields went up in flames. Punishments and night watchmen did not help; Javanese peasants sometimes shot burning arrows over the heads of guards, who received a severe beating for any arson occurring under their watch.[81] Although the forced cultivation system did not involve the systematic cruelty of the Cuban, Brazilian, and Louisiana plantation economies, it was attended by violence. Moreover, it inflicted hardship and even many deaths as the imposition of sugar—and, even more so, indigo—cultivation contributed to the famines that raged through Java in the mid-1840s. The spread of diseases accelerated as throughout Java forced cultivation engendered mobility, for example to encampments surrounding the sugar factories where between one and two thousand workers and their families lived in packed conditions. Annual mortality rates in Java were much lower than in the sugar plantations of Cuba and Louisiana, but the forced cultivation system likely raised overall death rates in Java by 10–30 percent.[82]

In fact, the colonial government did acknowledge that the existing system of sugar production put too much of a burden on the landowning farmers. In 1847, not coincidentally after three years of famines in Java, it made the vacuum pan mandatory for sugar factories under government contract. This would extract more sugar from the cane and thus enhance the output per acre with the same amount of work. The colonial government also decided to relieve the landowning peasants from the burden of cane harvesting and obliged factories to hire waged laborers, who became easier to recruit over time because of Java's rapid population growth. In the 1860s, conscription was abolished for the growing of cane, which now became a matter of negotiation between factory owners and their surrounding villages.[83] What followed, however, was not what one might call a free labor market, because factories did not negotiate with individual farmers and did not hire workers on an individual basis. Everything went via village heads and other Javanese notables, who received a bonus from factories for each worker and each plot of land they provided. Meanwhile, land was declining in availability because of Java's rapid population growth, and an increasing share of peasant income came from working in the sugar factories. In fact, as early as by the mid-nineteenth century, around 56 percent of the agricultural workers in the proximity of factories had some much-needed side employment in the sugar economy.[84]

Java's Agricultural Involution

The forced cultivation system turned Java into the second largest cane sugar exporter after Cuba. Decisive factors were the abundance of labor resulting from a combination of rapid population growth and the Dutch colonizers' ability to manipulate Java's village economies and enlist local elites in their project of colonial exploitation. Sugar in Java did not open up new frontiers but stayed embedded within the village economies, in contrast to the Caribbean region where soil exhaustion usually resulted in rapidly expanding sugar frontiers and putting land to fallow after having depleted the soil. Java's colonial sugar production was therefore not only socially but also ecologically unique.

In China, Egypt, and later in the Caribbean islands crop rotation had served early on to slow the exhaustion of the soil by cane cultivation. In Java, crop rotation was applied to the maximum effect by embedding cane cultivation in the existing system of wet rice (*sawah*) cultivation. While cane exhausted the soil, rice contributed to its regeneration. Hence, alternation of the two crops not only enabled cane cultivation on a relatively small acreage with a limited amount of fertilizer, but it also allowed for a remarkable growth of output per acre. Every year, tens of thousands of hectares of paddy fields were turned into cane fields, for which the dams of *sawah* cultivation had to be erased. Fences were put up to protect the young plants against wild animals, and bridges and roads had to be completely reconstructed after every sugar campaign as they were ruined by the heavy carts filled with cane.

However, this relentless pursuit of the highest output per acre sharply conflicted with the colonial government's policy of reducing the burden it had imposed on Java's population under the forced cultivation system. Not for nothing it had discontinued its arduous forced indigo cultivation and gradually abolished conscription for the growing of cane.[85] The obvious next step in this direction was to abandon the system of alternation and instead plant cane for several consecutive harvests on the same plot before rotating it. In preparation for this step in the early 1850s, a government committee interviewed all local officials including village heads as well as some farmers involved in cane growing to find out whether such a measure would be welcomed. To the surprise of the colonial officials the peasantry and village heads overwhelmingly pointed out that the existing practice should be maintained because it was the most efficient use of scarce land in terms of the growing cycles of cane and wet rice. Clearing the field from the cane stubbles after each harvest—necessary to give new infant sugar cane plants a chance to grow—was considered to be more cumbersome than restoring the semiaquatic paddy fields, which simply drowned the stubbles.[86]

Both ecologically and socially, the wet rice lands were central to how the cultivation system had embedded the sugar sector in rural Java. Since forced cultivation was imposed on villages and within villages only upon landownership—and of wet rice lands in particular—it encouraged village elites to have as many villagers as possible owning a small share in these often communal wet rice lands to spread the burden of the work assigned to each village.[87] This had resulted in a complex and increasingly labor-intensive system of *sawah* sharing among villagers and between villages and the sugar industry. This embedding of capitalist sugar production inspired Clifford Geertz in his famous work *Agricultural Involution* to classify Java's sugar industry as a centaur: a combination of highly sophisticated cane processing and increasingly labor-intensive cane growing on ever more densely populated wet rice lands.[88]

This involution, as a socioecological development, was hard if not impossible to reverse. In the 1860s, Dutch liberals had tried to ban shared (or communal) landownership and foster private property in order to bring rural Java under the sway of capitalism. Their ideal was to create a strong farmer class owning all the land who would push out marginal farmers, who in turn would become a true rural proletariat of "free" wage earners. This would, however, not only have required a complete transformation of rural society, reversing thirty years of forced cultivation, but also involved the separation of wet rice and cane cultivation.[89] Sugar factories were not at all inclined to move to dry land as this would severely reduce the yields per acre, and village elites definitely benefited from the status quo. Thus, the fates of the sugar factories and *sawah* agriculture continued to be entwined. When the sugar industry had become Java's dominant agricultural industry in the early decades of the twentieth century, in some residencies more than half of the *sawah* lands within five kilometers of a factory were occupied by cane.[90]

For contemporary onlookers, what happened in Java was as paradoxical as what had transpired in in Cuba. In their view, the most advanced industrial cane sugar complexes in the world, rather than having embraced the economic rationalities of free land and labor markets, relied on atavistic communal land use and slavery, respectively. But this precisely shows how much sugar is the product of an agro-industry, in which factory and field increasingly became two different worlds—a centaur, as Geertz famously observed. Whereas the factories all over the world converged on the same design, cane fields exhibited a stunning diversity. Java's immensely labor-intensive cane cultivation moved in the complete opposite direction to Cuba's, where little incentive existed for innovation in cane cultivation or the adoption of age-old measures such as crop rotation and limiting the number of ratoons. Fertile land was abundant and labor shortages were most pressing during the harvest, when workers were almost literally worked to death.

In their relentless quest to save on labor, the Cuban planters brutalized nature and instead of felling trees and ploughing they burned forests to obtain new cane fields. The sugar frontier ruthlessly crushed ancient trees, ignoring stern warnings about the devastating environmental consequences of this rapid deforestation. As early as the 1840s, over fifty thousand hectares of trees were disappearing every year.[91] Trees were needed for many aspects of sugar production, not only for construction work and for boxes to transport sugar but for fuel wood as well. Planters initially did not feed their huge steam-driven crushers and vacuum pans with bagasse and coal. Massive felling of trees for fuel forced them to replace their factories regularly as they rapidly ran out of forest on their land. In 1860, Cuba's sugar industry had 120,000 hectares in direct use and occupied an area of 800,000 hectares, compared to just 28,000 hectares in Java. Forty years later, the figures stood at 1.7 million hectares and 122,000, respectively.[92] By that time, most of Cuba was deforested and the island faced the same ecological problems of the earlier sugar frontiers. Droughts, flooding, and soil exhaustion all occurred on an island that was once famous for its soil fertility.

Diminishing rainfall caused by deforestation was a serious problem that was raised by Álvaro Reynoso as early as the 1860s. He was the director of the Chemical Institute in Havana. Born near the city he held a doctor's degree in medicine from a Parisian university. He made it his mission to

convert Cuban planters to more sustainable cultivation methods and recommended improved tilling, fertilization, and irrigation, along with annual
planting instead of many years of ratooning. It was up to the planters, he
argued, to use their potential labor surplus beyond the sugar campaign, the
zafra, to bring agriculture onto a more sustainable footing and abandon
their slash-and-burn practices.[93]

Reynoso's warnings fell on deaf ears in his native land, but it was a different story in Java, where his translated pamphlet outlining a new system
of cane planting became known by almost everyone in the sugar-producing
districts. The application of Reynoso's system in Java involved more than
hundred thousand men digging trenches and building up the soil between
them in ridges. An equally large army of Javanese women then took to the
fields to sow infant cane plants in the trenches. After four months of growth,
the men threw the soil of the ridges into the trenches, resulting in cane
that was deeply rooted in the soil and wind resistant.[94] The rapid growth
of Java's population of marginal peasants facilitated an incredibly labor-
intensive cane sugar industry with one of the highest yields per acre anywhere. In the 1920s, an average of 7.7 workers managed a hectare of cane
in Java against an average of 0.5 workers in Cuba, which represented the
two extremes of the global sugar industry. Each ton of Java sugar required
3.5 times the labor needed in Cuba but only half the amount of land.[95]

Industrialization and Forced Labor

When Britain took the lead in the abolition of slavery in 1834, few perhaps
would have expected plantation slavery to endure for most of the nineteenth
century. Slavery at sugar plantations not only persisted, it even slightly increased, during a period dubbed "the second slavery" by Dale Tomich.[96]
By the mid-nineteenth century, about eight hundred thousand enslaved
toiled in cane fields, half of whom were in Cuba and almost a third in
Brazil.[97] Even after slavery was abolished in Louisiana in 1864, almost half
of the world's cane sugar exports were still produced by slave labor. An additional quarter of those exports came from indentured labor.[98] Forms of
slavery or coercion continued, often barely disguised. Workers could be
bought in Africa and "redeemed" as *engagés* in Réunion, for instance, a practice that was severely censured by British authorities—to little avail.[99] In
Java, the forced cultivation system was phased out from the 1860s onward,

but, as we have seen, this did not change much for the Javanese peasants who continued to be summoned by village elites to grow cane for the factories.

Since the mechanization of cane fields made little progress prior to the World War II, much of the world's sugar production relied on a variety of coercive conditions: slavery, forced cultivation, indentured labor, anti-vagrancy laws, or outright starvation, as was the case in Barbados. This not only belied Saint-Simonian optimism that mechanization would phase out arduous and coerced manual agricultural labor, but it also exposed the mis-guided belief that industrialization would be incompatible with slave-based production systems. Again, the crux of the matter is that Java and Cuba would never have achieved their dominant position as cane sugar ex-porters without coerced field labor.

When the well-informed economist John Elliott Cairnes (1823–1875) argued that slave-based economies were incapable of raising labor produc-tivity, he mistakenly attributed this to coerced conditions rather than to the limited options to mechanize cane and cotton fieldwork. But he was right to warn that in order for slave-based economies to grow, they would need to enslave ever more people. No friend of slavery or colonialism—Cairnes was an Irishman, after all—he predicted in the first year of the American Civil War in his book *Slave Powers* that a victory of the pro-slavery Confed-erates would unleash a revival of the slave trade. Hence, economies such as those of the southern United States were inherently aggressive and expan-sionist, Cairnes argued, reiterating an earlier observation by Alexis de Toc-queville in his famous *Democracy in America*.[100] Early nineteenth-century liberal capitalist optimism that the inferior labor regime of slavery was a dying institution gave way to the fear that it posed a real political and mil-itary threat to more advanced economies—a fear that was fully warranted, as the American Civil War would tragically prove.

Indeed, Cairnes and his contemporaries were not entirely wrong about industrialization and slavery being ultimately incompatible. Sugar estates had always employed skilled enslaved workers, but they were often remu-nerated to reduce the risk of sabotage. Or, as happened in preindustrial mills in Brazil, free workers of African-European descent were hired for crucially important tasks such as the supervision of the boiling process or the pack-aging of sugar.[101] Still, enslaved workers were employed at strategic positions in mills in spite of the risks. This was for the obvious reason that in the tropics white skilled labor was usually scarce and expensive, until at least the mid-nineteenth century. Derosne wrote in his *Sugar* that Cuba's most advanced factory, which was owned by Don Wenceslao de Villa-Urrutia, employed just one white sugar master in the early 1840s.[102] Likewise, in Louisiana enslaved worked not only as carpenters, but also as accountants, steam-driven machine operators, or might even run the plantation.[103] These enslaved professionals acquired an authority, however, that was hardly commensurable with their enslaved condition. Moreover, with a growing influx of European workers later in the nineteenth century, having enslaved laborers and free European workers working alongside each other handling the machines turned out to be a source of irritation. Spanish immigrants who came to work at Cuba's sugar estates, for instance, agitated against slavery on the factory floor as they felt that it pulled down their own wages and status.[104]

Over the course of the nineteenth century, coerced labor conditions in factories ultimately disappeared, whereas workers in the field continued to be subjected to harsh physical discipline. As a general trend, the unity of field and factory that existed in the plantations was lost when the factory became a different operation, drawing its cane from ever wider areas. The end of slavery would encourage the emergence of smallholder cane growing on former plantation islands. In Mauritius, estates sold land to their emancipated slaves as did the Jamaican estates, as well as to many workers returning from the construction of the Panama Railway. This happened to a lesser extent in Barbados. Planters in Tobago, St. Lucia, Grenada, and the French Antilles started to introduce a *métayer* system, a way of sharecropping in which estate owners provided land and seedlings to workers who shared in the agricultural risks and profits. In Tobago, for example, where such a system was introduced in 1843 and became widespread by 1845, the laborer received one acre to cultivate and harvest cane. Albeit a measure born out of the poverty of estate owners, it nevertheless empowered former enslaved according to contemporary observer and the same effect was evident in St. Lucia, where a small métayer cooperative was established in 1843.[105] In Trinidad, meanwhile, a smallholder class emerged among the growing settler Indian population because almost 80 percent of these migrants stayed after the completion of their contract. Thousands of these smallholders delivered their cane to the Saint Madeleine sugar central, which had been built in 1872 and was the largest factory in the West Indies.[106] But even if on some Caribbean islands, and Mauritius, a class of dependent small cane farmers emerged, cane fields still needed growing armies of seasonal laborers for the harvest. These laborers were now the worst off in the world of sugar and would bear the brunt of the severe sugar crisis of 1884.

7

Crisis and Wonder Cane

THE INDUSTRIAL REVOLUTION THOROUGHLY reshaped the world's sugar production, transport, and markets. It was, however, a slow revolution that followed a convoluted and incremental trajectory. Capital shortages, planters' conservatism, fragile technology, and particularly the impossibility of mechanizing harvesting prolonged slavery and engendered new forms of coerced labor. Meanwhile, Chinese and Indian peasant sugars easily maintained themselves on the global market, thanks to the costs of living in Asia being so much lower than in the Americas. And, not surprisingly, Java's factories, which combined cheap labor and high capital intensity emerged in the early twentieth century as the world's most competitive sugar industry.

Mass consumption accelerated the globalization of sugar production and the integration of markets. From the 1840s, imperial governments and colonial administrations assumed a key role in the introduction of the vacuum pans and centrifuges. A revolution in transport followed when the invention of the Bessemer process reduced the steel price by five times over the second half of the nineteenth century. This allowed sugar centrals to construct railway systems carrying cane from ever longer distances to their crushers. In the most advanced sugar producing regions, miles of railway tracts began linking fields to the factories. Steel also allowed for cheap sugar transports across the globe, creating an entirely new geography of food production and trade. Within the North-Atlantic realm, the labor-abundant European countryside switched from wheat to beet after the continent had become flooded by US cereals. In contrast to its treatment of wheat farmers, Europe would staunchly defend its beet sugar industry with import tariffs and export subsidies against steeply declining prices on the global market.

Taikoo Sugar Refinery, located at Quarry Bay, Hong Kong, was one of the largest sugar refineries in the world in 1895. Much of the sugar processed there came from Java.

Throughout the nineteenth century, sugar plantations had rapidly changed hands, resulting in select groups of wealthy owners. In some locations, metropolitan capital took over almost all estates, as was the case in British Guiana, where a few large British metropolitan merchant houses had dominated since the 1850s. More often, however, successful colonial sugar bourgeoisie aligned themselves with metropolitan industrial interests and the world of high finance, while colonial administrations facilitated the development of infrastructure and labor recruitment. The large sugar centrals inexorably replaced the old estates with their mills, slave quarters, and planters' mansions. From these terribly noisy factories, many kilometers of narrow-gauge railroad stretched into the fields bringing in tons of cane stalks that was transformed into sacks of almost-white sugar within a matter of hours. Not only was the exterior architecture of these large cane-processing factories identical for every industrial cane sugar belt in the world, so were their interiors, and this also applied to a large extent to the beet sugar factories. These impressive industrial complexes fed the even larger refineries in the north Atlantic ports and, to a lesser extent, in Asia. Through their close contacts with their respective governments, refiners secured import tariffs on high-grade sugars that deterred sugar factories in the colonies from building refineries nearby. Instead, large compounds appeared on the waterfronts of New York, Hong Kong, and London that operated using increasingly standardized technology, disgorging massive volumes of nearly white crystalline sugar.[1]

The cane fields, meanwhile, exhibited a stunning diversity of operations, varying from Cuba's neglected plots surrounded by vandalized forests to the meticulously dug Reynoso trenches in Java. The cane fields, and the beet fields for that matter, shared an almost unsatisfiable demand for laborers. They could be indentured workers from China and India or impoverished migrants from Spanish or Polish Galicia, Madeira, Java and Madura, Haiti, Barbados, the arid hinterlands of west India, or Sicily. Every year growing numbers of laborers walked hundreds of kilometers to Europe's beet fields or to Java's cane fields. Their wages were squeezed to the bare minimum, while the factories converged to a single model, as did their output: shining white sugar crystals. Meanwhile, factory staff were increasingly better paid and shared in the welfare provisions that became customary in the North Atlantic world, and enjoyed the luxuries of tennis courts and swimming pools that appeared near their factories.

Concentration and Cartelization

In spite of rapidly rising consumption, sugar prices showed a persistent downward trend. This was not just because of the opening up of new fertile frontiers in Cuba, Louisiana, and Java with a massive mobilization of enslaved or otherwise coerced labor. At least as important was the astonishing growth of the beet sugar industry. It emerged from the margins of the global sugar market within a matter of decades. In the early 1860s, volumes started soaring and, urged by its alarmed refiners who feared the importation of refined German beet sugar, Britain brought France, Belgium, and the Netherlands to the negotiating table in Paris in 1864, where they agreed on ceilings on import tariffs and export bounties.[2]

The truce was a short one, however, because the output of beet sugar factories ballooned due to the export subsidies provided by the most powerful European nations to help their farmers convert over a million hectares of land from wheat to beet. The beet leaves and pulp fed the cattle, which in turn provided dairy and meat for Europe's rapidly growing urban populations. But above all, the beet sugar industry offered much needed agricultural employment, requiring three to four times as many workers as for dairy or wheat farming during the growing and harvesting season.[3] This labor came from countries such as Poland where the number of landless peasants quadrupled in the final decades of the nineteenth century. Across Europe, rural proletarians in their millions became the labor reservoir the beet industry could tap. Beet sugar production in Europe exploded, with Germany's production alone quintupling in the fifteen years preceding the global sugar crisis of 1884.[4]

Soon, Europe was swimming in sugar and, if the market had been allowed to do its work, German factories would have forced many of their less advanced French counterparts to quit. However, in the 1870s, France was still recovering from a humiliating military defeat by Germany's armies. Captivated by a spirit of revanchism against Europe's leading beet sugar exporter, the French government was determined to boost beet sugar exports and catch up with Germany. French consumers were called upon to spend a few cents more to protect the jobs of the country's hundred thousand beet workers.[5] Other European countries such as Austria-Hungary and Russia joined this race of subsidies, or bounties as they were called at the time. Germany did not relent, however, and spent most of its tax revenue from sugar on export bounties. In fact, German consumers paid extra for their sugar to subsidize the sugar on British kitchen tables.[6]

This structural overproduction led to a tremendous fall in sugar prices on the global market in 1884, which was followed by another halving of its price over the next fifteen years. In almost every sugar-producing region, regardless of whether it grew beet or cane, the decline of the number of sugar factories and refineries accelerated dramatically. This decline was felt in Europe and in the United States, as well as throughout the British and French Caribbean sugar colonies, and in Puerto Rico, Pernambuco, Louisiana, and South Africa. Even in Cuba, which had the most advanced sugar industry in the world at the time, consolidation accelerated after 1884. Powerful sugar producers such as Edwin F. Atkins, a Boston refiner who had a residence in Cuba, built an impressive sugar empire by absorbing defaulting mills. No less spectacular was the sugar business of Julio de Apezteguía y Tarafa, who was born on the island and had been trained as an engineer in Barcelona. His sugar central, Constancia, had a capacity of twenty thousand tons per year by 1890—more than the entire island of Jamaica.[7]

Across the globe, both cane and beet sugar producers as well as refiners responded to the declining margins of profit by upscaling their operations and creating cartels. In the sugar cane belts, the Java Sugar Syndicate, the Hawaiian Sugar Planters' Association, and the Louisiana Sugar Planters Association emerged as prominent examples. In the United States refiners united to form the notorious "Sugar Trust," whereas in Germany, Austria-Hungary, the Netherlands, and Belgium, sugar producers and refiners forged cartels or mergers. In the Ukraine, the beet sugar belt of Czarist Russia, the sugar producers, predominantly wealthy aristocratic families, cartelized and, with government support, dumped their sugar abroad, in Persia, for instance. Earlier on in the nineteenth century, cheap beet sugar from the Ukraine had already hampered the development of Persia's cane sugar industry; now it also destroyed an infant beet sugar industry set up with Belgian assistance for the country's sugar-craving people.[8] In Austria-Hungary, the sugar factories and refiners united in a cartel to widen their margins of profit at the expense of consumers and beet farmers, who sharply protested this power grab.[9] In the Netherlands, twenty years of relentless merging and closing of less profitable factories resulted in the Central Dutch Sugar Society in 1919. This consolidation even crossed national boundaries, because a driving force behind it was Paul Wittouck, the largest sugar industrialist of Belgium and leader of the Tirlemontoise sugar refinery, but also owner of factories in the Netherlands.[10]

Declining prices and the search for economies of scale drove cartelization and concentration of the sugar sector around the world. But for the cane sugar sector it was also attended by a drastic financial restructuring, as credit was still based upon advances on crops to be planted, the fragility of which became palpably clear in 1884. The dwindling sugar prices of the previous year had caused an unprecedented and devastating credit crunch. In sugar colonies, local banks that had provided credit to sugar factories were pulled asunder, sometimes with the entire sugar sector, as happened in Tobago.[11] Most dramatically, however, the entire financial infrastructure supporting Java's sugar industry was on the verge of collapse.

The banks in the Netherlands were initially reluctant to start a rescue operation, leading to frantic telegram correspondence between the colonial government in Batavia, the Dutch government in The Hague, and the Amsterdam bankers. Thirty million guilders (£3 million) were hastily assembled to recapitalize the cultivation banks that supplied the advances to the sugar planters.[12] The Java sugar industry was simply too big to fail for the Netherlands, as its collapse would have caused an immediate and immense impoverishment of large parts of Java at a time when peasant revolts were already occurring in its poorest provinces. Once the dust settled, the leverage of the Java sugar industry over colonial policies appeared only to have grown, because metropolitan banks had heavily invested in their survival. Not surprisingly, the sugar factories pointing out their eminent importance to the colonial economy succeeded in having export duties on Java sugar first suspended and, in 1894, abolished altogether.[13]

Java's sugar industry survived not least thanks to its technologically advanced stage on the eve of the 1884 crisis, which was true also for the industries of British Guiana and Trinidad. Through massive metropolitan investments coupled with an unstinting influx of indentured laborers, these two West Indian colonies had leapfrogged to the vanguard of sugar capitalism. More investment into, and further concentration of, the sugar industry would follow after 1884. By 1900, over 70 percent of British Guiana's sugar industry was controlled by its four largest companies. The most prominent of these, Booker & McConnell, would eventually own most of British Guiana's sugar economy for a large part of the twentieth century. Likewise, in Trinidad, one firm, the Colonial Company, would come to dominate the island. In the early twentieth century its massive St. Madeleine factory owned or controlled cane lands that had once fed a hundred mills. Both in British Guiana and Trinidad, factories squeezed labor costs either by lowering wages or reducing the price of the cane they bought from smallholders.[14]

Indeed, workers usually paid a heavy price for the thorough restructuring of the sugar sector. Shifting the burden of the crisis to workers did not go unresisted, however, and strikes and cane fires broke out in many fields.[15] Others who still had their homesteads returned to their farms or their own *trapiches* (small pre-industrial mills) after wage cuts. Quite a few workers turned their backs on state-of-the-art factories in Peru, Puerto Rico, the Dominican Republic, and Brazil.[16]

The Resilience of the Colonial Sugar Bourgeoisie

Historians have marked the year 1884 as the moment at which power was transferred from the colonies to the metropolitan traders and banks in London, Amsterdam, Paris, and New York. In the context of rampant imperialism had that brought large parts of the earth under European or US flags, industrialized countries invested hugely in commodity production across their colonized territories. The sugar crisis of 1884 undeniably ruined many planters, and metropolitan banks had to be called upon to recapitalize estates. These creditors imposed their control over the sugar factories' operations. And yet this did not unavoidably result in a transfer of property to Europe or the United States and was definitely not the end of the colonial sugar bourgeoisie.

The sugar bourgeoisie did not disappear, only the historians wrongly interpreted the conversion of family estates into stockholding corporate enterprises at the turn of twentieth century as takeovers by companies in the colonial mother countries.[17] In reality, many powerful and family-owned cane *and* beet sugar factories were turned into limited liability companies while staying in family hands. The prominent Klein Wanzleben beet sugar estate in Saxony, for instance, founded by Matthias Rabbethge and his son-in-law Julius Giesecke, was incorporated when its founders died in 1881 and 1885, respectively. The firm continued to be a family enterprise, however, led by Matthias's grandsons. Likewise, the second generations of Hawaiian sugar planters incorporated their business to avoid the dispersion of property over many family members, who also began to live in many different places.[18] The Vicinis in the Dominican Republic and prominent families in Puerto Rico and Cuba also incorporated their sugar enterprises, both to protect themselves against inheritance tribulations and to attract new capital. The Goytisolo family, based in Barcelona but with extensive sugar property in Cuba, for instance, decided to incorporate their property in 1893 to attract new capital from the United States to further develop their sugar central and to finance the construction of expensive railroads to carry the cane to the factory.[19]

Family ownership proved to be remarkably resilient. In Java, by 1910 half of the 177 sugar factories had been in the same family for two or even three generations. In addition, another twenty-two factories were owned by established Indo-Chinese bourgeois families. In the same year, Puerto Rico's local bourgeoisie still controlled 57.4 percent of the sugar coming from their island's sugar centrals.[20] In Guadeloupe and Martinique, the Creole families might have been seriously indebted to the Colonial Credit Bank (Crédit Foncier Colonial), but, being much better trained than their grandfathers, they had taken back the management of their factories from the Cail & Cie engineers. Even the seriously impoverished West Indies planters released themselves from their British creditors and redirected their exports to the rapidly growing US market.[21] In Barbados, large estates and commercial houses merged the plantation and trading sectors into vertically and horizontally concentrated conglomerates, which largely replaced the absentee owners, who owned only 7.4 percent of the land by 1930.[22]

The colonial bourgeoisie as a class yielded little to metropolitan interests, but the crisis of 1884 and nearly two decades of declining prices mercilessly punished overambitious expansion schemes financed with expensive credit. The tragedy that befell Khedive Isma'il the Magnificent in Egypt in the late 1870s (see Chapter 5) would repeat itself on a smaller scale in the Dominican Republic, Puerto Rico, and Cuba: overconfident local investors and local governments lost their assets to overseas European or US banks. Prominent planters lost their estates as a consequence of misfortune, mismanagement, or the ravages of the Cuban War of Independence (1895–1898). However, metropolitan investors were usually keen to keep estates going.[23] When Don Leonardo Igaravídez's impressive sugar central in Puerto Rico went asunder due to the factionalism and corruption in Puerto Rican society, metropolitan banking interests and Cail & Cie—whose money was in the machines—desperately tried to save it, albeit to no avail.[24]

Since metropolitan banks and other investors considered the colonial bourgeoisie as clients and not as competitors, plantation owners became more deeply embedded in networks that had access to imperial political and financial centers.[25] The mobility of these families, who often lived in both worlds, further blurred the boundaries between the colonial and metropolitan domains. Leading figures in the Cuban sugar industry, such as the aforementioned Edwin F. Atkins or the Spaniard Manuel Rionda, might live part of the year in the United States, but would definitely be near their estates during the harvest.[26] These links generated circuits of capital, people, and knowledge between metropolitan centers and sugar frontiers. The largest sugar plantation owner in Peru, the Gildemeister family who came to the country in the 1840s, continued to be as much German as Peruvian, drawing their capital and engineers from Germany.[27] It was not exceptional, moreover, that marriages between members of colonial and metropolitan bourgeoisie forged links between planter networks and the high finance of Amsterdam or Wall Street.[28]

Even planters' families who had lived for generations near or on their sugar estates followed the latest styles and fashions from Europe. Rich planters could often be found among tourists in Paris, Venice, or Switzerland. Planters in Cuba passed their time in New York, Paris, or Spain between two harvests.[29] A Louisiana planter was likely to meet colleagues from Java or Cuba at such trips. Europe was also a popular retirement destination for planters. Successful Cuban or Puerto Rican entrepreneurs settled in Barcelona after handing over the management of their estates to the next generation. Some locations were true enclaves, such as Begur on the Spanish Costa Brava, where hardly any families without relatives in Cuba lived.[30] Members of wealthy Dutch planters' families retired in The Hague, even if they had been born in Java and only occasionally been in the Netherlands before. Barbadian planters whose families had lived there for many generations called England home. Members of British Guiana planter families, meanwhile, traveled back and forth between their plantations and their mansions in England.

Planters sent their children to high schools and universities in the United States, England, France, Spain, or the Netherlands, and this included the mestizo-Chinese sugar bourgeoisie in the Philippines and Java.[31] Even in Brazil, which had its own universities, wealthy sugar planters sent their sons and sometimes daughters to England and France for education.[32] Sometimes this was just for reasons of snobbery, but quite often planters registered their sons at the best agricultural schools or universities to be trained in tropical agriculture. This allowed them to stay in charge of their factories and maintain the confidence of their creditors.

While one source of the sugar bourgeoisie's strength was their orientation toward European high culture and education, another was the way in which they had developed their family clans into impressive business networks. This was not any different from how the bourgeoisie generally operated in the nineteenth century. New York's economic elite at the time, for instance, were equally family-based and just as held together by marriages as the creole sugar planters of Central Java, Mauritius, Puerto Rico, Cuba, Hawaii, the Philippines, and the Franco-American planters of Louisiana.[33] In case rich daughters did not find a wealthy partner, they might lead and administer estates, and sometimes even stayed in control of their property after marriage, as was the case in Louisiana. In

Brazil, daughters were married within their own families to prevent family property being split up and to avoid adventurers freshly arrived from Portugal getting their hands on it.[34]

Wealth accumulated through marriage in turn created hierarchies within the planters' networks, which usually acknowledged one or more leaders. In Hawaii, for instance, it was Samuel Northrup Castle (1808–1894), the bookkeeper of the mission, who had arrived as a twenty-eight-year-old in 1836 on a ship from Boston. After the missionary assignment had been completed, he started a banking agency together with Amos S. Cooke in 1851. During his long life, Castle became a driving force in the emerging Hawaiian sugar industry, providing capital and equipment and forging relations with refiners in San Francisco. He supported the plantations run by the other children of the missionaries, known as the "haole Big Five," and was appointed to the king of Hawaii's Privy Council in 1863.[35]

The most powerful sugar bourgeois families were among the richest of their respectively countries. The largest slave owners in Louisiana, for instance, had over a thousand enslaved and total property worth over $1 million. Others might own a number of huge factory compounds with extensive railway tracks running into the cane fields. The Kervéguens of Réunion, for example, owned no less than half of the island's cane fields, a collection of estates that covered thirty thousand hectares. In Peru, the Larco family (of Italian provenance) and the Gildemeisters (of German origin) emerged as the dominant landowners after the global sugar crisis of 1884. After the bankruptcy of Víctor Larco in 1927—he had overextended his sugar empire—the Gildemeister family took over his extensive property through which they controlled almost the entire Chicama sugar belt of Peru.[36] Indubitably, the wealthiest sugar barons were among the richest people on earth. This applied as much to the Lascelles and Beckfords in late eighteenth-century England as to the Venezuelan-born Terry Adan, probably the wealthiest man in Cuba in the nineteenth century, who had about $25 million to his name when he died in Paris in 1886. His children married into Europe's high nobility, just as one of the Lascelles had married the daughter of the British king, George V.

The colonial bourgeoisie was a network of families who, if not clannish, clearly thought in terms of insiders and outsiders. They managed to prevail against the most powerful external menaces. The haole Big Five did so in a spectacular manner. They successfully resisted Claus Spreckels, a leading sugar refiner in California, whose ambition was to dominate the entire Hawaiian sugar production.

Spreckels, once a penniless immigrant from Germany, had managed to build an impressive sugar business in California. Prior to his ascendency as a sugar magnate, he had made a modest fortune as a beer brewer. When the American Civil War ruined Louisiana's sugar estates, he started sugar refining in California with Philippine sugar and applied German technology. His sugar refinery yielded him a fortune within a matter of years, part of which he reinvested to lease forty thousand acres of Crown land on one of the Hawaiian islands. Shrewdly exploiting the indebtedness of members of the royal family, he obtained his land by lending them the money to help them out of their financial trouble, which was decried as land grabbing by local newspapers, probably owned by his haole adversaries.[37]

Spreckels invested half a million dollars in a thirty-mile irrigation canal; built a state-of-the-art factory that managed to use the still-wet green bagasse for heating, brought to the factory with an automatic conveyor; introduced railroad haulage; and installed electric light as early as in 1881. With his own shipping company, he tied this estate as well as those of the haole families to his factory in California, unscrupulously creating a shipping monopoly between Honolulu and San Francisco for freight and passengers.[38] To the government of Hawaii, which was dominated by the haole plantocracy, Spreckels must have seemed like an encircling force. Partly via his local partner Irwin & Co., Spreckels controlled almost half of the sugar crop of Hawaii. He also owned more than 50 percent of the public debt of the kingdom and was the true power behind the throne.[39]

But Spreckels was not invulnerable. While the crisis of 1884 hit all Hawaiian plantations, Spreckels's interests had been hurt particularly hard, and allegedly only survived by defrauding shareholders. At least this was the opinion of a journalist for the *San Francisco Chronicle,* for which he almost paid with his life when one of Spreckels's son went berserk and shot him. This was the first sign of Spreckels's waning power in Hawaii, and must have encouraged the haole Big Five to wrestle the kingdom from his financial stranglehold by enlisting a huge loan from London financiers in 1886.[40] They reconquered lost terrain and by 1898 the Spreckels's plantations were nearly all in the hands of the haole firms of Castle & Cooke and Alexander &

Baldwin.[41] A few years later, the families broke Spreckels' shipping monopoly, and in 1910 Spreckels's ocean line itself came into their hands, completing their control over the Hawaiian sugar sector.[42]

Again, the way in which the haole colonial bourgeoisie recuperated their position was not unique, as we have seen with regard to Barbados and Guadeloupe. The Filipino planter class, which consisted of a merging of ethnic Chinese business families with Filipino landed interests, made an even more impressive comeback under the US administration in the early twentieth century. When US investors revamped the Philippine sugar industry and concentrated it in a small number of highly capitalized sugar centrals in the early years of the twentieth century, the Filipino sugar elites created a banking vehicle to bring these factories into their hands. In the 1930s, Filipinos owned 94 percent of the sugar land and controlled 51 percent of the sugar production by the sugar centrals; an additional 20 percent of production was in Spanish hands. A tight network of Filipino sugar entrepreneurs had emerged who would rule the country for most of the twentieth century.[43]

Members of the wealthy planter and banking families had always assumed prominent political roles in England and the Netherlands, but in the sugar-producing countries such as Peru, the Dominican Republic, and the Philippines, the political and economic power of the sugar barons was far more pervasive. It created, to use Violeta B. Lopez-Gonzaga's word, "sugarlandias," where almost every aspect of life was under the sway of the powerful sugar planter families, who were deeply rooted locally but at the same time integrated into the global sugar economy.[44] Such a family was the Chinese Filipino Lopez family, whose business history began in the 1830s in Philippine textile manufacturing and who made a fortune on the sugar frontier of Negros, where they owned the largest sugar mill in the Philippines in the early twentieth century. One member of this family would become vice-president under Ferdinand Marcos.[45] In Peru, the sugar planters were part of the national oligarchy that ruled the country from the late nineteenth century until 1931, and between 1900 and 1919 two sugar barons were elected president.[46] In the Dominican Republic, the son of Juan Bautista Vicini, the founder of the family's prominent sugar business, was president of the state from 1922 to 1924. He negotiated the Americans' withdrawal from the quagmire they found themselves in after occupying his country in 1916.[47]

Java Sugar for Asia

Although the colonial bourgeoisie mostly weathered the crisis of 1884—as did their counterparts in Europe's beet sugar industry—their ranks had thinned, and their world had changed profoundly. Sugar industrialists in Louisiana, Java, and Hawaii were forced to refashion their old associations or institutions they had founded in the 1840s and 1850s, as we saw above. These new associations had greater influence than the old ones, including with regard to labor recruitment and wages. These organizations launched their own well-established professional and scientific journals and set up experimental sugar stations.

Java, now the world's second largest cane sugar exporter, was eminently successful in reorienting itself after the crisis of 1884. From 1875 to 1927, its exports increased more than tenfold, a growth that was attended by a complete shift in destinations for its sugar. After being pushed out of Europe by beet sugar protectionism, and having no chance to compete on an increasingly protected US market, Java's sugar industry pulled off a most remarkable accomplishment: conquest of major Asian markets. By the mid-1920s, these had become the main destination of Java sugar, with 40 percent going to India and another 40 percent to China and Japan.[48]

Like any rapidly industrializing country, Japan began to get used to sugar and made its first steps toward establishing its own sugar industry. Sweets were an artisanal product until the late nineteenth century, but they became increasingly popular and entered Japan's streets through sweet-sellers.[49] An attempt to establish a beet sugar industry in Hokkaido, the colonized island immediately north of its archipelago, failed despite help from German technicians. Japan did, however, obtain its own refining capacity, thanks to Tosaburo Suzuki, originally a poor candy maker, who persevered in his pursuit to produce crystalline sugar. Suzuki read every relevant scientific publication he could lay his hands on and asked university students to translate the parts he could not understand. In 1890, he managed to build his first sugar-refining machine, and in 1896 he founded the Nihon Sugar Refining Company.[50] Together with the giant refiners of China's coastal cities as well as the Greek multinational commodity traders the Ralli brothers, this company became a major customer of Java sugar and accessed precious sugar technology through the purchase of one of the biggest sugar factories in Java. By the 1920s, Japanese investors owned five sugar factories on the island.[51]

In the late nineteenth century, artisanal candy makers became an increasingly common sight in Japan's streets, as depicted in this 1893 painting, *The Ameya,* by the US artist Robert Frederick Blum.

Sugar was a case in point of how Asian financial and merchant capitalism developed independently from London, the world's financial capital of that time. A group of three merchant houses—two in Java (Maclaine Watson & Co. in Batavia, McNeill & Co. in Semarang) and Maclaine Fraser & Co. in Singapore—weaned themselves off from British banking to become truly Asian-based and emerged from the 1870s as the largest European sugar-trading house in Asia, increasingly tuned to Asian markets. It became the chief provider of Java sugar to China's east coast refineries of Butterfield & Swire and to India via the Ralli brothers. In the wake of the 1884 sugar crisis, Maclaine Watson & Co. bought up half of Java's sugar harvest and at points during the early twentieth century even controlled two-thirds.[52]

Java's rapidly growing capacity to produce almost pure sugar—that is, a product that is about 99 percent sucrose—catered to growing urban demand in Asia.[53] Thanks to its purity, it could easily be adapted to please local taste and preferences—in India by mixing it with gur or molasses and in China by grinding the crystals to powder. The British refineries of Butterfield & Swire and Jardine Matheson & Co. on China's east coast discontinued their purchases from Guangdong in 1907 and switched to suppliers from Java. Sugar exports to China and Japan became so substantial that a consortium of Dutch shipping companies sponsored by the government of the Netherlands Indies opened a direct shipping line for transport.[54] Java's sugar industry outcompeted not only Chinese peasant sugar but also the stagnating industries in the Philippines and Thailand.[55] Even the large and modern Penang Sugar Estates Ltd. in British Malaya were converted to rubber production as they could no longer compete with Java sugar.[56] Java's factories had splendidly survived the sugar crisis of 1884, and its bourgeoisie had emerged as more powerful than ever, but let us not forget that much of this victory had been achieved at the expense of the Javanese peasantry, whose income declined.[57]

Global Cane, Global Disease

The financial crisis that raged over the world's sugar belts in 1884 was solved expeditiously by a major injection of fresh metropolitan capital, bringing scrutiny from banks over sugar factories. In Java, another crisis would soon overshadow the financial crisis. In 1883, planters noticed that their Black Cirebon cane sometimes suffered from a disease that gave it the appearance of lemon grass, for which it was called "sereh disease" (*sereh* means "lemon grass"). It would take years to eradicate this disastrous pest, but eventually the fight against this and other diseases would usher in revolutionary cane varieties with enhanced sucrose yields. However, these new varieties would go on to spread throughout the cane-growing world and lead to serious overproduction, which would again shake the foundations of the world's financial systems in the late 1920s.

Plant diseases had become worldwide menaces since the global search for the highest-yielding varieties had reduced the number of cane varieties being planted to a handful and opened to the door for a single disease to wreak havoc on cane fields across the globe. Plant diseases traveled with the speed of steam ships to ruin cane fields ten thousand kilometers apart. The traditional farming wisdom of maintaining biodiversity had been completely ignored in most places, but not in the Indian countryside. Members of India's Agricultural and Horticultural Society had tried in vain to disseminate Otaheite cane in the 1840s—farmers had stuck to their own motley collections of cane varieties. Their canes gave low yields, but their genetic diversity substantially reduced the risk of losing the entire harvest to diseases, which often target specific specimens. Conversely, the colonial bourgeoisie's mindset was all about finding the silver bullet of the highest-yielding cane. Otaheite, having traveled around the globe since Louis-Antoine, Comte de Bougainville, discovered it in Tahiti in 1767, dominated the cane fields in the Caribbean region and the Latin American mainland. Yet its success also led to its downfall. An epidemic of red rot began in Mauritius and Réunion in 1840 and spread across the cane-growing world over the next thirty years, to Brazil (1860), Cuba (1860s), Puerto Rico (1872), Queensland (1875), and the West Indies (1890s), where it caused the loss of 20–50 percent of the harvest.[58]

By that time, an alternative cane under the name Black Cirebon had already made its way from Java to the Americas. It arrived in the Dutch Antilles in the late eighteenth century, from where it rapidly spread throughout the Caribbean region—it probably reached Cuba as early as 1795—and somewhat later to Louisiana (where it received the name Louisiana Purple). Another Java cane variety, the White Priangan (or Cristalina), spread from the famous Buitenzorg (Bogor) botanical garden in the 1840s to Cuba, Argentina, Louisiana, Puerto Rico, and Taiwan, and was widely present in Brazil, Mauritius, and Peru in the late nineteenth and early twentieth centuries. It was easy to cultivate and kept yielding after significant ratooning, which was particularly important for Cuba, which was always short of labor.[59]

However, Black Cirebon and Cristalina were just as vulnerable to diseases as Otaheite. A pest such as sereh disease posed an almost insurmountable problem for planters.[60] Developing new resistant varieties would be the solution pursued today, but in the nineteenth century it was still widely believed that cross-breeding resistant cane varieties was impossible as cane putatively only reproduced itself asexually. A few specialists, however, remembered some quickly abandoned experiments to breed cane in the 1850s in Java, Hawaii, and Barbados, at a time when Mendelian biology had not yet informed agricultural science. Now, the sereh disease crisis spurred new attempts at the cross-pollination of flowering plants. Dr. F. Soltwedel at the Semarang experimental station in Java succeeded at this in 1886.[61] Breeding cane hybrids began in the final years of the nineteenth century and had produced revolutionary high-yielding hybrids by the 1920s, boosting global sugar production and thus sharply lowering sugar prices. Indeed, this success would lead to an even greater calamity, as noted above.[62]

Nevertheless, the immediate effect of the search for resistant cane varieties was a further tightening of planter networks, which were already held together by family bonds. In Java, thirty factories pooled funds to open Java's first experimental station in 1885 and hire the most gifted scientists to combat plant disease. Java would eventually maintain three experimental sugar stations that were funded via factory membership fees and without any government subsidies. In these years, the conversion of family estates into public limited companies and the increasing technical, botanical, and chemical specialization brought a managerial class to the fore, operating with a technocratic and science-based sense of superiority and fostering further concentration of economic power. The technocratic logic of disease control bound the sugar estates together in a disciplined format, which went in tandem with factories closely coordinating their recruitment mechanisms and labor control.

The modern sugar conglomerates therefore resulted from the disciplining effects of stiff global competition in markets with continually declining prices, the permanent danger of plant disease epidemics wreaking havoc, and the challenges of controlling labor and organizing labor recruitment. Technology and science uniformized production and disciplined planters. The experimental stations prescribed best practices for handling plant material to avoid contamination. Hygiene regulations spread from Java to Louisiana, and the young cane was handled with the greatest care to avoid new pests obliterating the green-waving fields.

A Wonder Cane: POJ 2878

The effective response by the Java sugar industry to sereh disease and its rapid recovery from the 1884 credit crunch attests to the resilience and innovative spirit of the colonial bourgeoisie. Java's planters, who did always everything in their power to enhance the yield per acre, took the lead. They were almost immediately followed, however, by Louisiana and Barbados, and the Franco-Mauritian planters, who had heavily influenced the research agenda of the famous Pamplemousses Botanical Garden since 1860 and established an agronomic station in 1892.[63] Across the globe, colonial bourgeoisie established and funded professional stations to conduct agricultural research and disseminate knowledge. Extensive breeding programs and other botanical research were facilitated by a rapidly growing number of experimental sugar stations, which appeared in Java (1885), Louisiana (1886), Barbados (1887), Mauritius (1892), Hawaii (1895), Cuba and Queensland (1900), Pernambuco (1910), Puerto Rico (1911), and Coimbatore (India) (1912).

Planters willingly supported their experimental stations but expected them to solve even the most intractable problems. Louisiana's planters, who had to cope with winter freezes and labor shortages, had set their hopes on the diffusion technology to revolutionize cane sugar manufacturing, just as it had done for beet sugar. The idea was to slice cane in the same way as beets and throwing the slices into hot water, allowing the sucrose to leave through the cell walls. Louisiana planters had come to know about this technology from experiments in Guadeloupe, which in turn had been inspired by the work of Mathieu Dombasle, a French beet sugar pioneer of the early nineteenth century.[64] In the 1880s, high-profile experiments were underway at the Magnolia plantation owned by Henry C. Warmoth, former governor of Louisiana and a key figure among the state's planters. Warmoth was sharply aware of the fact that in an open market Louisiana's sugar could not compete with Cuba's.

Warmoth traveled to Germany and France to see with his own eyes the diffusion process in operation at beet sugar factories. Moreover, he obtained the full cooperation of the chief chemist of the US Department of Agriculture, Harvey Wiley, for his experiments. Sugar planters across the globe began to hear about putatively successful experiments with diffusion technology for cane, particularly with the latest model vacuum pan, the one developed by the Louisiana engineer Rillieux, who now lived in Paris.[65] At Wiley's suggestion, an experimental station was established near New Orleans in 1885, staffed by Harvard-trained chemists who hoped to bring the technology swiftly to the world's sugar vanguard. Diffusion would never work for cane on a commercial basis, however. It used excessive energy while ruining the bagasse for fuel purposes. A deeply disappointed Warmoth sold his sugar estate and factory in 1888. Nonetheless, of lasting value was the experimental station, which trained sugar chemists who gave factories more control over cane processing. This training was institutionalized in the form of a school in

1891, which within a matter of years was also attended by students from Cuba, Puerto Rico, Spain, and Colombia.[66]

Meanwhile, the Pasuruan experimental station in Java emerged as the global center of cane research. Staffed by sixty researchers and assistants in 1929, it achieved world fame for its successful hybridization program crossing "wild" resistant canes with those in use, which stopped the global spread of devastating mosaic disease. Originating in Java, this disease appears to have entered the Americas through Argentina, from where it spread all over the Caribbean region and to Louisiana.[67] After fifteen years of experimentation with indigenous and exotic canes, an astonishing breakthrough came with the POJ 2878 cane in 1921—POJ is the acronym of the Dutch name of the experimental station in East Java: Proefstation Oost-Java.

This tremendously consequential cane variety was not only resistant to mosaic disease but also high-yielding—a true cane revolution. Well before its formal introduction in 1926, it was widely disseminated in Louisiana

A worker at Indonesia's Pasuruan Experimental Station isolates a female cane flower after cross-pollination, circa 1920s. The development of improved cane varieties through cross-breeding was a significant accomplishment of the late nineteenth century.

and Puerto Rico. In Louisiana, the POJ cane restored the cane harvest that had sunk by a dramatic 85 percent since 1911. Japanese industrialists, who owned five sugar factories in Java in the 1920s, brought POJ 2878 with other POJ varieties to their colony Formosa (Taiwan). Between the 1930s and the 1950s, the Pasuruan hybrids dominated cane fields in the Americas as well as in Java, Mauritius, and Taiwan. In India, the experimental station in Coimbatore, established in 1912, mixed POJ variants with its own hybrids and in the Philippines the Pasuruan variants together with Hawaiian canes replaced its indigenous canes in the 1930s.[68]

The POJ canes came to dominate even in the Caribbean region, where initially a hybrid developed by Bovell's Barbados botanic station had saved sugar estates in the British West Indies and was then further disseminated to the Danish Virgin Islands, as well as Guadeloupe and Martinique. In Puerto Rico, this cane covered 40 percent or more of the cane fields at its peak.[69] However, the Barbados varieties did not reach Cuba, by far the most important sugar producer in the Caribbean region. While being keen industrialists, the Cuban owners of sugar factories were simply not interested—many of them did not grow cane themselves but bought it from cane farmers. Edwin F. Atkins, owner of an extensive acreage under cane in Cuba, thought otherwise, however. After the ravaging Cuban War of Independence (1895–1898) he consulted with scientists at Harvard University and established the Harvard Botanical Station for Tropical Research and Sugar Cane Investigation at his Soledad estate. Yet its new cane varieties, dubbed "Harvard," never saw the Cuban cane farms.[70] The Cuban sugar factories and estates changed their minds, however, when mosaic disease wreaked havoc on their fields while the POJ varieties continued to give high elsewhere. From then on, the POJ varieties increasingly supplanted Cristalina, and they stood in 63 percent of Cuba's cane fields by 1943.

Even though the Pasuruan canes made a larger imprint than the Barbados hybrids, the histories of both testify to how scientific knowledge was being disseminated at a global scale. Most notably, colonial boundaries were crossed in multiple directions. Experimental stations in Pasuruan, Bogor, Coimbatore, and Barbados—backed up by metropolitan institutions like Kew Gardens in London or Wageningen Agricultural University in the Netherlands—for obvious reasons were loyal to their respective sponsors. However, individual scientists exchanged material whether or not the authorities liked it, and when the Dutch colonial authorities banned the export of precious plant material in 1930, for instance, it was already too late.

The global impact of the introduction of new cane varieties or innovations in combatting pests turned individual cane experts into celebrities, whose expertise was solicited across the globe. Walter Maxwell was one such expert. After receiving his training in Germany, he became the director of the Louisiana experimental station. In 1895, he was hired by Hawaiian planters for their newly established experimental station, who must have congratulated themselves with this coup.[71] But Hawaii would not be Maxwell's final workplace. Urged by local sugar refiners, the government of Queensland invited Maxwell to inspect their sugar fields, which suffered from exhaustion and thus rapidly declining yields. He assessed the cultivation methods as crude and recommended establishing three experimental stations. The government not only heeded his advice but also offered him the directorship of the stations, which he accepted.[72] To complete the circle of staff exchange, the Hawaiian experimental station hired A. J. Mangelsdorf, a scientist at the Pasuruan station, to develop a cane hybridization program in 1926.

As if there was no knife-edge competition among sugar producers, scientists collaborated with their colleagues abroad whenever the opportunity emerged. They traveled widely, as they had done since the days of the legendary German emperor Frederick Barbarossa, who recruited sugar makers from Syria to Sicily, where he held court. In the twentieth century, the names of the most outstanding experts, such as the Dutchman Hendrik Coenraad Prinsen Geerligs, were known by all cane manufacturers around the world. He published literally hundreds of articles and dozens of books on sugar chemistry as well as authoritative studies on the global cane sugar industry. Together with colleagues from Cuba, the main rival of Java, he tried to avert a disaster of global proportions by drafting plans for managed reductions of sugar production in the course of the 1920s. His obituary describes him rightfully as a scientist who served the sugar industry of the entire world.[73]

8

Global Sugar, National Identities

By THE END OF THE NINETEENTH CENTURY, industrial cane- and beet-processing technology had become increasingly standardized. In the fields as well, best practices forged ahead thanks to scientific journals and experimental stations. Yet while science spread all over the globe and capital could be wired within a matter of hours, labor always entailed extensive physical mobility. Sugar attracted millions of people to harvest the fields of cane or beet, radically changing the social fabric of the countryside. We have already seen this scenario unfold in the seventeenth century when the influx of enslaved Africans in the West Indies and French Antilles turned those islands from European settlements into plantation belts and reduced European settlers to minority populations within a matter of years. Since then, sugar's potential to radically change the ethnic composition of entire societies had only magnified. Over the course of the nineteenth century, global sugar production grew tenfold, unleashing huge immigration flows toward cane and beet fields.

Resistance against mass migrations of impoverished sugar workers reached its climax at the turn of the twentieth century, but it had been brewing since the late eighteenth century. At that time, the abolitionists had advanced the notion that slavery, plantations, and violence went together in the same way as smallholder agriculture, peace, and stability. The dichotomy of peaceful smallholder sugar production versus violent oppressive plantation production had shaped Benjamin Rush's open letter to Thomas Jefferson, in which he proposed to substitute maple sugar for cane plantation sugar (see Chapter 3). It had emerged as a serious policy matter since Achard wrote his manual on the production of beet sugar that reached almost every corner of Europe in 1811 (see Chapter 4). Various authors subscribed to his moral preference for beet over cane sugar as a national, indigenous cultivation unstained by slavery or the "coolie trade."

At the end of the nineteenth century, sugar emerged as an issue of national or political identity also because of the changing modes of production and consumption expressing themselves in contested relations between farms and factories, between traditional sugars and factories, and between rural and urban consumption. White centrifugal sugar became the standard for urban consumption, whereas raw sugars continued to be widely consumed in the countryside, at that time the residence of most of the world's population. Until the 1870s, most sugar was still unrefined, and was crucially part of the agricultural cycles in many parts of the world, contributing significantly to rural income and hence to rural resilience. Indian peasants, for instance, had notably rebuffed British industrialization of sugar production in their country. Gur still prevailed over industrial centrifugal sugar in South Asia by the mid-twentieth century, and Latin America at that time had more than a hundred thousand small preindustrial mills producing raw sugar. The old preindustrial ways of sugar production survived very well in the countryside, defying the drive toward upscaling sugar production as a result of declining sugar prices on the world market.

Without doubt, the long shadows of slavery pervasively shaped the political cultures and institutions of some of the world's major cane sugar-producing regions. It is not that long ago, in fact as late as the mid-nineteenth century, that slavery still accounted for half of the world's cane sugar exports. In the Americas, the cause of abolition hung in the balance in these years. Slaveholders in Cuba and the southern states of the United States, if they had aligned, might have swung the pendulum toward a consolidation of their position. This was far from hypothetical, and President James Monroe had already contemplated it in 1822, when Latin America was in turmoil and Cuba was considered to be of paramount interest to the United States.[1]

James Buchanan, a Democrat whose political base was solidly in the southern states, had advocated the purchase of Cuba from Spain throughout his career as secretary of state, as US ambassador to Britain, and as president of the United States (1857–1860).[2] In this pursuit, Buchanan was warmly supported by the planters of Louisiana, whose mouthpiece, *De-Bow's Review,* argued in 1850, "There is a well fixed and almost universal conviction upon the minds of our people, that the possession of Cuba is indispensable to the proper development and security of the country."[3] Clearly, the slaveholders in America's southern states would welcome the annexation of the rich island of Cuba because it would tilt the balance toward the slaveholding states within the United States, if only the resistance against such a move by the northern states could be overcome. This was a big "if" because in 1860, on the eve of the Civil War, President Buchanan himself had stated he was in favor of the emancipation of Cuba's enslaved to stop the illicit slave trade. No doubt, he spoke under pressure from his supporters in the northern US states and not in the interest of the sugar producers in Louisiana and Cuba.[4]

When the cannons of the American Civil War roared, the Irish economist Cairnes, whom we met in Chapter 6, warned in his book *Slave Powers* about the danger of what he regarded as atavistic but violent economic systems based on slavery gaining the upper hand. If the South had won the Civil War and aligned with Cuba—and Brazil for that matter—slaveholders indeed would have emerged as the dominant political force in the Americas. As it happened, the South's capitulation had immediate and compelling repercussions for Cuba because it forced American ships, the suppliers of enslaved Africans to Cuba, to quit their trafficking.[5] The Cuban planters realized that the days of slavery were numbered and the industrially advanced among them now preferred a full imposition of the ban on the slave trade. Having lost their quest to become part of the United States and no longer in need of Spanish protection for their illegal slave trade, the republican spirit that had been silenced since the days of Simon Bolivar now reawakened. Cuba's Ten Years' War (1868–1878) was a defining moment in the island's national identity, which was centered around a shared cross-racial sense of Cuban belonging. That enslaved workers had been part of the insurrectionist troops eroded the social basis of the institution of slavery. Abolition started spontaneously in parts of Cuba in 1868, was followed by apprenticeship in 1880, after which full emancipation was completed by 1886.[6]

Sugar versus Republicanism

The American Civil War and Cuba's Ten Years' War violently revealed a fundamental tension between the institution of slavery and republican nationalism striving for an inclusive citizenship. When Simon Bolivar and his followers had taken up the cause of abolition in 1816 to obtain Haiti's support for his military liberation campaign against Spain, they still cherished a narrow sense of nationhood, one that was based upon an imagined white creole (that is America-born) European identity, if not entirely in racial terms then at least in cultural ones. But this exclusiveness still resisted extensive plantation slavery, if only because it entailed the vast outnumbering of white creole populations. Apparently, the best way to combine sugar production with white republicanism was to tap the flows of millions of Europeans migrating from their continent after 1850. Yet few European immigrants would accept indentureship, and sugar plantations could only exist with underpaid and subservient labor. The tension, or even incompatibility, between white settler republicanism and plantation economies not only pertained to Cuba, Louisiana, and Brazil, but also to the Dominican Republic, Argentina, and Australia, which had no history of slave-based sugar production and emerged as new sugar producers in the course of the nineteenth century.

In Cuba, the world's largest cane sugar exporter, the question of how to overcome the contradiction between plantation and republic had long occupied the minds of the island's elites. In the 1840s, David Turnbull, the British consul in Cuba and a dedicated abolitionist, observed that "the great object of the Creole patriots of Cuba is at once to increase the white population, and render the further imports of Africans unnecessary."[7] Among these patriots was, surprisingly, Francisco de Arango y Parreño (see Chapter 4), who at the end of his life came to regret that the Cuban economy and elite had become so dependent upon slavery. To save Cuba's Iberian character, he made a passionate plea to break down racial prejudice, alongside the gradual manumission of enslaved and a real ban on the slave trade. The same man who had made an excursion to Britain in 1788 to learn how to develop a Cuban slave trade and who had urged Madrid not to ban the slave imports to Cuba, despite its treaty with Britain, now realized that slave emancipation was not only unavoidable but also vital to preserve Cuba culturally as a Hispanic island.[8]

At the time that Turnbull made his observations in Cuba, Brazil's Historical and Geographical Institute held a contest on how to write the country's history. The winner, Karl Friedrich Philipp von Martius, admitted in his essay that Brazil's society was a confluence of migrants from three continents, but insisted that its whites had a civilizing duty, particularly because the Africans brought as slaves impeded the nation's progress and actually should never have been introduced.[9] Indeed, like the Brazilian Francisco Soares Franco had noted twenty years earlier, when Brazil had just become an independent monarchy, that the "colored caste" was dominant in Brazil. To "whiten" Brazil, which Soares saw as a necessity, immigration from Europe was of great importance. The black Brazilian, in his view, should be banished to the mines and plantations of the interior.[10] It could not have been put more bluntly than by Martius and Soares: the African contingent of the Brazilian population had either to be "diluted" or removed far from public sight.

Just like the elites in Cuba, Brazilian intellectuals became opposed to immigration that did not originate from Europe. They fiercely denounced attempts by Brazilian planters in the early 1870s to import Chinese indentured laborers to solve their growing labor shortages after the slave trade was banned. This would not happen because Britain, already alarmed by horrific stories of the "coolie" trafficking to Peru and Cuba, used its influence in China to sabotage the plan. Although some Japanese workers were hired, Brazil predominantly reoriented itself toward sponsored migration of Italians and other Europeans.[11] As a result, a dual Brazil emerged for which the census of 1890 defined the south, with its center in São Paulo, as consisting of a white majority and the northeast, the old sugar belt, as being dominated by people of African descent.[12]

What happened in Brazil fit a general pattern in the Americas as cheap steamship connections enabled tens of millions of Europeans and Asians to migrate across oceans in search of industrial and agricultural work. Almost a third of Europe's population emigrated between the Irish Potato Famine of 1845 and the 1920s, which changed the racial composition of societies in the Americas and Australasia. Moreover, the influx of Europeans was attended by exclusionary policies regarding immigrants from other continents. After Brazil's government began to sponsor massive white immigration in the aftermath of its sugar dominance, Cuba took a similar trajectory after the Ten Years' War had prepared the ground for gradual abolition, which ushered in the transition from plantations to a system of central sugar factories and cane farmers known as *colonos*. Massive white immigration followed. Between the Ten Years' War and the late 1920s, about 1.3 million Spanish immigrants entered Cuba and although many of them would subsequently return, it would change the country's racial composition decisively from 50 percent officially registered as white by the mid-nineteenth century to 70 percent in the 1920s.[13]

The elites of the Dominican Republic, who had achieved a short-lived independence from neighboring Haiti in 1821 but had come under its rule again between 1822 and 1844, were probably most radical in their anti-African standpoint. They embraced a discourse that privileged the national identity of Hispanidad, or Latinidad, different from the Anglo-Saxon culture though still European. This ideology was championed by the poet Joaquin Balaguer, who ended his long political career as president of the Dominican Republic in the late twentieth century. Historically more important, however, was his role as the chief ideologue of Rafael Trujillo's dictatorship that lasted from 1930 to 1961. During this regime, census registrations were manipulated to fabricate a declining black population and a growing share of "mulatto" and "mestizo" residents.[14] Sugar was instrumental in this fierce assertion of Hispanidad. Since the 1880s, Cuban, American, and Dominican planters had brought the island into sugar production, for which they hired growing numbers of Afro-Caribbean workers. The Dominican political elite tried to block this influx but, in contrast to Cuba, they did not manage to hire workers from Spain. They sought instead to encourage the immigration of aspiring cane smallholders from the Canary Islands and to settle them as cane farmers, a scheme which largely failed because a decent standard of living in the sugar sector was not on offer.[15]

Argentina faced the same conundrum as the Dominican Republic, but its sugar planters, like those of Australia, had less trouble combining an emerging sugar industry with fostering a white identity. Argentina emerged as a major sugar producer just as it erased from its history the important African populations who were severely diminished through negligence and abuse over the course of the nineteenth century. Whitening Argentina was a policy inspired, worded, and implemented by Domingo F. Sarmiento, the country's president from 1868 to 1874, who looked to immigration from Europe to bring civilization to his country. In his *Facundo: Civilization y Barbarie* (Facundo: Civilization and Barbarism) (1845), he recorded his travels over the country's endless pampas, deploring them as a barbarous emptiness waiting to be civilized through river transport, the telegraph, and railways.[16] During Sarmiento's presidency, a railway was constructed from Buenos Aires all the way to Tucumán in the northwest, opening it up as a cane sugar frontier. It catapulted Argentina among the top ten sugar producers in the world. French commercial interests, headed by Fréderic Baron Portalis, also a representative of Fives-Lille—the partner company of Cail & Cie—built refineries in Buenos Aires. This further strengthened the political clout of the Argentinian sugar industry, which formed the Argentine Sugar Association in 1894.[17]

The Argentine sugar millers insisted on maintaining tariff walls against imports of cheap sugar from Cuba, Java, and Brazil.[18] Their sugar, they claimed, was racially as white as Queensland sugar, whereas other producers still employed enslaved or servile laborers. Indeed, Australia had reconstructed its sugar plantations in Queensland in the face of increasing recruitment costs and a diminishing flow of Melanesian indentured laborers, which was the consequence of their terrible mistreatment in the cane fields. Queensland turned to white smallholder producers who provided central sugar factories with cane and blocked non-European agricultural labor at the turn of the twentieth century. In Tucumán, however, the situation was comparable to the Spanish Caribbean islands. Land distribution was extremely skewed, with big estates that had given up their own mills as well as a large population of small cane growers and tenant farmers. Among the latter were Italian and Spanish immigrants without citizen status and uncertain titles on their land. Much of the cane was harvested by about fifty thousand seasonal workers, mostly of Amerindian descent.[19] In fact, one of the few things Tucumán had in common with Queensland was that this Australian sugar frontier also hired thousands of Italian immigrants, who were treated as second-class citizens, if they were citizens at all.[20]

More or less simultaneously with the planters in Australia and Cuba, the haole Big Five planters of Hawaii began importing European laborers as part of their ambition to turn their islands into a white settlers' republic and bring it under the US flag. Their goal was to have their sugar counted as a domestic US product, which would eliminate the existing tariffs. But with the exception of the sixteen thousand Portuguese workers who came to the cane fields of Hawaii between 1878 and 1911, recruitment of European workers ended in recrimination. The 365 Polish Galicians, for instance, who arrived in 1898 had been promised employment in crafts but were sent instead to the cane fields under indentured conditions and browbeaten by German overseers.[21] No more Galicians came. Recruiters from Hawaii then traveled to Puerto Rico, where the majority of inhabitants were categorized as white under the US administration. After a long voyage, five thousand came but soon felt cheated like the workers from Europe before them. From then on, the Hawaiian planters relinquished their ambition to create a "Caucasian" workforce. Since US policies of Asian exclusion had prohibited Chinese labor immigration and made Japanese labor immigration almost impossible in 1907, they began recruiting workers in the Philippines, an American colony at that time. This was not an instantaneous success, however. Desperate for labor, the Hawaiian planters even used their old missionary network to hire seven thousand Christian Koreans, an illicit operation according to Korean law.[22]

Sugar estates struggled with exclusionist immigration policies because they could only offer a pittance for grueling work, which few European emigrants to the Americas were prepared to do. Meanwhile, smallholder cane cultivation for sugar centrals had proved to be a viable alternative, and more efficient than the plantation model at that. This system emerged in Australia, Argentina, Cuba, Puerto Rico, Trinidad, and Mauritius. In Louisiana, the cotton planters had initially allowed smallholder farming but the sugar plantocracy tenaciously resisted not only African American but also smallholder cane farming by Italian immigrants.[23] In Hawaii, it was considered but never implemented, also because planters had adamantly opposed it. Louisiana and Hawaiian plantocracies fiercely opposed both economic and political democratization.

Trapped between the "race to the bottom" of wages on the one hand and the exclusionary immigration policies toward Asian immigrants on the other, sugar plantations in the white settler republics found a way out by recruiting Europeans from the most impoverished regions of the continent who would be less capable of asserting their rights. This meant the sugar producers had it both ways: they could lobby for tariffs guarding their sugar as being grown by free white labor while maintaining their exploitative plantation system. The fact that these migrants came from the economic periphery of Europe made it easy to impose on them racialized markers and keep them in subordinate positions. And thus, after the abolition of slavery, the racial categorization of workers proliferated throughout the world's cane and beet sugar frontiers. Sugar played its role in forging fine-grained racial categorizations within the racial construction of whiteness.

Louisiana: The Reconstruction of a Plantation

Republicanism and plantation-wise sugar production proved to be irreconcilable in Louisiana more than anywhere else in the world, since the United States had become the first nation to allow practically universal male suffrage. The Fifteenth Amendment of 1870 gave the African American majority of Louisiana the same near universal voting rights as white Americans, which in theory empowered them to outvote the plantocracy. This situation was profoundly different from Brazil or Cuba, where literacy and tax assessment criteria kept suffrage down to about 3 percent of the population in the final decade of the nineteenth century.[24]

Not surprisingly, the white economic elites in Louisiana, and other Southern states for that matter, did everything in their power to exclude the African Americans from exerting their citizenship rights. After the devastating Civil War, Louisiana's planters gradually managed to restore their supremacy, which was instrumental in their quest to suppress wages and labor resistance. After the highly irregular elections of 1877, they regained control over the state legislature and in that year the wealthiest sugar planters established the Louisiana Sugar Planters' Association, which like its counterparts in Hawaii and Java, used its disciplined membership and political clout as a formidable vehicle to suppress workers' rights.[25]

In the early 1870s, labor shortages had helped sugar workers in Louisiana to improve their position.[26] But through tightening their control of the state's repressive institutions, the planters succeeded in shifting the burden of the 1884 crisis onto the workers. They ruthlessly put down challenges to their power, which did come as former slaves responded to the restoration of plantation society not only by going to the North but also by striking.[27] The Knights of Labor, an interracial US labor organization, called a strike at the beginning of the cane harvest in November 1887 for which it rallied ten thousand workers. The planters retaliated by sending their militias out, killing or wounding three hundred people, an atrocity that went down in history as the Thibodaux Massacre. Next came the notorious segregationist Jim Crow laws, culminating in severe restrictions on the voting rights of the African Americans by 1900. This helped planters to keep wages down in spite of permanent labor shortages and continue their trucking system (plantation shops) as well as scrip payment, which continued from the time of slavery as means to isolate workers from the regular economy.[28]

What had happened earlier in the Caribbean region, when planters managed to obtain funds to import labor from India, now occurred in Louisiana: oppression of local labor was complemented with labor immigration. The political and economic elite of Louisiana started to hire Italians, from Sicily in particular, which was facilitated by trade contacts between New Orleans, with its sizable Italian community, and Palermo. Soon, chaotic scenes of thousands of newly arrived migrant workers housed in makeshift boarding facilities spread throughout New Orleans. In the late nineteenth century, an average of sixty thousand Sicilians entered the Louisiana cane fields every year, supplemented by much smaller contingents from a wide range of European countries as well as Mexicans.[29]

The importation of workers and ruthless suppression of African American labor resistance facilitated Louisiana's sugar industry's astonishingly fast recovery from the debris of the war, even if its prewar output was still not matched in the 1880s.[30] Nonetheless, the planters brimmed with confidence and were ready to take on the challenge of rapidly declining sugar prices. This spirit was expressed in a new journal launched under the auspices of the Louisiana Sugar Planters Association in 1888, shortly after the Thibodaux Massacre. Its opening article stated that the Louisiana planters through "constantly adopting new methods and devices for increased economy, increased yield and improved quality, have set before the world an example of energy and earnestness never before attained in the agriculture and mechanics of sugar."[31]

This rationalization set in motion a separation between mill and field and thus the introduction of the sugar central. Three-quarters of Louisiana's mills disappeared after the 1884 crisis, but of the remaining factories 75 percent became equipped with vacuum pans. By 1930, just seventy sugar centrals remained in Louisiana, which in addition to their own extensive fields harvested cane from farms, overwhelmingly plantations that had given up their mills. The most successful pioneer of this transformation was the wealthy merchant Leon Godchaux, a native Frenchman who had arrived as a poor peddler in New Orleans. After having bought his first plantation in the midst of the Civil War, he rapidly expanded his engagement in sugar production by taking over property from defaulting planters to whom he had provided credit to get their plantations back on their feet. Thus, Godchaux became a towering figure in Louisiana and was known as the Sugar King of the South. In 1916, the Godchaux factory in

It took many years of failed attempts to develop reliable mechanical sugar cane harvesters. This 1938 photograph shows Louisiana planter Allen Ramsey Wurtele operating an experimental harvester of his own invention.

Reserve, Louisiana—at that time owned by his heirs—processed cane from ten thousand acres and produced an almost pure white sugar, which was praised for its cleanliness.[32]

However, the rapid modernization of Louisiana's sugar factories did not solve the labor shortages in the cane fields. Since the state's plantocracy did not tolerate smallholder cane growing, 83 percent of the cane fields were still tended by wage laborers in 1910. Many Italian cane workers who had saved enough money left the cane sugar belt and bought land via railroad concessions. Alternatively, they sought employment in New Orleans, which had had a sizable Italian population since the early nineteenth century. Moreover, Italian immigration to Louisiana cane fields was seriously hampered after xenophobic hatred had culminated in the lynching of prominent Italian residents in New Orleans in 1891, which led to severe diplomatic repercussions between the United States and Italy.[33]

Upholding the plantation model instead of moving toward smallholder cane growing made it almost impossible to attract and keep significant numbers of European workers in the cane fields of Louisiana and Hawaii. Mechanization became imperative. Haulage was already partially mechanized in the 1880s, and in 1889 the first experiments with mechanical cane cutting were conducted at Louisiana's Magnolia estate. At the turn of the twentieth century, various machines were tested at Louisiana's experimental station at Audubon, although these harvesters would not become a common sight until World War II.[34] Incidentally, Hawaii applied even more rigorous labor-saving methods through the application of fertilizer in irrigation water and allowing the planters to ratoon their cane for at least eight years, and still achieved the world's highest yield per acre.[35] Ultimately, the old ambition to release mankind from arduous work in the cane fields by mechanization was achieved not by humanitarian principles but white-supremacist identity politics.

Competence and Whiteness

Through the ascendancy of the sugar central, field and factory became increasingly separated worlds, and this was accompanied by a reinforcing of racial boundaries. The sugar factories and fields were in fact a microcosm of what was happening on the global scale, as European mass emigration, colonial expansion throughout Africa and Asia, and the democratization of European and North American societies all fed a sense of superiority among European societies and their offshoots. Indeed, democracy, imperialism, and racism were no strangers to each other.[36] For plantation societies, segregation was a matter of survival in the age of advancing democracy because any unconditional acceptance of democratic norms and civil rights would undermine their very existence.

In Brazil and Cuba, extreme inequality was shored up by suffrage being confined to just 3 percent of the population. For the Louisiana plantocracy, however, the situation was far more complicated, because US political institutions were based upon egalitarian principles. Since it was not in the plantocracy's power to go against the grain, they sought to confine egalitarianism within clear racial boundaries. Witnessing the advance of egalitarian democratic principles the Louisiana planters fiercely spoke out against any blurring of racial boundaries as the greatest threat to "the harmony and compactness of Southern society." Such was the argument of the Louisiana planters' magazine *DeBow's Review* in 1861, in the midst of the Civil War.[37] That harmony, the magazine argued, was based upon the social and economic complementarity of the "African negro . . . whose mission on earth

seems to be to become the servant of the Caucasian race . . . each occupying its own appropriate sphere—the one constituting the labor class, the
other the supervisory and intellectual class."[38]

This notion of the "appropriate spheres" was new in 1861, and it prefigured
the time of the sugar centrals and the era of Jim Crow, which eventually
produced the notorious concept of segregation.[39] The idea of appropriate
spheres made headway not only in Louisiana but in many plantation societies through the mass emigration of Europeans that introduced a balance
between male and female migrants, enabling racial separations in the private
and intimate spheres. Meanwhile, science infused sugar production, shifting
the balance from relying on the experience held by enslaved, who until then
had performed almost every task on sugar estates, to hiring formally educated specialists. That this education was only accessible to white employees
solidified the racial hierarchy, which was also guiding the layout of the factory complex. The housing of expatriate and at least nominally white staff in
compounds clearly separated them from the local workers.

This situation was radically different from the time Europeans had lived
amidst their enslaved on the plantations and had been prone to assimilate
to a certain extent their culture. Even fully white children born in plantation societies did not escape from this as they were raised not only by their
mothers but also by enslaved—or by Javanese domestic servants in Java.
Thus, the worlds of the enslaved and their masters merged in the minds of
planters' children. In all colonies, the resulting "indigenization" of their
children was something the planters wanted to undo by sending them back
to the mother country, preferably before puberty. The prominent late
eighteenth-century planter and writer Edward Long, whose family was
linked with Jamaica for generations but who himself was born and raised
in England before going to his family plantation, insisted that planters
should send their children to school in England. This would remove them
from the degenerating influences of plantation society, which was an issue
of concern in every colonial society.[40]

This was rather wishful thinking, however. In reality, by the early nineteenth century a complex social structure had emerged in most colonial
societies in which wealth, gender, and education had become social markers
in addition to skin color. Although for white women it was rarely socially
or even legally allowed to live with a free man of color, for white men an
interracial relationship would rarely cause social ostracism.[41] It was accepted

without much ado as the logical outcome of the male bias among European immigrants, one that existed in the Americas until at least the mid-nineteenth century and in Asian colonies until the turn of the twentieth century. Racial mixture in Brazil, Java, or Puerto Rico was not that much of an impediment to social advantage, as long as it was not too apparent. It could not be otherwise in a creole society such as Java's, where at the end of the nineteenth century the majority of its European residents had Asian foremothers and European soldiers as forefathers.[42] In eighteenth-century Jamaica, it has been suggested that 90 percent of the white plantation employees had a slave mistress.[43] Many people who were considered to be white could still have one or more African ancestors. This was also accepted to a certain extent. Bryan Edwards explains that in late eighteenth-century Jamaica, persons with only one African great grandmother were considered to be fully equal to white subjects, and persons with only one African great-great grandmother were considered to be white.[44]

Moreover, inheritance empowered planters' children. It allowed women to marry "up" the racial hierarchy, an ambition that existed in almost every plantation society. This was a realistic option, since rich planters' daughters had the money and newcomers to the colony had a white skin but were usually without means. In Brazil, Gilberto Freyre—the great sociologist of its plantation past and prophet of a multiracial future—observed that planters favored their daughters of color to their sons as they could marry off the former to "clerks" coming from Portugal.[45] Even in Louisiana, it was noted in the 1850s that there were colored planters, probably of French or Spanish descent. Rich colored girls of Louisiana, and from elsewhere as well, received the best possible education at home and even abroad to enhance their chances of a good match.[46]

Across the globe, the colonial sugar bourgeoisie carefully protected and cultivated their status within the European social and cultural hierarchy. They usually had assembled their wealth within a few generations and sometimes falsified their family histories to overwrite the unpleasant fact that they were of common stock and quite often of somewhat mixed descent. The bourgeoisie shipped over all the luxuries from Europe, enjoyed the best of Europe on their visits there, and spent lavishly not only on vulgarities but also on high culture.[47] Every planters' community of some importance had a theatre, and sometimes a magnificent opera such as the one in Cienfuegos (Cuba) donated by the tycoon Terry Adan. As John

Mawe had observed during his travels through Brazil in the early years of
the nineteenth century, "A taste for music is general; there are few houses
without the guitar, and all of the respectable families have their piano-
fortes."[48] Thanks to the mass production of upright pianos, invented in 1826,
and mass printing, Beethoven's sonatas, Chopin's mazurkas, and Schumann's
Kinderszenen (Scenes from Childhood) became familiar to thousands of bourgeois families around the world.

For most of the nineteenth century, a good upbringing and wealth still
provided access to a "whiteness" that was culturally defined. But times
changed, and biological whiteness increasingly became considered to be
a prerequisite for cultural competence—indeed, as Louisiana's *DeBow's
Review* had pointed out, the whites' role was "supervisory."[49] At the time of
the Jim Crow laws in the US South, the "one drop of blood" dogma began
to replace the earlier intricate taxonomy defining the shades of color linking
black and white. As a consequence, even fair-haired and blue-eyed people
could be considered black because of their ancestry. In the novel *Madame
Delphine* (1881) by George Washington Cable, the great chronicler of creole
New Orleans, makes the reader feel the cruel and tragic consequence of
this axiom: Delphine could only marry off her fair-haired daughter to a
rich white man, a smuggler in fact, by denying that she was her mother.[50]

The US South was just an extreme example of a global trend as the belief
in white superiority made itself felt all over the world and permeated both
European and US imperialism. But it did not go unresisted. It evoked a
counterdiscourse by anti-colonial movements as well as by the elites of
Latin American countries such as in Brazil, Mexico, and even to a certain
extent in the Dominican Republic, who had embraced the ideal of creolization. The Brazilian sociologist Giberto Freyre denounced modern capitalism as segregationist and anti-democratic and saw it as an even greater
social threat than the legacies of the old plantation societies. He did not
romanticize the plantation, as did the white elites of the US South; he portrayed Brazilian slave holders with all their appalling cruelty. At the same time,
however, he celebrated the creole culture that emanated from plantation
societies.[51] Thus, he posited a powerful counternarrative of an inclusive "racial democracy." This echoed the work of his contemporary, the Mexican
intellectual and politician José Vasconcelos, who wrote about the confluence of people from all over the globe in Latin America promising the future
of a "cosmic race."[52]

The Resilience of Peasant Sugar in Latin America

By prophesying a creolized identity, Freyre and Vasconcelos took direct aim at the rise of white racism in the 1930s, which from their perspective was inextricably linked to imperialism and modern industrial capitalism. This discourse now included the materiality of nonindustrial sugar. Raw sugar (*rapadura*) became embraced, for instance, as part of Brazil's culinary tradition as appears from an anecdote told by Freyre about Francisco de Assis Chateaubriand, a colorful Brazilian politician, media magnate, and, in the late 1950s, ambassador to the United Kingdom. At one of his formal dinners, Assis Chateaubriand served his English guests rapadura as part of the dessert with freshly flown-in pineapple.[53] After European fashions had been imported for so long into Brazil, Chateaubriand must have felt that it was time to bring a little Brazilianness to Europe.

The ambassador might have aimed to surprise his guests with a tinge of exoticism, but this was also an expression of a shared sentiment among Latin American intellectuals. Vasconcelos and the painter Diego Rivera—famous for his murals merging elements from Aztec symbols, Cubism, and Communism—praised *piloncillo* (Mexican raw sugar) as a sign of cultural integrity and independence from the United States.[54] Lazaro Cárdenas, who was of Amerindian descent and served as president of Mexico from 1934 to 1940, drank his coffee with this sugar. For Mexican immigrants in the United States, piloncillo was one of the things that maintained their relations with home. Although three times as expensive as industrial beet sugar in most of the United States, it continued to be favored on festive occasions by Mexican migrants, including beet workers.[55]

At different levels, raw sugar was one of the symbols of independence of Latin America from the dominant North Atlantic world, signifying the resilience of small-scale cottage sugar making against large industries. This desire for autonomy would see a revival as a result of the "small is beautiful" movement in the 1970s. One may also perceive the resilience of peasant sugar as a forerunner of today's global movements for farmer autonomy in the face of capitalist large-scale agricultural enterprise, of which Via Campesina, the worldwide movement of small- and medium-scale peasant farmers, is a prominent example. Peasant sugar has proven its resilience widely in Latin America and India, as well as in East Africa, where the Indian way of sugar making was introduced by Indian immigrants.[56]

From their position, governments usually hated peasant sugar for being difficult to tax and inefficient because of the loss of sucrose involved during milling. Sugar experts such as Wynn Sayers, who was affiliated with India's experimental station in Pusa in the early twentieth century, condemned it as wasteful, inefficient, and outdated.[57] Governments were also suspicious of peasant mills as they often produced sugar or molasses for local illicit distilleries. Nonetheless, peasant sugar had the immense advantage that it contributed significantly to rural income, in contrast to corporate mono-cropping. And although peasants extracted less sucrose from the cane, their advantage was that they could do the milling in the slack season after other crops had been harvested, and their simple implements could be locally manufactured and repaired. British industrialists in India had encountered this resistance in the nineteenth century, and it still existed in the twentieth. Despite government loans to modernize Brazil's sugar industry, in the 1940s a third of Brazil's sugar, for instance, was being produced by 55,000 small mills—the majority not producing more than three tons.[58]

In every rural area where Indians, Iberians, or Chinese had introduced their mills, peasants continued to produce their cottage sugar. Hawaiians and Puerto Ricans consumed relatively raw sugar: the Dominican Republic had its *mielo* (confusing because *mielo* means "honey"), Belize its *dulce,* and the Philippines its muscovado (in the Visayas) or *panocha* (in the Tagalog region). Throughout Latin America, peasants produced sugar under a variety of names such as rapadura, piloncillo, or panela. A crude palm sugar was the most common sugar in the Malay world and was also widespread in Indochina and India.[59] In Egypt, peasant-owned crushers continued to produce their own coarse sugars and molasses, in defiance of the massive sugar industrialization project of the country's rulers, the khedives.[60] Even in Java, sugar making based upon the old Chinese methods survived into the twentieth century, defying the sugar industry's consistent attempts to eliminate it.[61]

In the United States, homemade glucose sweeteners had been part of rural life since sorghum grass was introduced in this country in the 1850s. The American food and sugar specialist Harvey Wiley recalled sorghum molasses being at the kitchen table when he was a boy in the late 1850s—and also that they were swiftly removed when the minister came calling.[62] Sorghum syrup was still considered to be the modest household's sugar at the time that industrial sugar and sweets flooded the American countryside in the early twentieth century. African American activists and scholars such as W. E. B. Dubois and Booker T. Washington lambasted it as an extravagance that seriously limited the economic independence of black rural workers.[63]

Peasant sugar continued to be widespread in Latin America and survived the industrialization of national sugar sectors. Tens of thousands of small mills—the trapiches introduced by Spanish and Portuguese and Spanish in the sixteenth and seventeenth centuries—existed even in countries where large centrifugal sugar factories dominated. In Guatemala, two-thirds of the sugar came from fourteen thousand producers of panela, with output peaking at forty-nine thousand tons in 1942. In Venezuela, many farmers grew cane on small plots, and by 1937 the average Venezuelan consumed 15.6 kilograms of such sugar, compared to 7.7 kilograms of centrifugal sugar. But no country in Latin America had as much panela as Colombia, where thousands of trapiches produced an estimated three hundred thousand tons per annum in the 1940s, equating to a per capita consumption of thirty kilograms. Sugar consumption in Colombia ranked at this time among the highest in the world.[64]

Tens of thousands of trapiches—simple roller mills introduced in the sixteenth century in Latin America—are still used today. Here, a modernized version makes both sugar cane juice and chocolate in Monteverde, Costa Rica.

Still, even if customers were prepared to pay more, the industrialization of the global sugar sector made progress. Sometimes migrations from the countryside to the cities eroded the basis of the peasant sugars. Today, the landscape of former panela-producing districts in Oaxaca, Mexico, is littered with the remnants of these mills.[65] In Pernambuco, likewise, the old *engenhos* rapidly disappeared after the 1950s when the sugar centrals began to dominate and merged into the big sugar conglomerates.[66] Nonetheless, at the turn of the twenty-first century there were still an estimated fifty thousand trapiches in operation in Latin America, and many of them, like those in South Asia, were motorized. Colombia was by far the largest producer with 1.3 million tons and twenty thousand trapiches, and panela was an incredibly important aspect of the rural economy. Today, Latin America's total production of peasant sugar is estimated at two million tons.[67]

The Evolution of India's Peasant Sugar

In the 1870s, most of the world's sugar was still the raw sugar produced by peasants around the globe. British India (today's Pakistan, India, and Bangladesh) alone produced about a third of world's sugar at that time. These extensive volumes of Indian sugar did, however, not appear in statistics, which took their data from industrial sugar syndicates and customs offices. Even at the turn of the twentieth century, India's colonial government could only report some rough estimates. Its sugar expert, Wynn Sayers, was not concerned since in his mind industrial capitalism was superior and hence owned the future of sugar production. As early as the late eighteenth century, sugar makers from the West Indies had ridiculed Indian sugar as being of a wretched character. Peasant sugar, indeed, quite often consisted of blackened lumps containing a lot of fibers, but the traditionally refined sugar, khandsari, reached British households until the 1880s. It was beloved for its fine grain that so readily dissolved in a cup of hot tea.[68]

The khandsari industry in India—as well as the outdated Barbadian sugar industry for that matter—received unexpected help from London's refiners in their fight against British entrepreneurs introducing centrifugal sugar production in India. This fact did not escape the British importers, who petitioned to remove the higher duties on the Mauritian, British Guiana, and Indian centrifugal sugar. Rebuffed by the British refiners who accused them of just serving the interests of a few industrialists in India at the detriment of the native sugar growers, one of the petitioners, Travers & Sons, retorted that India's sugar production was of a terrible quality, and that this cane-abundant country had to import centrifugal sugar from Mauritius.[69]

Asked for their opinion on this petition, experts from the government of India made the pointed argument that Travers & Son completely ignored the role gur played in the Indian rural economy and its firm place in the Indian diet. One of these experts, an agricultural officer, replied to Travers & Sons' scathing judgment of Indian sugar firstly by stating that all Indian consumers held suspicions about industrial sugar because of its use of bovine bone charcoal. But most importantly, people were used to the taste of gur, and this would not change. As the agricultural officer wrote, "The compost known as gur has a peculiar flavor which is absent from machine-made sugars, and the tastes of a most conservative people [i.e., Indians] will require to be changed before the local markets of India really open to the European sugar manufacture."[70]

Industrial sugar was unable to replace the beloved traditional Indian sugars and their manufacturing *did* innovate in a way that fit the crucial role of sugar in the social fabric of India's rural societies. Peasant sugar production first of all started to expand with the large irrigation projects initiated in Madras 1830s and 1840s, in Punjab in the 1850s, and in Orissa as well as in the hinterland of Bombay in the 1860s. Irrigation not only made large areas suited for cane but also saved a lot of human and animal power because water no longer had to be carried from wells to the land.[71]

The next large-scale innovation was a portable crusher that replaced the pestle-and-mortar mill, which had spread throughout the Ganges plains with the first wave of sugar commercialization in the thirteenth and fourteenth centuries. The better mortars were made of stone, but most were hollowed pieces of wood or an old tree trunk. The cane first had to be chopped into shorter pieces before it could be crushed, which together with a dirty mortar caused excessive fermentation. In the south of India, the roller mills were in use, and these caused less fermentation, dirt, and loss of sucrose content. Punjab, an important sugar exporter to Afghanistan and Central Asia, had reached a rather advanced stage of sugar production by the early nineteenth century. Here, the same mill that was in use in the West Indies existed, namely one consisting of two *horizontally* placed rollers set in a right angle with two other wheels to allow oxen to turn the mill.[72]

However, the hard vermin-resistant Indian cane varieties ruined the wooden-roller mills, which often broke down and had to be replaced every five years. The pestle-and-mortar mill continued in use therefore until Walter Thomson and James Mylne introduced a solution that would produce a tidal wave of innovations in India's rural sugar making. Thomson and Mylne were the owners of a firm in Shahabad (North Bihar) and had established a zamindari, a noble landholding, in the aftermath of the Great Rebellion of 1857–1858 on several square miles of erased jungle that had given shelter to rebel holdouts. In its role as tax collector and landlord as well as trader and processor of raw sugar, the firm had a direct interest in better-quality raw sugar (gur) and improved yields for the Indian *ryot* (peasant), which they generously estimated was 1.5 tons per acre at best.[73]

Seeing peasants struggling with the newly introduced wooden-roller mills, Thomson and Mylne decided to develop an iron-roller mill, which they named after their estate, Beheea. It produced much more juice from the cane than the pestle and mortar and was transportable, meaning it could be brought into the field. Farmers bought them collectively or moneylenders or zamindars rented them out. Between 1874 and 1891, an estimated 250,000 of these mills came in use—a resounding success. Soon a third roller was added, and in the twentieth century motor power was applied, replacing the bullocks that were often too weak to put the device at its maximum crushing pressure.[74]

In the early eighteenth century, Taiwan was still the world's largest sugar exporter, but with the Beheea mill, India leaped ahead of Taiwan technologically. The British consular attaché W. Wykeham Myers had tried in vain to introduce a portable iron cane mill on the island in 1890. In contrast to the Indian context, money lenders were not interested in improving output and the result was that, after the global sugar crisis of 1884, Taiwanese sugar exports stagnated, despite growing demand from Japan. The Taiwanese procedures of sugar pressing, boiling, and claying—with mud scraped from the bottom of the sewage—did not at all conform to late nineteenth-century standards, but they nonetheless proved very hard to change.[75] Five years after Wykeham Myer's report, the Japanese conquerors would fully replace this local sugar manufacturing with state-of-the-art factories.

In India, the evolution of the peasant sugar making would continue. Improving the boiling process was an absolute necessity according to Mylne, who recounted that on one of his tours of sugar-making sheds he saw "literally no grain, but lumps of hardened treacle instead."[76] His firm came with a new tinned boiling pan—soon known as the Rohilkhand Bel—to replace the earthenware that could never be entirely cleaned and hence prevented much of the juice from crystallizing. Then, in the early twentieth century a third major innovation arrived in the Indian countryside in the shape of a portable centrifuge to separate the molasses from sugar crystals. The design was borrowed from Chinese sugar makers in British Malaya, who probably had adapted and simplified European technology. By replacing the old method of applying waterweed, it resulted in considerable increases in higher-quality gur at modest cost.

The final step involved the improvement of the cane itself, for which India established an experimental cane station in Coimbatore in 1912. This was difficult at first because the use of local cane varieties and ways of planting were based upon sound peasant knowledge of risk reduction. Nevertheless, soon the motley collections of cane gave way to high-yielding varieties. Better cane together with improved processing allowed for a doubling of the amount of gur produced per hectare to about two tons. In some regions of India it even reached five tons. This enhanced efficiency helped traditional sugars to withstand the pressures from industrialists in India who felt encouraged to start sugar factories by a stiff hike in the tariff on Java sugar from 5 to 25 percent between 1916 and 1925. Actually, two of the three centrifugal factories that arose in the Bombay Deccan in the 1920s failed, unable to compete with the still cheap Java sugar and declining gur prices.[77]

Meanwhile the traditional refiners, the khandsari workshops, rather than being pushed aside by industrial mass production, would double their output in the 1920s. They achieved this through adopting industrial innovations in a way that fit their scale. Just as small iron crushers had conquered the Indian countryside, small centrifuges did away with the old method of waterweed put on the raw sugar mass to trickle down the molasses. The khandsari workshops had always had a distinct advantage over the big industrial factories in the form of their networks of agents contracting with middle-class peasants who could spare some land. They could even rely on poor marginal or even landless peasants to help with the harvest. Modern khandsaris now had their own staff in the field where they oversaw the tinned boiling pans that produced a much cleaner sugar (known as jaggery) that they could put in their centrifuges right away. Sure, the modernized khandsari sugar still cost 50 percent more than Java sugar, but its taste was what people were used to. Just like in Latin America, consumers were prepared to pay more for a product that was part of their own culinary tradition.[78]

Moreover, much like in Latin America, Indian rural sugars also fit an anti-imperialist narrative. The Indian nationalist movement, and Gandhi himself, famously supported cottage production, which directly furthered the cause of India's traditional sugar. The government of India did its part to encourage small-scale industries by giving a tax rebate to factories employing less than fifty people.[79] Surely, white arrogance invoked a counter-discourse of indigenous autonomy and tradition, but precisely because of this we should not overstate the contrast between the traditional and modern sugar industries. Throughout the history of sugar, new technologies had crossed cultural boundaries and every society had eagerly adopted them if they fit their specific social and cultural settings. Neither should we romanticize traditional industries. Historically, khandsari workshops belonged to the earliest capitalist firms, and in the early twentieth century, under the guise of tradition, they exploited workers even more than the industrial sugar factories, which had to deal with labor unions. In the countryside, the peasantry that grew the cane was still just as exploited by the big landlords, the zamindars. Still, gur making can be considered as a vestige of a peasant autonomy, or even a world beyond capitalism, in which farmers could decide whether or not to grow cane, whether or not to make gur, and whether or not it stayed within their own neighborhood.

Meanwhile, Indian nationalism was certainly not married to traditional crafts. Businesspeople were prominently active in the Indian National Congress, and its leader Jawaharlal Nehru envisioned a catching up with Western modernity. The colonial authorities who were less invested in industrialization than in rural welfare, which they considered of paramount importance for the colonial political order. Industrial sugar production nonetheless gained ground, and an overproduction of cane was forecast as higher-yielding varieties made headway. By 1930, this looming overproduction had become an immediate threat to the livelihood of the 5.5 percent of the Indian population deriving at least part of their income from cane growing. The government decided to stop the influx of Java sugar to protect the prospering gur and khandsari sectors. As a complementary policy,

Sugar boiling in Punjab, Pakistan, 2010. Throughout South Asia, farmers continue to make their own raw sugar.

it began encouraging the domestic sugar industry—not to replace the traditional sectors but in an effort to absorb the overabundant cane.

At any rate, even if sugar factories offered the same price for cane as for gur, peasants might still prefer to produce their own raw sugar to preserve their independence.[80] This explains, for instance, why the head of Birla Corporation, India's largest industrial sugar producer, complained in the late 1950s about the shortage of cane supplies for one or more of his seven sugar factories in the cane-rich states of Bihar and Uttar Pradesh.[81] The situation worsened in 1978 when India's government abandoned the price controls on sugar that had guaranteed farmers a decent cane price. At that point, many of them returned to their own cottage gur production.

In the mid-1980s, over half of Indian cane was still used for the traditional gur and the slightly more refined jaggery, whereas the big industrialists processed a mere 30–35 percent. In these years of low sugar prices on the global market when factories struggled to find money for maintenance let alone modernization, the peasant sugars proved to be very competitive.[82] In Pakistan, almost a third of the sugar produced was still gur in 1995; and as much as 60 percent of all cane in Bangladesh has gone into gur or jaggery in recent years.[83] The traditional sugars received an additional boost in South Asia as white refined sugar came under increased scrutiny as a health menace. The raw sugars with their fibers and additional nutrients could boast better taste and provide, according to one of the many advertisements citing a medical professional, many health benefits: "Since it is rich in many vital vitamins and minerals, jaggery boosts immunity, keeps the body warm, helps treat cold and cough and controls the temperature of the body. This natural sweetener has been a great go-to ingredient in India since time immemorial."[84]

9

American Sugar Kingdom

FOR MOST OF THE NINETEENTH CENTURY, sugar was the primary import of the United States. In terms of value, it accounted for 15 percent of what passed the country's customs.[1] Although the United States was not short of fertile land and its white elites controlled a large enslaved population until the Civil War, domestic cane sugar production had always fallen way short of demand. Obviously, only the country's most southern states were warm enough to grow sugar cane. In the more temperate states the soil was often conducive to beet cultivation, but in those land-abundant and labor-scarce states, there was no room for laborious crops that had to compete with cheap imports.[2] Sugar cultivation was therefore more or less confined to Louisiana and, to a much smaller extent, Texas, where it was initiated by Anglo-Americans in the 1820s when the state was still part of Mexico.

Florida is a major sugar belt today, but for centuries its potential for sugar production remained unfulfilled. The Spanish had made failed attempts at cane cultivation in 1565, and British settlers fared no better in the late eighteenth century.[3] After Florida had become part of the United States in 1819, twenty-two plantations emerged along the east coast, some of which operated with state-of-the-art crushers and boiling equipment. But it all ended tragically for these planters when in 1835 the Native American Seminoles and maroons joined forces to destroy some of these plantations.[4] Meanwhile, American ships plowed every ocean to obtain sugar. Merchants from Salem, Massachusetts, in particular—already involved in the sugar trade throughout the Caribbean region including Cuba, Martinique, and Guadeloupe—built a world-spanning network to obtain sugar from Hawaii, Canton, the Philippines, Cochin-China, and Penang.[5]

Few were worried when the Civil War all but ruined the Louisiana sugar industry and postponed the likelihood of sugar self-sufficiency even further. Sugar prices generally declined and the United States controlled many of its sugar suppliers in an informal way. The sugar sector of Hawaii was run by the haole Big Five (see Chapter 7), who had managed to obtain free access for their sugar on the US market through the Reciprocity Treaty in 1875. The US East Coast refiners purchased most of their sugar from the nearby Caribbean region, where the US Navy maintained a robust presence.

When the United States transitioned from an agrarian to an industrial nation at the end of the nineteenth century, it seemed even less desirable to produce commodities such as unrefined sugar domestically. The McKinley Tariff Act of 1890 boosted America's industrial interests by reducing duties on the import of raw commodities. It was a victory also for the country's sugar refiners who had become a major political force and who drew much of their sugar from outdated Caribbean mills.[6] This happened to the chagrin of the Hawaiian producers, whose sugar exports had grown by a factor of ten since the Reciprocity Treaty had allowed their sugar to enter America duty free. The McKinley Act eliminated their advantage over Caribbean raw sugar, whereas the bounty provided by the same law to domestic sugar producers was clearly to their disadvantage.[7] The Louisiana sugar planters rejoiced: having reinstated white supremacy and found new supplies of labor, they now reveled in their subsidies and converted to the vacuum pan within a matter of years.

The McKinley Act exhibited some similarities with the Cobdenist legislation that forty years earlier had spurred Britain's quest to open up sugar frontiers in Peru and the Philippines, as well as rice frontiers in Burma and Siam. But unlike Britain, the United States established both financial and military control over their sugar suppliers. In 1893, the haole families in Hawaii instigated a revolution to depose the Hawaiian queen, clearing the path toward annexation, which would mean their crop would be treated as a domestic product.[8] In the same year as Hawaii's annexation in 1898, the United States engaged in a full-scale war with Spain. It occupied Cuba, Puerto Rico, and the Philippines after having bloodily suppressed Philippine independence, which had been declared in the wake of a Spanish defeat. This colonial expansion was followed by a number of military interventions in the Dominican Republic, Haiti, Nicaragua, and a new one in Cuba.

The United States had no ambitions for a formal colonial empire and did not confer statehood on its new dominions. Hawaii had to wait almost sixty years after its annexation before officially becoming one of the fifty US states, and Puerto Rico still has not been granted US statehood to this day. Ad hoc legislation regulated trade relations between the United States and its dependencies, which in turn became subject of intense lobbying by economic interests—sugar producers, in particular. Hawaii obtained free access to US markets, but only for its raw sugars, whereas Puerto Rico—a de facto colony fiercely protested by the beet sugar industry—saw its tariffs abolished in 1901.[9] The Philippines, whose leaders surrendered to US troops in 1901, obtained free access to the US market for its commodities in 1909. This would elevate the then waning Philippine cane sugar exports to the fourth-largest in the world by the mid-1920s. The real struggle, however, was about the status of occupied Cuba, with its immense production capacity. Cuba's elite traditionally might have preferred annexation, but since this island—just two hundred miles from Florida—was such an important sugar supplier to the United States, such a prospect was massively resisted by the US refiners and beet sugar factories. Moreover, Cuba's tragedy—as well as that of a dozen other Caribbean and Central American nations—was that the United States did not need to annex this island to control its economy.

In addition to its territorial occupations, the United States deployed a new style of colonialism that operated via control of banking facilities, which has become known as "dollar diplomacy"—but the marines were never far away, of course. This diplomacy, moreover, was not about bankrolling but about taking over the ramshackle and often barely existing bank systems of Caribbean nations, and sometimes holding these countries' customs as liens. Thus, the Dominican Republic, an independent state for most of the nineteenth century, was drawn into the US orbit as early as 1893. Not unlike Puerto Rico and Egypt, its eagerness to modernize and build an industrial sugar sector had resulted in an overdependency on foreign banks, which received the Dominican Republic's customs in lien.[10] The end result was the forfeit of political independence: an insurrection by Dominican guerillas pulled the United States even further into the country, and by 1916 the Dominican Republic found itself occupied by US marines. Neighboring Haiti had already come under US rule the year before.

Indeed, sugar played a key role in how these territories were formally or informally subordinated to the United States, which by the late nineteenth century had become the single largest sugar-consuming country in the world. Thanks to its conquests and the annexation of Hawaii, the United States could in principle draw almost all its sugar cane from its own imperial orbit and most notably from Cuba, which provided 62 percent of the US sugar needs in the 1920s.[11] At that time, the United States and its dependencies accounted for more than half of the world's centrifugal sugar production. Eric Williams, the author of the seminal book *Capitalism and Slavery* (1944), coined the term "American Sugar Kingdom" to capture the entwining of US imperial policies and the country's soaring demand for sugar.

It was a contentious and highly unstable kingdom, however, contested not only by America's Hispanic Caribbean dependencies whose creole populations resisted massive imports of cheap Afro-Caribbean immigrant labor by American-owned sugar factories, but also within the United States itself. White nationalists had discovered sugar beet as a source of income for white rural America, and they opposed annexation of newly conquered territories with their large nonwhite populations. They also blamed the existing cartel of American sugar refiners that drew their sugar from these dependencies for setting the United States on the path of colonialism. They fought against corporate capitalism, against the influx of Asian contract labor in Hawaii, California, and potentially in Cuba, and posed as the champions of the white American settler. Thus, sugar not only shaped US colonialism but also played a part in defining the battle lines of immigration debates.

In 1897, with the annexation of Hawaii looming large, Herbert Myrick, the mouthpiece of US white farmer interests published a treatise that included a map presenting sugar from these Pacific pearls potentially conquering all the markets of the western half of the United States. The text above the map reads "Shall the American Farmer Be Sacrificed to the Hawaiian Sugar Monopoly and the New York Trust?"[12] "The Trust" was the name given to the powerful consortium of the American sugar refiners. Quite a few Americans must have seen through this propaganda, as most of them lived in the East at that time. But some might have been swayed by Myrick's argument that in these years of agricultural depression the United States should create its own beet sugar industry and that it constituted a crime to import cane sugar, a "coolie-grown" product.

To be sure, while white nationalists railed against the Trust and "coolies," they had no qualms about the moral implications of imperialism. The Democratic member of Congress Francis G. Newlands, like Myrick a white supremacist and champion of beet sugar, even saw the annexing Cuba and Hawaii as the quickest way to destroy the influx of "coolie sugar," as it would automatically extend the US Chinese Exclusion Act of 1882 to these islands.[13] This Act was indeed extended to both Cuba and the Philippines and the door was further closed on Asian immigration to US territory when in 1907 the influx of Japanese workers, mostly coming via Hawaii, was stopped as well. With Newlands on their side, beet sugar interests convinced US Congress not to skip tariffs on Cuban sugar, and to restrict US land purchases in Puerto Rico and the Philippines to a maximum of 500 acres and 1,024 hectares, respectively, so as to deter US sugar companies developing big plantations in these territories.

Meanwhile, Newlands had successfully lobbied for the US Land Reclamation Act of 1902, which carried his name and was aimed at opening up millions of acres for farmers through irrigation and land deeds.[14] Beet growers were notably included. Critics of protectionism warned that this beet sugar populism would entail high costs for American consumers and was utterly unnecessary as the tropics produced more than enough sugar. With sugar prices so volatile, why should the United States be involved in producing a commodity under highly competitive conditions with all the labor problems involved? "Let the tropics carry this burden," one observer quipped.[15]

At the turn of the twentieth century, US sugar policies were the result of two big competing interests. The Trust lobbied for low tariffs on imports of raw sugar and high tariffs on imports of refined sugar. As a rule, they opposed annexation of the newly acquired territories to prevent them from exporting high-grade sugar duty-free to the US market. The refiners were opposed by noisy white nationalist populists advocating the cause of the American beet growing farmers and tariff protection for domestically produced sugar. Soaring sugar consumption mitigated the tensions between

US beet sugar producers fiercely resisted efforts by American sugar refiners, known as the Trust, who lobbied on behalf of duty-free imports of Cuban raw sugar. As the creator of this 1902 cartoon saw it, though, Cuban farmers would be squeezed no matter the outcome of this tug of war. From left to right: Henry T. Oxnard of American Beet Sugar Company, President Theodore Roosevelt, a Cuban cane farmer, House Majority Leader Sereno E. Payne, and the Trust's Henry O. Havemeyer.

domestic beet and overseas cane sugar, but they would not disappear, and US governments throughout the twentieth century struggled to find a balance between these two highly organized interests.

The Trust

In the late 1880s, American sugar refiners forged a cartel that became known under the simple but ominous name of "the Trust." It would dominate US sugar policies for almost half a century. This massive concentration of power was driven by the rapid advance of sugar technology and continually declining sugar prices, which had transformed an industry of hundreds of artisanal workshops spread over many cities into a handful of capital-intensive factories at only a few locations directly on the waterfront. In this "gilded age" of rapid economic growth, New York emerged as the center of gravity of sugar refining, and it was no coincidence that the Trust emerged there.

While the American Sugar Kingdom was a mixture of interests that involved the most powerful banks such as J. P. Morgan and City Bank, its core was a tight network of New York bourgeois families that were as dynastic and class conscious as the colonial sugar bourgeoisie had been.[16] Henry O. Havemeyer was the figurehead of the Trust and is remembered as one of the most "colorful" captains of industry. He belonged to an illustrious dynasty of sugar refiners. His grandfather was a German sugar baker who together with his brother had migrated to New York. Henry's father, Frederick C. Havemeyer, was the first of three generations of leading sugar refiners, and his father's cousin, William F. Havemeyer, was an influential banker and three times mayor of New York—as well as a sugar refiner.

When Henry's father had learned his trade, it was still a time-consuming artisanal craft, but the introduction of the centrifuge changed the refining process almost overnight. Since sugar prices continually declined, scale was everything, and Henry's father invested massively in the new centrifugal refining technology, which he obtained from his ancestral Germany. In 1876, his refinery employed a thousand men and women who produced a hundred million pounds of refined sugar a year.[17] The unskilled dangerous work in these plants, which were replete with inflammable material and where the temperature could reach fifty degrees Celsius, was first done by Irish and German immigrants and then by Poles and Lithuanians.

The East Coast waterfront refiners experienced boom times in the 1870s, when they received government subsidies to expand their exports of refined sugar and benefited from low tariffs on raw sugar by importing increasing quantities of dark-looking raw sugar from the often-outdated Caribbean mills.[18] In these years, Frederick C. Havemeyer and his sons acquired the reputation of being unscrupulous businessmen. They instructed the modern mills in British Guiana, for instance, to darken their sugar to mislead customs officers, who supposedly would take it for a low-grade sugar and thus apply a milder tariff. Also, large quantities of sugar reportedly arrived at its factory without going through customs, which was easy since the new Havemeyer plant, like many other state-of-the-art refineries, was located right on the waterfront.[19]

The days of high profits came to an end, however, when the United States abandoned its bounty policy in 1886. This was in response to fierce protests by the British refiners, who saw US sugar flooding the English market, which was also reeling from German beet sugar being dumped on it.

Confined to the domestic market again, America's East Coast refiners saw their margins dwindle, which forced them to negotiate among themselves a cap on their output. It was at that time that the third-generation Havemeyers rose to prominence, with Henry O. Havemeyer as their leader. Inspired by the success of John D. Rockefeller's Standard Oil Trust, he embarked on a project to unite all American refiners into one corporation. The first step was not taken by him, however, but by his second cousins—the sons of New York's mayor William F. Havemeyer—and their manager John F. Searles.[20] When the latter had brought Henry O. Havemeyer in, others joined and, as a result, the Sugar Refineries Company was established in 1887 with the participation of almost all the leading players in the American world of sugar. It included, for instance, Edwin F. Atkins, the big sugar planter in Cuba who also owned a refinery in Boston (see Chapter 7). The Oxnard brothers, another big name in American sugar, sold their refinery to the Trust to start an ambitious new beet sugar adventure in California and the Midwest.

Having gathered seventeen of the twenty-three refineries in the United States under its wings and secured a capital of $44 million, this new company all but eliminated competition, for which it became known as "the Trust." It rapidly widened its margins of profit by removing excess capacity by closing obsolete refineries. This raised the price of refined sugar, and, as a near-monopolist, the Trust could bring down the price at which it purchased sugar. The American Sugar Refining Company—the official name of the Trust after 1890—ranked sixth largest among the select group of twelve companies that set the Dow Jones Average at that time.[21]

The Trust often operated on the edges of the law, and it perpetrated major legal offences, ranging from illegal transport arrangements with the New York Central Railway Company to multiple cases of defrauding customs. Its most consequential transgression, the violation of US antitrust legislation, went unpunished, however. Rudolf Hilferding, at the time the chief ideologist of the German Social Democrats and the inventor of the word *Finanzkapital,* therefore cited the Trust as a prime example of capitalist excess. Indeed, the Trust's 1895 victory over the US government in the courts marked a crucial moment in US business history. This happened after the Trust had incorporated itself in New Jersey, the only state where such a cartel could find a legal basis, and the federal government rushed to annul this incorporation as in violation of the

Sherman Anti-Trust Act (1890). The Supreme Court found in favor of the Trust, which was a ruling of momentous consequence because it opened the gates for an unprecedented wave of mergers that led to what became known as "corporate America."[22]

Not surprisingly, the Trust made many enemies, ranging from America's largest coffee firm, the Arbuckle Brothers, to the Louisiana sugar producers, who felt exploited by it and spoke of having to "pay tribute." Leon Godchaux, Louisiana's largest sugar miller, decided to build his own refinery to release himself from the Trust's thrall.[23] However, the Trust's most epic battle was fought with Claus Spreckels, whom we met in Chapter 7. This California refiner at that time controlled half of Hawaii's sugar harvest and flatly refused to be absorbed into the Trust. Although Spreckels's sugar enterprise was much smaller than the Trust's, his unwillingness to join was still a tough nut to crack for the latter, because of his vertically integrated business of refining, shipping, and overseas sugar estates. The Trust got more than it bargained for when it bought the American Sugar Refinery of California from Henry Oxnard, Spreckels's local competitor, and used this acquisition to undersell Spreckels's sugar. The latter could retaliate thanks to his control of half of Hawaii's sugar supplies, which enabled him to set the price for most of the raw sugar arriving in California.[24] While following the Trust and reducing the price of his refined sugar, he raised the price of his own Hawaiian raw sugar, which was for him just a matter of bookkeeping. His move inflicted considerable losses to the Trust's refinery in California, however, which had little alternative but to buy Spreckels's expensive Hawaiian sugar.

Spreckels even went on the offensive on the East Coast and built a factory in Philadelphia, said to be the largest in the world at the time. To open his plant, he came all the way from San Francisco by private train and was hailed as a hero by enthusiastic crowds at every station. The Trust, and "capitalist robber barons" in general, had become widely unpopular and the public apparently considered Spreckels as the valiant underdog struggling for what was their cause too, conveniently ignoring the fact that he was cut from the same cloth as Havemeyer. After all, when Claus Spreckels died in 1908, his business empire was worth over $50 million.[25]

Eventually, the Trust and Spreckels realized that they had to negotiate a settlement to end their costly price war. The agreement, signed on March 4, 1892, gave the Trust 45 percent of Spreckels's Philadelphia plant, whereas the two competing California plants—Spreckels's factory and the plant that the Trust had bought from Henry Oxnard—were merged and split equally between Spreckels and the Trust.[26] As Burnley put it in his history of American captains of industry that appeared in 1901, "Mr. Henry Osborne Havemeyer is the king of the Eastern forces, and Mr. Claus Spreckels is the monarch of the Western battalions."[27]

Now that the antagonism between the sugar giants had subsided, Spreckels and Oxnard lobbied together against the annexation of Hawaii to prevent refined sugar from these islands entering the United States duty-free. Havemeyer, Oxnard, and Spreckels joined forces to lobby for the fiercely protectionist Dingley Act of 1897, which further raised the tariffs on refined sugar also in response to the massive imports of bounty-fed (export-subsidized) beet sugar from Germany. This Act simultaneously favored the imports of relatively raw Caribbean sugar, which was crucial for the profitability of the Trust's refineries, and protected the infant domestic beet sugar industry.[28] The antagonism between beet and cane was a thing of the past in the United States when the Dingley Act ushered in an expansion of the Trust into the US beet sugar industry, in which it achieved a controlling position of 79 percent by 1907. Ironically, Myrick, who had fulminated against the Trust, had through his lobbying for protectionist legislation created the space for the Trust's massive diversification.

The Sorghum Craze

Since the beginning of the Civil War, powerful voices in the northern states had urged a weaning off from cane sugar and sought alternative sweeteners suited to a more temperate climate. When the Civil War ruined the cane fields of Louisiana, the federal government established the United States Department of Agriculture (USDA), which immediately began experimenting with beet sugar, although it doubted whether this sector could ever compete with imports from Europe. Another crop, sorghum, seemed to be far more promising as a source of sugar. This botanical cousin of sugar cane took only three months to mature and, in contrast to cane, also thrived in drier and more temperate climates.

By the mid-nineteenth century, planters, chemists, and speculators around the world, from India to the United States, were in a race to produce crystalline sorghum sugar. Until then, this crop had rarely come into view as a replacement for cane, although it had been known in China as sweetener for time immemorial. In Europe, only the famous botanist Pietro Arduino had tried to make crystalline sugar from this crop—in his garden near Florence after he had obtained a specimen in 1766.[29] Interest was rekindled in 1851 when the French consul in Shanghai sent some seeds to France. Simultaneously and independently, Leonard Wray, a sugar planter who would live in almost every continent of the world, became an advocate for sorghum sugar both in Europe and the United States.[30] After having published his widely circulated *Practical Sugar Planter* in 1848, Wray had moved from the Malay Peninsula to Natal where misfortune led to bankruptcy in 1852. He thought his luck had changed, however, after he discovered that in Zulu villages people chewed sweet *imphee* (the Zulu name for African sorghums). In 1854, he wrote a treatise on how to crystallize the syrup from this imphee. A French translation of his work helped him obtain 2,500 acres of land in Algeria from Napoleon III.[31]

Wray did not depart for Algeria, however, and instead traveled to the United States in 1856, where he obtained a patent for his proposed method of extracting crystallized sugar from sorghum juice. Impressed, the former governor of South Carolina James Henry Hammond invited him to conduct experiments on his estate, but no crystalline sugar appeared. This was because the juice mostly consisted of glucose and not much sucrose.[32] However, since crystals did emerge after letting the juice rest for a couple of weeks, a flurry of publications hailed sorghum as the silver bullet that deliver the United States from both sugar imports and Louisiana's slave sugar. Henry Steel Olcott's book, *Sorgho and Imphee* (1857), which included Wray's paper on the subject, went through eight reprints in a year, ushering in thousands of experiments—at least according to Olcott himself—in the United States alone. None of these produced crystalline sugar, but many farmers were perfectly happy with the glucose syrup from sorghum. Although less sweet than sugar, it served its purpose in many country homes.[33]

The outbreak of the Civil War in 1860 further fanned the sorghum craze, and one of the first deeds of the newly established USDA was to order new sorghum seed from China. After the capitulation of the Confederates, enthusiasm for this crop subsided somewhat, but it was then reinvigorated by the same USDA. Harvey Wiley, who would become a major figure in the history of US sugar and food in general, was the department's chief chemist and responsible officer for this project. He accepted the challenge and set his eyes on diffusion technology (i.e., releasing sucrose through the cell walls), which he not only wanted to introduce into sorghum factories but also into the cane sugar industry of Louisiana (see Chapter 7). Since diffusion technology had turned Europe's beet sugar industry into a success, Wiley visited a number of European beet sugar factories in the winter of 1885–1886 to see the process with his own eyes. He managed to reduce the production costs of sorghum sugar, but profitable production remained a chimera.[34]

Beet Sugar

At the time as when sorghum sugar experiments were failing to deliver, California bustled with experiments to extract sweeteners from almost every crop, including watermelons. Beet sugar won the day, however, after Californians with German and French roots visited Europe to study its manufacturing.[35] Among them was Claus Spreckels. After having conducted some experiments in the 1870s, he broadened the scope of his sugar principality to take in beet sugar in the next decade, a diversification that was part of his two-front battle both with the haole planters in Hawaii and the Trust. In 1887, he visited a beet sugar factory in Magdeburg in Germany, brought machinery as well as seedlings back to California, and built a factory in Watsonville, the largest sugar plant in the United States at that time.[36]

In the same year, the Oxnard brothers, Spreckels's competitors in California, traveled to Europe. Their father had been a Louisiana sugar planter and refiner who had wisely sold his possessions on the eve of the Civil War and restarted his business in Massachusetts. After Henry Oxnard and his brother had sold their Brooklyn refinery to the Trust, they sailed to France, home of their ancestors. There they bought French machinery and hired technicians with the intention of starting a beet sugar factory in Nebraska.[37] Former Harvard classmates of Henry Oxnard also established beet sugar factories in Nebraska and Wyoming, and after the McKinley Tariff Act was adopted in 1890, the Oxnard brothers themselves built two additional factories: one in Nebraska and another in Chino, California.[38] It was beyond doubt, Henry O. Havemeyer pointed out, that McKinley Act had been instrumental in the rise of the beet sugar industry in the United States. It is equally true, however, that this legislation was the result of the propaganda and lobbying by Newlands, Myrick, Oxnard, and Spreckels.[39]

It was a lobby, moreover, that appealed to the popular idea of the US frontier moving westward, with railroads and irrigation opening up immense tracts of land for agriculture, including sugar beet cultivation. The Carey Act of 1894, which facilitated private enterprise to construct immense irrigation works, boosted the beet sugar industry in Utah, Michigan, and the Great Plains. In the 1890s, engineers set up camps in the North Platte Valley, crossing Colorado, Wyoming, and Nebraska. Extensive negotiations over water rights preceded the digging of hundreds of miles of canals, irrigation tunnels, the construction of impressive dams, and the blowing up of mountains. It was the largest irrigation project of the United States at the time and took twenty years to complete.[40]

Three years after the Carey Act, US beet sugar manufacturing received an additional boost from the Dingley Act of 1897, which put up a steep tariff wall against German beet sugar. On top of that, there was the temporary elimination of Cuba's sugar industry during the island's War of Independence. This dramatically changed the math in favor of the nascent US beet sugar industry. Anticipating this new tariff regime, Spreckels again traveled to Germany in 1896 to study the latest developments in beet sugar processing and to order equipment for an immense beet sugar complex in California's Salinas Valley, half of the capital coming from the Trust. This new factory increased the US beet sugar output by eight times and turned California into the nation's leading beet sugar producer. Spreckels gave his name to the industrial town surrounding the factory. Meanwhile, the Oxnard brothers, aided by New York banking capital, rapidly expanded their business to Colorado, and later to the Red River Valley in Minnesota.[41]

In 1902, the year that the Newlands Reclamation Act further advanced irrigation schemes in the dry regions of America's West, Henry O. Havemeyer himself entered the scene in a rather surprising alliance with the Church of Jesus Christ of Latter-day Saints (LDS Church). Fifty years after their failed beet sugar adventure in the 1840s (see Chapter 4), the Mormons had embarked on their second attempt to produce beet sugar. They sought to replenish their badly diminished funds after the confiscation of property and persecution by the federal state for the crime of polygamy. Initially, the leaders of the LDS Church believed in the promise of sorghum, but what they learned from experiments in Kansas was enough to put that idea to rest. Beet it would be, and Mormon farmers learned how beet cultivation fit their agricultural cycle and provided useful by-products, such as cattle fodder. The success of the first Mormon beet sugar factory whetted the appetite of the LDS Church leaders for expansion, and while considering this step the name of Havemeyer came up as a potential partner. It surely caused discomfort of some of the apostles of the LDS Church, who feared this outside and unscrupulous influence.[42]

Havemeyer, who was already convinced of the potential of the beet sugar industry, saw a unique business asset in the LDS Church, which instilled its farmer members with the sense that beet cultivation was their religious duty—the best guarantee of steady supplies. In 1902, he bought half the shares of the LDS Church's sugar company at a generous price and supplied the chemistry, engineering, and agronomic expertise that enabled the Mormons to build two additional factories in Idaho. The three companies were merged into one in 1907, which expanded its operations into Washington, Oregon, and Nevada. The business methods of the Trust-LDS combination were such, however, that they elicited an investigation by the Democratic-led House of Representatives in 1911. The upshot was that Charles W. Nibley, the Mormon leader of the Utah-Idaho Sugar Company, was forced to buy the Trust out. Unrepentant, Nibley continued to bar competitors from Utah and Idaho, which allowed him to keep beet prices low and sugar prices artificially high. Eventually he was forced to bow down, however—by his own beet farmers who shed their docility and threatened to sow another crop if the beet prices stayed at the same dismal level.[43]

The Trust, Wall Street, and Manuel Rionda

When Henry O. Havemeyer died in 1907, followed one year later by Claus Spreckels Sr., the contours of the American Sugar Kingdom had been drawn, stretching from the Pacific to the Caribbean region and encompassing beet and cane farming, processing and refining. The Dingley Act of 1897 had opened the door for the domestic beet sugar industry in which the Trust would soon become engaged, one year later US military expansion into the Caribbean region opened another door for the Trust's sugar interests. Through building and buying factories in Cuba and Puerto Rico, the Trust procured raw sugar, which it could import under a regime of low import tariffs to its refineries on the East Coast and then sell the product on the protected US market. The American Sugar Kingdom was intimately connected with Wall Street financial circles and had to walk the line between domestic beet sugar interests and the country's geopolitical commitments to opening its domestic market to its dependent territories, whose sugar production was increasingly dominated by the Trust.

Interestingly, the first steps in the expansion into actual sugar production in the Caribbean region had been taken well before the Spanish-American War of 1898. In 1890, Henry O. Havemeyer and his cousin Charles Senff, accompanied by their spouses, visited Cuba to prepare the purchase of land and to build a large factory. This Trinidad Sugar Company would start operations two years later. The visitors were welcomed by Edwin F. Atkins, who, through his Boston refinery, was a member of the Trust. We met Atkins in Chapter 7 as the prominent American sugar planter who had brought Harvard's botanical expertise to Cuba for cane improvement. The timing of Havemeyer's visit was in anticipation of the Foster-Cánovas Act of 1891 that led to the Reciprocity Treaty between Cuba and the United States, for which Atkins himself had lobbied.[44]

A scion of a family involved in the Cuban sugar trade since 1838, Atkins had expanded his business from trade and refining to actual sugar production. His Soledad Alegre Sugar Company in Cuba had gobbled up land from his insolvent debtors from the 1880s, and by 1894 it was one of the largest sugar estates in the world with five thousand acres under cane. This was just the beginning. In the 1920s, Atkins controlled the production of over half a million tons of sugar, or about one-eighth of Cuba's total sugar output. From 1866, he had always resided on his estate during the harvest, but for the rest of the year he lived in the United States as a member of the economic elite, sitting on the board of the Union Pacific Railroad with J. P. Morgan for instance. Atkins was involved in all major political decisions of Washington regarding Cuba. He had access to congressmen, senators, foreign secretaries, and presidents of the United States, and was consulted by them.[45]

The audacious plan of Atkins and Havemeyer was to turn parts of Cuba into sugar plantations on a much grander scale than what Spreckels had achieved in Hawaii. But a devastating war dashed these hopes, at least temporarily. In 1894, trade negotiations between the United States and Spain broke down, to which the Americans responded by slapping a 40 percent tariff on raw sugar and a 48 percent tariff on refined sugar. Spain retaliated by imposing heavy duties on US imports in Cuba. The hardship inflicted by these two measures on Cuba's population sparked off the devastating Cuban War of Independence that lasted until 1898. As Atkins's deeply shocked associate P. M. Beal wrote in 1895, "It has been a perfect roaring hell of fires all the way to the hills of Trinidad and the sea, and one could see nothing but smoke and smoldering ruins, groups of poor people on foot, the women with their little ones in their arms fleeing for safety."[46] In the end, the war sent two hundred thousand Cubans to their graves and left two-thirds of the island's sugar plantations destroyed and deserted. It would take the Cuban sugar industry years to recover.[47]

The occupation of Cuba by US troops in 1898 initially seemed to give the Trust an excellent chance to resume its expansion in the Cuban sugar industry. However, the Cuban War of Independence and the Dingley Act had given the infant American beet sugar sector a unique opportunity to emerge. Its industrialists now feared that the Cuban sugar industry would be put on its feet again by American capital and they fiercely resisted the renewal of the Reciprocity Treaty with Cuba. Henry Oxnard, the beet sugar baron, was one of the leaders of this resistance. At that time, the Trust had not yet united the beet and cane sugar sectors and hence he found himself opposed by Edwin Atkins and Henry O. Havemeyer, who had joined Leonard Woods—Cuba's governor-general between 1898 and 1901—in a campaign for free trade with this island. Obviously, Atkins and Havemeyer were keen to avoid a repetition of the 1894 trade war, which had sparked the insurrection that had reduced much of Cuba's sugar industry to ashes. They lost their reciprocity bid, however, and although Cuba obtained preferential access for its sugar to the US market, its new rather ambivalent trade status and depressed global sugar prices created a wait-and-see attitude among US investors for a couple of years.[48]

By 1906, however, Havemeyer had concluded that Cuba was safe and attractive enough to invest. He did this directly via the Trust, but also participated in the National Sugar Refining Company (NSRC), which was led by James Howell Post and his cousin Thomas Andrews Howell. With Havemeyer's help, the NRSC was reorganized in 1906 with a large minority share in the hands of the Trust, a share which was however reduced to 25 percent after an anti-trust ruling in 1922. At that time, the NRSC was one of the most powerful players in Cuba, where it produced over 450,000 tons of sugar per year—over 11 percent of the country's total output—and had factories in Puerto Rico and the Dominican Republic as well.[49]

US capital massively flowed into Cuba during World War I, when the destruction of part of the European beet sugar industry and the depredations by submarines on commercial shipping drove sugar prices up. The island's sugar industry entered a phase of frenzied growth and an even more crazy land-grabbing bonanza. The Trust, NSRC, and the United Fruits Company bought extensive tracts of land in Cuba for a pittance and rapidly cleared massive areas of forest. The large-scale American companies anxiously guarded their independence and, in contrast to the Cuban-owned centrals, grew their own cane and kept field and factory integrated.[50] By 1924, the US nationals—who may have included persons of Cuban origin who had fled the war of 1895–1898—owned 62.5 percent of the island's sugar production. Most importantly, the American share was dominated by the Trust and within this share at least 40 percent was held by Atkins and the Howell cousins.[51]

While the foregoing reveals a massive concentration of refiners' and bankers' interests, it was just part of an even more entangled story. During World War I, the interests of the Cuban colonial bourgeoisie and those of Wall Street began to merge, a fusion that was personified by Cuba's largest sugar broker and sugar magnate, the Spaniard Manuel Rionda, head of the Czarnikow-Rionda firm. In Cuba, his firm took care of much of the international sales of the sugar harvest.

The origins of the Czarnikow-Rionda's firm lead us to Germany. In 1861, Julius Caesar Czarnikow, a Prussian, established himself as a sugar broker and as an associate of the London-based Schroder house. This extensive merchant family originated from Hamburg, where it had made its fortune in the sugar trade two generations before. It also had become the most important investor in the Cuba's railway system (see Chapter 5).[52] Empowered by the Schroders Czarnikow imported the first beet sugar for the London market as well as sugar from Java and Egypt. Later on he also obtained a dominant position in the sales of West Indian sugar and diverted about two-thirds of it from Britain to the United States.[53] He opened an office in New York in 1891, the year of the adoption of the short-lived Reciprocity Treaty between the United States and Cuba. Julius Caesar

Czarnikow had done his two first names justice by emerging as probably the largest sugar broker in the world.

Manuel Rionda joined Czarnikow's New York firm in 1897. Rionda was born in Spain but also member of a family of sugar traders in Cuba. After the death of Czarnikow in 1909, his New York office was reorganized and renamed Czarnikow-Rionda, with Manuel Rionda as its president. Five years later, this firm was selling 40 percent of Cuba's sugar.[54] The Rionda family also acquired a number of sugar factories in Cuba, a plant for the production of cellulose from cane bagasse, and a wallboard factory; arranged credit and insurances to millers; and supplied jute bags as well as machinery. This family engaged in almost every facet of the Cuban sugar business.

Being a true sugar tycoon by now and having established excellent contacts with New York's high finance, Manuel Rionda used the opportunity of the wartime sugar scarcity to launch a major coup by establishing the Cuba Cane Sugar Corporation in 1915, which bought seventeen sugar factories in Cuba. He added Horace O. Havemeyer and Claus August Spreckels Jr. to the company's executive board and obtained firm backing from the Wall Street banks, J. P. Morgan in particular. Rionda's daring initiative drew Wall Street into a central position in Cuba's sugar production, a role that had already been growing since 1914 when raw sugar was added to the New York stock exchange in response to the discontinuation of the London and Hamburg exchanges and future trading. Futures trading pertained to the advance purchase of commodities at a fixed price, reducing the risks for producers and traders of sudden price hikes or falls, which in 1846 and 1884 had wreaked havoc in the world of sugar.[55]

From a Cuban perspective, Rionda's initiative to give Wall Street such a large stake in Cuba's sugar industry was quite a gamble, and risked a selling out to American capitalists, but Rionda defended it as a means to create the necessary economies of scale and enhance the staying power of the Cuban sugar industry in a rough international market. For a global sugar broker like Rionda it was a natural thing to align with high finance in a relationship that was purely transactional. He was acting just like his deceased partner Czarnikow had done when he exchanged London for New York, when the latter city became the world's financial center. The Riondas did not fit any national categories, apart from having Spanish passports.[56] It was not their lack of national loyalty, however, that would backfire on them but the difficulty of managing such an unwieldy conglomerate of sugar factories. When the global sugar shortages during and after World War I suddenly turned into a glut in 1921, Rionda's Cuban Cane Sugar Company suffered severe losses and fell more or less into the hands of its bankers. In fact, after the devastating year of 1921 US banks took over the Hispanic-Cuban banking system and financed almost two-thirds of the milling capacity, managed all credit facilities for the mills, and dominated many other sectors of the Cuban economy.[57]

Conquests in the Caribbean Region

At no moment in history was Cuba more closely tied to the United States than in the mid-1920s. Cuba owed much of its prosperity to its location adjacent to a consumer market as large as the United Kingdom, France, Italy, Belgium, the Netherlands, and Germany combined. In fact, the Americans consumed twice as much sugar per capita as the Europeans. Thanks also to massive immigration from Spain and rapid natural growth, Cuba's population increased from 1.6 million in 1899 to almost 4 million in 1930. In the *Book of Cuba* (1925), the island was portrayed as wealthier than any other Latin American country apart from Argentina. Mortality rates were low, literacy high, the telephone system was state-of-the-art, the island had an international airport, and the streets saw more automobiles than almost every other Latin American country.[58]

Alongside the Trust and its affiliate the NSRC, other processors of cane and cane sugar set their eyes on Cuba too. Since the late nineteenth century, the growth of the beverage, candy, and chocolate industries had been explosive, and for these sugar constituted a substantial part of the cost price. It thus became attractive to produce sugar themselves in order to hedge market volatilities and circumvent potential price machinations by the Trust. One of the pioneers integrating the entire chain from cane field to chocolate bar was the industrialist Milton Snavely Hershey. He came from Philadelphia, the American "capital of sweets," where in 1851 the first revolving steam pan cookers had revolutionized the laborious process of producing candies. Whereas until the mid-nineteenth century the artisanal candy workshops produced a few kilos per day at best, the new factories disgorged tons of candies within a week.[59]

Hershey belonged to the type of legendary self-made entrepreneur who had known hunger as a child and experienced a string of failures before reaching industrial stardom. His first big success came when he managed to make caramels less sticky and chocolate more mellow with the right doses of the right cow milk, qualities for which the Hershey bars are still famous today.[60] By 1912 his factory had eighteen acres of floor space and, being a massive purchaser of sugar, he began considering how to circumvent the Trust and NSRC. The matter became more urgent during World War I, when war shortages of sugar threatened to cripple his business. Hershey decided to buy his own hacienda in Cuba in 1916, established a huge central sugar factory, and as a lasting legacy constructed an electrified railway from Matanzas to Havana for the transport of his sugar to the port. He domiciled himself part of the year in Cuba, which increasingly became a pleasure island for American millionaires, including for his friend Henry Ford, who explored options in Cuba for producing cane-based ethanol for his cars. Since the sugar was for his own factory, Hershey preferred to refine his sugar in Cuba. He did not load it in jute bags but in special rail cars to be shipped to the port of Philadelphia, from where they were hauled to his factory.[61] But even Hershey could not escape the collapse of sugar prices in 1921, and he was forced to hand over most of his possessions in Cuba and Pennsylvania to the National City Bank of New York. Hershey regained control over his mortgaged business, however, in the Roaring Twenties, the golden days for sweets, beverages, and ice creams.[62]

The American refiners, industrialists such as Hershey, and brokers such as Rionda had brought Wall Street to the vanguard of Caribbean expansion. This was not an entirely new development though, as ties between Wall Street and the key figures in US sugar corporations had been strong for many years. To a certain extent, they were part of the same family networks that made up the New York bourgeoisie. At the turn of the twentieth century, both James Howell Post and Henry O. Havemeyer were on the board of the National City Bank, and the latter's son Horace sat on the board of the New York Bankers Trust, which was controlled by J. P. Morgan.[63] But after World War I, the banks became directly involved in financing the Caribbean sugar industry. The City Bank, for instance, extensively financed sugar factories and sustained considerable losses in the wake of the 1921 collapse of sugar prices. A quarter of the Cuban mills, including much of Hershey's property, fell into its hands, and as it had to write off $25 million of the $60 million in outstanding loans. City Bank turned these immense sugar possessions into the General Sugar Company, but this would not become profitable.[64]

Meanwhile, the US government furthered Wall Street's interests by allowing banks to open branches throughout the Caribbean region and Central America. In Cuba, Puerto Rico, Haiti, the Dominican Republic, and a number of Central American states, City Bank, J. P. Morgan, and Chase had branches that actually performed the task of central banks in absence of domestic financial infrastructures. These banks pursued a policy of pushing out European financial interests from Haiti and the Spanish Caribbean islands. In this endeavor, they were supported by the US government, which used the banks to financially control these severely indebted countries as well as to avoid European creditor nations sending their gunboats, as they had done when Venezuela defaulted.[65]

Since the 1910s, Puerto Rico had come under the sway of the same Wall Street sugar oligarchy as Cuba and its sugar exports exploded from forty thousand tons in 1899 to over a million in 1929. In terms of value, sugar made up 60 percent of its exports between 1911 and 1940. Of these sugar exports, about 60 percent were owned in the 1920s by the big four US corporations, with James Howell Post, Horace O. Havemeyer, and their allied Wall Street banks in commanding positions.[66] These conglomerates did not entirely eliminate the local sugar bourgeoisie, however. Old planters' families still benefited hugely from cane farming for US-owned sugar centrals, which could send their sugar duty-free to the US market. Larger and smaller cane farmers, often united through family ties, sometimes forged associations to improve their harvest and negotiate with the factories.[67] They delivered their cane to US corporations, which were not allowed to own more than five hundred acres, although these companies massively evaded the landowning limitation—which was left unpunished by the government of Puerto Rico and the US Congress.[68]

Yet Puerto Rico offered limited space for cane growing, and hence the big US corporations started cane farms in the Dominican Republic, which was just eighty kilometers away, to feed the Puerto Rican factories. The Dominican Republic had ample land and neighboring Haiti had an abundance of labor. Cheap cane from the Dominican Republic entered the US market duty-free via the sugar centrals of Puerto Rico, making it an immensely profitable business for the Trust. Turning the Dominican Republic into a cane farm for the Puerto Rican factories owned by the Trust and its affiliates involved the dispossession of the local peasantry, which in turn stirred a guerrilla war that saw control of the eastern part of the Dominican Republic wrestled from its government. That the guerrillas occupied the Romana estate (owned by the South Porto Rico Sugar Company with Horace O. Havemeyer on the board) must have hastened the occupation of the Dominican Republic by US marines in May 1916. From then on, the Trust and NSRC, both backed by Wall Street, expanded their interests. They no longer confined themselves to cane farming; they began operating sugar factories in the Dominican Republic as well.[69]

The history of the American Sugar Kingdom entailed the control over the sugar production chain by the American East Coast refiners and the entwining of sugar and banking interests, and was facilitated by the control of Wall Street over most of the Hispanic Caribbean financial sectors. It opened up sugar frontiers in blatant disregard of customary land rights, engendering violent confrontations with local rural populations. The lease of a large tract of Crown land in Hawaii by Spreckels in 1876 was already denounced as an act of land grabbing, but it paled by how the sprawling American sugar plantations were violating land rights forty years later. Moreover, these twentieth-century violations had involved the military on more than one occasion.

In the Dominican Republic the displacement of many small farmers by sugar plantations had incited peasant rebellions since the 1890s, including a sustained guerrilla against the American marines.[70] In eastern Cuba, Afro-Cubans rose up in 1912 and took to the cities to destroy the municipal archives that recorded, and hence legitimized, the dispossession of their land. The US Army was called upon to help protect the sugar factories, while the Cuban troops ruthlessly isolated the population in concentration camps, slaughtering those who refused to be interned or had not been interned in time. Most victims had not been involved in any act of violence or vandalism.[71] It was among the peasants in eastern Cuba, still engaged in ongoing struggles against land grabbing in the 1950s, that Castro would find a basis for his guerilla war that eventually would bring him to power.[72]

The violence of the American Sugar Kingdom spread beyond the Caribbean region. In 1908, the US administration had cleared the way for the expansion of the sugar industry on the Philippine island Negros by squashing the resistance of the local leader, Pap Issio, who led a peasant revolt against the sugar factories for grabbing all the land and not leaving sufficient room for food crops.[73] The US military occupation of Nicaragua between 1909 and 1933 enabled the gobbling up of thousands of acres of Chichigalpa land for sugar production, and was spurred by the staggering US demand during World War I. In 1926, a full-blown revolt erupted in which the compounds of the huge San Antonio factory were demolished and its distillery set ablaze.[74]

One of the most brazen acts of land grabbing happened when Horace Havemeyer opened a factory in the Philippine island of Mindoro that was constructed on an estate of twenty-two thousand hectares. Havemeyer had bought this huge estate from the government, which had dispossessed its owners, a religious order of friars, as part of its policy to redistribute large idle landholdings among landless peasants. This transgression of land reform—and violation of the 1,024 hectares maximum set for US investors—was decried in Washington as an "auctioning off of the Philippines," but to no avail.[75] In every aspect except for admitting it, the United States had become a colonial power itself.

Florida, the Domestic Cane Sugar Frontier

Massive amounts of land were cleared for growing cane or beet for the almost insatiable demand of American consumers. Peasants were dispossessed, forests devastated, and mountains were blown up. Ultimately, the American sugar frontier entailed a direct attack on Florida's famous wetlands, the Everglades. In his populist crusade against the influx of "coolie sugar," Myrick had already mentioned the subtropical swamps as the domestic southern frontier, which in addition to the Midwest frontier, would achieve US self-sufficiency in sugar.[76] He was joined by Harvey Wiley, who published a glowing report about the potential of Florida's wetlands for raising cane. Half a century after the tragic end of a promising sugar industry on Florida's east coast, dredges arrived on the peninsula to convert wetlands into fertile cane land. A consortium of investors from the north of the United States, assembled by Hamilton Disston, began draining a massive nine million acres north of the Everglades, ignoring the rights of the original inhabitants.[77]

The building of Florida's first factory with state-of-the-art equipment started in 1888. However, this pioneering enterprise suffered from a host of ecological and climatic disasters ranging from cane borer to an early frost. In 1895, Disston's megalomaniac land reclamation project went broke, and he died a year later—some said he committed suicide. In 1900, his factory was dismantled and the equipment sold off.[78]

In the early 1920s, Florida sugar production still seemed so unrealistic that the Cuban sugar tycoon Manuel Rionda shrugged off the idea that his business had anything to fear from it.[79] He might have changed his mind somewhat when, a few years later, a new major enterprise, Bohr Dahlberg's Southern Sugar Company, acquired 130,000 acres along the southern shore of Lake Okeechobee. Dahlberg was not a sugar man but the owner of Calotex, a firm that produced insulation material from bagasse. He invested in the best and most advanced methods and introduced the wonder cane POJ 2778 into Florida after it was brought to America by the Dutch sugar scientist E. W. Brandes. He had come from Pasuruan, in Java, to be employed at the US Department of Agriculture. Struggling with labor shortages and as an industrialist pur sang, Dahlberg asked Allis Chalmers, the famous Wisconsin producer of orange tractors, to construct fourteen cane harvesters based upon the pioneering Australian-patented Falkiner cane mower. It was a daring initiative because the machines were still technically prototypes, and they were mothballed only a few years later during the Great Depression when wages declined. At that time Dahlberg's Southern Sugar Company had come in the hands of Charles Stewart Mott, the vice-president of the General Motors Corporation.[80]

Alongside corporate capital, local farmers tried their luck with cane, hoping to profit from the sugar shortages during World War I. Frank W. Heiser had mobilized farmers to grow cane for his Fellsmere Sugar Company but drainage problems killed his enterprise in 1917. On the eve of the Great Depression, Heiser tried again, operating his new venture on a shoestring with rusty parts of dilapidated factories brought in from Louisiana and Cuba.[81] Undeterred by a freezing winter in 1934 that ruined much of the cane, Heiser attracted investors to build a refinery, and two years later the first sacks filled with "Florida Crystals" left this plant.

For another twenty-five years, sugar production in Florida trudged on, hampered by bad weather, plant disease, and chronic labor shortages. Florida's big moment arrived, however, in 1959 when Castro's revolutionaries came to power. With Cuba's sugar exports to the United States blocked, Florida's acreage under cane almost quintupled within five years, and at the turn of the twenty-first century Florida accounted for 20 percent of US sugar needs.[82]

The American Sugar Kingdom was run by a select and often intermarried group of sugar traders and refiners. It had become increasingly entwined with Wall Street and, to some extent, with the beverage and candy industries. It became entangled in colonial policies, mingled with local potentates, and was complicit in land grabbing, tax evasion, and severe exploitation of workers. The inroads of sugar into the Everglades marked the apotheosis and synthesis of this history. In the sugar frontier of Florida, American populism, finance capital, land grabbing, ecological destruction, and the colonial bourgeoisie would all come together. After the Cuban Revolution in 1959, almost the entire Rionda family moved to Florida, as did many other members of Cuba's sugar elite. Alfonso Fanjul Estrada, nephew of the legendary Manuel Rionda, was at that time the leader of the family and was married to Lillian Rosa Gomez-Mena, a bond which united the two wealthiest Cuban sugar families. In Florida, Alfonso Fanjul began to rebuild his business almost from scratch on four thousand acres in Pahokee: "By barge they brought sections of three small sugar mills from Louisiana, reassembled them into the Osceola mill."[83] Within two years, their sugar business was up and running again. At present, the key figures in the buoyant sugar industry of Florida are the two sons of Alfonso Fanjul and grandnephews of Manuel Rionda. Today, the sprawling Fanjul holding company owns in a strategic partnership with the Sugar Cane Growers Co-operative of Florida the world's largest sugar producer, American Sugar Refining.

10

Rising Protectionism

To UNDERSTAND ONE OF THE MAJOR CAUSES of our contemporary over-consumption of sugar, we need to go back to the sugar crisis of 1884, which ruined hundreds of sugar factories around the world. The crisis was the result of an ongoing disruption of the global sugar market, particularly through the revolutionary expansion of Europe's beet sugar. It is crucial to understand that this industry was in no way globally competitive. Its rapid growth was in fact driven by European farmers, who massively shifted from wheat to beet when cheap cereals from the Americas flooded Europe. In the second half of the nineteenth century, Europe's beet sugar output climbed from an inauspicious two hundred thousand to five million tons. The share of beet sugar in global centrifugal production increased from slightly over a third in 1870 to over 60 percent in the final years of the nineteenth century.[1] By then, Europe's exports had reached such tremendous volumes that they glutted the global sugar market. Europe's largest beet sugar–producing countries exacerbated global overproduction by taxing domestic sugar consumption to subsidize exports. Germany led this bounty race. In 1898, of the 1.7 million tons of sugar it produced, only seven hundred thousand was absorbed by the home market.[2]

Overproduction was the consequence not only of seismic shifts in the global agricultural markets and national protectionism, but also of scientific progress in the beet sugar industry, similar to what we have seen in the cane sugar sector. In the course of the nineteenth century, Germany had moved ahead of France as the botanical and technological center of beet sugar cultivation and manufacture. Within Germany, the region around Magdeburg (contemporary Sachsen-Anhalt) dominated, producing 65 percent of all German sugar.[3] And here Matthias Rabbethge Jr., a son of

Sugar factory in Klein Wanzleben, Germany, 1923. Founded and owned by the Rabbethge family of beet sugar producers, the Klein Wanzleben concern was globally renowned as a developer of improved sugar beet seeds.

the founder of the Klein Wanzleben sugar factory, unstintingly worked to improve the quality and sucrose content of beets. This had resulted in the Original Kleinwanzlebener variety, the seeds of which were sown in about a third of the world's beet fields. Known today as KWS, the company Rabbethge founded, is the world's fourth largest seed producer, active in seventy countries.[4] In the decades around 1900, major figures in the world of sugar did apprenticeships at the Klein Wanzleben sugar factory or other factories near Magdeburg. Claus Spreckels, the king of sugar in the US West; Walter Maxwell, the leader of experimental stations in Louisiana, Hawaii, and Queensland; and S. C. van Musschenbroek, the driving force behind the creation of Java's Pasuruan experimental station, were all students of the German beet sugar industry.[5]

Toward the Brussels Convention (1902)

The rapid development of the Continental beet sugar industry had alarmed British refiners as early as the 1860s. They usually cared little about the provenance of their sugar as long as it was low-grade, but this was not the case with beet sugar which entered England in refined form. At their instigation, the British government gathered Europe's major sugar producers in Paris in 1864 with the aim of regulating sugar production in Europe and suppressing bounties and duties—all in aid of ending overproduction. The conference failed, however, as would three subsequent attempts, allowing the situation to fester and ultimately culminate in the global sugar crisis of 1884. Four years later, in 1888, Britain, Germany, the Netherlands, Russia, Spain, and Italy gathered in Brussels for a new attempt—which also failed— to rein in overproduction. Conspicuously absent was the United States, which at that time was building its own sugar kingdom.

The aim of the Brussels conference of 1888 was to abolish tax rebates on exports, which had led to perverse market effects. As one contemporary observer remarked, "Every householder in [Britain] gets good sugar at less than one-half the price paid for it in the countries where it is made."[6] Not surprisingly, Germany's manufacturing industry had grown impatient with the high cost of their country's bounty system, and the British government had begun to feel uncomfortable about its dependency on a few foreign producers. The towering British liberal statesman John Ewart Gladstone noted, for instance, that states had moved beyond protecting their markets and begun crippling the industries of other nations through "concealed subsidies."[7] Britain's prime minister, Lord Salisbury, observed, "It was in the power of a foreign Government, by a simple turn of the screw, so to artificially cheapen the production side as to make the prosecution of the industry on this side a matter of impossibility."[8] No doubt, the British government was convinced of the need to rein in dumping, and the Brussels conference of 1888 resulted in a treaty. Yet its ratification in the British Parliament failed due to the combined resistance of market liberals and the confectionery industry, whose interests were obviously not aligned with those of the refiners.[9]

Meanwhile, the global sugar market would only become further warped. France caught up with Germany as a beet sugar producer after it had copied the latter's bounty system in 1885, which came with animosity and much at the expense of the French taxpayer because its industry was less efficient than Germany's. Under this system, France's production had quadrupled by 1900 and, as a side effect, redirected the sugar exports of the French Antilles to the refineries of the Sugar Trust in the United States. Bounties also pushed up the production of Austria-

Hungary and the Ukraine.[10] Increasing expenditures on export premiums had to be offset with taxation on sugar for the internal market, which created a vicious circle of increasing production at the expense of consumption, further fueling dumping practices.

One might be inclined to think that globalization leads to open markets, and the late nineteenth century was indeed a moment of intense globalization. The sugar market, however, went against the tide and experienced a chain reaction of protectionist measures. Since the 1880s, a sugar tariff and bounty (subsidy) war had erupted among the European powers, which crossed the Atlantic Ocean and involved the United States as well. After Britain had forced the United States to quit dumping refined sugar on its market in 1886, the United States itself became the target of German beet sugar dumping in the mid-1890s. This was not entirely unprovoked, as Germany felt compelled to act after Havemeyer's Trust had convinced the US government to raise the duties on sugar imports.[11] According to Julius Caesar Czarnikow, the world's leading sugar broker at that time, German sugar producers had an additional agenda, namely to undersell and eliminate the West Indian sugar industry that catered to the same US market.[12]

The US retaliation to German dumping came with the Dingley Act of 1897, which eliminated in a single stroke the market for a quarter of German sugar exports and gave, as we saw in Chapter 9, the beet sugar factories of the Oxnard brothers, Claus Spreckels, and the Mormons a tremendous boost.[13] It also had wide-ranging international repercussions, as European sugar producers sought new outlets and set their sights on Asia's markets. They could reach these markets at relatively low cost, since their white refined sugar did not deteriorate during long-distance transport and their steamships had huge holds which often went empty to Asia to collect tropical commodities. As a result, both in India and in southeast China, local sugars came under the threat of bounty-fed European beet sugar.

Since India was of paramount interest to the British Empire, London did not ignore reports about the threat of beet sugar dumping in this colony as it had done with the less important West Indies. After receiving reports about shipments of white sugar coming from Trieste and Hamburg to India, Britain quickly intervened. Secretary for the Colonies Joseph Chamberlain backed the new viceroy of India, Lord Curzon, to impose countervailing duties against the bounty-fed sugar entering Karachi, Bombay, and Calcutta. Lord Curzon was advised that the buoyant and modernizing gur

sector, a key component of India's rural economy that undergirded the colonial order, should not be exposed to the dumping of European beet
sugar. In early 1899, Curzon hammered the countervailing duty through
the legislative council of India. Indeed, Chamberlain, the champion of imperial interests, had handsomely outflanked the Cobdenist majority in the
government of which he was part.[14]

But this obviously did not stop the global tariff war, and new rounds of
bounties from Germany and Austria-Hungary followed, which were pre-
dictably encountered by British duties. In 1901, Britain further raised the
stakes by threatening to fully compensate the bounties with duties. This
nudged the beet-exporting countries to sign the Brussels Convention of
1902, which ended the vicious circle of export premiums of beet sugar and
retaliatory measures. The share of beet sugar in the world market soon fell
considerably, from 62 percent in 1897 to about 50 percent on the eve of
World War I, a historic achievement.[15] An additional major accomplishment was that the Brussels Convention became monitored by a new International Sugar Council, which would prove to be the model for stabilizing
international commodity markets for most of the twentieth century. Most
famously, this institution would inspire French foreign minister Robert
Schuman's proposal of a European Coal and Steel Community in 1950.
Schuman's successful scheme laid the foundation for today's European
Union.[16]

The lasting legacy of the Brussels Convention, however, was that it increased the ongoing compartmentalization of the global sugar market. First,
Europe continued to be practically closed to cane sugar to protect its more
expensive beet sugar.[17] Second, in December 1902, ten months after the
signing of the Brussels Convention, the United States ratified its Reciprocity
Treaty with Cuba, which fit its objective of diminishing its reliance on West
Indies sugar. The United States correctly anticipated that West Indian sugar
would now be redirected from US refineries to British ones.[18] Britain pon-
dered retreating to its own colonies for its sugar purchases and began to
regret that it had not negotiated preferential treatment for imports from
its hard-hit West Indian territories. This sentiment only increased after
Britain discovered that the Brussels Convention had made the sugar market
much more volatile. It faced a shocking price hike of 80 percent on its domestic market in 1911. In addition to making economic sense, sugar self-
sufficiency presented itself as a moral duty because the West Indies had sent

soldiers to fight in World War I. This intra-imperial solidarity could now be rewarded through sugar trade policy.[19]

Another consequence of the end of beet sugar dumping was that Europe's beet sugar factories and their national sugar policies turned inward, with continental Europe turning into a major domestic sugar market. Before the Brussels Convention, cheap beet sugar imports had boosted sugar consumption in the United States and Britain, whereas in the beet sugar–exporting countries consumption was suppressed through sugar taxes.[20] After 1902, consumption in France and Germany received a boost from the reduction of sugar taxes, which were no longer needed to pay for dumping practices. Moreover, powerful beet sugar interests, represented for instance by the German Sugar Association, began lobbying for additional government measures to enhance national sugar consumption. It persuaded the German War Department, for instance, to prescribe "a daily sugar ration for recruits to take with their morning coffee."[21]

The Brussels Convention was an exemplary success for its international regulation of the sugar trade, but it did not stop the tripartition of the world of sugar into continental Europe's expanding beet sugar interests, the American Sugar Kingdom, and an emerging British imperial sugar sector. Within their protected domains, sugar industries successfully lobbied their governments to strengthen their domestic position by encouraging consumption. In the early years of the twentieth century, the full consequences of this configuration—including its perverse effect of artificially enhanced consumption—were not yet visible, but they would endure and cement the domination of the world of sugar by the Global North.

The Brussels Convention stopped the influx of beet sugar into Asia, allowing the Java sugar factories to become the largest industrial complex of Southeast Asia. It also helped the Cuban sugar industry to recover from the ravages of war. Nonetheless, the sugar factories of Java remained barred from European markets, and Cuba's position as the world's largest sugar exporter remained under permanent threat from US beet sugar interests. While cane sugar could be produced at lower cost than beet sugar, it was grown in territories that did not have the political power to enforce fair competition. This would be the harsh reality for the entire twentieth century.

Nonetheless, by 1908 Java had secured a large Asian market for its higher-grade sugars, which accounted for more than half of its sugar exports by

1924.[22] In addition to considerable Japanese demand, Java's sugar exports found an immense and rapidly growing market in India, where centrifugal production of white sugar was still in its infancy. One would have expected Java's sugar factories to experience serious headwinds because of ongoing rumors in India that Java's factories used bovine bone charcoal in their filters, which was actually no longer the case. Apparently, the low price of imported sugar was enough to induce Indian retailers, bakers, and lemonade makers to ignore their concerns about impurities and bone charcoal, and they began to mix imported sugar with Indian sugar.[23] Moreover, at a time when the Swadeshi independence movement was growing, it was not opportune to advertise a replacement of the "traditional" taste for a foreign one. In India, sugar coming from Java was first pulverized and washed with gluey water to give it a more domestic appearance before being retailed, as a representative of the Java sugar producers reported when he visited a workshop in Karachi in 1931. The representative was there at the invitation of Java's second largest sugar exporter, the Kian Gwan firm, which had offices all over Asia, including in Karachi and Bombay.[24] Indeed, in spite of its racialized management, in many respects the Java sugar industry was an Asian sugar complex.

The Clash of the Sugar Giants

Although the Brussels Convention would serve as the basic model to regulate the global sugar market well into the 1970s, its regime did not survive World War I. Britain withdrew from it in 1913, giving itself the power to put preferential tariffs on sugar from its own colonies and gradually turn its 90 percent dependence on foreign sugar into imperial self-reliance.[25] After World War I, the rapid expansion of production capacity in Java and particularly Cuba in response to shortages resulted in structural overproduction when the European beet sugar industry recovered and started to grow again.[26]

Czechoslovakia, and its eastern region of Slovakia in particular, emerged as a prominent beet sugar exporter after World War I. It was blessed with an excellent soil for beet and an abundance of potash, a fertilizer that was lavishly applied to the land. Beets, furthermore, perfectly fit the annual agricultural calendar, in which other crops such as potatoes were harvested earlier. Abundant low-wage labor in this densely populated and poor rural country and the availability of sufficient oxen compensated a relatively low level of mechanization in the fields. Growers were supported by a tightly organized and highly scientific industrial complex, together forming a Sugar Syndicate of growers, manufacturers, and refiners all operating under government auspices. The system was backed up by experimental stations and supported by a substantial downstream industry producing chocolate and candies, as well as distilleries. The molasses and the beet pulp, finally, made valuable cattle fodder.[27]

Meanwhile, the European sugar industry increased its efficiency and profitability through concentration, vertical integration (combining processing and refining), diversification into by-products, and expansion into Eastern and Southern Europe. The most spectacular example of this were the beet sugar factories in Southern Germany that were united into the South German Sugar Company in 1926. Four years later, most of the shares were surprisingly no longer in German hands. They were owned by the Italian industrial chemist Ilario Montesi, the son of a railway worker who was a leading figure in an Italian-Belgian consortium. Montesi had the strength of the Tirlemontoise factory behind him. They were the largest and one of the oldest Belgian industrial refiners, which also possessed factories in the Netherlands. Since sugar production in Belgium and the Netherlands fell under the restrictions of the Brussels Convention, this company had begun building beet sugar factories in northern Italy, Romania, and Bulgaria, where the convention did not apply, and where sugar consumption was low but increasing. In 1927, Montesi bought out his Belgian partners and started to acquire shares in the South German Sugar Company; by 1930 he owned 82.5 percent of probably the largest German sugar firm.[28]

In the meantime, a surplus of sugar was flooding into a shrinking open sugar market, which made up a mere 25 percent of global production by the late 1920s.[29] A bitter battle would now be fought by the world's main sugar exporters: Cuba, Java, and Europe's beet sugar–producing nations. Java seemed to hold the best cards as it was able to produce sugar at just £10 per ton and was serving a huge and expanding Asian market, whereas Cuba had to sell at £11.5 and the European beet sugar factories could do no better that £16 per ton.[30] The producers in the Global South were, however, subject to colonial forces, and the colonizing powers would always favor their domestic producers—a fact which the Java's sugar producers failed to remember. They also bore a particular responsibility for escalating tensions through their refusal to compromise. Rather than face the reality that they were in the same boat as Cuba, they considered Cuba as their adversary and more vulnerable than themselves in case of an all-out sugar war.[31]

Meanwhile, Gerardo Machado, Cuba's newly elected president, was already grappling with massive labor unrest resulting from diminishing export income, to which he responded with brutal oppression. At the same time, he was a nationalist who despised the 1901 Platt Amendment, which had given the United States a veto over Cuba's foreign policies. Not being a sugar man, he recognized the need for diversification of the island's economy. In 1926, shortly after assuming office, Machado, decided to cut back Cuba's sugar production by 10 percent to counter declining sugar prices, although this measure also entailed a serious risk of unrest among workers and *colonos,* the Cuban farmers who provided cane to the factories.[32] This reduction was, however, part of a three-pronged strategy. The first aim was to make sugar production profitable again; the second to protect the *colonos* from being outcompeted by the big US-owned sugar plantations that could produce at a lower cost price; and the third was to free up land and resources for other commodities so as to become less dependent on sugar. As an additional benefit, at least in the eyes of the Cuban nationalists, it would stem the influx of Caribbean immigrant labor.

Machado was also keenly aware that Cuba was now struggling with the severe consequences of mass deforestation by the sugar industry. The sugar bonanza that had erupted during World War I had been devastating for Cuba's remaining forests. On Cuba's eastern frontier, cane was planted between recently felled trees since the factories no longer bothered to haul these away. While in 1815 Cuba's forests still covered 80 percent of the island, in 1926 that figure was just 20 percent. A sharp decline in rainfall necessitated the construction of huge irrigation works during World War II. Today, almost 78 percent the arable land on this once so fertile island is in poor to very poor condition. When Machado signed the Forest Protection Act in order to at least save the forests in the highlands in 1926, it was in fact already too late to save Cuba from ecological disaster.[33]

For Machado to achieve his objectives, he had to bring the other large exporters, namely the European beet sugar producers and the Java sugar factories, to the negotiating table. In early 1927, Europe's beet sugar producers had organized themselves into the International Commission of European Sugar Beet Growers (Confédération Internationale des Betteraviers Européens [CIBE]), a powerful organization which still exists today.[34] The economic ideas of members of Cuban sugar elites such as Manuel Rionda, whom we met in Chapter 9, and those of the CIBE were in accord. The European beet sugar producers primarily wanted to keep their markets closed for cane sugar, and Cuba was keen to preserve its preferential access to the US market. Both therefore preferred quota systems rather than free competition to balance the global sugar market.[35] Java's sugar producers, however, still saw room for expansion into the Asian markets, which they considered to be theirs. In their view, the predicament of the Cuban sugar industry ought to be solved by Wall Street, which had a considerable stake in it. Meanwhile, and as expected, Machado felt the heat of labor unrest and the fading support of the *colonos*. It became a matter of survival for his regime to reach an agreement on the comprehensive reduction of the global sugar exports in order to stop the fall of sugar prices.

In 1927, Machado sent the prominent Cuban sugar businessman Colonel Miguel Tarafa—a friend of the Riondas—to Europe in an effort to get the three largest sugar exporters in the world—Czechoslovakia, Java, and Cuba—around the table. On his voyage to Europe, Tarafa studied the brochure of the eminent Dutch sugar expert Prinsen Geerligs entitled "Project of the Reconstruction of the Brussels Convention of 1902." But reviving the Brussels Convention would prove to be even more of a Herculean task than its crafting had been, because in 1902 concessions were sought from the governments of beet sugar–producing countries, who possessed diversified industrial economies and for whom beet was just one of their economic interests. Now, Tarafa had to persuade the sugar producers of Java, who were a dominant force in the Netherlands Indies, to make concessions with little to offer in return. He therefore conferred first in Paris with the beet sugar producers of Poland, Czechoslovakia, and Germany, who expressed their willingness to reach an agreement.[36] With this mandate, he traveled to Amsterdam, where he was received by three representatives of the United Java Sugar Producers, who told him flatly that shrinking the acreage of cane to be planted in Java for 1929 was out of the question. In 1929, Tarafa made a second attempt, and while he managed to forge an agreement between Cuba, Germany, Czechoslovakia, and Poland on production cuts, he again did not obtain approval from Java's producers, which made the deal of little value.[37]

In the meantime Herbert Hoover was elected to the White House and during his campaign he had promised to protect the interests of US farmers. The 1929 Wall Street Crash provided him with the necessary arguments to adopt tough protectionist measures, which came in the form of the Smoot-Hawley Tariff Act of 1930. The Act raised the tariffs on sugar imports, among other things, and was signed by the president despite a thousand economists petitioning him not to, and despite agreeing in personal conversations with a desperate Henry Ford and an equally alarmed director of J. P. Morgan that it was an utterly counterproductive and thus stupid Act. Threatened by growing US protectionism and facing the intransigence of the Java Sugar Producers Association, the Cuban government attempted to enter the Chinese market. Shanghai newspapers reported plans for a joint Cuban-Chinese refinery in their city, for which Cuba would provide part of the capital and the technological expertise. US business circles took it as an ominous sign that Cuba was no longer willing to leave the Chinese market to the Java sugar producers. The Java factories, mostly family property and generally in excellent financial health, declared their readiness to fight if Cuba started carving out a market in Asia.[38]

Throughout 1929, Java's sugar producers were deaf to pleas for compromise, trusting in their growing markets in China and India and the fact that they had managed to further reduce production and freight costs. Instead, they tried at all costs to keep Cuba out of the Asian markets, which turned out to be a serious mistake. They shipped large quantities of cheap sugar "West of Suez" in retaliation to Cuba's attempts to enter markets in Asia. This action dramatically backfired when much of this sugar found its way back to British India and China to compete with the Java sugar that had been delivered earlier to the local trading houses at the normal prices. The arrival of sugar that had been dumped on the market led to outrage among importers and refiners of Java sugar. British India made a formal complaint about it at a meeting of the Economic Committee of the League of Nations in Geneva in June 1929, which was convened to discuss the problems of the global sugar market.[39]

While the Java sugar industrialists were making enemies in Cuba and India, they had no friends in Europe or the United States either. The European beet sugar producers had a clear interest in carving up the global sugar market. Prinsen Geerligs had experienced this in Geneva when, in his capacity of the representative of the Java sugar industry, he crossed swords with Erich Rabbethge, the representative of the German and European beet sugar producers. This member of the family whose Original Kleinwanzlebener variety of beet grew in a third of the world's fields, fiercely defended European protectionism. Over the course of the 1920s, the US beet sugar industry defended with increasing success their interests against cane sugar imports, too.

The only reason why US beet sugar interests did not prevail was that it would have severely hurt the interests of the Wall Street financiers of the Caribbean sugar industry. These financiers took matters in their own hands and approached the Wall Street lawyer Thomas L. Chadbourne to design a reorganization of the Cuban sugar industry. He was a true representative of the entwined financial-industrial sugar interests of the American Sugar Kingdom and a prominent shareholder in US investments in Cuba. On the other hand, he was also a far-sighted businessman with genuine concern for the global economic system. He had expressed serious reservations, for instance, about the punitive war reparations imposed on Germany at the Versailles Conference of 1919, and even admitted during the Great Depression that capitalism was on trial.[40]

Chadbourne convened a committee of Wall Street and Cuban sugar interests that fleshed out a gentlemen's agreement with beet sugar producers in the United States, as well as cane sugar producers in Puerto Rico, Louisiana, and even the Philippines. It was agreed to keep production in pace with the growth of US consumption. Armed with this stabilization scheme, Chadbourne confidently opened negotiations with European beet and the Java sugar producers.[41] Sugar prices, meanwhile, were at a level that was pushing even the Java sugar industry into the red. Nevertheless, Java's sugar producers were not ready to receive Chadbourne with open arms. They felt strong enough to play hard ball with Wall Street, knowing they were the cheapest sugar producer in the world and serving an immense and growing Asian market. Protests in India against their dumping barely reached the ears of Java's producers.

Java's producers expected that the Dutch banks who financed them would not yield to US pressure and keep Chadbourne far away from Amsterdam. But he arrived in the city soon after; a clear sign that the Dutch bankers had wired their willingness to talk. After a couple of negotiating sessions, the executives of the Netherlands Trading Society announced that it had agreed to restrict sugar cultivation in Java from 1932 onward—with which the Java producers of course had to comply.[42] With the Dutch on board, Chadbourne headed to Brussels to convince the European beet sugar producers to reduce their output. Germany proved to be the most reluctant partner, but Chadbourne cleared this hurdle by visiting Berlin. By the end of February 1931, he had accomplished his mission to achieve voluntary production restrictions by the major sugar exporters. The Chadbourne Plan was expeditiously institutionalized through the International Sugar Council, which would hold office in The Hague. The Brussels Convention seemed to have been revived.

Chadbourne had brilliantly succeeded, but it was not enough to tame the tempests that ravaged the global sugar market in the early 1930s. Cuba continued to be threatened by US beet sugar producers and Java's loss of the Indian market was unavoidable, as we have seen, since new cane varieties allowed India to dispense with imports. Moreover, the Indian National Congress was assuming co-responsibility for India's economic policies and fostered no sympathy for the colonial and, as it had learned, racist sugar complex of Java. In the late 1920s, these factories had refused to welcome Indian management trainees at their compounds for the unspoken but obvious reason that doing so would blur the racial divisions on their estates. The Indian National Congress's local branches had already urged local traders to stop buying Java sugar. Such a boycott was no longer necessary, however. In 1931, grievances relating to dumping by the Java sugar producers were submitted as testimony to the Indian Tariff Board, and in 1932 the Indian government raised the import duties on refined sugar by 25 percent, amounting to a prohibitive tariff. The Indian market was now irretrievably lost to the Java sugar industry.[43]

When it rains it pours, and that was definitely the case for the Java sugar industry. Japan now also detached itself from Java, sugar having developed its own sugar industry in Taiwan by reshaping the island's Chinese peasant mode of production with a thousand wooden roller mills into an industrial sugar belt, with forty-eight factories drawing cane from the peasantry. By 1929, the island had a fully developed sugar sector, producing 745,000 metric tons of sugar per year that not only supplied Japan's market but also began to drive out Java sugar from China.[44] And then came the third major setback: China's Kuomintang government imposed a high import tariff of 50 percent on sugar from Java and Taiwan.[45]

In Cuba, meanwhile, the situation was hardly less desperate. To restore profitability, Wall Street financiers were keen to reduce Cuban production to 2.3 million tons, which was less than half from where it once stood. However, the Cuban *colonos,* who were the backbone of the Machado regime, revolted against the bankers of Wall Street, who were seen as keeping Cuba in their iron grip, and demanded a partial lifting of the quota. As a well-informed Dutch newspaper in Java observed, "M Machado *cannot* further reduce the harvest, because there is no money, there is large-scale hunger and misery in Cuba. Sugar must be produced to bring money to Cuba's population, to survive and to prevent their general uprising."[46]

The Chadbourne Plan now needed urgent revision to prevent its imminent collapse and the complete destruction of the world's two largest industrial cane sugar complexes. First of all, the division of the US market had to be renegotiated to ensure Cuba's access. Next, the deep suspicions Java and Cuba held about each other needed to be overcome. Chadbourne forged ahead, guided by the belief that the only way to end the devastating protectionist wave was to establish fair price setting, which unavoidably entailed production restrictions. The second iteration of the scheme, agreed after tortuous negotiations at the end of March 1932, allotted fixed export quotas to the major sugar producers. For Java, however, this brought no relief, because its potential to compete with its low cost prices of 2 cents per pound was curtailed by the fact that producers were not allowed to sell their sugar beneath of 2.5 cents per pound according to this agreement. The European CIBE and the American Sugar Kingdom had thrown the Java sugar industry under the bus.[47] In no way could it find new markets beyond Asia, which became increasingly self-reliant regarding sugar.

Huge volumes of sugar from the 1931 harvest became stuck in the warehouses of Java's port cities. One Java sugar factory after the other was mothballed or taken apart, and European employees were laid off by the thousand. The eastern salient of Java that once had attracted impoverished people from Central Java and the adjacent island of Madura now slid into hunger and misery. The once so proud Java sugar industry saw some of its factories sold off to India and its warehouses set on fire to destroy the sugar that under the Chadbourne agreement was no longer allowed to enter the market. By 1935, Java's production had dwindled to half a million tons—one-sixth of its production in 1930.[48] The people of Java, so many of whom relied on by-employment at this industry, suffered immensely, but, as expected, did not revolt.

In stark contrast and as many had predicted, the social unrest in Cuba that followed the production restrictions culminated in a revolution and the ousting from power of President Machado in 1933, who had firmly held the reins of power for many years, degenerating from a democratically elected politician into a brazenly corrupt and dictatorial ruler. What can be said for Machado, however, is that he put much of his political capital into putting ceilings on Cuban sugar production with the aim of diversifying the country's economy, strengthening the position of its sugar producers vis-à-vis the American banks, and assisting the hard-pressed Cuban sugar farmers. He had become the victim of the global sugar battles, which he had desperately tried to pacify. He was succeeded by a university professor, Ramón Grau San Martín, who came to power through a coup. After barely a hundred days, he was removed by Colonel Fulgencio Batista y Zaldivar, who would remain Cuba's most powerful politician until 1959, when he was ousted by Fidel Castro.

Meanwhile, it had become abundantly clear to the new US president, Franklin Roosevelt, that barring so much of Cuba's exports from the US market was not a wise policy at all. Although he had little sympathy for the Cuban sugar industry, which he considered to be overcapitalized and in the thrall of Wall Street, he was no friend of the domestic beet sugar industry either, because its demands for protectionism hurt industrial exports to commodity-producing countries such as Cuba.[49] Roosevelt focused on calibrating the various interests within the American Sugar Kingdom. The Jones-Costigan Act signed in 1934 was designed to help the hard-hit local beet sugar sector and the beet workers, and to provide better access for Cuban sugar to the US market. This improved economic conditions in Cuba and thus give US products a better market there.[50]

Still, domestic interests prevailed in this agreement, and the US refiners succeeded in keeping the import tariffs on refined Cuban sugar. The American beet sugar producers also obtained a production restriction on the Philippines, forcing it to destroy 60 percent of its sugar harvest of 1934, although the Roosevelt administration saw to it that the Philippines were financially compensated.[51] Ultimately, Roosevelt's New Deal entailed a retreat of the American Sugar Kingdom. It included the end of the colonialist Platt Amendment imposed on Cuba in 1902, a clear path toward Philippine independence, and a military withdrawal from Nicaragua and Haiti. It also nipped the emerging sugar industry in Haiti in the bud, which perfectly suited the interests of the US sugar corporations in the Hispanic Caribbean who drew their cheap labor from this deeply impoverished republic.[52]

Sugar behind Tariff Walls

In 1937, five years after the collapse of the Java sugar industry, the Pasuruan experimental station celebrated its fiftieth anniversary. A jubilee issue of a local newspaper, devoted to the festive occasion, highlighted the station's role in bringing Java's sugar industry to global prominence. The special issue conveyed some regret about the generosity with which Pasuruan had shared the fruits of its research with desperate sugar producers around the world, whose cane fields were being destroyed by plant diseases.[53] The rapid spread of the POJ 2878 wonder cane, such a hopeful sign of international collaboration to combat plant diseases and safeguard global food production, had quickly emerged as a structural factor in overproduction, as Manuel Rionda, the Spanish-Cuban sugar tycoon had already concluded in 1927.[54] POJ 2878's dominance had resulted in the dismal sight of dumping and the ruin of sugar economies; it was, by extension, one of the causes of the Wall Street Crash of 1929.

Chadbourne's valiant attempts to rescue global sugar capitalism from the jaws of protectionism were embedded in this tradition of internationalism. But it was also an internationalism that had abandoned the principle of free trade and now tried to find a balance between demand and supply through quotas, to the detriment of cane sugar producers that were economically capable of outcompeting beet sugar. After Wall Street had failed to prod the League of Nations into bringing the Chadbourne agreement under its auspices, some progress toward international, legally underpinned coordination was made with the International Sugar Agreement of 1937. It was supervised by the International Sugar Council, an intergovernmental institute with an office in The Hague and entrusted with the authority to impose punitive sanctions. However, this institution, of which revised versions continued to exist until 1977, could not reverse the marginalization of the open world market for sugar after the decline of Java and Cuba and the refusal of the US and European governments to reduce protections for their domestic sugar producers. The CIBE emerged as the model for other powerful agricultural lobbies that would three decades later shape the European Economic Community's—and subsequently the European Union's—common agricultural market, shielding Europe's farmers from global competition.[55]

The fundamental weakness of the International Sugar Agreement was its premise that sugar was a global commodity, when governments were increasingly treating it as a national staple. Countries one after another established tariff walls to protect and foster their own sugar industries. Creating price stability on their national markets led to a further shrinking of the international market, which engendered its volatility.[56] India led this trend toward protectionism, and Mexico, South Africa, Egypt, and Brazil followed suit by comprehensively modernizing their industries behind protective walls. Their industrial production rapidly increased and, in the case of Egypt, attracted farmers who in the 1920s had been driven back to their peasant sugar making when the factories had not been able to offer attractive prices for their cane.[57] In 1933, Brazil's President Gétulio Vargas established the Institute of Sugar and Alcohol to assist the hard-hit local sugar industry and stabilize prices. Indeed, it went so far as to partially integrate the sugar and energy sectors by making the addition of ethanol to gasoline mandatory.[58]

While the governments of Mexico, India, Egypt, and Brazil embarked on a planned development of their national sugar sectors, China started to build its own sugar industry. Just as we saw in the decades of upheaval after the revolutions in France and Haiti, expertise was transferred and this time even entire factories were taken apart and shipped to new frontiers in Florida, India, or China. China's warlords and the Kuomintang government could rely on the extensive Chinese diaspora in Southeast Asia and Java in particular to advance these ventures. In the early 1930s, the Chinese business communities in Java began intensifying their relationship with the Kuomintang government, with the Chinese-Indonesian tycoon Oei Tiong Ham, who had five sugar factories in Java by 1940, playing a prominent role.[59] Although these strengthened ties between the Chinese business communities in Java and China were greeted with understandable apprehension by the Java sugar industry, other commercial interests dominated, and eventually the colonial government itself sent a mission to China. As a collaborative project between Chinese business leaders in Java and high colonial government officials, this mission explored the potential of the huge Chinese market and was a clear indication of how much the power of the once mighty Java sugar industry had waned by the mid-1930s[60]

British Imperial Sugar Policies

In the late nineteenth century, Britain still influenced international sugar agreements, and the Brussels Convention was a crowning event of its economic diplomacy. By the 1920s, however, it was no longer the world's leading power, and it withdrew behind the fences of its still impressive empire. The idea of an imperial market was already propagated by Joseph Chamberlain's Tariff Reform League, founded in 1903, but since the consumer had to bear the costs, it did not stir much enthusiasm at that time. The Great Depression of the 1930s, however, made the British people ripe for a "shopping for the empire" campaign.[61] The British imperial sugar policies aimed at stable supplies of sugar, which had been seriously interrupted during World War I, while alleviating the plight of the West Indies, which had lost their American market. From less than 10 percent of its total sugar imports on the eve of World War I, Britain's sugar imports from its colonies grew to over 50 percent in the 1930s. In addition, Britain developed its own beet sugar industry partly with Dutch technology and Dutch co-ownership, which eventually would meet over a third of its national demand.[62] Reminiscent to the old sugar policies, the sugar colonies were discouraged, however, from investing in the latest technology that would have enabled them to produce an almost pure sugar, the so-called factory white, a policy which placated the British refiners.[63]

British endeavors to build an imperial or commonwealth economy with a division of tasks in which the dominions grew or mined the commodities to pay for the manufactured goods produced by Britain allowed the refiner Tate & Lyle to become one of the world's leading sugar producers. Much like the Havemeyers in New York (see Chapter 9), Henry Tate, who gave his name to the famous Tate Gallery in London, made his fortune at the time that the refining business transformed from an artisanal into a mass production. Born in 1819, Tate was originally a grocer owning six shops at the age of forty when he decided to enter the sugar business. In 1875, he signed a contract with David Martineau, a big name in sugar technology, as well as with the German Pfeifer Langen Company to obtain access to their patents and produce sugar in small cubes rather than conical sugar leaves.[64]

The sugar giant Tate & Lyle emerged in 1921, the result of a merger with the company founded by Abram Lyle, a Glasgow sugar refiner and the producer of Golden Syrup (a product that still exists today). This invention had saved his firm when sugar prices collapsed in 1884.[65] Within the British Empire and later the Commonwealth, Tate & Lyle would dominate the construction and planning of sugar factories, cane milling, molasses trade, sugar refining, and the marketing of sugar. It achieved, for instance, a dominant position in the West Indies at the end of the Great Depression. It took over the already heavily concentrated sugar industry in Trinidad and revived the ailing Jamaican sugar industry, which also received considerable investment from the US United Fruit Company.[66]

Tate & Lyle's only serious rival in Britain and the British West Indies was Booker McConnell. This firm's history dated back to 1815, the year of Napoleon's final defeat at Waterloo and the year that the British took over Demerara from the Dutch, who had created the tropical sugar polder below sea level. Josias Booker landed there first as plantation manager and later started a merchant firm together with his brothers. In 1835, he established a shipping line between Liverpool and Georgetown, the capital of British Guiana. John McConnell, who had started as a clerk working for Booker and his brothers in 1845, would eventually become the owner of this firm, which after 1890 operated under the name Booker McConnell. Originally a set of merchants and moneylenders backed up by British capital, the company acquired an impressive sugar conglomerate.[67] On the eve of World War II, the firm was joined by the even older British Guiana planter family of the Campbells, who had also started as traders before acquiring extensive plantation property in the 1780s when many West Indian planters defaulted. From the early 1950s, Jock Campbell would be in charge of Booker McConnell, and in 1969 established the prestigious Booker Prize.

11

The Proletariat

WHEN AMERICAN INDUSTRIALISTS ESTABLISHED the Central Aguirre sugar factory in Puerto Rico in 1899, they replaced the old mill and hacienda with state-of-the-art technology and built a complete village with houses for their expatriate employees. Compounds like this one could be found throughout the Caribbean region at the time, and also in colonial Java. Featuring all the modern conveniences and often including a swimming pool and a tennis court, these factory villages reflected existing notions of how to organize racial segregation in the sugar cane industry.[1] The cane workers, of course, would never enter such villages, and the expatriate workers had no need to ever leave them.

The sugar factory compound exemplified how industrialization had socially separated field and factory since the mid-nineteenth century, when enslaved were still operating the mills or working side by side with European technicians. The factory operations had now become the exclusive domain of well-paid staff. Managerial positions were filled almost exclusively by expatriates trained at vocational schools or even universities, enjoying generous salaries and sharing in the company's profits. A small class of locally hired staff for the factories—laboratory assistants and so on—received much lower wages, but they were still high compared to local standards. Next came the cane farmers. The majority of these had just a few hectares under cane, but there was usually a powerful minority consisting of big landowners. Most of the work was done by an immense army of cane harvesters—as well as beet workers for that matter—paid the bare minimum. In sum, by the early twentieth century a tripartition between factory staff, farmers, and cane harvesters had become the norm.

Sugar factory complex with housing for European employees, Central Java, circa 1935. Beginning in the late nineteenth century, cane sugar factories routinely included residential facilities for their expatriate staff.

Seasonal migrant laborers now began replacing indentured labor in the Americas, which still existed in many colonial cane fields at the turn of the twentieth century. In Natal, in South Africa they did, for instance. Here, mortality rates and the length of working days were not any better than in Cuba during the days of slavery. On Natal's Reynold's estate dozens of workers committed suicide due to the terrible conditions.[2] An outraged nationalist movement in India now demanded an end to indentured labor emigration. This was granted by the government of India in 1917, after over a million Indian troops had fought to defend the British Empire in World War I. Too often, however, the abolition of one abusive system only led to the adoption of another almost equally bad. When, for instance, the importation of Chinese workers into Peru was banned in 1874, they were quickly replaced by Japanese workers. And when such workers complained about "slave-like conditions," seasonal laborers were recruited from the hinterland and kept enthralled in debt via the financial tricks of the big sugar companies.[3]

The increasing availability of seasonal labor allowed employers to dispense with indentured labor, saving them considerable recruitment costs. Soaring global sugar consumption coupled with still incredibly labor-intensive harvesting required legions of such laborers. Historians of the industrial world have always put the spotlight on urban entrepreneurship, but the world economy would have come to a halt if millions had not grown and harvested cane and other export crops. In Java and Cuba alone, which accounted for half of the world's cane sugar exports, the industry employed over 1.7 million workers. Another six million worked in India's cane fields, and an unknown number in fields in other parts of the world such as China and mainland Latin America.[4] At the turn of the twentieth century, an estimated 1.2 million people, the majority consisting of women and children, populated the beet fields during the planting and harvesting season.[5] All in all, in the 1920s over ten million people stood in the world's beet and cane fields, most of whom for only part of the year. Nonetheless, sugar involved the work of more than 2 percent of the world population, which translated to 6–8 percent of all the world's households.

Young women were historically a critical source of labor in Javanese cane fields, supplying hundreds of thousands of workers every year. Here, women work a cane field in Tegal, Java, circa 1890.

The harvesters especially were the wretched of the earth, often driven by debts, drought, overpopulation, or all three combined. Cheap transport enabled massive seasonal migration flows. Trains carried hundreds of thousands of migrants to the sugar and tobacco fields of East Java, for instance, where daily wages were about 20–30 percent above the island's average. Besuki, the thinly populated residency (province) in East Java, was turned into a massive sugar and tobacco plantation belt. Hundreds of thousands came to settle there from other parts of Java and the adjacent island of Madura. They were joined by large numbers of seasonal laborers. Every year these would come by boat from Madura, for instance, and then walk to the sugar factories. In west India, seasonal workers traveled with their cattle from the dry hinterlands of the Bombay Deccan to the irrigated cane fields; seasonal workers came to Pernambuco in Brazil and to Tucumán in Argentina every year. The Philippines saw extensive migrations from the northwestern Ilocano provinces to the cane fields of Luzon's heartlands, and later on even to the sugar island of Negros, where in the 1940s at least fifty thousand male seasonal migrants were employed.[6] The Hawaiian planters recruited 160,000 Japanese between 1885 and 1907 when the United States and Japan made their Gentlemen's Agreement to stop Japanese labor immigration.[7] The Hawaiian planters then managed to recruit a total of 130,000 Filipinos, facilitated by the fact that the Philippines had become US territory after 1898.

Meanwhile, sugar-producing states recruited a growing number of Europeans to counterbalance the influx of Asian, Polynesian, or Afro-Caribbean workers. In Louisiana, every year about sixty thousand Sicilians came to the cane fields in the late nineteenth century to be joined by smaller contingents from a multitude of nations.[8] Hawaii brought 25,000–30,000 people categorized as "Caucasian" to work in the cane fields. Cuba, however, implemented the most radical engineering of its immigration to protect the country's Hispanic identity. Between 1882 and 1898, it attracted and often sponsored over half a million Spanish immigrants and another 750,000 arrived over the next twenty-five years. This considerably strengthened the European-settler character of Cuba, although labor shortages persisted because in the early twentieth century only 40 percent of the Spanish migrants stayed.[9] The immigrants mostly came from Spanish Galicia, Asturias, and the Canary Islands, but thousands also arrived from Poland, Ukraine, Italy, Turkey, and Syria.

The government of the Dominican Republic, where American companies operated large cane farms, tried to stem the influx of cane workers from Haiti and the West Indies by issuing vagrancy laws to force Dominicans to work on the plantations. They also sought to attract workers from Puerto Rico, who were considered to be Hispanics, and even tried to recruit labor from India. It was all to no avail, however, as the number of West Indian workers only increased and continued to grow after 1912, even though all immigrants except "Caucasians" had to apply for permission to enter the country. Fines for illicitly importing workers and prohibitively high prices for immigration permits for Haitians and West Indians were widely circumvented by the sugar industry. West Indians might be stopped in the ports, but they could easily disembark elsewhere on the coast. Tens of thousands of Haitians came without formal permission through the porous border that ran across the island. In 1916, the US began a military occupation and administration of the Dominican Republic and immediately rescinded the restrictive migration regulations to boost the sugar industry.[10]

Rafael Trujillo, dictator of the Dominican Republic from 1930 until his assassination in 1961—when the CIA allegedly had had enough of him—had it both ways: he allowed cheap Haitian labor in for the sugar sector while framing his country as a "Mulatto" and "Hispanic" republic. Shortly after having agreed on a border with his Haitian counterpart in 1936 at a conference in which the two presidents showered each other with words of friendship and cooperation, Trujillo sent his soldiers to the borderlands to launch the genocide of fifteen thousand ethnic Haitian Dominicans to underscore the Hispanic character of the Dominican Republic. His militarizing of the border area, meanwhile, cynically served the economic objective of catching undocumented Haitian immigrants and directing them toward the sugar estates.[11]

Eventually, Afro-Caribbeans came to the cane fields of Cuba as well, when labor shortages emerged during World War I. About 180,000 individual workers arrived from Haiti—which was under US occupation from 1915 to 1929—and were joined by 140,000 British West Indians, mostly from Jamaica, all in search of alternative employment after the completion of the Panama Canal in 1914.[12] Many entered the harbor of Santiago de Cuba at the eastern tip of the island, which was only a few hundred kilometers from Haiti and Jamaica but others landed undocumented elsewhere on Cuba's eastern coast.[13] In addition, thousands more came from all over the

Caribbean region and ten thousand from China—the Chinese Exclusion Act was lifted for the occasion. They were all treated as second-rate and low-paid workers.[14]

Meanwhile, rapid population growth in Europe's countryside resulted in millions of farms too small to make a living from and millions of rural workers without any land at all. Seasonal agricultural and rural migration toward the beet fields allowed peasants to keep their land and sometimes extend their property. Saxony received hundreds of thousands of workers from overpopulated rural areas in Poland and Galicia. Their conditions were not any better than those of the seasonal workers in Cuba. They were not free to change employer and under legal compulsion to return after the harvest. Through their identity papers, which listed their own name and their employer, they were kept under surveillance. Female labor dominated the beet fields, the women working in gangs under supervision of a man.[15]

Meanwhile, workers from the deeply impoverished Flemish countryside went to the beet fields of adjacent northern France.[16] They worked thir-

Polish workers weeding a beet field in Funen, Denmark, 1913. Twentieth-century US and European planters relied heavily on immigrant workers to tend beet fields and gather the harvest.

teen to fourteen hours a day and slept in stables, but they could earn five times more than as farm hands in Flanders. The men also brought their women and children, emptying schools and defying the law on compulsory education. Luckier workers found employment in the beet sugar factories, where they sometimes could climb the social ladder, although they too had to work eighteen-hour workdays during the harvest.[17] When better-paid factory work was not an option, European beet workers' families tried their luck across the ocean when they had assembled sufficient money to buy boat tickets. Facilitated by cheap steamship connections, Europeans from the impoverished countryside traveled all the way to the beet sugar belts of the US Midwest, where many of them would eventually settle.[18]

Whereas in industrialized societies workers were allowed to unionize, which often improved their conditions, in the sugar cane belts oppression intensified as the colonial bourgeoisie passed the burden of depressed global sugar prices on to the laborers in the field. Workers hired under indentured labor contracts were not in any position to protest the hardships imposed upon them following the sugar crisis of 1884. In Hawaii, for instance, employers reacted to low sugar prices by no longer paying the fares of their indentured Japanese workers across the Pacific.[19] If not indentured, many workers were still subject either to informal coercion, as was the case in Java or in the Philippine island of Negros, or to Louisiana's appalling racialized labor oppression. Sometimes slavery even resurfaced, for instance at the sugar-producing haciendas of Mexico's southern Yucatan. The much mistreated source of labor there were the Yaquis, the native American population of Sonora in the north of Mexico, who were deported en masse to Yucatan as chattel slaves after their failed revolt in the 1880s.[20]

Even if cane or beet field workers were not exposed to outright oppression, they were left behind by the emerging labor unions, which initially were only present in the factories. Field workers nonetheless resisted underpayment and oppression by their bosses, as they had always done. The oldest and most common way for seasonal workers to defend their interests was by traveling and working in labor gangs under a leader who negotiated on their behalf. Through acting as a collective, they could apply leverage to the factories who relied on the gangs to get the harvest done. Madurese, Haitian, and Philippine cane cutters as well as Mexican beet workers in California, all formed labor gangs under their own headmen.[21]

Arson had been another weapon resorted to by workers since the earliest Atlantic slave plantations. Cane is highly inflammable when ready for harvesting. The air around cane fields would regularly be full of thick smoke. In Cuba, these fires were particularly frequent during years of crisis such as the Ten Years' War (1868–1878), the War of Independence (1895–1898), and the Great Depression (1929–1939). Sugar factories suffered considerable losses through arson and usually failed to identify the culprits. In the 1920s, sugar factories in Java addressed the problem of cane fires ignited by disgruntled small peasants and cane cutters by hiring an extensive private police force to guard the fields during harvest.[22]

In the 1880s, strikes in cane fields were recorded across the globe. Servile laborers struck in dozens of sugar and indigo estates in Java, and many others simply quit.[23] In Martinique, unsuccessful strikes occurred in 1885 after employers halved their wages. Fifteen years later, strikes broke out again, resulting in the killing of ten strikers in a clash with a small military force at one factory. The outrage about this bloodshed forced the factories to negotiate with the workers as the island's administration did not have the means to suppress such a large movement.[24] There was also blood spilled in Suriname, where plantations faced fierce labor resistance after 1884. After two hundred furious workers had killed the director of the Marienburg plantation for lowering their wages and not taking their demands for better wages seriously, an army platoon arrived and killed twenty-four workers.[25] This tragedy was the result of years of frustration about shrinking wages and extensive and arbitrary punishments under the indentured labor system.

Heavy police and even military suppression occurred throughout the Caribbean region and prevented any sustained action to bring wages on par with rising prices. Labor unrest continued to hold the West Indies in its grip in the 1890s, on a scale alarming enough for London to send an investigative Royal Commission.[26] Interestingly, the investigators recommended diversifying crops and breaking up plantations, rightfully pointing out that smallholder production of sugar was cheaper. The commission did not see much of a future for the West Indian sugar industry, however, because of the relentless beet sugar dumping—this was a few years before the Brussels Convention. It made the pointed argument that Britain could not dodge its responsibility for a black population whose ancestors it had carried to this part of the world.[27] This did not result in concrete improvements, however. Wages stayed frozen, and in 1905 a dockworkers' strike in the harbor of Georgetown in British Guiana rapidly spread to sugar plantations. The deadly clashes that followed were the culmination of thirty years of stagnant wages and hardship. What started as a strike became an uprising that could only be suppressed with the assistance of hastily dispatched warships and marines.[28]

At the turn of the twentieth century, more and more cane workers began to unite to demand better wages and working conditions. The aftermath of World War I and the Russian Revolution of 1917 produced a wave of workers' activism in the sugar industry across the globe, although most unions were suppressed. Nonetheless, communist labor organizations continued to appeal to immigrant beet and cane workers because they upheld the ideal of international and thus interethnic solidarity against employers who used ethnic divides to weaken labor resistance. In the end, the impressive waves of labor activism during the Great Depression yielded mixed results, because the position of immigrant field workers was weakened by mass unemployment. Yet the misery in the cane and beet fields exposed how sugar monocropping had brought about alarming vulnerability and persistent poverty to large populations. This resulted in a number of reports and investigations in the 1930s that addressed the structural problems of the world's sugar belts, such as lack of economic diversification, malnutrition, glaring rural social inequalities, and overpopulation. These publications would lay the groundwork for the birth of the academic discipline of development economics in the 1950s and 1960s, as we will see below.

Discrimination in the US and German Beet Fields

In 1902, both Henry Oxnard, the beet sugar baron, and Herbert Myrick, the populist propagandist for beet sugar, testified to the Ways and Means Committee of the US Congress on the subject of a possible reciprocity treaty with Cuba.[29] They feared with real justification that sugar producers in the United States would be no match for Cuba's factories, which could rely on hundreds of thousands of impoverished Caribbeans for the seasonal harvest. Myrick, and the populist senator Francis G. Newlands for that matter, were right about the word "coolie" being used pejoratively to refer to migrant laborers without any rights. But the two conveniently ignored that within the American Sugar Kingdom the buoyant beet sugar industry relied as much on immigrant labor as the Caribbean cane fields did. Eastern Europeans came to Michigan and Japanese laborers disembarked in California, where they were hired in great numbers at the beet sugar farms. From here they moved further into the interior of the United States. Mexicans, meanwhile, took the train to California and Texas but also increasingly to the North as far as to Michigan, where about fifteen thousand Mexican workers worked in the beet fields by about 1930.[30]

Wealthy countries usually did not have the labor force to work in the cane or beet fields, and this pertained to the United States to the same extent as to Germany or France, whose own rural populations had moved to the cities. Rural workers stood at the bottom of the labor hierarchy and their protection lagged behind industrial labor regulations and welfare provisions. The conditions of immigrant beet workers were even worse. They were usually not paid daily wages but on the basis of fulfilled tasks, which were taken on by entire families. The immigrant workers could expect little from local labor unions that were primarily worried about the depressing effect on wages by the influx of impoverished newcomers.

Such concerns were raised in the United States as well as in Germany, with its massive presence of predominantly Polish seasonal beet workers, and even in Cuba when tens of thousands of workers from Haiti and the West Indies came to the cane fields.[31] None other than the famous German sociologist Max Weber concluded disapprovingly after his research on the rural labor market in eastern Germany that it was in the interest of the Junkers, the landowning aristocratic families that each owned hundreds of acres of beet land, to import Polish workers to weaken the position of the German labor class.[32] The same thing was done by employers in almost every sugar belt in the United States. American labor unions were therefore just as worried about the influx of foreign laborers as Weber. The Mexican anthropologist Manuel Gamio, one of the first to conduct systematic research on Mexican migration to the United States, observed in 1926 that the American Federation of Labor was hostile to Mexican immigration because without the influx of these laborers, "the American worker would receive higher wages than he does."[33]

Again, Weber and the American Federation of Labor seriously misjudged how little immigrant labor markets and national labor markets interacted, because neither in the United States nor in Prussia was local labor available in sufficient numbers for the beet fields. In Cuba too, cane cutting was increasingly left to immigrant laborers. But it was also true that employers saw a distinct advantage in hiring "aliens" who lacked the protection citizens enjoyed, and in the United States the Mexican seasonal beet workers were never supposed to settle and had to travel back and forth. Precisely because of this, they were exempted from the mandatory literacy test that was part of the US Immigration Act of 1917.[34] Indeed, the question for employers and governments was not whether or not to allow Polish workers into Germany or Mexican workers into the United States, but how to prevent them from settling.

The Mexicans who began to arrive in the United States from the end of World War I experienced an increasingly restrictive migration regime. They were considered to be a captive labor force, culturally distinct and, according to the US census of 1930, a separate race. Store and barber shops put up signs saying "No Mexicans Allowed."[35] The racist argument that Mexicans could never become settlers cynically ignored the fact that so many of them had become US citizens after the United States had expanded its borders over almost half of the Mexican territory in the 1840s. Tragically, these racist attitudes culminated in a wave of xenophobic frenzy in the early years of the Great Depression, when at least four hundred thousand and possibly as many as 1.8 million Mexicans and Mexican Americans were rounded up and deported in blatant disregard of whether they were American citizens or not, putatively to make room for American unemployed.[36]

Many beet farmers and factories tried to shield their workers from the deportation craze. The Great Western Sugar Company urged its workers to stay out of the cities during winter, where they ran a higher risk of deportation, and promised them work for the next season. Such desperation proved that the US beet sugar sector could not exist without Mexican workers and belied Newlands's propaganda that lauded beet sugar as "white native" sugar. In the early 1930s, over half of the beet workers in the United States were Mexicans or Americans of Mexican descent.[37]

Although desperately needed, the Mexican men, women, and children who came to the beet fields lived under harsh conditions. Their work was organized in such a way that family heads actually became subcontractors, bringing their children into the field as well. Families did backbreaking work twelve hours a day, earning just $340 per harvesting season. Since this was an income for 6.4 persons on average, it gave individual workers less than what cane cutters earned in Cuba or Hawaii. Children, sometimes as young as seven years old, handled sharp knives, and chronic malnutrition meant they were usually much smaller than the average child of their age group. Having for many years referred to the vices attending the Cuban plantation system to urge protection of the domestic sugar industry, the beet sugar producers were eventually called to account in the 1930s. Concerns raised by human rights activists resulted in provisions in the Jones-Costigan Act of 1934 and the Sugar Act of 1937 that federal subsidies would only be available for American beet farmers who paid the minimum wage set by the secretary of agriculture and did not employ children under the age of fourteen in the fields.[38]

Started as a temporary measure to address urgent labor shortages at the end of World War I, Mexican labor immigration became an enduring and indispensable part of American economic life, with all the attendant racism and political hypocrisy. During World War II, the Mexican beet workers were again desperately needed, because the government decided to allow the acreage under sugar beet to grow by 25 percent, just when many farm hands had been conscripted into the army. Sugar at that time was a strategic commodity, not just for consumption but also as the raw material for acetone, a key item for ammunition. In 1942, the United States and Mexico signed the Mexican Farm Labor Agreement, which became known as the Bracero program. The agreement brought about 63,000 Mexican workers across the border to supplement the 33,000 interned Japanese Americans who were put to work in the cane fields of Oregon, Utah, Idaho, Montana, and Colorado.[39] Although the "white nativist" beet sugar propaganda spread by Myrick and Newlands never degenerated into genocide as did Trujillo's anti-Africanism, it was equally hypocritical: open racism served to deny workers' rights and was co-responsible for the mass deportations of Mexicans and Mexican Americans of the early 1930s.

Labor Resistance in Hawaii and California

The concerns of Weber, Cuban intellectuals, and the American Federation of Labor that immigrant laborers were taking jobs away from the natives were not justified. However, bringing in immigrant labor was an effective weapon for employers determined to degrade their workers' hard-won right to unionize. That the national labor unions saw the immigrants as unfair competitors further facilitated employers in pitting different ethnic groups of workers against each other. The beet sugar employers in California and the Hawaiian Sugar Planters' Association (HSPA) were true masters in this respect. While driven by the desire to be a white American settlers' colony and to sell their sugar as "domestic," the haole sugar planters relied on cheap disenfranchised labor in order to stay competitive on the US market, where they had to compete with Cuban sugar imports. Victor Clark, the US commissioner on labor conditions in Hawaii, had harsh words to say about this opportunism in his report for Congress in 1915: "The policy pursued by the United States and by the Territory of Hawaii toward Immigration has always been both inconsistent and opportunistic. When times were good and sugar prospects bright the Territory turned to Europe for new settlers and tried to foster small farming and to increase its citizen population. When times were bad and the future of the sugar industry uncertain employers centered attention exclusively upon cheap Asiatic labor."[40]

Haole opportunism would reach new heights a few years after Clark's harsh verdict, when the HSPA petitioned Congress to lift the ban on Chinese labor imports. Actually, a precedent in this area had already been set for Cuba's booming sugar industry during World War I. But this time it was less about shortages and more about muzzling labor activism. The HSPA petition came in the aftermath of a four-month mass strike among the 10,354 Filipino and 24,791 Japanese plantation workers. On Capitol Hill, the Hawaiian planters played the card of the Asian threat, portraying the strike as an attempt by the Japanese residents of Hawaii to take over the islands from the Americans.[41] Although the House Committee on Immigration and Naturalization consented to consider "an emergency remedy for the acute labor shortage in Hawaii," the HSPA must have regretted that they brought their case to Washington because labor organizations were also invited, and they highlighted the blatant opportunism on the part of the HSPA, just as Clark had. Those at Washington included George W. Wright, the president of the Central Labor Council of Honolulu, the forerunner of the local chapter of the American Federation of Labor. In his letter to the House committee, he promised to resist "flooding the plantations with a horde of coolies."[42] Paul Scharrenberg, member of California's Commission of Immigration and Housing and a local union leader hit the final nail in the coffin: "Mr. Chairman, I desire to enter a protest against the importation of laborers from any country who are to be held in peonage."[43]

Besides divide-and-rule, intimidation of labor leaders was a common fea-
ture in US beet and cane fields. In Hawaii, the HSPA regularly evicted
strikers from their plantation lodges, once even in the midst of the 1918
influenza pandemic, forcing workers to sleep in the streets of Honolulu.[44]
Police officers could easily be bought, as happened in Puerto Rico, and they
even used their guns against strikers, which occurred at a demonstration of
the Japanese-Mexican workers union in Oxnard's Chinatown in 1903.[45]
Violence was provoked and used as pretext to arrest union leaders, as happened to Pablo Manlapit, the Philippine labor leader in Hawaii who was
railroaded into prison. His rights were violated by a legal system thoroughly
corrupted by the all-powerful haole planters. To avoid harsher punishment,
he accepted exile in California. Hawaii's governor, Wallace R. Farrington,
who was responsible for making extradition conditional on parole, came
to the pier to wish Manlapit bon voyage. Manlapit did not blame the
governor, knowing that he had to follow the instructions of the haole
plantocracy.[46]

Communism and International Labor Solidarity

Against the backdrop of the divide-and-rule policies of employers and the
wariness of national labor unions to accept migrant workers as their members, communist activists who campaigned for international workers'
solidarity made headway among cane and beet workers. The October Revolution in Moscow in 1917 reverberated widely through the world of sugar
and ignited widespread labor activism against high sugar prices, tremendous
profits for sugar factories, and real wages being depressed by inflation.
Strikes occurred in places as far away as Peru, the Dominican Republic,
Cuba, Puerto Rico, Hawaii, the West Indies, and Java. Demands often
involved eight-hour workdays and for wage hikes to compensate for inflation during the World War I.[47] Colonial governments, impressed by the
spirit of self-determination unleashed by US president Woodrow Wilson
and by the establishment of the League of Nations, acted with some restraint toward this labor unrest. In 1919, the Indonesian labor union of sugar
workers, which boasted a thirty-thousand-strong membership, was recognized by the colonial government as a legitimate representative of labor.[48]
In the West Indies, meanwhile, revolutionary fervor was fueled by soldiers
returning from the front in Europe; their demands were now much harder

to ignore. Labor unions were accordingly legalized in Jamaica in 1919, and one year later in Trinidad.

In the 1920s, extensive labor migration in the Caribbean region carried Spanish anarchism, Garveyism (i.e., the movement founded by the Jamaican Marcus Garvey calling for black self-reliance and Pan-Africanism), and communism to almost every Caribbean sugar island. Cuba, the world's largest cane sugar producer with labor immigrants from all over the region, emerged as the center of communist labor activism and the defied systematic repression of the authorities. Strikes had already occurred in 1917 demanding an eight-hour workday plus the recognition of labor unions, but they were quickly suppressed with the help of US marines.[49] In 1924, new strikes broke out with the same demands and this time they expanded from the Cuban factories into the fields. They were squashed a few months later by the new government of Gerardo Machado, yet the communist organizers miraculously kept a functioning union intact, which in 1933 would play a prominent role in the ousting of Machado.[50]

In Southeast Asia as well, communist movements faced state persecution that was often instigated by plantation owners. In the Netherlands Indies (or colonial Indonesia), a strike on the eve of the sugar harvest by the radical socialist railway union was quickly suppressed, and this ushered in a general clampdown on labor unions. Colonial Indonesia still had the largest communist movement in Southeast Asia, but it was eliminated after an untimely insurrection in 1926, which ushered in a spate of oppressive measures. New weapons were added to the policing arsenal, such as the gathering of 160,000 fingerprints by Java's Sugar Syndicate to detect known political propagandists among the labor force in the factories and among the *mandurs* (headmen) in the field.[51] After the communist party was liquidated in Indonesia, a tremendous setback for the movement, it managed to gain a serious foothold in the Philippine countryside. Hunger and oppression by the Philippine landlords, or hacenderos, provoked widespread resistance, manifesting itself in the torching of many a cane field. Here, communist rebellion became endemic, and in the 1930s the Hukbalahap guerrillas emerged in the sugar and rice belts of Luzon, where landlessness and poverty had become rampant.[52]

Whereas in Southeast Asia radical labor activism was suppressed and went mostly underground, in the Caribbean region, and in Cuba in particular, it actually drove political change. Thousands went to the cities in "caravans of hunger," as they were called by contemporaries.[53] Strikes broke out in 1933, and the communist National Confederation of Cuban Workers played a central role in forging cross-national solidarity. This was explicitly advocated by the Caribbean bureau of the Communist International (Comintern) and the Communist Party of the United States, both of which directed their attention to the sugar industry around 1930. From August to October 1933, field and mill workers in Cuba, with active participation and leadership of literate and vocal Jamaicans often seconded by Haitians, seized factories and estates and established soviets. The Cuban communist labor movement continued its opposition against the first presidency of Ramón Grau San Martín (September 1933–January 1934) when it started to deport 150,000–200,000 Caribbean immigrant workers as part of his "Cuban national"-oriented policies, which were rooted in nineteenth-century aspirations of a Hispanic white Cuba.[54]

Meanwhile, anti-American feelings erupted throughout the Hispanic Caribbean. Offices of US banks were the most visible emblems of US imperialism, which was held at least partly responsible for the misery of the Great Depression. Some regional offices of Wall Street banks became the targets of bombs. Trujillo, the dictator of the Dominican Republic, cynically used anti-American sentiment to appropriate much of City Bank's assets. Cuba's Machado had seized upon growing discontent with US dominance and imposed additional taxes on US banks and companies to prop up the finances of his regime that was suffering from declining sugar prices. At least this is how City Bank felt about it.[55]

The people of Puerto Rico had particularly good reason to blame US corporations and banks for their misery. The vertical integration of the most important Puerto Rican central sugar factories with US refiners' interests backed up by J. P. Morgan and the City Bank left only a tiny share of profits in Puerto Rico. These were further reduced by the factories selling their sugar to the affiliated refineries in the United States down the chain well below market prices. Puerto Rico lost substantial tax income through such accounting tricks, as the outraged treasurer of this US territory detailed when he took his case to court.[56]

Exposure of these machinations added to the growing anti-imperialist mood in Puerto Rico, where about a quarter of the laboring population worked in the sugar industry earning a pittance. On top of this, they had to pay industrialized-world prices for foodstuffs and clothing.[57] Puerto

Rico's dismal situation was extensively detailed by a report of the Brookings Institution, which had been commissioned by Victor Clark, who had made a distinguished career reporting on labor issues in the Philippines, Indonesia, and Hawaii. The impoverished Puerto Ricans, incensed by how their island was defrauded by Wall Street interests, followed Cuba with strikes in 1933–1934.[58]

The desperate hunger of the masses played into the communists' hands. The vice-president of the US United Fruit Company, a major investor in Cuba, noticed in 1934 that "U.S. tariff policies have ruthlessly destroyed [Cuba's] very life. . . . The great mass of her people are underfed and underclothed. They are so beset with the consequent unrest that they are easy prey to communists who are flooding to Cuba."[59] Cuba's new strongman, Fulgencio Batista, shrewdly exploited the fears of corporate America by intensifying government control over the sugar industry and the country's economy at large. He gave the waged workers a share in the sugar profits and granted them an eight-hour workday.[60] But while Cuban workers benefited from Batista's policies to alleviate their economic plight, the large migratory rural proletariat coming from Haiti and Jamaica faced a new round of expulsions in 1937.[61]

The cane workers expelled from Cuba brought their familiarity with communist activism back to the Caribbean region. In October 1931, a hunger riot occurred in the capital of Suriname, Paramaribo, and a leftist labor movement emerged with strong communist influences; it was immediately suppressed by the authorities. Poverty and misery fueled widespread protests on sugar estates in Trinidad, Jamaica, Guiana, Barbados, and Saint Vincent. Protesters took to the streets throughout the region in the 1930s. Hunger marches occurred across the French, British, Spanish, and Dutch Caribbean.[62] Strikes erupted at the Booker McConnell sugar estates in British Guiana in 1934, and labor unrest would continue in the years after. In 1935, starving people raided potato fields in Barbados and their desperation and anger culminated in an island-wide rebellion two years later.[63] Elsewhere in the British Empire, in Mauritius, workers and smallholders rose up when wages and payments for cane fell. Cane fields went up in flames and one clash at a sugar factory resulted in several casualties.[64]

But the most sustained and successful movement of sugar workers within the British Empire emerged in Jamaica, where the Great Depression had forced thirty thousand people home, mainly from Cuba. Some carried valuable first-hand experience in organizing workers with them. The sugar factories became a flashpoint in the Jamaican labor movement. A large sugar strike erupted at the Frome factory owned by Tate & Lyle (see Chapter 10), which held 61,500 acres of land in Jamaica and treated its workers as disposable. Cane fires flared up, police were rushed to the factory, and the ensuing confrontation resulted in several casualties and dozens of wounded. Leaders and workers now felt that they were fighting not only for better wages but also against racism and international imperialism, typified at that time by the Italian invasion of Ethiopia. More strikes, meetings, and demonstrations with thousands of people followed. In this atmosphere, the arrest of their leader, Alexander Bustamante, only served to make him a celebrity.[65] His Industrial Trade Union, formed in 1938, achieved its first major victory in 1941 with an island-wide sugar contract for workers after a long strike. It was a significant win, although insufficient to fully address the miserable conditions of the field workers.[66]

Last but not least, the US beet sugar fields—and the Hawaiian cane fields for that matter—became sites of labor activism that made important gains against discrimination and the oppression of labor unionism. Labor activism received a boost from the Roosevelt administration and from the Jones-Costigan Act of 1934, which tied the granting of sugar quotas to improving labor conditions.[67] Both in California and the Midwest, interracial labor unionism emerged, as it had done in Cuba, to protect the interests of the migrant workers neglected by national organizations. The communist Cannery and Agricultural Workers Industrial Union led over 37,000 agricultural and packing workers, both Mexican nationals and Mexican Americans, in numerous strikes against appallingly low wages.[68] The employers, in this case the beet-growing farmers associated with the Oxnard factory, responded by using police repression and hiring thugs to deny "Mexican peons" the right to unionize. They thought they would be able to fall back on their usual divide-and-rule tactics, replacing Mexican workers with Filipinos who were reluctant to join the radical union. Their reservations melted away, however, when Filipino activists discovered they were not safe from mob violence either.[69]

Yet the position of the labor unions for beet and cane workers in the United States was structurally weak. The acreage planted with beet had shrunk substantially, and itinerant workers were desperately in search of work. In the Great Lakes region, factories simply refused to negotiate with the unions representing the beet workers, hiding behind the fact that not they but the subcontractors were the real employers of the workers.[70] E. J. Eagen, the director of the National Labor Relations Board, which was established in 1935 to safeguard labor rights, visited Hawaii for nine months in 1937–1938 and arrived at the damning but hardly surprising conclusion that the planters practically owned the islands.[71]

Cane and beet workers had become a radical force for change during the Great Depression, but despite the sugar protectionism of Britain and the United States, which allowed for some improvement in labor conditions in Jamaica, Cuba, and the United States, the overall position of rural immigrant workers remained precarious. Even if they were allowed to organize—in colonial Indonesia the right to do so was all but extinct— they usually remained outside the mainstream labor movement. Nonetheless, labor resistance, the rising expectations of workers in the course of the 1930s, and particularly the glaring discrepancy between the promises of early welfare policies and the grim realities of the cane and beet fields, created an urgent sense of crisis that would be addressed by a new economic paradigm.

The Birth of Development Economics

The millions of the seasonal workers in the world's cane or beet fields could barely subsist, and their makeshift housing was invariably unhealthy. Even the Mexican families who could afford a car—sometimes sponsored by their employer[72]—to drive to the beet fields in California, to the Midwest, or to Michigan still lived in shacks and their children had to perform exhausting, dirty, and dangerous fieldwork. The seasonal Polish beet workers in German Saxony might be worse off than the seasonal cane workers in Cuba, although the latter were still lodged in the same barracks where enslaved had lived, and their conditions were equated with those of slavery by critical observers. Even before the Great Depression, poverty had struck the world's cane and beet fields and sugar exporters were trapped in a situation of declining prices. The Caribbean plantation-dominated economies were criticized for their lack of industrialization and dependency on the United States by the eminent Cuban historian Ramiro Guerra y Sánchez in his *Sugar and Population in the Antilles,* which was published in 1927.[73]

The sugar crisis that evolved in the late 1920s was the second of its kind within half a century. The aftermath of the crisis of 1884, which had lingered for about twenty years, had been a dismal period for most cane sugar-producing areas in the world. The Brussels Convention of 1902 had raised the prospect for improvement because it forced beet sugar producers to scale down exports of their bounty-fed sugar. It had, however, mainly benefited the Cuban and Java sugar industries, which rapidly expanded their production. Most smaller sugar-producing colonies languished, particularly in the Caribbean region.

In the 1930s, economists and politicians recognized that the world had too many sugar producers, which was making their future look grim—not only in the Caribbean region but in Southeast Asia as well. In the once prosperous sugar districts of East Java, people were now starving. All over Java, death rates went up and the physical strength of laborers diminished because of undernourishment. Workers in the Philippine cane fields were often underfed as well, and population pressures turned conditions desperate in the most densely parts of the Philippine countryside.[74]

The sugar crisis of the 1930s led to calls for government intervention to combat severe poverty through fostering manufacturing and food production instead of furthering the growth of commodity exports. There were different models and ideological orientations involved, but all shared the same ambition of finding a third way between unhinged capitalism and communism. Fabianism, a moderate form of democratic socialism that originated in late nineteenth-century England, rapidly gained political momentum in the British Empire from India to the West Indies and was propagated by both the leading nationalist Jawaharlal Nehru, later Prime Minister of India, and the economist John Maynard Keynes. In the United States, the New Deal managed to reach the cane and beet fields. In Brazil and Mexico, and later Argentina, strong charismatic presidents advanced corporatism, and various degrees of revolutionary fervor led to governments organizing society as a body in which different sectors, and capital and labor in particular, had to cooperate in harmony.

In Cuba, Batista steered a course of economic populism in his two-front struggle against American sugar interests and the revolutionary party of his rival Grau. In 1938, he even allowed the Communist Party and labor unions to come out of hiding, where they had been since the strikes of 1933–1934. He sought their support for the simple reason that they were the enemies of Grau.[75] When Batista visited the United States in his quest for lower US import tariffs, he announced that he would travel to revolutionary Mexico too and publicly toyed with the idea of nationalizing the Cuban sugar industry. All of this was to outmaneuver the Grau nationalists and the sugar oligarchs.[76] Meanwhile, in Puerto Rico, Luis Muñoz Marín founded the Popular Democratic Party in 1937, taking aim at the power of the big American companies dominating the island's sugar sector. After four years of campaigning, he managed to form a government with the specific mission of land reform and the strict implementation of the five-hundred-acre limit for US-owned land.[77]

Even the most export-oriented commodity-producing economies such as colonial Indonesia considered encouraging small industry, a policy that had hitherto been swept aside by pressure from the powerful sugar industry intent on keeping living standards low in rural Java so that it could continue to obtain land and labor cheaply. In a major effort to raise rural income, the colonial government decided to stop cheap rice imports from Thailand, Burma, and Vietnam in order to protect the Java rice market. This indeed breathed new life in Java's crippled manufacturing sector.[78] Diversification of the tropical economies had to guide future policies, concluded Bob van Gelderen, a prominent Dutch economist, former head of the Statistical Bureau of the Netherlands Indies and a social democrat. In his book, published in 1939, he showed how the collapse of the Java sugar industry had opened the door to a more diversified development of the island's rural economy.[79]

In the same year that Van Gelderen's book appeared, the young economist and later Nobel Prize winner William Arthur Lewis published his essay *Labour in the West Indies: The Birth of a Workers' Movement* with the Fabian Society. Like Van Gelderen, Lewis was motivated by the traumatic conditions of mass unemployment, malnutrition, and even hunger in the plantation societies during the Great Depression.[80] In the years that followed, Lewis further developed his analysis of the economic predicament of plantation societies. Eventually, in his famous article "Economic Development with Unlimited Supplies of Labour" published in 1954, he would succinctly explain why the global sugar industry combined exceptionally high productivity gains with poverty for its workers: "workers in the sugar industry continue to walk barefooted and to live in shacks, while workers in wheat enjoy among the highest living standards in the world. The reason is that wages in the sugar industry are related to the fact that the subsistence sectors of tropical economies are able to release however many workers the sugar industry may want, at wages which are low, because tropical food production per head is low."[81]

Lewis made the crucial point that low productivity in food agriculture was one of the underlying factors of low wages. The corollary of this was that improving domestic agriculture was a key ingredient in economic development.[82] In addition, Lewis pointed to the lasting legacies of plantation societies, such as gross inequality, racial divisions, and lack of upward mobility.[83] He related these conditions to the unfavorable position of commodity-producing countries. At the core of the current economic system were the imperial and financial centers that Lewis argued were oligopolistic economic structures—we may think here of cartels of refiners and producers such as Havemeyer's Trust or Germany's South German Sugar Company—whereas the periphery was exporting to highly competitive markets. He saw the world divided between core and periphery countries, terms he took from the Argentine economist Raúl Prebisch and which would become key notions for postwar development economics.[84] Sugar provided an eminent example of Lewis's theory. After all, the number of sugar-exporting countries had grown rapidly over the nineteenth century, whereas the core countries and major markets had organized themselves in three major blocks.

This configuration, Lewis maintained, was making it increasingly difficult to escape from the vicious circle of poverty and overproduction and was dooming attempts to improve the lot of the millions of cane cutters. Conversely, the availability of millions of cane cutters had postponed mechanization in the field. In the past, slavery and deceitful recruitment of indentured labor had been necessary to obtain labor for sugar estates; in the twentieth century the conditions seen in Barbados by the mid-nineteenth century had become general: labor had become abundant in plantation societies. The upshot was that labor migration from the waning sugar belts in particular had grown massively and spread in many different directions.

The birth of development economics and the emergence of labor movements in the Global South more or less coincided, and both seemed to promise the end of colonial economic relationships. The British Empire provided crucial examples. Lewis's *Labour in the West Indies* (1939) appeared in the same year that the Royal Moyne Commission investigated the labor riots in the West Indies. A new Fabian wind blew through the British Commonwealth, and not only the West Indies. In Mauritius, London tried to steer the colonial administration away from its symbiosis with the Franco-Mauritian plantocracy and "law and order" labor repression. In the most intensely colonized parts of the British Empire, the beginnings of a welfare policy became visible.[85]

In 1927, the eminent Cuban historian Ramiro Guerra y Sanchez had decried the dire consequences of centuries of plantation economies in the Caribbean. He specifically took aim at the latifundia, the large landholdings, and the sugar centrals, which he held responsible for the immiseration of the once so fertile Caribbean region. His was an economic-nationalist agenda aimed at bringing landownership to cultivators, who should be Cubans. Guerra y Sanchez strongly opposed the importation of the seasonal workers from elsewhere from the Caribbean region—a common theme among Cuban intellectuals.[86] His *Azúcar y población en las Antillas* (Sugar and Population in the Antilles) is one of the first critical appraisals of plantation economies.

In Brazil, where the government of Getulio Vargas had introduced corporatist social policies, social scientists conducted field studies in Pernambuco, with Gilberto Freyre and Josué de Castro being among the most prominent. Freyre's fieldwork was partly thwarted by the planters, but he still managed to produce the seminal book *The Mansions and the Shanties* (1936). Freyre criticized the appalling inequality in his country and was adamant that tuberculosis and other diseases were not predicated on race— an existing prejudice among the Brazilian elite—but the result of the living conditions in the shanties. The cause of all this poverty, he emphasized, was that "at the end of the nineteenth century millions of Brazilians did not possess one foot of land, in contrast to the few thousand owners of factories, ranches, rubber plantations, coffee groves and cane fields."[87]

The most devastating summary of all the destruction caused by plantation agriculture came from the Brazilian nutritionist Josué de Castro, however. In *The Geography of Hunger* (1952), he made an equally grandiose as dismal tour d'horizon, explaining hunger as a political phenomenon and arguing that the surface of the earth offered more than enough to feed all the people of the world adequately. But monocropping in northeastern Brazil and Cuba and the US domination over the Caribbean had brought malnutrition. Even in the US South, 73 percent of the population was malnourished in spite of natural abundance.[88] De Castro insisted that "soil erosion and the erosion of human potential, are the disastrous results of a single factor: the plantation system."[89] This system had destructive reverberations in the industrial world too. The foreword to De Castro's book was written by the famous British nutritionist Lord John Boyd Orr. He would later become the director-general of the FAO (United Nations Food and Agricultural Organization) and a Nobel Prize winner. In 1936, he had deeply embarrassed the British government by estimating that half of the British population suffered from malnutrition.[90] The relationship between plantation capitalism and malnutrition in both poor and rich nations was pointed out in unequivocal terms by the world's most prominent nutritionists.

De Castro is less remembered today than his fellow Brazilian Celso Furtado, who became one of the most prominent scholars of colonial underdevelopment and the so-called dependency school. Like all pioneers in development economics, both men pointed to the deep historical roots of economic inequality and the unfair trading relations that suppressed commodity prices and hampered industrialization in colonies or former colonies. In his doctoral thesis completed in 1948, Furtado argued that Brazil had been the victim of declining prices for commodities, especially sugar, since the early nineteenth century. Brazil's victimhood was aggravated by lack of protection for its industry and lack of access on the world market for its industrial products. Furtado contrasted rural Brazilians, dominated by the vicissitudes of the plantations, with the prospering independent farmers populating most of North America. He thus added his voice to those of Thomas Jefferson and Benjamin Rush in the eighteenth-century and Francis G. Newlands and the Cuban nationalist historian Guerra y Sanchez in the twentieth, asserting that the wealth of a nation stemmed from independent farmers. All of these figures decried the extensive plantation economies in the Americas.[91]

Three years after having completed his thesis on the colonial economy of Brazil, Furtado started to work at United Nations Economic Commission for Latin America and the Caribbean, which was then headed by Raúl Prebisch. Meanwhile, the old sugar belt of Pernambuco had become such a poverty zone that an alarmed President John F. Kennedy, already stirred by the revolution in Cuba, mentioned northeast Brazil in particular when he launched his Alliance for Progress in 1961, a development collaboration program for Latin America. Furtado tried as minister for planning and head of the ambitious Superintendency of the Northeast to convince landlords to cede parts of their underutilized landholdings in return for government-funded irrigation projects. Furtado encountered fierce resistance, however, and eventually had to flee the country after the military coup of 1964.[92]

Clearly, since the 1930s the impoverishment of the cane sugar belts had not only become a humanitarian concern but also a pressing political liability, considering the revolutionary potential of the oppressed workers in depressed monocrop economies. These dismal conditions were the outcome of both local and global vested interests blockading more equitable conditions in the world of sugar. The histories of both the Brussels Convention and the Chadbourne Plan had demonstrated how necessary and at the same time how difficult it was to avoid overproduction and protectionism, which warped the global sugar market. Prebisch would play a crucial role in reviving Chadbourne's work by coordinating the international sugar market in his capacity as founding secretary-general of the United Nations Conference on Trade and Development.

12

Failed Decolonization

ONE OF THE FEW POSITIVE OUTCOMES of the economic cataclysm and the deep misery of the 1930s was the birth of the new discipline of development economics. It identified the malign legacies of centuries of plantation capitalism, in which sugar had played such a prominent role. Its scholars influenced policies of individual governments and international organizations to bring some justice to the cane fields and some order to the global sugar market. Reminiscent of how slave resistance at the turn of the nineteenth century had precipitated the end of the Caribbean slave-based plantation system, workers' resistance during the 1930s had forced governments to intervene in agricultural labor relations. Sugar workers' unions managed to cross the racial divisions created by their employers. Workers' expectations rose in the late 1930s when the world was finally recovering from the Great Depression. They had seen the spectacle of modern consumption and wanted their share, as the Moyne Report had concluded with regard to the West Indies in 1939.[1] The British government had found the content of that report so explosive—it was wartime after all—that it waited to publish it until 1945. Its message had not lost its relevance, however, and it guided Britain to establish a new relationship with its Caribbean dominions. A similar urgency was felt by the leaders of France.

Labor had made its demands felt, but in the poor cane plantation belts its position had been weakened because it was no longer in short supply. And indeed where it was, employers had an increasing range of options to accelerate mechanization, which had stalled during the Great Depression. Sugar producers throughout the United States responded to the emboldened position of labor by thoroughly mechanizing their field work. Having to pay the world's highest wage for cane work, Hawaii saved labor in all stages of production and this went as far as throwing fertilizer in irrigation water. Its plantations succeeded in quadrupling the output per worker to 129 tons between 1945 and 1957, which was 2.5 times that of Florida and five times that of the US beet sugar sector.[2]

The United States was leading mechanization, but Australia, the Caribbean region, and Mauritius invested in labor-saving equipment too. This ranged from cane-planting machines to tractors or caterpillars with ploughs, and from mechanical cane harvesters to switching to bulk shipping instead of using sacks. Even in cane harvesting, the most difficult part of the operation, mechanization made headway after decades of failed attempts. And still the challenges were formidable as the strain on harvesting machinery was intense and each terrain required its own technology. For the hills of Hawaii, for instance, a bulldozer, and not a mower, was developed that raked the cane four inches below the surface and loaded the stalks with leaves, stones, and mud on lorries. In Florida, the orange Allis Chalmer cane harvester was initially sucked into the soft soil. In Cuba, hundreds of pieces of equipment arrived from the Soviet Union in the 1960s, but the overwhelming majority of these badly constructed machines broke down. It took another ten years before their technical deficiencies were overcome.[3]

The Louisiana cane fields were the first where mechanical cane harvesters became a common sight. The need to mechanize became urgent during World War II, when workers left for nearby industries and for the Texas and Mississippi Gulf ports. Driven by acute sugar shortages, the US government allowed the Louisiana planters a free hand to grow as much sugar as they could. In these years, the number of tractors, used for ploughing, weeding, fertilizing, and cane loading doubled. Incredibly, 354 machines had replaced eighteen thousand cane cutters and handled half the harvest by 1946.[4] Meanwhile, the war and concomitant labor shortages also sped up mechanization in the US beet fields. Everywhere, tractors appeared for planting and weeding while experiments with mechanical beet harvesters were underway. Small airplanes sprayed poison to exterminate the weeds growing between the beet plants, and mechanical harvesting had become universal by 1952.[5]

Mechanization fundamentally changed the arithmetic of the world of sugar, particularly because it made it much easier for high-income countries

to compete with low-wage countries. To understand the impact of mechanization, one only needs to compare the half ton of sugar produced by an
eighteenth-century Caribbean enslaved with the almost three hundred times
greater output per operator in the fully mechanized cane belt of Hawaii in
the late 1950s.[6] Lower-income countries were disadvantaged in this race
not only because they were short of capital but also because cane cutting
was a meagre but indispensable source of income for so many. In the West
Indies and Cuba, workers and unions massively resisted the mechanization of cane mowing. In Cuba, workers even put pales in the fields to stop
the still experimental cane harvesters in the 1930s, and sabotage continued
into the 1950s. Some imported machines did not even pass the country's
customs if the officers were on the side of the cane workers.[7]

Besides workers' resistance and the reluctance of governments to put tens
of thousands of workers out of employment, mechanical harvesting had
distinct operational disadvantages, such as the vulnerability of the machines
and the fact that they devoured not only cane but also trash, dirt, and even
dead animals, which all ended up in the cane crushers.[8] Often, manual harvesting continued to be cheaper, and this pertained not only to poorer
countries such as India and Brazil. Even in Queensland, Australia, which
together with Louisiana was the first cane sugar region to construct a mechanical cane harvester, the machines were initially too expensive for
farmers. Instead, thousands of Italian and Maltese immigrants still came
to Australia's cane fields.[9] Florida managed to postpone mechanized cane
harvesting until the 1980s by exploiting cane cutters from Jamaica and Haiti.
According to an appalled columnist in the *Washington Post*, cane cutting
was the "nation's most dangerous and grueling occupation." Another investigative journalist denounced housing and living conditions as absolutely
below US standards. Only after the labor unions took the big sugar corporations to court for dodging the US minimum wage—and after HIV spread
alarmingly through this sugar belt—did the mechanized cane harvesters
enter the fields.[10]

Overall, however, mechanization advanced the fastest in the wealthy
countries. Tariff walls shielded firms in the United States and Europe from
competition from cheaper sugar producers in the Global South and provided a safe environment for major investments. Protectionism thus prevented a massive transfer of sugar production from Europe and the United
States to developing countries, which indeed flew in the face of the spirit

of the 1944 Bretton Woods Agreement, which had aimed to reverse the devastating protectionism that had engulfed the world economy since the late 1920s. Initially, the plan had been to complement the Bretton Woods institutions, such as the World Bank and the International Monetary Fund, with the International Trade Organization (ITO). This was an ambitious scheme launched by the same John Maynard Keynes who had designed the Bretton Woods institutes. The ITO's aim was to stabilize international trade and global commodity markets, but when it was completed in Havana in 1946 and ready for ratification, the US Congress refused to sign. The abortive ITO revealed the fundamental rift between the interests of the developing countries in market stabilization and the insistence of the most advanced industrial nations on having cheap commodities and protecting their own agricultural producers. Hence, the international trade framework that was adopted, the General Agreement on Tariffs and Trade—the forerunner of World Trade Organization—did not cover the global commodity markets when it went into effect in 1948.

The failure of ITO did, however, lead to a dusting off the International Sugar Agreement that had resulted from the Chadbourne negotiations during the Great Depression. For that purpose, a conference was held in London in 1953 under the auspices of the United Nations. The choice of location annoyed the United Nations staff, who made a formal objection that London, heavily bombed during World War II, was not yet able to house a major international conference. Their real concern, obviously, was that the city was the capital of the British Commonwealth, and therefore anything but neutral territory. Just one year earlier, in December 1951, Britain had created its own internal protected market via the Commonwealth Sugar Agreement (CSA), which gave its dominions exclusive access to the British market with guaranteed prices. Yet the British government had the backing of the United States, and enough political expertise to snatch the initiative away from the United Nations and protect its own interests. British civil servants adroitly prodded the delegates of sugar-exporting and sugar-importing countries into compliance, and the Commonwealth's sugar producers would continue to enjoy protection.[11]

In fact, Britain's insistence on its CSA and the United States' perseverance regarding its quota system severely undermined the outcomes of the conference and were perceived as blatantly unfair by sugar exporters. Cuba, for example, had every reason to object and when on New Year's Day 1959

Fidel Castro's communists took over, they rejected any restrictions on its sugar exports as the product of "sugar barons and imperialist U.S. financiers." Cuba insisted that countries should make room for imports—in other words that beet sugar production had to be curtailed.[12] That did not happen, however, and in the 1960s protectionism shored up sugar prices behind the tariff walls of the wealthy sugar-producing countries while pushing them down on the world market by 33–50 percent.[13]

The same old conflict that had held the world of sugar in its grip since the 1860s now threatened to eliminate the international sugar market altogether. At this point, three prominent officials in the world of international trade and agriculture made a valiant attempt to rescue it by resurrecting the International Sugar Agreement in 1968. They were Ernest Jones Parry, the executive director of the council overseeing the International Sugar Agreement, Albert Viton, one of the directors of the United Nations Food and Agriculture Organization, and Raúl Prebisch, who later became secretary-general of the United Nations Conference on Trade and Development, which was established in 1964 to coordinate international commodity policies. The International Sugar Agreement crafted by these three experts was only a limited and temporary success, however. The European Economic Community (EEC), the forerunner of the European Union (EU), sabotaged a renewed agreement in 1977 by not signing it and giving itself a free ride, reckoning that the other signatories would comply with restrictions. Further negotiations to revive the scheme in 1984 ended in disagreement on where the massive excess production of twenty million tons had to be capped.[14] One year later, the global sugar market would collapse again, wreaking social chaos in many cane sugar belts. As we will see below, this catastrophe also pulled asunder national projects in the Global South designed to leave colonial times behind and create more equitable conditions in the cane fields.

Sugar beyond Colonialism: The Cooperatives

The faltering attempts in the international political arena to create a more stable and fair global sugar market cast their shadow on, and eventually doomed, attempts to give cane farmers in the so-called developing countries their fair share. In these attempts, cooperatives were considered to be crucial. Grasping the spirit and issues of the time, the 1961 encyclical of

Pope John XXIII titled "Mater et Magistra" explicitly encouraged farmers' cooperatives.[15] In the case of cane sugar, this call chimed well with the structural trend toward sugar centrals coupled with smallholder farming. This trend began in Australia, Mauritius, the Caribbean region, and Mexico after the revolution of 1911. A few decades later Puerto Rico embarked on a comprehensive land redistribution scheme, which brought haciendas and land controlled by the big US sugar companies either into the hands of government-owned farms or the landless clients of the landlords, the hacenderos.[16] This shift toward smallholder cane cultivation would continue throughout the twentieth century until by 1990 more than 60 percent of the world's cane sugar was grown on plots averaging less than five hectares. Cane cultivation usually happened in combination with other crops to allow the soil to recover.[17] Sugar beet was even more commonly grown on small plots.

However, farmers almost invariably found themselves in a weaker position than the factories, because both cane and beet are highly perishable and must be processed almost immediately after harvesting. This means a close coordination between field and factory is required, leaving little room for the "independent" smallholders to decide when and where to deliver their harvest. To square the desired circle of "synchrony without subordination," cane farmers' cooperatives emerged across the globe either as a countervailing power to factories or as owners of the mills themselves.

In the early twentieth century, the first cooperative cane mills emerged in Australia financed by the Queensland government after cane switched from being a plantation crop that used Melanesian labor to one that was the sole preserve of white farmers. At that time, beet farmers in Europe were fighting back against the industrialists who tried to control them, and they often won. Dutch beet farmers, for example, founded a cooperative sugar beet factory in 1899 in response to cartelization efforts by the factories, which would soon be followed by another six.[18] Today, 60 percent of the Dutch beet sugar is produced by a single cooperative. In France, two big cooperatives, Tereos and Cristal, dominate the market. Germany's two beet sugar giants, Südzucker and Nordzucker, are corporations where the farmers hold the majority of the shares.[19] In the case of Südzucker, this involved a forty-year battle with the industrialists, until, in 1988, thirty thousand beet famers emerged victorious and obtained a majority interest in this sugar and food giant.[20]

Even in the United States, where corporate capitalism had dominated the sugar sector since the late nineteenth century, the sugar cooperative emerged as a viable model. In Louisiana, where most planters had become cane growers supplying central sugar factories, a group of farmers established the state's first cooperative mill in 1932, and by the mid-1960s cooperatives processed about a quarter of Louisiana's cane.[21] In Florida, where a farmers' cooperative had pioneered sugar production before World War II, cane farmers chartered their cooperative in 1960, encouraged by the US boycott of Cuba after Castro came to power. Today, it is a powerful vertically integrated business that works closely with the Fanjul brothers' Florida Crystals Corporation. Almost as spectacular was the transfer of the American Crystal Sugar Company, established by Oxnard in 1898, to a farmers' cooperative, which became the largest beet sugar producer in the United States in the early 1970s. Confronted with a company that retrenched and closed factories to raise efficiency while heaping rising transport costs on the farmers, beet growers took their fate in their own hands, bought the shares, and turned the company into a cooperative.[22]

These developments stood in striking contrast to the Global South, where in the 1970s many cooperatives faltered, and some national projects utterly discredited the cooperative philosophy by oppressing instead of empowering farmers. Things had seemed to start well, with sugar cooperatives mushrooming in India. In the hinterland of Bombay, a cooperative sugar industry developed as an offshoot from an even older cooperative system dating from the 1870s, when a steep decline in global cotton prices after the American Civil War impoverished the countryside. To stop the influx of destitute peasants from the hinterland to Bombay, the city's government and private capitalists began promoting village cooperatives to improve conditions in the countryside. Their efforts complemented an extensive canal project irrigating vast tracts of land. Credit systems enabled farmers to obtain iron plows and crushers, and a rapidly growing number of the latter had combustion motors after 1910.[23] Over time, thriving cane-grower cooperatives managed to assemble the necessary capital to build factories themselves and cut out the Bombay capitalists.

In northern India, in Bihar and Uttar Pradesh, a slightly different type of cooperative emerged in the 1930s as a countervailing power to the dozens of factories built by Indian capitalists and British managing agencies—

corporations financing and managing a set of companies. These enterprises initially used intermediary agents to negotiate with local farmers and get them to quit making gur and grow cane for their factories instead. This way of operating was rather cumbersome and inefficient. At some stations, trains carrying cane passed each other in opposite directions, clearly not heading for the most nearby factory. Not surprisingly, members of the Indian Sugar Committee who had made a study trip to Java in 1920 had seen an egg of Columbus in the *areaal*, the designated circle around each Java factory from which other factories were forbidden to buy cane. This was, however, a thoroughly colonial model, invented as part of Java's forced cultivation system (1830–1870; see Chapter 6) that put the cane farmers at the mercy of the factories. In northern India, however, the farmers' cooperatives became the solution as they were mandated to negotiate on behalf of their members with the industrialists about the price to be paid for the cane. Both farmers and factories benefited as a few thousand cooperatives carried out development work, disseminated new cane varieties, and provided chemical fertilizers.[24]

The successful sugar farmers' cooperatives across the globe became models for governments aiming for more egalitarian and democratic conditions in the countryside. In the case of Mexico, the development of cooperatives was combined with the splitting up of large landholdings. However, in contrast to India, Europe, and the United States, the initiative did not come from the farmers, and the factory owners continued to constitute a formidable factor in Mexican politics, allowing them to control the sugar market.[25] Sugar workers were even worse off in Peru, when the army officers who took over the government in 1969 also took over many large estates, including Gildemeister's gigantic Casa Grande (see Chapter 7). Rather than being driven by a desire for rural reform, their aim was to break the opposition these large landowners posed to their rule. The big "Casa Cooperativa" sign on the roof of a former landowner's mansion was just a gold ring in a pig's snout. The ugly reality was one of saddling smallholders with heavy debt as the Peruvian government shifted the bill for compensating the big landowners onto their shoulders.[26] Suharto's regime in Indonesia even more brazenly abused the cooperative philosophy. It inherited a dilapidated sugar industry struggling to procure cane. Euphemistically calling its program Intensified Smallholder Cane, Suharto's government restored the central role of the village head in designating land for cane cultivation—echoing the forced cultivation system of the colonial days—and the village elites resumed their role of controlling land and labor on behalf of the sugar factories.[27]

Nevertheless, even if genuinely motivated to empower peasants, the tasks assigned to the cooperatives were unrealistic given declining sugar prices, staggering rural underemployment, and factories that often went decades without maintenance. After Jamaica's independence in 1962, for instance, the government took over the outdated and inefficient factories of Tate & Lyle as well as those of the United Fruit Company and handed the cane fields over to twenty-three cooperatives. This was in way a triumph for the government of Michael Manley, the son of Norman Manley, who had been one of the leaders of the big strikes of the 1930s and first premier of Jamaica. Having succeeded his father, Michael became a leading voice for the Global South—or the "Third World," to use the terminology of that time. He tried to steer his country away from colonial dependency, and his message to the workers of the cane cooperatives was "You must understand that you are becoming the pioneers of socialism."[28] The government's project to introduce social justice in the sugar sector unfortunately began in the context of sharply declining sugar prices after their peak in 1974.

The governments of the developing countries could not shield their cooperatives from dwindling world market prices because, in contrast to their counterparts in the wealthy nations, they could not afford to subsidize their sugar sector over periods of many years. The Indian government was forced to abandon price controls in 1978 after four years of rapidly declining sugar prices on the world market. In northern India, factories desperately tried to cut costs, for instance by doctoring the scales and economizing on maintenance. The increased frequency of stoppages kept farmers waiting sometimes for many hours at the factory gates. Disgruntled, they either went back to gur production or switched to other crops. The least fortunate tried to find work elsewhere in India. In Maharashtra, the cooperative factories did survive, but at the expense of the small peasants. The cooperatives' leadership—composed of the biggest farmers—had enough leverage over the peasantry to blockade their return to gur production. Assisted by the World Bank, the Maharashtra factories achieved the highest cane yield per acre in the world from over five hundred thousand hectares on the Deccan Plateau in the late 1970s.[29]

The World Bank planned and financed the restructuring of ailing sugar industries across the Global South, from Indonesia to Jamaica, and although the agency did not appear to be prejudiced against cooperatives, its assistance invariably led to a concentration of power to the detriment of smallholder cane growers. Big landholding farmers and factories shared an interest in exploiting the immense armies of cane cutters, who were usually not included in the cooperative schemes. Indeed, the demise of the cooperative ideal in the Global South was not only the result of sharply declining sugar prices; it was also rooted in persistent rural inequalities as well as authoritarian tendencies in some of the newly independent nations. Sugar plantocracies could disappear overnight through nationalizations of their properties, as happened in Cuba and Java in the late 1950s, but this did not help rural populations, particularly not if the military took over, as happened in the 1960s in Indonesia and Peru. The Dominican Republic dictator Rafael Trujillo decided to take personal possession of the country's sugar industry and owned most of it by 1957.[30]

In the Philippines, Ferdinand Marcos, although not a military man, was still a dictator and usurper of the economic power of the Philippine sugar bourgeoisie. He was installed by the Lopez family, the hugely successful Negros sugar planters who had diversified their business over time.[31] However, after Marcos became president he sidelined Fernando Lopez, who had obtained the vice-presidency as part of the deal, and started to appropriate the family's possessions by imprisoning Fernando's nephew, the crown prince of the family's sugar business. Outsiders like Marcos and Trujillo, the latter a former cattle thief and military man, were definitely not part of a sugar bourgeoisie. They used their office as president to raid the sugar industry just as the Mamluk sultan Barsbay had raided the Karimi bourgeois in early fifteenth-century Egypt (see Chapter 2).[32] Against the brute force of despots, the sugar bourgeoisie was defenseless. However, in contrast to the Mamluk sultans, the modern dictators were ousted after decades of infamous rule and the old colonial sugar bourgeoisie made a comeback. In the Philippines, Marcos was succeeded by Corazon Aquino, member of an influential sugar family. The Philippine Lopez family recovered from the Marcos regime, as did the Vicinis of the Dominican Republic, who would return from exile after Trujillo's assassination in 1961.

Winners and Losers in the British
Commonwealth Sugar Agreement

The attempt of Michael Manley to put Jamaica's sugar industry on a more equitable footing soon collapsed under the weight of a heavily distorted international sugar market. As noted above, prices peaked in 1974 and then went steeply downward. Moreover, in that year Britain's imperial protectionist sugar policies ended, and it had become palpably clear that it was not the overseas cane-growing territories that held the best cards but the big corporations. This was an outcome few would have expected in 1949, when the British government decided to nationalize the sugar giant Tate & Lyle, which was ferociously resisted by the company. It started a public relations campaign, printing on every packaged item, on every truck, and on every leaflet handed out by shopkeepers to customers the slogan "Tate Not State," which was uttered by a cartoon character called "Mr. Cube."

The government was forced to give in and the nationalization was called off, but its message was clear: sugar was a matter of both public and imperial interest. The Commonwealth Sugar Agreement (CSA) was introduced in 1951, guaranteeing sugar producers stable prices that were on average 25 percent above the world market, which was the outcome of the social reform and protectionism that the Fabians had advocated for the West Indies.[33] As we saw in Chapter 11, William Arthur Lewis had published his report—about the alarming conditions of these sugar colonies—with the Fabian Society on the eve of World War II. Over time, the CSA turned out to be more beneficial to Tate & Lyle and Booker McConnell, however, than to the poor in Fiji, Mauritius, and the West Indies.

Jock Campbell, the head of Booker McConnell, Fabian, and later a Labour politician, acted as the chief negotiator on behalf of the sugar industry in the forging of the CSA. He bridged the old planter class and the sunset days of the British Empire, considering it his generation's mission to help the colonies achieve economic independence. In charge of the dominant sugar producer of British Guiana, he knew and conversed with leading Caribbean intellectuals such as C. L. R. James and the cousins Alexander Bustamante and Norman Manley, rival political leaders of the Jamaican people since the late 1930s. Campbell had luncheons with Eric Williams, the famous author of *Slavery and Capitalism* and Trinidad's prime minister for twenty-five consecutive years from 1956.[34] More adversarial, but still mutually respectful, was Campbell's relationship with Cheddi Jagan, who had been a dentist and communist labor activist before serving as chief minister and then premier of British Guiana, ultimately becoming president of Guyana at the end of his life.

Jagan could only see an economic future for British Guiana with a thoroughly decolonized economy. He was right in maintaining that the CSA would not accomplish its aim of a smooth transition for its sugar colonies toward economic independence. In the case of his country almost half its exports consisted of sugar, much more than Jamaica's (12 percent). Jagan's critique pertained even more to Mauritius and Fiji, which in the 1970s relied on sugar for 59 percent and 89 percent, respectively, of their export income.[35] In the end, the cynical outcome of the CSA was that increased living standards in a number of sugar islands blocked their road to industrialization. After all, newly industrializing countries could only carve out a share in the global market if their wages ranked among the lowest in the world, as Nobel Prize winner James Meade explained when discussing options for economic diversification in Mauritius in the early 1960s.[36]

While Nobel Prize winners Lewis and Meade as well as a range of outstanding Caribbean intellectuals all advocated an industrialization policy to replace sugar, Britain's sugar policies continued to treat its overseas territories as providers of raw materials and agricultural commodities, allowing big companies such as Tate & Lyle and Booker McConnell to expand a sugar production that was actually too expensive for the world market.[37] Their sheer size also gave these companies immense leverage over West Indian governments. Tate & Lyle was the largest sugar producer in Jamaica, and in Trinidad it controlled all shipping and 80–90 percent of the milling, whereas in British Guiana Booker McConnell acted as state within a state, controlling 80 percent of sugar production and all bulk storage, as well as shipping facilities.[38] Even if their estates in the West Indies made losses, these were more than compensated by generous profits downstream from their shipping, refining, and retail divisions. The World Bank accurately observed in 1975 that the considerable vertical integration of Tate & Lyle "makes it conceivable that the profits will be concentrated at the end of the chain," which was in Britain. Indeed, only 10 percent of Tate & Lyle's turnover came directly from the West Indies. It drew most of its income from its dominance of the British sugar market.[39]

With the discontinuation of the CSA in 1974, and the governments of the West Indies reluctant to go along with the cost-saving mechanization of cane harvesting, Tate & Lyle and Booker McConnell felt it was time to leave. They were happy to sell their factories to the governments of the newly independent West Indies, burdening them with the problem of a one-sided economy while staying in control of access of West Indies sugar to the European market.[40] Something similar happened in Fiji. The Colonial Sugar Refining Company, based in Sydney and since 1926 the sole owner of Fiji's factories, maintained complete control over the agricultural process, exploiting the smallholder cane growers. After an intervention by the British government in favor of the smallholders in 1973, the company was happy to leave Fiji and pursue a diversification of its business in Australia.[41]

Clearly, governments of the countries supplying the raw or basic materials in the commodity chain found themselves in a weak position because the transnational corporations distributed agricultural risks over different countries and mitigated them through vertical integration and product diversification. The West Indian governments, all on the verge of independence or already independent, now found themselves trapped between the British corporations, who were keen to get rid of their factories, and mounting worker discontent, which became visible on the streets but also led to an increasing number of cane fires.

After Tate & Lyle and Booker McConnell withdrew from the West Indies, they found a new field of operations in the African countries that were also part of the British Empire and its successor, the Commonwealth of Nations. African societies that had always lived without sugar now began consuming it, and a growing number of African countries used their conducive climate and rapidly growing labor force to start producing sugar themselves. As an additional incentive, increasing sugar consumption came with rising imports and thus deteriorating foreign exchange. The African governments hoped to avoid such a loss by building their own sugar factories.[42] For this, they had to rely, however, on the investments and expertise of the big companies, and here Tate & Lyle and Booker McConnell saw their opportunity.

Reminiscent of how Henry O. Havemeyer had orchestrated the expansion of the American Sugar Kingdom in the Caribbean region, Henry Tate put the Franco-Mauritian René Leclezio in charge of building a sugar branch within the sprawling London and Rhodesian Mining and Land Company (Lonhro) in the early 1960s. Lonhro was run by the unscrupulous corporate raider Tiny Rowland, who had befriended many African leaders. Leclezio established a diverse set of businesses in decolonizing British Africa and had sugar factories across the continent when he retired in 1997.[43]

In the age of decolonization, the sugar firms that had dominated in colonial times no longer put their capital in factories but embraced a new business model of selling their expertise to aspiring sugar producers throughout Asia and Africa. Ownership of factories was now risky, as the Amsterdam Trading Society (Handels Vereeniging Amsterdam [HVA]), once a major plantation owner in colonial Indonesia, found out to its cost. Insecure about its position in Indonesia, where its factories would indeed be nationalized in 1958, the HVA started building several sugar factories in Ethiopia in 1951, based on a remarkable contract between Haile Selassie, the lion of African anti-colonialism, and one of the Netherlands' biggest

Work proceeds at the Handels Vereeniging Amsterdam (HVA) sugar cane plantation, Wonji, Ethiopia, 1969. Once one of the largest plantation enterprises in colonial Indonesia, HVA made a new start in Ethiopia after the end of Dutch colonial rule.

colonial enterprises. The scheme converted the wetlands along the Awash River for sugar cane cultivation, with an estimated thirty thousand Ethiopian families depending on the company for their income. But the HVA would lose out again when, in the wake of a communist revolution, its Ethiopian assets were nationalized in 1974.

Firms such as the HVA, Booker McConnell, and Tate & Lyle insulated themselves against the risk of nationalization by retreating to consultancy and management assignments. As monopolists of technical and managerial expertise, these companies took advantage of the financial support offered by development aid schemes.[44] Paying lip service to the politically correct smallholder model, consultants operated factories like any other viable sugar enterprise by establishing their dominance over the field to ensure sufficient cane supplies. They designed schemes that subordinated smallholders in a way that would never have been accepted from foreign companies, but became acceptable under the guise of nationalized property and cooperative schemes. HVA operated as consultant in thirty countries in the Global South, mostly in sugar. Behind the scenes, Tate & Lyle and Booker McConnell opened up new sugar frontiers in Africa, which at the turn of the twenty-first century radically outcompeted the Caribbean region with yields per hectare ranking among the highest in the world.[45]

At the end of the day, the CSA had facilitated a massive transfer of sugar production from the West Indies to Africa, orchestrated by the British sugar giants. The old sugar colonies, meanwhile, had to reorient themselves. In 1970, two years after independence, the Mauritian government decided to establish export-processing zones, which had the double advantage of giving it preferential access to European markets as well as access to Hong Kong capital, turning the island into an "Indian Ocean Tiger" economy.[46] In fact, the East Asian Tiger economy of Taiwan owed much of its success to the resurrection of its sugar sector after World War II. The Taiwan Sugar Corporation, relying on the state-organized farmers' cooperative, was the island's main source of foreign exchange and government revenue in the 1950s, and thus accumulated vital investment capital for its owner, the government.[47] Taiwan, and Mauritius to some extent, reached prosperity, but in general the establishment of export zones, which usually operated under mild tax regimes, perpetuated the enclave economies of plantations, allowing companies to siphon off profits.

Similar reorientations were underway within the shrinking American Sugar Kingdom. The Philippines notoriously developed extensive enclaves for textiles and electronics populated by underpaid female workers. According to critical observers in the mid-1980s, the Caribbean region had become a paradise for transnational corporations, which hopped from island to island in search of the lowest sweatshop wages, and eventually disappeared to even lower-wage countries. Felipe Vicini, member of the powerful Dominican sugar family, disavowed this industrialization as a misnomer—it did not bring true industrial development but temporary work that would be gone as soon as companies found cheaper labor elsewhere.[48]

Meanwhile, the colonial sugar bourgeois families of Hawaii, Mauritius, Barbados, the Dominican Republic, Puerto Rico, and the Philippines successfully diversified their businesses toward real estate, textiles, infrastructure, tourism, and the media. Eugenio Lopez, the brother of the vice-president under Marcos, emerged as a leading newspaper publisher and ship owner.[49] In the British dominions, the powerful families moved away from sugar or at least diversified into tourism or other economic sectors. Even the Franco-Mauritian plantocracy that still owned all the island's sugar factories at the turn of the twenty-first century successfully invested in other sectors.[50] For the former British sugar colonies, as well as for Puerto Rico, the Dominican Republic, and Martinique, tourism became the new frontier, one of a more durable character than the sweatshops and the subcontracting segments of transnational corporations. The windmills that crushed cane for three centuries now appear as logos on the napkins of luxury hotel resorts in the Caribbean.[51] However, tourism and offshore industry did not remotely compensate for the loss of employment through the demise of the sugar industry. Mass emigrations from the Caribbean islands are an enduring legacy of their past as sugar colonies.

The Two Remaining Sugar Empires

The resolute determination of the sugar empires to shield themselves from international competition explains much of why the dreams and ambitions of the young development economists of the 1930s did not materialize. Protectionism had only grown worse since World War II. By 1976, only

25 percent of the world's sugar production was exported, and half of this was under regimes of preferential treatment, mainly maintained by the United States, EEC (later EU) and the Soviet-led Council for Mutual Economic Assistance (Comecon), which purchased much of Cuba's sugar, shielding the island from the decline in sugar prices after 1974.[52]

Particularly detrimental to the international sugar market were the sugar policies of the EEC, through which it had become the world's second largest sugar exporter. Its Common Agricultural Policy, established in 1962, guaranteed for its farmers a minimum so-called intervention price for sugar ranging from 50 percent to 100 percent above world market prices—but only for fixed quota. Sugar beyond that volume did not receive any subsidy but could be freely disposed of on the world market. The intervention prices allowed efficient producers, and the huge European beet sugar cooperatives in particular, to compensate the losses they incurred from their dumping on the world market. Although the EEC provided the sugar producers in the Global South—mainly former European colonies—some access to its market, this happened through a quota system intended to set a ceiling on their production because every additional kilogram of sugar they exported fell under the regime of severely depressed world market prices.

Europe's sugar empire became even more formidable after the accession of the United Kingdom to the EEC in 1973. The consolidation of this single European sugar empire took place two years later through the Lomé Convention, which gave eighteen African, Caribbean, and Pacific countries access to this European market. The former British colonies—including Mauritius, Fiji, Guyana, Jamaica, and Swaziland—could export a fixed amount of sugar to the EEC. Much of this went through Tate & Lyle, thanks to a premium system for sugars destined for Britain in which the firm held a quasi-monopoly.[53] Together with Booker McConnell, it had comfortably positioned itself as gatekeeper for the cane sugar of the former British colonies on the European markets, which made it even easier for these two companies to sell off their West Indian factories. For the cane sugar–producing countries in question, the Lomé convention was a mixed blessing, however, because it pushed them even further in the direction of monoculture. Mauritius did escape this fate, as we have seen, but Fiji rapidly moved down this road; within three years after the Lomé convention, its acreage under cane had doubled.[54]

Big sugar business was fed by export subsidies and obtained the space to grow through the establishment of an internal free market with the EEC—the EU from 1993—which geographically expanded after the fall of the Soviet Union. It resulted in a massive concentration of sugar interests across national borders, which until then had been blocked by national governments. In 1991, the Italian Feruzzi group acquired the French Béghin-Say refineries, through which they became the largest sugar corporation in Europe. Meanwhile, Südzucker took over the Belgian company Tirlemontoise, outmaneuvering both Feruzzi and Tate & Lyle, which had both shown interest, and became Germany's largest food corporation when they then acquired the Schöller group. Südzucker also followed the EU's eastward expansion through investments in Hungary, the Czech Republic, and Poland. After the fall of the Iron Curtain, Südzucker's Austrian partner Agrana rapidly built factories in countries that had once belonged to the Austrian-Hungarian Empire.[55]

Through this concentration, a handful of powerful agro-industrial complexes represented 335,000 farmers and 40,000 factory workers at the turn of the twentieth-first century. Moreover, the economic and political clout of these conglomerates was enhanced by their diversification; groups like Associated British Foods and Südzucker were among the top retail food companies in the EU. These formidable, entrenched interests made it difficult for Brussels to adjust to the World Trade Organization's policies, which would see agrarian subsidies and dumping of agricultural products disappear.[56]

The other remaining sugar empire, that of the United States, calibrated domestic beet sugar interests against geopolitical exigencies to maintain cane sugar import quotas for its client states. By and large, the postwar architecture of the US sugar policies, also known as the Sugar Program, was still rooted in the Jones-Costigan Act of 1934, which had tried to reconcile the conflicting forces competing for their share in its domestic market. The Act had kept consumer prices within limits, helping Cuba to recover and assisting the US territories of Hawaii, the Philippines, Puerto Rico, and the Virgin Islands.[57] After a temporary abandonment of the quota system during World War II, the Republican-controlled Congress reinstated the Sugar Quota Act in 1947, which greatly favored domestic US producers at the expense of consumers who had to foot a yearly bill of $300 million in the mid-1950s.[58] Initially, Cubans saw their conditions improve, which was

partly a reward for helping the United States out with increased production during the war, but this was soon threatened by the increasing
US domestic production and the reconstruction of the Philippine sugar
industry.[59]

Unwisely, the United States used the Cuban sugar quota as leverage to
keep control over the country's sugar industry and restrain attempts by the
Cuban government to limit the number of American staffers at US-owned
factories.[60] Secretary of State George Marshall, the father of the postwar
aid program that had reconstructed Europe, warned that such policies in
combination with reduced access to the US market might inflict political
chaos on the island. Reiterating Marshall's warning, the US State Department pointed out in 1955 that the perversion of Cuba's economic interests
only aided twenty-five thousand active communists. One year later, the
Eisenhower administration nonetheless reduced the Cuban quota to its
prewar level, to which Cuba reacted by exploring its options for selling sugar
to the Soviet Union, knowing that this would alarm the United States. In
this way, Batista started a relationship with Russia that would eventually
help Castro's regime to survive.[61]

In 1962, Cuba's sugar quota was handed over to other Latin American
countries, despite warnings by the chair of the Senate Foreign Relations
Committee James Fulbright that this would only keep Castro in power.[62]
This redistribution of Cuba's quota actually propped up *three* unpalatable
dictators. Ignoring the call for sanctions against the Trujillo regime by the
Organization of American States, the United States increased the Dominican Republic's quota to more than 15 percent, and the Philippines' quota
was enlarged too.[63] This engendered a neocolonial situation for the latter
country, with a bloated noncompetitive sugar sector that directly benefited
Marcos.

In many ways, the postwar US sugar policies perpetuated the entan-
glement of sugar and the geopolitics of the American Sugar Kingdom,
which the governments of the Caribbean and Latin America countries
knew very well how to exploit. Sugar lobbyists hired by these countries
were queueing up in Washington. Trujillo went one step further by in-
viting the House Agricultural Committee to his country for a junket.
Relatives of the chairman and some committee members were not shy in
taking up his offer.[64] Clearly, the quota system came with corruption
and huge costs for consumers, and the large sugar estates in the United

States reaped most of the benefits. The agricultural economist Gale Johnson concluded that it was therefore better to import sugar from Brazil, with its tremendous capacity for expansion.[65]

While Johnson's advice was seemingly taken to heart when the US government abandoned the protectionist quota system in 1974, this only occurred because global sugar prices temporarily spiked in that year. Eight years later, when global prices had fallen far below US domestic prices, it was reinstated and resumed its role as a political tool as well. Revolutionary Nicaragua was punished by President Ronald Reagan and saw its sugar quota reduced by 90 percent in 1983.[66] In the end, however, it would not be economics that would curtail this politicized quota system but a spectacular development in the chemistry of sweeteners, one which was as revolutionary as the introduction of beet sugar.

High-Fructose Corn Syrup and Its Consequences

The name of this spectacular development was high-fructose corn syrup (HFCS). Since the 1930s, scientists had tried to convert glucose into the sweeter sucrose, a repetition of the quest for the silver bullet that had marked the sorghum craze during the Civil War. Since abandoning the attempt to extract sucrose from sorghum grass, chemistry had advanced tremendously. Two Japanese scientists discovered in 1966 how to convert glucose into a sweetener—dubbed HFCS—that was 55 percent fructose. Through further improvements in the chemical process, the cost price of HFCS fell at least 30 percent below those of beet and cane sugars in the 1970s, and while it was only being used in pastry, cereal, and dairy products, it could potentially fully replace sugar in beverages. In 1979, Coca-Cola started using HFCS in the US market and soon after half the company's sweetener needs were met by this syrup. Perversely, the protectionism that had maintained US domestic sugar prices at a level four times higher than at the world market gave a tremendous boast to this cheap sweetener. HFCS appeared in practically all soft drinks and made up half the volume of all sweeteners in the United States by 1998.[67]

HFCS made the world's largest sugar importer almost self-sufficient within a decade and also wiped out parts of the US beet sugar industry. But above all, it severely rocked the international sugar market, which already suffered from overproduction. World sugar prices fell dramatically from \$2.60 per kilogram at their peak in 1974 to just \$0.06 in 1985.[68] This collapse deeply affected the lives of millions of cane workers, not the least those in the US client states. The Dominican Republic saw its recently increased sugar quota severely curtailed, causing additional misery to tens of thousands of Haitian seasonal cane workers.[69] The Philippine sugar industry, which had exported almost exclusively to the United States, plunged into a deep crisis. Wages in the Philippine sugar sector were already so low that the strategy of the Marcos regime to eliminate widespread labor resistance by the mechanization of planting, weeding, and harvesting had failed.[70] On Negros, monocropping had made land for food crops so scarce that religious and labor leaders begged President Marcos to make 10 percent of the island's arable land available for it, but planters resisted and quipped that workers could grow food in tin cans.[71] HFCS turned an already miserable situation into a full-blown famine, giving Negros the name of the Ethiopia of Southeast Asia. In the end, however, HFCS would be an important factor pulling the Marcos regime down.

The sharp drop in sugar prices and the declining US demand for sugar imports not only severely hurt the domestic beet sugar industry and the sugar industries of the Philippines and the Dominican Republic, it also spelled the end of even the highly efficient sugar industry in Hawaii, still owned by the haole great-grandchildren of the missionaries. An additional factor here was that cheap flights brought mass tourism, pushing up wages and making sugar production no longer profitable. The last haole sugar factory stopped its operations in 2016. Likewise, Trinidad and Tobago ceased to be a sugar exporter, the majority of Jamaica's factories closed their gates, and the sugar industry of Martinique was more or less dismantled.[72] Even the Barbados plantocracy, which had held the island in its firm grip for centuries, was brought to its knees, and the island's future now lay with tourism, not sugar.[73]

HCFS wreaked havoc throughout the cane belts in the Global South, where only the most efficient sugar producers survived, usually through vertical integration and often by catering to domestic markets with both sugar and ethanol. On the island of Negros, the old haciendas were transformed into agro-industrial complexes supplying the Philippine market.[74] In Brazil, vertical integration had been underway since the 1960s, when the manufacturers had established a cooperative structure, or rather a syndicate, under the name of Copersucar, turning the country into the world's largest ethanol producer after the United States. Big companies acquired vast tracts of land and dominated the sugar landscape in Brazil. Alcohol production furthered monocropping, large landownership, dubious welfare effects, and terrible labor conditions for seasonal laborers.[75] In India, which along with Brazil leads the world's sugar production, the same processes of vertical integration and conversion to ethanol took place. The government of the state of Maharashtra in India rescued the cooperative factories with subsidies, but above all by making the mixing of ethanol with gasoline mandatory.[76] In northern India, private enterprise bought and refurbished the rundown state-owned factories and eliminated the corrupt cooperatives in the 1990s. Firms such as Birla, whose seven factories are fed with cane from three hundred thousand farmers, and the Hindustan Petrol Company won over the peasantry by generously providing fertilizer, chemicals, offering advice, and buying their cane.[77]

Meanwhile, the International Monetary Fund insisted on the privatization of state-owned factories in Mexico. As a result, in the 1990s soft drink giants such as PepsiCo and Coca-Cola started processing half of Mexico's sugar. To reduce costs, they launched an assault on smallholder cultivation, insisting it stood in the way of mechanization and thus the supply of cheap cane. Diving cane prices left the cane growers indebted, forcing them to sell their land. Numerous cane growers escaped this fate by switching to growing cattle food or blackberries, which actually made them better off.[78] The buying up of sugar estates and mills by big energy and beverage corporations completed the reversal of the decolonization of sugar production in the Global South.

Sugar's failed decolonization is a tale of unrealized potential as the hopes raised during the Great Depression of a better and more equitable future for commodity producers through crop diversification and cooperative production were dashed within a matter of decades. It was not entirely unforeseen, however. When the critics of the plantation economies of the 1930s advocated smallholder cane growing and economic diversification of the plantation economies, they were acutely aware that the suppliers of the cane sugar were many and that demand was controlled by a few powerful players. The distorted global sugar market underlay the demise of the sugar cooperatives in the Global South. The structural adjustment programs that were imposed in the 1980s and that prioritized market freedom and privatization offered a palliative instead of a remedy. They ushered in, moreover, in a cynically one-sided withdrawal of the state: at the same time that India abandoned price controls on sugar, which sent its once nationalist project of industrial sugar production with cooperatives into a tailspin, the sugar cooperatives and sugar corporations in the Global North, grown fat thanks to tariff walls, would set their sights on the Global South, as we will see in the next chapter.

13

Corporate Sugar

BY THE 1980S SUGAR HAD ENTERED a corporate age in which globalization, deregulation of markets, and the growing power of transnational corporations set the tune. Sugar production and consumption had grown spectacularly across the globe. Yet the international trade in sugar waned. Since the 1920s, the sugar industry had become increasingly attuned toward domestic consumption, and fifty years later this made up 75 percent of its markets. At that point, the production of high-fructose corn syrup (HFCS) in Japan and the United States, so detrimental to sugar producers in the Global South, was just about to begin.[1]

As we have seen, national interests and protectionism provide the explanation for the decline in the international trade in sugar. In the days of Adam Smith, protectionism was denounced as unfair and even complicit in inhuman institutions such as slavery. It was, moreover, perceived as the favorite strategy of weaker nations to shield their inefficient economies from competition. History has shown, however, that in the case of sugar it was not the weakest economies but the most powerful—those of the United States, the European Union (EU), and Japan—that committed themselves to highly protectionist sugar policies. This should not be surprising as the history of sugar demonstrates time and again how industrial capitalism has been tremendously facilitated by the state, not least through stiff tariffs and generous export subsidies. The role of the state in the development of global capitalism has only grown over time, and this has definitely been the case with regard to sugar. This, in turn, explains the present paradoxical situation in which heavy protectionism allows huge transnational corporations to develop and dominate the world of sugar.

Through a combination of massive subsidies and stiff tariffs on imports, the EU enabled its companies to export, or rather dump, millions of tons of sugar on the world markets. At the turn of the twenty-first century, the EU had a 17 percent share in the global exports of raw sugar (and 30 percent share of white refined sugar exports), only surpassed by Brazil, with a share of 26 percent. Thailand and Cuba followed, with 9 and 8 percent respectively.[2] For Oxfam, one of the world's most prominent nongovernmental development agencies, the situation was crystal clear in 2004: "Europe dumps around five million tons of excess sugar on world markets each year, artificially depressing prices and depriving efficient developing country producers of potential revenue."[3]

In the United States, meanwhile, domestic sugar and sweetener interests won out over the geopolitical clientelism that had been a crucial element in the American Sugar Kingdom. It has been estimated that a thorough reform of the sugar policies of both the United States and the EU would have allowed countries in the Global South to fetch prices up to a third higher on average in the 1990s. The Caribbean sugar estates would have been able to secure prices up to 68.2 percent higher, and many of them would not have perished.[4]

While in Europe and the United States big sugar corporations flourished behind tariff walls, governments across the Global South decided to relinquish protections, and cooperative projects in particular. International consultancy firms and the World Bank restructured their sugar industries, which usually happened at the expense of smallholders and cooperatives. This opened the door for transnational sugar corporations. These, however, were no longer exclusively based in the Global North but also in Southern Africa, Thailand, China, and Latin America. Nonetheless, a declining number of multinationals control both the input (e.g., fertilizer, seeds) as well as the output (e.g., beverages, food, and fuel) of the sector. Hundreds of millions of farmers and a much larger number of consumers are dependent upon a shrinking pool of food corporations that increase their wealth by widening the gap between farmer and consumer prices.[5]

Meanwhile, the acreage under cane rapidly expanded as governments in the Global South, and the big producers such as Brazil, India, and Thailand, embraced ethanol production to save their industry from being destroyed by sugar dumping and protectionism of the industrialized countries. This has burdened the world with immense ecological costs and consumer households subsidize the sector to the tune of $50 billion annually.[6] The trend away from plantation to smallholder sugar cultivation has been reversed in favor of capital-intensive plantation enterprises that are akin to mining companies, geared toward getting the maximum energy out of the soil at minimal cost.

The Plight of the Cane Cutters

Since the global economic order did not change in favor of the commodity-producing former colonies, it is not surprising that at the turn of the twenty-first century the International Labor Organization observed that poverty among the cane workers seemed to be universal.[7] Migrants from impoverished hinterlands or poor adjacent islands continue to do the dirty, dangerous and physically exhausting work of cane cutting. In the past they came from Madura to East Java, from Jamaica and Haiti to Cuba, or from the highlands of Puerto Rico to its southern coast. Today, migrants come from the dryer districts of West India to the cane belts of Maharashtra or South Gujarat, from northeastern Brazil to the sugar belt of the state of São Paulo, from the highlands of Peru to the coast, or from Haiti to the Dominican Republic. Keeping labor migrants in debt bondage to their recruiters and employers is as ubiquitous as in the past among contemporary large-scale sugar plantations throughout Asia, Latin America, and Southern Africa. In Mozambique, for instance, recruiters still drive to villages and round up workers, just as they did a century ago when sugar production started there.[8]

The big sugar firms dodge their legal obligations, such as paying the minimum wage, by recruiting through subcontractors. These practices went not unresisted by workers and unions, but the latter faced immense hurdles in trying to organize workers. Throughout the cane belts in the Global South, unions urged governments to hold factories accountable for violating existing labor laws and for hiding behind intermediaries who recruit and pay the workers.[9] The unions' negotiating position often crumbled, however, under the weight of advancing mechanization. The mere threat of mechanical cane harvesters entering the fields was often enough to keep wages at an extremely depressed level. As a result, until recently modern machines have been rarely seen in the cane fields of the Global South.

Cane cutters with their machetes have become a disposable com-modity, working under conditions barely superior to those of slaves in the eighteenth century; thousands suffer from injuries and die from kidney disease caused by permanent serious dehydration.[10] Some of the most notorious abuses of cane workers in the twenty-first century have occurred in the plantations of the Dominican Republic. Shockingly, the gruesome chapter of ethnic cleansing and mass murder at the border with Haiti by the Trujillo regime in the 1930s was just the beginning (see Chapter 11). In 2007, when the Dominican Republic still had the largest share of the much-reduced US sugar quota, two explosive documenta-ries brought the terrible treatment of Haitian cane workers to American audiences.[11] The first, *The Price of Sugar,* was directed by the American Bill Haney and documented the plight of the cane workers at the estates of the prominent Vicini family.[12] The second, *Sugar Babies,* was directed by the highly regarded American Cuban filmmaker Amy Serrano. Ser-rano succinctly summarized the mistreatment of the Haitian laborers in an interview: "If an ox is hurt, the veterinarian is called immediately to take care of it, but not the doctor if the Haitian is injured."[13] Sugar in-terests, represented by among others the ambassador of the Dominican Republic to the United States, did not hesitate to condemn *Sugar Babies* after its theatrical release on a Florida university campus. Its subsequent deselection from the 2008 Miami International Film Festival was hardly surprising, since one of the biggest sugar producers in the Dominican Republic is the Fanjul family, who reside in Florida.[14]

In Brazil as well, violence and oppression dominated the cane fields. De-spite the end of twenty-one years of military rule in 1985, the landed inter-ests remained strong enough to stall land reform, and their violent intimi-dation of labor leaders made unions skeptical about their chances of ending lawlessness in the countryside. Much of the labor was hired via *empreit-eiros* (subcontractors), who kept the workers in debt bondage and enabled employers to evade taxes and other social benefits—a practice also rampant in the cane fields of western India, another major sugar belt.[15] Although cane cutters are no longer whipped and tortured like the enslaved in the past, they are still considered disposable, and after twelve years their bodies are usually broken by the work. Amnesty International observed as recently as in 2008 that cane workers in Brazil were living in "conditions analogous to slavery."[16]

Deployment of mechanical harvesters in the cane fields of the Global South is usually not the result of humanitarian concerns and stems rather from the cold calculation of corporations that it is cheaper to mechanize than to give in to workers' demands. In western India, mechanical cane harvesters entered the fields in the early twenty-first century after cane cutters' increasingly effective collective action against their exploitation, undoing their hard-won gains in basic benefits. Much of the cane harvesting is done manually, however, precisely because wages are so low.[17] In Brazil, mechanization of cane harvesting was driven by environmental concerns. Large-scale cane burning, done to speed up manual harvesting, left the state of São Paulo under dense smoke. Begun under President Fernando Henrique Cardoso and expedited under his successor Luiz Inácio Lula da Silva, mechanization was presented as part of a new "social and green" contract between producers and the government.[18] It is understandable that governments were now aiming for radical change in the cane fields, even though in the case of Brazil the mechanization of cane harvesting was driven at least as much by the massive complaints about the smoke pollution as by concerns about the appalling labor and living conditions of the cane cutters.[19]

In western India, the inhuman labor conditions that attend manual cane cutting continue, according to a recent Oxfam report. It presents the same dismal picture of the conditions of the 1.5 million seasonal migrant workers in Maharashtra as Jan Breman described almost half a century ago in his much-quoted field research in South Gujarat. Or, as another author has remarked, workers' pay permitted a family only "to maintain itself at the barest animal level of subsistence."[20] At present, working days still range from twelve to eighteen hours, and while the men cut the cane, women have to carry bundles weighing forty to forty-five kilograms. Cane workers in Gujarat and Maharashtra are kept in a permanent debt cycle as they have to live on advances charged at high interest rates during the harvest, just like half a century ago.[21]

The End of the Sugar Bourgeoisie?

As the fate of the *Sugar Babies* documentary clearly demonstrates, the old familial ownership and business networks are still robustly present in today's world of sugar transnationals. The colonial sugar bourgeoisie adapted itself handsomely to a new corporate phase of capitalism. This process started in the late nineteenth century, when the worlds of sugar and high finance began to merge via appointments in the companies' respective boards. The leaders of these worlds belonged to prominent bourgeois families such as the Morgans, the Havemeyers, and the Spreckels, who had risen to the most powerful positions at the turn of the twentieth century. In Germany, prominent sugar-producing families such as the Rabbethges sat on the board of banks as well, whereas Südzucker, the largest sugar company in Germany, was represented on the supervisory board of the Deutsche Bank.[22]

The world sugar business was highly personal and dominated by a limited number of powerful families for most of the twentieth century. The prominent sugar firms such as Tate & Lyle, Spreckels, Czarnikow-Rionda, and Maclaine Watson, the latter based in Java, were all family businesses.[23] Some firms were ruled as dynasties, without being named after a family. In the prominent Klein-Wanzleben Seed Company, for instance, the Rabbethge-Giesecke family never surrendered their leading role, miraculously surviving the utter chaos of World War II and the partition of Germany. In 1945, the British smuggled the family together with sixty tons of their beet seed from the Russian-occupied Klein Wanzleben to their occupation zone in Germany. Today's chair of the supervisory board of the Kleinwanzlebener Seed Company is Andreas J. Büchting, son of Joanne Rabbethge and Carl-Ernst Büchting, who were both great grandchildren of Matthias Rabbethge, the founder of the company.

The global sugar trade was strongly family-based, with members placed at the nodal points of sprawling commercial networks. This trend could be seen as early as in the fourteenth century, the days of the Egyptian Karimi and the German Ravensburger traders (see Chapter 2). This business model proved to be so resilient because it is conducive to preserving the most valued company secrets, including those that involve politically sensitive transactions. It facilitates fast decisions and without external shareholders profits are kept within the company, boosting growth. Moreover, the shrinking and increasingly distorted global sugar market left room for politically savvy sugar traders who not only knew everything about sugar and markets but also fostered personal relationships with influential politicians and heads of state.

The Cuban sugar magnate Julio Lobo definitely belonged in this category. In 1934, on his way to supplant Manuel Rionda as Cuba's most important sugar trader, Lobo outwitted US sugar traders, leading to sugar prices on the New York Stock Exchange going through the roof. The sugar trade had to be temporarily suspended as a result.[24] Lobo became by far the largest sugar trader in the American Sugar Kingdom, and in 1959 he rescued Cuba's sugar economy from being strangled by the United States—because of Castro's takeover—by selling a large quantity of sugar to France. He refused, however, an offer from Che Guevara to become part of Castro's regime, and went into exile, living his final years out in a small apartment in Madrid.

At that time, another daring global sugar trader was waiting in the wings, someone who had no qualms about working with Fidel Castro. Maurice Varsano, owner of the French firm Sucres et Denrées (Sucden), emerged as a major international sugar operator when he struck the deal with Lobo for the Cuban sugar imports to France and assisted Castro to find new markets in Japan and North Africa. Through his friendships with Castro and the leaders of a number of newly independent countries, Varsano gained a reputation for being *the* sugar trader of the Global South. He was reportedly one of the architects of the Sugar Protocol established by the 1975 Lomé Convention, which gave former colonies access to the European market. But as a new Havemeyer, he also allegedly played a key role in the ongoing cartelization of the European beet sugar producers. Today, under the leadership of Varsano's son Serge, Sucden is the most important broker of Russian sugar and owns cane fields in Southeast Asia—including in Vietnam—as well as in Brazil. The company currently controls about 15 percent of the global sugar trade.[25]

Brilliant and daring individual sugar traders such as Varsano, and before him Czarnikow, Rionda, and Lobo, obtained huge chunks of the global sugar trade by astutely reading the volatile sugar geopolitics. Nonetheless, the room for these traders to stage spectacular coups has shrunk since the 1980s. While in 1934 Lobo's bravado and market knowledge could still derail the futures trade and ruin US commodity traders, he would have been no match for today's computers. Since the 1980s, the highly oligopolistic commodity trade has been financed by ten to fifteen banks in New York, Frankfurt, London, Geneva, and Tokyo. Trading offices follow by satellite everything that is relevant regarding harvests, and couple this with the information systems of the banks, of which they are subsidiaries. About 40 percent of all the global sugar trade runs through computers in Swiss offices.[26]

Meanwhile, the old refiner dynasties would retreat together with the US and British sugar empires they once dominated. The Havemeyer family sold its sugar company in 1969. Booker McConnell and Tate & Lyle left the imperial sugar business a few years after Britain gave up its Commonwealth sugar policies and joined the European Economic Community, the forerunner of the European Union, in 1973. The former would transform into a wholesale giant, whereas the latter eventually would find a position in a highly specialized niche of artificial sweeteners. Jock Campbell retired as president of Booker McConnell in 1979, and a year later Saxon Tate, the last family member to head Tate & Lyle, was sidelined from daily management. A new type of manager came at the helm, trained in the corporate business of permanent mergers and reorganizations rather than steeped in the shaping of imperial sugar markets.[27]

Compared to the imperial traders and the refiners in particular, the colonial sugar bourgeoisie appeared to be far more resilient. Prominent families such as the Lopezes in the Philippines, the Rionda-Fanjuls, and the Rabbethges survived wars and revolutions and rebuilt their empires within a few decades. They were crucially not confined to a particular ethnicity or religion and preserved their independence, even if they aligned themselves high finance. These old families were joined by new family firms in the Global South. And just like in Europe and the United States, the majority of these powerful sugar producers owed much of their growth to the protective tariffs or subsidies of national governments. "The mother of all trusts is the customs tariff bill," Henry O. Havemeyer famously noted at the turn of the twentieth century, and this was no less true a century later.

The third largest sugar corporation in the world, the Mitr Phol Group, is mainly owned by the Thai Vongkusolkit family. It started sugar production in 1956 and received massive government support. The company now has factories in Guangxi (China), Laos, Queensland, and Cambodia.[28] The Birla firm—the huge Indian sugar producer we met in Chapter 8—is still in family hands after four generations. The founder of this sprawling enterprise started as an opium and later cotton trader in 1860 in Mumbai. His grandson and great-grandson maintained warm relations with Mahatma Gandhi, Prime Minister Jawaharlal Nehru, and the latter's daughter Indira Gandhi, who also was prime minister. The Indian National Congress has consistently supported the rise of an Indian entrepreneurial class, and the seven Birla sugar factories that were built in Uttar Pradesh and in Bihar in the 1930s were one of the fruits of this economic nationalism.[29]

The most remarkable history about the mobility and flexibility of the colonial and now postcolonial sugar bourgeoisie brings us at last to the world's largest sugar company: the Florida-based ASR Group, which has refineries and factories in ten different countries. It emerged through a strategic partnership between the Sugar Cane Growers Cooperative of Florida and the Florida Crystals Corporation of the Fanjul brothers. On the group's website, a timeline is presented going far back into the nineteenth century. It includes the beginnings of William Havemeyer in New York, the first plant of Henry Tate, and the first Fanjul factory in Cuba. This spectacular concentration of the businesses of the old sugar giants began in 1963 when the Spreckels family sold its shares in its sugar operations to the American Sugar Refining Company of the Havemeyers, who in turn sold their interests to investment bankers in 1969. In 1988, Tate & Lyle became the new owner, seizing this golden opportunity to buy the refineries for "a bargain price" because HFCS had severely diminished their value.[30] Through this transaction, the company owned 36 percent of the US refining capacity— but not for long. In the course of the 1990s it switched focus to artificial sweeteners and nonsweet sugars.[31] As a result, the entire American Sugar Refining Company complex plus components of the Tate & Lyle company ended up in the hands of the ASR Group, and thus . . . the Fanjul brothers.[32] This yet again testifies to the family-based character of the corporate world of sugar and the resilience of the colonial sugar bourgeoisie: the refineries of Havemeyer's Trust and the Tate & Lyle refineries in Britain are now all partly owned by the Fanjuls, who carry Spanish and American passports and were once among the most prominent colonial bourgeois of Cuba.

Sugar Giants Unchained

Protectionism fostered the sugar giants but in the current age of corporate capitalism it seems they no longer need the state to protect them. This became palpably clear when Europe started dismantling its sugar empire in 2005 after Australia, joined by Thailand and Brazil, had successfully appealed to the World Trade Organization against sugar dumping by the EU. European food industries using sugar unsurprisingly applauded the verdict, and EU officials acknowledged that a product with relatively little added value compared to other food stuffs was not worth an escalation of trade conflicts.[33] Meanwhile, the dismantling of the EU sugar empire also entailed the end of the sugar quota under the Lomé Convention, leading to the collapse of smaller sugar producers in the Global South that had enjoyed privileged access to the European market. Brazil, Thailand, and Southern African countries were the winners. While the EU's raw sugar exports declined by 80 percent between 1999 and 2019, Brazil's exports almost tripled and Thailand's more than doubled. In addition, since 2007 sugar exports by Mozambique, Swaziland, and Malawi have grown massively thanks to them being among the lowest-cost producers of sugar.[34]

Europe's big sugar corporations easily shrugged off the abolition of the subsidy regime for European beet sugar producers. On September 30, 2017, the day that marked the end of the EU sugar quota system, Phil Hogan, the European Agricultural Commissioner, confidently stated, "Producers will now have the opportunity to expand their trade on global markets."[35] Actually, they already had done so, thanks also to the European Commission itself. In the years before the bounties dried up, Brussels had made €5.4 billion available to restructure its sugar sector and facilitate its global expansion. Südzucker, which had emerged as the largest sugar company in continental Europe, started to import raw Mauritian sugar in 2008 partly to compensate the beet sugar quotas it had to surrender under the new EU sugar policies.[36] Tereos, the cooperative owned by twelve thousand French sugar beet producers, became the sole sugar producer in Réunion in 2010. It also moved into the Brazilian sugar production—in partnership with Sucden—and started producing in Mozambique.[37]

Meanwhile, the British food and retail giant Associated British Foods (ABF) staged a spectacular expansion in Southern Africa, securing a majority share in Illovo, the continent's largest sugar producer, in 2006. ABF owns well-known brands such as Ovaltine and Primark, controls two-thirds of the British sugar market, and its four separate sugar concerns span Southern Africa, China, and Europe.[38] Illovo had originated in South Africa, where it first benefited from the protected South African market under Apartheid and then expanded into Southern Africa when that regime was defeated. A major move was its purchase in 1997 of Lonhro from its founder, the Franco-Mauritian René Leclezio (see Chapter 12). The fattened

Illovo fish was subsequently swallowed completely by ABF, which became its full owner in 2016. Through that and other acquisitions, ABF is now the second largest sugar producer in the world, after Florida's ASR Group.[39]

In contrast to the EU, which gradually abolished its protectionist sugar policies, the United States *expanded* its tariff zone through the North American Free Trade Agreement (1994–2020) to include Mexico and Canada, which discriminated against more efficient producers at the expense of consumers.[40] The Cato institute, a libertarian US think tank, did not mince its words about it: "the unfortunate reality is that the price of sugar and the sources of its production are determined in this country as much by bureaucrats and politicians as by consumers and producers."[41] The lobbies for protection and subsidies at the expense of the taxpayer are extremely powerful. As Alec Wilkinson, a journalist who investigated Florida's cane belt in the 1980s, observed, "A congressman from the Northeast has said that the growers of sugar cane and sugar beets and the growers of corn have together organized Congress as effectively as has the National Rifle Association."[42] Yet this political influence does not go uncontested. Since the 1990s, Florida's ASR Group has come under increasing criticism from an unlikely alliance of environmentalists, Coca-Cola, and chocolate producer Hershey, who allege that it is destroying the environment and keeping sugar prices high at the expense of the American taxpayer.[43]

Under attack, the sugar industries strengthened their defenses by donating to political parties. The Fanjul brothers have given generously to both the Republicans and the Democrats to keep the price supports in place and "prevent the dumping of foreign sugar."[44] Senator Marco Rubio from Florida, heavily supported by the state's sugar interests, defended protectionist policies—termed "corporate welfare" by critics—with the argument that without them the American sugar industry would be wiped out by the Brazilians.[45] Still, his sponsors will probably not lose any sleep over such a prospect, because the ASR Group could just as easily survive the removal of tariffs as the big European sugar corporations did in 2005. No taboos existed regarding international expansion as far as Alfonso Fanjul was concerned, who revealed in 2014 his desire to invest in Cuba when the time was ripe. He was booed as a traitor, but what else would one expect from a transnational corporation, even from one that owed so much to American protectionism?[46]

The rapid expansion of the area under cane in Brazil, Southern Africa, and Southeast Asia impelled sugar industries to reconsider their relationship with the empires that had provided them so much "corporate welfare." Tate & Lyle did so with the EU, although it still reportedly received more than a third of the €6 billion in agricultural subsidies doled out by the latter until 2012.[47] Yet this company was actively pro-Brexit. One of its former executives was David Davis, a prominent Conservative and ardent propagandist for leaving the EU. In the 1970s and 1980s he was assigned with the task of restructuring parts of Tate & Lyle after the company had failed to acquire a substantial interest in the beet sugar industry in continental Europe. Moreover, its attempt to produce HFCS for the European market was effectively quashed by the European Commission, which took the side of the European beet sugar industry and imposed a ceiling on HFCS of 5 percent of total sweetener production. More recently, the quota under the Lomé Convention has been removed, eliminating the power base of Tate & Lyle as a sugar refiner.[48] In his capacity as Brexit negotiator from 2016 to 2018, Davis finally had his chance to settle his scores with the EU.

What also put Tate & Lyle in the pro-Brexit camp was its feud with the other sugar behemoth, ABF, which controlled the British beet sugar industry and has been favored by the EU's sugar policies. Tate & Lyle apparently hoped to restore its leading position in cane sugar by creating open access for tropical cane sugar in Britain at the expense of the country's beet sugar sector, which after all could not compete with Brazilian, Australian, or Southern African cane sugar. In a 2020 interview with the *Guardian,* Paul Kenward, director of the food and sugar giant ABF, rubbed salt in the wounds of Tate & Lyle, saying that it was a British imperial flagship in name only, because since 2010 its refineries had been the property of "a guy in Miami." By "guy," of course, Kenward meant the Fanjul brothers. Moreover, in its attempt to regain some of its old status as a sugar importer in Britain, Tate & Lyle may find competition from Chinese and American firms on the sugar frontiers, for instance in the Amazonian region. Greenpeace has already accused the company of importing cheap Brazilian sugar produced under unacceptable social and ecological conditions, which does not sit well with its stated policy of responsible entrepreneurship.[49]

Totalitarian Capitalism or Green Capitalism?

The transnational corporate regime entails an unprecedented expansion of sugar frontiers in Southern Africa, Brazil, China, and Southeast Asia driven by staggering global sugar consumption as well as a growing demand for ethanol. Global sugar production has reached a point where it extracts so much carbohydrate from the soil and causes so much collateral environmental damage that comparisons with mining operations come to mind. The combination of ethanol production and rapidly expanding new consumer markets, such as in China, pushes sugar frontiers into the ecologically most vulnerable parts of the world.

In spite of being the world's third largest producer, China still has to import soaring volumes of sugar, which will only increase in size. Since average consumption in China is only a quarter of Europe's, even with a stagnant Chinese population, catching up with the most developed markets would quadruple its consumption.[50] The China Oil and Foodstuff Corporation, the largest state-owned food-processing corporation, is responsible for 50 percent of China's sugar imports and, according to its website, belonged among the top five sugar traders in the world in 2017.[51] Not surprisingly, it has also emerged as one of the leading sugar and ethanol producers in Brazil.

Huge sugar companies from Europe, China, Thailand, and the United States now run massive and highly capitalized sugar- or ethanol-producing estates. In Indonesia, for instance, new frontiers have been opened up outside Java, where sugar production was historically concentrated. The immense advantage for the Indonesian state is that this mode of production entails no complicated negotiations with farmers, cooperatives, or village heads, which had presented major challenges in the postcolonial Javanese countryside. Where smallholder cane growers still exist on the new sugar frontiers of the Global South, they do so as clients of vertically integrated corporations, which can clearly be seen in Southern Africa, one of the most competitive and fast-growing sugar regions in the world. The big sugar companies owning the sugar factories work with farmers, but they favor the larger landowners who start to exploit the poorer ones, a mechanism we have already encountered in western India.[52]

With soaring demand for sugar and ethanol and yields per hectare growing sluggishly, cane gobbles up ever more land; global acreage under cane doubled between 1960 and 1985, for instance. And expansion is being further driven by subsidies on biofuel, which have turned Brazil and the United States into the world's largest ethanol producers.[53] In Pernambuco, for instance, the area under cane almost doubled between 1970 and the late 1980s, a growth almost exclusively geared to the production of ethanol. Staggering fertilizer use, disastrous deforestation, and water pollution have gone hand in glove with the complete marginalization of small farmers, a diminishing availability of land for food production, and thus rising food prices.[54] Tragically, the conversion of forest to cane fields for ethanol will only result in more carbon emissions (taking into account a diminished capacity to absorb these emissions) than the fossil fuel alternative.[55] Moreover, extensive cane farming needs tremendous amounts of water, further jeopardizing already fragile ecological systems. In the Maharashtra sugar belt in western India, for instance, a drop in rainfall caused severe water shortages in the 2010s.[56]

The race for agro-fuels may bring large swathes of land in Africa, the Philippines, Brazil, and Indonesia into the hands of foreign companies. Land grabbing, land hoarding, and dispossession of communal land has always attended sugar cane cultivation, as we have seen in Java, the Dominican Republic, and Cuba. But these practices have grown exponentially since sugar cane has been developed into a crop for both food and fuel. Not only are rainforests felled at a speed reminiscent of what was happening in Cuba a century ago, agrarian communities are ruthlessly forced into ethanol production, such as in the Luzon province of Isabela or in Aceh (Sumatra). A consistent pattern has emerged whereby huge swaths of land are declared idle when they are in fact inhabited and cultivated. Corporations clear the land with the local military on their side.[57] Usually little can be done, although occasionally powerful international organizations such Amnesty intervene, for instance on behalf of seven hundred Cambodian families forcibly evicted from their homes in 2008–2009. Amnesty finally won the court case—eleven years later.[58] Amnesty's public statement on the case presents a chilling account of corporate land grabbing by the Mitr Phol Group's local subsidiary, which hired military forces who "destroyed farmland and bulldozed, burned and razed hundreds of homes to the ground in order to clear land for the sugar plantation."[59]

A glimmer of hope is that the horrific images of physical abuse of cane cutters, land grabbing, and ecological devastation published by human rights organizations and global environmental nongovernmental organizations are shaming the sugar multinationals into action. When Illovo, for instance, became deeply entangled in land rights and forced labor issues in Southern Africa, its British mother company ABF felt obliged to publicly state its condemnation of such practices.[60] Owners of the leading brands are feeling the pressure of a growing public awareness about the social and environmental consequences of their production methods. To deflect this public scrutiny, companies have started aligning themselves with smallholder sugar producers to provide "added value" to their brands. The German sugar corporation Nordzucker, for example, obtained a Fairtrade certificate for its "Sweet Family" cane sugar. Likewise, in 2008 Tate & Lyle was allowed to retail sugar obtained from cooperatives in Belize under the Fairtrade label.[61] The additional operational costs of the Belize cane fields were only a fraction of the company's turnover, but it earned the right to advertise itself as a Fairtrade company in supermarkets in Britain and abroad.

"Green capitalism" is indeed making headway as a business model and now guides the official presentation of the world's most important sugar firms from Taiwan to Florida.[62] A video presentation by the Sugar Cane Growers Cooperative of Florida, the partner of the Fanjuls' Florida Crystals, shows the Everglades and includes the following narration: "We understand that caring for the land is good for business—and we operate with great awareness that the land we farm is ecologically sensitive."[63] The viewers are treated to a shiny presentation by a high-tech company that claims to care about people and the environment. We see sugar bags with the Domino brand logo, introduced a century ago by Horace Havemeyer. In reality, the Florida sugar industry has a reputation for having obstructed adequate measures to protect the environment and improve water quality for decades.[64] In the 1990s, the Fanjul brothers were accused of using their personal contacts with President Bill Clinton to postpone a clean-up operation initiated by Vice-President Al Gore. Alfonso Fanjul had direct telephone access to the president, which allowed him to interrupt a rendezvous with Monica Lewinsky, allegedly to object to the levying of a government tax to rescue the Everglades.[65]

Obviously, the big sugar corporations do care about their reputations and shrewdly adopt the language of ecological responsibility. They are happy to produce niche products for socially conscious consumers but their core business continues to rely on the public perception that food should be cheap.[66] What has emerged is a set of high-end supermarket chains that connect smallholder and environmentally friendly production with wealthy and socially conscious consumers. The vast majority of supermarkets, however, stock cheap food in bulk that is produced by exploiting both the environment and farmers in the Global South.[67] In 2018, a mere two hundred thousand tons of sugar were sold under the Fairtrade label, which amounted to a minute 0.017 percent of the total global production of 171 million tons.[68]

Nonetheless, a silver lining is that the marketing units of the big corporations are recognizing that the winds are changing. Much like the abolition movement, in which a rise of consumer consciousness coupled with local resistance was crucial, today's environmental justice movements in the Global South combined with consumer awareness are developing into an increasingly effective Fairtrade movement. This movement may bring about a new regime of food production comparable to what we saw two centuries ago in the early nineteenth century when a new regime emerged in the shape of industrial sugar capitalism. But we are not there yet. Sugar is still overwhelmingly produced in bulk and at minimum cost, leading often to appalling labor conditions and catastrophic environmental damage. The sugar industry is also, of course, a prime cause of the obesity and type 2 diabetes epidemics.

14

Sweeter Than Nature

For most of its sprawling history, sugar has been a luxury beyond the reach of the vast majority of people. Just 150 years ago, global sugar consumption was only a tenth of what it is today. From 1.8 kilograms per capita in 1850, it rapidly increased to 5.1 kilograms in 1900 and 12.3 kilograms in 1930, after which it stagnated until the early 1950s. It then soared toward twenty kilograms per capita in the 1990s.[1] Meanwhile, the differences in consumption among countries are huge. In the late 1990s, per capita sugar consumption in China was a modest seven kilograms a year, in India it amounted to 15.4 kilograms, whereas in middle-income sugar-producing countries such as Brazil, Cuba, and Mexico it exceeded forty kilograms.[2]

The big leap that sugar made from being consumed in tiny amount by most people to being a key commodity in a globalized food industry occurred in less than a century and could only happen through the emergence of powerful corporate sugar industries. Gale Johnson, the prominent agricultural economist, concluded in 1974 in his damning evaluation of the American Sugar Program—the protectionist US quota system—that humanity's sweet tooth is just only marginally based on old cultural traditions and overwhelmingly caused by a "high level of protection for what is generally acknowledged to be a high-cost industry."[3] Sugar, high-fructose corn syrup (HFCS), and other bulk sweeteners are massively present in branded and heavily marketed foods and beverages. Most consumers are unaware of the full extent of sugar's presence. Cigarettes, for example, contain sweetening tobacco—first introduced by Reynolds just before World War I in its blended Camel cigarettes—which makes it easier to inhale nicotine deep in the lungs.[4] Beverages are advertised as "sports drinks," despite the fact that they are often 90 percent water and 10 percent sugar. Companies must spend enormous sums on advertising to survive in an extremely competitive environment.

How Banting Was "Buried"

That sugar makes fat was recognized long before it became available in sufficient quantities to have serious public health effects. In 1845, the respectable medical journal the *London Lancet* published a long article on the causes of obesity and diabetes mellitus, identifying sugar and starch as culprits. To make his point, the author of the article quoted from the *Cyclopedia of the Practice of Medicine* that had appeared ten years earlier in 1835: "Thus the negroes of the West Indies, and the Chinese slaves [sic], sometimes acquire enormous size during the sugar season by drinking the cane juice."[5] The *Cyclopedia* goes on to give historical examples of obesity in other cultures derived from deliberate intakes of huge amounts of sugar and starch. No doubt, the relationship between carbohydrates, obesity, and diabetes was established well before sugar was an item of mass consumption in Europe.

Prior to the nineteenth century, obesity caused by excessive sugar consumption occurred rarely in Europe and the United States, and was only mentioned in passing. For example, the Dutch doctor Steven Blankaart fulminated as early as in the seventeenth century against extensive sugar consumption of his rich countrymen. He was more focused on tooth decay and gout, however.[6] Interestingly, by the mid-nineteenth century doctors had found a high incidence of gout in India—about 7 percent—in a population that had always led the world in sugar consumption.[7] But it was only much later that the relationship between gout and sugar was firmly established. At any rate, prior to the introduction of the vacuum pan and the centrifuge, sugar was still too expensive in Europe and the United States to be a possible cause of obesity and diabetes. According to Jean-Anthelme Brillat-Savarin, the famous early nineteenth-century culinary expert, no food ingredient was as widely used as sugar, but it was equally certain that "sugar only hurts the purse." He definitely acknowledged the relationship between starchy diets and obesity, but with regard to sugar he only noticed that it caused swollen bellies among children.[8]

Until the mid-nineteenth century, corpulence was a problem confined to the well-to-do. The wealthiest few percent in Britain consumed eight to ten times as much sugar per head as the rest of the population.[9] Among these wealthy Britons, obesity became recognized as a problem, and one sufferer became fully convinced that he would have died if he had not abandoned sugar. In a pamphlet entitled *Letter on Corpulence, Addressed to the Public*, which appeared in 1863, William Banting, a high-end undertaker who served Britain's elite, including the royal family, wrote how he had heeded the advice of his general practitioner and eliminated most of the starch and sugar from his diet. This had returned him to a normal weight. Banting's pamphlet was reprinted four times in subsequent decades and served as the starting point for many dietary concepts. In some countries, "Banting" became near-synonymous with being on diet.[10]

In these years, other publications appeared that were even more straightforwardly anti-sugar. One of these, entitled *On Corpulence, its Diminution and Cure without Injury to Health* and authored by John Harvey in 1864, took a more rigorous stance: "sugar in all its forms; at every meal and wherever met with, forbid it altogether."[11] Although contemporaries might have found this advice extreme, most would have agreed that sugar ought to be consumed in moderation. Thomas Nichols, for instance, the author of *Eating to Live: The Diet Cure: An Essay on the Relations of Food and Drink to Health, Disease and Cure* (1877), felt that the Banting diet was overdoing things, but he nonetheless urged his readers to abstain from excess sugar and eat natural and fresh food.[12]

Banting's publication disappeared from the public eye in the early twentieth century when within medical science the discourse about sugar and obesity gave way to another about sugar as an energy provider. Yet German and Austrian medical scientists continued to express concerns about sugar and identified obesity as a hormonal regulatory disorder, which, as nutritionists would point out almost a century later, was directly related to high sugar consumption. Regrettably, as Gary Taubes notes, this strand of research "evaporated" during World War II. German-language scientific literature was hardly read in the Anglophone world after the war.[13]

Throughout the twentieth century, the sugar industry eagerly contributed to the "burial" of Banting, notably by sponsoring academic nutritional research that put the blame for cardiovascular diseases on fat, which deflected from the need to reduce sugar intake. John Yudkin, the nutritionist who singled out sugar as responsible for the rapid growth of obesity and related diseases such as hypertension and cardiovascular disease, would pay a heavy price for going against the grain. His book *Pure, White, and Deadly* (1972) made him an outsider in the academic community, despite his perfectly sensible argument that the human metabolism was not evolutionary equipped to deal with large quantities of sucrose. It would be decades before Yudkin was rehabilitated. In 2007, Taubes paid him tribute, as well as, tellingly, Banting, in his book *Good Calories, Bad Calories*.[14] Yudkin's book was republished in 2012 with a foreword by the prominent nutritionist Robert Lustig, whose 2009 lecture pointing out the dangers of sugar went viral and who is highly critical about the influence of the sugar industry on medical science.[15]

Much of the advertising and lobbying of the sugar, food and beverage industries is to obfuscate the fact that sugar is an important cause of obesity and type 2 diabetes. It is in many ways analogous to how the tobacco industry sowed confusion with pseudo-scientific arguments and glamorous advertising about a habit the unhealthiness of which had always been clear. However, while it is easy to trace the different medical histories of smokers and nonsmokers, nonsugar consumers barely exist, if at all. Conducting longitudinal studies testing two populations would be both costly and utterly unethical. Hence, medical history and ethnography are key to a better understanding of the impact of rising sugar consumption. Nutritionists have gratefully turned to historical data, showing that ceteris paribus—at least for food—obesity, type 2 diabetes, and cardiovascular diseases rose once sugar became a mass commodity. Yudkin, for instance, included a graph in his landmark article published in *Nature* showing how British sugar consumption soared after the duties on slave sugar were abolished in the 1850s. Nutritionists also pointed to medical data from the early twentieth century revealing a substantial increase in hypertension in the United States. They discovered that hospital doctors were diagnosing an alarmingly rising number of type 2 diabetes patients back then.[16] Indeed, this upsurge coincided with staggering increases in sugar consumption.

In general, countries that had been familiar with sugar for many centuries ranked among the highest consumers. India is a case in point. And indeed in the diets of enslaved and later plantation workers, sucrose—from cane stalks, juice, or molasses—was one of the few nutrients present in

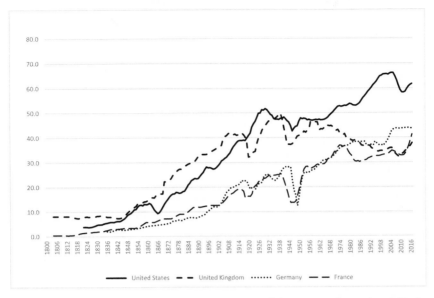

Annual sugar and sweetener consumption per capita, in kilograms, in four industrialized countries, 1801–2017 (five-year moving average).

sufficient quantities.[17] The average inhabitant of Tehran—Persia was an ancient sugar producer after all—seems to have consumed over twenty kilograms of sugar by the end of the nineteenth century.[18] Turkey, another country fond of sugar for many centuries, consumed twice as much sugar as Italy in the early twentieth century, for instance. However, within Italy consumption varied widely too. It ranged from 16.1 kilograms in Venice and Tuscany, old centers of sugar trade, to a mere 320 grams in the south, where living standards were much lower but also cultural and culinary traditions differed.[19] In late nineteenth-century France, it was estimated that wealthier families consumed 21.5 kilograms per capita per year while the rest of the population consumed less than a kilogram. French farmers preferred cheese and salt, and even the artisanal Parisian workers consumed a modest three to four kilograms per year.[20]

At the start of the twentieth century, the United States led global sugar consumption but was followed relatively closely by Australia, Western Europe, India, the Middle East, and Latin America. All these countries left most of Asia and Africa far behind, and in Central Africa sugar was practically unavailable.[21] In sum, sugar consumption is not only a matter of wealth and availability; historically developed consumption patterns are at least as important. In the late nineteenth century, the United States and England consumed twice as much sugar as France and Germany, both wealthy countries with, as we have seen, large beet sugar industries. After sugar consumption in Germany had significantly increased in the late eighteenth century, it then grew at a slow pace, despite the country's rapidly developing beet sugar industry. This was the upshot of the domestic sugar taxes that had to compensate for Germany's export bounties on sugar (see Chapter 10). Moreover, while elsewhere in Europe the upper and middle classes rapidly increased their sugar consumption, their counterparts in Germany believed that sugar extracted calcium and minerals from the body, which German doctors considered to be crucial to one's health. Incidentally, this explains the country's thriving spa economy.[22]

The situation could not have been more different in Britain and the United States. Throughout the nineteenth and twentieth centuries, candies ranked prominently among the items responsible for the soaring sugar consumption in these countries. Many children were small wage earners who happily spent some of their pennies on these sweets. Yet candies were considered a health threat early on, not for causing caries or obesity but for usually being replete with dangerous additives. In 1830, the world's most respected medical journal *The Lancet* warned against these poisonous sweets.[23] Few proletarians will have perused this journal, however, and candies were available everywhere. Apart from the shops, two hundred candy vendors populated the streets of London by the mid-nineteenth century, and they were joined by about five hundred sellers of muffins and crumpets. These vendors alone used about 125 tons of treacle and white sugar per annum.[24]

By this time, sugar had drawn the attention of Puritan traditions in the United States. In the 1830s, the Presbyterian minister Sylvester Graham prescribed vegetarianism and the avoidance of stimulants. including sugar. His back-to-nature guidelines became highly influential among the American avant-garde. The Seventh-Day Adventists committed themselves to a vegetarian diet devoid of stimulants. Two adherents, the Kellogg brothers, developed cornflakes for the guests of their famous Battle Creek Sanitarium, where people tried to recover from their bad eating habits. The cornflakes were triumphantly served as a healthy alternative to the fat- and sugar-loaded breakfasts of the day, despite not being particularly healthy. Will Keith Kellogg further compromised his health credentials when profit seeking led him into adding sugar to his cornflakes when he started mass-producing them in 1907. Things have apparently not improved since then. In 2011, Kellogg's and Quaker children's breakfast cereals were found to be among the sweetest on the market, containing up to 55 percent sugar according to a US Environmental Working Group study.[25]

Eventually, puritanism and the temperance movement did more to encourage the consumption of sugar than mitigate it. In the early nineteenth century, tea was the icon of the temperance movement, whose adherents became known as "teatotalers." But with tea came sugar, and not only sugar but also sweets and cakes. Quakers figured prominently in the industry of sweets, induced by their avoidance of alcohol. In 1824, John Cadbury, a Quaker who was also active in the temperance movement, opened a shop in Birmingham selling tea and coffee; he later started selling cocoa and making drinking chocolate. Quakers also turned Philadelphia into the "capital of sweets" by the late eighteenth century, a tradition that led to Hershey's chocolate empire at the turn of the twentieth century.[26] For Muslims and Mormons, of course, alcohol is forbidden. Probably not coincidentally, sugar is generously consumed among these faiths and, among the Mormons, to an alarming extent.[27] Indeed, it seems that sugar and alcohol act as each other's substitute. As Taubes observes in his bestselling *The Case against Sugar:* "sugar can allay the physical craving for alcohol."[28]

In the United States, growing societal disapproval of alcoholic beverages went along with ubiquitous advertisements for everything sweet and the introduction of new beverages. Coca-Cola, for instance, was invented in 1886 by the apothecary John S. Pemberton in response to the prohibition of alcohol in his town of Atlanta, Georgia. This drink, which contained cocaine until the year 1905, received its iconic bottle in 1915, when the product became massively retailed. Both the beverage and candy industry enormously expanded during US Prohibition from 1920 to 1933, precisely at the time the introduction of the assembly line dramatically lowered the price of candy making.[29] As a result, the year 1936 saw a record annual candy consumption of 16 pounds per capita, making these sweets the eighth largest "food" item at the time.[30]

Soda fountain, Boston, 1913. Beginning in the mid-nineteenth century, soda fountains spread rapidly in the United States, popularizing the consumption of sweetened carbonated beverages.

Mass beverages such as Coca-Cola, innovations such as soda fountains and ice creams in cones, became widely available in the United States. The low and still declining sugar prices allowed ice cream makers and producers of chocolate bars such as Cadbury and Hershey to reach the masses. Small, packaged cakes and desserts entered the US market as well.[31] In the 1920s, Harry Burt Sr. created a chocolate-coated vanilla ice cream bar on a stick together with his son. These "Good Humor" bars were sold from white trucks with bells and became famous far beyond America when they be-

came the subject of a Little Golden Book in 1964. Considering this revolution in the production of all these treats and the persistence of anti-alcohol
policies, it is not difficult to see the link with a soaring sugar intake and
concomitant diseases. The US diabetes death rate in the 1930s was already
five times as high as it was in 1880.[32]

In Germany and France, the beet sugar factories realized that sugar consumption was lagging behind that of the United States and Britain, and
they hired a small army of medical experts to convince consumers about
the necessity of sugar as a source of energy. Initially their efforts were to
little avail because of high sugar prices and consumers not yet being accustomed to extensive sugar consumption. The beet sugar factories' campaign
to raise sugar consumption became far more successful after the Brussels
Convention of 1902, however, when they could prod their governments into
lowering taxes on their product.[33] After being forced to quit dumping, the
producers now tried to funnel their sugar into their home markets.

The German and French beet sugar industrialists were convinced that
people could be taught to love sugar. Not coincidentally, in the same year
that the Brussels Convention was signed Alfred Steinitzer published "Die
Bedeutung des Zuckers als Kraftsstoff für Tourisit, Sport under Militär-
dienst" ("The Importance of Sugar as Fuel for Tourism, Sports, and Military
Service"), which was sponsored by the sugar industry. The industry printed
posters, postcards, and paper bags with the slogan "Sugar Gives Energy" to
be distributed by grocery stores. In France, the sugar industry was boosted
by scientists claiming that the laboring classes were not getting enough calories to provide them with the necessary energy to perform their work. Most
French people, and particularly those living in the countryside, still considered sugar a bourgeois frivolity. Even in Paris, one in four men and one in
five women did not yet consume sugar on a daily basis in 1905. While French
authorities seemed to accept the idea that a healthy diet involved a sugar
intake of an annual twenty-five kilograms per capita, instead of the actual
fourteen to fifteen kilograms then being consumed, such an elevated level
did not accord with the French taste. A proposal to sweeten baguettes
demonstrated how little confidence there was in getting the general population accustomed to more sugar.[34] In Germany, industrial workers' began to
consume rice porridge, puddings, and other sweet foods that became available in the early years of the twentieth century, but in many German farm
houses sugar consumption was still seen as a wasteful sin.[35]

It would be garrisons and battlefields that played a decisive role in raising sugar consumption. The French army began introducing coffee and tea with a drop of sugar in daily rations in the 1870s.[36] In Germany platoons of soldiers underwent trials in the final years of the nineteenth century to test whether sugar would enhance their endurance, which apparently was the case. From then on, they received sugar cakes and other sweets in their rations to strengthen their resilience. During World War I, the German army rapidly increased its purchase of sugary products, particularly marmalade, to replace more nutritional components that became increasingly scarce.[37]

US soldiers sent to the tropical territories brought under US rule at the turn of the twentieth century were given sugar in abundance. Easily digestible calories kept them on their feet, particularly if they suffered from diarrhea in the tropics. Rations increased over time; US soldiers who were sent to Europe in 1917 consumed a quarter pound of sugar per day, plus candies. Sugar again appeared in larger quantities in the soldiers' backpacks in World War II.[38] The rations of Japanese soldiers followed the examples of European and American armies with increasing amounts of sugar, which was possible because Japan's colonial expansion had turned Taiwan into its sugar provider. Through the national confectionery industry, the often-undernourished Japanese soldiers were extensively provided with sweets in the 1930s and 1940s.[39]

Food Standards and Mass Consumption

While the sugar industry's propaganda pushed sugar as a necessary energy provider it also benefited from increasing public concerns about bacteria, vermin and adulteration. This anxiety was a combination of the development of chemistry and microbiology as well as the increasing distance between producers and consumers—varying from tea plucked in China to milk from the countryside for urban dwellers.[40] A growing awareness of the importance of good hygiene advanced the cause of packaged and industrially processed food, with key beneficiaries being Lipton tea in England and Borden condensed milk in the United States. While such items rapidly spread throughout the urban and industrial world, this happened particularly fast and comprehensively in the United States, and to this day the country continues to heavily influence standards of global food consumption.

Borden's sweetened condensed milk is a pertinent example of how food preservation, mass consumption, and an elevated sugar intake became entangled. On the eve of the American Civil War, Gail Borden succeeded in producing condensed milk on an industrial scale, which enabled the Union Army to supply soldiers with milk that did not turn sour in the hot climate of the South. Borden's invention also found an eager market in the cities, where milk was often adulterated, contributing to a child mortality reportedly higher than elsewhere in the industrial world.[41] With the rise of the United States as a global power, condensed milk spread as a global product and mixed with sugar into a caramel paste it turned into the widely popular dulce de leche in Latin America, the Philippines, and Spain. Condensed milk became a universal ingredient, ranging from the artisanal sweetened and thickened milk popular in India to the caramel paste put on bread in numerous homes.[42]

Sweetening of food became commonplace in the emerging mass food industry, which gained the immense advantage of being considered as trusted and hygienic at the time that the United States, for instance, notoriously lacked hygiene standards and the addition of poisonous substances and dilution of milk, honey, and sweets occurred frequently. While the adding of poisonous coloring material such as aniline, chromium, copper, and other metals to children's sweets was widespread at the time—and not confined to the United States—candies were nonetheless being consumed in immense quantities by Americans at the end of the nineteenth century.[43] Harvey Wiley, we met him as the foremost US sugar expert in Chapter 7, became a crusader against the adulteration of sweeteners and food in general. He was the main architect of the Pure Foods and Drugs Act of 1906, the enforcement of which was put in the hands of his own agency, the US Department of Agriculture (USDA). Thanks also to Wiley's unstinted efforts, we find it completely normal today that packaged foods and beverages list their ingredients. Consumers became educated about the importance of buying standardized, unadulterated food, not only for their own health but also because consuming food of a trusted quality underwrote their middle-class status. The less beneficial side effect was a growing preference for industrially processed food, which was poor in terms of vitamins and usually loaded with carbohydrates.

Industrially bottled beverages and canned food increasingly passed as healthy food at the time that fresh vegetables and fruit were considered by domestic economists as pointless luxuries for the ordinary working-class American, whereas fat and sugar were lauded as extremely efficient energy suppliers.[44] Sugar obviously was a most efficient energy transmitter, as travelers in India had known for two thousand years and patients in Egyptian and Crusader hospitals had known a millennium ago. The first US dietary guidelines of 1917 considered a healthy diet to consist of 52 percent carbohydrates, which legitimized a high sugar intake and allowed even candy to be counted as food.[45] Vitamins were only discovered and identified as crucially important after 1912, even though it was long established as a fact that vegetables and fruits were indispensable to preserving people's health. Obviously, different standards were applied to the lower classes than what Thomas Nichols had prescribed for the middle and upper classes in Victorian England in 1877.

The market for cheap sweeteners was immense, and industry was now capable of providing them. Industrially manufactured glucose syrup, for instance, replaced the old molasses as the poor people's sugar, which had become increasingly inedible as sugar factories managed to extract almost all sucrose from the juice. Glucose syrup nonetheless had to overcome public skepticism, which sometimes equated it with sawdust, but it won the day because it was cheap, not poisonous, and could be manufactured in almost unlimited quantities.[46] Franz O. Matthiessen, a nephew of Henry O. Havemeyer and owner of a gigantic sugar refinery in Chicago, carried glucose production into a new phase by establishing the Glucose Sugar Refining Company in 1897. After a merger, this became known as the Corn Products Refining Company, which introduced the Karo brand of corn syrup with a massive advertisement campaign in 1903.[47]

Growing public awareness of the dangers of unhygienic and poisonous food also led to industrial white sugar becoming the preferred kind of sugar, even though Wiley, in his authoritative work *Foods and Their Adulteration* (1917), expressed his puzzlement about consumers' preference for this sugar, a "dead white product which is now in vogue."[48] But he should not have been surprised as raw sugar had become increasingly suspect at the time the notion of bacteria was introduced. Moreover, it was widely advertised in the 1890s that the sugar beetle was found in bags of raw sugar arriving at the harbors of the United States. Refiners jumped on any story about bacteria and insects in raw sugar to prod the public into switching to their white sugar. Henry O. Havemeyer launched the Eagle and Crystal Domino brands of white granulated sugar in 1900. Twenty years later, his son Horace had individual sugar cubes wrapped in paper being served in chic restaurants, which helped to define Domino sugar as up-market, classy, and hygienic.[49]

Sugar marketing now associated white granulated sugar with purity, science, and hygiene, a strategy that had global influence. In India the highly refined industrial Java sugar was propagated in one newspaper as pure and thus higher-caste sugar in the 1920s. Yet it was admitted that "notwithstanding the spread of education conservative India is not yet converted to the extent as to intelligently adopt better and purer food products in preference to the crude and harmful indigenous supplies."[50] At any rate, across the globe the food industry boomed as it could now disgorge millions of standardized packaged items of guaranteed quality. Branding came with mass advertisement, and mass advertisement with print capitalism that forged nations as communities, which not only shared information and values but also "national" brands, such as Coca-Cola, Domino, Kellogg's, and Karo. All these famous trademarks became part of American national identity and the American way of life—and cultural exports to the world.

In addition to being trusted and popular, many of these brands were successful as convenience food that saved time in the household. This trend had started as early as the 1860s, when baking powder, a combination of refined flour and sugar, came on the market as a basic ingredient for home baking.[51] This was easy to use in a cast iron stove, which was present in most households of moderate means at the time. When fewer women baked their own bread, cake mix became a new and promising niche for flour companies. The standard taste and texture, and the reliability of the product as long as the directions on the box were followed, made cake mix an item present in almost every household in industrial societies.[52] Sugar also found its way into instant puddings such as Jell-O, to which only water needed to be added.[53]

When the United States entered World War I, sugar had become part of a vast array of its foodstuffs and now extended to canned vegetables, a whole range of flavoring extracts and, last but not least, condensed milk. Herbert Hoover, the official in charge of the wartime Food Administration, feared that rationing sugar consumption would lead to a revolt as "sugar was a sort of binding material on which our cuisine largely revolves."[54] Despite global sugar shortages caused by the war, rationing was not applied and US sugar consumption actually rose.[55] Increasingly, foods containing sugar have become cheaper and easier to retail than "non-sugared" food.[56] This is partly because sugar preserves food, whereas healthy fiber reduces the shelf life of products, as Robert Lustig has pointed out. This is a fact sugar refiners have known for almost two thousand years.[57]

Mass advertising pushed industrial food as socially acceptable, and in these foodstuffs liquid invert sugars (sucrose dissolved into glucose and fructose) were generously added because of their powerful preserving qualities. Moreover, sugar was cheap and thus gave producers of sweetened products generous margins of profitability. Sugar was no longer advertised as sugar per se but in the form of the numerous edible items that contained sugar. Through multiple channels, the sugar industry managed to normalize the consumption of sugar-loaded cakes, sweets, and beverages, but also tomato ketchup, cornflakes, and so on. Authors of American cookbooks found jobs with big food corporations. Recipes in popular magazines featured mass-produced convenience foods.[58] Children were enticed with cartoons and later through television adds to consume candies and sweetened beverages and food. Over time, advertisements became ever more sophisticated in evocating pleasure, desire, and prestige. Coca-Cola, which traveled with the GIs during World War II, later became part of the US presence across the globe with bottling plants appearing in even the poorest regions.[59]

Struggling against Obesity

The history of how sugar became ubiquitous in American food and beverages can be read as an extreme version of what happened elsewhere in the world. As the industrial center of the world, the United States exported its consumption patterns in a variety of sometimes unexpected ways. In 1899, for instance, the Japanese migrant Taichiro Morinaga returned from the United States, where he had studied the production of confectionery, to develop the first industrial candy company in Japan.[60] Sweets became part of popular Japanese cookbooks that sometimes appeared in issues of hundred thousand copies or more. Japan would introduce confectionery in Korea after it occupied the country in 1910. With growing sugar supplies from Java and its own colony of Taiwan, Japan's government began propagating sugar as cheap calories for its rapidly urbanizing industrial workforce. Even more so than in nineteenth-century England, cheap sugar was considered the fuel for Japan's imperial project. The government advanced sugar in the 1920s as food for a nation that needed to be strong.[61]

Sugar consumption was also promoted through the Americanization of advertising culture. Since sugar-stuffed food was part of the American way of life, its consumption was globally disseminated through the US film industry. Ironically, the same film industry set the new bodily norm of slimness, which dominated illustrated advertisements at a time when tuberculosis had receded through better food and more hygienic living conditions. If slimness until then had tended to be associated with suffering from this deadly disease, it obtained a completely new connotation in the years just before World War I.[62] At that time, the cigarette industry exploited women's awareness that sweets made you fat to open up the female market for cigarettes. They competed with sweets by advertising that cigarettes make women slim: "Reach for a Lucky [Strike] instead of a sweet."[63]

Excessive consumption of sugar, and more broadly of carbohydrates, was definitely a subject of concern for the American middle class. At the turn of the twentieth century, for instance, the *Boston Cooking School Magazine* had warned that "sugar is needed to supply heat and energy, but the dietaries in most families and institutions are apt to contain too much starch and sugar and too little protein."[64] The highly influential Good Housekeeping Institute also warned against too much sugar. In the 1920s, its magazine *Good Housekeeping* had a circulation of about a million copies, and after World War II this ballooned up to five million. The magazine's careful approach to sugar is even more remarkable because of the two highly familiar names connected with this monthly. The first was Herbert Myrick, the populist propagandist for domestic sugar who was also the president of Phelps Publishing Company, which specialized in farmers' periodicals. In this capacity he was the director of the Good Housekeeping Company from 1900 to 1911 and publisher of *Good Housekeeping*. The second was Harvey Wiley.

From 1912 to 1930, Wiley acted as director of the Good Housekeeping Institute research department. *Good Housekeeping* offered him a widely influential platform, making him the food scientist of middle-class America who put the woman in the kitchen to make her marriage a success and her family happy by good cooking. Like Myrick, Wiley was too much engaged with the US sugar industry to be a complete adversary of sugar. In the highly influential *Good Housekeeping Cook Book,* which he authored together with

Mildred Maddocks and which was first published in 1914, the word "sugar" occurs 211 times. It nonetheless included this stern warning: "The sugars which enter so largely into the desserts are food products, but minister only to the production of heat and energy and the formation of fat. The deposition of adipose matter is the Nemesis which follows the over-eater."[65] There was not a shred of doubt for this chemist and champion of the American sugar industry that sugar was "adipose matter."

In addition to sugar being identified as fattening, the relationship between dental decay and sugar was established by an extensive study conducted by the Ohio dentist Weston A. Price, published in 1939. Worried about rapidly deteriorating dental health in his own practice, he had concluded from his travels around the globe that "primitive" people—who in fact included inhabitants of sequestered mountain villages in Switzerland—had better teeth than "civilized" ones.[66] One year after Price's publication, excessive tooth decay appeared as the most important reason for rejecting 40 percent of the first million drafted for US military service.[67] Sugar and candies in particular became a concern for both doctors and teachers, not only in the United States but in England as well, where sweets ruined the teeth of generations of children.[68] As early as in 1930, the advice was given to hand out fruits and nuts to children instead of candies. Teachers advocated for making nutrition part of school curricula and called for improvements to the quality of school lunches. But they also acknowledged that they fought an uphill battle against a food industry that could spend millions of dollars on advertising.[69]

Sugar was put on notice in the 1930s, but its industrialists stood ready to deal with any threat to their existence. When the USDA advised the government in 1942 that the wartime scarcity of sugar need not be seen as a health threat and that other foodstuffs had far more nutritional value, the sugar industry went up in arms. As a result of its lobbying, the US Congress did not impose a tax on soft drinks.[70] Furthermore, raw sugar producers and refiners from every corner of US territory convened under the leadership of the president of the National Sugar Refining Company to launch a publicity offensive. The Sugar Research Foundation was established in 1943 and, although a public relations vehicle, it was able to attract an associate professor from the Massachusetts Institute of Technology as its director. One of his main tasks was to counter the work of dietitians and other professionals warning against the dangers of sugar.[71] When in 1947 the wartime sugar rationings were gradually abolished, the Sugar Research Foundation was called upon to advocate sugar as part of a healthy diet, just as French and German beet sugar industries had tried to sell sugar as a nutritional item rather than a luxury fifty years before. As the editors of the magazine *Sugar*, the mouthpiece of the American sugar industry, wrote in 1947, "Steps must be taken to correct the 'psychology of scarcity' that has been created in the minds of the consuming public by government agencies and private institutions over the past five years."[72]

When Ancel Keys's argument that cholesterol was the cause of cardiovascular diseases won the day in the 1950s, the sugar industry gratefully jumped on the bandwagon of fat being the main problem of our diet. The Sugar Research Foundation sponsored a project by three Harvard professors, one of them being Mark L. Hegsted, who would play a major role in US food policies in the next decades. The research was published in 1967 and prominently contributed to deflecting attention from the health risks of sugar by identifying saturated fats as the prime cause of cardiovascular diseases.[73] This seemed to be corroborated when Keys published his magnum opus, a seven-country study, in 1980. Keys's research was fundamentally flawed, however, as it violated a basic statistical rule. So intent was he on proving that fat was the determining factor in cardiovascular diseases that he omitted this equally important fact: that sugar intake also grew considerably over the course of the period covered by his research. That sugar is also a cause of cardiovascular and metabolic diseases seemed not to have been mainstream knowledge at the time—nor that cardiovascular diseases, diabetes, and obesity are related. It is only rather recently that the record has been set straight. In 2013, Sanjay Basu, Robert Lustig, and colleagues demonstrated through econometric analysis that "sugar appears to be uniquely correlated to diabetes prevalence."[74]

Meanwhile, between 1950 and 1980, the number of bottles of soft drink consumed per capita increased 7.5 times in the United States. Vending machines, often put in schools in return for sponsorships, overwhelmingly offered sweet stuff.[75] What had happened to soldiers at the turn of the twentieth century was now inflicted on children. Obviously, the younger that people get accustomed to a high sugar intake, the better it is for the beverage and sugar industries. In the 1970s, the average daily calorie intake from sugar had reached 500–550 kilocalories in the United States, as well as in Britain for that matter, but for many people that figure stood at 1,000–1,500 kilocalories, which is half the amount an adult person needs. Meanwhile, milk consumption in the United States saw a 22.5 percent drop between 1970 and 1997.[76]

The data were already alarming when in 1974 an editorial in *The Lancet* identified obesity as "the most important nutritional disease in the world." The message needed time to sink in even in the United States, where the attention of the political class had just been directed to the persistence of hunger in the country. Few realized, however, that because of the cheapness of carbohydrates obesity was lurking behind hunger and malnutrition. Increasing purchasing power for the poorest layers of the population would not yet give them access to healthy food but only to cheap, industrial bulk food. Indeed, in the twentieth century the working poor were no longer hungry; they had shifted within a generation from undernourishment to calorie abundance.[77]

Guidelines for Sugar Intake

The proceedings of the Senate Select Committee on Nutrition and Human Needs illustrate how rapidly this transition from hunger to obesity could happen. Established in 1968 to address the existence of hunger in America under the chairmanship of George McGovern, the committee soon felt compelled to shift its focus to obesity, and its deliberations resulted in *Dietary Goals for the United States,* known as the McGovern Report, in 1977. This gave much prominence to fat as a cause of cardiac and vascular diseases, and proposed a considerable increase in carbohydrates to reduce saturated and monounsaturated fats.[78] The main consultant was Mark L. Hegsted, a scholar who had publicly condemned Yudkin as a "health threat" and one of the three Harvard nutritionists who had received the grant from the US sugar industry for research identifying saturated fats as the cause of cardiac diseases. Although it was a blatant ethics violation to leave out the sugar industry from its acknowledgments—a fact probably not known to the select committee—Hegsted did not behave merely as a lackey of the sugar factories. The McGovern Report came with a guideline reducing the intake of refined and processed sugar by 45 percent to 10 percent of the daily calorie intake, a recommendation which would become a bone of contention in the decades to follow.[79]

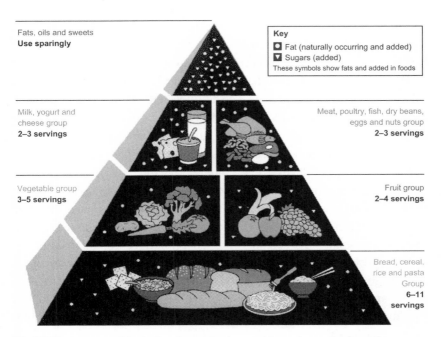

Fats, oils and sweets
Use sparingly

Key
☐ Fat (naturally occurring and added)
▼ Sugars (added)
These symbols show fats and added in foods

Milk, yogurt and
cheese group
2–3 servings

Meat, poultry, fish, dry beans,
eggs and nuts group
2–3 servings

Vegetable group
3–5 servings

Fruit group
2–4 servings

Bread, cereal,
rice and pasta
Group
**6–11
servings**

The US Department of Agriculture's 1992 food pyramid was the result of an effort to encourage a more balanced diet. The project was almost destroyed by food-industry lobbyists, who had no interest in promoting reduced intake of fat and sugar. Meanwhile nutritionists were critical of the high recommended consumption of carbohydrates, as indicated at the base of the pyramid.

Under the Reagan administration, the struggle against obesity suffered serious blows; HFCS was allowed to bring sugar prices down while the protectionist Sugar Program—that had been discontinued in 1974—was reinstated to shore up the domestic sugar industry. This unleashed increasing quantities of carbohydrates in the daily menu.[80] It also derailed a 1980s USDA project to develop a new set of guidelines, the so-called Food Pyramid, as a successor of the earlier tables of the Basic Seven food groups guidelines of 1943 and Basic Four of 1956. The nutritionist Luise Light was hired to head this venture, but she was dismayed when the end result was far more the product of the food lobby than of nutritionists. She and her team had recommended reducing the intake of refined grains and saturated fats and maximizing free sugar intake (i.e., sugars that are refined or processed and include honey and fruit juices) at 10 percent of the daily energy intake. But after Light had submitted her Food Guide to the secretary of agriculture, it was not made public until 1992, when it was more or less turned upside down. All instances of "less" had been changed "moderate." Yet even this substantial modification of the original guidelines—designed as a pyramid by a marketing bureau—elicited a firestorm from the food industry, so intense that even these not very healthy guidelines barely survived. Whistleblowers and prominent nutritionists such as Marion Nestle—who was actually unenthusiastic about the pyramid—should be credited for its rescue.[81]

Meanwhile, consumption patterns developed in a far unhealthier direction than what was prescribed in the guidelines. Briefly, sweet beverages and fried potatoes took the space that according to the guidelines belonged to milk and green vegetables. As Yudkin put it, "good foods were being crowded out by the nutritionally inferior, sugar-based, foods."[82] Attempts to stop this trend, as through the World Health Organization (WHO) report on *Diets, Nutrition, and the Prevention of Chronic Diseases* that appeared in 1990, put the sugar and beverage industry up in arms. The WHO's report recommended an annual intake of free sugars of fifteen to twenty kilograms, which was half of what was consumed in large parts of the world.[83]

In the 1990s, the global sugar industry managed to become an accredited stakeholder of the WHO, which made their input or advice mandatory. But even more threatening, the sugar industry put the US Congress and the administration of George W. Bush under pressure to scupper US funding for the WHO if it refused to omit a guideline setting a maximum of 10 percent on daily intake of free sugars from its report to be published in 2003. The guideline nevertheless stayed in the report and was underlined by the WHO's concern over the high intake of sweetened beverages by children in many countries.[84] Nonetheless, a fierce US lobby prevented the 10 percent maximum from being explicitly endorsed in 2004 by the World Health Assembly, the governing body of the WHO consisting of its member states. Instead, it recommended a rather vague "limiting" of the levels of free sugars. Ignoring this lukewarm support of its governing body, the WHO would continue to formulate the guideline to reduce the share of free sugar in the daily energy intake *below* 10 percent.[85]

Many of these free sugars are put in beverages, and over the past century the battlefront against obesity has shifted from the kitchen, where it was in Wiley's days, to the beverage industry. By the end of the twentieth century,

56 percent of the sweetener market in the United States was occupied by HFCS, which was massively applied to beverages.[86] Since sugar-sweetened beverages do not satisfy one's hunger, they do not reduce the intake of other calories and are therefore a major cause of obesity. Children are obviously particularly vulnerable in this respect. In 2010, the World Health Assembly therefore unanimously adopted recommendations regarding advertising sweetened beverages and a similar call to restrict misleading advertisements. In 2016, a recommendation followed to introduce a tax on sugary beverages.[87]

Whatever guidelines the WHO issues, however, they can have no impact unless national governments implement them, and they often fail to do so. The US Senate Finance Committee discussed a proposal to tax sugar-sweetened beverages in 2009 to co-fund Obamacare, but it did not make it to the Senate floor. The state of New York failed to impose an 18 percent tax on nondiet soft drinks and beverages with less than 70 percent juice content.[88] Michael Bloomberg's initiative to introduce a sugar tax in New York during his tenure as mayor did not succeed, nor his proposal to the USDA to run a pilot to remove sugared beverages from the Supplemental Nutrition Assistance Programs, formerly known as the Food Stamp Program. Bloomberg then poured millions of dollars into a campaign to introduce a sugar tax in Chicago. He was successful this time—but the measure was repealed within two months.[89] Cynically, this happened because the sugar tax was *too* effective in reducing the sales of these beverages, as was also proven elsewhere in the United States. In Berkeley, the sugared beverage tax introduced in 2014 led to a halving of consumption there by 2017, for instance. And when Philadelphia taxed sugared beverages in 2017, it reduced consumption by about 42 percent.[90] That taxation works should not surprise us. After all, in the late nineteenth century German and French domestic consumption had stayed at a relatively low level when consumers had to pay for the dumping of beet sugar abroad.

Still, one argument against a tax on high-sucrose beverages is that it may lead to substitution of other unhealthy foods and, undeniably, that this tax hits low-income groups the hardest.[91] Fiscally discouraging sugar consumption may nonetheless be the only option for governments such as of Mexico, a middle-income country where one in three adults is overweight and where cardiovascular disease is the leading cause of mortality. This situation is a direct consequence of the US beverage industry, including

Coca-Cola, owning more than half of Mexico's sugar factories, coupled with a glaring absence of clean tap water. Children have soft drinks at breakfast and the cheapness of these products pushes healthier food and fruits out.[92] In 2013, Mexico managed to levy a one-peso tax per liter on sugary beverages, and seven years later the state of Oaxaca took another important step by banning the sales of sugary drinks and junk food to children.[93]

The European Union also considered a taxation on calorie-rich soft drinks, and some countries even implemented it. Denmark was one of these, but the measure lasted for only fifteen months. In July 2015, the British Medical Association, supported by sugar tax campaigners such as Action on Sugar and the renowned chef Jamie Oliver, pressured the British government to introduce a tax related to the sugar content of beverages in 2016.[94] By 2018, Britain, Portugal, Catalonia, six local jurisdictions in the United States, Chili, Mexico, France, Finland, Hungary, Brunei, Thailand, the United Arab Emirates, and Saudi Arabia had some form of sugar tax. The food industry, meanwhile, is lobbying as hard as it can against such measures, and it is much more powerful than the tobacco industry because sugar is part of almost every industrially processed food item. The enormous power of the industry is no doubt partially responsible for the absence of support in Germany for a sugar tax, despite half of its population suffering from overweight and 20–25 percent from pathological obesity. It may also explain why European health ministers agreed in 2015 on a timid 10 percent reduction of free sugar intake by 2020. The results of "collaboration" between governments and the food industry are invariably underwhelming. In the Netherlands, agreements between the government and food industry envisaged a reduction of sugar intake by a minute 2 percent of consumption that still exceeded an annual forty kilograms per capita.[95]

While the sugar industry has done everything it can over the past 150 years to deflect sound dietary advice and used its financial power to influence politicians, the media, and scientists, there have always been publicists and scientists who challenged its power in the face of retribution. Tate & Lyle actively worked to marginalize Yudkin as a nutritional specialist, labeling his book *Pure, White and Deadly* as "science fiction."[96] Marion Nestle disclosed in the 2007 edition of *Food Politics* that two weeks before the publication of the first edition in 2002, three highly critical reviews had been posted on the Amazon website.[97] The long arm of the sugar industry went even further. The Swiss publicist Al Imfeld lost his job as director of the study center sponsored by the supermarket chain Migros after he invited Yudkin for a lecture. Imfeld was not a man to be silenced, however, and exposed the malign influence of the sugar industry in his book *Sugar*.[98]

Robert Lustig and his colleagues have pointed out time and again that the medical and nutritional sciences alone cannot win the battle against obesity because they are hopelessly outgunned by formidable, vested interests whose tactic it is to sow confusion about scientific findings. As a result, it seems to be less obvious that sugar causes obesity today than it was 150 years ago at the time of Banting, the undertaker of the British royals. Sugar was always a luxury, and from a nutritional perspective an unnecessary additive. The idea that we need sugar for energy, an argument any working man or woman would have ridiculed in the nineteenth century, is something that had to be sold to the public via advertisements, by putting sugar in soldiers' rations, and, most brazenly, by placing vending machines in schools. Governments today allow interest groups to corrode their primary duty of protecting the health and safety of their citizens.

The beverage and sugar industries claim that preventing obesity is the responsibility of the individual consumer, and to underscore their point they advertise their brands with images of people playing sports and working outs. In 2015, the *New York Times* reported how Coca-Cola had sponsored researchers who concluded that lack of exercise rather than sugar was the main cause of obesity.[99] The marketing strategy of advertising its drinks as belonging to a lifestyle filled with sport and fitness is copied from the tobacco industry, or perhaps the other way round.[100] The silver lining, however, is that in contrast to the tobacco industry, the beverage producers can resort to the alternative of nonsucrose sweeteners, although it should be admitted that their positive contribution to the battle against obesity is still not clear.[101]

The Corporate Sweetener Business

Beet-, cane-, and starch-processing industries all have their own and often competing interests, but they tend to unite when they see their businesses endangered, whether at the national level or by international organizations, such as the WHO. They also have a joint adversary in the powerful beverage industry, which, if it fits its agenda, attacks the Fanjul brothers and has no qualms about skipping sucrose sweeteners or putting beet or cane farmers out of business, as the case of HFCS has shown. Ironically, it was Roberto Goizueta, refugee from Cuba and grandson of a Spanish sugar miller, who as CEO of Coca-Cola shifted to HFCS and saved his company 20 percent of its production costs in one fell swoop.[102]

Even more challenging than HFCS are the noncaloric sweeteners, whose entrance onto world markets has not surprisingly been resisted tooth and nail by beet and cane sugar producers. The emergence of artificial sweeteners opened a new arena of industrial lobbying and created a new advertising language, as they had a distinct interest in impressing upon the public that sucrose made you fat and that you therefore buy their product. The cane and beet sugar sectors immediately joined forces in resistance. When in the mid-1950s sugar consumption in the United States entered a downward slope thanks to the introduction of artificial sweeteners, Cuban cane farmers, the Sugar Research Foundation, the Czarnikow-Rionda Company, and American sugar workers forged an unlikely coalition and targeted their considerable lobbying power at the US Congress to fight the advance of artificial sweeteners.[103]

This was not the first battle against artificial sweeteners, however. At the turn of the twentieth century, the German government had banned saccharine from the ordinary consumer market under pressure from the sugar beet industry. Saccharine, which is made from coal tar, was discovered in 1879 by Russian-born Constantine Fahlberg, who was educated in Germany as a chemist and was affiliated to Johns Hopkins University in the United States. He patented the production process, returned to Germany, and together with his uncle built a factory near Magdeburg, more or less in the lion's den of the world's beet sugar interests. Touted as a miraculous discovery, particularly for patients of diabetes, it attracted instant and wide press coverage. In 1901, saccharine, which is five hundred times as sweet as sucrose, occupied 5 percent of the German sugar market in terms of "sweetener power," and emerged as a serious competitor for beet sugar. Fahlberg became a wealthy man. However, at that stage, the German Reichstag, in deference to the beet sugar producers, duly enacted a law confining saccharine production for medical purposes. After the signing of the Brussels Convention that severely restricted beet sugar output, the country's sugar industry convinced the government to further ban saccharine production and again the government obliged and assigned its manufacturing to a single factory.[104]

Most European countries followed Germany's example with the notable exception of Switzerland, where artificial sweetener research contributed to the rise of the chemical giant Sandoz.[105] Swiss chemists staffed the laboratories of Monsanto, where they produced a number of chemical substitutes such as vanillin, coumarin, and caffeine. Established in 1901 in St. Louis, this chemical behemoth had started as a saccharine producer for Coca-Cola.[106] In the early years of the twentieth century, many soft drinks in the United States contained saccharine produced by Monsanto.

Saccharine became one of the targets of Harvey Wiley's crusade against adulterants. He succeeded in having Coca-Cola abandon this sweetener and actually all diet colas (this continued until 1962). He found it repugnant to extract a sweetener from coal and to produce a substance without any nutritional value that he deemed near-poisonous. In 1911, Wiley's Department of Food Inspection decided that adding saccharine was unhealthy and lowered food value. Ironically, when he had tried to convince President Theodore Roosevelt on this point a few years before, the president himself had just been prescribed saccharine by his doctor to prevent diabetes. Nonetheless, Wiley's opinion was enshrined in the law that saccharine could not replace sugar and that each package containing this sweetener had to carry the message that it was added for dieting purposes.[107] During World War I, when sugar shortages threatened, the environment might have seemed conducive to more extensive use of saccharine, but it remained an additive for dieting purposes only in the United States. Only after World War II did its application rapidly spread through low-calorie beverages, which occupied 10 percent of the beverage market in 1964.[108]

The fact that saccharine had an unpleasant aftertaste made it vulnerable to competition from other artificial sweeteners. Cyclamate, marketed as Sucaryl, was a liquid sweetener launched in 1950. It was advertised as tasting delightful "while keeping your waist in shape."[109] Indeed, this advertising shows that the American public at the time were well aware of the fattening power of sugar. Big chemical industries began to produce cyclamate in bulk, and it flowed into beverage production lines. This was serious business, as the average American had between four and five sodas per week. Unsurprisingly, the American Sugar Association and the Sugar

Research Foundation launched a crusade against cyclamate. Although there was no proof that it was carcinogenic—unless consumed in ridiculously high quantities—the US Food and Drug Administration (FDA) banned it in 1969, in the same year that it was allowed in a number of European countries. The public campaign against cyclamate had done its work.[110]

With cyclamate out of the way, the beverage industry had to fall back on saccharine, but this sweetener fell victim to another improperly conducted test with rats, which were fed enormous quantities of it. In 1972, the FDA removed saccharine from the list of safe additives and five years later packaging of foods containing this sweetener had to show a health warning. The struggle went on until 2000, when the US Congress abolished this regulation.[111]

A new calorie-free sweetener arrived in 1974, two years after the FDA had withdrawn saccharine from the list of safe additives. This sweetener, aspartame, would have a checkered career, particularly because Searle, the company that had developed it, had submitted manipulated testing data to the FDA. Nutritionists started a campaign against aspartame, joined by Ralph Nader, the well-known consumer and civil rights activist. Investigations resulted in the devastating conclusion that Searle's laboratory had doctored their testing logbooks.[112] Aspartame was banned in 1975, but not for good. Donald Rumsfeld, the former—and future—secretary of defense, was hired as president of Searle and one of his tasks was to have the ban rescinded. His chance came when, as a member of Ronald Reagan's first transition team, he could arrange for the appointment of a new director at FDA, who magically lifted the ban on aspartame for table consumption and in food.[113]

In 1981, aspartame was approved by the FDA, but by that time the patent was almost expired, a problem that was dealt with by members of the Senate who reportedly had received campaign funding from the Searle family. With a prolonged patent, Searle was eventually sold for a good price to Monsanto in 1985, at that time a highly lucrative chemical firm with excellent connections with members of Congress.[114] Although all restrictions on aspartame were lifted by the FDA in 1986, the passing of so many years left the name of this sweetener tainted. This was to all appearances neither deserved nor warranted, as expert assessment did not find any health risks involved in its consumption. New tests by the Italian researcher Morando Soffriti and his team that claimed carcinogenic effects have been rejected by the European Food Safety Authority as flawed, because the quantities fed to the rats were more suited to elephants.[115]

With the reputation of three artificial sweeteners shredded, the road was cleared for a fourth one: sucralose, sold under the brand name Splenda. The American Sugar Association aimed to quickly crush this sweetener by brandishing it as a "chlorinated artificial sweetener," referring to the fact that sucralose contains chloride. This was nonsense, however, because this sweetener had nothing in common with the unpleasantly smelling stuff in swimming pools. Sucralose was patented in Britain in 1976 by Tate & Lyle, which developed a production site for it in Alabama together with the pharmaceutical giant Johnson & Johnson. This fit the transformation of Tate & Lyle from a bulk sugar giant into a nutrition specialist in the 1990s, advertising itself as a company "helping with low calorie solutions." Splenda became a cash cow, conquering 60 percent of the US artificial sweetener market.[116] What spoiled the party somewhat for Tate & Lyle was a painful defeat when it litigated against an infringement of its sucralose patent by Chinese factories. The Chinese won thanks to the testimony of one of the researchers involved in the invention of this sweetener, the prominent chemist Bertram Fraser-Reid, who was born in Jamaica and a descendant of enslaved Africans.[117] Where he grew up, Tate & Lyle was known to be responsible for oppressive labor relations, particularly in the 1930s. There is an irony here.[118]

Decades of struggle to bring noncaloric sweeteners on the market demonstrate the power of the cane and beet sugar producers, but also the immense corporate interests involved. It took years for noncaloric sweeteners to find a market and once they had, their producers did not hesitate to push competitors out. This also happened to stevia, which in contrast to all the other noncaloric sweeteners could not be discarded as artificial. After stevioside had been isolated by French chemists in 1931, it took another thirty-nine years until this product was introduced commercially. Japan that has banned artificial sweeteners introduced it in 1970 and since then is widely used in this country. In the United States, however, the FDA moved aggressively against stevia in the 1980s. Rumor had it that the US ban on this sweetener was instigated by Monsanto, the owner of NutraSweet since 1985. Monsanto did everything within its considerable power to expand its market share and fight the growing popularity of stevia. Brazil would experience its muscle when it approved this sweetener as early as in 1988 in its struggle against obesity and type 2 diabetes, while maintaining its ban on artificial sweeteners. Monsanto did not take this lightly and pressured this country to allow aspartame, cyclamate, and saccharine in diet drinks as well.[119]

Although the WHO had already given the green light for stevia in 1990 and it had been endorsed by the Atkins low carbohydrate diet, it would take another eighteen years before in the United States the FDA accepted stevia as a sweetener. Belgium, Italy, and Spain followed in 2010, and one year later stevia was approved for the entire EU. Although it has an unpleasant aftertaste and is much more expensive than artificial sweeteners, it became a real success, entering Coca-Cola, Sprite, and Nestea to reduce the sugar content in these beverages by 30 percent. The French sugar giant Tereos began to sell stevia-based sugar products to food and drink makers in several EU countries.[120] Tate & Lyle took up the challenge to develop stevia without an unpleasant aftertaste and began work on its own brand, called Tasteva, which became a key element in the company's shift toward nonsucrose sweeteners. To free up capital for this purpose, it sold its five starch-based glucose factories in Europe to Syral (a subsidiary of Tereos) in 2007.[121] It also sold its sugar refineries in the United States, and finally its molasses distribution branch in 2010, marking the end of its historic role as a British sugar giant. Its CEO Javed Ahmed explained the abandonment of the molasses trade as a transaction that provided the company with the capital to further specialize in food ingredients, and of course low-calorie food ingredients in particular.[122]

Tate & Lyle, the paragon of sugar capitalism, had again sensed the turning of the tide, and has probably secured its survival for the decades to come. Given the overwhelming academic consensus that links high sucrose intake with type 2 diabetes and cardiovascular diseases, the world is looking for artificial sweeteners to stop an immense tragedy in the making.[123] India, the cradle of sugar, counted 77 million people with diabetes in 2019, China 116.4 million, and in the sugar island of Mauritius 22 percent of the population suffers from the disease.[124] These alarming figures appeared half a century after Yudkin had raised the alarm bell and 150 years after Banting wrote his *Letter on Corpulence, Addressed to the Public.*

Conclusion

In RELATIVELY SHORT PERIOD OF TIME, white crystalline sugar has evolved from a luxury into an utterly unremarkable item in our daily lives. Almost undetectably, our taste has become adjusted to an amazing level of sweetness in much of our food. This overabundance has not only resulted in a global health crisis but is also entangled with a history of environmental destruction, racism, and sharp global inequalities. It is the outcome of seven hundred years of global capitalism, going right back to the days of the Egyptian Mamluk rulers and the prominent Venetian Corner family, as well as to the days of famous explorers Ibn Battuta and Marco Polo, and even further back in history to the impressive sugar complex of Abwaz in Persia, the ruins of which astonished and puzzled the British Army officer Robert Mignan. It is a history full of inhuman abuse, ecological destruction, countermovements, resistance, protests, and obliterating wars between different sugar producers—but it is also one of tremendous ingenuity, entrepreneurial spirit, and optimism.

Already an important sector in the preindustrial world, in the nineteenth century sugar was what oil would become in the twentieth: a key commodity representing immense value in global trade and involving a labor force of legions. In the early twentieth century, maybe 6–8 percent of all the world's households derived part of their income from producing sugar. Meanwhile, the manufacturing, refining, and trading of sugar became increasingly concentrated into immensely powerful conglomerates. Henry O. Havemeyer's Sugar Trust was one of the twelve companies setting the Dow Jones index. The European beet sugar industry was instrumental in shaping the forerunner of the European Union's Common Agricultural Policies, which in turn ruined the sugar economies of a number of developing countries and selectively bloated others. Throughout history, the sugar industry has shifted the costs of adaptation to workers and consumers, and often raised its margins of profit well beyond the average while drowning the rich and middle-income countries in calories. Such a powerful industry will hardly accept limits to its growth, and will continue its relentless expansion through the opening up of new frontiers for ethanol production, with even graver environmental consequences.

The sugar industry represents the two faces of capitalism: progressive and innovative on the one hand but also indifferent to social and ecological consequences so long as these do not harm business. While the sugar industry speaks the truth when it claims that a modest consumption of its product does not endanger one's health and that sugar is not an addictive stimulant like nicotine, the point is that the sugar sector, as well as the food industry of which it is a major part, has an interest in adding excessive sugar to food, and it is not capable of self-regulation. The sugar industry maximizes its profits and shifts the health and ecological costs to society at large. The immense power of the sugar conglomerates makes us consumers pay for protective tariffs, for overconsumption, for staggering health insurance costs, and for repairing environmental damage.

Yet as we have seen throughout this book, it would be fundamentally wrong to blame the sugar industry alone for unhinged capitalism. Sven Beckert pointed out in *The Empire of Cotton* that we tend to overlook the crucial role of increasingly powerful states in facilitating capitalists, which makes capitalism less impervious to change than we often assume. After all, governments rely on their electorates to keep power.[1] History has shown that sugar capitalism can change course if confronted by social resistance or consumer choices putting pressure both on industry and government. At the same time, these responses were invariably partial, and every change for the better created new problems and contradictions. For hundreds of years, soil exhaustion ushered in the opening up of new frontiers and thus the destruction of ever larger tracts of land. The winning of the battle against cane diseases at the end of the nineteenth century ushered in the overproduction of cane sugar during the Great Depression. Sugar quota and tariff systems may have solved problems for the wealthy countries, but they made the global market highly volatile and extremely inequitable.

Today, the sugar industry is responding to a rising consumer awareness about health and ecology, but it will not easily change a business model in which pure quantity, and thus market share, determines success. Massive advertising budgets can polish the industry's image to make it shine for even the most critical consumer, a phenomenon known as "greenwashing." If consumers are voicing concerns about ecology, the food industry will advertise its ecological credentials; if fiber is advertised as being important to a healthy diet, it will be added to their favorite sugar-laden food and drinks.

Nonetheless, we may be witnessing a transformation even more fundamental than during the Depression years, when massive labor resistance and revolutionary upheaval resulted in development economics and sugar cooperatives. The current turn toward green capitalism can be compared with the social movements at the turn of the nineteenth century. At that time, the world saw a confluence of social resistance by enslaved with consumer movements that maintained that eating slave-produced sugar was cannibalism and condemned its production system as not making economic sense. Resistance is mounting against the current corporate sugar regime, which, when unrestrained, is grossly destructive, particularly when it involves the annihilation of indigenous communities. Similar to two hundred years ago, protests and resistance are emerging on a global scale, both among consumers and people whose rights are grossly violated by the ever-expanding sugar frontiers. The Fairtrade movement is effectively linking consumer awareness with environmental justice movements, and of course with health concerns.

Sugar has been so central in the history of capitalism that the sugar industry today resembles the Gordian knot. Massive environmental, health, and humanitarian problems have accumulated through the unrelenting expansion of the sugar frontiers. It requires tremendous political will to reform a system that has evolved over the past seven hundred years and to impose a global limit of twenty kilograms of free sugar per person per year, as recommended by the World Health Organization (WHO), as well as a ban on growing cane just for fuel. It is an ironical, if not a cynical, reality that after such a long history of intense state-intervention in sugar production, the majority of democratically elected governments are so reticent to take the measures that would implement the WHO guidelines. It is nonetheless within the power of legislative bodies to accomplish a change on the magnitude of the abolition of the slave trade by British Parliament in 1807. Sure, this decision did not bring a cane workers' paradise—far from it—but it did mark the beginning of a long struggle against slavery and coerced labor. Every new phase of capitalism will entail new disappointments and new challenges ahead. A ban on excessive addition of sugar to food and drinks would only be the start of this much-needed change, but it would make a monumental improvement to human health and the environment—in addition to saving consumers money. Transformative changes to legislation are needed desperately to cut the Gordian knot of overproduction, overexploitation, and overconsumption in the world of sugar.

NOTES

ACKNOWLEDGMENTS

IMAGE CREDITS

INDEX

Notes

Introduction

1. Stanley L. Engerman, "Contract Labor, Sugar, and Technology in the Nineteenth Century," *Journal of Economic History* 43, no. 3 (1983): 651.

2. Patrick Karl O'Brien, "Colonies in a Globalizing Economy, 1815–1948," in *Globalization and Global History*, ed. Barry K. Gills and William R. Thompson (Hoboken, NJ: Taylor and Francis, 2012), 237–238.

3. Sidney W. Mintz, *Sweetness and Power: The Place of Sugar in Modern History* (Harmondsworth, England: Penguin, 1986), 158.

4. For a historical perspective on capitalism, see, for example, Jürgen Kocka, "Durch die Brille der Kritik: Wie man Kapitalismusgeschichte auch Schreiben Kann," *Journal of Modern European History* 15, no. 4 (2017): 480–488.

5. Aseem Malhotra, Grant Schofield, and Robert H. Lustig, "The Science against Sugar, Alone, Is Insufficient in Tackling the Obesity and Type 2 Diabetes Crises—We Must Also Overcome Opposition from Vested Interests," *Journal of the Australasian College of Nutritional and Environmental Medicine* 38, no. 1 (2019): a39.

6. One publication covering data of 165 countries forecasts that by 2030, 7.7 percent of the global population will suffer from type 2 diabetes. Praveen Weeratunga et al., "Per Capita Sugar Consumption and Prevalence of Diabetes Mellitus—Global and Regional Associations," *BMC Public Health* 14, no. 1 (2014): 1.

7. On the definition of bourgeoisie, see also Christof Dejung, David Motadel, and Jurgen Osterhammel, *The Global Bourgeoisie: The Rise of the Middle Classes in the Age of Empire* (Princeton, NJ: Princeton University Press, 2020), 8. Beckert adds three economic criteria defining bourgeoisie, namely that their power is derived from capital, that they do not work for wages themselves, and that they do not perform manual work and employ labor. Sven Beckert, *The Monied Metropolis: New York City and the Consolidation of the American Bourgeoisie, 1850–1896* (Cambridge: Cambridge University Press, 2001), 6–7.

1. Asia's World of Sugar

1. Robert Mignan, *Travels in Chaldea, Including a Journey from Bussorah to Bagdad, Hillah, and Babylon, Performed on Foot in 1827* (London: H. Colburn and R. Bentley, 1829), 304.

2. Mignan, *Travels in Chaldea,* 309; Carl Ritter, *Über die geographische Verbreitung des Zuckerrohrs . . .* (Berlin: Druckerei der k. Akademie, 1840), 1.

3. Alexander Burnes, *Travels into Bokhara: Being the Account of a Journey from India to Cabool, Tartary and Persia . . . in the Years 1831, 1832, and 1833,* vol. 2 (London: J. Murray, 1834), 453–454.

4. W. Heyd and Furcy Raynaud, *Historie du commerce du Levant au moyen age,* vol. 2 (Wiesbaden, Germany: Otto Harrassowitz, 1885–1886), 681; Mohamed Ouerfelli, *Le sucre: Production, commercialisation et usages dans la Méditerranée médiévale* (Leiden: Brill, 2008), 19–21; Ritter, *Über die geographische,* 67.

5. Tsugitaka Sato, *Sugar in the Social Life of Medieval Islam* (Leiden: Brill, 2015), 23.

6. Duarte Barbosa, *A Description of the Coasts of East Africa and Malabar, in the Beginning of the Sixteenth Century,* trans. Henry E. J. Stanley (London: Hakluyt Society, 1866), 14.

7. Ritter, *Über die geographische,* 20.

8. Richard H. Major, *India in the Fifteenth Century: Being a Collection of Narratives of Voyages to India . . .* (London: Hakluyt Society, 1857), 27; Jean-Baptiste Tavernier, *Travels in India: Translated from the Original French Edition of 1676 . . . ,* 2 vols. (London: Macmillan, 1889); see esp. 1:275, 386, 391; and 2:264.

9. Ulbe Bosma, *The Sugar Plantation in India and Indonesia: Industrial Production, 1770–2010* (Cambridge: Cambridge University Press, 2013), 38–39.

10. Lallanji Gopal, "Sugar-Making in Ancient India," *Journal of the Economic and Social History of the Orient* 7, no. 1 (1964): 65.

11. Edmund Oskar von Lippmann, *Geschichte des Zuckers: Seit den ältesten Zeiten bis zum Beginn der Rübenzucker-Fabrikation: ein Beitrag zur Kulturgeschichte* (Berlin: Springer, 1929), 160–161.

12. Sucheta Mazumdar, *Sugar and Society in China: Peasants, Technology, and the World Market* (Cambridge, MA: Harvard University Press, 1998), 22, 26–27. Ji Xianlin thinks that the art of sugar making through boiling cane juice might have been known in China before 400 A.D. Ji Xianlin, *A History of Sugar* (Beijing: New Starr Press, 2017), 72, 78–80.

13. F. Buchanan, *A Journey from Madras through the Countries of Mysore, Canara, and Malabar . . . ,* vol. 1 (London: Cadell and Davies, 1807), 157–158.

14. Francis Buchanan, *A Geographical, Statistical and Historical Description of the District of Dinajpur in the Province of Bengal* (Calcutta: Baptist Mission Press, 1833), 301–307.

15. Bosma, *The Sugar Plantation,* 40.

16. Irfan Habib, *Economic History of Medieval India, 1200–1500* (Delhi: Longman, 2011), 127; Ritter, *Über die geographische,* 32.

17. S. Husam Haider, "A Comparative Study of Pre-Modern and Modern Stone Sugar Mills (Distt. Agra and Mirzapur)," *Proceedings of the Indian History Congress* 59 (1998): 1018–1019; B. P. Mazumdar, "New Forms of Specialisation in Industries of Eastern India in the Turko-Afghan Period," *Proceedings of the Indian History Congress* 31 (1969): 230.

18. Jan Lucassen, *The Story of Work: A New History of Humankind* (New Haven, CT: Yale University Press, 2021), 176–177.

19. Scott Levi, "India, Russia and the Eighteenth-Century Transformation of the Central Asian Caravan Trade," *Journal of the Economic and Social History of the Orient* 42, no. 4 (1999): 529; R. H. Davies, *Report on the Trade and Resources of the Countries on the North-Western Boundary of British India* (Lahore: Government Press, 1862), 8–9; Anya King, "Eastern Islamic Rulers and the Trade with Eastern and Inner Asia in the 10th–11th Centuries," *Bulletin of the Asia Institute* 25 (2011): 177; Burnes, *Travels into Bokhara,* 2:429.

20. Duarte Barbosa, *The Book of Duarte Barbosa: An Account of the Countries Bordering on the Indian Ocean and Their Inhabitants [Mansel L. Dames],* vol. 2 (London: Hakluyt Society, 1918), 112, 146; Barbosa, *A Description,* 60–69, 80; Ralph Fitch, "1583–1591 Ralph Fitch," in *Early Travels in India 1583–1619,* ed. William Foster (London: Humphrey Milford, Oxford University Press, 1921), 24; François Bernier, *Travels in the Mogul Empire A.D. 1656–1668: A Revised and Improved Edition Based upon Irving Brock's Translation by Archibald Constable* (Westminster, England: Archibald Constable, 1891), 283, 428, 437, 441, 442.

21. Johannes de Laet quoted in Frederic Solmon Growse, *Mathurá: A District Memoir,* vol. 1 (North-Western Provinces' Government Press, 1874), 115.

22. Haripada Chakraborti, "History of Irrigation in Ancient India," *Proceedings of the Indian History Congress* 32 (1970): 155; Habib, *Economic History,* 194–195.

23. Mazumdar, *Sugar and Society,* 142; Joseph Needham, Christian Daniels, and Nicholas K. Menzies, *Science and Civilisation in China,* vol. 6, *Biology and Biological Technology,* pt. 3, *Agro-Industries: Sugarcane Technology* (Cambridge: Cambridge University Press, 2001), 303–306.

24. Lady Fawcett, Charles Fawcett, and Richard Burn, *The Travels of the Abbé Carré in India and the Near East, 1672 to 1674,* vol. 1 (London: Hakluyt Society, 1947), 178; Barbosa, *A Description,* 60, 69, 155; John Fryer, *A New Account of East-India and Persia . . . Being Nine Years Travels, Begun 1672 and Finished 1681 . . .* (London: Chiswell, 1698), 105; Tomé Pires, Armando Cortesão, and Francisco Rodrigues, *The Suma Oriental of Tomé Pires: An Account of the East, from the Red Sea to Japan, Written in Malacca and India in 1512–1515 . . .* (London: Hakluyt Society, 1944), 92; Barbosa, *The Book,* 1:64, 107, 188.

25. Ibn Battúta, *Travels in Asia and Africa, 1325–1354* (London: George Routledge and Sons, 1929), 282.

26. Needham, Daniels, and Menzies, *Sugar Cane Technology*, 185; Billy K. L. So, *Prosperity, Region, and Institutions in Maritime China: The South Fukien Sugar Cane Pattern, 946–1368* (Cambridge, MA: Harvard University Asia Center / Harvard University Press, 2000), 71.

27. Françoise Sabban, "Sucre candi et confiseries de Quinsai: L'essor du sucre de canne dans la Chine des Song (Xe–XIIIes.)," *Journal d'Agriculture traditionnelle et de Botanique appliquée* 35, no. 1 (1988): 209; Françoise Sabban, "L'industrie sucrière, le moulin à sucre et les relations sino-portugaises aux XVIe–XVIIIe siècles," *Annales. Histoire, Sciences sociales* 49 (1994): 836; Mazumdar, *Sugar and Society*, 29–30; Needham, Daniels, and Menzies, *Sugar Cane Technology*, 92; So, *Prosperity*, 65–66; Paul Wheatley, "Geographical Notes on Some Commodities Involved in Sung Maritime Trade," *Journal of the Malayan Branch of the Royal Asiatic Society* 32, no. 2 (186) (1959): 87; Ju-Kua Chau, *Chau Ju-Kua: His Work on the Chinese and Arab Trade in the 12th and 13th Centuries, Entitled Chu-fan-dii*, trans. Friedrich Hirth and W. W. Rockhill (St. Petersburg: Imperial Academy of Sciences, 1911), 49, 53, 61, 67.

28. Daniels and Daniels claim that this boiling of bagasse—the residue left after the juice has been extracted—allowed sucrose to leave the cell walls, a diffusion process. John Daniels and Christian Daniels, "The Origin of the Sugarcane Roller Mill," *Technology and Culture* 29 (1988): 524n.110. They refer to the eye-witness account of Eckeberg, "A Short Account of Chinese Husbandry," in Pehr Osbeck, *A Voyage to China and the East Indies . . . and an Account of the Chinese Husbandry, by Captain Charles Gustavus Eckeberg*, trans. John Reinhold Forster, F.A.S., vol. 2 (London: Benjamin White, 1771), 197. However, neither Sabban nor Mazumdar mention the diffusion process; they do mention the pressing of juice from the boiled bagasse. Sabban, "Sucre candi," 202; Mazumdar, *Sugar and Society*, 129–130.

29. Sato, *Sugar in the Social Life*, 49; Marco Polo, *The Book of Ser Marco Polo the Venetian concerning the Kingdoms and Marvels of the East . . .* , trans. and ed. Henry Yule and Henri Cordier, 2 vols (London: Murray, 1903), 1:intro., 98; 2:226.

30. Angela Schottenhammer, "Yang Liangyao's Mission of 785 to the Caliph of Baghdād: Evidence of an Early Sino-Arabic Power Alliance?," *Bulletin de l'École française d'Extrême-Orient* 101 (2015): 191, 208, 211; Xianlin, *A History of Sugar*, 127–128.

31. Mazumdar, *Sugar and Society*, 162–163; Sabban, "L'industrie sucrière," 843; Needham, Daniels, and Menzies, *Sugar Cane Technology*, 95–98.

32. Daniels and Daniels, "The Origin," 528; Mazumdar, *Sugar and Society*, 152–158. For the theory that in the Americas the three-roller vertical mill was developed from the three-roller horizontal mill, see Sabban, "L'industrie sucrière," 824, 829, 831.

33. Mazumdar, *Sugar and Society*, 160–161.

34. Chin-Keong Ng, *Boundaries and Beyond: China's Maritime Southeast in Late Imperial Times* (Singapore: NUS Press, 2017), 104, 239–240.

35. Darra Goldstein, *The Oxford Companion to Sugar and Sweets* (Oxford: Oxford University Press, 2015), 372, 467.

36. Data assembled by Nagazumi and quoted in George Bryan Souza, "Hinterlands, Commodity Chains, and Circuits in Early Modern Asian History: Sugar in Qing China

and Tokugawa Japan," in *Hinterlands and Commodities,* ed. Tsukasa Mizushima, George Bryan Souza, and Dennis Owen Flynn (Leiden: Brill, 2015), 34.

37. Ng, *Boundaries and Beyond,* 227–228.

38. By the mid-seventeenth century, Taiwan's Chinese population of 21,500 was 93 percent adult males. See "Generale missiven van gouverneurs-generaal en raden aan heren XVII der Verenigde Oostindische Compagnie," II, Grote Serie 112, 354–355, http://resources .huygens.knaw.nl/voctaiwan. In addition the VOC archives mention that kongsias (kongsis) were involved in sugar production: "VOC, *Dagregisters van het Kasteel Zeelandia, Taiwan,* July 12, 1655, fol. 669, http://resources.huygens.knaw.nl/voctaiwan.

39. Chin-Keong Ng, *Trade and Society: The Amoy Network on the China Coast, 1683–1735* (Singapore: NUS Press, 2015), 104, 134; Mazumdar, *Sugar and Society,* 300; John Robert Shepherd, *Statecraft and Political Economy on the Taiwan Frontier: 1600–1800* (Stanford, CA: Stanford University Press, 1993), 159; Xianlin, *A History of Sugar,* 376.

40. Robert B. Marks and Chen Chunsheng, "Price Inflation and Its Social, Economic, and Climatic Context in Guangdong Province, 1707–1800," *T'oung Pao* 81, fasc. 1/3 (1995): 117; Guanmian Xu, "Sweetness and Chaozhou: Construction of Tropical Commodity Chains on the Early Modern China Coast, 1560s–1860s" (MA thesis, Chinese University of Hong Kong, 2017), 57–59; Guanmian Xu, "From the Atlantic to the Manchu: Taiwan Sugar and the Early Modern World, 1630s–1720s," *Journal of World History* 33, no. 2 (2022): 295; Xianlin, *A History of Sugar,* 347, 414.

41. Osbeck, *A Voyage to China,* 2:297.

42. Mazumdar, *Sugar and Society,* 173–177. See also Yukuo Uyehara, "Ryukyu Islands, Japan," *Economic Geography* 9, no. 4 (1933): 400.

43. Yasuzo Horie, "The Encouragement of 'Kokusan' (國產) or Native Products in the Tokugawa Period," *Kyoto University Economic Review* 16, no. 2 (36) (1941): 45, 47; Souza, "Hinterlands," 41–42; Laura Mason, *Sweets and Candy: A Global History* (London: Reaktion Books, 2018), 18; Goldstein, *The Oxford Companion,* 777.

44. Tansen Sen, "The Formation of Chinese Maritime Networks to Southern Asia, 1200–1450," *Journal of the Economic and Social History of the Orient* 49, no. 4 (2006): 426; Craig A. Lockard, "'The Sea Common to All': Maritime Frontiers, Port Cities, and Chinese Traders in the Southeast Asian Age of Commerce, ca. 1400–1750," *Journal of World History* 21, no. 2 (2010): 229–230.

45. Xianlin, *A History of Sugar,* 261, 263, 274.

46. See Guanmian Xu, "The 'Perfect Map' of Widow Hiamtse: A Micro-Spatial History of Sugar Plantations in Early Modern Southeast Asia, 1685–1710," *International Review of Social History* 67, no. 1 (2021): 97–126.

47. Mazumdar, *Sugar and Society,* 68; John A. Larkin, *Sugar and the Origins of Modern Philippine Society* (Berkeley, CA: University of California Press, 1993), 21.

48. Agustin de la Cavada y Méndez de Vigo, *Historia geográfica, geológicos y estadísticos de las Islas de Luzon, Visayas, Mindanao y Jolo: Y los que Correspónden a las Islas Batanes,*

Calamianes, Balabac, Mindoro, Masbate, Ticao y Burias, Situadas al n. so. y s. de Luzon, vol. 2 (Manila, Philippines: Imp. de Ramirez y Giraudier, 1876), vol. 2, 410.

49. Larkin, *Sugar and the Origins,* 22, 25–26; Nathaniel Bowditch and Mary C. McHale, *Early American-Philippine Trade: The Journal of Nathaniel Bowditch in Manila, 1796* (New Haven, CT: Yale University, Southeast Asia Studies / Cellar Book Shop, Detroit, 1962), 31n.14.

50. Lockard, "'The Sea Common,'" 237.

51. Pierre Poivre, *Voyages d'un philosophe ou observations sur les moeurs et les arts des peuples de l'Afrique, de l'Asie et de l'Amérique,* 3rd ed. (Paris: Du Pont, 1796), 89.

52. John Crawfurd, *Journal of an Embassy from the Governor General of India to the Courts of Siam,* vol. 1 (London: S. and R. Bentley, 1828), 474; Ritter, *Über die geographische,* 40; John White, *History of a Voyage to the China Sea* (Boston: Wells and Lilly, 1823), 251, 260–261.

53. A. D. Blue, "Chinese Emigration and the Deck Passenger Trade," *Journal of the Hong Kong Branch of the Royal Asiatic Society* 10 (1970): 80.

54. Jean-Baptiste Pallegoix, *Description du royaume Thai ou Siam,* vol. 1 (Paris: Mission de Siam, 1854), 80–82.

55. James Carlton Ingram, *Economic Change in Thailand since 1850* (Stanford, CA: Stanford University Press, 1955), 4, 123–124; Jacob Baxa and Guntwin Bruhns, *Zucker im Leben der Völker: Eine Kultur- und Wirtschaftsgeschichte* (Berlin: Bartens, 1967), 155.

56. Jean-Paul Morel, "Aux Archives Pusy La Fayette: Les archives personnelles de Pierre Poivre. Mémoire sur la Cochinchine," no. 25 (April 2020): 8, http://www.pierre-poivre.fr/Arch-pusy-D.pdf; Pierre Poivre, *Voyages d'un Philosophe,* 90.

57. Bosma, *The Sugar Plantation,* 47–48.

58. James Low, *A Dissertation on the Soil & Agriculture of the British Settlement of Penang, or Prince of Wales Island . . . Including Province Wellesley on the Malayan Peninsula . . .* (Singapore: Singapore Free Press Office, 1836), 49–58.

59. Jan Hooyman, *Verhandeling over den Tegenwoordigen Staat van den Landbouw in de Ommelanden van Batavia* (Batavia: Bataviaasch Genootschap der Konsten en Wetenschappen, 1781), 184; P. Levert, *Inheemsche Arbeid in de Java-Suikerindustrie* (Wageningen, the Netherlands: Veenman, 1934), 55–56.

60. B. Hoetink, "So Bing Kong: Het Eerste Hoofd der Chineezen te Batavia (1619–1636)," *Bijdragen tot de Taal-, Land- en Volkenkunde van Nederlandsch-Indië* 73, nos. 3–4 (1917): 373–376; Tonio Andrade, "The Rise and Fall of Dutch Taiwan, 1624–1662: Cooperative Colonization and the Statist Model of European Expansion," *Journal of World History* 17, no. 4 (2006): 439–440.

61. Andrade, "The Rise and Fall," 445–447; Hui-wen Koo, "Weather, Harvests, and Taxes: A Chinese Revolt in Colonial Taiwan," *Journal of Interdisciplinary History* 46, no. 1 (2015): 41–42; Xu, "From the Atlantic," 8, 11.

62. Hooyman, *Verhandeling over den Tegenwoordigen Staat,* 225, 238–239; Margaret Leidelmeijer, *Van Suikermolen tot Grootbedrijf: Technische Vernieuwing in de Java-Suikerindustrie in de Negentiende Eeuw* (Amsterdam: NEHA, 1997), 74, 324.

63. J. J. Reesse, *De Suikerhandel van Amsterdam: Bijdrage tot de Handelsgeschiedenis des Vaderlands, Hoofdzakelijk uit de Archieven verzameld,* vol. 1 (Haarlem: J. L. E. I Kleynenberg, 1908), 169; see Ghulam Nadri, "The Dutch Intra-Asian Trade in Sugar in the Eighteenth Century," *International Journal of Maritime History* 20, no. 1 (2008): 63–96.

64. "Generale missiven van gouverneurs-generaal en raden aan heren XVII der Verenigde Oostindische Compagnie," III, Grote Serie 125, 645, 743, http://resources.huygens.knaw.nl; Norifumi Daito, "Sugar Trade in the Eighteenth-Century Persian Gulf" (PhD diss., Leiden University, 2017), 23, 37, 68; Nadri, "The Dutch Intra-Asian Trade," 76–77; James Silk Buckingham, *Travels in Assyria, Media, and Persia, Including a Journey from Bagdad by Mount Zagros, to Hamadan, the Ancient Ecbatani . . . ,* vol. 2 (London: Colburn and Bentley, 1830), 115, 117, 170.

65. Daito, "Sugar Trade," 44, 47.

66. A. Mesud Kucukkalay and Numan Elibol, "Ottoman Imports in the Eighteenth Century: Smyrna (1771–72)," *Middle Eastern Studies* 42, no. 5 (2006): 730; James Justinian Morier, *Journey through Persia, Armenia, and Asia Minor, to Constantinople, in 1808 and 1809* (London: Longman, Hurst, 1812), 171–172; Sébastien Lupo, "Révolution(s) d'échelles: Le marché levantin et la crise du commerce marseillais au miroir des maisons Roux et de leurs relais à Smyrne (1740–1787)" (PhD diss., Université Aix-Marseille, 2015), 580.

67. Burnes, *Travels into Bokhara,* 2:436.

68. William Milburn, *Oriental Commerce: Containing a Geographical Description of the Principal Places in the East Indies, China, and Japan, with their Produce, Manufactures, and Trade . . . ,* vol. 2 (London: Black, Parry, 1813), 307, 547. For the exports to the United States, Persia, and Arabia in 1805, I have assumed a price of 5 rupees per maund (37.22 kilograms). See also *East-India Sugar: Papers Respecting the Culture and Manufacture of Sugar in British-India: Also Notices of the Cultivation of Sugar in Other Parts of Asia* (London: E. Cox and Son, 1822), app. 4, 4.

69. Depending upon the quality and price (ranging from 3.5 to 6.5 rupees per maund), exports from Bombay and Surat across the western Indian Ocean must have been between 2,200 and 4,000 tons, and along the coast of western India between 3,100 and 5,800 tons. Milburn, *Oriental Commerce,* 1:148, 211–212, 223; William Milburn and Thomas Thornton, *Oriental Commerce . . .* (London, 1827), 41, 119.

70. Based upon 3.5 rupees per maund. Milburn, *Oriental Commerce,* 1:155, 221.

71. Based upon 5 rupees per maund. Milburn, *Oriental Commerce,* 1:217. See also Milburn and Thornton, *Oriental Commerce,* 169.

72. Hosea Ballou Morse, *The Chronicles of the East India Company: Trading to China, 1635–1834* (Cambridge, MA: Harvard University Press, 1926), 249–250, 272, 385.

73. Milburn and Thornton, *Oriental Commerce*, 307, 327, 349, 515.

74. J. W. Davidson, *The Island of Formosa: Historical View from 1430 to 1900* . . . (New York: Paragon Book Gallery, 1903), 445, 446, 457.

75. Mazumdar, *Sugar and Society*, 351, 356–357, 383; Robert Marks, *Rural Revolution in South China: Peasants and the Making of History in Haifeng County, 1570–1930* (Madison: University of Wisconsin Press, 1984), 107; Jack. F. Williams, "Sugar: The Sweetener in Taiwan's Development," in *China's Island Frontier Studies in the Historical Geography of Taiwan*, ed. Ronald G. Knapp (Honolulu: University of Hawaii Press, 1980), 220.

2. Sugar Going West

1. Tsugitaka Sato, *Sugar in the Social Life of Medieval Islam* (Leiden: Brill, 2015), 34–36.

2. Mohamed Ouerfelli, *Le sucre: Production, commercialisation et usages dans la Méditerranée médiévale* (Leiden: Brill, 2008), 81.

3. Sato, *Sugar in the Social Life*, 40–45.

4. Subhi Labib, *Handelsgeschichte Ägyptens im Spätmittelalter (1171–1517)* (Wiesbaden, Germany: Franz Steiner Verlag, 1965), 319–320.

5. Eliyahu Ashtor, "Levantine Sugar Industry in the Later Middle Ages: An Example of Technological Decline," in *Technology, Industry and Trade: The Levant versus Europe, 1250–1500*, ed. Eliyahu Ashtor and B. Z. Ķedar (Hampshire, England: Ashgate, 1992), 240.

6. See, for example, Judith Bronstein, Edna J. Stern, and Elisabeth Yehuda, "Franks, Locals and Sugar Cane: A Case Study of Cultural Interaction in the Latin Kingdom of Jerusalem," *Journal of Medieval History* 45, no. 3 (2019): 316–330; Judith Bronstein, *The Hospitallers and the Holy Land: Financing the Latin East, 1187–1274* (Woodbridge, England: Boydell and Brewer, 2005).

7. Edna J. Stern et al., "Sugar Production in the ʿAkko Plain from the Fatimad to the Early Ottoman Periods," in *The Origins of the Sugar Industry and the Transmission of Ancient Greek and Medieval Arab Science and Technology from the Near East to Europe*, ed. K. D. Politis (Athens: National and Kapodistriako University of Athens, 2015), 89–93; Hamdan Taha, "Some Aspects of Sugar Production in Jericho, Jordan Valley," in *A Timeless Vale: Archaeological and Related Essays on the Jordan Valley in Honour of Gerrit van der Kooij on the Occasion of His Sixty-Fifth Birthday*, ed. Eva Kaptijn and Lucas Pieter Petit (Leiden: Leiden University Press, 2009), 181, 186–187.

8. Eliyahu Ashtor, *Levant Trade in Later Middle Ages* (Princeton, NJ: Princeton University Press, 1983), 17–18.

9. Bethany J. Walker, "Mamluk Investment in Southern Bilad Al-Sham in the Eighth / Fourteenth Century: The Case of Ḥisban," *Journal of Near Eastern Studies* 62, no. 4 (2003): 244; Laparidou Sofia and M. Rosen Arlene, "Intensification of Production in Medieval Islamic Jordan and Its Ecological Impact: Towns of the Anthropocene," *The Holocene* 25, no. 10 (2015): 1687–1688.

10. Ashtor, *Levant Trade*, 52–53.

11. A. T. Luttrell, "The Sugar Industry and its Importance for the Economy of Cyprus during the Frankish Period," in *The Development of the Cypriot Economy: From the Prehistoric Period to the Present Day*, ed. Vassos Karageorghis and Demetres Michaelides (Nicosia: Printed by Lithographica, 1996), 168; Ashtor, *Levant Trade*, 39.

12. Luttrell, "The Sugar Industry," 166.

13. Ellen Herscher, "Archaeology in Cyprus," *American Journal of Archaeology* 102 (1998): 351–352; Marie-Louise von Wartburg, "The Medieval Cane Sugar Industry in Cyprus: Results of Recent Excavation," *Antiquaries Journal* 63, no. 2 (1983): 304, 309, 312, 313.

14. Darra Goldstein, *The Oxford Companion to Sugar and Sweets* (Oxford: Oxford University Press, 2015), 767.

15. Stuart J. Borsch, *The Black Death in Egypt and England: A Comparative Study* (Austin: University of Texas Press, 2010), 24.

16. Labib, *Handelsgeschichte*, 421.

17. Ashtor, *Levant Trade*, 102, 131–132.

18. Walker, "Mamluk Investment," 249; John L. Meloy, "Imperial Strategy and Political Exigency: The Red Sea Spice Trade and the Mamluk Sultanate in the Fifteenth Century," *Journal of the American Oriental Society* 123, no. 1 (2003): 5.

19. Nelly Hanna, *Artisan Entrepreneurs in Cairo and Early-Modern Capitalism (1600–1800)* (New York: Syracuse University Press, 2011), 44.

20. Ronald Findlay and Kevin H. O'Rourke, *Power and Plenty: Trade, War, and the World Economy in the Second Millennium* (Princeton, NJ: Princeton University Press, 2009), 132.

21. Ibn-al-'Auwām, *Le Livre de l'Agriculture par . . .*, trans. J. J. Clément-Mullet, vol. 1 (Paris: Albert L. Hérold, 1864), 365–367.

22. Ouerfelli, *Le sucre*, 180, 192–194; Adela Fábregas García, *Producción y comercio de azúcar en el Mediterráneo medieval: El ejemplo del reino de Granada* (Granada: Editorial Universidad de Granada, 2000), 151–163.

23. Ouerfelli, *Le sucre*, 25.

24. Stephan R. Epstein, *An Island for Itself: Economic Development and Social Change in Late Medieval Sicily* (Cambridge: Cambridge University Press, 2003), 210–215; Carmelo Trasselli, *Storia dello Zucchero siciliano* (Caltanissetta, Italy: S. Sciascia, 1982), 115–174.

25. Mohamed Ouerfelli, "L'impact de la production du sucre sur les campagnes méditerranéennes à la fin du Moyen Âge," *Revue des Mondes musulmans et de la Méditerranée*, no. 126 (2012): para. 34.

26. Ashtor, "Levantine Sugar Industry," 246–257. Ashtor attributes the lower price to better milling technology, but this is based upon a misinterpretation of the Sicilian *trapeto* as a three-roller mill instead of an edge-runner mill.

27. Aloys Schulte, *Geschichte der grossen Ravensburger Handelsgesellschaft, 1380–1530*, 2 vols. (Stuttgart: Deutsche Verlags-Anstalt, 1923), 1:17, 21, 31.

28. Schulte, *Geschichte der grossen Ravensburger*, 2:176–177.

29. Stern et al., "Sugar Production," 109.

30. Alberto Vieira, "The Sugar Economy of Madeira and the Canaries, 1450–1650," in *Tropical Babylons: Sugar and the Making of the Atlantic World, 1450–1680,* ed. Stuart B. Schwartz (Chapel Hill: University of North Carolina Press, 2004), 65.

31. Juan Manuel Bello León and María Del Cristo González Marrero, "Los 'otros extranjeros' catalanes, flamencos, franceses e ingleses en la sociedad canaria de los siglos XV y XVI," *Revista de Historia Canaria* 179 (1997): 11–72; 180 (1998): 16, 55–64.

32. Ouerfelli, *Le sucre,* 51–52; Stern et al., "Sugar Production," 99.

33. Luttrell, "The Sugar Industry," 166; von Wartburg, "The Medieval Cane Sugar Industry," 301.

34. Jason W. Moore, "Madeira, Sugar, and the Conquest of Nature in the 'First' Sixteenth Century, Part II: From Regional Crisis to Commodity Frontier, 1506–1530," *Review (Fernand Braudel Center)* 33, no. 1 (2010): 11–13; Stefan Halikowski Smith, "The Mid-Atlantic Islands: A Theatre of Early Modern Ecocide?," *International Review of Social History* 55, suppl. 18 (2010): 65–67; Vieira, "The Sugar Economy of Madeira," 45.

35. María Luisa Frabellas, "La producción de azúcar en Tenerife," *Revista de Historia (Tenerife)* 18, no. 100 (1952): 466; Vieira, "The Sugar Economy of Madeira," 45; Felipe Fernandez-Armesto, *The Canary Islands after the Conquest: The Making of a Colonial Society in the Early Sixteenth Century* (Oxford: Oxford University Press, 1981), 65, 91, 106.

36. Frabellas, "La producción de azúcar," 456; J. H. Galloway, *The Sugar Cane Industry: An Historical Geography from Its Origins to 1914* (Cambridge: Cambridge University Press, 1989), 57.

37. von Wartburg, "The Medieval Cane Sugar Industry," 314n.22.

38. Ouerfelli, "L'impact," paras. 14–15, 20, 22, 27; Fernandez-Armesto, *The Canary Islands,* 97–98.

39. Ouerfelli, *Le sucre,* 270–271.

40. Vieira, "The Sugar Economy of Madeira," 75. For the ecological problems that were concomitant to sugar production on the Atlantic islands, see Halikowski Smith, "The Mid-Atlantic Islands," 63–67.

41. Ritter, *Über die geographische* 103; M. Akif Erdoğru, "The Servants and Venetian Interest in Ottoman Cyprus in the Late Sixteenth and the Early Seventeenth Centuries," *Quaderni di Studi Arabi* 15 (1997): 104–105.

42. Ouerfelli, *Le sucre,* 23–24; Jacqueline Guiral-Hadziiossif, "La diffusion et la production de la canne à sucre: XIIIe-XVIe siècles," *Anuario de Estudios Medievales / Consejo Superior de Investigaciones Científicas* 24 (1994): 225–226; Sato, *Sugar in the Social Life,* 38.

43. Ouerfelli, *Le sucre,* 126–127; Luttrell, "The Sugar Industry," 167. There is mention of thousands of enslaved workers at the royal sugar plantations of Cyprus, but without further corroboration this is not very plausible. Benjamin Arbel, "Slave Trade and Slave Labor

in Frankish Cyprus (1191–1571)," in *Cyprus, The Franks and Venice, 13th–16th Centuries*, ed. Benjamin Arbel (Aldershot, England: Variorum, 2000), 161.

44. Ouerfelli, "L'impact," para. 8. Sato also denies the presence of slaves in the sugar sector in Morroco. Sato, *Sugar in the Social Life*, 39. See also David Abulafia, "Sugar in Spain," *European Review* 16, no. 2 (2008): 198.

45. Fernandez-Armesto, *The Canary Islands*, 202.

46. Sidney W. Mintz, *Sweetness and Power: The Place of Sugar in Modern History* (Harmondsworth, England: Penguin, 1986), 78.

47. Paul D. Buell, "Eurasia, Medicine and Trade: Arabic Medicine in East Asia—How It Came to Be There and How It Was Supported, Including Possible Indian Ocean Connections for the Supply of Medicinals," in *Early Global Interconnectivity across the Indian Ocean World*, vol. 2, *Exchange of Ideas, Religions, and Technologies*, ed. Angela Schottenhammer (London: Palgrave Macmillan, 2019), 270–293.

48. Woodruff D. Smith, *Consumption and the Making of Respectability, 1600–1800* (London: Routledge, 2002), 266n.84; Edmund Oskar von Lippmann, *Geschichte des Zuckers: Seit den ältesten Zeiten bis zum Beginn der Rübenzucker-Fabrikation: ein Beitrag zur Kulturgeschichte* (Berlin: Springer, 1929), 274–275.

49. Ouerfelli, *Le sucre*, 587; Sato, *Sugar in the Social Life*, 92–94.

50. My translation. Lippmann, *Geschichte des Zuckers*, 245–254, 290.

51. Lady Fawcett, Charles Fawcett, and Richard Burn, *The Travels of the Abbé Carré in India and the Near East, 1672 to 1674*, vol. 1 (London: Hakluyt Society, 1947), 46.

52. Wendy A. Woloson, *Refined Tastes: Sugar, Confectionery, and Consumers in Nineteenth-Century America* (Baltimore, MD: Johns Hopkins University Press, 2002), 67.

53. John Fryer, *A New Account of East-India and Persia . . . Being Nine Years Travels, Begun 1672 and Finished 1681 . . .* (London: Chiswell, 1698), 223.

54. Sucheta Mazumdar, *Sugar and Society in China: Peasants, Technology, and the World Market* (Cambridge, MA: Harvard University Press, 1998), 41.

55. Lippmann, *Geschichte des Zuckers*, 224–225; Jean Mazuel, *Le sucre en Egypte: étude de géographie historique et economique* (Cairo: Société Royale de Géographie d'Égypte, 1937), 11–12; Sato, *Sugar in the Social Life*, 58, 123–125; Ashtor, "Levantine Sugar Industry," 232.

56. Eddy Stols, "The Expansion of the Sugar Market in Western Europe," in *Tropical Babylons: Sugar and the Making of the Atlantic World, 1450–1680*, ed. Stuart B. Schwartz (Chapel Hill: University of North Carolina Press, 2004), 237; John Whenham, "The Gonzagas Visit Venice," *Early Music* 21, no. 4 (1993): 542n.75; Edward Muir, "Images of Power: Art and Pageantry in Renaissance Venice," *American Historical Review* 84, no. 1 (1979): 45.

57. Sato, *Sugar in the Social Life*, 29, 166–167; Ouerfelli, *Le sucre*, 570–571.

58. Quotation in Philip Lyle, "The Sources and Nature of Statistical Information in Special Fields of Statistics: The Sugar Industry," *Journal of the Royal Statistical Society. Series*

A (General) 113, no. 4 (1950): 533; Jon Stobart, *Sugar and Spice: Grocers and Groceries in Provincial England 1650–1830* (Oxford: Oxford University Press, 2016), 30–31.

59. See, for example, Félix Reynaud, "Le mouvement des navires et des marchandises à Port-de-Bouc à la fin du XVe siècle," *Revue d'Histoire économique et sociale* 34, nos. 2–3 (1956): 163.

60. Tobias Kuster, "500 Jahre kolonialer Rohrzucker—250 Jahre europäischer Rübenzucker," *Vierteljahrschrift für Sozial- und Wirtschaftsgeschichte* (1998): 485.

61. Quoted in John Yudkin, *Pure, White and Deadly* (London: Penguin, 2012), 128–129. See also Alain Drouard, "Sugar Production and Consumption in France in the Twentieth Century," in *The Rise of Obesity in Europe: A Twentieth Century Food History,* ed. Derek J. Oddy, P. J. Atkins, and Virginie Amilien (Farnham, England: Ashgate, 2009), 123n.21.

62. Noël Deerr, *The History of Sugar,* vol. 1 (London: Chapman and Hall, 1949), 113, 193–200, 235–236.

63. Laura Mason, *Sweets and Candy: A Global History* (London: Reaktion Books, 2018), 10–11.

64. In China, for example, the manufacture of confectioneries came with the introduction of cane sugar in the seventh century. See Joseph Needham, Christian Daniels, and Nicholas K. Menzies, *Science and Civilisation in China,* vol. 6, *Biology and Biological Technology,* pt. 3, *Agro-Industries: Sugarcane Technology* (Cambridge: Cambridge University Press, 2001), 68.

65. G. D. J. Schotel and H. C. Rogge, *Het Oud-Hollandsch Huisgezin der Zeventiende Eeuw Beschreven,* 2nd ed. (Leiden: Sijthoff, 1905), 52, 224, 242–243, 270; Yda Schreuder, *Amsterdam's Sephardic Merchants and the Atlantic Sugar Trade in the Seventeenth Century* (London: Palgrave Macmillan, 2019), 108.

66. Goldstein, *The Oxford Companion,* 745–747.

67. See Jay Kinsbruner, *Petty Capitalism in Spanish America: The Pulperos of Puebla, Mexico City, Caracas, and Buenos Aires* (Boulder, CO: Westview Press, 1987), 3, 7; Goldstein, *The Oxford Companion,* 72.

68. See Reiko Hada, "Madame Marie Guimard: Under the Ayudhya Dynasty of the Seventeenth Century," *Journal of the Siam Society* 80, no. 1 (1992): 71–74.

69. Lallanji Gopal, "Sugar-Making in Ancient India," *Journal of the Economic and Social History of the Orient* 7, no. 1 (1964): 67; R. H. Davies, *Report on the Trade and Resources of the Countries on the North-Western Boundary of British India* (Lahore: Government Press, 1862), 1:clx, clxi.

70. Daito, "Sugar Trade," 15, 17.

71. Alexander Burnes, *Travels into Bokhara: Being the Account of a Journey from India to Cabool, Tartary and Persia . . . in the Years 1831, 1832, and 1833,* 3 vols. (London: J. Murray, 1834), 2:167, 168, 436; Davies, *Report on the Trade,* 1:clx, clxi.

72. Ibn Battúta, *Travels in Asia and Africa, 1325–1354* (London: George Routledge and Sons, 1929), 57.

73. James P. Grehan, *Everyday Life and Consumer Culture in Eighteenth-Century Damascus* (Seattle: University of Washington Press, 2016), 116–118; Ju-Kua Chau, *Chau Ju-Kua: His Work on the Chinese and Arab Trade in the 12th and 13th Centuries, Entitled* Chu-fan-dii, trans. Friedrich Hirth and W. W. Rockhill (St. Petersburg: Imperial Academy of Sciences, 1911), 140.

74. Jacob Baxa and Guntwin Bruhns, *Zucker im Leben der Völker: Eine Kultur- und Wirtschaftsgeschichte* (Berlin: Bartens, 1967), 19.

75. The debate about whether or not the Native Americans also boiled maple syrup is inconclusive because of a lack of relevant archaeological data antedating the European presence in North America. See Margaret B. Holman, "The Identification of Late Woodland Maple Sugaring Sites in the Upper Great Lakes," *Midcontinental Journal of Archaeology* 9, no. 1 (1984): 66. For Mason, the question is unresolved; see Carol I. Mason, "Prehistoric Maple Sugaring Sites?," *Midcontinental Journal of Archaeology* 10, no. 1 (1985). See also Matthew M. Thomas, "Historic American Indian Maple Sugar and Syrup Production: Boiling Arches in Michigan and Wisconsin," *Midcontinental Journal of Archaeology* 30, no. 2 (2005): 321; John G. Franzen, Terrance J. Martin, and Eric C. Drake, "*Sucreries* and *Ziizbaakdokaanan:* Racialization, Indigenous Creolization, and the Archaeology of Maple-Sugar Camps in Northern Michigan," *Historical Archaeology* 52, no. 1 (2018): 164–196.

76. Mazumdar, *Sugar and Society,* 15; Goldstein, *The Oxford Companion,* 39–40, 419, 529–530.

77. Guanmian Xu, "From the Atlantic to the Manchu: Taiwan Sugar and the Early Modern World, 1630s–1720s," *Journal of World History* 33, no. 2 (2022): 293.

78. The total sugar production of the Caribbean colonies stood at just below 250,000 tons in 1790 according to Deerr, *The History of Sugar,* 1:239. For 1790, I have taken the figure of 120 million people in the thirteen countries identified as Western European in Angus Maddison, *The World Economy. A Millennial Perspective (Vol. 1). Historical Statistics (Vol. 2)* (Paris: OECD, 2006), https://www.stat.berkeley.edu/~aldous/157/Papers/world_economy .pdf. The population of the United States at that time was about four million. I assume that Latin America was self-sufficient in sugar.

79. Kenneth Pomeranz, *The Great Divergence: Europe, China, and the Making of the Modern World Economy* (Princeton, NJ: Princeton University Press, 2000), 120–122; George Bryan Souza, "Hinterlands, Commodity Chains, and Circuits in Early Modern Asian History: Sugar in Qing China and Tokugawa Japan," in *Hinterlands and Commodities,* ed. Tsukasa Mizushima, George Bryan Souza, and Dennis Owen Flynn (Leiden: Brill, 2015), 31.

80. Deborah Jean Warner, *Sweet Stuff: An American History of Sweeteners from Sugar to Sucralose* (Washington, DC: Smithsonian Institution Scholarly Press / Rowman and Little-field, 2011), 32.

81. In 1770, annual sugar consumption in the thirteen colonies must have been about 1.5 kilograms per capita; see John J. McCusker, *Essays in the Economic History of the Atlantic World* (London: Routledge, 2014), 322. However, the United States imported an additional

eleven liters of molasses per capita per year, most of which went into rum. See John J. Mc-Cusker and Russell R. Menard, *The Economy of British America, 1607–1789* (Chapel Hill: University of North Carolina Press, 1991), 290.

82. Goldstein, *The Oxford Companion,* 518–519, 528–529.

83. Maud Villeret, *Le goût de l'or blanc: Le sucre en france au XVIIIe siècle* (Rennes: Presses Universitairs, 2017), 258.

84. Banquet letters are a traditional confection made from almonds, formed in the shape of letters.

85. Steven Blankaart, *De Borgerlyke Tafel* (Amsterdam: J. ten Hoorn, 1683), 41–42, 102.

86. Villeret, *Le goût de l'or blanc,* 261.

87. Goldstein, *The Oxford Companion,* 777.

88. For India see, for example, H. R. Perrott, "The Family Budget of an Indian Raiyat," *Economic Journal* 22, no. 87 (1912): 497. For Turkey, see Julius Wolf, *Zuckersteuer und Zuckerindustrie in den europäischen Ländern und in der amerikanischen Union von 1882 bis 1885, mit besonderer Rücksichtnahme auf Deutschland und die Steuerreform Daselbst* (Tübingen: Mohr Siebeck, 1886), 5. For Persia, see *Encyclopaedia Iranica,* s.v. "Sugar," last modified July 20, 2009, http://www.iranicaonline.org/articles/sugar-cultivation.

89. Ralph A. Austen and Woodruff D. Smith, "Private Tooth Decay as Public Economic Virtue: The Slave-Sugar Triangle, Consumerism, and European Industrialization," *Social Science History* 14, no. 1 (1990): 99. Richardson gives slightly different figures but still in the same order of magnitude, namely, from 4.6–6.5 pounds in 1710 to 23.2 pounds in 1770. David Richardson, "The Slave Trade, Sugar, and British Economic Growth, 1748–1776," *Journal of Interdisciplinary History* 17, no. 4 (1987): 748.

90. Richardson, "The Slave Trade," 751–752; Stobart, *Sugar and Spice,* 12, 53.

91. Guillaume Daudin, "Domestic Trade and Market Size in Late-Eighteenth-Century France," *Journal of Economic History* 70, no. 3 (2010): 736; Austen and Smith, "Private Tooth Decay," 101.

92. Louis-Sébastien Mercier, *Tableau de Paris . . . ,* vol. 1 (Amsterdam, 1783), 227–229; Haim Burstin, *Une Révolution à l'Oeuvre: Le Faubourg Saint-Marcel (1789–1794)* (Seyssel, France: Champ Vallon, 2005), 332.

93. George Rudé, *The Crowd in the French Revolution* (Oxford: Oxford University Press, 1960), 96–97, 114–115, 230.

94. Martin Bruegel, "A Bourgeois Good?: Sugar, Norms of Consumption and the Labouring Classes in Nineteenth-Century France," in *Food, Drink and Identity: Cooking, Eating and Drinking in Europe since the Middle Ages,* ed. Peter Scholliers (Oxford: Berg, 2001), 106.

95. Hans Jürgen Teuteberg and Günter Wiegelmann, *Der Wandel der Nahrungsgewohnheiten unter dem Einfluss der Industrialisierung* (Göttingen: Vandenhoeck and Ruprecht, 1972), 239.

96. Ulrich Pfister, "Great Divergence, Consumer Revolution and the Reorganization of Textile Markets: Evidence from Hamburg's Import Trade, Eighteenth Century," Working

Paper 266 (London: London School of Economics and Political Science, 2017), 37, 47; Teuteberg and Wiegelmann, *Der Wandel der Nahrungsgewohnheiten,* 304–305.

97. Klaus Weber, "Deutschland, der atlantische Sklavenhandel und die Plantagenwirtschaft der Neuen Welt," *Journal of Modern European History* 7, no. 1 (2009): 60.

98. Erika Rappaport, *A Thirst for Empire: How Tea Shaped the Modern World* (Princeton, NJ: Princeton University Press, 2017), 49.

3. War and Slavery

1. David Harvey, "The Spatial Fix—Hegel, Von Thunen, and Marx," *Antipode* 13, no. 3 (1981): 1–12.

2. Fernando Ortiz, *Cuban Counterpoint: Tobacco and Sugar* (New York: Vintage Books, 1970), 268.

3. Klaus Weber, "Deutschland, der atlantische Sklavenhandel und die Plantagenwirtschaft der Neuen Welt," *Journal of Modern European History* 7, no. 1 (2009): 41–42; Julia Roth, "Sugar and Slaves: The Augsburg Welser as Conquerors of America and Colonial Foundational Myths," *Atlantic Studies* 14, no. 4 (2017): 439–441.

4. Genaro Rodríguez Morel, "Esclavitud y vida rural en las plantaciones azucareras de Santo Domingo, siglo XVI," *Genaro Anuario de Estudios Americanos* 49 (1992): 6. On the introduction of the two-roller horizontal mill, see also Anthony Stevens-Acevedo, "The Machines That Milled the Sugar-Canes: The Horizontal Double Roller Mills in the First Sugar Plantations of the Americas" (unpublished manuscript, 2013).

5. Ward J. Barrett, *The Sugar Hacienda of Marqueses del Valle* (Minneapolis: University of Minnesota Press, 1970), 11.

6. I base the figure of 2,000–2,500 tons on the fact that the Spanish Americas counted over fifty ingenios and at least a handful of trapiches, as identified in Lorenzo E. López y Sebastián and Justo L. del Río Moreno, "Comercio y transporte en la economía del azucar antillano durante el siglo XVI," no. 49 (1992). For the sugar production of Hispaniola in the sixteenth century, see López y Sebastián and Río Moreno, "Commercio y transporte," 29–30; Mervyn Ratekin, "The Early Sugar Industry in Española," *Hispanic American Historical Review* 34, no. 1 (1954): 13.

7. See I. A. Wright, "The History of the Cane Sugar Industry in the West Indies V," *Louisiana Planter and Sugar Manufacturer* 63, no. 15 (1919). Sugar imports in Seville sharply dropped in the 1580s; see Huguette Chaunu and Pierre Chaunu, *Séville et l'Atlantique: 1506–1650: Première partie: Partie statistique* (Paris: S.E.V.P.E.N., 1956), VI_2, pp. 1004–1005, table 702.

8. Arlindo Manuel Caldeira, "Learning the Ropes in the Tropics: Slavery and the Plantation System on the Island of São Tomé," *African Economic History,* no. 39 (2011): 48–49.

9. H. A. Gemery and J. S. Hogendorn, "Comparative Disadvantage: The Case of Sugar Cultivation in West Africa," *Journal of Interdisciplinary History* 9, no. 3 (1979): 431, 447–449.

10. Christopher Ebert, *Between Empires: Brazilian Sugar in the Early Atlantic Economy, 1550–1630* (Leiden: Brill, 2008), 22, 152; Eddy Stols, *De Spaanse Brabanders of de Handelsbetrekkingen der Zuidelijke Nederlanden met de Iberische wereld 1598–1648* (Brussels: Paleis der Academiën, 1971), 102–103.

11. J. H. Galloway, "Tradition and Innovation in the American Sugar Industry, c. 1500–1800: An Explanation," *Annals of the Association of American Geographers* 75, no. 3 (1985): 339. For the capacity of the Brazilian mills, see Stuart B. Schwartz, "A Commonwealth within Itself," in *Tropical Babylons: Sugar and the Making of the Atlantic World, 1450–1680,* ed. Stuart B. Schwartz (Chapel Hill: University of North Carolina Press, 2004), 165.

12. Kit Sims Taylor, "The Economics of Sugar and Slavery in Northeastern Brazil," *Agricultural History* 44, no. 3 (1970): 272.

13. For the output per enslaved, see Stuart B. Schwartz, "Introduction," in *Tropical Babylons: Sugar and the Making of the Atlantic World, 1450–1680,* ed. Stuart B. Schwartz (Chapel Hill: University of North Carolina Press, 2004), 19. See also "Trans-Atlantic Slave Trade—Estimates," Slave Voyages, accessed January 20, 2022, https://www.slavevoyages .org/assessment/estimates; Noël Deerr, *The History of Sugar,* vol. 1 (London: Chapman and Hall, 1949), 112.

14. Yda Schreuder, *Amsterdam's Sephardic Merchants and the Atlantic Sugar Trade in the Seventeenth Century* (London: Palgrave Macmillan, 2019), 52.

15. Kristof Glamann, *Dutch-Asiatic Trade: 1620–1740* (The Hague: Nijhoff, 1958), 153.

16. Schreuder, *Amsterdam's Sephardic Merchants,* 108.

17. J. J. Reesse, *De Suikerhandel van Amsterdam: Bijdrage tot de Handelsgeschiedenis des Vaderlands, Hoofdzakelijk uit de Archieven verzameld,* vol. 1 (Haarlem: J. L. E. I Kleynenberg, 1908), 132–133.

18. Markus P. M. Vink, "Freedom and Slavery: The Dutch Republic, the VOC World, and the Debate over the 'World's Oldest Trade,'" *South African Historical Journal,* no. 59 (2007): 23, 30.

19. José Antônio Gonsalves de Mello, G. N. Visser, and B. N. Teensma, *Nederlanders in Brazilië (1624–1654): De Invloed van de Hollandse Bezetting op het Leven en de Cultuur in Noord-Brazilië* (Zutphen, the Netherlands: Walburg Pers, 2001), 183, 185.

20. Henk den Heijer, "The Dutch West India Company, 1621–1791," in *Riches from Atlantic Commerce: Dutch Transatlantic Trade and Shipping, 1585–1817,* ed. Johannes Postma and Victor Enthoven (Leiden: Brill, 2003), 88; quoted from Hermann Wätjen, *Das holländische Kolonialreich in Brasilien: Ein Kapitel aus der Kolonialgeschichte des 17. Jahrhunderts* (Gotha, Germany: Justus Perthes, 1921), 316–323.

21. Heijer, "The Dutch West India Company," 88.

22. "Generale missiven van gouverneurs-generaal en raden aan heren XVII der Verenigde Oostindische Compagnie," II, Grote Serie 112, pp. 613, 706, 758; III Grote Serie 125, pp. 238, 363, digital version at http://resources.huygens.knaw.nl/; Guanmian Xu, "From the Atlantic

to the Manchu: Taiwan Sugar and the Early Modern World, 1630s–1720s," *Journal of World History* 33, no. 2 (2022): 3.

23. Larry Gragg, *Englishmen Transplanted: The English Colonization of Barbados, 1627–1660* (Oxford: Oxford University Press, 2007), 19.

24. "Trans-Atlantic Slave Trade—Estimates"; William A. Green, "Supply versus Demand in the Barbadian Sugar Revolution," *Journal of Interdisciplinary History* 18, no. 3 (1988): 411; Schreuder, *Amsterdam's Sephardic Merchants,* 102–103.

25. Matthew Edel, "The Brazilian Sugar Cycle of the Seventeenth Century and the Rise of West Indian Competition," *Caribbean Studies* 9, no. 1 (1969): 30.

26. Green, "Supply versus Demand," 405; Richard Ligon, *A True & Exact History of the Island of Barbados . . .* (London: H. Moseley, 1657), 85–86.

27. Schreuder, *Amsterdam's Sephardic Merchants,* 113, 134, 146, 156.

28. Christian J. Koot, *Empire at the Periphery: British Colonists, Anglo-Dutch Trade, and the Development of the British Atlantic . . .* (New York: New York University Press, 2011), 187.

29. Herbert I. Bloom, *The Economic Activities of the Jews in Amsterdam in the Seventeenth and Eighteenth Centuries* (Williamsport, PA: Bayard Press, 1937), 37.

30. Gyorgy Novaky, "On Trade, Production and Relations of Production: The Sugar Refineries of Seventeenth-Century Amsterdam," *Tijdschrift voor Sociale Geschiedenis* 23, no. 4 (1997): 476; Jan van de Voort, "De Westindische Plantages van 1720–1795: Financiën en Handel" (Eindhoven, the Netherlands: De Witte, 1973), 26; Schreuder, *Amsterdam's Sephardic Merchants,* 230, 234, 239–240, 243–245, 252.

31. David Watts, *The West Indies: Patterns of Development, Culture and Environmental Change since 1492* (Cambridge: Cambridge University Press, 1998), 219–223; Galloway, "Tradition and Innovation," 342.

32. Matthew Parker, *The Sugar Barons: Family, Corruption, Empire, and War in the West Indies* (New York: Walker, 2012), 143.

33. Cecilia Ann Karch, "The Transformation and Consolidation of the Corporate Plantation Economy in Barbados: 1860–1977" (PhD diss., Rutgers University, 1982), 158.

34. Holing must have started by about 1670; see Peter Thompson, "Henry Drax's Instructions on the Management of a Seventeenth-Century Barbadian Sugar Plantation," *William and Mary Quarterly* 66, no. 3 (2009): 579. Menard mentions that later in the seventeenth century holing was replaced by digging trenches. Russell R. Menard, *Sweet Negotiations: Sugar, Slavery, and Plantation Agriculture in Early Barbados* (Charlottesville: University of Virginia Press, 2014), 71.

35. Justin Roberts, "Working between the Lines: Labor and Agriculture on Two Barbadian Sugar Plantations, 1796–97," *William and Mary Quarterly* 63, no. 3 (2006): 580–582, 584; Robert Hermann Schomburgk, *The History of Barbados* (London: Longman, Brown, Green and Longmans, 1848), 166n.1.

36. Thomas D. Rogers, *The Deepest Wounds: A Labor and Environmental History of Sugar in Northeast Brazil* (Chapel Hill: University of North Carolina Press, 2010), 32–33. Ligon presents in his book (published in 1657) a highly informative drawing of a Barbadian sugar mill, which shows us five cauldrons, a mill, and the boiling house as a careful designed integrated plant. Ligon, *A True & Exact History,* 84–85.

37. Mohamed Ouerfelli, *Le sucre: Production, commercialisation et usages dans la Méditerranée médiévale* (Leiden: Brill, 2008), 270–271.

38. Parker, *The Sugar Barons,* 46–51.

39. B. W. Higman, "The Sugar Revolution," *Economic History Review* 53, no. 2 (2000): 213.

40. See Roberts Justin, "Surrendering Surinam: The Barbadian Diaspora and the Expansion of the English Sugar Frontier, 1650–75," *William and Mary Quarterly* 73, no. 2 (2016): 225–226.

41. Schreuder, *Amsterdam's Sephardic Merchants,* 181. See also Samuel Oppenheim, "An Early Jewish Colony in Western Guiana, 1658–1666, and Its Relation to the Jews in Surinam, Cayenne and Tobago," *Publications of the American Jewish Historical Society,* no. 16 (1907): 95–186.

42. Michel-Christian Camus, "Le Général de Poincy, premier capitaliste sucrier des Antilles," *Revue française d'Histoire d'Outre-Mer* 84, no. 317 (1997): 122.

43. Mordechai Arbell, "Jewish Settlements in the French Colonies in the Caribbean (Martinique, Guadeloupe, Haiti, Cayenne) and the 'Black Code,'" in *The Jews and the Expansion of Europe to the West, 1450–1800,* ed. Paolo Bernardini and Norman Fiering (New York: Berghahn Books, 2001), 288–290; Guy Josa, "Les industries du sucre et du rhum à la Martinique (1639–1931)" (PhD diss., Université de Paris, 1931), 12, 33–34.

44. Abdoulaye Ly, "La formation de l'économie sucrière et le développement du marché d'esclaves africains dans les Iles françaises d'Amérique au XVIIe siècle," *Présence Africaine,* no. 13 (1957), 20–21, no. 16 (1957), 120n.14, 125.

45. Alex Borucki, David Eltis, and David Wheat, "Atlantic History and the Slave Trade to Spanish America," *American Historical Review* 120, no. 2 (2015): 440.

46. Galloway also points to other factors, such as worsening agricultural conditions caused by droughts. J. H. Galloway, "Northeast Brazil 1700–50: The Agricultural Crisis Re-Examined," *Journal of Historical Geography* 1, no. 1 (1975): 21–38.

47. Taylor, "The Economics of Sugar," 270n.13. See also Henry Koster, *Travels in Brazil* (London: Printed for Longman, Hurst, Rees, Orme, and Brown, 1816), 348–349.

48. Shawn W. Miller, "Fuelwood in Colonial Brazil: The Economic and Social Consequences of Fuel Depletion for the Bahian Recôncavo, 1549–1820," *Forest & Conservation History* 38, no. 4 (1994): 183, 186, 189–190; Koster, *Travels in Brazil,* 346, 358, 360.

49. Although Deerr just assumes that two-thirds of the enslaved people transported from Africa were destined for sugar plantations, his assumption may well be accurate. Noël Deerr,

The History of Sugar, vol. 2 (London: Chapman and Hall, 1950), 284. See also B. W. Higman, *Slave Population and Economy in Jamaica, 1807–1834* (Kingston, Jamaica: University of the West Indies Press, 1995), 243–244.

50. Deerr, *The History of Sugar,* 1:239. For the numbers of enslaved transported from East Africa to Saint Domingue, see David Eltis and David Richardson, *Atlas of the Transatlantic Slave Trade* (New Haven, CT: Yale University Press, 2015), 248.

51. Roberts, "Working between the Lines," 569, 579, 581.

52. C. L. R. James, *The Black Jacobins: Toussaint L'Ouverture and the San Domingo Revolution* (New York: Vintage, 1989), 392.

53. Roberts, "Working between the Lines," 560–561; Jennifer L. Morgan, *Laboring Women: Reproduction and Gender in New World Slavery* (Philadelphia: University of Pennsylvania Press, 2004), 147–149; Ligon, *A True & Exact History,* 48.

54. Mello, Visser, and Teensma, *Nederlanders in Brazilië,* 142, 148–152.

55. Labat quoted in Judith Ann Carney and Richard Nicholas Rosomoff, *In the Shadow of Slavery: Africa's Botanical Legacy in the Atlantic World* (Berkeley: University of California Press, 2011), 110; Dale Tomich, "Une petite Guinée: Provision Ground and Plantation in Martinique, 1830–1848," in *The Slaves Economy: Independent Production by Slaves in the Americas,* ed. Ira Berlin and Philip D. Morgan (London: Frank Cass, 1991), 71.

56. Edmund Oskar von Lippmann, *Geschichte des Zuckers: Seit den ältesten Zeiten bis zum Beginn der Rübenzucker-Fabrikation: ein Beitrag zur Kulturgeschichte* (Berlin: Springer, 1929), 503–504.

57. J. R. Ward, *British West Indian Slavery, 1750–1834: The Process of Amelioration* (New York: Oxford University Press, 1991), 22–24, 151–155; J. S. Handler and R. S. Corruccini, "Plantation Slave Life in Barbados: A Physical Anthropological Analysis," *Journal of Interdisciplinary History* 14, no. 1 (1983): 75, 78.

58. Jean Baptiste Labat, *Nouveau voyage aux isles de l'Amerique: Contenant l'histoire naturelle de ces pays, l'origine, les moeurs, la religion & le gouvernement des habitans anciens & modernes,* vol. 3 (Paris: Chez Guillaume Cavelier pere, 1742), 356–358.

59. John Gabriel Stedman, *Reize in de Binnenlanden van Suriname,* 2 vols. (Leiden: A. en J. Honkoop, 1799), 2:200.

60. Jerome S. Handler and Diane Wallman, "Production Activities in the Household Economies of Plantation Slaves: Barbados and Martinique, Mid-1600s to Mid-1800s," *International Journal of Historical Archaeology* 18, no. 3 (2014): 449, 450, 454–456, 461; Carney and Rosomoff, *In the Shadow,* 76–79, 106, 132; Hilary McD. Beckles, "An Economic Life of Their Own: Slaves as Commodity Producers and Distributors in Barbados," in *The Slaves Economy: Independent Production by Slaves in the Americas,* ed. Ira Berlin and Philip D. Morgan (London: Frank Cass, 1991), 32–34.

61. Carney and Rosomoff, *In the Shadow,* 76–79.

62. Gilberto Freyre, *The Mansions and the Shanties (Sobrados e Mucambos): The Making of Modern Brazil* (New York: A. A. Knopf, 1968), 186, 189.

63. Handler and Wallman, "Production Activities," 458–460.

64. Sweeney, "Market Marronage: Fugitive Women and the Internal Marketing System in Jamaica, 1781–1834," *William and Mary Quarterly* 76, no. 2 (2019): 201.

65. Robert Robertson, *A Detection of the State and Situation of the Present Sugar Planters: Of Barbadoes and the Leward Islands* (London: J. Wilford, 1732), 44; Stedman, *Reize*, 1:142.

66. Ligon, *A True & Exact History*, 50–51; Vincent Brown, *The Reaper's Garden: Death and Power in the World of Atlantic Slavery* (Cambridge, MA: Harvard University Press, 2010), 132–133.

67. William Beckford, *Remarks upon the Situation of Negroes in Jamaica: Impartially Made from a Local Experience of Nearly Thirteen Years in That Island . . .* (London: Printed for T. and J. Egerton, 1788), 23.

68. Stedman, *Reize,* 2:203.

69. Daniel E. Walker, *No More, No More: Slavery and Cultural Resistance in Havana and New Orleans* (Minneapolis: University of Minnesota Press, 2004), 14–15.

70. Londa Schiebinger, *Plants and Empire: Colonial Bioprospecting in the Atlantic World* (Cambridge, MA: Harvard University Press, 2004), chap. 3.

71. Robertson, *A Detection of the State,* 49.

72. Hilary Beckles, *Afro-Caribbean Women and Resistance to Slavery in Barbados* (London: Karnak House, 1988), 69–70.

73. Caldeira, "Learning the Ropes," 59; Deerr, *The History of Sugar,* 2:318.

74. Morgan, *Laboring Women,* 175.

75. Menard, *Sweet Negotiations,* 112, 20. For counterfeiting, see Beckles, *Afro-Caribbean Women,* 63.

76. Jerome S. Handler and Charlotte J. Frisbie, "Aspects of Slave Life in Barbados: Music and Its Cultural Context," *Caribbean Studies* 11, no. 4 (1972): 8.

77. See, for example, Stuart B. Schwartz, *Slaves, Peasants, and Rebels: Reconsidering Brazilian Slavery* (Urbana: University of Illinois Press, 1992), chap. 4. See also Richard Price, *Maroon Societies: Rebel Slave Communities in the Americas* (Baltimore, MD: Johns Hopkins University Press, 1979); Vincent Brown, *Tacky's Revolt: The Story of an Atlantic Slave War* (Cambridge, MA: Harvard University Press, 2022).

78. Stedman, *Reize,* 2:13–14.

79. Laurent Dubois, *Avengers of the New World: The Story of the Haitian Revolution* (Cambridge, MA: Harvard University Press, 2005), 55, 62.

80. See, for example, Douglas Hall, *In Miserable Slavery: Thomas Thistlewood in Jamaica, 1750–86* (London: Macmillan, 1989).

81. Zachary Macaulay and Margaret Jean Trevelyan Knutsford, *Life and Letters of Zachary Macaulay* (London: E. Arnold, 1900), 8.

82. See Dave Gosse, "The Politics of Morality: The Debate Surrounding the 1807 Abolition of the Slave Trade," *Caribbean Quarterly* 56, nos. 1–2 (2010): 127–138; Katherine Paugh, *Politics of Reproduction: Race, Medicine, and Fertility in the Age of Abolition* (New York: Oxford University Press, 2017), 26, 31–36, 42–43.

83. Alex van Stipriaan, *Surinaams Contrast: Roofbouw en Overleven in een Caraïbische Plantagekolonie 1750–1863* (Leiden: KITLV, 1993), 323; Nicole Vanony-Frisch, "Les esclaves de la Guadeloupe à la fin de l'Ancien Régime d'après les sources notariales (1770–1789)," *Bulletin de la Société d'Histoire de la Guadeloupe*, nos. 63–64 (1985): 52–53; S. D. Smith, *Slavery, Family, and Gentry Capitalism in the British Atlantic: The World of the Lascelles, 1648–1834* (Cambridge: Cambridge University Press, 2010), 284. Craton and Greenland cite a natural decrease rate (deaths minus births) of 2 percent by 1783. Michael J. Craton and Garry Greenland, *Searching for the Invisible Man: Slaves and Plantation Life in Jamaica* (Cambridge, MA: Harvard University Press, 1978), 85.

84. Karol K. Weaver, "'She Crushed the Child's Fragile Skull': Disease, Infanticide, and Enslaved Women in Eighteenth-Century Saint-Domingue," *French Colonial History* 5 (2004): 94.

85. Richard B. Sheridan, *Doctors and Slaves: A Medical and Demographic History of Slavery in the British West Indies, 1680–1834* (Cambridge: Cambridge University Press, 1985), 238; Ward, *British West Indian Slavery*, 16.

86. Parker, *The Sugar Barons*, 208.

87. Selwyn H. H. Carrington, *The Sugar Industry and the Abolition of the Slave Trade, 1775–1810* (Gainesville: University Press of Florida, 2002), 73; Bryan Edwards, *The History, Civil and Commercial, of the British Colonies in the West Indies . . .*, vol. 2 (London: Printed for John Stockdale, 1793), 451, 493.

88. Richard S. Dunn, "The English Sugar Islands and the Founding of South Carolina," *South Carolina Historical Magazine* 101, no. 2 (2000): 142–144, 146.

89. For the biography of Christopher Codrington III, see James C. Brandow, *Genealogies of Barbados Families: From Caribbeana and the Journal of the Barbados Museum and Historical Society* (Baltimore, MD: Genealogical Publishing, 2001), 222–224.

90. Jean Baptiste Labat and John Eaden, *The Memoirs of Pere Labat, 1693–1738* (London: Constable, 1931), 214.

91. Daniel Defoe, *The Complete English Tradesman, etc.*, 2nd ed., vol. 1 (London: Printed for Charles Rivington at the Bible and Crown in St. Paul's Church-yard, 1727), 316.

92. T. G. Burnard, "'Prodigious Riches': The Wealth of Jamaica before the American Revolution," *Economic History Review* 54, no. 3 (2001): 508.

93. Smith, *Lascelles*, 102–118.

94. Parker, *The Sugar Barons*, 265.

95. Alex van Stipriaan, "Debunking Debts: Image and Reality of a Colonial Crisis: Suriname at the End of the 18th Century," *Itinerario* 19, no. 1 (1995): 75; Smith, *Lascelles*, 106;

Bram Hoonhout, *Borderless Empire: Dutch Guiana in the Atlantic World (1750–1800)* (Athens: University of Georgia Press, 2020), 50, 169.

96. Smith, *Lascelles,* 104; Hoonhout, *Borderless Empire,* 170.

97. Klas Rönnbäck, "Governance, Value-Added and Rents in Plantation Slavery-Based Value-Chains," *Slavery & Abolition* 42, no. 1 (2021): 133.

98. Smith, *Lascelles,* 77–78, chap. 6.

99. S. D. Smith, "Gedney Clarke of Salem and Barbados: Transatlantic Super Merchant," *New England Quarterly* 76, no. 4 (2003): 540–541.

100. Amy Frost, "The Beckford Era," in *Fonthill Recovered: A Cultural History,* ed. Caroline Dakers (London: UCL Press, 2018), 63–64.

101. Richard B. Sheridan, "The Wealth of Jamaica in the Eighteenth Century," *Economic History Review* 18, no. 2 (1965): 308–309; Lillian Margery Penson, *The Colonial Agents of the British West Indies: A Study in Colonial Administration, Mainly in the Eighteenth Century . . .* (London: F. Cass, 1971), 228; Richard B. Sheridan, *Sugar and Slavery* (Aylesbury, England: Ginn, 1976), 60. See also Andrew J. O'Shaughnessy, "The Formation of a Commercial Lobby: The West India Interest, British Colonial Policy and the American Revolution," *Historical Journal* 40, no. 1 (1997): 71–95.

102. The 2019 movie is referred to here, not the sequel that came out in 2022.

103. Carrington, *The Sugar Industry,* 70–72.

104. David Richardson, "Slavery and Bristol's 'Golden Age,'" *Slavery & Abolition* 26, no. 1 (2005): 48–49.

105. Madge Dresser, "Squares of Distinction, Webs of Interest: Gentility, Urban Development and the Slave Trade in Bristol c.1673–1820," *Slavery & Abolition* 21, no. 3 (2000): 31–32; David Pope, "The Wealth and Social Aspirations of Liverpool's Slave Merchants of the Second Half of the Eighteenth Century," in *Liverpool and Transatlantic Slavery,* ed. David Richardson, Anthony Tibbles, and Suzanne Schwarz (Liverpool: Liverpool University Press, 2007), 170.

106. The figure of three hundred thousand enslaved people is based upon an estimated productivity per enslaved worker in the West Indies of five hundred kilograms sugar and the actual output of the West Indies of about 150,000 tons in the first five years of the nineteenth century. See Selwyn H. H. Carrington, "'Econocide'—Myth or Reality?—The Question of West Indian Decline, 1783–1806," *Boletín de Estudios Latinoamericanos y del Caribe,* no. 36 (1984): 2; Ward, *British West Indian Slavery,* 91.

107. Rönnbäck, "Governance," 144.

108. This "millstone argument" was repeated later by historians. Robert Paul Thomas, "The Sugar Colonies of the Old Empire: Profit or Loss for Great Britain?," *Economic History Review* 21, no. 1 (1968): 37. According to Coelho, "The costs of the British colonies in the [British West Indies] were borne by the consumers of sugar and the taxpayers." Philip R. P. Coelho, "The Profitability of Imperialism: The British Experience in the West Indies 1768–1772," *Explorations in Economic History* 10, no. 3 (1973): 278.

109. J. F. Wright, "The Contributions of Overseas Savings to the Funded National Debt of Great Britain, 1750–1815," *Economic History Review* 50, no. 4 (1997): 658.

110. Joseph E. Inikori, "Slavery and the Development of Industrial Capitalism in England," *Journal of Interdisciplinary History* 17, no. 4 (1987): 778–781, 788–789; Ralph Davis, "English Foreign Trade, 1660–1700," *Economic History Review* 7, no. 2 (1954): 291–292.

111. Barbara L. Solow, "Caribbean Slavery and British Growth," *Journal of Development Economics* 17, nos. 1–2 (1985): 111.

112. See Guillaume Daudin, "Profitability of Slave and Long-Distance Trading in Context: The Case of Eighteenth-Century France," *Journal of Economic History* 64, no. 1 (2004): 144–171.

113. See, for example, Daron Acemoglu, Simon Johnson, and James Robinson, "The Rise of Europe: Atlantic Trade, Institutional Change, and Economic Growth," *American Economic Review* 95, no. 3 (2005): 546–579.

114. See Ronald Findlay, "'The Triangular Trade' and the Atlantic Economy of the Eighteenth Century: A Simple General-Equilibrium Model," Essays in International Finance No. 177, Princeton University, International Finance Section, Department of Economics, 1990; Knick Harley, "Slavery, the British Atlantic Economy, and the Industrial Revolution," in *The Caribbean and the Atlantic World Economy: Circuits of Trade, Money and Knowledge, 1650–1914*, ed. Adrian Leonard and David Pretel (London: Palgrave Macmillan, 2015), 173–174.

115. Guillaume Daudin, *Commerce et prospérité: La France au XVIII siècle* (Paris: Presses de l'Université Paris-Sorbonne, 2005), 367–368. The figure of 9 percent is based on the assumption that 75 percent of the French re-exports of extra-European imports came from the Antilles.

116. This rough estimate is based on Klas Rönnbäck, "Sweet Business: Quantifying the Value Added in the British Colonial Sugar Trade in the 18th Century," *Revista de Historia Económica* 32, no. 2 (2014): 233. Rönnbäck calculated 2.8 percent of GDP for 1759 and 3.1 percent for 1794–1796, but one should deduct the average planters' gross surpluses because the colonies by definition ought not to be counted for Britain's GDP. The maintenance cost of garrisons and the navy should be added, calculated at £0.41 million by Thomas, "The Sugar Colonies," 38. In addition, there is the slave trade, which Engerman assumes made up 0.54 percent of Britain's GDP by the end of the eighteenth century. Two-thirds of this 0.54 percent can be attributed to sugar. See Stanley L. Engerman, "The Slave Trade and British Capital Formation in the Eighteenth Century: A Comment on the Williams Thesis," *Business History Review* 46, no. 4 (1972): 440. For France, the 3.5 percent is based upon sugar making up 39 percent of the value of the commerce based on the French Antilles. See Pierre Emile Levasseur, *Histoire du Commerce de la France* (Paris: Librarie nouvelle de droit et de jurisprudence, 1911), 488; Daudin, *Commerce et prosperité*, 367–368.

117. Paul M. Bondois, "Les centres sucriers français au XVIIIe siècle," *Revue d'Histoire économique et sociale* 19, no. 1 (1931): 57, 60; Paul M. Bondois, "L'Industrie sucrière française

au XVIIIe siècle: La fabrication et les rivalités entre les raffineries," *Revue d'Histoire économique et sociale* 19, no. 3 (1931): 338, 346.

118. Maud Villeret, *Le goût de l'or blanc: Le sucre en france au XVIIIe siècle* (Rennes: Presses Universitairs, 2017), 80.

119. Stipriaan, "Debunking Debts," 72, 78–79; Van de Voort, "De Westindische Plantages," 26, 260–61.

120. Van de Voort, "De Westindische Plantages," 260–261; Reesse, *De Suikerhandel van Amsterdam,* 1:57–58.

121. C. Sigmond, Sjoerd de Meer, and Jan Willem de Boezeman, *Een Zoete Belofte: Suikernijverheid in Dordrecht (17de–19de eeuw)* (Dordrecht, The Netherlands: Historische Vereniging Oud-Dordrecht, 2013), 72–190, 192.

122. Pepijn Brandon and Ulbe Bosma, "De Betekenis van de Atlantische Slavernij voor de Nederlandse Economie in de Tweede Helft van de Achttiende Eeuw," *Tijdschrift voor Sociale en Economische Geschiedenis* 16, no. 2 (2019): 45, annex x, xii. See also Tamira Combrink, "From French Harbours to German Rivers: European Distribution of Sugar by the Dutch in the Eighteenth Century," in *La diffusion des produits ultra-marins en Europe (XVIe–XVIIIe siècles),* ed. Maud Villeret and Marguerite Martin (Rennes: Presses Universitaires de Rennes, 2018).

123. Van de Voort, "De Westindische Plantages," 260–261; Pepijn Brandon and Ulbe Bosma, "Slavery and the Dutch Economy, 1750–1800," *Slavery & Abolition* 42, no. 1 (2021): 63.

124. Astrid Petersson, *Zuckersiedergewerbe und Zuckerhandel in Hamburg im Zeitraum von 1814 bis 1834: Entwicklung und Struktur Zweier wichtiger Hamburger Wirtschaftzweige des vorindustriellen Zeitalters* (Stuttgart: F. Steiner, 1998), 53, 56.

125. Tsugitaka Sato, *Sugar in the Social Life of Medieval Islam* (Leiden: Brill, 2015), 177–178; Sébastien Lupo, "Révolution(s) d'échelles: Le marché levantin et la crise du commerce marseillais au miroir des maisons Roux et de leurs relais à Smyrne (1740–1787)" (PhD diss., Université Aix-Marseille, 2015), 580.

126. Deerr, *The History of Sugar,* 1:193–203, 235–236, 239–240.

127. Benjamin Lay, *All Slave-Keepers that Keep the Innocent in Bondage, Apostates Pretending to Lay Claim to the Pure & Holy Christian Religion . . .* (Philadelphia: Printed by Benjamin Franklin for the author, 1837), 32, 37, 40, 151. See also Marcus Rediker, *The Fearless Benjamin Lay: The Quaker Dwarf Who Became the First Revolutionary Abolitionist* (Boston: Beacon Press, 2018).

128. Julie L. Holcomb, *Moral Commerce Quakers and the Transatlantic Boycott of the Slave Labor Economy* (Ithaca, NY: Cornell University Press, 2016), 32.

129. Roy L. Butterfield, "The Great Days of Maple Sugar," *New York History* 39, no. 2 (1958): 159–160.

130. Holcomb, *Moral Commerce,* 67–69.

131. See Benjamin Rush, "An Account of the Sugar Maple-Tree of the United States, and of the Methods of Obtaining Sugar from It . . . ," *Transactions of the American Philosophical Society* 3 (1793): 64–81.

132. Poivre quoted in Benjamin Rush, *An Address to the Inhabitants of the British Settlements in America, upon Slave-Keeping* (Boston: John Boyles, for John Langdon, 1773), 8. See also Pierre Poivre, *Voyages d'un philosophe ou observations sur les moeurs et les arts des peuples de l'Afrique, de l'Asie et de l'Amérique,* 3rd ed. (Paris: Du Pont, 1796), 90.

133. Rush, *An Address,* 30.

134. Holcomb, *Moral Commerce,* 38–40, 67; Seymour Drescher, *The Mighty Experiment: Free Labor versus Slavery in British Emancipation* (New York: Oxford University Press, 2002), 18, 21, 31.

135. William Fox, *An Address to the People of Great Britain on the Propriety of Abstaining from West India Sugar and Rum* (London; Philadelphia: D. Lawrence, 1792), 4.

136. Troy Bickham, "Eating the Empire: Intersections of Food, Cookery and Imperialism in Eighteenth-Century Britain," *Past & Present,* no. 198 (2008): 82, 86, 89–90.

137. Ortiz, *Cuban Counterpoint,* 42.

138. Jon Stobart, *Sugar and Spice: Grocers and Groceries in Provincial England 1650–1830* (Oxford: Oxford University Press, 2016), 60–62.

139. Wilberforce quoted in Charlotte Sussman, "Women and the Politics of Sugar, 1792," *Representations* 48 (1994): 64.

140. Fox, *An Address,* 11.

141. K. P. Mishra, "Growth of Sugar Culture in Eastern U.P. (1784–1792)," *Proceedings of the Indian History Congress* 41 (1980): 594, 597–598; N. P. Singh, "Growth of Sugar Culture in Bihar (1793–1913)," *Proceedings of the Indian History Congress* 45 (1984): 588–589; Shalin Jain, "Colonial Expansion and Commodity Trade in Banares, 1764–1800," *Proceedings of the Indian History Congress* 63 (2002): 499; Kumkum Chatterjee, *Merchants, Politics and Society in Early Modern India: Bihar, 1733–1820* (Leiden: Brill, 1996), 48–50.

142. Elizabeth Boody Schumpeter, *English Overseas Trade Statistics, 1697–1808* (Oxford: Clarendon Press, 1976), table XIII; Ulbe Bosma, *The Sugar Plantation in India and Indonesia: Industrial Production, 1770–2010* (Cambridge: Cambridge University Press, 2013), 17, 58.

143. See John Prinsep, *Strictures and Occasional Observations upon the System of British Commerce with the East Indies . . .* (London: J. Debrett, 1792).

144. East India Sugar: Papers Respecting the Culture and Manufacture of Sugar in British India : also Notices of the Cultivation of Sugar in Other Parts of Asia (London: Printed by Order of the Court of Proprietors of the East India Company by E. Cox and Son, Great Queen Street, 1822), app. I, 211.

145. Bosma, *The Sugar Plantation,* 50–51.

146. Macaulay and Knutsford, *Life and Letters of Zachary Macaulay,* 21.

147. David Geggus, "Jamaica and the Saint Domingue Slave Revolt, 1791–1793," *The Americas* 38, no. 2 (1981): 219.

148. Geggus, "Jamaica," 222.

149. David Geggus, "The Cost of Pitt's Caribbean Campaigns, 1793–1798," *Historical Journal* 26, no. 3 (1983): 703

150. Geggus, "The Cost", 705.

151. *Kentisch Gazette,* November 14, 1794.

152. Carrington, "'Econocide,'" 25, 44. Figure derived from Schumpeter, *English Overseas Trade Statistics, 1697–1808,* table XVIII.

153. David Beck Ryden, "Does Decline Make Sense?: The West Indian Economy and the Abolition of the British Slave Trade," *Journal of Interdisciplinary History* 31, no. 3 (2001): 365, 368, 370–371; Carrington, "'Econocide,'" 35.

154. Deerr, *The History of Sugar,* 1:59.

155. Bosma, *The Sugar Plantation,* 46–48, 63.

156. Petersson, *Zuckersiedergewerbe,* 91, 124–161; Otto-Ernst Krawehl, *Hamburgs Schiffs- und Warenverkehr mit England und den englischen Kolonien 1814–1860* (Köln: Böhlau, 1977), 323, 325; Richard Roberts, *Schroders: Merchants and Bankers* (Basingstoke, England: Macmillan, 1992).

4. Science and Steam

1. Plinio Mario Nastari, "The Role of Sugar Cane in Brazil's History and Economy" (PhD diss., Iowa State University, 1983), 43; Gilberto Freyre, *New World in the Tropics: The Culture of Modern Brazil* (New York: Alfred A. Knopf, 1959), 72.

2. Alex van Stipriaan, *Surinaams Contrast: Roofbouw en Overleven in een Caraïbische Plantagekolonie 1750–1863* (Leiden: KITLV, 1993), 139. Most of the labor productivity increase—and in the case of Suriname and Barbados a reversal of productivity decline— happened after 1790, which coincided with the introduction of the Otaheita cane in these years. Ward, *British West Indian Slavery,* 7, 91, 132, 190; David Eltis, Frank D. Lewis, and David Richardson, "Slave Prices, the African Slave Trade, and Productivity in the Caribbean, 1674–1807," *Economic History Review* 58, no. 4 (2005): 684–685; Alex van Stipriaan, "The Suriname Rat Race: Labour and Technology on Sugar Plantations, 1750–1900," *New West Indian Guide* 63, nos. 1–2 (1989): 96–97, 101–102.

3. See Sven Beckert, *Empire of Cotton: A Global History* (New York: Alfred A. Knopf, 2014).

4. Padraic X. Scanlan, "Bureaucratic Civilization: Emancipation and the Global British Middle Class," in *The Global Bourgeoisie: The Rise of the Middle Classes in the Age of Empire,* ed. Christof Dejung, David Motadel, and Jürgen Osterhammel (Princeton, NJ: Princeton University Press, 2019), 145.

5. Dorothy Burne Goebel, "The 'New England Trade' and the French West Indies, 1763–1774: A Study in Trade Policies," *William and Mary Quarterly* 20, no. 3 (1963): 337.

6. Franklin W. Knight, "Origins of Wealth and the Sugar Revolution in Cuba, 1750–1850," *Hispanic American Historical Review* 57, no. 2 (1977): 249.

7. Eltis, Lewis, and Richardson, "Slave Prices," 683–684.

8. See William Belgrove, *A Treatise upon Husbandry or Planting, etc.* (Boston: D. Fowle, 1755).

9. S. D. Smith, *Slavery, Family, and Gentry Capitalism in the British Atlantic: The World of the Lascelles, 1648–1834* (Cambridge: Cambridge University Press, 2010), 124–125; Olwyn M. Blouet, "Bryan Edwards, FRS, 1743–1800," *Notes and Records of the Royal Society* 54 (2000): 216.

10. Ward, *British West Indian Slavery,* 208–209.

11. See Jerome S. Handler and JoAnn Jacoby, "Slave Medicine and Plant Use in Barbados," *Journal of the Barbados Museum and Historical Society,* no. 41 (1993): 74–98.

12. See James Grainger, *An Essay on the More Common West-India Diseases . . .* (London: T. Becket and P. A. De Hondt, 1764).

13. See Susana María Ramírez Martín, "El legado de la real expedición filantrópica de la Vacuna (1803–1810): Las Juntas de Vacuna," *Asclepio* 56, no. 1 (2004); Richard B. Sheridan, *Doctors and Slaves: A Medical and Demographic History of Slavery in the British West Indies, 1680–1834* (Cambridge: Cambridge University Press, 1985), 249–267.

14. W. A. Green, "The Planter Class and British West Indian Sugar Production, before and after Emancipation," *Economic History Review* 26, no. 3 (1973): 454; J. H. Galloway, "Tradition and Innovation in the American Sugar Industry, c. 1500–1800: An Explanation," *Annals of the Association of American Geographers* 75, no. 3 (1985): 334–351; Christopher Ohm Clement, "Settlement Patterning on the British Caribbean Island of Tobago," *Historical Archaeology* 31, no. 2 (1997); Michael J. Craton and Garry Greenland, *Searching for the Invisible Man: Slaves and Plantation Life in Jamaica* (Cambridge, MA: Harvard University Press, 1978), 15.

15. Green, "The Planter Class," 449–450.

16. Jerome S. Handler and Diane Wallman, "Production Activities in the Household Economies of Plantation Slaves: Barbados and Martinique, Mid-1600s to Mid-1800s," *International Journal of Historical Archaeology.* 18, no. 3 (2014): 450, 461; Judith Ann Carney and Richard Nicholas Rosomoff, *In the Shadow of Slavery: Africa's Botanical Legacy in the Atlantic World* (Berkeley: University of California Press, 2011), 131; Dale Tomich, "Une petite Guinée: Provision Ground and Plantation in Martinique, 1830–1848," in *The Slaves Economy: Independent Production by Slaves in the Americas,* ed. Ira Berlin and Philip D. Morgan (London: Frank Cass, 1991), 70, 73, 86; Sheridan, *Doctors and Slaves,* 195, 207, 213.

17. Charles Mozard quoted in James E. McClellan and Vertus Saint-Louis, *Colonialism and Science: Saint Domingue in the Old Regime* (Chicago: University of Chicago Press, 2010), 160.

18. Richard A. Howard, "The St. Vincent Botanic Garden—The Early Years," *Arnoldia* 57, no. 4 (1997): 12–14.

19. Edward Brathwaite, *The Development of Creole Society in Jamaica 1770–1820* (Oxford: Clarendon Press, 1978), 84.

20. Richard Harry Drayton, *Nature's Government: Science, Imperial Britain, and the "Improvement" of the World* (New Haven, CT: Yale University Press, 2000), 94–95.

21. Stipriaan, *Surinaams Contrast,* 171; Galloway, "Tradition and Innovation," 341.

22. See, for example, Ward J. Barrett, *The Sugar Hacienda of Marquess del Valle* (Minneapolis: University of Minnesota Press, 1970), 45–46.

23. Galloway, "Tradition and Innovation," 341; Stuart George McCook, *States of Nature: Science, Agriculture, and Environment in the Spanish Caribbean, 1760–1940* (Austin: University of Texas, 2002), 79–80.

24. Drayton, *Nature's Government,* 104, 110.

25. Adrian P. Thomas, "The Establishment of Calcutta Botanic Garden: Plant Transfer, Science and the East India Company, 1786–1806," *Journal of the Royal Asiatic Society of Great Britain & Ireland* 16, no. 2 (2006): 171–172.

26. Matthew Parker, *The Sugar Barons: Family, Corruption, Empire, and War in the West Indies* (New York: Walker, 2012), 271.

27. Seymour Drescher, *The Mighty Experiment: Free Labor versus Slavery in British Emancipation* (New York: Oxford University Press, 2002), 20.

28. McClellan and Saint-Louis, *Colonialism and Science,* 226–227.

29. Hans Groot, *Van Batavia naar Weltevreden: Het Bataviaasch Genootschap van Kunsten en Wetenschappen, 1778–1867* (Leiden: KITLV, 2009), 52, 101.

30. Groot, *Van Batavia,* 78–79, 105; McClellan and Saint-Louis, *Colonialism and Science,* 226.

31. See Jan Hooyman, *Verhandeling over den Tegenwoordigen Staat van den Landbouw, in de Ommelanden van Batavia* (Batavia: Bataviaasch Genootschap der Konsten en Wetenschappen, 1781), 239.

32. J. J. Tichelaar, "De Exploitatie eener Suikerfabriek, Zestig Jaar Geleden," *Archief voor de Java-Suikerindustrie* 33, no. 1 (1925): 265–266; Margaret Leidelmeijer, *Van Suikermolen tot Grootbedrijf: Technische Vernieuwing in de Java-Suikerindustrie in de Negentiende Eeuw* (Amsterdam: NEHA, 1997), 76–79, 110.

33. David Lambert, *White Creole Culture, Politics and Identity during the Age of Abolition* (Cambridge: Cambridge University Press, 2010), 50; Brathwaite, *The Development of Creole Society,* 83–84; Edward Long, *The History of Jamaica; or, General Survey of the Ancient and Modern State of That Island with Reflections on Its Situation, Settlements, Inhabitants, Climate, Products, Commerce, Laws and Government,* vol. 1 (London: Lowndes, 1774), 436–437.

34. William Whatley Pierson, "Francisco de Arango y Parreño," *Hispanic American Historical Review* 16, no. 4 (1936): 460.

35. Dale Tomich, "The Wealth of Empire: Francisco Arango y Parreño, Political Economy, and the Second Slavery in Cuba," *Comparative Studies in Society and History* 45, no. 1 (2003): 7; *Wikipedia,* s.v., "Francisco de Arango y Parreño," accessed April 9, 2022, https://en.wikipedia.org/wiki/Francisco_de_Arango_y_Parre%C3%B1o.

36. Ada Ferrer, *Freedom's Mirror: Cuba and Haiti in the Age of Revolution* (New York: Cambridge University Press, 2016), 23; David Murray, "The Slave Trade, Slavery and Cuban Independence," *Slavery & Abolition* 20, no. 3 (1999): 112.

37. Ferrer, *Freedom's Mirror,* 33–36; Francisco de Arango y Parreño, *Obras,* vol. 1 (Havana: Impr. Enc. Rayados y Efectos de Escritorio, 1888), 47–51.

38. See "Discurso sobre la agricultura de la Habana y medios de fomentarla," in Arango y Parreño, *Obras,* 1:53–112; Antonio Benítez Rojo, "Power / Sugar / Literature: Toward a Reinterpretation of Cubanness," *Cuban Studies* 16 (1986): 9–31.

39. Alain Yacou, "L'expulsion des Français de Saint-Domingue réfugiés dans la région orientale de l'Île de Cuba (1808–1810)," *Cahiers du Monde hispanique et luso-brésilien,* no. 39 (1982): 50.

40. Carlos Venegas Fornias, "La Habana y su region: Un proyecto de organizacion espacial de la plantacion esclavista," *Revista de Indias (Madrid)* 56, no. 207 (1996): 352; María M. Portuondo, "Plantation Factories: Science and Technology in Late-Eighteenth-Century Cuba," *Technology and Culture* 44 (2003): 253; Antón L. Allahar, "The Cuban Sugar Planters (1790–1820): 'The Most Solid and Brilliant Bourgeois Class in All of Latin America,'" *The Americas* 41, no. 1 (1984): 49.

41. Tomich, "The Wealth of Empire," 23; Francisco de Arango y Parreño, *Obras,* vol. 2 (Havana: Impr. Enc. Rayados y Efectos de Escritorio, 1889), 214, 220–221; Rafael Marquese and Tâmis Parron, "Atlantic Constitutionalism and the Ideology of Slavery: The Cádiz Experience in Comparative Perspective," in *The Rise of Constitutional Government in the Iberian Atlantic World: The Impact of the Cádiz Constitution of 1812,* ed. Scott Eastman and Natalia Sobrevilla Perea (Alabama: University of Alabama Press, 2015), 184.

42. Matt D. Childs, *The 1812 Aponte Rebellion in Cuba and the Struggle against Atlantic Slavery* (Chapel Hill: University of North Carolina Press, 2009), 4, 22, 79, 157; Ferrer, *Freedom's Mirror,* chap. 7.

43. Alexander von Humboldt, *Essai politique sur l'Île de Cuba* (Paris: Librairie de Gide fils, 1826), 309.

44. Oliver Lubrich, "In the Realm of Ambivalence: Alexander von Humboldt's Discourse on Cuba (Relation historique du voyage aux régions équinoxiales du nouveau continent)," *German Studies Review* 26, no. 1 (2003): 71; Humboldt, *Essai politique,* 323–329; Ferrer, *Freedom's Mirror,* 27.

45. Irina Gouzévitch, "Enlightened Entrepreneurs versus 'Philosophical Pirate,' 1788–1809: Two Faces of the Enlightenment," in *Matthew Boulton: Enterprising Industrialist of the Enlightenment,* ed. Kenneth Quickenden, Sally Baggott, and Malcolm Dick (New York: Routledge, 2013), 228; Venegas Fornias, "La Habana y su region," 353; Jennifer Tann, "Steam

and Sugar: The Diffusion of the Stationary Steam Engine to the Caribbean Sugar Industry 1770–1840," *History of Technology* 19 (1997): 70.

46. Noël Deerr, *The History of Sugar*, vol. 2 (London: Chapman and Hall, 1950), 537, 540, 543.

47. Michael W. Flinn, *The History of the British Coal Industry*, vol. 2 (Oxford: Clarendon Press, 1986), 228.

48. For a detailed overview of the number of Boulton & Watt, Fawcett & Littledale, and Rennie machines and their destinations in the Caribbean, see Tann, "Steam and Sugar," 71–74, 79. For Smith Mirrlees in Glasgow, see Annie Wodehouse and Andrew Tindley, *Design, Technology and Communication in the British Empire, 1830–1914* (London: Palgrave Pivot, 2019), 94. Steam-powered crushers were practically absent in Brazil until the 1860s; see J. H. Galloway, "The Sugar Industry of Pernambuco during the Nineteenth Century," *Annals of the Association of American Geographers* 58, no. 2 (1968): 296.

49. Luis Martinez-Fernandez, "The Sweet and the Bitter: Cuban and Puerto Rican Responses to the Mid-Nineteenth-Century Sugar Challenge," *New West Indian Guide* 67, nos. 1–2 (1993): 49; Alexander von Humboldt, *The Island of Cuba. Translated from the Spanish, with Notes and a Preliminary Essay by J. S. Thrasher* (New York: Derby & Jackson, 1856), 271.

50. John Alfred Heitmann, *The Modernization of the Louisiana Sugar Industry: 1830–1910* (Baton Rouge: Louisiana State University Press, 1987), 10; Lawrence N. Powell, *The Accidental City: Improvising New Orleans* (Cambridge, MA: Harvard University Press, 2013), 258–260.

51. E. J. Forstall, "Louisiana Sugar," *De Bow's Review* 1, no. 1 (1846): 55–56.

52. Beckert, *Empire of Cotton*, 220.

53. Andrew James Ratledge, "From Promise to Stagnation: East India Sugar 1792–1865" (PhD diss., Adelaide University, 2004), 379, app. 4, table 1.

54. Tann, "Steam and Sugar," 65.

55. Ulbe Bosma, "Het Cultuurstelsel en zijn Buitenlandse Ondernemers: Java tussen Oud en Nieuw Kolonialisme," *Tijdschrift voor Sociale en Economische Geschiedenis* 2, no. 1 (2005): 24; Leidelmeijer, *Van Suikermolen*, 142.

56. José Guadalupe Ortega, "Machines, Modernity and Sugar: The Greater Caribbean in a Global Context, 1812–50," *Journal of Global History* 9, no. 1 (2014): 12.

57. Jacob Baxa and Guntwin Bruhns, *Zucker im Leben der Völker: Eine Kultur- und Wirtschaftsgeschichte* (Berlin: Bartens, 1967), 100, 102, 112, 131.

58. Herbert Pruns, *Zuckerwirtschaft während der Französischen Revolution und der Herrschaft Napoleons* (Berlin: Verlag Dr. Albert Bartens KG, 2008), 457–458.

59. Achard cited in Baxa and Bruhns, *Zucker im Leben*, 130.

60. Dubuc, "Of Extracting a Liquid Sugar from Apples and Pears," *Belfast Monthly Magazine* 5, no. 28 (1810): 378–379; H. C. Prinsen Geerligs, *De Ontwikkeling van het Suikergebruik* (Utrecht: De Anti-Suikeraccijnsbond, 1916), 8.

61. *Gazette nationale ou le Moniteur universel,* March 12, 1810, p. 286; June 22, 1810, p. 684.

62. Wilhelm Stieda, *Franz Karl Achard und die Frühzeit der deutschen Zuckerindustrie* (Leipzig: S. Hirzel, 1928), 44, 46–47, 60–61.

63. M. Aymar-Bression, *L'industrie sucrière indigène et son véritable fondateur* (Paris: Chez l'Auteur et les principaux Libraires, 1864), 15.

64. My translation. *Gazette nationale ou le Moniteur universel,* January 3, 1812, p. 13.

65. S. L. Jodidi, *The Sugar Beet and Beet Sugar* (Chicago: Beet Sugar Gazette Company, 1911), 2; H. D. Clout and A. D. M. Phillips, "Sugar-Beet Production in the Nord Département of France during the Nineteenth Century," *Erdkunde* 27, no. 2 (1973): 107; Baxa and Bruhns, *Zucker im Leben,* 135, 138–139.

66. Baxa and Bruhns, *Zucker im Leben,* 149.

67. Napoléon-Louis Bonaparte, *Analyse de la Question des Sucres . . .* (Paris: Administration de librairie, 1843), 5.

68. Roland Villeneuve, "Le financement de l'industrie sucrière en France, entre 1815 et 1850," *Revue d'Histoire économique et sociale* 38, no. 3 (1960): 293.

69. Aymar-Bression, *L'industrie sucrière indigène,* 23.

70. Tobias Kuster, "500 Jahre kolonialer Rohrzucker—250 Jahre europäischer Rübenzucker," *Vierteljahrschrift für Sozial- und Wirtschaftsgeschichte* (1998): 505; Manfred Pohl, *Die Geschichte der Südzucker AG 1926–2001* (Munich: Piper, 2001), 29.

71. Baxa and Bruhns, *Zucker im Leben,* 175–176, 186–187; Stieda, *Franz Karl Achard,* 165.

72. Susan Smith-Peter, "Sweet Development: The Sugar Beet Industry, Agricultural Societies and Agrarian Transformations in the Russian Empire 1818–1913," *Cahiers du Monde russe* 57, no. 1 (2016): 106–107, 120; A. Seyf, "Production of Sugar in Iran in the Nineteenth Century," *Iran* 32 (1994): 142.

73. Harvey Washington Wiley, *The Sugar-Beet Industry: Culture of the Sugar-Beet and Manufacture of Beet Sugar* (Washington, DC: Government Printing Office, 1890), 31.

74. Edward Church, *Notice on the Beet Sugar: Containing 1st; A Description of the Culture and Preservation of the Plant. 2d; An Explanation of the Process of Extracting Its Sugar . . .* (Northampton, MA: J. H. Butler, 1837), iv; Warner, *Sweet Stuff,* 88; Torsten A. Magnuson, "History of the Beet Sugar Industry in California," *Annual Publication of the Historical Society of Southern California* 11, no. 1 (1918): 72.

75. Church, *Notice on the Beet Sugar,* 54.

76. Deborah Jean Warner, *Sweet Stuff: An American History of Sweeteners from Sugar to Sucralose* (Washington, DC: Smithsonian Institution Scholarly Press / Rowman and Littlefield, 2011), 89–90.

77. Matthew C. Godfrey, *Religion, Politics, and Sugar: The Mormon Church, the Federal Government, and the Utah-Idaho Sugar Company, 1907–1921* (Logan: Utah State University Press, 2007), 21–24.

78. Leonard J. Arrington, "Science, Government, and Enterprise in Economic Development: The Western Beet Sugar Industry," *Agricultural History* 41, no. 1 (1967): 3.

5. State and Industry

1. See Conrad Friedrich Stollmeyer, *The Sugar Question Made Easy* (London: Effingham Wilson, 1845).

2. Ulbe Bosma and Jonathan Curry-Machado, "Two Islands, One Commodity: Cuba, Java, and the Global Sugar Trade (1790–1930)," *New West Indian Guide* 86, nos. 3–4 (2012): 238–239.

3. Walter Prichard, "Routine on a Louisiana Sugar Plantation under the Slavery Regime," *Mississippi Valley Historical Review* 14, no. 2 (1927): 175.

4. Sidney Mintz, "Cañamelar: The Subculture of a Rural Sugar Plantation Proletariat," in *The People of Puerto Rico: A Study in Social Anthropology* by Julian Haynes Steward et al. (Urbana: University of Illinois Press, 1956), 337.

5. José Guadalupe Ortega, "Machines, Modernity and Sugar: The Greater Caribbean in a Global Context, 1812–50," *Journal of Global History* 9, no. 1 (2014): 10.

6. Franz Carl Achard, D. Angar, and Charles Derosne, *Traité complet sur le sucre européen de betteraves: Culture de cette plante considérée sous le rapport agronomique et manufacturier* (Paris: chez M. Derosne: chez D. Colas, 1812), viii–x.

7. M. Aymar-Bression, *L'industrie sucrière indigène et son véritable fondateur* (Paris: Chez l'Auteur et les principaux Libraires, 1864), 17; J. Flahaut, "Les Derosne, pharmaciens parisiens, de 1779 à 1855," *Revue d'Histoire de la Pharmacie* 53, no. 346 (2005): 228.

8. Jean-Louis Thomas, *Jean-François Cail: Un acteur majeur de la première révolution industrielle* (Chef-Boutonne, France: Association CAIL, 2004), 15–23, 30.

9. Thomas, *Jean-François Cail*, 37, 85.

10. Ortega, "Machines, Modernity," 16.

11. J. A. Leon and Joseph Hume, *On Sugar Cultivation in Louisiana, Cuba, &c. and the British Possessions* (London: John Ollivier, 1848), 40–41, 58–60, 65; Nadia Fernández-de-Pinedo, Rafael Castro, and David Pretel, "Technological Transfers and Foreign Multinationals in Emerging Markets: Derosne & Cail in the 19th Century," Working Paper, Departamento de Análisis Económico, Universidad Autonoma de Madrid, 2014, 22.

12. Thomas, *Jean-François Cail*, 92.

13. Hugh Thomas, *Cuba; or, the Pursuit of Freedom* (London: Eyre and Spottiswoode, 1971), 117; Ortega, "Machines, Modernity," 18–19.

14. Ulbe Bosma, *The Making of a Periphery: How Island Southeast Asia Became a Mass Exporter of Labor* (New York: Columbia University Press, 2019), 75.

15. Margaret Leidelmeijer, *Van Suikermolen tot Grootbedrijf: Technische Vernieuwing in de Java-Suikerindustrie in de Negentiende Eeuw* (Amsterdam: NEHA, 1997), 159; Aymar-Bression, *L'industrie sucrière indigène*, 20–21.

16. Leidelmeijer, *Van Suikermolen,* 138, 152.

17. Roger G. Knight, *Sugar, Steam and Steel: The Industrial Project in Colonial Java, 1830–1850* (Adelaide, Australia: University of Adelaide Press, 2014), 139–141; Ulbe Bosma, "The Cultivation System (1830–1870) and Its Private Entrepreneurs on Colonial Java," *Journal of Southeast Asian Studies* 38, no. 2 (2007): 285.

18. Ulbe Bosma and Remco Raben, *Being "Dutch" in the Indies: A History of Creolisation and Empire, 1500–1920* (Singapore: NUS Press, 2008), 106–124.

19. Great Britain Parliament and House of Commons, *The Sugar Question: Being a Digest of the Evidence Taken before the Committee on Sugar and Coffee Plantations . . .* (London: Smith, Elder, 1848), 40; Ulbe Bosma, *The Sugar Plantation in India and Indonesia: Industrial Production, 1770–2010* (Cambridge: Cambridge University Press, 2013), 67.

20. John Alfred Heitmann, *The Modernization of the Louisiana Sugar Industry: 1830–1910* (Baton Rouge: Louisiana State University Press, 1987), 33, 35.

21. Lawrence N. Powell, *The Accidental City: Improvising New Orleans* (Cambridge, MA: Harvard University Press, 2013), 346.

22. Heitmann, *The Modernization,* 16–19, 42; J. Carlyle Sitterson, *Sugar Country: The Cane Sugar Industry in the South 1753–1950* (Lexington: University of Kentucky Press, 1953), 147.

23. Mark Schmitz, *Economic Analysis of Antebellum Sugar Plantations in Louisiana* (New York: Arno Press, 1977), 39.

24. J. Carlyle Sitterson, "Financing and Marketing the Sugar Crop of the Old South," *Journal of Southern History* 10, no. 2 (1944): 189; Sitterson, *Sugar Country,* 200–202; Richard J. Follett, *The Sugar Masters: Planters and Slaves in Louisiana's Cane World, 1820–1860* (Baton Rouge: Louisiana State University Press, 2007), 35.

25. Daniel Rood, *The Reinvention of Atlantic Slavery: Technology, Labor, Race, and Capitalism in the Greater Caribbean* (Oxford: Oxford University Press, 2020), 36; Sitterson, *Sugar Country,* 148–150; Schmitz, *Economic Analysis,* 35, 39–40; Follett, *The Sugar Masters,* 34, 36; Judah Ginsberg, *Norbert Rillieux and a Revolution in Sugar Processing* (Washington, DC: American Chemical Society, 2002).

26. Ortega, "Machines, Modernity," 19–21; Deerr presents a slightly different story, see Noël Deerr, *The History of Sugar,* vol. 2 (London: Chapman and Hall, 1950), 569.

27. Albert Schrauwers, "'Regenten' (Gentlemanly) Capitalism: Saint-Simonian Technocracy and the Emergence of the 'Industrialist Great Club' in the Mid-Nineteenth Century Netherlands," *Enterprise & Society* 11, no. 4 (2010): 766; Knight, *Sugar, Steam,* 63–91.

28. Dale Tomich, "Small Islands and Huge Comparisons: Caribbean Plantations, Historical Unevenness, and Capitalist Modernity," *Social Science History* 18, no. 3 (1994): 349.

29. Victor Comte de Broglie quoted in Victor Schoelcher, *Histoire de l'esclavage pendant les deux dernieres années,* vol. 2 (Paris: Pagnerre, 1847), 399.

30. Victor Schoelcher, *Des colonies françaises: Abolition immédiate de l'esclavage* (Paris: Pagnerre, 1842), xxiii.n.2.

31. Paul Daubrée, *Question coloniale sous le rapport industriel* (Paris: Impr. de Malteste, 1841), 8, 55–56.

32. A. Chazelles, *Émancipation—Transformation: Le système anglais—le système français: Mémoire adressé à la Chambre des Députés à l'occasion du projet de loi concernant le régime des esclaves dans les colonies françaises* (Paris: Imprimerie de Guiraudet et Jouaust, 1845), 18.

33. Chazelles, *Emancipation—Transformation*, 47.

34. Chazelles, *Emancipation—Transformation*, 56.

35. Thomas, *Jean-François Cail*, 192–193, 195; Christian Schnakenbourg, "La création des usines en Guadeloupe (1843–1884)," *Bulletin de la Societé d'Histoire de la Guadeloupe*, no. 141 (2005): 25–26. Using a slightly different definition of *usine*, Thomas mentions ten sugar centrals in Guadeloupe and two in Martinique.

36. Nelly Schmidt, "Les paradoxes du developpement industriel des colonies françaises des Caraibes pendant la seconde moitie du XIX siècle: Perspectives comparatives," *Histoire, Économie et Société* 8, no. 3 (1989): 321–322.

37. Henry Iles Woodcock, *A History of Tobago* (London: Frank Cass, 1971), 107, 190, app.

38. William A. Green, *British Slave Emancipation: The Sugar Colonies and the Great Experiment 1830–1865* (Oxford: Clarendon Press, 2011), 200; Claude Levy, *Emancipation, Sugar, and Federalism: Barbados and the West Indies, 1833–1876* (Gainesville: University Press of Florida, 1979), 95.

39. Jean-François Géraud, "Joseph Martial Wetzell (1793–1857): Une révolution sucrière oubliée à la Réunion," *Bulletin de la Société d'Histoire de la Guadeloupe*, no. 133 (2002): 44–45.

40. Alessandro Stanziani, *Labor on the Fringes of Empire: Voice, Exit and the Law* (Basingstoke, England: Palgrave Macmillan, 2019), 187.

41. Géraud, "Joseph Martial Wetzell," 57; Andrés Ramos Mattei, "The Plantations of the Southern Coast of Puerto Rico: 1880–1910," *Social and Economic Studies* 37, nos. 1–2 (1988): 369; Peter Richardson, "The Natal Sugar Industry, 1849–1905: An Interpretative Essay," *Journal of African History* 23, no. 4 (1982): 520.

42. Thomas, *Jean-François Cail*, 204–205; Fernández-de-Pinedo, Castro, and Pretel, *Technological Transfers*, 22.

43. Sudel Fuma, *Un exemple d'impérialisme éccomique dans une colonie française aux XIXe siècle—l'île de La Réunion et la Société du Crédit Foncier Colonial* (Paris: Harmattan, 2001), 31.

44. Schnakenbourg, "La création," 36, 54–55.

45. W. J. Evans, *The Sugar-Planter's Manual: Being a Treatise on the Art of Obtaining Sugar from the Sugar-Cane* (Philadelphia: Lea and Blanchard, 1848), 171–173.

46. Dale Tomich, "Commodity Frontiers, Spatial Economy, and Technological Innovation in the Caribbean Sugar Industry, 1783–1878," in *The Caribbean and the Atlantic World*

Economy Circuits of Trade, Money and Knowledge, 1650–1914, ed. Adrian Leonard and David Pretel (London: Palgrave Macmillan, 2015), 204.

47. Anthony Trollope, *West Indies and the Spanish Main* (London: Chapman and Hall, 1867), 183, 202.

48. Noël Deerr, *The History of Sugar,* vol. 1 (London: Chapman and Hall, 1949), 194; Richard B. Sheridan, "Changing Sugar Technology and the Labour Nexus in the British Caribbean, 1750–1900, with Special Reference to Barbados and Jamaica," *New West Indian Guide* 63, nos. 1–2 (1989): 74.

49. Deerr, *The History of Sugar,* 2:577; Luis Martinez-Fernandez, "The Sweet and the Bitter: Cuban and Puerto Rican Responses to the Mid-Nineteenth-Century Sugar Challenge," *New West Indian Guide* 67, nos. 1–2 (1993): 50.

50. Victor H. Olmsted and Henry Gannett, *Cuba: Population, History and Resources, 1907* (Washington, DC: US Bureau of the Census, 1909), 131, 143; Bosma, "The Cultivation System," 280–281. For an estimate of the total population of Java, see Bosma, *The Making of a Periphery,* 29.

51. David Turnbull, *Travel in the West Cuba: With Notices of Porto Rico, and the Slave Trade* (London: Longman, Orme, Brown, Green, and Longmans, 1840), 129–130.

52. See J. Curry-Machado, "'Rich Flames and Hired Tears': Sugar, Sub-Imperial Agents and the Cuban Phoenix of Empire," *Journal of Global History* 4, no. 1 (2009): 33–56.

53. Oscar Zanetti Lecuona and Alejandro García Alvarez, *Sugar and Railroads: A Cuban History, 1837–1959* (Chapel Hill: University of North Carolina Press, 1998), 25, 78, 95–96; Turnbull, *Travel in the West Cuba,* 175; Thomas, *Cuba,* 123.

54. Thomas, *Cuba,* 118–119. Fraginals believes 8.3 percent of Cuba's sugar output was produced by vacuum pans by 1860, but this could be an underestimation. Manuel Moreno Fraginals, *El ingenio: El complejo economico social cubano del Azucar* (Havana: Comisión Nacional Cubana de la UNESCO, 1964), 119. See also J. G. Cantero et al., *Los ingenios: Colección de vistas de los principales ingenios de azúcar de la isla de Cuba* (Madrid: Centro Estudios y Experimentación de Obras Públicas, 2005).

55. Jonathan Curry-Machado, *Cuban Sugar Industry: Transnational Networks and Engineering Migrants in Mid-Nineteenth Century Cuba* (Basingstoke, England: Palgrave Macmillan, 2011), 67; Bosma, "The Cultivation System," 290.

56. J. Carlyle Sitterson, "Hired Labor on Sugar Plantations of the Ante-Bellum South," *Journal of Southern History* 14, no. 2 (1948): 200–201; Sitterson, *Sugar Country,* 65.

57. Knight, *Sugar, Steam and Steel,* 56, 60n.109; Dale Tomich, "Sugar Technology and Slave Labor in Martinique, 1830–1848," *New West Indian Guide* 63, nos. 1–2 (1989): 128.

58. Schnakenbourg, "La création," 39–41, 58, 71, 73; Schmidt, "Les paradoxes," 314, 325.

59. Raymond E. Crist, "Sugar Cane and Coffee in Puerto Rico, I: The Rôle of Privilege and Monopoly in the Expropriation of the Jibaro," *American Journal of Economics and Sociology* 7, no. 2 (1948): 175.

60. Charles Ralph Boxer, *The Golden Age of Brazil, 1695–1750: Growing Pains of a Colonial Society* (Berkeley: University of California Press, 1962), 150; Fernando Ortiz, *Cuban Counterpoint: Tobacco and Sugar* (New York: Vintage, 1970), 278–279; Schoelcher, *Des colonies françaises,* 296.

61. Richard Pares, *Merchants and Planters* (Cambridge: Cambridge University Press, 1960), 44.

62. Pares, *Merchants and Planters,* chap. 4; S. D. Smith, *Slavery, Family, and Gentry Capitalism in the British Atlantic: The World of the Lascelles, 1648–1834* (Cambridge: Cambridge University Press, 2010), chap. 6.

63. See Bram Hoonhout, "The Crisis of the Subprime Plantation Mortgages in the Dutch West Indies, 1750–1775," *Leidschrift* 28, no. 2 (2013): 85–100.

64. Sitterson, "Financing and Marketing," 189.

65. "Havana," *Bankers' Magazine* (1846–1847): 243; Richard A. Lobdell, *Economic Structure and Demographic Performance in Jamaica, 1891–1935* (New York: Garland, 1987), 321–322.

66. Lobdell, *Economic Structure,* 321.

67. In Cuba, the position of the creditors was enhanced during the 1850s by the abandonment of the *privilegio de ingenio,* which prevented the property of the mill, including enslaved, to be seized by creditors upon default. In the French sugar colonies, this happened through the new hypothecary law of 1848 and in the West Indies through the Incumbered Estates Act of 1854. The government of Brazil had tried to reform the mortgage law in 1846. See Martinez-Fernandez, "The Sweet and the Bitter," 56; Christian Schnakenbourg, "La disparition des 'habitation-sucreries' en Guadeloupe (1848–1906): Recherche sur la désagrégation des structures préindustrielles de la production sucrière antillaise après l'abolition de l'esclavage," *Revue française d'Histoire d'Outre-Mer* 74, no. 276 (1987): 265–266; Nicholas Draper, "Possessing People," in *Legacies of British Slave-Ownership: Colonial Slavery and the Formation of Victorian Britain* by Catherine Hall et al. (Cambridge: Cambridge University Press, 2014), 43; Peter L. Eisenberg, *The Sugar Industry in Pernambuco: Modernization without Change, 1840–1910* (Berkeley: University of California Press, 1974), 73.

68. Trollope, *West Indies,* 130; Alexander von Humboldt, *The Island of Cuba. Translated from the Spanish, with Notes and a Preliminary Essay by J. S. Thrasher* (New York: Derby and Jackson, 1856), 281; Franklin W. Knight, *Slave Society in Cuba during the Nineteenth Century* (Madison: University of Wisconsin Press, 1970), 119; Edwin Farnsworth Atkins, *Sixty Years in Cuba: Reminiscences . . .* (Cambridge: Riverside Press, 1926), 52.

69. Thomas, *Cuba,* 137; Martín Rodrigo y Alharilla, "From Periphery to Centre: Transatlantic Capital Flows, 1830–1890," in *The Caribbean and the Atlantic World Economy: Circuits of Trade, Money and Knowledge, 1650–1914,* ed. Adrian Leonard and David Pretel (London: Palgrave Macmillan, 2015), 221–222.

70. While Kervéguen also used the Wetzell pans, from the 1850s onward he shifted to the Derosne & Cail vacuum pans, as did other large sugar planters on Réunion. See

Jean-François Géraud, *Kerveguen Sucrier* (Saint-Denis: Université Réunion, n.d.); Fuma, *Un exemple d'impérialisme*, 54–55, 64, 75.

71. Draper, "Possessing People," 43; R. W. Beachey, *The British West Indies Sugar Industry in the Late 19th Century* (Oxford: B. Blackwell, 1957), 36–38.

72. Levy, *Emancipation, Sugar, and Federalism*, 55.

73. See also Nicholas Draper, "Helping to Make Britain Great: The Commercial Legacies of Slave-Ownership in Britain," in *Legacies of British Slave-Ownership: Colonial Slavery and the Formation of Victorian Britain* by Catherine Hall et al. (Cambridge: Cambridge University Press, 2014), 83, 95, 102.

74. Alan H. Adamson, *Sugar without Slaves: The Political Economy of British Guiana, 1838–1904* (New Haven, CT: Yale University Press, 1972), 202–203; Beachey, *The British West Indies*, 69, 95.

75. Ryan Saylor, "Probing the Historical Sources of the Mauritian Miracle: Sugar Exporters and State Building in Colonial Mauritius," *Review of African Political Economy* 39, no. 133 (2012): 474; Arthur Jessop, *A History of the Mauritius Government Railways: 1864 to 1964* (Port Louis, Mauritius: J. E. Félix, 1964), 2.

76. Draper, "Helping to Make Britain Great," 95. For the compensation funds to resident and absentee slave owners, see the Database of the Centre for the Study of the Legacies of British Slavery, https://www.ucl.ac.uk/lbs/project/details/; Richard B. Allen, *Slaves, Freedmen and Indentured Laborers in Colonial Mauritius* (Port Chester, NY: Cambridge University Press, 1999), 123–127; Bosma, *The Sugar Plantation*, 85n.159; Richard B. Allen, "Capital, Illegal Slaves, Indentured Labourers and the Creation of a Sugar Plantation Economy in Mauritius, 1810–60," *Journal of Imperial and Commonwealth History* 36, no. 2 (2008): 157.

77. G. William Des Voeux, *My Colonial Service in British Guiana, St. Lucia, Trinidad, Fiji, Australia, New-Foundland, and Hong Kong with Interludes . . .* (London: John Murray, 1903), 212–225, 279.

78. Galloway, "The Sugar Industry of Pernambuco," 300–302; Manuel Correia de Andrade, *The Land and People of Northeast Brazil* (Albuquerque: University of New Mexico Press, 1980), 71.

79. Jean Mazuel, *Le sucre en Egypte: Étude de géographie historique et economique* (Cairo: Société Royale de Géographie d'Égypte, 1937), 32; Claudine Piaton and Ralph Bodenstein, "Sugar and Iron: Khedive Ismail's Sugar Factories in Egypt and the Role of French Engineering Companies (1867–1875)," *ABE Journal*, no. 5 (2014): paras. 7 and 8.

80. F. Robert Hunter, *Egypt under the Khedives, 1805–1879: From Household Government to Modern Bureaucracy* (Cairo: American University in Cairo Press, 1999), 40; Kenneth M. Cuno, "The Origins of Private Ownership of Land in Egypt: A Reappraisal," *International Journal of Middle East Studies* 12, no. 3 (1980): 266.

81. Piaton and Bodenstein, "Sugar and Iron," para. 9, p. 13; *Institution of Civil Engineers, Minutes of Proceedings of the Institution of Civil Engineers with Abstracts of the Discussions* (London: 1873), 37.

82. See Piaton and Bodenstein, "Sugar and Iron," para. 29.

83. Thomas, *Jean-François Cail*, 105–106, 135.

84. Maule, *Le sucre en Egypte*, 40–44; Barbara Kalkas, "Diverted Institutions: A Reinterpretation of the Process of Industrialization in Nineteenth-Century Egypt," *Arab Studies Quarterly* 1, no. 1 (1979): 33.

6. Slavery Stays

1. Cuba was followed by Brazil (82,000 tons), India (60,000 tons to England but also unknown quantities within Asia), Java (60,000 tons), Louisiana (49,460 tons), Mauritius (36,599 tons), Puerto Rico (36,515 tons), and British Guiana (35,619 tons). Noël Deerr, *The History of Sugar*, vol. 1 (London: Chapman and Hall, 1949), 112, 126, 203, 249.

2. Zachary Macaulay, *A Letter to William W. Whitmore, Esq. M.P. . . .* (London: Lupton Relphe, and Hatchard and Son, 1823), 2–4.

3. Harold E. Annett, *The Date Sugar Industry in Bengal: An Investigation into Its Chemistry and Agriculture* (Calcutta: Thacker Spink, 1913), 289.

4. Ulbe Bosma, *The Sugar Plantation in India and Indonesia: Industrial Production, 1770–2010* (Cambridge: Cambridge University Press, 2013), 29.

5. Ulbe Bosma and Jonathan Curry-Machado, "Two Islands, One Commodity: Cuba, Java, and the Global Sugar Trade (1790–1930)," *New West Indian Guide* 86, nos. 3–4 (2012): 239.

6. Jerome S. Handler and JoAnn Jacoby, "Slave Names and Naming in Barbados, 1650–1830," *William and Mary Quarterly* 53, no. 4 (1996): 702, 725; Colleen A. Vasconcellos, *Slavery, Childhood, and Abolition in Jamaica, 1788–1838* (Athens: University of Georgia Press, 2015), 72–74.

7. Jerome S. Handler and Charlotte J. Frisbie, "Aspects of Slave Life in Barbados: Music and Its Cultural Context," *Caribbean Studies* 11, no. 4 (1972): 11, 38–39.

8. John B. Cade, "Out of the Mouths of Ex-Slaves," *Journal of Negro History* 20, no. 3 (1935): 333–334; Richard J. Follett, *The Sugar Masters: Planters and Slaves in Louisiana's Cane World, 1820–1860* (Baton Rouge: Louisiana State University Press, 2007), 220.

9. Jan Jacob Hartsinck, *Beschryving van Guiana, of de Wilde Kust, in Zuid-America . . .* (Amsterdam: G. Tielenburg, 1770), 910, 913; John Gabriel Stedman, *Reize in de Binnenlanden van Suriname*, 2 vols. (Leiden: A. en J. Honkoop, 1799), 2:205.

10. My translation. Victor Schoelcher, *Des colonies françaises: Abolition immédiate de l'esclavage* (Paris: Pagnerre, 1842), 14.

11. Cade, "Out of the Mouths," 297–298.

12. J. Wolbers, *Geschiedenis van Suriname* (Amsterdam: H. de Hoogh, 1861), 455–456.

13. Claude Levy, *Emancipation, Sugar, and Federalism: Barbados and the West Indies, 1833–1876* (Gainesville: University Press of Florida, 1979), 20.

14. Hilary McD. Beckles, "The Slave-Drivers' War: Bussa and the 1816 Barbados Slave Rebellion," *Boletín de Estudios Latinoamericanos y del Caribe,* no. 39 (1985): 95, 102–103; Michael Craton, "Proto-Peasant Revolts? The Late Slave Rebellions in the British West Indies 1816–1832," *Past & Present,* no. 85 (1979): 101.

15. The estimates range from 13,000 to 30,000 enslaved people involved. Craton, "Proto-Peasant Revolts?," 106; Richard B. Sheridan, "The Condition of the Slaves on the Sugar Plantations of Sir John Gladstone in the Colony of Demerara, 1812–49," *New West Indian Guide* 76, nos. 3–4 (2002): 248.

16. *Legacies of British Slavery Database* s.v., "John Gladstone," accessed January 27, 2022, http://wwwdepts-live.ucl.ac.uk/lbs/person/view/8961.

17. Sheridan, "The Condition of the Slaves," 256, 259; Anya Jabour, "Slave Health and Health Care in the British Caribbean: Profits, Racism, and the Failure of Amelioration in Trinidad and British Guiana, 1824–1834," *Journal of Caribbean History* 28, no. 1 (1994): 4, 7, 10–13.

18. Zachary Macaulay, *East and West India Sugar, or, A Refutation of the Claims of the West India Colonists to a Protecting Duty on East India Sugar* (London: Lupton Relfe and Hatchard and Son, 1823), 44; Macaulay, *A Letter to William W. Whitmore,* 31.

19. Bosma, *The Sugar Plantation,* 64.

20. Robert Montgomery Martin, *Facts Relative to the East and West-India Sugar Trade, Addressed to Editors of the Public Press, with Supplementary Observations* (London, 1830), 5–6.

21. James Cropper, *Relief for West-Indian Distress, Shewing the Inefficiency of Protecting Duties on East-India Sugar, and Pointing Out Other Modes of Certain Relief* (London: Hatchard and Son, 1823), 27.

22. Anonymous, "A Picture of the Negro Slavery Existing in the Mauritius," *Anti-Slavery Monthly Reporter* (1829): 375, 378–379.

23. Bosma, *The Sugar Plantation,* 61.

24. Elizabeth Heyrick, *Immediate, Not Gradual Abolition: or, an Inquiry into the Shortest, Safest, and Most Effectual Means of Getting Rid of West Indian Slavery* (Boston: Isaac Knapp, 1838), 24.

25. Holcomb, *Moral Commerce,* 42, 43, chap. 4, 107; Ruth Ketring Nuermberger, *The Free Produce Movement: A Quaker Protest against Slavery* (Durham, NC: Duke University Press, 1942), 77–79.

26. See Seymour Drescher, "History's Engines: British Mobilization in the Age of Revolution," *William and Mary Quarterly* 66, no. 4 (2009): 737–756; J. Quirk and D. Richardson, "Religion, Urbanisation and Anti-Slavery Mobilisation in Britain, 1787–1833," *European Journal of English Studies* 14, no. 3 (2010): 269.

27. Levy, *Emancipation, Sugar, and Federalism,* 55.

28. Hilary McD. Beckles, *Great House Rules: Landless Emancipation and Workers' Protest in Barbados, 1838–1938* (Kingston, Jamaica: Randle, 2004), 45; Cecilia Ann Karch, "The

Transformation and Consolidation of the Corporate Plantation Economy in Barbados: 1860–1977" (PhD diss., Rutgers University, 1982), 200; Levy, *Emancipation, Sugar, and Federalism*, 113, 115–116, 127.

29. G. E. Cumper, "A Modern Jamaican Sugar Estate," *Social and Economic Studies* 3, no. 2 (1954): 135.

30. William G. Sewell, *The Ordeal of Free Labor in the British West Indies* (New York, 1863), 204; W. A. Green, "The Planter Class and British West Indian Sugar Production, before and after Emancipation," *Economic History Review* 26, no. 3 (1973): 458–459.

31. Deerr, *The History of Sugar*, 1:198–199.

32. Thomas C. Holt, *The Problem of Freedom: Race, Labor, and Politics in Jamaica and Britain, 1832–1938* (Baltimore, MD: Johns Hopkins University Press, 1992), 278, 317; Karch, "The Transformation," 193; O. Nigel Bolland, *On the March: Labour Rebellions in the British Caribbean, 1934–39* (Kingston, Jamaica: Ian Randle, 1995), 158.

33. West India Royal Commission, *Report of . . . with Subsidiary Report by D. Morris . . . (Appendix A), and Statistical Tables and Diagrams, and a Map (Appendix B)* (London: H. M. Stationery Office, by Eyre and Spottiswoode, 1897), 140–142.

34. Bosma, *The Sugar Plantation*, 71, 78; Andrew James Ratledge, "From Promise to Stagnation: East India Sugar 1792–1865" (PhD diss., Adelaide University, 2004), 240.

35. Bosma, *The Sugar Plantation*, 67–68.

36. Bosma, *The Sugar Plantation*, 79.

37. Lynn Hollen Lees, *Planting Empire, Cultivating Subjects: British Malaya, 1786–1941* (New York: Cambridge University Press, 2019), 25–26.

38. Leone Levi, *On the Sugar Trade and Sugar Duties: A Lecture Delivered at King's College, London, Feb. 29, 1864* (London: Effingham Wilson, 1864), 12–13. For data on sugar imports in Britain, see James Russell, *Sugar Duties: Digest and Summary of Evidence Taken by the Select Committee Appointed to Inquire into the Operation of the Present Scale of Sugar Duties* (London: Dawson, 1862), app. 1, 87.

39. Seymour Drescher, *The Mighty Experiment: Free Labor versus Slavery in British Emancipation* (New York: Oxford University Press, 2002), 205; Tâmis Parron, "The British Empire and the Suppression of the Slave Trade to Brazil: A Global History Analysis," *Journal of World History* 29, no. 1 (2018): 8.

40. Anthony Trollope, *West Indies and the Spanish Main* (London: Chapman and Hall, 1867), 101.

41. Bosma, *The Sugar Plantation*, 83.

42. See Leslie Bethell, "The Mixed Commissions for the Suppression of the Transatlantic Slave Trade in the Nineteenth Century," *Journal of African History* 7, no. 1 (1966): 79–93; David R. Murray, *Odious Commerce: Britain, Spain and the Abolition of the Cuban Slave Trade* (Cambridge: Cambridge University Press, 2002); Arthur F. Corwin, *Spain and the Abolition of Slavery in Cuba, 1817–1886* (Austin: University of Texas Press, 1967), 112–113, 118–119.

43. Richard Huzzey, "Free Trade, Free Labour, and Slave Sugar in Victorian Britain," *Historical Journal* 53, no. 2 (2010): 368–372.

44. Julius Wolf, *Zuckersteuer und Zuckerindustrie in den europäischen Ländern und in der amerikanischen Union von 1882 bis 1885, mit besonderer Rücksichtnahme auf Deutschland und die Steuerreform Daselbst* (Tübingen: Mohr Siebeck, 1886), 71.

45. Demy P. Sonza and Nicholas Loney, *Sugar Is Sweet: The Story of Nicholas Loney* (Manila: National Historical Institute, 1977), 53, 59–60.

46. Violeta Lopez-Gonzaga, "The Roots of Agrarian Unrest in Negros, 1850–90," *Philippine Studies* 36, no. 2 (1988): 162, 165; Nicholas Loney, José María Espino, and Margaret Hoskyn, *A Britisher in the Philippines, or, The Letters of Nicholas Loney: With an Introduction by Margaret Hoskyn and Biographical Note by Consul José Ma. Espino* (Manila: National Library, 1964), xx, xxi; Filomeno V. Aguilar, *Clash of Spirits: The History of Power and Sugar Planter Hegemony on a Visayan Island* (Honolulu: University of Hawaii Press, 1998), 107, 110–117, 128; Sonza and Loney, *Sugar Is Sweet,* 53, 59–60, 100.

47. Shawn W. Miller, "Fuelwood in Colonial Brazil: The Economic and Social Consequences of Fuel Depletion for the Bahian Recôncavo, 1549–1820," *Forest & Conservation History* 38, no. 4 (1994): 190–191.

48. John Richard Heath, "Peasants or Proletarians: Rural Labour in a Brazilian Plantation Economy," *Journal of Development Studies* 17, no. 4 (1981): 272; David A. Denslow, "Sugar Production in Northeastern Brazil and Cuba, 1858–1908," *Journal of Economic History* 35, no. 1 (1975): 262; J. H. Galloway, "The Sugar Industry of Pernambuco during the Nineteenth Century," *Annals of the Association of American Geographers* 58, no. 2 (1968): 291–300.

49. David Eltis, "The Nineteenth-Century Transatlantic Slave Trade: An Annual Time Series of Imports into the Americas Broken Down by Region," *Hispanic American Historical Review* 67, no. 1 (1987): 122–123. Tomich presents a slightly higher estimate of 387,000 enslaved over the same period of time. Dale Tomich, "World Slavery and Caribbean Capitalism: The Cuban Sugar Industry, 1760–1868," *Theory and Society* 20, no. 3 (1991): 304.

50. Tomich, "World Slavery," 304.

51. Manuel Moreno Fraginals, "Africa in Cuba: A Quantitative Analysis of the African Population in the Island of Cuba," *Annals of the New York Academy of Sciences* 292, no. 1 (1977): 196, 199–200; Franklin W. Knight, *Slave Society in Cuba during the Nineteenth Century* (Madison: University of Wisconsin Press, 1970), 76, 82.

52. Luis A. Figueroa, *Sugar, Slavery, and Freedom in Nineteenth-Century Puerto Rico* (Chapel Hill: University of North Carolina Press, 2005), 98–102.

53. David Turnbull, *Travel in the West Cuba: With Notices of Porto Rico, and the Slave Trade* (London: Longman, Orme, Brown, Green, and Longmans, 1840), 53.

54. Aisha K. Finch, *Rethinking Slave Rebellion in Cuba: La Escalera and the Insurgencies of 1841–1844* (Chapel Hill: University of North Carolina Press, 2015), 69.

55. See Joao José Reis, *Slave Rebellion in Brazil the Muslim Uprising of 1835 in Bahia* (Baltimore, MD: Johns Hopkins University Press, 1993); Thomas Ewbank, *Life in Brazil:*

Or, a Journal of a Visit to the Land of the Cocoa and the Palm . . . (New York: Harper & Brothers, 1856), 438–441. See also Manuel Barcia Paz, *West African Warfare in Bahia and Cuba: Soldier Slaves in the Atlantic World, 1807–1844* (Oxford: Oxford University Press, 2016); Finch, *Rethinking Slave Rebellion*, 48, 78–80, 227.

56. Antón Allahar, "Surplus Value Production and the Subsumption of Labour to Capital: Examining Cuban Sugar Plantations," *Labour, Capital and Society* 20, no. 2 (1987): 176–177.

57. *American Slavery as It Is: Testimony of a Thousand Witnesses* (New York: American Anti-Slavery Society, 1839), 35–39; Rebecca J. Scott, *Degrees of Freedom: Louisiana and Cuba after Slavery* (Cambridge, MA: Harvard University Press, 2008), 23; Follett, *The Sugar Masters*, 77; Peter Depuydt, "The Mortgaging of Souls: Sugar, Slaves, and Speculations," *Louisiana History* 54, no. 4 (2013): 458.

58. Frederick Law Olmsted, *A Journey in the Seaboard Slave States: With Remarks on Their Economy* (New York: Dix and Edwards, 1856), 694.

59. Olmsted, *A Journey,* 675, 689; J. Carlyle Sitterson, *Sugar Country: The Cane Sugar Industry in the South 1753–1950* (Lexington: University of Kentucky Press, 1953), 99; Follett, *The Sugar Masters*, 201; Roderick A. McDonald, "Independent Economic Production by Slaves on Louisiana Antebellum Sugar Plantations," in *The Slaves' Economy: Independent Production by Slaves in the Americas,* ed. Ira Berlin and Philip D. Morgan (London: Frank Cass, 1991), 186, 190.

60. Daniel E. Walker, *No More, No More: Slavery and Cultural Resistance in Havana and New Orleans* (Minneapolis: University of Minnesota Press, 2004), 28; Albert Bushnell Hart, *Slavery and Abolition, 1831–1841* (New York: Harper and Bros., 1906), 114–115.

61. Herbert Aptheker, *Essays in the History of the American Negro* (New York: International Publishers, 1945), 62.

62. See Victor Schoelcher, *L'arrêté Gueydon à la Martinique et l'arrêté Husson à la Guadeloupe* (Paris: Le Chevalier, 1872); Ryan Saylor, "Probing the Historical Sources of the Mauritian Miracle: Sugar Exporters and State Building in Colonial Mauritius," *Review of African Political Economy* 39, no. 133 (2012): 471.

63. For Hawaii, see Gary Okihiro, *Cane Fires: The Anti-Japanese Movement in Hawaii* (Philadelphia: Temple University Press, 1991), 15; Joan Casanovas, "Slavery, the Labour Movement and Spanish Colonialism in Cuba, 1850–1890," *International Review of Social History* 40, no. 3 (1995): 373–374.

64. B. W. Higman, "The Chinese in Trinidad, 1806–1838," *Caribbean Studies* 12, no. 3 (1972): 26–28, 42; Alan H. Adamson, *Sugar without Slaves: The Political Economy of British Guiana, 1838–1904* (New Haven, CT: Yale University Press, 1972), 42.

65. Madhavi Kale, "'Capital Spectacles in British Frames': Capital, Empire and Indian Indentured Migration to the British Caribbean," *International Review of Social History* 41, suppl. 4 (1996): 123.

66. Saylor, "Probing the Historical Sources," 471; Great Britain Parliament and House of Commons, *The Sugar Question: Being a Digest of the Evidence Taken before the Committee on Sugar and Coffee Plantations . . .* (London: Smith, Elder, 1848), 34.

67. Walton Look Lai, *Indentured Labor, Caribbean Sugar: Chinese and Indian Migrants to the British West Indies, 1838–1918* (Baltimore, MD: Johns Hopkins University Press, 2003), 157–158, 184–187; R. W. Beachey, *The British West Indies Sugar Industry in the Late 19th Century* (Oxford: B. Blackwell, 1957), 107.

68. J. H. Galloway, *The Sugar Cane Industry: An Historical Geography from Its Origins to 1914* (Cambridge: Cambridge University Press, 1989), 175.

69. G. W. Roberts and J. A. Byrne, *Summary Statistics on Indenture and Associated Migration Affecting the West Indies, 1834–1918* (London: Population Investigation Committee, 1966), 127.

70. Roberts and Byrne, *Summary Statistics,* 127.

71. John McDonald and Ralph Shlomowitz, "Mortality on Chinese and Indian Voyages to the West Indies and South America, 1847–1874," *Social and Economic Studies* 41, no. 2 (1992): 211; Watt Stewart, *Chinese Bondage in Peru: A History of the Chinese Coolie in Peru, 1849–1874* (Chicago: Muriwai Books, 2018), 17–22, 37–38.

72. Lisa Lee Yun, *The Coolie Speaks: Chinese Indentured Laborers and African Slaves in Cuba* (Philadelphia: Temple University Press, 2009), 17, 29, 31, 83, 84, 140, 148, 149.

73. Peter Klaren, "The Sugar Industry in Peru," *Revista de Indias* 65, no. 233 (2005): 37; Michael J. Gonzales, "Economic Crisis, Chinese Workers and the Peruvian Sugar Planters 1875–1900: A Case Study of Labour and the National Elite," in *Crisis and Change in the International Sugar Economy 1860–1914,* ed. Bill Albert and Adrian Graves (Norwich, England: ISC Press, 1984), 188–189, 192.

74. Bosma, *The Sugar Plantation,* 93–94.

75. See G. R. Knight, "From Plantation to Padi-Field: The Origins of the Nineteenth Century Transformation of Java's Sugar Industry," *Modern Asian Studies,* no. 2 (1980): 177–204.

76. J. Van den Bosch, "Advies van den Luitenant-Generaal van den Bosch over het Stelsel van Kolonisatie," in *Het Koloniaal Monopoliestelsel Getoetst aan Geschiedenis en Staatshuishoudkunde,* ed. D. C. Steijn Parvé (Zalt-Bommel, the Netherlands: Joh. Noman en Zoon, 1851), 316–317.

77. Knight, "From Plantation to Padi-Field," 192; G. H. van Soest, *Geschiedenis van het Kultuurstelsel,* 3 vols. (Rotterdam: Nijgh, 1871), 2:124–125, 145.

78. Jan Luiten van Zanden, "Linking Two Debates: Money Supply, Wage Labour, and Economic Development in Java in the Nineteenth Century," in *Wages and Currency: Global Comparisons from Antiquity to the Twentieth Century,* ed. Jan Lucassen (Bern: Lang, 2007), 181–182.

79. Ulbe Bosma, "Migration and Colonial Enterprise in Nineteenth Century Java," in *Globalising Migration History.,* ed. Leo Lucassen and Jan Lucassen (Leiden: Brill, 2014), 157.

80. Saylor, "Probing the Historical Sources," 471.

81. Van Soest, *Geschiedenis van het Kultuurstelsel,* 3:135.

82. See Pim de Zwart, Daniel Gallardo-Albarrán, and Auke Rijpma, "The Demographic Effects of Colonialism: Forced Labor and Mortality in Java, 1834–1879," *Journal of Economic History* 82, no. 1 (2022): 211–249.

83. Bosma, *The Sugar Plantation,* 100–118.

84. Ulbe Bosma, "The Discourse on Free Labour and the Forced Cultivation System: The Contradictory Consequences of the Abolition of Slave Trade for Colonial Java 1811–1863," in *Humanitarian Intervention and Changing Labor Relations: The Long-Term Consequences of the British Act on the Abolition of the Slave Trade (1807),* ed. M. van der Linden (Leiden: Brill, 2010), 410–411; Bosma, *The Sugar Plantation,* 111.

85. Bosma, "The Discourse," 413.

86. Bosma, "The Discourse," 413–414.

87. Bosma, *The Sugar Plantation,* 112.

88. See Clifford Geertz, *Agricultural Involution: The Process of Ecological Change in Indonesia* (Berkeley: University of California Press, 1966).

89. Ulbe Bosma, "Multatuli, the Liberal Colonialists and Their Attacks on the Patrimonial Embedding of Commodity Production of Java," in *Embedding Agricultural Commodities: Using Historical Evidence, 1840s–1940s.,* ed. Willem van Schendel (London: Routledge, 2016), 46–49.

90. Arthur van Schaik, "Bitter and Sweet: One Hundred Years of the Sugar Industry in Comal," in *Beneath the Smoke of the Sugar-Mill: Javanese Coastal Communities during the Twentieth Century,* ed. Hiroyoshi Hiroyoshi Kano, Frans Hüsken, and Djoko Suryo (Yogyakarta, Indonesia: Gadjah Mada University Press, 2001), 64.

91. Josef Opatrný, "Los cambios socio-económicos y el medio ambiente: Cuba, primera mitad del siglo XIX," *Revista de Indias* 55, no. 207 (1996): 369–370, 384.

92. Michael Zeuske, "Arbeit und Zucker in Amerika versus Arbeit und Zucker in Europa (ca. 1840–1880); Grundlinien eines Vergleichs," *Comparativ* 4, no. 4 (2017): 62. For Java, see Handelingen van de Tweede Kamer der Staten-Generaal, *Koloniaal Verslag* (1900), 89. Reinaldo Funes Monzote, *From Rainforest to Cane Field in Cuba an Environmental History since 1492* (Chapel Hill: University of North Carolina Press, 2008), 133, 144–153, 171.

93. See Alvaro Reynoso, *Ensayo sober el cultivo de la caña de azucar* (Madrid, 1865); Funes Monzote, *From Rainforest to Cane Field,* 154–155.

94. J. Sibinga Mulder, *De Rietsuikerindustrie op Java* (Haarlem: H. D. Tjeenk Willink, 1929), 39.

95. Bosma, *The Sugar Plantation,* 159–160.

96. See Dale Tomich, "The Second Slavery and World Capitalism: A Perspective for Historical Inquiry," *International Review of Social History* 63, no. 3 (2018): 477–501.

97. In Louisiana, 139,000 of the total 229,000 enslaved worked on sugar plantations; in Cuba, about 300,000; in Puerto Rico 50,000; and in Suriname 18,000. For Brazil, Galloway assumes that most of the 350,000 slaves in the northeastern part of the country were employed on sugar plantations. Reis claims that for the *zona da mata* in Pernambuco almost 70 percent of the enslaved population was directly involved in the sugar economy, and that enslaved workers were also involved in sugar production near Rio de Janeiro. A figure of 280,000 for Brazil therefore seems a reasonable assumption. J. H. Galloway, "The Last Years of Slavery on the Sugar Plantations of Northeastern Brazil," *Hispanic American Historical Review* 51, no. 4 (1971): 591; Jaime Reis, "Abolition and the Economics of Slaveholding in North East Brazil," *Boletín de Estudios Latinoamericanos y del Caribe,* no. 17 (1974): 7.

98. Stanley L. Engerman, "Contract Labor, Sugar, and Technology in the Nineteenth Century," *Journal of Economic History* 43, no. 3 (1983): 651. Note that Engerman's table is not complete; exports from the Philippines, India, and China are missing, for example.

99. Alessandro Stanziani, *Labor on the Fringes of Empire: Voice, Exit and the Law* (Basingstoke, England: Palgrave Macmillan, 2019), 201–202.

100. John Elliott Cairnes, *The Slave Power* (New York: Carleton, 1862), 46, 137, 142–143.

101. Stuart B. Schwartz, *Slaves, Peasants, and Rebels: Reconsidering Brazilian Slavery* (Urbana: University of Illinois Press, 1992), 44–47; Manuel Correia de Andrade, *The Land and People of Northeast Brazil* (Albuquerque: University of New Mexico Press, 1980), 64, 66.

102. Schoelcher, *Des colonies françaises,* 158; Dale Tomich, "Sugar Technology and Slave Labor in Martinique, 1830–1848," *New West Indian Guide* 63, nos. 1–2 (1989): 128; David R. Roediger and Elizabeth D. Esch, *Production of Difference: Race and the Management of Labor in U.S. History* (Oxford: Oxford University Press, 2012), 43.

103. Roediger and Esch, *Production of Difference,* 43; Follett, *The Sugar Masters,* 119–120.

104. Casanovas, "Slavery, the Labour Movement," 368–369; Daniel Rood, *The Reinvention of Atlantic Slavery: Technology, Labor, Race, and Capitalism in the Greater Caribbean* (Oxford: Oxford University Press, 2020), 10, 34.

105. Henry Iles Woodcock, *A History of Tobago* (London: Frank Cass, 1971), 189; Woodville K. Marshall, "Metayage in the Sugar Industry of the British Windward Islands, 1838–1865," in *Caribbean Freedom: Economy and Society from Emancipation to the Present: A Student Reader,* ed. Hilary McD. Beckles and Verene Shepherd (Kingston, Jamaica: Ian Randle, 1996), 65, 67, 75–76.

106. Karen S. Dhanda, "Labor and Place in Barbados, Jamaica, and Trinidad: A Search for a Comparative Unified Field Theory Revisited," *New West Indian Guide* 75, nos. 3–4 (2001): 242; Roberts and Byrne, *Summary Statistics,* 129, 132.

7. Crisis and Wonder Cane

1. For Hong Kong, see Jennifer Lang, "Taikoo Sugar Refinery Workers' Housing Progressive Design by a Pioneering Commercial Enterprise," *Journal of the Royal Asiatic Society Hong Kong Branch* 57 (2017): 130–157.

2. George Martineau, "The Brussels Sugar Convention," *Economic Journal* 14 (1904): 34.

3. Klaus J. Bade, "Land oder Arbeit? Transnationale und interne Migration im deutschen Nordosten vor dem Ersten Weltkrieg" (PhD diss., University of Erlangen-Nuremberg, 1979), 277–278.

4. E. Sowers, "An Industrial Opportunity for America," *North American Review* 163, no. 478 (1896): 321; George Martineau, "The Statistical Aspect of the Sugar Question," *Journal of the Royal Statistical Society* 62, no. 2 (1899): 297.

5. Julius Wolf, *Zuckersteuer und Zuckerindustrie in den europäischen Ländern und in der amerikanischen Union von 1882 bis 1885, mit besonderer Rücksichtnahme auf Deutschland und die Steuerreform Daselbst* (Tübingen: Mohr Siebeck, 1886), 3–4; Martineau, "The Statistical Aspect of the Sugar Question," 298–300.

6. John Franklin Crowell, "The Sugar Situation in Europe," *Political Science Quarterly* 14, no. 1 (1899): 89, 97, 100.

7. César J. Ayala, "Social and Economic Aspects of Sugar Production in Cuba, 1880–1930," *Latin American Research Review* 30, no. 1 (1995): 97, 99; *Wikipedia*, s.v. "Julio de Apezteguía y Tarafa," accessed January 27, 2022, https://es.wikipedia.org/wiki/Julio_de_Apeztegu%C3%ADa_y_Tarafa.

8. Roger Munting, "The State and the Beet Sugar Industry in Russia before 1914," in *Crisis and Change in the International Sugar Economy 1860–1914,* ed. Bill Albert and Adrian Graves (Norwich, England: ISC Press, 1984), 26; Martineau, "The Statistical Aspect of the Sugar Question," 314; A. Seyf, "Production of Sugar in Iran in the Nineteenth Century," *Iran* 32 (1994): 140, 142–143.

9. Em Hromada, *Die Entwicklung der Kartelle in der österreichisch-ungarischen Zuckerindustrie* (Zurich: Aktien-Buchdruckerei, 1911), 52–99.

10. Martijn Bakker, *Ondernemerschap en Vernieuwing: De Nederlandse Bietsuikerindustrie, 1858–1919* (Amsterdam: NEHA, 1989), 119–121, 125–128.

11. R. W. Beachey, *The British West Indies Sugar Industry in the Late 19th Century* (Oxford: B. Blackwell, 1957), 115; Richard A. Lobdell, *Economic Structure and Demographic Performance in Jamaica, 1891–1935* (New York: Garland, 1987), 327; Benito Justo Legarda, *After the Galleons: Foreign Trade, Economic Change and Entrepreneurship in the Nineteenth-Century Philippines* (Quezon City, Philippines: Ateneo de Manila University Press, 2002), 320–326.

12. Ulbe Bosma and Remco Raben, *Being "Dutch" in the Indies: A History of Creolisation and Empire, 1500–1920* (Singapore: NUS Press, 2008), 260–261.

13. Bijlagen Handelingen der Tweede Kamer 1894–1895 [150.1–7], "Schorsing der Heffing van het Uitvoerrecht van Suiker in Nederlandsch-Indië" [Suspension of export duties on sugar from the Netherlands Indies].

14. C. Y. Shephard, "The Sugar Industry of the British West Indies and British Guiana with Special Reference to Trinidad," *Economic Geography* 5, no. 2 (1929): 152–153; Alan H. Adamson, *Sugar without Slaves: The Political Economy of British Guiana, 1838–1904* (New Haven, CT: Yale University Press, 1972), 190–192, 212.

15. See, for example, O. Nigel Bolland, *On the March: Labour Rebellions in the British Caribbean, 1934–39* (Kingston, Jamaica: Ian Randle, 1995), 179.

16. Teresita Martinez Vergne, "New Patterns for Puerto Rico's Sugar Workers: Abolition and Centralization at San Vicente, 1873–92," *Hispanic American Historical Review* 68, no. 1 (1988): 53–59.

17. One of the most prominent being J. S. Furnivall, *Netherlands India: A Study of Plural Economy* (Cambridge: Cambridge University Press, 1939), 196–199.

18. Carol A. MacLennan, *Sovereign Sugar: Industry and Environment in Hawaii* (Honolulu: University of Hawaii Press, 2014), 100–101.

19. See, for example, Andrés Ramos Mattei, "The Plantations of the Southern Coast of Puerto Rico: 1880–1910," *Social and Economic Studies* 37, nos. 1–2 (1988): 385. See also Martín Rodrigo y Alharilla, "Los ingenios San Agustín y Lequeitio (Cienfuegos): Un estudio de caso sobre la rentabilidad del negocio del azúcar en la transición de la esclavitud al trabajo asalariado (1870–1886)," in *Azúcar y esclavitud en el final del trabajo forzado: Homenaje a M. Moreno Fraginals,* ed. José A. Piqueras Arenas (Madrid: Fondo de Cultura Económica, 2002): 252–268; César J. Ayala, *American Sugar Kingdom: The Plantation Economy of the Spanish Caribbean, 1898–1934* (Chapel Hill: University of North Carolina, 1999), 102.

20. Humberto García Muñiz, *Sugar and Power in the Caribbean: The South Porto Rico Sugar Company in Puerto Rico and the Dominican Republic, 1900–1921* (San Juan, Puerto Rico: La Editorial, 2010), 69; Ulbe Bosma, "Sugar and Dynasty in Yogyakarta," in *Sugarlandia Revisited: Sugar and Colonialism in Asia and the Americas, 1800–1940,* ed. U. Bosma, J. R. Giusti-Cordero, and R. G. Knight (New York: Berghahn Books, 2007), 90.

21. Christian Schnakenbourg, "La création des usines en Guadeloupe (1843–1884)," *Bulletin de la Societé d'Histoire de la Guadeloupe,* no. 141 (2005): 63–64, 71–74; Beachey, *The British West Indies,* 33.

22. Cecilia Karch, "From the Plantocracy to B.S. & T.: Crisis and Transformation of the Barbadian Socioeconomy, 1865–1937," in *Emancipation IV: A Series of Lectures to Commemorate the 150th Anniversary of Emancipation,* ed. Woodville Marshall (Kingston, Jamaica: Canoe Press, 1993), 38–43.

23. *Wikipedia,* s.v. "Julio de Apezteguía y Tarafa." See also Rodrigo y Alharilla, "Los ingenios."

24. Teresita Martínez-Vergne, *Capitalism in Colonial Puerto Rico: Central San Vicente in Late Nineteenth Century* (Gainesville: University Press of Florida, 1992), 74, 90–92, 98–100.

25. See Roger Knight, "Family Firms, Global Networks and Transnational Actors," *Low Countries Historical Review* 133, no. 2 (2018): 27–51.

26. John Paul Rathbone, *The Sugar King of Havana: The Rise and Fall of Julio Lobo, Cuba's Last Tycoon* (New York: Penguin, 2010), 69. See also Edwin Farnsworth Atkins, *Sixty Years in Cuba: Reminiscences . . .* (Cambridge: Riverside Press, 1926).

27. Peter F. Klarén, *Modernization: Dislocation, and Aprismo: Origins of the Peruvian Aprista party, 1870–1932* (Austin: University of Texas Press, 1973), 15.

28. See, for example, García Muñiz, *Sugar and Power,* 149–155.

29. William Kauffman Scarborough, *Masters of the Big House: Elite Slaveholders of the Mid-Nineteenth-Century South* (Baton Rouge: Louisiana State University Press, 2003), 40; Atkins, *Sixty Years in Cuba,* 50.

30. Martín Rodrigo y Alharilla, "From Periphery to Centre: Transatlantic Capital Flows, 1830–1890," in *The Caribbean and the Atlantic World Economy: Circuits of Trade, Money and Knowledge, 1650–1914,* ed. Adrian Leonard and David Pretel (London: Palgrave Macmillan, 2015), 218, 225; Mattei, "The Plantations of the Southern Coast," 374–375.

31. For abundant visual proof, see, for example, Peter Post and M. L. M. Thio, *The Kwee Family of Ciledug: Family, Status and Modernity in Colonial Java* (Volendam, the Netherlands: LM Publishers, 2019).

32. Gilberto Freyre, *Order and Progress: Brazil from Monarchy to Republic* (New York: Knopf, 1970), 279–280; Gilberto Freyre, *The Mansions and the Shanties (Sobrados e Mucambos): The Making of Modern Brazil* (New York: A. A. Knopf, 1968), 355.

33. Sven Beckert, *The Monied Metropolis: New York City and the Consolidation of the American Bourgeoisie, 1850–1896* (Cambridge: Cambridge University Press, 2001), 33.

34. Freyre, *Mansions,* 97; Scarborough, *Masters of the Big House,* 107, 124.

35. *Haole* refers to descendants of these missionaries (or of other American and European immigrants). Castle & Cooke, *The First 100 Years: A Report on the Operations of Castle & Cooke for the Years 1851–1951* (Honolulu, 1951), 10; MacLennan, *Sovereign Sugar,* 88–89.

36. Klarén, *Modernisation,* 16–20.

37. Jacob Adler, *Claus Spreckels: The Sugar King in Hawaii* (Honolulu: Mutual, 1966), 52, 54, 63–65.

38. Jacob Adler, "The Oceanic Steamship Company: A Link in Claus Spreckels' Hawaiian Sugar Empire," *Pacific Historical Review* 29, no. 3 (1960): 257, 259, 261–262; Adler, *Claus Spreckels,* 73–78, 112–26.

39. Adler, *Claus Spreckels,* 99, 158, 183.

40. Adler, *Claus Spreckels,* 159–213.

41. MacLennan, *Sovereign Sugar,* 95–96; Adler, *Claus Spreckels,* 83–85.

42. US Congress, *National Labor Relations Act: Hearings before the United States House Special Committee to Investigate National Labor Relations Board, Seventy-Sixth Congress, Third Session, on May 2, 3, 1940. Volume 22* (Washington, DC: Government Printing Office, 1973),

4525–4226; Adler, "The Oceanic Steamship Company," 269; Adler, *Claus Spreckels,* 127; Castle & Cooke, *The First 100 Years,* 27–28.

43. Filomeno V. Aguilar, *Clash of Spirits: The History of Power and Sugar Planter Hegemony on a Visayan Island* (Honolulu: University of Hawaii Press, 1998), 207–208.

44. See Violeta B. Lopez Gonzaga, *Crisis in Sugarlandia: The Planters' Differential Perceptions and Responses and Their Impact on Sugarcane Workers' Households* (Bacolod City, Philippines: La Salle Social Research Center, 1986).

45. Alfred W. McCoy, "Sugar Barons: Formation of a Native Planter Class in the Colonial Philippines," *Journal of Peasant Studies* 19, nos. 3–4 (1992): 114.

46. Peter Klaren, "The Sugar Industry in Peru," *Revista de Indias* 65, no. 233 (2005): 39.

47. Ellen D. Tillman, *Dollar Diplomacy by Force: Nation-Building and Resistance in the Dominican Republic* (Chapel Hill: University of North Carolina Press, 2016), 189.

48. Rudolf Freund, "Strukturwandlungen der internationalen Zuckerwirtschaft: Aus dem Institut für Weltwirtschaft und Seeverkehr," *Weltwirtschaftliches Archiv* 28 (1928): 32.

49. Barak Kushner, "Sweetness and Empire: Sugar Consumption in Imperial Japan," in *The Historical Consumer: Consumption and Everyday Life in Japan, 1850–2000,* ed. Penelope Francks and Janet Hunter (New York: Palgrave Macmillan, 2012), 131–132.

50. Kozo Yamamura, "The Role of the Merchant Class as Entrepreneurs and Capitalists in Meiji Japan," *Vierteljahrschrift für Sozial- und Wirtschaftsgeschichte* 56, no. 1 (1969): 115–118; Johannes Hirschmeier, *The Origins of Entrepreneurship in Meiji Japan* (Cambridge, MA: Harvard University Press, 2013), 266–267.

51. G. R. Knight, *Commodities and Colonialism: The Story of Big Sugar in Indonesia, 1880–1942* (Leiden: Brill, 2013), 46.

52. See G. Roger Knight, *Trade and Empire in Early Nineteenth-Century Southeast Asia: Gillian Maclaine and His Business Network* (Roydon, England: Boydell Press, 2015), 170.

53. Usually, the purity of sugar is expressed in degrees of polarization. Factory white sugar is close to 99° polarization and pure sugar is about 100°.

54. Bosma, *The Sugar Plantation,* 169–171; Robert Marks, *Rural Revolution in South China: Peasants and the Making of History in Haifeng County, 1570–1930* (Madison: University of Wisconsin Press, 1984), 107.

55. See, for example, James Carlton Ingram, *Economic Change in Thailand since 1850* (Stanford, CA: Stanford University Press, 1955), 124–125.

56. Lynn Hollen Lees, *Planting Empire, Cultivating Subjects: British Malaya, 1786–1941* (New York: Cambridge University Press, 2019), 24–37, 175.

57. See Ulbe Bosma and Bas van Leeuwen, "Regional Variation in the GDP Per Capita of Colonial Indonesia 1870–1930," *Cliometrica* (2022). https://doi.org/10.1007/s11698-022-00252-x.

58. O. Posthumus, "Java-Riet in het Buitenland," *Archief voor de Suikerindustrie in Ned.-Indië* 36, no. 2 (1928): 1149; Shephard, "The Sugar Industry," 151; Peter Griggs, "'Rust'

Disease Outbreaks and Their Impact on the Queensland Sugar Industry, 1870–1880," *Agricultural History* 69, no. 3 (1995): 427; Ulbe Bosma and Jonathan Curry-Machado, "Turning Javanese: The Domination of Cuba's Sugar Industry by Java Cane Varieties," *Itinerario: Bulletin of the Leyden Centre for the History of European Expansion* 37, no. 2 (2013): 106.

59. Posthumus, "Java-Riet in het Buitenland," 1150; Bosma and Curry-Machado, "Turning Javanese," 107.

60. *De Locomotief,* January 24, 1885.

61. D. J. Kobus, "Historisch Overzicht over het Zaaien van Suikerriet," *Archief voor de Suikerindustrie in Ned.-Indië* 1 (1893): 17.

62. A. J. Mangelsdorf, "Sugar Cane Breeding: In Retrospect and in Prospect," in *Proceedings of the Ninth Congress of the International Society of Sugar Cane Technologists,* ed. O. M. Henzell (Cambridge: British West Indies Sugar Association, 1956), 562.

63. W. K. Storey, "Small-Scale Sugar Cane Farmers and Biotechnology in Mauritius: The 'Uba' Riots of 1937," *Agricultural History* 69, no. 2 (1995): 166.

64. J. A. Leon and Joseph Hume, *On Sugar Cultivation in Louisiana, Cuba, &c. and the British Possessions* (London: John Ollivier, 1848), 15–18.

65. Roger G. Knight, *Sugar, Steam and Steel: The Industrial Project in Colonial Java, 1830–1850* (Adelaide, Australia: University of Adelaide Press, 2014), 194–195.

66. John A. Heitmann, "Organization as Power: The Louisiana Sugar Planters' Association and the Creation of Scientific and Technical Institutions, 1877–1910," *Journal of the Louisiana Historical Association* 27, no. 3 (1986): 287, 291; J. Carlyle Sitterson, *Sugar Country: The Cane Sugar Industry in the South 1753–1950* (Lexington: University of Kentucky Press, 1953), 255–257.

67. Stuart George McCook, *States of Nature: Science, Agriculture, and Environment in the Spanish Caribbean, 1760–1940* (Austin: University of Texas, 2002), 87–88.

68. Bosma and Curry-Machado, "Turning Javanese," 109; T. Lynn Smith, "Depopulation of Louisiana's Sugar Bowl," *Journal of Farm Economics* 20, no. 2 (1938): 503; Thomas D. Rogers, *The Deepest Wounds: A Labor and Environmental History of Sugar in Northeast Brazil* (Chapel Hill: University of North Carolina Press, 2010), 104.

69. See J. H. Galloway, "Botany in the Service of Empire: The Barbados Cane-Breeding Program and the Revival of the Caribbean Sugar Industry, 1880s–1930s," *Annals—Association of American Geographers* 86, no. 4 (1996).

70. See Leida Fernandez-Prieto, "Networks of American Experts in the Caribbean: The Harvard Botanic Station in Cuba (1898–1930)," in *Technology and Globalisation: Networks of Experts in World History,* ed. David Pretel and Lino Camprubi (London: Palgrave Macmillan, 2018), 159–188.

71. Association Hawaiian Sugar Planters and A. R. Grammer, *A History of the Experiment Station of the Hawaiian Sugar Planters' Association, 1895–1945* (Honolulu: Hawaiian Sugar Planters' Association, 1947), 183.

72. Peter Griggs, "Improving Agricultural Practices: Science and the Australian Sugarcane Grower, 1864–1915," *Agricultural History* 78, no. 1 (2004): 13, 21.

73. W. P. Jorissen, "In Memoriam Dr. Hendrik Coenraad Prinsen Geerligs: Haarlem 23. 11. 1864—Amsterdam 31. 7. 1953," *Chemisch Weekblad: Orgaan van de Koninklijke Nederlandse Chemische Verenging* 49, no. 49 (1953): 905–907.

8. Global Sugar, National Identities

1. Hugh Thomas, *Cuba; or, the Pursuit of Freedom* (London: Eyre and Spottiswoode, 1971), 100.

2. Anthony Trollope, *West Indies and the Spanish Main* (London: Chapman and Hall, 1867), 131.

3. J. D. B. De Bow, "The Late Cuba Expedition," *Debow's Review: Agricultural, Commercial, Industrial Progress and Resources* 9, no. 2 (1850): 173.

4. *New York Times,* August 24, 1860.

5. Leslie Bethell, "The Mixed Commissions for the Suppression of the Transatlantic Slave Trade in the Nineteenth Century," *Journal of African History* 7, no. 1 (1966): 92.

6. Joan Casanovas, "Slavery, the Labour Movement and Spanish Colonialism in Cuba, 1850–1890," *International Review of Social History* 40, no. 3 (1995): 377–378. See Rebecca J. Scott, "Gradual Abolition and the Dynamics of Slave Emancipation in Cuba, 1868–86," *Hispanic American Historical Review* 63, no. 3 (1983): 449–477.

7. David Turnbull, *Travel in the West Cuba: With Notices of Porto Rico, and the Slave Trade* (London: Longman, Orme, Brown, Green, and Longmans, 1840), 261.

8. Francisco de Arango y Parreño, *Obras,* vol. 2 (Havana: Impr. Enc. Rayados y Efectos de Escritorio, 1889), 649–658; David Murray, "The Slave Trade, Slavery and Cuban Independence," *Slavery & Abolition* 20, no. 3 (1999): 121.

9. Lilia Moritz Schwarcz, *The Spectacle of the Races: Scientists, Institutions, and the Race Question in Brazil, 1870–1930* (New York: Hill and Wang, 1999), 128.

10. Gilberto Freyre, *The Mansions and the Shanties (Sobrados e Mucambos): The Making of Modern Brazil* (New York: A. A. Knopf, 1968), 388–389.

11. Gilberto Freyre, *New World in the Tropics: The Culture of Modern Brazil* (New York: Alfred A. Knopf, 1959), 128–131.

12. Schwarcz, *The Spectacle of the Races,* 10.

13. Alejandro de la Fuente, "Race and Inequality in Cuba, 1899–1981," *Journal of Contemporary History* 30, no. 1 (1995): 135.

14. April J. Mayes, *The Mulatto Republic: Class, Race, and Dominican National Identity* (Gainesville: University Press of Florida, 2015), 115; Edward Paulino, *Dividing Hispaniola: The Dominican Republic's Border Campaign against Haiti, 1930–1961* (Pittsburgh: Pittsburgh University Press, 2016), 150, 159.

15. Mayes, *The Mulatto Republic,* 44, 80.

16. Aarti S. Madan, "Sarmiento the Geographer: Unearthing the Literary in Facundo," *Modern Language Notes* 126, no. 2 (2011): 266.

17. J. H. Galloway, *The Sugar Cane Industry: An Historical Geography from Its Origins to 1914* (Cambridge: Cambridge University Press, 1989), 187–188.

18. Donna J. Guy, "Tucuman Sugar Politics and the Generation of Eighty," *The Americas* 32, no. 4 (1976): 574; Henry St John Wileman, *The Growth and Manufacture of Cane Sugar in the Argentine Republic* (London: Henry Good and Son, 1884), 12.

19. Patricia Juarez-Dappe, "*Cañeros* and *Colonos:* Cane Planters in Tucumán, 1876–1895," *Journal of Latin American Studies* 38, no. 1 (2006): 132–133; Daniel J. Greenberg, "Sugar Depression and Agrarian Revolt: The Argentine Radical Party and the Tucumán Cañeros' Strike of 1927," *Hispanic American Historical Review* 67, no. 2 (1987): 310–311; Oscar Chamosa, *The Argentine Folklore Movement: Sugar Elites, Criollo Workers, and the Politics of Cultural Nationalism, 1900–1955* (Tucson: University of Arizona Press, 2010), 79–80, 82–83; Adrian Graves, *Cane and Labour: The Political Economy of Queensland Sugar Industry, 1862–1906* (Edinburgh: Edinburgh University Press, 1993), 26, 33, 77–78, 89, 126, 248.

20. Maria Elena Indelicato, "Beyond Whiteness: Violence and Belonging in the Borderlands of North Queensland," *Postcolonial Studies: Culture, Politics, Economy* 23, no. 1 (2020): 104; N. O. P. Pyke, "An Outline History of Italian Immigration into Australia," *Australian Quarterly* 20, no. 3 (1948): 108.

21. Tadeusz Z. Gasinski, "Polish Contract Labor in Hawaii, 1896–1899," *Polish American Studies* 39, no. 1 (1982): 20–22; Edward D. Beechert, *Working in Hawaii: A Labor History* (Honolulu: University of Hawaii Press, 1985), 86–87, 119, 124–139.

22. Wayne Patterson, "Upward Social Mobility of the Koreans in Hawaii," *Korean Studies* 3 (1979): 82, 89.

23. Sven Beckert, *Empire of Cotton: A Global History* (New York: Alfred A. Knopf, 2014), 287.

24. Joseph L. Love, "Political Participation in Brazil, 1881–1969," *Luso-Brazilian Review* 7, no. 2 (1970): 7; Inés Roldán de Montaud, "Política y elecciones en Cuba durante la restauración," *Revista de Estudios Politicos,* no. 104 (1999): 275.

25. Scott, *Degrees of Freedom: Louisiana and Cuba after Slavery* (Cambridge, MA: Harvard University Press, 2008), 70; Rick Halpern, "Solving the 'Labour Problem': Race, Work and the State in the Sugar Industries of Louisiana and Natal, 1870–1910," *Journal of Southern African Studies* 30, no. 1 (2004): 22.

26. J. C. Rodrigue, "'The Great Law of Demand and Supply': The Contest over Wages in Louisiana's Sugar Region, 1870–1880," *Agricultural History* 72, no. 2 (1998): 160.

27. Paolo Giordano, "Italian Immigration in the State of Louisiana: Its Causes, Effects, and Results," *Italian Americana* 5, no. 2 (1979): 165; J. P. Reidy, "Mules and Machines and Men: Field Labor on Louisiana Sugar Plantations, 1887–1915," *Agricultural History* 72, no. 2 (1998): 184.

28. Rebecca J. Scott, *Degrees of Freedom,* 85, 93, 189–99; Halpern, "Solving the 'Labour Problem,'" 23.

29. J. Vincenza Scarpaci, "Labor for Louisiana's Sugar Cane Fields: An Experiment in Immigrant Recruitment," *Italian Americana* 7, no. 1 (1981): 20, 27, 33–34; Giordano, "Italian Immigration," 165; Reidy, "Mules and Machines," 188.

30. Mark D. Schmitz, "Postbellum Developments in the Louisiana Cane Sugar Industry," *Business and Economic History* 5 (1976): 89.

31. Anonymous, "Salutatory," *Louisiana Planter and Sugar Manufacturer,* 1888, 1.

32. Mark Schmitz, "The Transformation of the Southern Cane Sugar Sector: 1860–1930," *Agricultural History* 53, no. 1 (1979): 274, 277; Anonymous, "Leon Godchaux," *Louisiana Planter and Sugar Manufacturer,* 1899, 305–306.

33. Giordano, "Italian Immigration," 168–172.

34. Reidy, "Mules and Machines," 189–190, 196; William C. Stubbs, "Sugar," *Publications of the American Economic Association* 5, no. 1 (1904): 80; J. Carlyle Sitterson, *Sugar Country: The Cane Sugar Industry in the South 1753–1950* (Lexington: University of Kentucky Press, 1953), 277, 394.

35. See John Wesley Coulter, "The Oahu Sugar Cane Plantation, Waipahu," *Economic Geography* 9, no. 1 (1933): 60–71.

36. This resonates with Ann Laura Stoler, "Sexual Affronts and Racial Frontiers: European Identities and the Cultural Politics of Exclusion in Colonial Southeast Asia," in *Tensions of Empire: Colonial Cultures in a Bourgeois World,* ed. Frederick Cooper and Ann Laura Stoler (Berkeley: University of California Press, 1997), 226.

37. A. Featherman, "Our Position and That of Our Enemies," *Debow's Review: Agricultural, Commercial, Industrial Progress and Resources* 31, no. 1 (1861): 31.

38. Featherman, "Our Position," 27.

39. See, in this respect, Ann Stoler, "Rethinking Colonial Categories: European Communities and the Boundaries of Rule," *Comparative Studies in Society and History* 31, no. 1 (1989): 134–161.

40. J. A. Delle, "The Material and Cognitive Dimensions of Creolization in Nineteenth-Century Jamaica," *Historical Archeology* 34 (2000): 57.

41. Lawrence N. Powell, *The Accidental City: Improvising New Orleans* (Cambridge, MA: Harvard University Press, 2013), 287–290.

42. Henry Koster, *Travels in Brazil* (London: Printed for Longman, Hurst, Rees, Orme, and Brown, 1816), 393–394; Elena Padilla Seda, "Nocorá: The Subculture of Workers on a Government-Owned Sugar Plantation," in *The People of Puerto Rico: A Study in Social Anthropology,* ed. Julian H. Steward (Urbana: University of Illinois Press, 1956), 274–275.

43. Colleen A. Vasconcellos, *Slavery, Childhood, and Abolition in Jamaica, 1788–1838* (Athens: University of Georgia Press, 2015), 43.

44. Bryan Edwards, *The History, Civil and Commercial, of the British Colonies in the West Indies . . . ,* vol. 2 (London: Printed for John Stockdale, 1793), 16–17.

45. Freyre, *Mansions*, 177.

46. Frederick Law Olmsted, *A Journey in the Seaboard Slave States: With Remarks on Their Economy* (New York: Dix and Edwards, 1856), 594, 635.

47. Edwin Farnsworth Atkins, *Sixty Years in Cuba: Reminiscences* . . . (Cambridge: Riverside Press, 1926), 46; Antonio Benítez Rojo, "Power / Sugar / Literature: Toward a Reinterpretation of Cubanness," *Cuban Studies* 16 (1986): 19.

48. John Mawe, *Travels in the Interior of Brazil: Particularly in the Gold and Diamond Districts of that Country* . . . (London: Longman, Hurst, Rees, Orme, and Brown, 1812), 281.

49. Featherman, "Our Position," 27.

50. George Washington Cable, *Madame Delphine: A Novelette and Other Tales* (London: Frederick Warne, 1881); Alice H. Petry, *A Genius in His Way: The Art of Cable's Old Creole Days* (Rutherford, NJ: Fairleigh Dickinson University Press, 1988), 32.

51. See Gilberto Freyre, *The Masters and the Slaves (Casa-Grande and Senzala): A Study in the Development of Brazilian Civilization,* trans. Samuel Putnam (New York: Knopf, 1946).

52. Freyre, *New World*, 92; Freyre, *Mansions,* 431. See also José Vasconcelos, *La raza cósmica: Misión de la raza iberoamericana, Argentina y Brasil* (México: Espasa-Calpe Mexicana, 1948).

53. Gilberto Freyre, *Order and Progress: Brazil from Monarchy to Republic* (New York: Knopf, 1970), xix.

54. April Merleaux, *Sugar and Civilization: American Empire and the Cultural Politics of Sweetness* (Chapel Hill: University of North Carolina Press, 2015), 108–115.

55. Edward E. Weber, "Sugar Industry," in *Industrialization of Latin America*, ed. L. J. Hughlett (New York: McGraw-Hill, 1946), 398; Merleaux, *Sugar and Civilization,* 114–119.

56. R. B. Ogendo and J. C. A. Obiero, "The East African Sugar Industry," *GeoJournal: An International Journal on Human Geography and Environmental Sciences* 2, no. 4 (1978): 343, 347.

57. Ulbe Bosma, *The Sugar Plantation in India and Indonesia: Industrial Production, 1770–2010* (Cambridge: Cambridge University Press, 2013), 197, 210.

58. Manuel Correia de Andrade, *The Land and People of Northeast Brazil* (Albuquerque: University of New Mexico Press, 1980), 81; Weber, "Sugar Industry," 393–394.

59. J. C. K., "The Sugar-Palm of East Indies," *Journal of the Royal Society of Arts* 59, no. 3048 (1911): 567–569; Charles Robequain, "Le sucre de palme au Cambodge," *Annales de Géographie* 58, no. 310 (1949): 189; D. F. Liedermoij, "De Nijverheid op Celebes," *Tijdschrift voor Nederlandsch Indië* 16, 2, no. 12 (1854): 360. See also Harold E. Annett, *The Date Sugar Industry in Bengal: An Investigation into Its Chemistry and Agriculture* (Calcutta: Thacker Spink, 1913).

60. Roger Owen, "The Study of Middle Eastern Industrial History: Notes on the Interrelationship between Factories and Small-Scale Manufacturing with Special References to Lebanese Silk and Egyptian Sugar, 1900–1930," *International Journal of Middle East Studies* 16, no. 4 (1984): 480–481.

61. Bosma, *The Sugar Plantation*, 191.

62. Mildred Maddocks and Harvey Washington Wiley, *The Pure Food Cook Book: The Good Housekeeping Recipes, Just How to Buy—Just How to Cook* (New York: Hearst's International Library, 1914), 3.

63. Merleaux, *Sugar and Civilization*, 133.

64. Weber, "Sugar Industry," 410–417.

65. Leigh Binford, "Peasants and Petty Capitalists in Southern Oaxacan Sugar Cane Production and Processing, 1930–1980," *Journal of Latin American Studies* 24, no. 1 (1992): 51–54; Manuel Moreno Fraginals, *El ingenio: El complejo economico social cubano del azucar* (Havana: Comisión Nacional Cubana de la UNESCO, 1964), 82.

66. John Richard Heath, "Peasants or Proletarians: Rural Labour in a Brazilian Plantation Economy," *Journal of Development Studies* 17, no. 4 (1981): 278; Andrade, *Land and People*, 86.

67. Gonzalo Rodriguez et al., *Panela Production as a Strategy for Diversifying Incomes in Rural Area of Latin America* (Rome: United Nations Food and Agriculture Organization, 2007), xvi, 10, 17.

68. Bosma, *The Sugar Plantation*, 86.

69. Bosma, *The Sugar Plantation*, 134–135; Leone Levi, *On the Sugar Trade and Sugar Duties: A Lecture Delivered at King's College, London, Feb. 29, 1864* (London: Effingham Wilson, 1864), 19–20.

70. Quoted in Bosma, *The Sugar Plantation*, 135.

71. Bosma, *The Sugar Plantation*, 136–137.

72. Alexander Burnes, *Travels into Bokhara: Being the Account of a Journey from India to Cabool, Tartary and Persia . . . in the Years 1831, 1832, and 1833*, 3 vols. (London: J. Murray, 1834), 1:44.

73. James Mylne, "Experiences of an European Zamindar (Landholder) in Behar," *Journal of the Society of Arts* 30, no. 1538 (1882): 704.

74. This section is derived from Bosma, *The Sugar Plantation*, 138–142, and app. I, 271.

75. J. W. Davidson, *The Island of Formosa: Historical View from 1430 to 1900 . . .* (New York: Paragon Book Gallery, 1903), 450, 457. The essay by Wykberg Myers is included in Davidson, *The Island of Formosa*, 449–451.

76. Mylne, "Experiences of an European Zamindar," 706.

77. Bosma, *The Sugar Plantation*, 146, 150, 205.

78. Bosma, *The Sugar Plantation*, 206.

79. Bosma, *The Sugar Plantation*, 206.

80. Bosma, *The Sugar Plantation*, 207–208.

81. Krishna Kumar Birla, *Brushes with History* (New Delhi: Penguin India, 2009), 594–595.

82. Bosma, *The Sugar Plantation*, 241–242.

83. "Background Study: Pakistan," *Proceedings of Fiji/FAO Asia Pacific Sugar Conference, Fiji, 29–31 October 1997,* https://www.fao.org/3/X0513E/x0513e23.htm; M. S. Rahman, S. Khatun, and M. K. Rahman, "Sugarcane and Sugar Industry in Bangladesh: An Overview," *Sugar Tech* 18, no. 6 (2016): 629.

84. Aashna Ahuja, "15 Jaggery (Gur) Benefits: Ever Wondered Why Our Elders End a Meal with Gur?," *NDTV Food,* August 24, 2018, https://food.ndtv.com/health/15-jaggery-benefits-ever-wondered-why-our-elders-end-a-meal-with-gur-1270883.

9. American Sugar Kingdom

1. Paul Leroy Vogt, *The Sugar Refining Industry in the United States: Its Development and Present Condition* (Philadelphia: Published for the University, 1908), 2.

2. J. Carlyle Sitterson, "Ante-Bellum Sugar Culture in the South Atlantic States," *Journal of Southern History* 3, no. 2 (1937): 179, 181–182, 187.

3. Gordon Patterson, "Raising Cane and Refining Sugar: Florida Crystals and the Fame of Fellsmere," *Florida Historical Quarterly* 75, no. 4 (1997): 412.

4. Lucy B. Wayne, *Sweet Cane: The Architecture of the Sugar Works of East Florida* (Tuscaloosa: University of Alabama Press, 2010), 3, 38–39, 98, 147.

5. Eleanor C. Nordyke and Richard K. C. Lee, *The Chinese in Hawaii: A Historical and Demographic Perspective* (Honolulu: East-West Center, 1990), 197; Carol A. MacLennan, *Sovereign Sugar Industry and Environment in Hawaii* (Honolulu: University of Hawaii Press, 2014), 85; Dorothy Burne Goebel, "The 'New England Trade' and the French West Indies, 1763–1774: A Study in Trade Policies," *William and Mary Quarterly* 20, no. 3 (1963): 344; Markus A. Denzel, "Der seewärtige Einfuhrhandel Hamburgs nach den 'Admiralitäts- und Convoygeld-Einnahmebüchern' (1733–1798): Für Hans Pohl zum 27. März 2015," *Vierteljahrschrift für Sozial- und Wirtschaftsgeschichte* 102, no. 2 (2015): 150. See Nathaniel Bowditch and Mary C. McHale, *Early American-Philippine Trade: The Journal of Nathaniel Bowditch in Manila, 1796* (New Haven, CT: Yale University, Southeast Asia Studies/Cellar Book Shop, Detroit, 1962).

6. C. Y. Shephard, "The Sugar Industry of the British West Indies and British Guiana with Special Reference to Trinidad," *Economic Geography* 5, no. 2 (1929): 151.

7. Sumner J. La Croix and Christopher Grandy, "The Political Instability of Reciprocal Trade and the Overthrow of the Hawaiian Kingdom," *Journal of Economic History* 57, no. 1 (1997): 172, 181.

8. La Croix and Grandy, "The Political Instability," 182–183.

9. César J. Ayala and Laird W. Bergad, "Rural Puerto Rico in the Early Twentieth Century Reconsidered: Land and Society, 1899–1915," *Latin American Research Review* 37, no. 2 (2002): 66–67.

10. April J. Mayes, *The Mulatto Republic: Class, Race, and Dominican National Identity* (Gainesville: University Press of Florida, 2015), 48–49.

11. Mark Schmitz, "The Transformation of the Southern Cane Sugar Sector: 1860–1930," *Agricultural History* 53, no. 1 (1979): 284.

12. Herbert Myrick, *Sugar: A New and Profitable Industry in the United States . . .* (New York: Orange Judd, 1897), 1.

13. April Merleaux, *Sugar and Civilization: American Empire and the Cultural Politics of Sweetness* (Chapel Hill: University of North Carolina Press, 2015), 33–38.

14. Merleaux, *Sugar and Civilization,* 36–37.

15. F. Schneider, "Sugar," *Foreign Affairs* 4, no. 2 (1926): 320; Frank R. Rutter, "The Sugar Question in the United States," *Quarterly Journal of Economics* 17, no. 1 (1902): 79.

16. See Sven Beckert, *The Monied Metropolis: New York City and the Consolidation of the American Bourgeoisie, 1850–1896* (Cambridge: Cambridge University Press, 2001).

17. Deborah Jean Warner, *Sweet Stuff: An American History of Sweeteners from Sugar to Sucralose* (Washington, DC: Smithsonian Institution Scholarly Press / Rowman and Littlefield, 2011), 8.

18. Christian Schnakenbourg, "La disparition des 'habitation-sucreries' en Guadeloupe (1848–1906): Recherche sur la désagrégation des structures préindustrielles de la production sucrière antillaise après l'abolition de l'esclavage," *Revue française d'Histoire d'Outre-Mer* 74, no. 276 (1987): 288.

19. Warner, *Sweet Stuff,* 23; Alfred S. Eichner, *The Emergence of Oligopoly: Sugar Refining as a Case Study* (Baltimore, MD: Johns Hopkins Press, 1969), 52–55.

20. Eichner, *The Emergence of Oligopoly,* 59, 65, 69, 72.

21. Eichner, *The Emergence of Oligopoly,* 84–87.

22. Eichner, *The Emergence of Oligopoly,* 16, 150, 152, 184–187.

23. J. Carlyle Sitterson, *Sugar Country: The Cane Sugar Industry in the South 1753–1950* (Lexington: University of Kentucky Press, 1953), 302, 312.

24. Jacob Adler, *Claus Spreckels: The Sugar King in Hawaii* (Honolulu: Mutual, 1966), 101.

25. Adler, *Claus Spreckels,* 29; "To Fight the Sugar Trust: Claus Spreckels as Belligerent as Ever and Ready for the Fray, *New York Times,* April 25, 1889; Eichner, *The Emergence of Oligopoly,* 153–154.

26. Eichner, *The Emergence of Oligopoly,* 166, 172.

27. James Burnley, *Millionaires and Kings of Enterprise: The Marvellous Careers of Some Americans Who by Pluck, Foresight, and Energy Have Made Themselves Masters in the Fields of Industry and Finance* (London: Harmsworth Brothers, 1901), 212.

28. Shephard, "The Sugar Industry," 151.

29. Henry Steel Olcott, *Sorgho and Imphee, the Chinese and African Sugar Canes: A Treatise upon Their Origin, Varieties and Culture, Their Value as a Forage Crop, and the Manufacture of Sugar . . .* (New York: A. O. Moore, 1858), 23.

30. Warner, *Sweet Stuff,* 145.

31. Olcott, *Sorgho and Imphee,* 27; C. Plug, "Wray, Mr Leonard Hume," in *S2A3 Biographical Database of Southern African Science,* accessed April 10, 2022, https://www.s2a3.org.za/bio/Biograph_final.php?serial=3197.

32. Olcott, *Sorgho and Imphee,* 228, 230–231.

33. Olcott, *Sorgho and Imphee,* iv, v, 243–245; Warner, *Sweet Stuff,* 146; Isaac A. Hedges and William Clough, *Sorgo or the Northern Sugar Plant* (Cincinnati, OH: Applegate, 1863), vi.

34. Warner, *Sweet Stuff,* 150, 153.

35. Leonard J. Arrington, "Science, Government, and Enterprise in Economic Development: The Western Beet Sugar Industry," *Agricultural History* 41, no. 1 (1967): 5.

36. Adler, *Claus Spreckels,* 25.

37. Warner, *Sweet Stuff,* 94; Alfred Dezendorf, "Henry T. Oxnard at Home," *San Francisco Sunday Call* 90, no. 40 (July 10, 1904).

38. Jack R. Preston, "Heyward G. Leavitt's Influence on Sugar Beets and Irrigation in Nebraska," *Agricultural History* 76, no. 2 (2002): 382–383.

39. Arrington, "Science, Government, and Enterprise," 15–17; Thomas J. Osborne, "Claus Spreckels and the Oxnard Brothers: Pioneer Developers of California's Beet Sugar Industry, 1890–1900," *Southern California Quarterly Southern California Quarterly* 54, no. 2 (1972): 119–121; Eichner, *The Emergence of Oligopoly,* 232.

40. Gerald D. Nash, "The Sugar Beet Industry and Economic Growth in the West," *Agricultural History* 41, no. 1 (1967): 29. See Preston, "Heyward G. Leavitt's Influence."

41. Anonymous, "American Beet Sugar Company," *Louisiana Planter and Sugar Manufacturer* 2, no. 17 (1899): 268; Eichner, *The Emergence of Oligopoly,* 243–244.

42. Matthew C. Godfrey, *Religion, Politics, and Sugar: The Mormon Church, the Federal Government, and the Utah-Idaho Sugar Company, 1907–1921* (Logan: Utah State University Press, 2007), 62–64.

43. Matthew C. Godfrey, "The Shadow of Mormon Cooperation: The Business Policies of Charles Nibley, Western Sugar Magnate in the Early 1900s," *Pacific Northwest Quarterly* 94, no. 3 (2003): 131; Godfrey, *Religion, Politics, and Sugar,* 65, chap. 3, 107–117; Eichner, *The Emergence of Oligopoly,* 239–240.

44. César J. Ayala, *American Sugar Kingdom: The Plantation Economy of the Spanish Caribbean, 1898–1934* (Chapel Hill: University of North Carolina, 1999), 36, 57.

45. See Edwin Farnsworth Atkins, *Sixty Years in Cuba: Reminiscences . . .* (Cambridge: Riverside Press, 1926), 108; Ayala, *American Sugar Kingdom,* 94.

46. Atkins, *Sixty Years in Cuba,* 186.

47. Mary Speck, "Prosperity, Progress, and Wealth: Cuban Enterprise during the Early Republic, 1902–1927," *Cuban Studies,* no. 36 (2005): 53.

48. Ayala, *American Sugar Kingdom,* 58–62; Antonio Santamaría García, "El progreso del azúcar es el progreso de Cuba: La industria azucarera y la economía cubana a principios del siglo XX desde el análisis de una fuente: *El Azúcar. Revista Industrial Técnico-Práctica,*" *Caribbean Studies* 42, no. 2 (2014): 74.

49. Ayala, *American Sugar Kingdom,* 80.

50. Robert B. Hoernel, "Sugar and Social Change in Oriente, Cuba, 1898–1946," *Journal of Latin American Studies* 8, no. 2 (1976): 229, 239.

51. Ayala, *American Sugar Kingdom,* 80, 94–95.

52. Muriel McAvoy, *Sugar Baron: Manuel Rionda and the Fortunes of Pre-Castro Cuba* (Gainesville: University Press of Florida, 2003), 22–23.

53. R. W. Beachey, *The British West Indies Sugar Industry in the Late 19th Century* (Oxford: B. Blackwell, 1957), 128–132.

54. McAvoy, *Sugar Baron,* 73.

55. E. M. Brunn, "The New York Coffee and Sugar Exchange," *Annals of the American Academy of Political and Social Science* 155 (1931): 112; McAvoy, *Sugar Baron,* 73.

56. McAvoy, *Sugar Baron,* 82–83, 95, 199; Ayala, *American Sugar Kingdom,* 88–89.

57. Rémy Herrera, "Where Is Cuba Heading? When the Names of the Emperors Were Morgan and Rockefeller . . . : Prerevolutionary Cuba's Dependency with Regard to U.S. High Finance," *International Journal of Political Economy* 34, no. 4 (2005): 33–34, 46.

58. Boris C. Swerling, "Domestic Control of an Export Industry: Cuban Sugar," *Journal of Farm Economics* 33, no. 3 (1951): 346; Speck, "Prosperity, Progress, and Wealth," 54.

59. Laura Mason, *Sweets and Candy: A Global History* (London: Reaktion Books, 2018), 71.

60. Michael D'Antonio, *Hershey: Milton S. Hershey's Extraordinary Life of Wealth, Empire, and Utopian Dreams* (New York: Simon and Schuster, 2006), 36–59.

61. D'Antonio, *Hershey,* 106–107, 131, 161–166.

62. Thomas R. Winpenny, "Milton S. Hershey Ventures into Cuban Sugar," *Pennsylvania History: A Journal of Mid-Atlantic Studies* 62, no. 4 (1995): 495.

63. Ayala, *American Sugar Kingdom,* 83–84, 95.

64. Peter James Hudson, *Bankers and Empire: How Wall Street Colonized the Caribbean* (Chicago: University of Chicago Press, 2018), 147, 189, 202.

65. See Hudson, *Bankers and Empire.*

66. Ayala, *American Sugar Kingdom,* 108, 112–115, 226–227, 240; Victor Selden Clark, *Porto Rico and Its Problems* (Washington, DC: Brookings Institution, 1930), 404, 431; Harvey S. Perloff, *Puerto Rico's Economic Future: A Study in Planned Development* (Chicago: University of Chicago Press, 1950), 136.

67. John Emery Stahl, "Economic Development through Land Reform in Puerto Rico" (PhD diss., Iowa State University of Science and Technology, 1966), 11–12; J. O. Solá, "Colonialism, Planters, Sugarcane, and the Agrarian Economy of Caguas, Puerto Rico, between the 1890s and 1930," *Agricultural History* 85, no. 3 (2011): 359–361; Javier Alemán Iglesias, "Agricultores independientes: Una introducción al origen de los colonos en el municipios de juncos y sus contratos de siembra y molienda, 1905–1928," *Revista de los Historiadores de la Región Oriental de Puerto Rico,* no. 3 (2019): 32–36.

68. Matthew O. Edel, "Land Reform in Puerto Rico, 1940–1959," *Caribbean Studies* 2, no. 3 (1962): 28–29.

69. Ellen D. Tillman, *Dollar Diplomacy by Force: Nation-Building and Resistance in the Dominican Republic* (Chapel Hill: University of North Carolina Press, 2016), 70; Ayala, *American Sugar Kingdom,* 106–107; Humberto García Muñiz, *Sugar and Power in the Caribbean: The South Porto Rico Sugar Company in Puerto Rico and the Dominican Republic, 1900–1921* (San Juan, Puerto Rico: La Editorial, 2010), 261, 330.

70. Bruce J. Calder, "Caudillos and Gavilleros versus the United States Marines: Guerrilla Insurgency during the Dominican Intervention, 1916–1924," *Hispanic American Historical Review* 58, no. 4 (1978): 657–658.

71. Louis A. Pérez, "Politics, Peasants, and People of Color: The 1912 'Race War' in Cuba Reconsidered," *Hispanic American Historical Review* 66, no. 3 (1986): 533–537.

72. Sara Kozameh, "Black, Radical, and *Campesino* in Revolutionary Cuba," *Souls* 21, no. 4 (2019): 298.

73. Serge Cherniguin, "The Sugar Workers of Negros, Philippines," *Community Development Journal* 23, no. 3 (1988): 188, 194.

74. Jeffrey L. Gould, "The Enchanted Burro, Bayonets and the Business of Making Sugar: State, Capital, and Labor Relations in the Ingenio San Antonio, 1912–1926," *The Americas* 46, no. 2 (1989): 167–168.

75. Volker Schult, "The San Jose Sugar Hacienda," *Philippine Studies* 39, no. 4 (1991): 461–462.

76. Myrick, *Sugar,* 19.

77. Gail M. Hollander, *Raising Cane in the 'Glades: The Global Sugar Trade and the Transformation of Florida* (Chicago: University of Chicago Press, 2009), 23.

78. See Pat Dodson, "Hamilton Disston's St. Cloud Sugar Plantation, 1887–1901," *Florida Historical Quarterly* 49, no. 4 (1971): 356–369.

79. Hollander, *Raising Cane,* 86.

80. John A. Heitmann, "The Beginnings of Big Sugar in Florida, 1920–1945," *Florida Historical Quarterly* 77, no. 1 (1998): 50–54; Geoff Burrows and Ralph Shlomowitz, "The Lag in the Mechanization of the Sugarcane Harvest: Some Comparative Perspectives," *Agricultural History* 66, no. 3 (1992): 67.

81. See Patterson, "Raising Cane," 416–418.

82. Gail M. Hollander, "Securing Sugar: National Security Discourse and the Establishment of Florida's sugar-producing region," *Economic Geography* 81 (2005): 252–253, 354.

83. "Alfonso Fanjul Sr.," in *Palm Beach County History Online,* accessed January 26, 2022, http://www.pbchistoryonline.org/page/alfonso-fanjul-sr.

10. Rising Protectionism

1. Noël Deerr, *The History of Sugar,* vol. 2 (London: Chapman and Hall, 1950), 490–491.

2. S. L. Jodidi, *The Sugar Beet and Beet Sugar* (Chicago: Beet Sugar Gazette Company, 1911), 3, 5; Rudolf Freund, "Strukturwandlungen der internationalen Zuckerwirtschaft: Aus dem Institut für Weltwirtschaft und Seeverkehr," *Weltwirtschaftliches Archiv* 28 (1928): 7–8; Em Hromada, *Die Entwicklung der Kartelle in der österreichisch-ungarischen Zuckerindustrie* (Zurich: Aktien-Buchdruckerei, 1911), 29.

3. Dirk Schaal, "Industrialization and Agriculture: The Beet Sugar Industry in Saxony-Anhalt, 1799–1902," in *Regions, Industries and Heritage: Perspectives on Economy, Society and Culture in Modern Western Europe,* ed. Juliane Czierpka, Kathrin Oerters, and Nora Thorade (Houndsmills, England: Palgrave Macmillan, 2015), 138.

4. "Future with Origin," KWS, accessed December 21, 2021, https://www.kws.com /corp/en/company/history-of-kws-future-with-origin/.

5. Roger G. Knight, *Sugar, Steam and Steel: The Industrial Project in Colonial Java, 1830– 1850* (Adelaide, Australia: University of Adelaide Press, 2014), 193.

6. Thomas Henry Farrer, *The Sugar Convention* (London: Cassell, 1889), 3.

7. Quoted in William Smart, *The Sugar Bounties: The Case for and against Government Interference* (Edinburgh: Blackwood and Sons, 1887), 47.

8. Farrer, *The Sugar Convention,* 47.

9. Philippe Chalmin, *The Making of a Sugar Giant: Tate and Lyle: 1859–1959* (Chur, Switzerland: Harwood Academic, 1990), 36–37.

10. George Martineau, "The Statistical Aspect of the Sugar Question," *Journal of the Royal Statistical Society* 62, no. 2 (1899): 308.

11. F. W. Taussig, "The Tariff Act of 1894," *Political Science Quarterly* 9, no. 4 (1894): 603.

12. Chalmin, *The Making of a Sugar Giant,* 37.

13. George S. Vascik, "Sugar Barons and Bureaucrats: Unravelling the Relationship between Economic Interest and Government in Modern Germany, 1799–1945," *Business and Economic History* 21 (1992): 338.

14. Overton Greer Ganong, "France, Great Britain, and the International Sugar Bounty Question, 1895–1902" (PhD diss., University of Florida, 1972), 258–261.

15. F. W. Taussig, "The End of Sugar Bounties," *Quarterly Journal of Economics* 18, no. 1 (1903): 130–131; Deerr, *The History of Sugar,* 2:491.

16. Fritz Georg Von Graevenitz, "Exogenous Transnationalism: Java and 'Europe' in an Organised World Sugar Market (1927–37)," *Contemporary European History* 20, no. 3 (2011): 258.

17. Martineau, "The Statistical Aspect," 321, 323.

18. B. Pullen-Burry, *Jamaica as It Is, 1903* (London: T. F. Unwin, 1903), 183.

19. E. Cozens Cooke, "The Sugar Convention and the West Indies," *Economic Journal* 17, no. 67 (1907): 315–322; Edward R. Davson, "Sugar and the War," *Journal of the Royal Society of Arts* 63, no. 3248 (1915): 263–266.

20. Paul Leroy Vogt, *The Sugar Refining Industry in the United States: Its Development and Present Condition* (Philadelphia: Published for the University, 1908), 90.

21. Vascik, "Sugar Barons," 339.

22. J. Van Harreveld, "Voortdurende Verschuiving van Ruwsuiker naar Wit-Suiker," *Archief voor de Suikerindustrie in Ned.-Indië* 33, no. 2 (1925): 1279.

23. Hendrik Coenraad Prinsen Geerligs, *De Rietsuikerindustrie in de Verschillende Landen van Productie: Historisch, Technisch en Statistisch Overzicht over de Productie en den Uitvoer van de Rietsuiker* (Amsterdam: De Bussy, 1931), 35–36.

24. Ulbe Bosma, *The Sugar Plantation in India and Indonesia: Industrial Production, 1770–2010* (Cambridge: Cambridge University Press, 2013), 171.

25. C. Y. Shephard, "The Sugar Industry of the British West Indies and British Guiana with Special Reference to Trinidad," *Economic Geography* 5, no. 2 (1929): 155.

26. Freund, "Strukturwandlungen," 34.

27. See Bessie C. Engle, "Sugar Production of Czechoslovakia," *Economic Geography* 2, no. 2 (1926): 213–229.

28. Quentin Jouan, "Entre expansion belge et nationalisme italien: La Sucrerie et Raffinerie de Pontelongo, image de ses époques (1908–1927)," *Histoire, Économie et Société* 34, no. 4 (2015): 76; Manfred Pohl, *Die Geschichte der Südzucker AG 1926–2001* (Munich: Piper, 2001), 129.

29. Bill Albert, "Sugar and Anglo-Peruvian Trade Negotiations in the 1930s," *Journal of Latin American Studies* 14, no. 1 (1982): 126–127.

30. Von Graevenitz, "Exogenous Transnationalism," 261.

31. C. J. Robertson, "Geographical Aspects of Cane-Sugar Production," *Geography* 17, no. 3 (1932): 179; Bosma, *The Sugar Plantation,* 159–160, 162.

32. Brian H. Pollitt, "The Cuban Sugar Economy and the Great Depression," *Bulletin of Latin American Research* 3, no. 2 (1984): 8, 13.

33. Anonymous, "Irrigation of Atrophy?," *Sugar: Including Facts about Sugar and the Planter and Sugar Manufacturer,* 41, no. 10 (1946): 26–28; Reinaldo Funes Monzote, *From Rainforest to Cane Field in Cuba an Environmental History since 1492* (Chapel Hill: University of North Carolina Press, 2008), 228, 229, 256, 261, 272.

34. The CIBE consisted of the national beet producer associations of Germany, Austria, Belgium, France, Hungary, Italy, Poland, and Czechoslovakia, with the Netherlands and Sweden as informal members. See Francois Houillier and Jules Gautier, *L'organisation internationale de l'agriculture: Les institutions agricoles internationales et l'action internationale en agriculture* (Paris: Libraire technique et economique, 1935), 164.

35. Michael Fakhri, *Sugar and the Making of International Trade Law* (Cambridge: Cambridge University Press, 2017), 92–93.

36. Houillier and Gautier, *L'organisation internationale,* 165.

37. Chalmin, *The Making of a Sugar Giant,* 151.

38. Bosma, *The Sugar Plantation*, 216.

39. Bosma, *The Sugar Plantation*, 217.

40. John. T. Flynn, "The New Capitalism," *Collier's Weekly* (March 18, 1933): 12.

41. Clifford L. James, "International Control of Raw Sugar Supplies," *American Economic Review* 21, no. 3 (1931): 486–489.

42. *De Indische Courant*, December 9, 1930.

43. Bosma, *The Sugar Plantation*, 217–218.

44. Arthur H. Rosenfeld, "Een en Ander omtrent de Suiker-Industrie in Formosa," *Archief voor de Suikerindustrie in Ned.-Indië* 37, no. 2 (1929): 1024–1026, translated from *International Sugar Journal*, 31, no. 369 (September 1929).

45. Cheng-Siang Chen, "The Sugar Industry of China," *Geographical Journal* 137, no. 1 (1971): 30.

46. *De Locomotief*, February 12, 1932.

47. See Von Graevenitz, "Exogenous Transnationalism"; Anno von Gebhardt, *Die Zukunftsentwicklung der Java-Zucker-Industrie unter dem Einfluß der Selbstabschließungstendenzen auf dem Weltmarkt* (Berlin: Ebering, 1937), 135; James, "International Control," 490–491.

48. Gebhardt, *Die Zukunftsentwicklung*, 56; Bosma, *The Sugar Plantation*, 220.

49. Gail M. Hollander, *Raising Cane in the 'Glades: The Global Sugar Trade and the Transformation of Florida* (Chicago: University of Chicago Press, 2009), 116.

50. Pollitt, "The Cuban Sugar Economy," 15–16.

51. Theodore Friend, "The Philippine Sugar Industry and the Politics of Independence, 1929–1935," *Journal of Asian Studies* 22, no. 2 (1963): 190–191.

52. Guy Pierre, "The Frustrated Development of the Haitian Sugar Industry between 1915 / 18 and 1938 / 39: International Financial and Commercial Rivalries," in *The World Sugar Economy in War and Depression 1914–40*, ed. Bill Albert and Adrian Graves (London: Routledge, 1988), 127–128.

53. *Soerabaiasch Handelsblad*, July 9, 1937, extra edition.

54. Muriel McAvoy, *Sugar Baron: Manuel Rionda and the Fortunes of Pre-Castro Cuba* (Gainesville: University Press of Florida, 2003), 203.

55. Von Graevenitz, "Exogenous Transnationalism," 278–279.

56. Fakhri, *Sugar*, 120; Kurt Bloch, "Impending Shortages Catch Sugar Consumers Napping," *Far Eastern Survey Far Eastern Survey* 8, no. 12 (1939): 141.

57. Eastin Nelson, "The Growth of the Refined Sugar Industry in Mexico," *Southwestern Social Science Quarterly* 26, no. 4 (1946): 275; Roger Owen, "The Study of Middle Eastern Industrial History: Notes on the Interrelationship between Factories and Small-Scale Manufacturing with Special References to Lebanese Silk and Egyptian Sugar, 1900–1930," *International Journal of Middle East Studies* 16, no. 4 (1984): 480–481.

58. Plinio Mario Nastari, "The Role of Sugar Cane in Brazil's History and Economy" (PhD diss., Iowa State University, 1983), 77–79; Barbara Nunberg, "Structural Change and

State Policy: The Politics of Sugar in Brazil since 1964," *Latin American Research Review.* 21, no. 2 (1986): 55–56.

59. Peter Post, "Bringing China to Java: The Oei Tiong Ham Concern and Chen Kung-po during the Nanjing Decade," *Journal of Chinese Overseas* 15, no. 1 (2019): 45.

60. H. Y. Lin Alfred, "Building and Funding a Warlord Regime: The Experience of Chen Jitang in Guangdong, 1929–1936," *Modern China* 28, no. 2 (2002): 200–201; Post, "Bringing China," 53–55; G. R. Knight, *Commodities and Colonialism: The Story of Big Sugar in Indonesia, 1880–1942* (Leiden: Brill, 2013), 150, 220.

61. Erika Rappaport, *A Thirst for Empire: How Tea Shaped the Modern World* (Princeton, NJ: Princeton University Press, 2017), 234–252.

62. H. D. Watts, "The Location of the Beet-Sugar Industry in England and Wales, 1912–36," *Transactions of the Institute of British Geographers,* no. 53 (1971): 98–99.

63. Albert, "Sugar and Anglo-Peruvian Trade," 127; C. J. Robertson, "Cane-Sugar Production in the British Empire," *Economic Geography* 6, no. 2 (1930): 135; Michael Moynagh, *Brown or White?: A History of the Fiji Sugar Industry, 1873–1973* (Canberra: Australian National University, 1981), 119.

64. Chalmin, *The Making of a Sugar Giant,* 75; Hermann Kellenbenz, *Die Zucker-wirtschaft im Kölner Raum von der Napoleonischen Zeit bis zur Reichsgründung* (Cologne: Industrie- und Handelskammer, 1966), 92.

65. Darra Goldstein, *The Oxford Companion to Sugar and Sweets* (Oxford: Oxford University Press, 2015), 307.

66. Carl Henry Fe, "Better Must Come: Sugar and Jamaica in the 20th Century," *Social and Economic Studies* 33, no. 4 (1984): 5.

67. David Hollett, *Passage from India to El Dorado: Guyana and the Great Migration* (Madison, WI: Fairleigh Dickinson University Press, 1999), 56–63.

11. The Proletariat

1. Sam R. Sweitz, "The Production and Negotiation of Working-Class Space and Place at Central Aguirre, Puerto Rico," *Journal of the Society for Industrial Archeology* 36, no. 1 (2010): 30.

2. Maureen Tayal, "Indian Indentured Labour in Natal, 1890–1911," *Indian Economic & Social History Review* 14, no. 4 (1977): 521–522, 526, 544; Duncan Du Bois, "Collusion and Conspiracy in Colonial Natal: A Case Study of Reynolds Bros and Indentured Abuses 1884–1908," *Historia: Amptelike Orgaan* 60, no. 1 (2015): 98–102.

3. Bill Albert, "The Labour Force on Peru's Sugar Plantations 1820–1930," in *Crisis and Change in the International Sugar Economy 1860–1914,* ed. Bill Albert and Adrian Graves (Norwich, England: ISC Press, 1984), 203, 206.

4. Ulbe Bosma and Jonathan Curry-Machado, "Two Islands, One Commodity: Cuba, Java, and the Global Sugar Trade (1790–1930)," *New West Indian Guide* 86, nos. 3–4 (2012):

253–254. For India see Ulbe Bosma, *The Sugar Plantation in India and Indonesia: Industrial Production, 1770–2010* (Cambridge: Cambridge University Press, 2013), 270.

5. Assuming an average yield of five tons of raw beet sugar per hectare in 1920 (extrapolated from four tons per hectare in 1890) and the need for at least one worker per hectare. See H. Paasche, *Zuckerindustrie und Zuckerhandel der Welt* (Jena, Germany: G. Fischer, 1891), 43.

6. Ulbe Bosma, *The Making of a Periphery: How Island Southeast Asia Became a Mass Exporter of Labor* (New York: Columbia University Press, 2019), 81–88.

7. Eleanor C. Nordyke, Y. Scott Matsumoto, *The Japanese in Hawaii: Historical and Demographic Perspective* (Honolulu: Population Institute, East-West Center, 1977), 164.

8. J. Vincenza Scarpaci, "Labor for Louisiana's Sugar Cane Fields: An Experiment in Immigrant Recruitment," *Italian Americana* 7, no. 1 (1981): 20, 33, 34; J. P. Reidy, "Mules and Machines and Men: Field Labor on Louisiana Sugar Plantations, 1887–1915," *Agricultural History* 72, no. 2 (1998): 188.

9. M. Bejarano, "La inmigración a Cuba y la política migratoria de los EE.UU. (1902–1933)," *Estudios Interdisciplinarios de América Latina y rl Caribe* 42, no. 2 (1993): 114.

10. Patrick Bryan, "The Question of Labour in the Sugar Industry of the Dominican Republic in the Late Nineteenth and Early Twentieth Century," *Social and Economic Studies* 29, nos. 2–3 (1980): 278–283; April J. Mayes, *The Mulatto Republic: Class, Race, and Dominican National Identity* (Gainesville: University Press of Florida, 2015), 83; Samuel Martínez, "From Hidden Hand to Heavy Hand: Sugar, the State, and Migrant Labor in Haiti and the Dominican Republic," *Latin American Research Review* 34, no. 1 (1999): 68.

11. Edward Paulino, *Dividing Hispaniola: The Dominican Republic's Border Campaign against Haiti, 1930–1961* (Pittsburgh: Pittsburgh University Press, 2016), 54; Richard Lee Turits, "A World Destroyed, a Nation Imposed: The 1937 Haitian Massacre in the Dominican Republic," *Hispanic American Historical Review* 83, no. 3 (2002): 590–591.

12. Jorge L. Giovannetti, *Black British Migrants in Cuba: Race, Labor, and Empire in the Twentieth-Century Caribbean, 1898–1948* (Cambridge: Cambridge University Press, 2000), Kindle, 44.

13. Louis A. Pérez, "Politics, Peasants, and People of Color: The 1912 'Race War' in Cuba Reconsidered," *Hispanic American Historical Review* 66, no. 3 (1986): 524–525.

14. César J. Ayala, *American Sugar Kingdom: The Plantation Economy of the Spanish Caribbean, 1898–1934* (Chapel Hill: University of North Carolina, 1999), 172; Barry Carr, "Identity, Class, and Nation: Black Immigrant Workers, Cuban Communism, and the Sugar Insurgency 1925–1934," *Hispanic American Historical Review* 78, no. 1 (1998): 83.

15. Klaus J. Bade and Jochen Oltmer, "Polish Agricultural Workers in Prussia-Germany from the Late 19th Century to World War II," in *The Encyclopedia of Migration and Minorities in Europe: From the 17th Century to the Present,* ed. Klaus J. Bade et al. (Cambridge: Cambridge University Press, 2011), 595–597.

16. Dirk Musschoot, *Van Franschmans en Walenmannen: Vlaamse Seizoenarbeiders in den Vreemde in de 19de en 20ste Eeuw* (Tielt, Belgian: Lannoo, 2008), 32–33, 38; E. Sommier,

"Les cahiers de l'industrie française: V: Le sucre," *Revue des Deux Mondes (1829–1971)* 2, no. 2 (1931): 354.

17. Musschoot, *Van Franschmans,* 51, 83, 111, 246; Christiaan Gevers, *De Suikergastarbeiders: Brabantse Werknemers bij de Friesch-Groningsche Suikerfabriek* (Bedum, the Netherlands: Profiel, 2019), 20.

18. Mark Wyman, *Round-Trip to America: The Immigrants Return to Europe, 1880–1930* (Ithaca, NY: Cornell University Press, 1993), 37–38, 129.

19. Gary Okihiro, *Cane Fires: The Anti-Japanese Movement in Hawaii* (Philadelphia: Temple University Press, 1991), 27.

20. Allan D. Meyers, "Material Expressions of Social Inequality on a Porfirian Sugar Hacienda in Yucatán, Mexico," *Historical Archaeology* 39, no. 4 (2005): 118. See John Kenneth Turner, *Barbarous Mexico: An Indictment of a Cruel and Corrupt System* (London: Cassell, 1911).

21. See, for example, Matthew Casey, "Haitians' Labor and Leisure on Cuban Sugar Plantations: The Limits of Company Control," *New West Indian Guide* 85, nos. 1–2 (2011): 14.

22. G. R. Knight, *Commodities and Colonialism: The Story of Big Sugar in Indonesia, 1880–1942* (Leiden: Brill, 2013), 199; Bosma, *The Sugar Plantation,* 190.

23. Bosma, *The Sugar Plantation,* 177.

24. Jacques Adélaïde-Merlande, *Les origines du mouvement ouvrier en Martinique 1870–1900* (Paris: Ed. Karthala, 2000), 113, 127, 139, 170, 173.

25. Rosemarijn Hoefte, "Control and Resistance: Indentured Labor in Suriname," *New West Indian Guide* 61, nos. 1–2 (1987): 8, 11–12.

26. R. W. Beachey, *The British West Indies Sugar Industry in the Late 19th Century* (Oxford: B. Blackwell, 1957), 153.

27. West India Royal Commission, *Report of the West India Royal Commission* (London: Printed for Her Majesty's Stationery Office by Eyre and Spottiswoode, 1897), 8, 17, 64, 66.

28. See Walter Rodney, "The Ruimveldt Riots: Demerara, British Guiana, 1905," in *Caribbean Freedom: Economy and Society from Emancipation to the Present: A Student Reader,* ed. Hilary McD. Beckles and Verene Shepherd (Kingston, Jamaica: Ian Randle, 1996), 352–358.

29. US Congress and House Committee on Ways and Means, *Reciprocity with Cuba Hearings before the Committee on Ways and Means, Fifty-Seventh Congress, First Session January 15, 16, 21, 22, 23, 24, 25, 28, 29, 1902* (Washington, DC: Government Printing Office, 1902), 175, 194.

30. Elizabeth S. Johnson, "Welfare of Families of Sugar-Beet Laborers," *Monthly Labor Review* 46, no. 2 (1938): 325; Dennis Nodín Valdés, "Mexican Revolutionary Nationalism and Repatriation during the Great Depression," *Mexican Studies* 4, no. 1 (1988): 3.

31. For Cuba, see Giovannetti, *Black British Migrants,* 56.

32. Max Weber, *Die Verhältnisse der Landarbeiter im ostelbischen Deutschland: Preussische Provinzen Ost- u. Westpreussen, Pommern, Posen, Schlesien, Brandenburg, Grossherzogtümer Mecklenburg, Kreis Herzogtum Lauenburg* (Leipzig: Duncker and Humblot, 1892), 491.

33. Manuel Gamio, *Mexican Immigration to the United State: A Study of Human Migration and Adjustment* (New York: Arno Press, 1969), 31.

34. Kathleen Mapes, *Sweet Tyranny: Migrant Labor, Industrial Agriculture, and Imperial Politics* (Urbana: University of Illinois Press, 2009), 128.

35. Dennis Nodín Valdés, "Settlers, Sojourners, and Proletarians: Social Formation in the Great Plains Sugar Beet Industry, 1890–1940," *Great Plains Quarterly* 10, no. 2 (1990): 118.

36. Jim Norris, *North for the Harvest: Mexican Workers, Growers, and the Sugar Beet Industry* (St. Paul: Minnesota Historical Society Press, 2009), 43n.7, 44.

37. Elizabeth S. Johnson, "Wages, Employment Conditions, and Welfare of Sugar Beet Laborers," *Monthly Labor Review* 46, no. 2 (1938): 325; Valdés, "Mexican Revolutionary," 4, 21–22.

38. Johnson, "Wages, Employment Conditions," 322.

39. Louis Fiset, "Thinning, Topping, and Loading: Japanese Americans and Beet Sugar in World War II," *Pacific Northwest Quarterly* 90, no. 3 (1999): 123.

40. Victor S. Clark, *Labor Conditions in Hawaii: Letter from the Secretary of Labor Transmitting the Fifth Annual Report of the Commissioner of Labor Statistics on Labor Conditions in the Territory of Hawaii for the Year 1915* (Washington, DC: Government Printing Office, 1916), 63.

41. Melinda Tria Kerkvliet, *Unbending Cane: Pablo Manlapit, a Filipino Labor Leader in Hawaii* (Honolulu: Office of Multicultural Student Services, University of Hawaii at Mānoa, 2002), 23–28; Okihiro, *Cane Fires,* 71–76, 84–98.

42. US Congress, House Committee on Immigration, and Naturalization, *Labor Problems in Hawaii. Hearings before the Committee on Immigration and Naturalization, House of Representatives, 67th Congress, 1st Session on H.J. Res. 158 . . . Serial 7—Part 1–2, June 21 to June 30 and July 7, July 22, 27 and 29, Aug. 1, 2, 3, 4, 10, and 12, 1921* (Washington, DC: Government Printing Office, 1921), 278–279.

43. US Congress, House Committee on Immigration, and Naturalization, *Labor Problems in Hawaii,* 361.

44. Kerkvliet, *Unbending Cane,* 25; Okihiro, *Cane Fires,* 52.

45. F. P. Barajas, "Resistance, Radicalism, and Repression on the Oxnard Plain: The Social Context of the Betabelero Strike of 1933," *Western Historical Quarterly* 35 (2004): 33; Tomás Almaguer, "Racial Domination and Class Conflict in Capitalist Agriculture: The Oxnard Sugar Beet Workers' Strike of 1903," *Labor History* 25, no. 3 (1984): 339.

46. Kerkvliet, *Unbending Cane,* 59–60.

47. See, for example, Humberto García Muñiz, *Sugar and Power in the Caribbean: The South Porto Rico Sugar Company in Puerto Rico and the Dominican Republic, 1900–1921* (San

Juan, Puerto Rico: La Editorial, 2010), 409; Albert, "The Labour Force on Peru's Sugar Plantations 1820–1930," 213–214.

48. Elsbeth Locher-Scholten, *Ethiek in Fragmenten: Vijf Studies over Koloniaal Denken en Doen van Nederlanders in de Indonesische archipel, 1877–1942* (Utrecht: Hes Publishers, 1981), 103.

49. Barry Carr, "Mill Occupations and Soviets: The Mobilisation of Sugar Workers in Cuba 1917–1933," *Journal of Latin American Studies* 28, no. 1 (1996): 134.

50. Oscar Zanetti, "The Workers' Movement and Labor Regulation in the Cuban Sugar Industry," *Cuban Studies,* no. 25 (1995): 185.

51. John Ingleson, *Workers, Unions and Politics: Indonesia in the 1920s and 1930s* (Leiden: Brill, 2014), 28.

52. For social conditions, see I. T. Runes, *General Standards of Living and Wages of Workers in the Philippine Sugar Industry* (Manila: Philippine Council Institute of Pacific Relations, 1939).

53. Carr, "Mill Occupations," 132–133.

54. Ken Post, *Arise Ye Starvelings: The Jamaican Labour Rebellion of 1938 and Its Aftermath* (The Hague: Nijhoff, 1978), 3; Alejandro de la Fuente, "Two Dangers, One Solution: Immigration, Race, and Labor in Cuba, 1900–1930," *International Labor and Working-Class History* 51 (1997): 43–45; M. C. McLeod, "Undesirable Aliens: Race, Ethnicity, and Nationalism in the Comparison of Haitian and British West Indian Immigrant Workers in Cuba, 1912–1939," *Journal of Social History* 31, no. 3 (1998): 604.

55. Hudson, *Bankers and Empire,* 217–218, 269.

56. Ayala, *American Sugar Kingdom,* 118.

57. Peter James Hudson, *Bankers and Empire: How Wall Street Colonized the Caribbean* (Chicago: University of Chicago Press, 2018), 264–265; Raymond E. Crist, "Sugar Cane and Coffee in Puerto Rico, II: The Pauperization of the Jíbaro; Land Monopoly and Monoculture," *American Journal of Economics and Sociology* 7, no. 3 (1948): 330; J. A. Giusti-Cordero, "Labour, Ecology and History in a Puerto Rican Plantation Region: 'Classic' Rural Proletarians Revisited," *International Review of Social History* 41 (1996): 53–82.

58. See Victor Selden Clark, *Porto Rico and Its Problems* (Washington, DC: Brookings Institution, 1930); Matthew O. Edel, "Land Reform in Puerto Rico, 1940–1959," *Caribbean Studies* 2, no. 3 (1962): 26; Hudson, *Bankers and Empire,* 263–267.

59. Quoted in Robert Whitney, *State and Revolution in Cuba: Mass Mobilization and Political Change, 1920–1940* (Chapel Hill: University of North Carolina Press, 2001), 119.

60. Robert Whitney, "The Architect of the Cuban State: Fulgencio Batista and Populism in Cuba, 1937–1940," *Journal of Latin American Studies* 32, no. 2 (2000): 442.

61. Whitney, *State and Revolution,* 155; Giovannetti, *Black British Migrants,* 240.

62. See, for example, Édouard de Lepine, *La crise de février 1935 à la Martinique: La marche de la faim sur Fort-de-France* (Paris: L'Harmattan, 1980); O. Nigel Bolland, *On the*

March: Labour Rebellions in the British Caribbean, 1934–39 (Kingston, Jamaica: Ian Randle, 1995), 280.

63. Bolland, *On the March,* 279–285, 340–356.

64. Jeremy Seekings, "British Colonial Policy, Local Politics, and the Origins of the Mauritian Welfare State, 1936–50," *Journal of African History* 52, no. 2 (2011): 162.

65. Post, *Arise ye Starvelings,* 350–351; Bolland, *On the March,* 299, 301, 312–313, 325.

66. Carl Henry Fe, "Better Must Come: Sugar and Jamaica in the 20th Century," *Social and Economic Studies* 33, no. 4 (1984): 21–22, 24.

67. Edward D. Beechert, *Working in Hawaii: A Labor History* (Honolulu: University of Hawaii Press, 1985), 272–273.

68. US Department of Labor, *Labor Unionism in American Agriculture* (Washington, DC: Government Printing Office, 1945), 83, 87.

69. Barajas, "Resistance, Radicalism," 37, 41–42, 48; Department of Labor, *Labor Unionism,* 96, 129; Carlos Bulosan, *America Is in the Heart: A Personal History* (Manila: National Bookstore, 1973), 195, 196.

70. Department of Labor, *Labor Unionism,* 59, 238–253, 387.

71. The Eagen report is included in *National Labor Relations Act: Hearings before the United States House Special Committee to Investigate National Labor Relations Board, Seventy-Sixth Congress, Third Session, on May 2, 3, 1940,* vol. 22 (Washington, DC: Government Printing Office, 1945), 4525–4526.

72. J. Norris, "Growing up Growing Sugar: Local Teenage Labor in the Sugar Beet Fields, 1958–1974," *Agricultural History* 79, no. 3 (2005): 301.

73. See Ramiro Guerra, *Azúcar y población en las Antillas* (Havana: Cultural, 1927), 86.

74. A. M. P. A. Scheltema, *The Food Consumption of the Native Inhabitants of Java and Madura: Done into English by A.H. Hamilton* (Batavia: Ruygrok / National Council for the Netherlands and the Netherlands Indies of the Institute of Pacific Relations, 1936), 62. See also Runes, *General Standards of Living;* Yoshihiro Chiba, "The 1919 and 1935 Rice Crises in the Philippines: The Rice Market and Starvation in American Colonial Times," *Philippine Studies* 58, no. 4 (2010): 540.

75. Samuel Farber, *Revolution and Reaction in Cuba, 1933–1960: A Political Sociology from Machado to Castro* (Middletown, CT: Wesleyan University Press, 1976), 85.

76. Whitney, "The Architect," 454, 459.

77. See Edel, "Land Reform."

78. Ulbe Bosma, "The Integration of Food Markets and Increasing Government Intervention in Indonesia: 1815–1980s," in *An Economic History of Famine Resilience,* ed. Jessica Dijkman and Bas Van Leeuwen (London: Routledge, 2019), 152–154.

79. J. van Gelderen, *The Recent Development of Economic Foreign Policy in the Netherlands East Indies* (London: Longmans, Green, 1939), 84.

80. William Arthur Lewis, *Labour in the West Indies the Birth of a Workers' Movement* (London: New Beacon Books, 1977), 16.

81. William Arthur Lewis, "Economic Development with Unlimited Supplies of Labour," *Manchester School of Economic and Social Studies* 22, no. 2 (1954): 183.

82. Norman Girvan, "W. A. Lewis, the Plantation School and Dependency: An Interpretation," *Social and Economic Studies* 54, no. 3 (2005): 215, 218; W. Arthur Lewis, *Growth and Fluctuations 1870–1913* (London: George Allen, 1978), 161, 200.

83. W. Arthur Lewis, *The Theory of Economic Growth* (London: Allen and Unwin, 1955), 410.

84. Lewis cited in Girvan, "W. A. Lewis," 205–206.

85. Seekings, "British Colonial Policy," 165.

86. Guerra, *Azúcar y población*, 117, 23.

87. Gilberto Freyre, *The Mansions and the Shanties (Sobrados e Mucambos): The Making of Modern Brazil* (New York: A. A. Knopf, 1968), 135–136, 407.

88. Josué de Castro, *Geography of Hunger: With a Foreword by Lord Boyd Orr* (London: Victor Gollancz, 1952), 113.

89. Castro, *Geography of Hunger*, 117.

90. Castro, *Geography of Hunger*, 198; John Boyd Orr, *Food Health and Income: Report on a Survey of Adequacy of Diet in Relation to Income* (London: Macmillan, 1937), 11.

91. Celso Furtado, *The Economic Growth of Brazil: A Survey from Colonial to Modern Times* (Berkeley: University of California Press, 1968), 109.

92. Manuel Correia de Andrade, *The Land and People of Northeast Brazil* (Albuquerque: University of New Mexico Press, 1980), 193–206.

12. Failed Decolonization

1. Walter Edward Guinness Moyne, *Royal Commission on West India Report* (London: Colonial Office, Great Britain, 1945), 422–423. For the French Antilles, see Charles Robequain, "Le sucre dans l'Union française," *Annales de Géographie* 57, no. 308 (1948): 340.

2. John Wesley Coulter, "The Oahu Sugar Cane Plantation, Waipahu," *Economic Geography* 9, no. 1 (1933): 64, 66; James A. Geschwender and Rhonda F. Levine, "Rationalization of Sugar Production in Hawaii, 1946–1960: A Dimension of the Class Struggle," *Social Problems Social Problems* 30, no. 3 (1983): 358.

3. Charles Edquist, *Capitalism, Socialism and Technology: A Comparative Study of Cuba and Jamaica* (London: Zed, 1989), 38–42, 45.

4. Robequain, "Le sucre dans l'Union française," 333; Joseph T. Butler Jr., "Prisoner of War Labor in the Sugar Cane Fields of Lafourche Parish, Louisiana: 1943–1944," *Louisiana History*, 14, no. 3 (1973): 284.

5. James E. Rowan, "Mechanization of the Sugar Beet Industry of Scottsbluff County, Nebraska," *Economic Geography* 24, no. 3 (1948): 176, 179; Jim Norris, "Bargaining for Beets: Migrants and Growers in the Red River Valley," *Minnesota History* 58, no. 4 (2002): 200, 202, 207.

6. J. A. Mollett, "Capital and Labor in the Hawaiian Sugar Industry since 1870: A Study of Economic Development," *Journal of Farm Economics* 44, no. 2 (1962): 386.

7. Edquist, *Capitalism, Socialism and Technology*, 32–33; Oscar Zanetti, "The Workers' Movement and Labor Regulation in the Cuban Sugar Industry," *Cuban Studies*, no. 25 (1995): 198, 202–203; John Paul Rathbone, *The Sugar King of Havana: The Rise and Fall of Julio Lobo, Cuba's Last Tycoon* (New York: Penguin, 2010), 185–186.

8. Alec Wilkinson, *Big Sugar: Seasons in the Cane Fields of Florida* (New York: Vintage, 1990), 72; George C. Abbott, *Sugar* (London: Routledge, 1990), 89.

9. David S. Simonett, "Sugar Production in North Queensland," *Economic Geography* 30, no. 3 (1954): 231.

10. Deborah Jean Warner, *Sweet Stuff: An American History of Sweeteners from Sugar to Sucralose* (Washington, DC: Smithsonian Institution Scholarly Press / Rowman and Littlefield, 2011), 78; Wilkinson, *Big Sugar*, 14–15; John A. Heitmann, "The Beginnings of Big Sugar in Florida, 1920–1945," *Florida Historical Quarterly* 77, no. 1 (1998): 61.

11. Albert Viton, *The International Sugar Agreements: Promise and Reality* (West Lafayette, IN: Purdue University Press, 2004), 31, 34.

12. Viton, *The International Sugar Agreements*, 84–96.

13. G. Johnson Harry, "Sugar Protectionism and the Export Earnings of Less Developed Countries: Variations on a Theme by R. H. Snape," *Economica* 33, no. 129 (1966): 34, 37. See also R. H. Snape, "Some Effects of Protection in the World Sugar Industry," *Economica* 30, no. 117 (1963): 63–73.

14. Michael Fakhri, *Sugar and the Making of International Trade Law* (Cambridge: Cambridge University Press, 2017), 199; Abbott, *Sugar*, 204–206.

15. Pope John XXIII, *Mater et magistra*, encyclical letter, *The Holy See*, May 15, 1961, https://www.vatican.va/content/john-xxiii/en/encyclicals/documents/hf_j-xxiii_enc_15051961_mater.html (sec. 143).

16. See Matthew O. Edel, "Land Reform in Puerto Rico, 1940–1959," *Caribbean Studies* 2, no. 3 (1962): 26–60.

17. Abbott, *Sugar*, 87.

18. Martijn Bakker, *Ondernemerschap en Vernieuwing: De Nederlandse Bietsuikerindustrie, 1858–1919* (Amsterdam: NEHA, 1989), 89.

19. See Bert Smit and Krijn Poppe, "The Position, Role and Future of Cooperative Sugar Refineries in the EU," in *Proceedings of the 74th International Institute of Sugar Beet Research Congress, Dresden, July 1–3, 2014* (Brussels: International Institute of Sugar Beet Research, 2014).

20. Manfred Pohl, *Die Geschichte der Südzucker AG 1926–2001* (Munich: Piper, 2001), 293–294.

21. See William R. Sharman, "Louisiana Sugar Co-Ops Help Raise Prosperity," *News for Farmer Cooperatives,* March 19, 1965.

22. "The Sugarbeet Growers Association Story," Red River Valley Sugarbeet Growers Association, accessed February 1, 2022, https://rrvsga.com/our-story/.

23. Ulbe Bosma, *The Sugar Plantation in India and Indonesia: Industrial Production, 1770–2010* (Cambridge: Cambridge University Press, 2013), 149–150.

24. Bosma, *The Sugar Plantation,* 207–208, 234, 241.

25. See, for example, Peter Singelmann, "The Sugar Industry in Post-Revolutionary Mexico: State Intervention and Private Capital," *Latin American Research Review* 28, no. 1 (1993): 61–88; Jack. F. Williams, "Sugar: The Sweetener in Taiwan's Development," in *China's Island Frontier Studies in the Historical Geography of Taiwan,* ed. Ronald G. Knapp (Honolulu: University of Hawaii Press, 1980), 228–229, 238.

26. James S. Kus, "The Sugar Cane Industry of the Chicama Valley, Peru," *Revista Geográfica,* no. 109 (1989): 61–66.

27. Bosma, *The Sugar Plantation,* 229.

28. Manley quoted in Carl H. Feuer, *Jamaica and the Sugar Worker Cooperatives the Politics of Reform* (Boulder, CO: Westview Press, 1984), 177.

29. Bosma, *The Sugar Plantation,* 239–248, 255, 256.

30. Michael R. Hall, *Sugar and Power in the Dominican Republic: Eisenhower, Kennedy, and the Trujillos* (Westport, CT: Greenwood Press, 2000), 5, 19, 21–22.

31. Mina Roces, "Kinship Politics in Post-War Philippines: The Lopez Family, 1945–1989," *Modern Asian Studies* 34, no. 1 (2000): 203.

32. Eliyahu Ashtor, "Levantine Sugar Industry in the Later Middle Ages: An Example of Technological Decline," in *Technology, Industry and Trade: The Levant versus Europe, 1250–1500,* ed. Eliyahu Ashtor and B. Z. Ķedar (Hampshire, England: Ashgate, 1992), 240, 242.

33. Vincent A. Mahler, "Britain, the European Community, and the Developing Commonwealth: Dependence, Interdependence, and the Political Economy of Sugar," *International Organization* 353 (1981): 477.

34. Clem Seecharan, *Sweetening 'Bitter Sugar': Jock Campbell, the Booker Reformer in British Guiana, 1934–1966* (Kingston, Jamaica: Ian Randle, 2005), 265.

35. Mahler, "Britain, the European Community," 480.

36. J. E. Meade, "Mauritius: A Case Study in Malthusian Economics," *Economic Journal* 71, no. 283 (1961): 525.

37. Richard L. Bernal, "The Great Depression, Colonial Policy and Industrialization in Jamaica," *Social and Economic Studies* 37, nos. 1–2 (1988): 44.

38. Philippe Chalmin, *The Making of a Sugar Giant: Tate and Lyle: 1859–1959* (Chur, Switzerland: Harwood Academic, 1990), 354–355; George L. Backford, "The Economics of

Agricultural Resource Use and Development in Plantation Economies," *Social and Economic Studies* 18, no. 4 (1969): 329, 331.

39. George L. Beckford and Cherita Girvan, "The Dynamics of Growth and the Nature of Metropolitan Plantation Enterprise," *Social and Economic Studies* 19, no. 4 (1970): 458–459. The World Bank quoted in Chalmin, *The Making of a Sugar Giant*, 375.

40. Al Imfeld, *Zucker* (Zurich: Unionsverlag, 1986), 72.

41. Michael Moynagh, *Brown or White?: A History of the Fiji Sugar Industry, 1873–1973* (Canberra: Australian National University, 1981), 124; David Merrett, "Sugar and Copper: Postcolonial Experiences of Australian Multinationals," *Business History Review* 81, no. 2 (2007): 218–223.

42. A. M. O'Connor, "Sugar in Tropical Africa," *Geography* 60, no. 1 (1975): 25.

43. See Jerry Gosnell, *Gallic Thunderbolt: The Story of René Leclézio and Lonrho Sugar Corporation* (Durban: Pinetown, 2004).

44. Samuel E. Chambua, "Choice of Technique and Underdevelopment in Tanzania: The Case of Sugar Development Corporation," *Canadian Journal of African Studies* 24, no. 1 (1990): 27–28, 30–31; Barbara Dinham and Colin Hines, *Agribusiness in Africa* (Trenton, NJ: Africa World Press, 1984), 172–173.

45. Abbott, *Sugar*, 104; Imfeld, *Zucker*, 60–63.

46. Tijo Salverda, "Sugar, Sea and Power: How Franco-Mauritians Balance Continuity and Creeping Decline of Their Elite Position" (PhD diss., Vrije Universiteit Amsterdam, 2010), 126.

47. "The Recovery of Taiwan Sugar Industry," *Taiwan Today*, March 1, 1952, https://taiwantoday.tw/news.php?unit=29,45&post=36816.

48. Tom Barry, Beth Wood, and Deb Preusch, *The Other Side of Paradise: Foreign Control in the Caribbean* (New York: Grove Press, 1984), 55–74 (Vicini quoted on p. 74).

49. Roces, "Kinship Politics," 190, 194, 195.

50. Salverda, "Sugar, Sea and Power," 119.

51. Grant H. Cornwell and Eve W. Stoddard, "Reading Sugar Mill Ruins: 'The Island Nobody Spoiled' and Other Fantasies of Colonial Desire," *South Atlantic Review* 66, no. 2 (2001): 137.

52. Jorge F. Perez-Lopez, "Cuban-Soviet Sugar Trade: Price and Subsidy Issues," *Bulletin of Latin American Research* 7, no. 1 (1988): 143; Gail M. Hollander, *Raising Cane in the 'Glades: The Global Sugar Trade and the Transformation of Florida* (Chicago: University of Chicago Press, 2009), 166.

53. Chalmin, *The Making of a Sugar Giant*, 474; Ben Richardson, *Sugar* (Cambridge: Polity, 2015), 76–77.

54. Thomas J. DiLorenzo, Vincent M. Sementilli, and Lawrence Southwick, "The Lomé Sugar Protocol: Increased Dependency for Fiji and Other ACP States," *Review of Social Economy* 41, no. 1 (1983): 37–38.

55. Pohl, *Die Geschichte,* 295–300, 313.

56. Pohl, *Die Geschichte,* 301.

57. D. Gale Johnson, *The Sugar Program: Large Costs and Small Benefits* (Washington, DC: American Enterprise for Public Policy, 1974), 9.

58. Harold A. Wolf, "Sugar: Excise Taxes, Tariffs, Quotas, and Program Payments," *Southern Economic Journal* 25, no. 4 (1959): 421.

59. David J. Gerber, "The United States Sugar Quota Program: A Study in the Direct Congressional Control of Imports," *Journal of Law & Economics* 19, no. 1 (1976): 113, 116.

60. See Thomas J. Heston, "Cuba, the United States, and the Sugar Act of 1948: The Failure of Economic Coercion," *Diplomatic History* 6, no. 1 (1982): 1–21.

61. Alan Dye and Richard Sicotte, "U.S.-Cuban Trade Cooperation and Its Unraveling," *Business and Economic History* 28, no. 2 (1999): 28. See also Willard W. Radell, "Cuban-Soviet Sugar Trade of Large Cuban Sugar Factories in the 1984 'Zafra,'" *Cuban Studies* 17 (1987): 141–155.

62. Thomas A. Becnel, "Fulbright of Arkansas v. Ellender of Louisiana: The Politics of Sugar and Rice, 1937–1974," *Arkansas Historical Quarterly* 43, no. 4 (1984): 301.

63. Thomas H. Bates, "The Long-Run Efficiency of United States Sugar Policy," *American Journal of Agricultural Economics* 50, no. 3 (1968): 525; Daniel M. Berman and Robert Heineman, "Lobbying by Foreign Governments on the Sugar Act Amendments of 1962," *Law and Contemporary Problems* 28, no. 2 (1963): 417.

64. Berman and Heineman, "Lobbying," 423–425.

65. Johnson, *The Sugar Program,* 58, 76.

66. Michael S. Billig, *Barons, Brokers, and Buyers: The Institutions and Cultures of Philippine Sugar* (Honolulu: University of Hawaii Press, 2003), 91.

67. Raul Fernandez, "Bitter Labour in Sugar Cane Fields," *Labour, Capital and Society* 19, no. 2 (1986): 245; Edward A. Evans and Carlton G. Davis, "US Sugar and Sweeteners Markets: Implications for CARICOM Tariff-Rate Quota Holders," *Social and Economic Studies* 49, no. 4 (2000): 16; Won W. Koo, "Alternative U.S. and EU Sugar Trade Liberalization Policies and Their Implications," *Review of Agricultural Economics* 24, no. 2 (2002): 350.

68. Brent Borrell and Ronald C. Duncan, "A Survey of the Costs of World Sugar Policies," *World Bank Research Observer* 7, no. 2 (1992): 172.

69. Scott B. MacDonald and F. Joseph Demetrius, "The Caribbean Sugar Crisis: Consequences and Challenges," *Journal of Interamerican Studies and World Affairs.* 28, no. 1 (1986): 44; Julie Lynn Coronado and Raymond Robertson, "Inter-American Development and the NAFTA: Implications of Liberalized Trade for the Caribbean Sugar Industry," *Caribbean Studies* 29, no. 1 (1996): 128–129.

70. Billig, *Barons,* 68.

71. Serge Cherniguin, "The Sugar Workers of Negros, Philippines," *Community Development Journal* 23, no. 3 (1988): 194.

72. Borrell and Duncan, "A Survey of the Costs," 176–178; MacDonald and Demetrius, "The Caribbean Sugar Crisis," 41–42.

73. Pamela Richardson-Ngwenya, "Situated Knowledge and the EU Sugar Reform: A Caribbean Life History," *Area* 45, no. 2 (2013): 190.

74. Michael S. Billig, "The Rationality of Growing Sugar in Negros," *Philippine Studies* 40, no. 2 (1992): 165.

75. Philippe Grenier, "The Alcohol Plan and the Development of Northeast Brazil," *GeoJournal* 11, no. 1 (1985): 64; C. R. Dabat, "Sugar Cane 'Plantations' in Pernambuco: From 'Natural Vocation' to Ethanol Production," *Review (Fernand Braudel Center)* 34, nos. 1–2 (2011): 134; Barbara Nunberg, "Structural Change and State Policy: The Politics of Sugar in Brazil since 1964," *Latin American Research Review*. 21, no. 2 (1986): 59.

76. See Madhav Godbole, "Co-Operative Sugar Factories in Maharashtra: Case for a Fresh Look," *Economic and Political Weekly* 35, no. 6 (2000): 420–424.

77. Bosma, *The Sugar Plantation,* 248–249, 260; "About Us," Birla Sugar, accessed April 17, 2022, https://www.indiamart.com/birla-sugarkolkata/aboutus.html.

78. Donna L. Chollett, "From Sugar to Blackberries: Restructuring Agro-Export Production in Michoacán, Mexico," *Latin American Perspectives* 36, no. 3 (2009): 82. See also Donna L. Chollett, "Renouncing the Mexican Revolution: Double Jeopardy within the Sugar Sector," *Urban Anthropology and Studies of Cultural Systems and World Economic Development* 23, nos. 2–3 (1994): 121–169.

13. Corporate Sugar

1. Donald F. Larson and Brent Borrell, *Sugar Policy and Reform* (Washington, DC: World Bank, Development Research Group, Rural Development, 2001), 3.

2. See Stephen Haley, *Sugar and Sweetener Situation and Outlook Report* (Washington, DC: Economic Research Service, US Department of Agriculture, January 2000), 24–39; Richard Gibb, "Developing Countries and Market Access: The Bitter-Sweet Taste of the European Union's Sugar Policy in Southern Africa," *Journal of Modern African Studies* 42, no. 4 (2004): 569, 570.

3. Penny Fowler and Rian Fokker, "A Sweeter Future: The Potential for EU Sugar Reform to Contribute to Poverty Reduction in Southern Africa," *Oxfam Policy and Practice: Agriculture, Food and Land* 4, no. 3 (2004): 4.

4. Gibb, "Developing Countries and Market Access," 578; Andrew Schmitz, Troy G. Schmitz, and Frederick Rossi, "Agricultural Subsidies in Developed Countries: Impact on Global Welfare," *Review of Agricultural Economics* 28, no. 3 (2006): 422; Won W. Koo, "Alternative U.S. and EU Sugar Trade Liberalization Policies and Their Implications," *Review of Agricultural Economics* 24, no. 2 (2002): 348.

5. Jan Douwe van der Ploeg, "The Peasantries of the Twenty-First Century: The Commoditisation Debate Revisited," *Journal of Peasant Studies* 37, no. 1 (2010): 18.

6. The figure of $56 billion as the total amount of subsidies is mentioned by Gawali Suresh, "Distortions in World Sugar Trade," *Economic and Political Weekly* 38, no. 43 (2003): 4513.

7. "ILO Global Farm Worker Issues," *Rural Migration News* 9, no. 4 (October 2003), https://migration.ucdavis.edu/rmn/more.php?id=785.

8. Alicia H. Lazzarini, "Gendered Labour, Migratory Labour: Reforming Sugar Regimes in Xinavane, Mozambique," *Journal of Southern African Studies* 43, no. 3 (2017): 621–622.

9. See, for example, "Colombia: Sugar Cane Harvesters Demand Rights at Work," International Trade Union Confederation, September 25, 2008, https://www.ituc-csi.org/colombia-sugar-cane-harvesters?lang=en.

10. Edward Suchman et al., "An Experiment in Innovation among Sugar Cane Cutters in Puerto Rico," *Human Organization Human Organization* 26, no. 4 (1967): 215. See also Allan S. Queiroz and Raf Vanderstraeten, "Unintended Consequences of Job Formalisation: Precarious work in Brazil's Sugarcane Plantations," *International Sociology* 33, no. 1 (2018): 128–146.

11. Julie Lynn Coronado and Raymond Robertson, "Inter-American Development and the NAFTA: Implications of Liberalized Trade for the Caribbean Sugar Industry," *Caribbean Studies* 29, no. 1 (1996): 128.

12. *Wikipedia* s.v., "The Price of Sugar (2007 Film)," accessed April 17, 2022, https://en.wikipedia.org/wiki/The_Price_of_Sugar_(2007_film); "Who Are the Richest Entrepreneurs in Central America and the Dominican Republic?," *Dominican Today,* June 29, 2020, https://dominicantoday.com/dr/economy/2020/06/29/who-are-the-richest-entrepreneurs-in-central-america-and-the-dominican-republic/.

13. Amy Serrano, "A Black Camera Interview: Documentary Practice as Political Intervention: The Case of "Sugar Babies": A Conversation With," *Black Camera* 22–23 (2008): 39.

14. Serrano, "A Black Camera Interview," 35.

15. Anthony W. Pereira, "Agrarian Reform and the Rural Workers' Unions of the Pernambuco Sugar Zone, Brazil 1985–1988," *Journal of Developing Areas* (1992): 173–175, 178, 188.

16. Eduardo Simoes and Inae Riveras, "Amnesty Condemns Forced Cane Labor in Brazil," *Reuters,* May 29, 2008, https://www.reuters.com/article/us-brazil-amnesty-cane/amnesty-condemns-forced-cane-labor-in-brazil-idUSN2844873820080528; Queiroz and Vanderstraeten, "Unintended Consequences," 137–138.

17. Dionne Bunsha, "Machines That Mow Down Migrants," *Dionne Bunsha* (blog), March 31, 2007, https://dionnebunsha.wordpress.com/2007/03/31/machines-that-mow-down-migrants; Saturnino M. Borras, David Fig, and Sofía Monsalve Suárez, "The Politics of Agrofuels and Mega-Land and Water Deals: Insights from the ProCana Case, Mozambique," *Review of African Political Economy* 38, no. 128 (2011): 221, 224.

18. Terry Macalister, "Sun Sets on Brazil's Sugar-Cane Cutters," *Guardian,* June 5, 2008, https://www.theguardian.com/environment/2008/jun/05/biofuels.carbonemissions.

19. See Jussara dos Santos Rosendo, "Social Impacts with the End of the Manual Sugarcane Harvest: A Case Study in Brazil," *Sociology International Journal* 1, no. 4 (2017): 121–125.

20. "Migrant Workers, Super-Exploitation and Identity: Case of Sugarcane Cutters in Gujarat," *Economic and Political Weekly* 23, no. 23 (1988): 1153. See also Jan Breman, "Seasonal Migration and Co-Operative Capitalism: The Crushing of Cane and of Labour by the Sugar Factories of Bardoli, South Gujarat," *Journal of Peasant Studies* 6, no. 1 (1978): 41–70; no. 2 (1979): 168–209.

21. Pooja Adhikari and Vani Shree, "Human Cost of Sugar: Living and Working Conditions of Migrant Cane Cutters in Maharashtra," Oxfam India Discussion Paper, February 3, 2020, https://d1ns4ht6ytuzzo.cloudfront.net/oxfamdata/oxfamdatapublic/2021-02/Human%20Cost%20of%20Sugar_Maharashtra%20Case-2.pdf?33ji.96dQfp5xHQ9svfwmnaSKE_ywIEC.

22. Manfred Pohl, *Die Geschichte der Südzucker AG 1926–2001* (Munich: Piper, 2001), 127.

23. See, for example, Alexander Claver and G. Roger Knight, "A European Role in Intra-Asian Commercial Development: The Maclaine Watson Network and the Java Sugar Trade c.1840–1942," *Business History* 60, no. 2 (2018): 202–230.

24. John Paul Rathbone, *The Sugar King of Havana: The Rise and Fall of Julio Lobo, Cuba's Last Tycoon* (New York: Penguin, 2010), 111–113.

25. Ulbe Bosma, "Up and Down the Chain: Sugar Refiners' Responses to Changing Food Regimes," in *Navigating History: Economy, Society, Knowledge and Nature,* ed. Pepijn Brandon, Sabine Go, and Wybren Verstegen (Leiden: Boston: Brill, 2018), 267; Al Imfeld, *Zucker* (Zurich: Unionsverlag, 1986), 77–82.

26. Frederick F. Clairmonte and John H. Cavanagh, "World Commodities Trade: Changing Role of Giant Trading Companies," *Economic and Political Weekly* 23, no. 42 (1988): 2156; Thomas Braunschweig, Alice Kohli, and Silvie Lang, *Agricultural Commodity Traders in Switzerland—Benefitting from Misery?* (Lausanne, Switzerland: Public Eye, 2019), 5.

27. Philippe Chalmin, *The Making of a Sugar Giant: Tate and Lyle: 1859–1959* (Chur, Switzerland: Harwood Academic, 1990), 668–671; "Sir Saxon Tate Bt," *Telegraph,* September 5, 2012.

28. "Foreign Business," Mitr Phol Group, accessed April 18, 2022, https://www.mitrphol.com/offshore.php.

29. Birla, *Brushes with History,* 5–7.

30. "History Timeline," ASR Group, accessed April 18, 2022, https://www.asr-group.com/history-timeline; Bosma, "Up and Down," 259, 266.

31. Gary W. Brester and Michael A. Boland, "Teaching Case: The Rocky Mountain Sugar Growers' Cooperative: 'Sweet' or 'Sugar-Coated' Visions of the Future?," *Review of Agricultural Economics* 26, no. 2 (2004): 291.

32. "Tate and Lyle Sugar Division Sold to US Company," *Agritrade,* August 7, 2010, https://agritrade.cta.int/en/layout/set/print/Agriculture/Commodities/Sugar/Tate-and-Lyle-sugar-division-sold-to-US-company.html.

33. Ben Richardson, *Sugar* (Cambridge: Polity, 2015), 204.

34. Alex Dubb, Ian Scoones, and Philip Woodhouse, "The Political Economy of Sugar in Southern Africa—Introduction," *Journal of Southern African Studies* 43, no. 3 (2017): 448; Haley, *Sugar and Sweetener Situation,* 24–39; United States Department of Agriculture, *Sugar: World Markets and Trade* (May 2022), 7, Foreign Agricultural Service, https://www.fas.usda.gov/data/sugar-world-markets-and-trade

35. Ben Richardson, "Restructuring the EU-ACP Sugar Regime: Out of the Strong There Came Forth Sweetness," *Review of International Political Economy* 16, no. 4 (2009): 674; European Commission, "EU Sugar Quota System Comes to an End," *CTA Brussels Office Weblog,* October 9, 2017, http://brussels.cta.int/indexa9a6.html?option=com_k2&view=item&id=15325:eu-sugar-quota-system-comes-to-an-end.

36. "Südzucker—Corporate Profile," *Agritrade,* September 27, 2014, https://agritrade.cta.int/en/Agriculture/Commodities/Sugar/Suedzucker-corporate-profile.html.

37. "Tereos—Corporate Profile," *Agritrade,* July 23, 2014, https://agritrade.cta.int/en/Agriculture/Commodities/Sugar/Tereos-corporate-profile.html.

38. Mark Carr, "AB Sugar's Modern Slavery Statement 2018," November 2018, https://www.absugar.com/perch/resources/abs-modern-slavery-statement-2018-2.pdf.

39. "Acquisition of Illovo Minority Interest Update," Associated British Foods, May 25, 2016, https://www.abf.co.uk/media/news/2016/2016-acquisition-of-illovo-minority-interest-update.

40. Coronado and Robertson, "Inter-American Development," 121, 134; J. Dennis Lord, "End of the Nation-State Postponed: Agricultural Policy and the Global Sugar Industry," *Southeastern Geographer* 43, no. 2 (2003): 287; "About Us," Alliance for Fair Sugar Policy, accessed January 27, 2022, https://fairsugarpolicy.org/about/.

41. Colin Grabow, "Candy-Coated Cartel: Time to Kill the U.S. Sugar Program," *Policy Analysis,* no. 837 (April 10, 2018): 2, https://www.cato.org/publications/policy-analysis/candy-coated-cartel-time-kill-us-sugar-program.

42. Alec Wilkinson, *Big Sugar: Seasons in the Cane Fields of Florida* (New York: Vintage, 1990), 79.

43. Gail M. Hollander, *Raising Cane in the 'Glades: The Global Sugar Trade and the Transformation of Florida* (Chicago: University of Chicago Press, 2009), 258.

44. Deborah Jean Warner, *Sweet Stuff: An American History of Sweeteners from Sugar to Sucralose* (Washington, DC: Smithsonian Institution Scholarly Press / Rowman and Littlefield, 2011), 80.

45. Zachary Mider, "Rubio's Deep Sugar Ties Frustrate Conservatives," *Bloomberg,* January 29, 2016, https://www.bloomberg.com/news/articles/2016-01-28/rubio-s-deep-sugar

-ties-frustrate-conservatives; Grabow, "Candy-Coated Cartel," 8; Timothy P. Carney, "At Kochfest, Rubio Defends Sugar Subsidies on National Security Grounds," *Washington Examiner,* August 2, 2015, https://www.washingtonexaminer.com/at-kochfest-rubio-defends -sugar-subsidies-on-national-security-grounds.

46. Peter Wallsten, Manuel Roig-Franzia, and Tom Hamburger, "Sugar Tycoon Alfonso Fanjul Now Open to Investing in Cuba under 'Right Circumstances,'" *Washington Post,* February 2, 2014.

47. Tim Lang and Michael Heasman, *Food Wars: The Global Battle for Minds, Mouths, and Markets,* 2nd ed. (London: Earthscan, 2004), table 8.4; "Tate & Lyle Europe (031583)," FarmSubsidy.org, accessed January 27, 2022, https://farmsubsidy.org/GB/recipient/GB47951 /tate-lyle-europe-031583-gb-e16-2ew/ source.

48. Scott B. MacDonald and F. Joseph Demetrius, "The Caribbean Sugar Crisis: Consequences and Challenges," *Journal of Interamerican Studies and World Affairs.* 28, no. 1 (1986): 37; "Flüssig ist billiger," *Spiegel,* October 3, 1976, http://www.spiegel.de/spiegel/print/d -41136649.html. See also E. K. Aguirre, O. T. Mytton, and P. Monsivais, "Liberalising Agricultural Policy for Sugar in Europe Risks Damaging Public Health," *BMJ (Online)* 351 (2015): h5085.

49. Dan Roberts, "Sweet Brexit: What Sugar Tells Us about Britain's Future outside the EU," *Guardian,* March 27, 2017, https://www.theguardian.com/business/2017/mar/27/brexit -sugar-beet-cane-tate-lyle-british-sugar; Michael Savage, "Brexit Backers Tate & Lyle Set to Gain £73m from End of EU Trade Tariffs," *Guardian,* August 8, 2020, https://www .theguardian.com/business/2020/aug/08/brexit-backers-tate-lyle-set-to-gain-73m-from -end-of-eu-trade-tariffs.

50. See ATO Guangzhou Staff, *People's Republic of China: Annual Chinese Sugar Production Growth Expected to Slow, Prices Rise,* GAIN Report Number: CH196006 (Guangzhou: US Department of Agriculture Foreign Agricultural Service, 2019); Y. R. Li and L. T. Yang, "Sugarcane Agriculture and Sugar Industry in China," *Sugar Tech* 17, no. 1 (2015): 1–8.

51. "Base in China, March onto the Global Scene," COFCO, accessed April 18, 2022, http://www.cofco.com/en/AboutCOFCO/; "Sugar," COFCO International, accessed April 18, 2022, https://www.cofcointernational.com/products-services/sugar/.

52. Fowler and Fokker, "A Sweeter Future," 23–30; Alan Terry and Mike Ogg, "Restructuring the Swazi Sugar Industry: The Changing Role and Political Significance of Smallholders," *Journal of Southern African Studies* 43, no. 3 (2017): 585, 592, 593; Emmanuel Sulle, "Social Differentiation and the Politics of Land: Sugar Cane Outgrowing in Kilombero, Tanzania," *Journal of Southern African Studies* 43, no. 3 (2017): 517, 528; P. James and P. Woodhouse, "Crisis and Differentiation among Small-Scale Sugar Cane Growers in Nkomazi, South Africa," *Journal of Southern African Studies* 43, no. 3 (2017): 535–549.

53. See P. Zuurbier et al., "Land Use Dynamics and Sugarcane Production," in *Sugarcane Ethanol: Contributions to Climate Change Mitigations and the Environment,* ed.

P. Zuurbier and J. van de Vooren (Wageningen, the Netherlands: Wageningen Academic Publishers, 2008): 29–62.

54. Thomas D. Rogers, *The Deepest Wounds: A Labor and Environmental History of Sugar in Northeast Brazil* (Chapel Hill: University of North Carolina Press, 2010), 182, 188, 199, 204, 210.

55. Ujjayant Chakravorty, Marie-Hélène Hubert, and Linda Nøstbakken, "Fuel versus Food," *Annual Review of Resource Economics* 1 (2009): 658.

56. See Adhikari and Vani Shree, "Human Cost of Sugar."

57. Carol B. Thompson, "Agrofuels from Africa, Not for Africa," *Review of African Political Economy* 35, no. 117 (2008): 517; Mohamad Shohibuddin, Maria Lisa Alano, and Gerben Nooteboom, "Sweet and Bitter: Trajectories of Sugar Cane Investments in Northern Luzon, the Philippines, and Aceh, Indonesia, 2006–2013," in *Large-Scale Land Acquisitions: Focus on South-East Asia,* ed. Christophe Gironde, Christophe Golay, and Peter Messerli (Boston: Brill-Nijhoff, 2016), 112–117; Borras, Fig, and Suárez, "The Politics of Agrofuels"; Marc Edelman, Carlos Oya, and Saturnino M. Borras, *Global Land Grabs: History, Theory and Methods* (Abingdon, England: Routledge, 2016); See Yasuo Aonishi et al., *Not One Idle Hectare: Agrofuel Development Sparks Intensified Land Grabbing in Isabela, Philippines: Report of the International Fact Finding Mission: May 29th–June 6th 2011: San Mariano, Isabela, Philippines* (Quezon City, Philippines: People's Coalition on Food Sovereignty, 2011); "ITOCHU and JGC Launch Large-Scale Bio-Ethanol Production and Power Plant Businesses in the Philippines," ITOCHU Corporation, accessed April 18, 2022, https://www.itochu.co.jp/en/news/press/2010/100408.html.

58. "Cambodia / Thailand: Court Ruling on Mitr Phol Watershed Moment for Corporate Accountability in SE Asia," Amnesty International, July 31, 2020, https://www.amnesty.org/en/latest/news/2020/07/court-ruling-mitr-phol-case-watershed-moment-for-se-asia-corporate-accountability/.

59. "Thailand: Evicted Cambodian Villagers Sue Giant Mitr Phol; Amnesty International Submits Third Party Intervention to Thai Court," Amnesty International, July 30, 2020, https://www.amnesty.org/en/documents/asa39/2806/2020/en/.

60. Blessings Chinsinga, "The Green Belt Initiative, Politics and Sugar Production in Malawi," *Journal of Southern African Studies* 43, no. 3 (2017): 511, 514; Carr, "AB Sugar's Modern Slavery Statement 2018."

61. "Tate & Lyle Sugar to Be Fairtrade," *BBC News,* February 23, 2008, http://news.bbc.co.uk/2/hi/uk_news/7260211.stm.

62. "Rooted in Sustainability," ASR Group, accessed April 18, 2022, https://www.asr-group.com/Sustainability-Report; "Sustainability," Taiwan Sugar Corp., accessed April 18, 2022, https://www.taisugar.com.tw/english/CP2.aspx?n=10960.

63. "Environment," Sugar Cane Growers Cooperative of Florida, accessed April 18, 2022, https://www.scgc.org/environment/.

64. See, for example, "Florida: Republican 'Green Governor' Seeks to Reverse Predecessor's Legacy," *Guardian,* January 23, 2019, https://www.theguardian.com/us-news/2019/jan/23/florida-governor-ron-desantis-water-reservoir-environment.

65. Kenneth Starr et al., *The Starr Report* (Washington, DC: Government Printing Office, 1998), 38; Marion Nestle, *Food Politics: How the Food Industry Influences Nutrition and Health* (Berkeley: University of California, 2002), 109–110; Hollander, *Raising Cane,* 252, 261.

66. Kristin Wartman, "Food Fight: The Politics of the Food Industry," *New Labor Forum* 21, no. 3 (2012): 76–77; Hans Jürgen Teuteberg, "How Food Products Gained an Individual 'Face': Trademarks as a Medium of Advertising in the Growing Modern Market Economy in Germany," in *The Rise of Obesity in Europe: A Twentieth Century Food History,* ed. Derek J. Oddy, P. J. Atkins, and Virginie Amilien (Farnham, England: Ashgate, 2009), 84.

67. Harriet Friedmann, "From Colonialism to Green Capitalism: Social Movements and Emergence of Food Regimes," in *New Directions in the Sociology of Global Development,* ed. Frederick H. Buttel and Philip D. McMichael (Bingley, England: Emerald Group Publishing, 2005), 251–253.

68. "Sweet News: Fairtrade Sugar Newsletter," April 2020, https://files.fairtrade.net/Fairtrade-Sugar-Newsletter_2_2020_external-edition.pdf.

14. Sweeter Than Nature

1. Sergey Gudoshnikov, Linday Jolly, and Donald Spence, *The World Sugar Market* (Cambridge: Elsevier Science, 2004), 11–12.

2. Won W. Koo, "Alternative U.S. and EU Sugar Trade Liberalization Policies and Their Implications," *Review of Agricultural Economics* 24, no. 2 (2002): 338.

3. D. Gale Johnson, *The Sugar Program: Large Costs and Small Benefits* (Washington, DC: American Enterprise for Public Policy, 1974), 6.

4. Carolyn Crist, "Few Smokers Know about Added Sugar in Cigarettes," *Reuters,* October 26, 2018, https://www.reuters.com/article/us-health-cigarettes-sugar-idUSKCN1N02UC; Robert Proctor, *Golden Holocaust: Origins of the Cigarette Catastrophe and the Case for Abolition* (Berkeley: University of California Press, 2011), 33–34.

5. William Watts, "On the Proximate Cause of Diabetes Mellitus," *The Lancet* 45, no. 1129 (1845): 438.

6. Steven Blankaart, *De Borgerlyke Tafel* (Amsterdam: J. ten Hoorn, 1683), 41–42, 102.

7. Gary Taubes, *The Case against Sugar* (London: Portobello Books, 2018), 240.

8. Jean Anthelme Brillat-Savarin, *Physiologie du goût ou méditations de gastronomie transcendante* (Paris: A. Sautelet, 1828), 106, 221.

9. Leone Levi, *On the Sugar Trade and Sugar Duties: A Lecture Delivered at King's College, London, Feb. 29, 1864* (London: Effingham Wilson, 1864), 12.

10. W. Banting, Letter on Corpulence: Addressed to the Public. with Prefatory Remarks by the Author Copious Information from Correspondents and Confirmatory Evidence of the Benefit of the Dietary System Which He Recommended to Public Notice. (London: Harrison & Sons, 1863).

11. John Harvey, *Corpulence, Its Diminution and Cure without Injury to Health* (London: Smith, 1864), 96.

12. Thomas Low Nichols, *Eating to Live: The Diet Cure: An Essay on the Relations of Food and Drink to Health, Disease and Cure* (London, 1877), 43–45.

13. Taubes, *The Case*, 116.

14. Gary Taubes, *Good Calories, Bad Calories* (New York: Knopf, 2007), ix, x.

15. John Yudkin, *Pure, White and Deadly* (London: Viking, 2012), vii.

16. John Yudkin, "Sugar and Disease," *Nature* 239, no. 5369 (1972): 197; Taubes, *The Case*, 6–7; Richard J. Johnson et al., "Potential Role of Sugar (Fructose) in the Epidemic of Hypertension, Obesity and the Metabolic Syndrome, Diabetes, Kidney Disease, and Cardiovascular Disease," *American Journal of Clinical Nutrition* 86, no. 4 (2007): 901; H. B. Anderson, "Diet in Its Relation to Disease," *Public Health Journal* 3, no. 12 (1912): 713.

17. Manuel Correia de Andrade, *The Land and People of Northeast Brazil* (Albuquerque: University of New Mexico Press, 1980), 99, 124; William Arthur Lewis, *Labour in the West Indies the Birth of a Workers' Movement* (London: New Beacon Books, 1977), 16; Deborah Jean Warner, *Sweet Stuff: An American History of Sweeteners from Sugar to Sucralose* (Washington, DC: Smithsonian Institution Scholarly Press / Rowman and Littlefield, 2011), 33.

18. *Encyclopædia Iranica* s.v., "Sugar," last modified July 20, 2009, https://www.iranicaonline.org/articles/sugar-cultivation.

19. C. J. Robertson, "The Italian Beet-Sugar Industry," *Economic Geography* 14, no. 1 (1938): 13–14.

20. Romuald Le Pelletier de Saint-Rémy, *Le questionnaire de la question des sucres* (Paris: Guillaumin, 1877), 216–220.

21. Charles Robequain, "Le sucre dans l'Union française," *Annales de Géographie* 57, no. 308 (1948): 323, 333; Koo, "Alternative U.S. and EU Sugar Trade," 338.

22. John Perkins, "Sugar Production, Consumption and Propaganda in Germany, 1850–1914," *German History* 15, no. 1 (1997): 25–30.

23. Wendy A. Woloson, *Refined Tastes: Sugar, Confectionery, and Consumers in Nineteenth-Century America* (Baltimore, MD: Johns Hopkins University Press, 2002), 36–37, 54, 55, 118.

24. Henry Mayhew, *London Labour and the London Poor*, vol. 1 (New York: Dover, 1968), 202–203.

25. Darra Goldstein, *The Oxford Companion to Sugar and Sweets* (Oxford: Oxford University Press, 2015), 758; Robert H. Lustig, *Fat Chance: Beating the Odds against Sugar, Processed Food, Obesity, and Disease* (New York: Penguin Group, 2013), 261; Paul Pestano, Etan Yeshua, and Jane Houlihan, *Sugar in Children's Cereals: Popular Brands Pack More Sugar Than Snack Cakes and Cookies* (Washington, DC: Environmental Working Group, 2011), 5.

26. Erika Rappaport, *A Thirst for Empire: How Tea Shaped the Modern World* (Princeton, NJ: Princeton University Press, 2017), 71–74, 81–82.

27. Philip B. Mason, Xiaohe Xu, and John P. Bartkowski, "The Risk of Overweight and Obesity among Latter-Day Saints," *Review of Religious Research* 55, no. 1 (2013): 132.

28. Taubes, *The Case*, 42.

29. Goldstein, *The Oxford Companion*, 87–88; Samira Kawash, *Candy: A Century of Panic and Pleasure* (New York: Faber and Faber, 2013), 85.

30. April Merleaux, *Sugar and Civilization: American Empire and the Cultural Politics of Sweetness* (Chapel Hill: University of North Carolina Press, 2015), 213.

31. Goldstein, *The Oxford Companion*, 87.

32. Irving V. Sollins, "Sugar in Diet Part I: An Educational Problem," *Journal of Educational Sociology* 3, no. 6 (1930): 345.

33. Perkins, "Sugar Production," 31.

34. Julia Csergo, "Food Consumption and Risk of Obesity: The Medical Discourse in France 1850–1930," in *The Rise of Obesity in Europe: A Twentieth Century Food History,* ed. Derek J. Oddy, P. J. Atkins, and Virginie Amilien (Farnham, England: Ashgate, 2009), 169–170; Martin Bruegel, "A Bourgeois Good?: Sugar, Norms of Consumption and the Labouring Classes in Nineteenth-Century France," in *Food, Drink and Identity: Cooking, Eating and Drinking in Europe since the Middle Ages,* ed. Peter Scholliers (Oxford: Berg, 2001), 107–110; Maurice Halbwachs, *L'évolution des besoins dans les classes ouvrières* (Paris: F. Alcan, 1933), 122.

35. Hans Jürgen Teuteberg and Günter Wiegelmann, *Der Wandel der Nahrungsgewohnheiten unter dem Einfluss der Industrialisierung* (Göttingen: Vandenhoeck and Ruprecht, 1972), 299.

36. Halbwachs, *L'évolution des besoins,* 122; Bruegel, "A Bourgeois Good?," 111.

37. Perkins, "Sugar Production," 32; Siegmund Ziegler, "Die Weltzuckerproduktion während des Krieges und der Zuckerpreis," *Weltwirtschaftliches Archiv* 15 (1919): 53–54; Kawash, *Candy,* 105.

38. Merleaux, *Sugar and Civilization,* 59, 65, 68–69; Kawash, *Candy,* 107.

39. Barak Kushner, "Sweetness and Empire: Sugar Consumption in Imperial Japan," in *The Historical Consumer: Consumption and Everyday Life in Japan, 1850–2000,* ed. Penelope Francks and Janet Hunter (New York: Palgrave Macmillan, 2012), 140–141.

40. Rappaport, *A Thirst for Empire,* 122, 139, 152.

41. Joe Bertram Frantz, "Infinite Pursuit: The Story of Gail Borden" (PhD diss., University of Texas, 1948), 68–69.

42. Laura Mason, *Sweets and Candy: A Global History* (London: Reaktion Books, 2018), 83–86.

43. Goldstein, *The Oxford Companion*, 753; Harvey Washington Wiley, *Foods and Their Adulteration: Origin, Manufacture, and Composition of Food Products: Infants' and Invalids' Foods: Detection of Common Adulterations* (Philadelphia: P. Blakiston's Son, 1917), 485.

44. Gail Hollander, "Re-Naturalizing Sugar: Narratives of Place, Production and Consumption," *Social & Cultural Geography* 4, no. 1 (2003): 64.

45. Kawash, *Candy*, 98, 112.

46. Kawash, *Candy*, 55, 67.

47. Warner, *Sweet Stuff*, 44, 109–119, 133.

48. Wiley, *Foods and Their Adulteration*, 470.

49. Warner, *Sweet Stuff*, 20, 24–25.

50. Ulbe Bosma, *The Sugar Plantation in India and Indonesia: Industrial Production, 1770–2010* (Cambridge: Cambridge University Press, 2013), 171.

51. Alice Ross, "Health and Diet in 19th-Century America: A Food Historian's Point of View," *Historical Archaeology* 27, no. 2 (1993): 47.

52. Goldstein, *The Oxford Companion*, 95–96.

53. Woloson, *Refined Tastes*, 214.

54. Merleaux, *Sugar and Civilization*, 106.

55. Ziegler, "Die Weltzuckerproduktion," 63, 65.

56. Merleaux, *Sugar and Civilization*, 19.

57. Lustig, *Fat Chance*, 172.

58. Goldstein, *The Oxford Companion*, 757.

59. Mark Pendergrast, *For God, Country, and Coca-Cola: The Definitive History of the Great American Soft Drink and the Company That Makes It* (London: Weidenfeld and Nicolson, 1993), 238.

60. Goldstein, *The Oxford Companion*, 737.

61. Kushner, "Sweetness and Empire," 135–136, 139.

62. K. Walden, "The Road to Fat City: An Interpretation of the Development of Weight Consciousness in Western Society," *Historical Reflections* 12, no. 3 (1985): 332.

63. Merleaux, *Sugar and Civilization*, 147; Kawash, *Candy*, 191.

64. Woloson, *Refined Tastes*, 194.

65. Mildred Maddocks and Harvey Washington Wiley, *The Pure Food Cook Book: The Good Housekeeping Recipes, Just How to Buy—Just How to Cook* (New York: Hearst's International Library, 1914), 11, 237.

66. See Weston A. Price, *Nutrition and Physical Degeneration* (Redland, CA: P. B. Hoeber, 1939); Merleaux, *Sugar and Civilization*, 221–222.

67. Taubes, *The Case*, 125.

68. Yudkin, *Pure, White and Deadly*, 127.

69. Sollins, "Sugar in Diet Part I," 342, 345–346; Irving V. Sollins, "Sugar in Diet Part II: An Experiment in Instruction in Candy Consumption," *Journal of Educational Sociology* 3, no. 9: 548.

70. *Revenue Revision of 1943: Hearings before the Committee of Ways and Means House of Representatives. Seventy-Eighth Congress. First Session, 1014–1031* (Washington, DC: Government Printing Office, 1943).

71. Hollander, "Re-Naturalizing Sugar," 65.

72. "Encourage Sugar Consumption," *Sugar (Including Facts about Sugar and the Planter & Sugar Manufacturer),* June 25–27, 1947.

73. Marion Nestle, "Food Industry Funding of Nutrition Research: The Relevance of History for Current Debates," *JAMA Internal Medicine* 176, no. 11 (2016): 1685–1686.

74. Sanjay Basu et al., "The Relationship of Sugar to Population-Level Diabetes Prevalence: An Econometric Analysis of Repeated Cross-Sectional Data," *PLoS ONE* 8, no. 2: e57873 (p. 6). For a concise description of the methodological flaws in Keys's project, see Lustig, *Fat Chance,* 111.

75. Yudkin, *Pure, White and Deadly,* 41; Pana Wilder, "No One Profits from Candy in the Schools," *Middle School Journal Middle School Journal* 15, no. 4 (1984): 18; Marion Nestle, *Food Politics: How the Food Industry Influences Nutrition and Health* (Berkeley: University of California, 2002), 197.

76. Nestle, *Food Politics,* 214.

77. Jonathan C. K. Wells, "Obesity as Malnutrition: The Role of Capitalism in the Obesity Global Epidemic," *American Journal of Human Biology* 24, no. 3 (2012): 272.

78. US Senate Select Committee on Nutrition and Human Needs, *Short Dietary Goals for the United States* (Washington, DC: Government Printing Office, 1977), 4, 5.

79. US Senate Select Committee on Nutrition and Human Needs, *Short Dietary Goals,* 4. I agree with Johns and Oppenheimer that the sugar industry might not have changed Hegsted's position on fat and sugar, but the latter's ethics breach is indefensible. See David Merritt Johns and Gerald M. Oppenheimer, "Was There Ever Really a 'Sugar Conspiracy'? Twists and Turns in Science and Policy Are Not Necessarily Products of Malevolence," *Science* 359, no. 6377 (2018): 747–750.

80. Lustig, *Fat Chance,* 169.

81. Nestle, *Food Politics,* 59, 66.

82. Yudkin, *Pure, White and Deadly,* 66.

83. WHO, *Diet, Nutrition, and the Prevention of Chronic Diseases: Report of a WHO Study Group* (Geneva: WHO, 1990), 94.

84. Sarah Boseley and Jean McMahon, "Political Context of the World Health Organization: Sugar Industry Threatens to Scupper the WHO," *International Journal of Health Services* 33, no. 4 (2003): 831–833; Joint WHO / FAO Expert Consultation on Diet, Nutrition and the Prevention of Chronic Diseases, *Diet, Nutrition and the Prevention of Chronic Diseases: Report of a Joint WHO/FAO Expert Consultation* (Geneva: WHO, 2003), 56–58, 66.

85. Geoffrey Cannon, "Why the Bush Administration and the Global Sugar Industry Are Determined to Demolish the 2004 WHO Global Strategy on Diet, Physical Activity and Health," *Public Health Nutrition* 7, no. 3 (2004): 369–380; David Stuckler et al., "Textual Analysis of Sugar Industry Influence on the World Health Organization's 2015 Sugars Intake Guideline," *Bulletin of the World Health Organization* 94, no. 8 (2016):

566–573; Boseley and McMahon, "Political Context"; WHO, *Guideline: Sugars Intake for Adults and Children* (Geneva: WHO, 2015), 4.

86. J. Putnam and J. Allshouse, "U.S. Per Capita Food Supply Trends," *Food Review* 21, no. 3 (1998): 1–10.

87. WHO, *Set of Recommendations on the Marketing of Foods and Non-Alcoholic Beverages to Children* (Geneva: WHO, 2010), http://www.who.int/dietphysicalactivity/publications /recsmarketing/en/index.html; WHO, "WHO urges Global Action to Curtail Consumption and Health Impacts of Sugary Drinks," news release, October 11, 206, https://www .who.int/news/item/11-10-2016-who-urges-global-action-to-curtail-consumption-and -health-impacts-of-sugary-drinks.

88. Alex Wayne, "Senate Panel Suggests Tax on Sweet Drinks to Pay for Health Care Overhaul," Commonwealth Fund, May 18, 2009, https://www.commonwealthfund.org /publications/newsletter-article/senate-panel-suggests-tax-sweet-drinks-pay-health-care -overhaul; Chen Zhen et al., "Habit Formation and Demand for Sugar-Sweetened Beverages," *American Journal of Agricultural Economics* 93, no. 1 (2011): 175.

89. Lustig, *Fat Chance,* 245; V.v.B., "Chicago's Soda Tax Is Repealed: A Big Victory for Makers of Sweet Drinks," *Economist,* October 13, 2017, https://www.economist.com /democracy-in-america/2017/10/13/chicagos-soda-tax-is-repealed.

90. Emi Okamoto, "The Philadelphia Soda Tax, while Regressive, Saves Lives of Those Most at Risk," *A Healthier Philly,* April 9, 2019, https://www.phillyvoice.com/philadelphia -soda-tax-regressive-saves-lives-most-at-risk; Chuck Dinerstein, "Soda Tax Continues to Decrease Sales, but There's No Evidence of Health Benefit," American Council on Science and Health, April 12, 2018, https://www.acsh.org/news/2018/04/12/soda-tax-continues-decrease -sales-theres-no-evidence-health-benefit-12829.

91. Zhen et al., "Habit Formation," 190.

92. Nathalie Moise et al., "Limiting the Consumption of Sugar Sweetened Beverages in Mexico's Obesogenic Environment: A Qualitative Policy Review and Stakeholder Analysis," *Journal of Public Health Policy* 32, no. 4 (2011): 468, 470; A. R. Lopez, "Mexico's Sugar Crusade Looking Forward," *Harvard International Review* 37, no. 3 (2016): 48–49.

93. Lawrence O. Gostin, "Why Healthy Behavior Is the Hard Choice," *Milbank Quarterly* 93, no. 2 (2015): 243; David Agren, "Mexico State Bans Sale of Sugary Drinks and Junk Food to Children," *Guardian,* August 6, 2020, https://www.theguardian.com/food/2020/aug /06/mexico-oaxaca-sugary-drinks-junk-food-ban-children#:~:text=The%20southern%20 Mexican%20state%20of,drinks%20and%20sweets%20to%20children.

94. See, for example, "The 2018 UK Sugar Tax," Diabetes.co.uk, January 15, 2019, https://www.diabetes.co.uk/nutrition/2018-uk-sugar-tax.html.

95. Gostin, "Why Healthy Behavior," 243, 245; Miguel Ángel Royo-Bordonada et al., "Impact of an Excise Tax on the Consumption of Sugar-Sweetened Beverages in Young People Living in Poorer Neighbourhoods of Catalonia, Spain: A Difference in Differences Study," *BMC Public Health* 19, no. 1 (2019): 1553; Wissenschaftliche Dienste Deutscher Bund-

estag, "Ausgestaltung einer Zuckersteuer in ausgewählten Ländern und ihre Auswirkung auf Kaufverhalten, Preise und Reformulierung Aktenzeichen," WD 5–3000–064 / 18 (Berlin Deutscher Bundestage 2018); Wissenschaftliche Dienste Deutscher Bundestag, "Studien zu gesundheitlichen Auswirkungen einer Zuckersteuer," WD 9 -3000–028 / 1 (Berlin: Deutscher Bundestage, 2018); Hans Jürgen Teuteberg, "How Food Products Gained an Individual 'Face': Trademarks as a Medium of Advertising in the Growing Modern Market Economy in Germany," in *The Rise of Obesity in Europe: A Twentieth Century Food History*, ed. Derek J. Oddy, P. J. Atkins, and Virginie Amilien (Farnham, England: Ashgate, 2009), 77; S. ter Borg et al., *Zout-, Suiker- en Verzadigd Vetgehalten in Levensmiddelen*, RIVM 2019–0032 (Bilthoven, the Netherlands: RIVM, 2019), 64.

96. Yudkin, *Pure, White and Deadly*, 168–169.

97. Nestle, *Food Politics*, 2013 edition, xi.

98. See Al Imfeld, *Zucker* (Zurich: Unionsverlag, 1986).

99. Anahad O'Connor, "Coca-Cola Funds Scientists Who Shift Blame for Obesity Away from Bad Diets," *New York Times*, August 9, 2015, https://well.blogs.nytimes.com/2015 /08/09/coca-cola-funds-scientists-who-shift-blame-for-obesity-away-from-bad-diets/?_r=1. See also C. Herrick, "Shifting Blame / Selling Health: Corporate Social Responsibility in the Age of Obesity," *Sociology of Health & Illness* 31, no. 1 (2009): 51–65.

100. See Aseem Malhotra, Grant Schofield, and Robert H. Lustig, "The Science against Sugar, Alone, Is Insufficient in Tackling the Obesity and Type 2 Diabetes Crises—We Must Also Overcome Opposition from Vested Interests," *Journal of the Australasian College of Nutritional and Environmental Medicine* 38, no. 1 (2019): a39; A. Malhotra, T. Noakes, and S. Phinney, "It is Time to Bust the Myth of Physical Inactivity and Obesity: You Cannot Outrun a Bad Diet," *British Journal of Sports Medicine* 49, no. 15 (2015): 967–968.

101. Lustig, *Fat Chance*, 192–194.

102. Pendergrast, *For God, Country*, 337.

103. Gail M. Hollander, *Raising Cane in the 'Glades: The Global Sugar Trade and the Transformation of Florida* (Chicago: University of Chicago Press, 2009), 164.

104. Perkins, "Sugar Production," 30–31.

105. Klaus Roth and Erich Lück, "Die Saccharin-Saga Ein Molekülschicksal," *Chemie in Unserer Zeit* 45, no. 6 (2011): 413–414.

106. *Britannica* s.v., "Monsanto," accessed April 17, 2022, https://www.britannica.com /topic/Monsanto-Company.

107. See Carol Levine, "The First Ban: How Teddy Roosevelt Saved Saccharin," *Hastings Center Report* 7, no. 6 (1977): 6–7.

108. Marvin L. Hayenga, "Sweetener Competition and Sugar Policy," *Journal of Farm Economics* 49, no. 5 (1967): 1364.

109. Klaus Roth and Erich Lück, "Kalorienfreie Süße aus Labor und Natur: Süß, süßer, Süßstoff," *Chemie in unserer Zeit* 46 (2012): 172.

110. Roth and Lück, "Kalorienfreie Süße," 173.

111. Warner, *Sweet Stuff,* 194.

112. Andrew Cockburn, *Rumsfeld: His Rise, Fall, and Catastrophic Legacy* (New York: Scribner, 2007), 64.

113. Robbie Gennet, "Donald Rumsfeld and the Strange History of Aspartame," *Huffington Post* May 25, 2011, https://www.huffpost.com/entry/donald-rumsfeld-and-the-s_b _805581.

114. Warner, *Sweet Stuff,* 211–212; Cockburn, *Rumsfeld,* 66–68.

115. "Findings on Risk from Aspartame Are Inconclusive, Says EFSA," CORDIS, May 8, 2006, https://cordis.europa.eu/article/id/25605-findings-on-risk-from-aspartame-are-incon clusive-says-efsa. New research by Morando Soffriti and his team has not changed the position of EFSA. See also Morando Soffritti et al., "Aspartame Administered in Feed, Beginning Prenatally through Life Span, Induces Cancers of the Liver and Lung in Male Swiss Mice," *American Journal of Industrial Medicine* 53, no. 12 (2010): 1197–1206.

116. Warner, *Sweet Stuff,* 212, 214.

117. See Bertram O. Fraser-Reid, *From Sugar to Splenda: A Personal and Scientific Journey of a Carbohydrate Chemist and Expert Witness* (Berlin: Springer, 2012).

118. It should be stressed that neither Henry Tate nor Abram Lyle were directly involved in slave owning; see "The Tate Galleries and Slavery," Tate, accessed January 13, 2022, https://www.tate.org.uk/about-us/history-tate/tate-galleries-and-slavery.

119. Linda Bonvie, Bill Bonvie, and Donna Gates, "Stevia: The Natural Sweetener That Frightens NutraSweet," *Earth Island Journal* 13, no. 1 (1997): 26–27.

120. Sybille de La Hamaide, "Miracle Sweetener Stevia May Have a Sour Note," *Reuters,* May 24, 2012, https://www.reuters.com/article/us-sugar-stevia/miracle-sweetener-stevia-may -have-a-sour-note-idUSBRE84M0Y120120523; "Commission Regulation (EU) No 1131/2011 of 11 November 2011 Amending Annex II to Regulation (EC) No 1333/2008 of the European Parliament and of the Council with regard to Steviol Glycosides," *Official Journal of the European Union,* November 12, 2011.

121. Thomas Le Masson, "Tate & Lyle vend 5 usines au sucrier français Tereos," *Les Echos,* May 10, 2007.

122. "Tate & Lyle Sells Molasses Unit," *Independent,* November 26, 2011, https://www .independent.co.uk/news/business/news/tate-amp-lyle-sells-molasses-unit-2143999.html.

123. Gandhi Sukhmani et al., "Natural Sweeteners: Health Benefits of Stevia," *Foods and Raw Materials* 6 (2018): 399.

124. International Diabetes Federation, *IDF Diabetes Atlas 9th Edition* (Brussels: International Diabetes Federation, 2019), 39–40, https://www.diabetesatlas.org/en/resources/.

Conclusion

1. Sven Beckert, *Empire of Cotton: A Global History* (New York: Alfred A. Knopf, 2014), 440.

Acknowledgments

In July 2001, a small group of scholars convened in Amsterdam. They came from Indonesia, Cuba, Australia, Puerto Rico and other parts the United States, and the Netherlands. I was one of the organizers of this workshop and our guest of honor was Professor Sidney Mintz. The workshop's objective was both simple and ambitious: to start a conversation among historians researching sugar production in Asia and in the Americas, fields of study that were not only geographically far apart but also intellectually distant. Mintz encouraged us to "rebalance" the Atlantic-centric bias in how we had been writing the history of sugar. It was the best possible start for my imaginary journey traversing almost the entire world.

Along the way, I could rely on excellent scholarship on almost every aspect of sugar. And I was never alone. Over the years, I talked at length with my friend and colleague Roger Knight about Java's colonial bourgeoisie. His knowledge of the Javanese sugar industry is unparalleled. I made friends with the initiators of the British Commodities of Empire program, resulting in publications with Jonathan Curry-Machado comparing the two largest cane sugar producers in Java and Cuba. From Jon I learned how the Java wonder cane POJ 2878 spread across the globe. Kathinka Sinha-Kerkhoff and Masoom Reza helped me familiarize myself with the history of sugar in India and provided invaluable help in accessing and obtaining research material. I remember sitting in front of a whiteboard with Sven Beckert, Mindi Schneider, and Eric Vanhaute, drawing a scheme to "periodize capitalism." In 2018, we were in downtown Amsterdam as fellows at the hospitable Netherlands Institute for Advanced Study. With Pepijn Brandon in the lead, we proved that slave-based commodities, and sugar in particular, made a significant contribution to the wealth of the Dutch

Republic. It became frontpage news in the Netherlands in 2019. Together with Kris Manjapra and Sascha Auerbach, I wrapped my mind around the question of how freedom looked from a plantation perspective. Guanmian Xu opened my eyes to the role of Taiwan in early modern sugar production. Norbert Ortmayr and Marcel van der Linden, along with Jonathan Curry-Machado and Sven Beckert, provided valuable insights on my manuscript.

I would like to thank the International Institute of Social History in Amsterdam, with its magnificent archive and library. For more than twenty years, my wonderful colleagues at the research department, at the reading room, and the collections department have provided the best possible intellectual environment. Jacques van Gerwen did his utmost to obtain precious material on the German beet and Dutch sugar industry.

I am grateful to the anonymous reviewers for their careful and constructive feedback. I thank Paul Vincent, Sherry Gerstein, and Simon Waxman for getting the text into much better shape. Last but not least, I thank Sharmila Sen for deciding that this story deserves to be read and for thinking through this project with me—how to write about sugar as the sweet stuff we never needed but which still shaped our world.

Image Credits

Index

Page numbers in *italics* refer to illustrations.